NELLA LARSEN
Novelist of the Harlem Renaissance

Thadious M. Davis

Nella Larsen
Novelist of the Harlem Renaissance

A Woman's Life Unveiled

Louisiana State University Press
Baton Rouge and London

Copyright © 1994 by Louisiana State University Press
All rights reserved
Manufactured in the United States of America
First printing
03 02 01 00 99 98 97 96 95 94   5 4 3 2 1

Designer: *Glynnis Phoebe*
Typeface: *Sabon*
Typesetter: *G & S Typesetters, Inc.*
Printer and binder: *Thomson-Shore, Inc.*

Library of Congress Cataloging-in-Publication Data
Davis, Thadious M., 1944–
    Nella Larsen, novelist of the Harlem renaissance: a woman's life
unveiled / Thadious M. Davis.
        p.   cm.
    Includes index.
    ISBN 0-8071-1866-4
    1. Larsen, Nella. 2. Afro-American women novelists—20th century—
Biography. 3. Afro-Americans in literature. 4. Harlem
Renaissance. I. Title.
PS3523.A7225Z63 1994
813'.52—dc20
    [B]   93-32515
                                                           CIP

Quotations from the New York Public Library employment file for Mrs. Nella L. Imes courtesy
The New York Public Library, Astor, Lenox and Tilden Foundations. Quotations from docu-
ments in the Carl Van Vechten Personal Collection courtesy Carl Van Vechten Papers, Rare
Books and Manuscripts Division, The New York Public Library, Astor, Lenox and Tilden
Foundations. Quotations from Serendipity Books Catalog 43, from the Lincoln School for
Nurses Collection, and from the Schomburg Clipping File courtesy Manuscripts, Archives and
Rare Books Division, Schomburg Center for Research in Black Culture, The New York Public
Library, Astor, Lenox and Tilden Foundations. Quotations from Arna Bontemps interview
with Ann Allen Shockley courtesy Ann Allen Shockley and the Fisk University Library's Black
Oral History Program. Quotations from Ethel Ray Nance interviews with Ann Allen Shockley
courtesy Glen Nance and the Fisk University Library's Black Oral History Program. Quota-
tions from the Papers of Thomas Elsa Jones courtesy Special Collections, Fisk University Library. Quotations from the Countee Cullen Collection courtesy the Amistad Research Center.
Quotations from documents and letters in the Hollis Burke Frissell Library courtesy Tuskegee
University Archives.

This publication has been supported by a grant from the National Endowment for the Humanities, an independent federal agency.

The paper in this book meets the guidelines for permanence and durability of the Committee
on Production Guidelines for Book Longevity of the Council on Library Resources. ⊚

In memory of my mother, Helen,
my grandmothers, Lelia and Evelyn,
and their will to live in beauty

Surely it is more interesting to belong to one's own time, to share its peculiar vision, catch that flying glimpse of the panorama which no subsequent generation can ever recover.

—*Nella Larsen*

CONTENTS

ILLUSTRATIONS

following page 186

Early photograph of Nellie Larsen, 1908

Lincoln School of Nurses graduating class of 1915

1928 publicity photograph for *Quicksand*

Nella Larsen Imes, *ca.* 1930

Elmer Imes in his laboratory, *ca.* 1935

Nella Larsen, March, 1932

Nella Larsen, August, 1932

Dorothy Peterson, Nella Larsen, and Sidney Peterson, 1932

Sidney and Dorothy Peterson, 1937

Larsen's 1928 Harmon Awards Bronze Medal in Literature

Nella Larsen, 1934

The Search for Nella Larsen

Of all the New Negro authors, Nella Larsen is the most elusive in the matters of biographical details, especially dates. Evidently there were certain things in her background which she felt were private, and she kept them that way. A few facts, however, have come to us, several taken from the book jacket of her first novel.

—Arthur P. Davis, From the Dark Tower:
Afro-American Writers, 1900–1960

WHEN I FIRST read Arthur Davis' words in 1974, I wondered how a popular writer, whose works had been widely reviewed in leading newspapers and journals of the 1920s, could leave behind so little factual information about herself. With only two novels, *Quicksand* (1928) and *Passing* (1929), Nella Larsen established a reputation as one of the three leading novelists of the New Negro, or Harlem, Renaissance. Along with Walter White and Jessie Fauset, she had carved out a special place for herself among the writers who would become the preeminent figures of early modern African-American literature: Langston Hughes, Countee Cullen, Zora Neale Hurston, Claude McKay, Rudolph Fisher, and Wallace Thurman.

Larsen, White, and Fauset began writing their first novels at the same time in 1922; White's *Fire in the Flint* and Fauset's *There Is Confusion* appeared in 1924. Two years later, White's second novel, *Flight,* was in print, but it was not until 1928 that Fauset's second novel, *Plum Bun,* and Larsen's first, *Quicksand,* were published. On the basis of both productivity and promise, however, Larsen matched White and Fauset by the end of the decade, when the three were the only New Negro authors to have written two novels published by major New York firms. Her acclaim, like White's, helped establish the novel as a creative form for New Negro writers, and her success, like Fauset's, focused attention on women as literary artists in a cultural movement of highly visible men, most of whom initially wrote poetry or short fiction.

The questions Arthur Davis raised about Nella Larsen were basic:

"When was she born? . . . When did she die? . . . We simply do not know, and there is no card for her in the morgue of the New York *Times*. There are no terminal dates for her in the card catalog of the Library of Congress."[1] Davis' speculations were not about the subtleties of interpretation or analysis, but about biographical facts that are usually verifiable in the twentieth century. Because Davis is one of the most respected critics of African-American literature, and one who has labored in the field since the 1930s, his admission of having to depend upon the insufficient information provided on the dust jacket of Larsen's first novel intrigued me almost as much as the absence of the usual biographical data. Nearly a decade later, he reiterated that he had been unable to uncover specific dates for Larsen's birth or death; he concluded, moreover, just as other scholars had, that she had literally disappeared from public view in the 1930s. Her meteoric rise to prominence at the end of the 1920s had been followed by almost as rapid a decline during which she did not publish another novel. Instead, she became the subject of rumors about her passing for white.

From the middle of the 1970s when Davis' *From the Dark Tower* appeared to the end of the decade when Robert Hemenway's *Zora Neale Hurston: A Literary Biography* (1977) went into a second printing, I waited for "facts" to surface about Nella Larsen. Adelaide Cromwell Hill, in an introduction to the 1971 Collier Books reprint of *Quicksand*, had already presented detailed information about some aspects of Larsen's life: her training as a nurse, her marriage, her fellowships and awards. Hill, a sociologist, sketched her subject's life and work from available primary documents and personal interviews, but acknowledged, "Nella Larsen's career has a mysterious quality." Hoyt Fuller had included only the barest essentials of Larsen's public record in his introduction to *Passing* in the same Collier African/American Library series of reprints, perhaps because, unlike Hill, he concentrated on the novel. Fuller nonetheless concluded that "Nella Larsen is virtually unknown and certainly rarely read."[2] By the end of the 1970s, however, his conclusion no longer applied, even though no one had permeated the mystery surrounding Larsen's career.

Even more than Jean Toomer, who renounced membership in a specifi-

---

1. Arthur P. Davis, *From the Dark Tower: Afro-American Writers, 1900–1960* (Washington, D.C., 1974), 98.

2. Adelaide Cromwell Hill, Introduction to *Quicksand*, by Nella Larsen (1928; rpr. New York, 1971), 15; Hoyt Fuller, Introduction to *Passing*, by Nella Larsen (1929; rpr. New York, 1971), 13.

cally black race for a place in a new racial order, Larsen became in the decades following the Harlem Renaissance a figure in the shadows. Her life and her novels were associated with "the tragic mulatto passing for white," a rubric that Sterling Brown used as an organizing category for discussing a group of novels in his 1937 study *The Negro in American Fiction*, but that subsequently became the primary way of approaching Larsen and her work in the criticism of Hugh M. Gloster (*Negro Voices in American Fiction*, 1948), Benjamin E. Mays (*The Negro's God as Reflected in His Literature*, 1949), and Robert Bone (*The Negro Novel in America*, 1958). Little more could be clearly ascertained about her vital statistics, the rest of her canon, her literary intentions, or her racial allegiance.

In the 1960s, Afrocentric literary studies, growing out of the civil rights struggle and the attendant Black Arts and Black Aesthetics movements, explored African-American cultural traditions with a renewed awareness of the importance of heritage. As the modern antecedent of the Black Arts movement, the Harlem Renaissance attracted much attention. Artists and thinkers of the 1920s and 1930s were investigated not simply because of their individual achievements, but because of their contributions to African-American culture and to a black cultural consciousness. W. E. B. Du Bois, James Weldon Johnson, Alain Locke, and Marcus Garvey, all from diverse political and philosophical positions, were linked with Toomer, Cullen, Hughes, Hurston, and Aaron Douglas in studies of the meaning and implications of the New Negro awakening. Lesser known figures, such as Thurman, Gwendolyn Bennett, Bruce Nugent, or Larsen, were not forgotten.

At the beginning of the 1970s and of the 1980s, two historians brought the world of the Harlem Renaissance and its major and minor actors to life. Nathan Irvin Huggins' *Harlem Renaissance* (1971) treated Larsen with a fresh focus on her exploration of the dilemma of the "cultured-primitive" and discovered in her rejection of "genteel formula" a "sharp dichotomy of realist and romantic." Although devoting less attention to Larsen than Huggins had a decade before, David Levering Lewis in *When Harlem Was in Vogue* (1981) also placed her within the activities of the Renaissance, but concluded that she remained "a figure of some mystery, luminous, unconventional, and in the end, perhaps one of those who found the vagaries of a white identity preferable to the pain of Africa."[3]

Discussions of Larsen invariably included some mention of the lack of

---

3. Nathan Irvin Huggins, *Harlem Renaissance* (New York, 1971), 157–61; David Levering Lewis, *When Harlem Was in Vogue* (New York, 1981), 231.

information about her life and career. George Kent, for instance, believed that "valuable light on the Renaissance may be shed by a more critical description of her intentions." Mary Helen Washington, adding the concerns of women's studies and feminist criticism, called Larsen the "Mystery Woman of the Harlem Renaissance" and asked why she did not leave "the greater legacy of the mature model, the perceptions of a woman who confronts the pain, alienation, isolation, and grapples with these conundrums until new insight has been forged from the struggle? Why didn't she continue to write after 1929?"[4]

By the time Washington articulated her questions in 1980, she and others were already engaged in a dialogue about the embedded feminist subjects of Nella Larsen's fiction, as well as about Larsen's own gendered meaning. Hortense Thornton had initiated the dialogue in 1973 with an early feminist treatment, "Sexism as Quagmire: Nella Larsen's *Quicksand*."[5] That dialogue, centered in gender identity, female achievement, sexual repression, and racial marginality, rekindled my interest in answering the basic questions posed by Arthur Davis and the more perplexing ones framed by Washington. For me, Larsen was transformed from the historical author of period pieces in the "passing" genre to a modern writer of complex, women-centered fiction.

For the next five years, I traced Nella Larsen through a quagmire of written records and oral testimonies that equaled the dramatic imagery in her first novel, *Quicksand*. Through city directories and telephone books in New York and Chicago, from departments of vital statistics in Illinois, New Jersey, New York, and Tennessee, out of letters, postcards, and photographs in research libraries, from school transcripts, employment records, fellowship and award applications, passport documents and census records, through old friends and older neighborhoods, over hundreds of miles, correspondence, and conversations, I tracked an elusive Nella Larsen.

In Chicago, files for Illinois authors at the Chicago Historical Society and the Newberry Library contained no record of her and no suggestion of her being a native of the state. In New York, the John Simon Guggenheim Memorial Foundation, though retaining her 1929 fellowship application and

4. George Kent, *Blackness and the Adventure of Western Culture* (Chicago, 1972), 29–30; Mary Helen Washington, "Nella Larsen: Mystery Woman of the Harlem Renaissance," *Ms.*, IX (December, 1980), 50.

5. Hortense Thornton, "Sexism as Quagmire: Nella Larsen's *Quicksand*," *CLA Journal*, XVI (March, 1973), 285–301.

her correspondence with Henry Allen Moe, secretary of the foundation during Larsen's tenure as a fellow, could not locate her for its annual updates on fellows after the late 1930s and had no record of her death. The Alfred A. Knopf publishing company no longer had records or copyrights for her, and her editor there, Harry Block, had moved to Mexico, where he had died some time ago. The Alfred A. and Blanche Knopf Collection at the University of Texas at Austin had in the Knopf publicity files only the standard author's information sheet that, in 1926, Larsen had filled incompletely in favor of a written statement that later appeared almost in full on the dust jacket of *Quicksand*.[6] These initial searches for materials in repositories outside of the James Weldon Johnson and the Carl Van Vechten collections at Yale University and the New York Public Library yielded little more than a few sketchy leads. But they confirmed Nella Larsen's construction of her gendered and racial self during a period when power relations within society did not generally allow for female or black self-construction.

Ironically, during that same period, the historical Nella Larsen attained renewed visibility as a woman novelist of consequence. African-American historians, novelists, and critics, such as Lewis, Alice Walker, and Cheryl Wall, all made references to Larsen, and in 1986, Deborah McDowell edited *Quicksand* and *Passing* for Rutgers University's American Women Writers Series. By the end of the 1980s, Hazel Carby had situated a reading of *Quicksand* as the conclusion of *Reconstructing Womanhood: The Emergence of the Afro-American Woman Novelist* (1987) and alerted a new generation of critics to Larsen's place in literary history. Not surprisingly, then, the January, 1990, issue of *PMLA* presented Ann E. Hostetler's "Aesthetics of Race and Gender in Nella Larsen's *Quicksand*" in the first special issue on African-American writing by that prominent journal. But the major biographical questions about Larsen's life remained unanswered; moreover, numerous misconceptions had become so entrenched that even careful scholars reinscribed them. In relying on published sources, one editor so questioned my correction of Larsen's dates of birth and death that she sent

6. David T. Thackery, Newberry Library, to Thadious Davis, September 25, 1984; Author's search of the catalogued holdings of the Newberry Library and the Chicago Historical Society, October 15 and 16, 1984, and June, 1985; Stephen L. Schlesinger, John Simon Guggenheim Memorial Foundation, to Thadious M. Davis, May 28, 1982, and June 16, 1982; Ashbel Green, Alfred A. Knopf, Inc., to Thadious M. Davis, November 5, 1981; William A. Knoshland, Alfred A. Knopf, Inc., to Thadious M. Davis, June 24, 1982, and March 15, 1988; John P. Chalmers, Harry Ransom Humanities Research Center, University of Texas Libraries, Austin, to Thadious M. Davis, June 29, 1982. All in possession of Thadious M. Davis.

an essay I had written out to a scholar for verification of Larsen's vital statistics.

Two factors complicate the search for information about Nella Larsen. First, she left no specific identification of her extended family that might be traced, and her single sibling, now dead, denied knowledge of her existence. Elmer Imes, the husband Larsen divorced in 1933, died in 1941, and the couple had no children. Second, she intentionally broke off communication in the 1930s with friends who knew her as a writer, and afterward she chose to spend much of the remainder of her life reclusively. By 1935, Harlem's surviving literati had lost all track of the promising novelist. Her colleagues and acquaintances after 1940 knew her almost exclusively as a nurse who revealed little of her private life or past experiences.

I discovered eventually that Nella Larsen herself was responsible for the mystery surrounding her life and career. She had created the limits of her known biography, just as she had later positioned the veil shrouding it from view. "Nella Larsen is a mulatto, the daughter of a Danish lady and a Negro from the Virgin Islands, formerly the Danish West Indies," she wrote for her 1926 author's publicity statement.[7] In completing that form for the Knopf biographic files, she had attached her own meaning to the directive: "Put down only such facts as you wish used in our publicity. If you prefer to write a letter giving the necessary data in narrative form, please do so, ignoring this questionnaire." Indeed, she chose to write seven paragraphs about her familial background, her formal education, and her employment history, which became the source of publicity statements about her life. They appeared on the dust jackets of her two novels, in contemporary reviews of her fiction, and subsequently in the texts of literary history and criticism that treated her writing career.

Perhaps the greatest tension in her life was between truth and meaning, or the transformation of truth into its signifiers and significations. I discovered, too, that little of what Larsen had written for Knopf was true in the strictest sense of her lived experiences, but that all of it was an accurate reflection of the felt meaning she accorded her own life. Her inventiveness revealed itself most fully in her creation of "Nella Larsen, novelist." Although it eventually manifested itself in the writing of fiction, her will to create began with her own self and personality.

---

7. Nella Larsen Imes, Author's statement for Alfred A. Knopf, Inc., November 24, 1926, in Alfred A. and Blanche Knopf Collection, Harry Ransom Humanities Research Center, University of Texas Libraries.

This book is an attempt to remove the aura of mystery and misconception from Nella Larsen's life and career without collapsing a complex existence into a single, emblematic script of race and gender. I seek to understand how a particular woman of color from a relatively obscure background, and with little formal education, had been able to transcend, however briefly, the barriers of race, gender, and class in order to pursue her own dream and become a writer—an award-winning novelist and a Guggenheim fellow. This is an attempt to read some patterns of meaning in her self-fashioning and silenced dream.

In exploring Larsen's development as an artist who was both female and African-American, I discuss culturally and racially specific phenomena that affected her creations and expressions: Chicago at the turn of the century; Harlem in the 1920s; work options for African-American women; class and color consciousness among African Americans; gender constraints in social institutions. These systemic topics relate to Larsen's life as inextricably interconnected with the external environment, cultural contexts, and social circumstances in which she and other "invisible" African Americans functioned during the first decades of the twentieth century. In the absence of abundant direct testimony, they serve as referential touchstones, reminders that if relatively invisible subjects are to become visible at all, their lives must be extrapolated from the social constructions and contextualities within which such individuals functioned. Larsen's internal psychological world was directly influenced by the broader exterior culture, its beliefs, attitudes, values, and prejudices, and by the social dynamics transforming and transformed by individual human agency.

While this exploration is based upon the limited materials and fragmentary testimonies left by Larsen herself, her husband, friends, acquaintances, and contemporaries, as well as upon some documents and records from public and private repositories, it proceeds from the belief that not all of the pressing questions about the "real *Nella Larsen*" within either material culture or historical moment can be answered definitively because *Nella Larsen* was not only an invented name, a public and private pseudonym, but also a self-created persona, willed and perpetuated from adolescence through old age by a woman who, for a short time at least, attained the meaning of her own daring self-invention.

Acknowledgments

This book has been a slow, painful learning process sustained by good colleagues and better friends who never ceased to be interested and responsive. During the many years of research and writing, some of its generous supporters have died; I particularly regret being unable to show Bruce Nugent, Darwin T. Turner, and Ethel Ray Nance a finished copy. I am especially indebted to my former colleagues at the University of North Carolina, Chapel Hill, Blyden Jackson, Louis D. Rubin, Jr., and Margaret Ann O'Connor, for reading early versions of the manuscript, and to Raymond Nelson, University of Virginia, for charitably and astutely reading a first draft. Virginia Whatley Smith, University of Alabama at Birmingham, and Mary Hughes Brookhart, North Carolina Central University, read chapters in progress. To them all, I owe a major debt of gratitude.

Several research assistants over the years located materials, checked sources, and kept me working: Paula Dale, Dorothy Wylie, Judith Brazinsky, and Steve Case (University of North Carolina); John D. Turner, Tracy D. Sharpley, Eleanor Alexander, Jennifer Campbell, and Yuko Matsukawa (Brown University). Small research grants from the National Endowment of the Humanities Summer Stipend Program, the University of North Carolina Faculty Development Fund, and the Newberry Library Short-term Fellowship-In-Residence enabled me to travel to collections and hire graduate assistants. Colleagues across the country shared information and gave me leads as well as encouragement: Mary Helen Washington, Bruce Kellner, David Levering Lewis, Nellie McKay, James Spady, John Hope Franklin,

Samuel W. Allen, Youra Qualls, Sue Houchins, Frankie Lea Houchins, Adelaide Cromwell Gulliver, Carla Peterson, Richard Long, Arthur P. Davis, Alonzo N. Smith, Eleanor Tignor, Hortense E. Thornton, Joe Weixlmann, Henry Louis Gates, Jr., Fahamisha Shariat (Patricia Brown), Marilyn Richardson, Peter B. Howard, G. James Fleming, Julian Mason, Townsend Ludington, Richard Robbins, Leatrice Taylor McKissack, Axel Hansen, Pearl Creswell and the late Isaiah Creswell, Edith Work, Rev. Jerome Wright, Charlie Mae Singleton, Minerva Johnson Hawkins, Nelson Fuson, Carole Martindale, Jean Blackwell Hutson, Helen Armstead Johnson, Erika Smilowitz, James Hatch, DeWitt Dykes, Eric Garber, Richard Newman, Mark J. Madigan, Barton St. Armand, Gerda Lerner and the participants in the Wingspread Conference on women's biography and autobiography, and more. Erma J. Smith, Johnea Kelly, and Patricia E. Sloan generously pointed out information about nursing and nurses's organizations; Alice Carper and Carolyn Lane graciously shared their experiences as Nella Larsen's nursing colleagues/friends and their memorabilia from her last years.

I owe an immeasurable debt to librarians, archivists, and curators: David Thackery, Tread Merrill, and the staff of the Newberry Library in Chicago; to Betty Kaplan Gubert, Diana Lachatanere, and the Schomburg Center for Research in Black Culture; to Genna Rae McNeil and Richard Newman formerly of the New York Public Library, and to the staff of the Astor, Lenox and Tilden Foundations, New York Public Library; to Patricia Willis, and the Beinecke Rare Book and Manuscript Library, Yale University, and David Schoonover, former Beinecke American Curator; to Archie Motley and Linda Evans at the Chicago Historical Society; to Linda Harvey, Hollis Burke Frissell Library, Tuskegee University; to the staffs of the Manuscript Division of the Library of Congress and of the National Archives; to Ann Allen Shockley, Beth Howse, Leslie M. Collins, and Marian Roberts, Fisk University Library; to John P. Chalmers, Special Collections of the University of Texas at Austin Library; to Esme E. Bhan, Moorland-Spingarn Research Center, Howard University; to Stephen L. Schlesinger, John Simon Guggenheim Memorial Foundation; and to Caroline Mann, Health Sciences Library, University of North Carolina, Chapel Hill, and especially to the librarians and staffs of Wilson and Davis Libraries, University of North Carolina, Chapel Hill.

I would also like to thank Julie Schorfheide, Louisiana State University Press, for her expert attention to details in copy editing and guiding the manuscript through production; Beverly Jarrett, University of Missouri Press, for initially supporting the manuscript at Louisiana State University

Press; James Olney and the LSU Press readers for their attention to a long manuscript; Robert Hemenway and Arnold Rampersad for the models of their scholarship and for sharing information about the writing of biography; and, in particular, Nell Irvin Painter and Leslie Catherine Sanders for reading, advising, and believing when my faith in the project faltered. Without their knowledge and personal kindness, I would have been unable to continue.

My sister Claudia Davis Webster in New Orleans, the Long family in North Carolina, Ellen and Morris Saks in New York, Bernadette and Anthony Chachere in California, JoAnn White and Monte Lloyd in Chicago, and Janie R. King in Nashville were all especially nurturing and supportive during my research trips. To them, to my students, and to everyone who believed that the manuscript would come to fruition and that Nella Larsen was worth the effort, I am sincerely forever grateful.

Abbreviations

CCC   Countee Cullen Collection, Amistad Research Center, Tulane University

CVV   Carl Van Vechten Personal Collection, New York Public Library

HFR   Records of the William E. Harmon Foundation, Library of Congress

JWJ   James Weldon Johnson Collection, Yale Collection of American Literature, Beinecke Rare Book and Manuscript Library, Yale University

         Note: Letters from Nella Larsen to Carl Van Vechten written before June 2, 1927, are cited as "Nella Imes to Carl Van Vechten"; letters written after that date are cited as "Nella Larsen Imes to Carl Van Vechten." However, all of the Imes–Van Vechten correspondence is filed under "Imes, Elmer S. and Nella (Larsen), Letters to CVV." Larsen's letters to Dorothy Peterson are all filed under "Larsen" and are therefore cited as "Nella Larsen to Dorothy Peterson." These letters can be found in the Dorothy Peterson Papers, Folder 27.

SCF   Schomburg Clipping File, Schomburg Center for Research in Black Culture, New York Public Library

WP   Booker T. Washington Papers, Library of Congress

WW, NAACP   Walter White Papers, NAACP Collection, Library of Congress

NELLA LARSEN
Novelist of the Harlem Renaissance

INTRODUCTION

The Mystery of Nella Larsen

ON MARCH 30, 1964, Nella Larsen Imes was found dead in her Manhattan apartment. The medical examiner determined the cause of death as being "acute congestive heart failure due to hypertensive and arteriosclerotic cardiovascular disease." Lamenting the lonely, unattended death, several acquaintances feared that she may have died as much as a week before the discovery. In identifying the body, a former co-worker informed the coroner's office that Mrs. Imes was a widow and a nurse who had lived alone on lower Second Avenue for twenty years.[1] Buried in the official report is the link between Nella Larsen Imes and Nella Larsen, novelist of the Harlem Renaissance.

Beginning in the 1940s, communication had been sparse from the Nella Larsen who had written *Quicksand* (1928) and *Passing* (1929). With a cryptic message delivered in reversed meaning, "I arrive at once," she disappeared from the world of prominent African-American New Yorkers.[2] Many believed that after writing about crossing the color line, she had opted to do so herself. Some observers of the literary scene in Harlem incorrectly placed her in Brooklyn, passing for white. Others assumed she had moved to a fast track in Bohemian Greenwich Village. In time she began to fade

1. Certificate of Death no. 156 64 107204, in Bureau of Vital Statistics, New York City Department of Health; Alice L. Carper and Carolyn Lane, interview with author, May 5, 1985.
2. Andrew G. Meyer to Thadious M. Davis, January 17, April 14, 1982, both in possession of Thadious M. Davis.

from memory, even of those who had associated with her at the height of her popularity. "I could not have known her really well as the name . . . brings up no picture!"[3] "For some reason I associate her with James Weldon Johnson and in particular with Mrs Johnson. . . . Perhaps they were both ladies of similar complexion and milieu."[4] Two of Larsen's friends from the early 1930s did not recognize that they had fused their memory of her with that of the actress Fredi Washington: "Nella had aquamarine eyes with yellow flecks; her eyes were most striking under heavy black brows and lashes."[5] By the 1960s, few witnesses to the Harlem Renaissance remembered with clarity the enigmatic woman, but few of them had forgotten that Nella Larsen was a novelist. Needed to answer the question of what happened to the writer are not jogs to sharpen memory, but keys to re-vision. *Re-vision* is Adrienne Rich's term for "the act of looking back, of seeing with fresh eyes, of entering an old text from a new critical direction."[6]

In the 1920s Nella Larsen had firmly anchored her identity in writing. She molded herself into a novelist at the historic moment when African Americans were poised for unprecedented literary accomplishment. From the beginning of her transformation from librarian into writer, she ranked novels at the highest level of creativity and positioned herself for achievement in that genre. The vocation became her primary means of individuation, and it provided a measure of stability to her often transformed identity. Her efforts toward writing and completing novels rather than short stories were comparable to refining her identity and reclaiming it from the dictates of others.

At the start of her career she had worked on a story of about six thousand words that she thought of sending to *Harper's,* but on reconsideration she remarked: "Now that it's done I am inclined to believe that I've squandered an idea that would have made a novel." In 1929 when both *Forum* and *Liberty* magazines asked her to submit short stories, her response was, "I can't write short stories."[7] After the appearance of *Quicksand* in 1928, "New Negro novelist" became the major aspect of her public identity and the primary axis of her self-meaning. Underlining the appositive *novelist* in

3. Zelma Corning Brandt to Thadious M. Davis, n.d. [postmarked December 30, 1983], *ibid.*

4. John Becker to Thadious M. Davis, July 14, 1982, *ibid.*

5. Andrew G. and Kay Meyer, interview with author, May 25, 1982.

6. Adrienne Rich, "When We Dead Awaken: Writing as Re-Vision," in *On Lies, Secrets, and Silence: Selected Prose, 1966–1978,* by Adrienne Rich (New York, 1979), 35.

7. Nella Larsen Imes to Carl Van Vechten, n.d. [postmarked June 29, 1927], in JWJ; Nella Larsen Imes to Carl Van Vechten, Saturday, July 28 [postmarked July 31, 1929], *ibid.*

newsclippings noting her attendance at social functions and forwarding the notices to friends, she imprinted her new identity upon her social world.[8] Although Larsen somewhat reluctantly accepted sharing the spotlight with Jessie Fauset as the only women novelists among the New Negroes of the 1920s, she recognized that she was without a female peer in the modernity and complexity of her fictional vision. Her autonomy in literary texts was a reflection of her capacity for survival.

Larsen flowered as an artist of the urban New York world and thrived on the social activity accompanying a literary career. In these milieux she embellished a self that had been severely diminished in childhood. "Literature is both the fruit and the nourishment of the imagination," Carolyn Heilbrun has said. "We must look to it not only for the articulation of female despair and constriction, but also for the proclamation of the possibilities of life."[9] Larsen imagined fresh possibilities for her own life and new mythologies of self in her novels. Her representations were of women seeking full expression of their racial, social, and sexual identities. The texts she created replicated the searches in her private and public interactions, but they served as well, by means of Larsen's self-referentiality, to demystify the urban, middle-class black woman.

In living out her own story, Larsen is suggestive of other women writers. Sandra Gilbert has pointed to the female's acts of self-definition in her writing and to "the most intimate conflicts of the self with the self, consciously inadmissible, are objectified in exotic psychodramas . . . the self splitting, doubling, mythologizing itself until it hardly seems any longer to have an existence within itself. . . . [W]e see the woman writer herself enacting the psychodrama in life as she had in art, becoming . . . the 'myth of herself.'"[10] Gilbert's examples might well include women of color: Angelina Grimké, Zora Neale Hurston, and Nella Larsen. Evolving throughout her life, Larsen's myth of herself took a definitive shape in her middle years.

Change and transformation demark Larsen's existence. She lived through the most eventful decades of the twentieth century, eventful for all of the American population but especially so for ethnic and racial minorities and for women.

Born Nellie Walker on April 13, 1891, in Chicago, she had for much of

8. See, for example, Nella Larsen to Dorothy Peterson, Tuesday 2nd [August, 1927], *ibid.*

9. Carolyn Heilbrun, *Reinventing Womanhood* (New York, 1979), 34.

10. Sandra Gilbert, "A Fine, White, Flying Myth: The Life/Work of Sylvia Plath," in *Shakespeare's Sisters: Feminist Essays on Women Poets,* ed. Sandra Gilbert and Susan Gubar (Bloomington, 1979), 249–50.

her life appropriated 1893, the year of the Columbian Exposition, popularly known as the Chicago World's Fair, as the year of her birth. She came of age in a city propelling itself into an unparalleled acceptance of urban modernity as progress. Her childhood was imprinted with modern buildings and technological inventions, public conveyances and paved thoroughfares. She bore the imprint, as well, of transformations of identity, possible given the fluidity of western and immigrant lives in an expanding city.

As Nellie Walker, Nellye Larson, Nellie Larsen, and as Nella Larsen, she witnessed immigrant communities striving for Americanization and amalgamation, for success and material comfort. A witness from behind the veil of color, she learned early in life that the limitations sometimes constricting the American dream for immigrants were exacerbated by race and gender. Her skin, the color of light "maple syrup,"[11] prevented her from assimilating into Chicago's Scandinavian community in which she lived as a child; her gender bound her to narrower choices for self-reliant mobility than her brown-skinned male counterparts. Her self-perception was shaped early by the reflection she saw in the eyes of others, particularly her parents. Denied access to the social and economic opportunities available to her white, immigrant relatives, she entered the world of African Americans, where she functioned without the resources and protection of family.

The paternal legacy that she carried out of Chicago was the emotional baggage of familial rejection and color consciousness, and her maternal legacy was emotional ambivalence toward women and African Americans. Her pain and unhappiness can be calculated in her profound dis-ease with African Americans and race and in her restless moves from city to city, from occupation to occupation, and in her persistent competition with other women. Her determination and will can be read in her indefatigable efforts to resist marginality and to create a coherent narrative of her life.

An unevenly textured continuity figures in her external development from nurse to housewife to librarian to novelist. Each phase, delimited by work, mirrors a shifting definition of self, but one constant in its referential urban space as the landscape for an enabling discourse of female identity. With little appreciation for life outside of cities and no nostalgia for the past, she encountered the South too late in her formative years and too early in her middle years to be impressed by its folklore or rural legacies. Her arrival in the New York of the 1910s anchored a fascination with urban existence emanating from her girlhood. While race and gender were the

11. Mary Rennels, New York *Telegram*, April 13, 1929, in SCF.

social constructions negatively affecting her youth, they recombined in New York to inspire an internal drive toward agency, visibility, and voice that went beyond mere survival. Her discovery of writing in the 1920s stabilized her adulthood—at least as far as any stabilization was possible for such a person at such a time—by giving shape and substance to a continuous authorial persona.

Sensitized to class position by her Chicago childhood, she found an emerging middle class of African Americans in the Bronx and Brooklyn, on Staten Island and Manhattan. Termed the "black bourgeoisie" by E. Franklin Frazier, this class differentiated itself from the generally poor, early twentieth-century African-American community by engaging in forms of conspicuous consumption and entertainment.[12] In order to compensate for exclusion from the dominant white population, the black bourgeoisie used behavioral codes and color snobbery to establish class distinction. White ancestry and Caucasian features became less crucial in determining membership in the social elite; the more important criteria for inclusion centered on occupation and income. Larsen encountered the black bourgeoisie in New York during a time of transition, when the criterion for inclusion was shifting away from physical appearance. Family background and color consciousness still pervaded much of the thinking about class position, but money, education, and professional status mattered as well.

Larsen sought access to this middle-class African-American world as an alternative to a dreary existence as a working-class female. Married in 1919 to a research physicist, Dr. Elmer Samuel Imes, she presented herself as the daughter of an interracial couple and as having been raised in an all-white Danish family. She disclosed little, however, about her past within a familial circle, and begged off identifying her relatives, suggesting that race separated her from them. Her self-representation was determined by an effort to retain a certain glamour about her unusual background.

In labeling herself a mulatto, she appropriated language less prevalent among African Americans but popular among West Indians, who used the term to distinguish themselves from the black masses and to evoke a class officially situated between whites and blacks in their native lands. Larsen projected both Danish and West Indian origins as a mark of uniqueness, even though she neither displayed an empathy with West Indians living in New York nor identified specific connections with West Indian relatives.

12. E. Franklin Frazier, *Black Bourgeoisie: The Rise of a New Middle Class* (New York, 1957), 198.

One Virgin Islander recalled, "She never attended our gatherings. We didn't know her family."[13] For Larsen, however, foreign markers of identity were crucial to her emancipatory strategy.

At the same time, Larsen's purported foreign origins deprived her of specificity and status among bourgeois African Americans who valued family background as a mainstay of identity. She avoided delineating family connections and could not, given the active network of the African-American elite, fabricate them. Well aware of what she left out of her public biography, she guarded her privacy. The secrets were willful but not negative, because she recognized that in concealing parts of her factual autobiography she sheltered her fragile subjective life. "To have no capacity for secrecy is to be out of control of how others see one; it leaves one open to coercion," Sissela Bok has said in demonstrating that "power comes through controlling the flow of information" about oneself or others and that secrecy is not by nature discreditable and negative.[14]

In blocking information about herself, Larsen engaged in various strategies to conceal and disguise not only her past but also her attitudes and emotions about that past. She attempted to protect both her personal and her psychological space. The dual territoriality of her self-defense through concealment caused her to establish an aura of mystery as a boundary around herself. Yet secrecy is a conflicted and ambivalent experience that has the potential to turn in against itself.[15] For Larsen, secrecy manifested in mystery as a boundary of self resulted in an isolation from that which she hoped to achieve in perpetrating her defensive concealments.

Throughout the 1920s she attempted to position herself socially by creating new versions of her life story, by creating discontinuous narratives that truncated portions of her life, excised and embellished others. Even though her sartorial style was rather flamboyant, her insistence on visibility was more muted than strident. In her various life stories, she manifested a desire for access to power connected to wealth, to middle-class comfort, to public life, to male privilege, to white people, and to artistic communities. Yet she interwove the more complicated results of such desire for a woman of color: the ravages of racism; the penalties extracted by patriarchy; the hypocrisies of the elite; the false promises of the American dream; and the female's ultimate breakdown.

13. G. James Fleming, telephone interview with author, October 16, 1983.

14. Sissela Bok, *Secrets: On the Ethics of Concealment and Revelation* (New York, 1982), 19–20.

15. *Ibid.*, 18.

By turns an iconoclast and a conventional lady, Larsen could be both self-assertive and self-effacing with those closest to her, especially her husband. In the early 1920s, she vacillated between desiring his prominence and resenting it, along with that of his religious family, whom she alternately satirized or conformed to. Although Larsen would not allow herself to be relegated to anonymity in social or familial gatherings, her lack of family credentials in a class-conscious circle of African Americans made her insecure about her position. Initially through her connection with Imes, she met all the right people in the literary and social community of upper-class African Americans. After she became a celebrity, she attended fashionable parties, openings, teas, and cabarets, yet she remained primarily an observer, highly visible, but rarely the center of attention. She was, according to one intimate, "very retiring. Imes's personality overshadowed hers. He was very outgoing." [16] More than once, she was called "aloof" or "standoffish" by those unable to calibrate her discomfort or its causes because of her sophisticated appearance. She moved with greater assurance outside the sphere dominated by Imes and his family, and gradually she gravitated toward the white world downtown. Her ambivalence toward the Imes name and insecurity around the family resulted in mood swings that made her seem unpredictable. Her emotions of desire and repulsion, however, followed an internal logic that exerted pressure on her behavior; the pressure, which Patricia Greenspan has labeled "the special motivational force of emotions," was fueled by rivalry with Imes and his family for acknowledgment of personal value.[17] Unwilling to define herself solely in terms of her husband's achievements and familial connections, she struggled to assert her own value, though she mistakenly calculated her value in the very terms, achievements and connections, that she renounced in Imes and others from his class.

Larsen moved in social circles with African Americans whose forebears had been lieutenant governors during Reconstruction (Jean Toomer, for instance), or diplomats and foreign consuls after the turn of the century (Dorothy Peterson), or who themselves were physicians (Rudolph Fisher, Alonzo DeG. Smith), scientists (Elmer Imes, St. Elmo Brady), Phi Beta Kappas (Jessie Fauset). She was enthralled by this African-American middle class that emerged out of a second generation of emancipated men and women or from several generations of free people of color; people who,

16. Richard Bruce Nugent, interview with author, April 30, 1983.

17. Patricia Greenspan, "A Case of Mixed Feelings: Ambivalence and the Logic of Emotion," in *Explaining Emotions*, ed. Amelie Oksenberg Rorty (Berkeley, 1980), 224.

alienated from the soil and its connotations with slavery, rose through church-affiliated and missionary schools and white educational institutions into the urban marketplace. The cities, New York, Philadelphia, Chicago, and Washington in particular, provided this generation with mobility and opportunity to achieve the goals set forth in the Fisk University catalogue: "preparation for high positions and large responsibilities."[18] Highly self-conscious, Larsen sought psychological refuge in the world of the black bourgeoisie, but she vacillated in her attitudes toward that very class.

The social configurations she mediated were egalitarian neither in class prescriptions nor in gender expectations. The fictions inscribed within her milieu made few allowances for a female's achievement outside her familial duties. Although ambivalent toward both race and gender, Larsen understood the dynamics of racism and sexism and fought against personal vulnerability to either. The odds, of course, were against her. In a field dominated by men, she was a woman who had the courage and the conviction not only to pursue her writing but to bring attention to it as well. Because she refused to remain silent about her recognition as a writer, she was painted as an aggravation and trivialized for boasting of her invitations to parties on Park Avenue, a sign of her acceptance by the white literati downtown. One member of her social group revealed a prevalent misogyny in referring to "painful Nella Imes. . . . [S]he thinks she is so much hell—I could have strangled her."[19]

In writing, Larsen discovered a female identity ostensibly free of race, though ultimately entrapped by it. The concealed self was layered in levels of autobiography that contained the facts of her private life and in levels of imaginative biography that revisioned her literal life in the struggles of her fictional characters. Trapped by the illusion that a stylish existence should not show signs of labor, she struggled privately with her craft and with overcoming what Sandra Gilbert and Susan Gubar have described as the female's "anxiety of authorship."[20]

During the mid-1920s, Larsen confirmed her growing interest in writing as a profession and in perfecting her new craft. In January and April, 1926, she published two short stories in *Young's Magazine.* "The Wrong Man"

18. *Catalogue of the Officers and Students of Fisk University, Nashville, Tennessee, 1907–1908* (Nashville, 1908), 7.

19. Harold Jackman to Countee Cullen, February 28, 1930, in CCC.

20. Sandra Gilbert and Susan Gubar, *The Madwoman in the Attic: The Woman Writer and the Nineteenth-Century Literary Imagination* (New Haven, 1979), 59.

and "Freedom" bore the pseudonym Allen Semi—Nella Imes in reverse. Three months after her second story appeared, she revealed that she was writing a novel: "How do these things get about? It is the awful Truth. But, who knows if I'll ever get through with the damned thing. Certainly not I." [21] Her statement became characteristic of her public observations about writing. She was committed to writing, but uncertain about her ability. As a protective measure, she assumed a nonchalant poise entirely characteristic of her milieu: a studied attitude of ennui to combat potential criticism.

While her efforts demonstrated a serious commitment to writing, Larsen would make light of her motives. "Heaven forbid that I should ever be bitten by the desire to write another novel!" she remarked after completing *Quicksand*.[22] Urbanity and sophistication dictated the assumption of ease and bravado in undertaking any task, whether simple or difficult. Shortly after tossing off the remark, she was at work on *Passing*. Because writing was never easy for her, she labored over drafting her fiction. A persistent subtext in Larsen's correspondence is the hard work that she expended in writing. "I *have* been working like a coloured person," she would stress. The refrain had calculated effect: assertion of a felicitous reality and subversion of perceived appearance. In February, 1928, while still enjoying the popularity of her first book, she was also determined to finish her second even if it required "going into retreat," because she had given herself a deadline that was only two months away. Unfortunately, she tended to create unreasonably short deadlines, which, following the success of the first two novels written under the same self-imposed restrictions, ultimately frustrated her. Driven by her ambition to become famous, and quickly, she disciplined herself to produce, but her creative work could not be reduced consistently to schedules. Although she would frequently relinquish social life for her work, she would also deny the implications of her sacrifice: "What I lack is self driving power," she complained just after having announced another of her "retreats."[23]

A mixture of certainty and doubt about her work never disappeared from her private observations about writing. In January, 1931, Larsen reported to Henry Allen Moe, secretary of the John Simon Guggenheim Memorial Foundation: "The work goes fairly well. A little slower than is usual for me.

21. Nella Imes to Carl Van Vechten, Wednesday [postmarked July 1, 1926], in JWJ.
22. Nella Imes to Carl Van Vechten, Monday, Seventh [March, 1927], *ibid.*
23. Nella Larsen Imes to Carl Van Vechten, Saturday [postmarked February 18, 1928], *ibid.*

But—I like it. Of course that means nothing because I really can't tell if it's good or not. But the way I hope and pray that it is is like a physical pain almost. I do so want to be famous." [24] The desire for fame characterizes her earliest comments about writing and attempts to publicize her achievement. The need for recognition fueled her will to create and to take risks in her writing that placed her in opposition to patriarchal prescriptions about appropriate texts for women.

At the same time, the mobility of her chosen class of African Americans combined with the opening of new roles available to women in the 1920s, from flapper to artist, to foster a reckless creativity in re-fashioning herself. She smoked in public, wore silk stockings and short dresses, mocked the religious conservatives and racial uplifters, played bridge, and drove a stylish automobile. More than anything else, she projected a propensity for modernity in an avant-garde attitude toward race, politics, sex, and religion, often ridiculing old-fashioned mores or manners regarding them. Her behavior expressed her resentment of confinement into race without ethnicity, into feminine roles without substance. She rebelled against the dominance of socially prominent others, yet she both sought and rejected social status as a goal and objective.

Her ability to function in this social domain may have affirmed her sense of self, but it also exacted a toll on her self-esteem. An outer mask disguised her anxieties about belonging. Concealing her vulnerability from the "smart set," she allowed few glimpses of a troubled private life. Although loneliness and pain would occasionally pierce her haughty façade, she was, as an old friend tactfully put it, "a good pretender." [25]

A diminutive five feet two inches tall, Nella Larsen was conscious of the value society placed on a female's looks and manners. Vain about her appearance and especially conscious of the premium of light skin among middle-class African Americans, she cultivated a dramatic feminine presence at a time when the novelist of color was expected to be a male. Her speaking voice was "like a muted violin" to which her audience would "have to listen." As one observer noticed, Larsen was "proud of her voice. She laughingly admit[ted] that it [was] acquired." [26] The acquired voice confirmed the existence of a polished woman with a lively intelligence, who understood

24. Nella Larsen Imes to Henry Allen Moe, January 11, 1931, in John Simon Guggenheim Memorial Foundation files, New York.

25. Carolyn Lane, interview with author, May 5, 1985.

26. Rennels, New York Telegram, April 13, 1929.

the necessity of reforming her social self to fit its mimetic world. Believing that inherited identity could be modified by social constructs and individual agency, she punctured the absurdities of life around her. Once when she encountered a pompous Englishman, she found herself tempted to ask, " 'Pardon me but are you the Lord Douglas who slept with Oscar Wilde?' "[27]

Not surprisingly, Larsen exhibited contradictory selves. On the one hand, she craved approval, and on the other she flaunted convention. She preferred being around people (in particular white people) who dismissed the significance of race in social intercourse. In the race-conscious Harlem in which "New Negro" racial pride was a distinguishing characteristic, she appeared to be aberrant, lacking sufficient understanding of the race. She enjoyed either ignoring or shocking the staid "race" people of New York, though she rarely did either publicly.

Just after the publication of *Quicksand*, the Women's Auxiliary of the NAACP planned to honor her at a tea, to which her response was "the good God only knows why"; her delight in the recognition could not be suppressed, yet she added that she "wanted very much the pleasure of refusing." But she could not disguise her delight in the recognition by Harlem's leading social arbiters, and she capitulated. What she sought surreptitiously was an escape from female powerlessness. As Carolyn Heilbrun has observed: "Power is the ability to take one's place in whatever discourse is essential to action and the right to have one's past matter."[28] Larsen's attempts to enter the contemporary discourses on race often backfired, in part because she never fully reconciled herself to the reality of her own past and to the compelling actuality of racial injustice. More positive was her refusal to see her gender or her lack of an official position in a race organization as a prohibition against expression of her ideas.

In 1929 after the appearance of *Passing*, she claimed that "recognition and liberation will come to the negro [sic] only through individual effort." She reiterated a position articulated the previous year when she held that "artistic" people "have a definite chance to help solve the race problem," though she had stressed then that neither of the two manuscripts she had promised Knopf after *Quicksand* would be "of the propaganda type." She associated "propaganda" with the work of the NAACP, and she tried to distance her art from pedantic racial appeals, because "propaganda," she

27. Nella Larsen Imes to Carl Van Vechten, Thursday 12th November, 1930, in JWJ.

28. Nella Larsen Imes to Carl Van Vechten, n.d. [postmarked May 1, 1928], *ibid.*; Carolyn Heilbrun, *Writing a Woman's Life* (New York, 1988), 18.

insisted, was not "the way to accomplish" the uplift of black people. Three years later, she praised George Schuyler's *Black No More* (1931) for its satire of the NAACP and the Garvey Movement, both of which she considered prone to rhetorical excesses in their advocacy of racial uplift.[29]

Larsen created an uproar among the black intelligentsia by allegedly telling a reporter that she did not "mind being shooed up the employes' entrance in hotels, because her Nordic side waits for such a situation; her negro [sic] side understands it." Her comments, negatively construed, quickly became the source of anger among Harlemites, three of whom "registered their protests (one very belligerently and indignantly)" because they understood her "to have stated that it is perfectly all right to send Negroes around to the back door." One of Larsen's friends at the NAACP, Walter White, reprimanded her for having told the reporter that she "didn't believe in propaganda."[30] Although Mary Rennels, the reporter, may have twisted Larsen's actual words to produce a better story, she was probably not too far off in representing Larsen's views as both simplistic and unconventional.

Confronted by the control exerted by conscientious race people, Larsen sought autonomy and power as a means of freeing herself. Her attempt was to speak with authority on matters of race, but her wisdom was not conventional enough for her striving middle-class acquaintances in Harlem, who were most vocal in expressions of racial pride and solidarity. Despite the evidence of her own formative years, one part of Larsen's being insisted on denying suffering caused by racist practices. She refused the passive role expected of her, but the cost of her refusal was great; she was labeled a racial renegade.

Believing that the racial beliefs adhered to by Harlemites were riddled with contradictions, she once asked a white confidant, Carl Van Vechten, whether he had ever noticed "that when Nordics talk against the admission of Negroes to their homes, etc., it is rank prejudice, but when we take the same attitude about white folks it is race loyalty?"[31] In taking a bemused stance toward matters of race, Larsen reflected an ironic vision of life, a willingness to dissent from acceptable racial discourse, and a complicated understanding of the arbitrariness of racial definitions. But in refusing to

29. Rennels, New York *Telegram,* April 13, 1929; Thelma E. Berlack, "New Author Unearthed Right Here in Harlem," New York *Amsterdam News,* May 23, 1928, p. 16; Nella Larsen Imes to Carl Van Vechten, March 3, 1931, in JWJ.

30. Rennels, New York *Telegram,* April 13, 1929, Nella Larsen Imes to Carl Van Vechten, n.d. [postmarked April 15, 1929], in JWJ.

31. Nella Imes to Carl Van Vechten, November 12, 1926, in JWJ.

follow the expected platitudes, she ran the risk of elevating her alliances with whites and emphasizing her difference from African Americans. Her interracial heritage, though ambiguous, was part of her self that she could neither deny nor obscure, not even for position within an elite African-American group after which she patterned her mature, sophisticated self.

Frequently, she presented herself as the object of her own wit. Her favorite description of herself is as a "poor coloured child."[32] The facetious self-description is ironically fitting. From 1925 until her disappearance, Larsen's health was delicate at best. She suffered from debilitating colds, flu, and grippe in winter, referring to the latter as "my old friend." She fared no better in summer when she lost all energy; as she observed in July, 1929, "I haven't been very well. . . . I always feel seedy in the summer." Bouts with pneumonia were not uncommon; in fact, soon after her arrival in Spain for the start of her writing fellowship (September, 1930), she contracted pneumonia, just as she did toward the end of her stay in France (August, 1931). So recurrent were her health problems that her husband considered sending her to California early in March, 1928, when he observed: "Nella has been sick again. She went out to play bridge last Friday night and spent the next three or four days in bed with a new cold—the fourth or fifth since Christmas." Several months later a newspaper account revealed the extent to which poor health had affected her life: "For three years . . . this little woman has had trouble with her health. She no longer goes out to business." At the height of her popularity as a Harlem writer, Larsen was bedridden for two weeks and attended by a local physician, Dr. Vernon Ayer.[33] This particular case of influenza caused her to cancel a talk scheduled for February 8, 1929, at the Harlem branch of the New York Public Library. Not only was the talk her first major speaking engagement, but it was also to occur within days of the announcement of the William E. Harmon Awards for Distinguished Achievement Among Negroes, for which she was a candidate.

Whether her illnesses were caused by a physical condition (by allergies, by a low resistance to infections, by a susceptibility to viruses) or by a psy-

32. See, for example, Nella Larsen Imes to Carl Van Vechten, "Home," n.d. [*ca.* April, 1928], Tuesday [postmarked March 5, 1930], and Sunday [postmarked May 11, 1930], all *ibid.*

33. Nella Larsen Imes to Carl Van Vechten, n.d. [postmarked March 19, 1928], in JWJ; Larsen Imes to Van Vechten, Saturday, July 28 [postmarked July 31, 1929], *ibid.;* Elmer Imes to Carl Van Vechten, n.d. [postmarked March 3, 1928], *ibid.;* Berlack, "New Author Unearthed"; New York *Amsterdam News,* February 26, 1929, p. 4.

chological condition (by stress, by emotional instability, by psychosomatic disorders), they recurred primarily during particularly stressful periods. They were one of the mechanisms she used to cope with her life. Frequent illness became a way of reiterating her own vulnerability as a person who needed care from others and a means of depicting her singular strength as one who routinely triumphed over great debilities. In either case, illness was a significant part of her strategy for survival.

Her representation of herself as a "poor coloured child" involved not only matters of health but relationships with others. Larsen desired friends and family. She rarely articulated the void left in her life by the absence of a supportive family, yet she was unable to put her loss behind her. The unresolved tension with her white mother and sister duplicated itself in her ambivalence toward other women. Seeking approval from male power-brokers as an exceptional female, she saw herself as being in competition with other women for finite rewards. Her friendships with Jessie Fauset, Gladys White (married to Walter White), Grace Nail Johnson (the wife of James Weldon Johnson), and other cultural or social leaders were tinged with envy and uncertainty, and they were relatively short-lived. Although their accomplishments differed, Fauset, White, and Johnson all functioned in highly visible public spaces that elevated Larsen's desire for recognition. Larsen was the most conflicted in her responses to the single and well-educated Fauset, who seemed on the surface to carry off her literary career with ease. But White, successful in hostessing innumerable high-profile social affairs while mothering two children, elicited Larsen's less veiled and most deflating criticism. Childless by choice or circumstance, Larsen was fascinated and repelled by White's obvious pleasure in motherhood. Rather than accepting the achievements of other women as signs that actualizing her own dreams was possible, or instead of reading their success as stemming from needs similar to hers, she responded with envy.[34]

The exception was her friendship with Dorothy Peterson, who epitomized much of what Larsen admired and desired. Peterson was a young, well-educated African-American woman who had spent much of her youth in Puerto Rico, where her father had worked for the American consulate. Fluent in Spanish and French, Peterson taught languages in the Brooklyn

---

34. "Behind the feeling of envy," Luise Eichenbaum and Susie Orbach have identified, "a person who is so deeply conflicted about her own wants and desires, that she is frightened by others' capacity to respond to theirs" (Luise Eichenbaum and Susie Orbach, *Between Women: Love, Envy, and Competition in Women's Friendships* [New York, 1988], 98–99).

public schools, but an inheritance from her grandmother gave her financial independence. Larsen confessed once to Peterson, who was in Europe on one of her frequent vacations abroad, "I do miss you very much and that is remarkable!!/because I'm not in the habit of missing people."[35] Given the great voids in her life, Larsen could not afford to miss people, or, more aptly, she rarely *admitted* to missing anyone. Peterson's outgoing and caring personality made her an unthreatening female friend. Larsen could confide her loneliness and her longings, but she would also fabricate stories and embellish her life to match the glamour she perceived in Peterson's. The friendship, though sometimes difficult, would inspire and sustain Larsen through her rise to prominence and her decline into obscurity.

Neither loneliness nor anger were easy expressions for Nella Larsen. Both emotions displayed a vulnerability she was usually determined to conceal. Yet Larsen had an explosive temper that she controlled in her youth and midlife but expressed more openly, if not always appropriately, as she grew older. She would "fly off," as one of her nursing colleagues remarked, but then just as quickly she would seem to forget about the irritant, return to a smooth, unruffled calm, and be heard humming under her breath.[36] Perhaps her ability to express anger was one healthy sign of her overcoming gender proscriptions in her old age.

Larsen understood well the behavior that was expected of a female in both social and literary spheres. She learned early in the 1920s to manipulate those expectations to her own benefit. Toward her writing she cultivated the appearance of being timid and self-deprecating, but she was adept at confident self-promotion. One historian of the Harlem Renaissance has called her "opportunistic," but surely her efforts on her own behalf may be read more positively than that.[37] She actively sought the support of leading New Yorkers, black and white, for the Harmon Awards in 1928 and 1929: James Weldon Johnson, W. E. B. Du Bois, Van Vechten, Lillian Alexander, Walter White, Blanche Knopf, Muriel Draper. Similarly, she carefully selected her references for her 1929 Guggenheim fellowship application because she knew that the foundation had not yet awarded a grant in creative writing to an African-American woman and she hoped to be the first. She recognized that the endorsement of influential individuals would significantly improve her chances as an African-American female, given the hold

35. Nella Larsen to Dorothy Peterson, Tuesday 19th [July, 1927], in JWJ.
36. Alice L. Carper, interview with author, May 5, 1985.
37. David Levering Lewis, *When Harlem Was in Vogue* (New York, 1981), 31.

that men with conventional notions of importance had over the literary establishment.

Larsen's friendship with Carl Van Vechten, though calculated to impress him and win his approval, revealed her longing for friends and for a defined place in society. At the end of the first three years of their acquaintance, she wrote, "I think you're the grandest friend that I've ever had, and I hope that I will never do anything to merit the withdrawal of your friendship." [38] While her reference was specifically to the support that the popular author and critic had provided for her writing, it also acknowledged the more personal aspects of his mentorship: his gifts of books, his notes of concern about her health, his invitations to social gatherings, his celebrations for her birthdays. A prolific and congenial correspondent, Van Vechten wrote to Larsen for over a decade beginning in 1924 when they met. His urbane letters "cheered" her; his celebrity status and hospitality added to her self-confidence. Particularly when her husband was away during the summers and Dorothy Peterson was abroad, Larsen depended on Van Vechten to avoid being "most beastly lonesome," as she put it. [39] She considered Van Vechten one of her few intimate friends to whom she could reveal the extent of her commitment to writing. Although she ingratiated herself to Van Vechten and was deferential to him and to prominent males involved in the Harlem Renaissance, she did not doubt that her success was the result of her own effort and talent, and she did not sacrifice her personality for their approval.

Larsen's need to write for publication intensified during the early years of the 1930s when her personal life became more troubled and she showed signs of major instability and neuroses. Part of the disorder of her middle life can be attributed to her realization that her chance for great achievement as a novelist had passed, that she was not destined to sustain celebrity status as an author. Writing had become one means of her maintaining her sanity and her balance; with the outlets for it gone, along with the few other resources for normalcy, she became erratic in behavior, vindictive in friendships, and obsessive about money. Her eccentricities were manifested in a fear of new places, an obsession with wearing a hat at all times, a reliance on medication, a delusion about her whiteness, and a fantasy of her youth in a loving family.

Often acting erratically, she nonetheless accomplished more than has

38. Larsen Imes to Van Vechten, Saturday [postmarked February 18, 1928], in JWJ.
39. Larsen Imes to Van Vechten, Saturday, July 28 [postmarked July 31, 1929], ibid.

been assumed, though perhaps not as much as she desired or intended. Larsen persisted in writing for a decade or more after the publication of her two novels and the one story ("Sanctuary," 1930) under her own name. A sensational divorce, physical ailments, a misguided romance, and economic pressures all distanced her from her former life in Harlem and her black and white associates in New York. Her will and persistence in writing throughout this traumatic time evidence the strength of her determination to create. The failure to publish her subsequent texts reiterates the familiar problems of outlet and audience for writers of color, particularly females. This circumstance beyond her control furthered a devastating personal isolation from which she never recovered.

That the once witty, energetic, and enterprising Nella Larsen, a woman gifted with the ability to write intelligent, psychological novels and to thrive on publicity, could spend her last twenty years in silence and social isolation may seem incredible. Yet, in fact, she spent nearly three decades of her life in obscurity, evidently suffering bouts of agoraphobia, and died alone in a studio apartment. In retrospect, it appears Larsen willed that her later existence would duplicate her fiction. She wrote the final script of her life into one of her initial publications, the short story "Freedom" (1926), and into her first novel, *Quicksand;* in both works, the protagonists disappear from their active lives into passive enactments of their own worst nightmares. She followed a process of change and transformation in which she manifested a determination for voice, for agency, and for visibility; that determination rendered her ultimate self-erasure—her act of removal from the known and the familiar—even more drastic than it might have been in another person's life.

If her latter years represent the exclusion of self from society and a division of self into discrete parts, they also are emblematic of the female writer whose disappearance from the struggle for creative voice and gender actualization is symptomatic not of defeat but of fracture. Life for Larsen was lived in counterdistinction to its stated meaning; against the grain of the smooth surface was the turbulent underside that she could not ultimately subdue, not even for the fictional art that gave her identity meaning and gave her hopes, as well as her fears, expression.

When Larsen died the spring of 1964, she had spent over thirty years alienated from her writerly self. Her life and career suggest the duality of talented women who, as Tillie Olsen has demonstrated, have had the "power and need to create, over and beyond reproduction," but who have "remained mute, or have never attained full capacity . . . because of circumstances, inner and outer, which oppose the needs of creation." Neither class privilege nor caste position could protect Larsen from the internal and external circumstances that would impede her art, circumvent her ambitions, fragment her personality, and, ultimately, end her writing. Her narratives, like her public life, would stop abruptly, present no viable solutions, and remain dominated by dissatisfaction. Her subtexts would remain consistent: fantasies of retaliation against her "white" parents, dreams of achieving unlimited success, and nightmares of oblivion in her own racial and gendered future. In 1926, Larsen noticed "the spirit inherent in us [African Americans], the urge, the sweet craving—for happiness and the better knowledge of unfulfillment, and our blindness to the reason."[40] She might well have applied the appraisal to herself. In the psychic split between her individual and group identity (whether that group is defined by gender or race) and in the personality breakdown between her public and private roles, the fiction and the writer herself were lost.

40. Tillie Olsen, *Silences* (New York, 1979), 17; Nella Imes to Carl Van Vechten, Wednesday, eleventh [postmarked August 12, 1926], in CVV.

I

A Woman's Life and Place, 1891 – 1919

I

Beginning in Chicago,
1891–1907

NELLA LARSEN'S FALLING out of place and concomitant seeking of place began in Chicago, where, within an immigrant social context, constricting circles of race and gender ran against the grain of opportunity and assimilation. Detached by color from the potentiality of the "melting pot" and circumscribed by sex to a limited sphere, Larsen began life in a disabling fluidity. The baby girl Nellie Walker, "Colored," entered the world on April 13, 1891. The first child of Mary Hanson Walker and Peter Walker, Nellie was born at home, 2124 Armour Avenue, in Chicago's Second Ward. Her twenty-two-year-old Danish mother gave birth unattended by a physician or a midwife; a local druggist, E. A. Lynn, filled out the statement of birth on May 10, 1891. Lynn failed to list the father's nationality, place of birth, or age, yet he knew that Peter Walker, a cook by occupation, was "Colored," and therefore designated the child "Colored" at birth.[1] Nellie Walker's racial designation, nearly a month after her birth, also rested upon her physical appearance; she was not visibly white.

"Nellie Walker" would become "Nella Larsen," but not before several transformations in name during the first decades of her life. While her name changed, her racial designation remained fixed and the source of the mystery at the center of her childhood in Chicago.

---

1. Return of Live Birth for Nellie Walker, May 10, 1891, in Records of Cook County, Certificate no. 16546, Office of the Cook County Clerk, Chicago. Elijah A. Lynn operated his business at 2506 Wabash Avenue and lived nearby at 2141 State Street (*Chicago City Directory*, 1891 [microfilm], Part 1, Reel 11, in Library of Congress).

A statement from 1926 in the Alfred A. Knopf publishing company's files of its authors reads:

> Nella Larsen is a mulatto, the daughter of a Danish lady and a Negro from the Virgin Islands, formerly the Danish West Indies. When she was two years old her father died and shortly afterward her mother married a man of her own race and nationality.
>
> Her formal education began at the age of eight. She and her half-sister child of the second marriage, attended a small private school, whose pupils were mostly the children of German or Scandinavian parents.[2]

This "official" biography presents the early life of Nella Larsen, who was about to become a published novelist. Or, does it? Nella Larsen submitted the biography. She wrote it herself in the third person and signed it "Nella Larsen (Imes)" on November 24, 1926. This Knopf author's statement, however, is not a personal autobiography but rather the public biography of the life that the author wanted known. It is an emblem of the distance between the Nella Larsen Imes writing in the 1920s and the child Nellie Walker growing up in Chicago during the 1890s.

The biographical statement appears detailed when actually it is sketchy, a mere outline of what Nella Larsen Imes's youth may have been. The few "facts" offered omit specifics. Names, places, and dates are missing. This version of her early life received verification and authentication from being printed on the dust jacket of *Quicksand* in 1928, and thereafter in publicity stories about the author and her work.

The authenticity of Larsen's brief autobiography has rarely been questioned, despite the author's having given contradictory stories about her background and family. In the statement for Knopf, which she knew would be published in whole or in part, she omitted her place of birth. Although she listed Chicago, Illinois, as her birthplace in applications for the Harmon Awards (1928, 1929), for the Guggenheim fellowship (1929), and for United States passports (1930, 1932), and gave Illinois as the state of her birth for her marriage license (1919), Nella Larsen apparently intended the omission for the publicity statement.

2. Nella Larsen Imes, Author's statement for Alfred A. Knopf, Inc., November 24, 1926, in Alfred A. and Blanche Knopf Collection, Harry Ransom Humanities Research Center, University of Texas Libraries, Austin.

At times during the 1920s, she fostered the fiction that she was a native of the Virgin Islands or Danish West Indies not only for whites eager to hear about cultural primitives, but also for blacks curious to learn about an instant celebrity. She delighted in rendering stories of her childhood in the exotic islands. "I went to lunch the other day," she revealed with amusement, "with some people I knew very little (ofays) [white people]. In the course of our talk it developed that they would have been keenly disappointed had they discovered that I was not born in the jungles of the Virgin Isles. So I entertained them with quite a few stories of my childhood in the bush, and my reaction to the tom-tom undertone in jazz. It was a *swell* luncheon."[3] For her frequent associates, Larsen also framed pictures of a childhood in the islands where her father was a Danish sea captain and her mother a black West Indian.[4] She draped her early life in the romantic appeal of the unusual, but the reality of her formative years as the biracial Nellie in Chicago was no less intriguing.

In addition to the certificate of birth, one of the public documentations of Nella Larsen's childhood is her elementary school records from the Zenos Colman School in Chicago. The Colman School was located at Dearborn and West 47th streets in 1900, when Daniel O'Connor served as its principal.[5] It was a public primary in the Chicago Public School System, and is still in existence on the original school grounds at 4655 Dearborn Street. Contrary to Nella Larsen's later claim, the Colman School has no history as a private school, though children of German and Scandinavian parents did in fact attend Colman along with those from other ethnic and racial groups who resided in the school's once multi-ethnic, multi-racial, and largely working-class district, because the Chicago public schools had been legally integrated since 1874. The Colman students came from an area centering on the north-south streets Dearborn, State, Michigan, and Indiana between 43rd and 50th. The school was in the Grand Boulevard section that was

3. Nella Larsen Imes to Carl Van Vechten, Friday, fourteenth [postmarked June 15, 1929], in JWJ. She is partly responsible for the confusion among contemporary critics about her birthplace. Hiroko Sato, "Under the Harlem Shadow: A Study of Jessie Fauset and Nella Larsen," in *The Harlem Renaissance Remembered,* ed. Arna Bontemps (New York, 1972), 82, incorrectly gives Larsen's birthplace as the Virgin Islands, as does Nathan Irvin Huggins, *Harlem Renaissance* (New York, 1971), 157, and David Levering Lewis, *When Harlem Was in Vogue* (New York, 1981), 231.

4. Andrew G. and Kay Meyer, interview with author, May 25, 1982.

5. See entry for Zenos Colman School, *Lakeside Directory of Chicago,* 1900, in Chicago Historical Society, Chicago.

bounded on the south by 51st Street and Hyde Park Boulevard, on the north by Pershing Road and 39th Street, on the east by Grand Boulevard (later South Parkway and now Martin Luther King Drive) and Cottage Grove Avenue, and on the west by Halsted Street. As African Americans gradually moved south from the area around State and 30th streets, the Grand Boulevard section would become home initially to African Americans in the upper-middle class and eventually to many others in the laboring classes.

The girl who entered Colman, however, was not Nellie Walker, but *Nellie Larson,* who was born on April 13, 1891 and lived at 4538 State Street with her father, Peter Larson. Peter Larson's name appears in the space marked "Father." No mother's name appears in the school's records; in fact, the spaces for both the mother's name and the guardian's name are not simply left blank, but are marked with an X.[6] Peter Larson and the school officials did not regard him as merely the guardian of Nellie Larson. The absence of the name of the child's mother suggests that the relationship of Peter Larson to Nellie Larson was more than that of stepfather. His presence, as opposed to the mother's absence, situates him as the child's primary public parent. Aside from the birth certificate, there are no records connecting Nellie to Mary Larson. Was Mary Larson illiterate and therefore unable to enter her name in her daughter's school records? Perhaps, but her possible illiteracy does not explain the absence of her name when a signature was not required and when the information was recorded by school officials. From Nellie's earliest years in public school, then, there is an unaccounted for distance between the child and the mother, and an obvious connection between the child and father whose own self-invention emerges from his public records.

The school registers for the Colman School during the period 1894 through 1903 are missing, but the register for the year 1903–1904 lists Nellie Larson as having entered the school at the age of nine and one-half and as being in the seventh grade from 1903 to 1904.[7] The next year, she completed the eighth grade at Colman.

On September 5, 1905, Nellie Larson entered the Wendell Phillips Junior High School at 244 East Pershing Road (39th Street), another public school in the Chicago system and located in an area with a concentration of African-American residents. The name recorded for her is *Nellye Larson.* Nellye

6. Nellie Larson, Elementary School Register records, Zenos Colman School, in Office of Former Student Records, Chicago Board of Education, Chicago.

7. Records of the Zenos Colman School, Chicago Board of Education.

Larson still resided at 4538 State Street with her father, Peter Larson, who was, as in the earlier school records, the only parent listed. Her initial vaccination was in 1901, which suggests that she entered Chicago's public school system for the first time in that year. Her date of birth is given as April 14, 1891, rather than April 13 of that year, and her age, upon entrance on September 5, 1905, is recorded as fourteen years and five months.[8]

Nellie Larson of the Colman School and *Nellye Larson* of Wendell Phillips are Nella Larsen's childhood selves. Larsen the novelist linked her education to the two Chicago schools despite some misrepresentation. As an adult applying on August 1, 1929, for the William E. Harmon Awards for Distinguished Achievement Among Negroes, she listed both schools in the record of her education.[9]

How did Nellie Walker become Nellie/Nellye Larson/Larsen? The transformation from *Nellie* to *Nellye* may be the simplest to explain. The change suggests that the young adolescent experimented with variant spellings of her given name. The spelling she preferred during high school was *Nellye,* which reflects the tendency of adolescents and teenagers to try out names for themselves that project a different image. Younger children, too, often pass through a stage during which they want to be called something other than their given names. For the young girl with a plain Anglicized name, *Nellye* lifted her identity out of the realm of the ordinary and out of lower-class connotations. The more exotic spelling of her given name would disappear in 1907 when Nellie Larson left the junior-high division at Wendell Phillips after two years to complete high school in the Normal School Department of Fisk University in Nashville. In that year, however, she assumed a Scandinavian spelling of her surname, *Larsen.* It would remain the spelling of choice throughout the remainder of her life, though the former spelling, *Larson,* would sometimes resurface from her official early school records. However, several of her Fisk records would list her as Nellie Walker Larsen, which suggests that her surname at birth remained part of her legal name and official documentation through her young adulthood.

The larger transformation, that of *Walker* to *Larson,* is less open to the preferences of the young girl, whose father registered her in public school as Nellie Larson rather than as Nellie Walker. This change in naming and iden-

8. See Wendell Phillips High School register for 1905–1906, entry no. 107, in Wendell Phillips High School, Chicago.

9. Nella Larsen Imes, Nomination blank, William E. Harmon Foundation Awards for Distinguished Achievement Among Negroes, 1929, in HFR.

tity is dependent upon an explanation of the fates of Nellie's parents, Peter Walker and Mary Hanson Walker.

As an adult, Nella Larsen claimed that her father was "a Negro from the Virgin Islands, formerly the Danish West Indies," and that he died when she was two years old. Peter Walker, Nellie's birth father, was twenty-eight years old when, on July 14, 1890, he and twenty-one-year-old Mary Hanson applied for a marriage license in Chicago.[10] When and whether the marriage took place are not part of the existing records.[11] Peter Walker is listed in the 1891 Chicago City Directory as a laborer residing at 2031 Armour Avenue;[12] in April, 1891, when his daughter was born, he was living at 2124 Armour. After 1891, he does not appear in the directory or in other public records of the city.

On February 6, 1894, Mr. Peter Larsen and Miss Marie Hansen of Chicago completed a marriage application, and the next day they were married by a "Minister of the Gospel." The minister performing the marriage is recorded both as John T. Hanson and John T. Hansen on the certificate; Marie is listed as Hansen on the application, but Hanson on the certificate. Was John Hanson/Hansen related to Marie Hanson/Hansen? A suggestive piece of information is that John T. Hanson/Hansen appears in the 1900 Illinois census as having been born in "St. Thomas, West India Islands" in August, 1864; his father was born in Denmark and his mother in France. In 1880, John Hanson immigrated to the United States from St. Thomas, one of the Danish West Indian Islands, now the Virgin Islands. Although she never identified the specific island, Nella Larsen claimed that her father was "a Negro from the Virgin Islands, formerly the Danish West Indies" in the Knopf statement; and she also told a newspaper reporter in 1928: "Her father, a Danish West Indian, died before she was old enough to know much about him. All of his people live in Denmark."[13] Could Peter Walker have

10. Larsen Imes, Author's statement for Alfred A. Knopf, Inc.; Marriage application, July 14, 1890, in Records of Cook County, no. 154616.

11. The application on July 14, 1890, remains on record in the Cook County clerk's office, but the marriage license was not returned for filing (Stanley T. Kusper, Cook County Clerk, State of Illinois, to Thadious M. Davis, September 12, 1989, in possession of Thadious M. Davis).

12. *Lakeside Directory of Chicago*, 1891 (microfilm), Part 2, Reel 11, in Library of Congress.

13. Marriage record, in Records of Cook County, no. 21424; *Twelfth Census, 1900: Illinois*, Enumeration District 56, Sheet 5, Line 1 (Microfilm reel 304), in Newberry Library, Chicago; Thelma E. Berlack, "New Author Unearthed Right Here in Harlem," New York *Amsterdam News*, May 23, 1928, p. 16.

been a native of St. Thomas? Did John Hanson/Hansen know Peter Walker from his native St. Thomas? Even more suggestive and pertinent is the question of whether there was a connection between Peter Walker and Peter Larsen.

Peter Larsen of Hanland, Shelby County, Iowa, was thirty-two years old and Marie Hansen of Chicago was twenty-seven at the time of their marriage. That Marie Hanson/Hansen is the same Mary Hanson who applied for a marriage license with Peter Walker in 1890 and who gave birth to Nellie Walker in 1891 is evident from public records. Less immediately evident is that Peter Larsen may be the same person as Peter Walker. Peter Walker, like Peter Larsen, would have been thirty-two in 1894. In 1910, when Peter Larsen and his wife, Marie, completed information for the Illinois census, both claimed to have been married for nineteen years. Yet if that were the case, their marriage would have taken place before the documented date, 1894. Peter and Marie Larsen's daughter Anna was seventeen at the time of the census, so it is entirely possible that they had moved the date of their marriage back to legitimize Anna's birth for the census. However, Marie Larsen also informed the census taker that she had given birth to one child and that she had one child surviving.[14] Since Anna is the daughter recorded as living in the household, she is the child to whom Marie Larsen refers.

What then of Nellie Walker Larsen? Why would her mother deny giving birth to her? The answer seemingly rests with Nellie's designation as "Colored" at birth. Both Peter and Marie Larsen listed themselves as "white" and "born in Denmark," but their race and country of origin would not have affected an acknowledgment of Marie's firstborn, Nellie, who was not living within the household at the time. While a mother can wash her hands of a child, especially one gone astray, and cut off contact with that child, a mother who denies giving birth to a child may be concealing something that in all likelihood has more to do with the mother than with the child. Nellie Larson of the public schools had no racial designation in either the Colman or the Wendell Phillips records, though Phillips was a school attended primarily by children of color. It is possible that Marie Larsen denied the child because of her husband, particularly if Peter Larsen no longer wanted the responsibility or the stigma of a stepdaughter of color, but Peter Larsen's, not Marie Larsen's, relationship to Nellie Larsen is the one publicly docu-

14. *Thirteenth Census, 1910: Illinois*, Ward 32, Sec. 47, Enumeration District 1389, Sheet 1, Line 57 (Microfilm reel 278), in Newberry Library.

mented by her school records, which suggest that he assumed a significant aspect of parenting involving her education and schools. The Larsens' concealment of a second daughter is complicated by their progress through Chicago of the 1890s from a racially mixed neighborhood to an all-white one.

A curious connection exists between the Chicago school records for Nellie Larson and Nella Larsen's later formulation of her school experience. It is suggestive of her need to explain her early years even while transforming them. The Colman records indicate that Nellie Larson entered school at the age of nine and a half. She was nearly ten, which was rather late for native-born children to begin school in Chicago, even at the turn of the century. In an unusual aspect of her author's biographical statement, Nella Larsen felt compelled to tell how old she was when she had first enrolled in elementary school or, as she put it, had begun her "formal education." She states that she was eight years old, which would have made her older than most entering students, but only slightly so. School attendance was compulsory for children over seven and under fourteen years of age, though children routinely began school at the age of six and those over fourteen and under sixteen were obliged under the Compulsory Attendance law to either attend school or be employed.[15] Larsen's inclusion is curious because none of the Knopf authors or the New Negro authors provided such information. She somehow felt the need to explain, even though no one would have known or cared about her "late entry" into grammar school. By the time she wrote the statement, she had erased two years from her age and adopted 1893 as the year of her birth. If those two years were to be added back on, they would advance the age at which Larsen claims to have started school. She would have been ten years old, the age that is more nearly that of the young Nellie Larson entering Colman at nine and a half. Where might she have spent those missing years?

The symbolic value of Nella Larsen's choice of 1893 as her birth year would not be lost on anyone familiar with Chicago during the 1890s and 1900s. The date marked the World's Columbian Exposition, the celebration which commemorated the four-hundredth anniversary of Columbus' arrival in the Americas and which thrust the city into its modern urban phase. Often considered the city's "greatest opportunity to display herself as a center of civilization," the Great Exposition featured everything from scientific inventions and the dynamo to household gadgets, from the fine arts and

15. See Chicago Board of Education, "Report of School Census, May 2, 1910," in Newberry Library, which surveys the previous decade.

architecture to the Ferris wheel and "Little Egypt." At the Women's Building in the "White City," the name given the World's Fair grounds, poet Harriet Monroe read from her "Columbian Ode," and society leader Mrs. Potter Palmer addressed the future: "Women as a sex have been liberated. . . . They now have time to think, to be educated, to plan and pursue careers of their own choosing. . . . Even more important than the discovery of Columbus is the fact that the general government has just discovered women."[16] At the same time, the exposition was infamous for its exclusion of African Americans from the celebrations and exhibits. Ida Wells-Barnett, one of the best-known African-American journalists of the time, led a group of women of color in a valiant fight against the discriminatory, racist practices. In choosing 1893 as her birth year, Nella Larsen may not have known of Mrs. Palmer's interpretation or of Ida Wells-Barnett's protest, but the public associative link between that year and the Great Exposition would not have been lost on her. More interesting in terms of the conundrum of her family, 1893 is the birth year of Larsen's younger sister, Anna, who replaced her as daughter within a white household.

Nellie Larson, who first entered the Colman School at the age of nine and one-half, had 1891 as a birth year and 1901 as the year of her vaccination. She would then have first enrolled in the Colman School in 1901, a year for which school registers are missing. That initial enrollment would be one year after the 1900 census lists one Nellie Larson as a child inmate of the Erring Woman's Refuge for Reform located at 5024 Indiana Avenue and within the South Side area where the Walkers and Larsons resided.[17] The listing suggests the possibility that Nellie Larson from the 1900 census and Nellie Larson from the Colman records may be the same child. It means, by extension, that Nella Larsen could well have spent a part of her early childhood in an institution from which she was later "rescued." Interestingly, in her semiautobiographical first novel Nella Larsen would portray her protagonist, Helga Crane, as having a sympathetic "Uncle Peter" who "rescued" her from a miserable childhood and sent her to school for six years.[18] Nella Larsen had exactly six years of education between 1901, when she

16. Edward Wagenknecht, *Chicago* (Norman, Okla., 1964), 6; Henry Justin Smith, *Chicago: A Century of Progress, 1833–1933* (Chicago, 1933), 104; Mrs. Potter Palmer, quoted in Smith, *Chicago*, 104.

17. *Twelfth Census, 1900: Illinois*, Soundex L625, and Enumeration District 1029, Sheet 21, Line 16 (Microfilm reel 285), in Newberry Library.

18. See Nella Larsen, *Quicksand*, in *"Quicksand" and "Passing,"* ed. Deborah E. McDowell (New Brunswick, 1986), 23.

entered Colman, and 1908, when she left Fisk after the 1907–1908 school year. Unfortunately, there is no way of ascertaining the precise connection between "Uncle Peter" and "Peter Walker" and "Peter Larsen," or between the female child enumerated with the residents of the Erring Woman's Refuge for Reform.

More information clarifying the earliest phase of Larsen's background may yet come to light. It seems plausible that Peter Walker, a cook, a laborer, and a man of color, could have fallen on hard times, and that in an effort to survive, he and his wife placed the visibly "colored," older of their two children in a home while the visibly "white" members of the family remained together. Were it to prove to be accurate, then the institutional background might explain several facets of Nella Larsen's personality and character. An institutional background with its emphasis on anonymity, regimen, uniformity, religion, and morality would gesture toward Larsen's aversion to conformity and to religion as an adult. It might also explain her sense of aloneness and her admission of the lack of affection in her earliest years, just as it might elucidate her love for material things, comfort, and luxury, as well as her need for recognition, fame, and a unique self for public consumption. This particular background, combined with Mary Hanson's (Marie Larsen's) rejection of her colored and possibly illegitimate child, also could set the stage for Nella Larsen's discomfort with and transformations of identity that are signaled by name changes throughout her life.

Peter Larson also begins to appear in public records in 1901. He is listed in the 1901 Chicago City Directory as a streetcar conductor, an occupation reserved for whites. The Chicago city directories for the years 1903 through 1907 list "Peter Larson, conductor," a resident of 4538 State Street.[19] Throughout the years of Nellie Larson's education in Chicago (1901 through 1907), she lived with her father at 4538 State Street, which remained the address of "Peter Larson, conductor" in the city directory. Neither father nor daughter appears in the 1900 census as residing at that address, and no comparable family grouping including a father Peter (Larson or Larsen) and daughter Nellie appears elsewhere in the 1900 Chicago-area enumerations. (The 4500 block of State Street at that time was still listed as part of the township of Lake, just as a number of other parts of the city—Cicero, Jefferson, Hyde Park—had retained separate township names after their annexation in 1889.) However, listings in the 1900 census for the

19. For Peter *Larson* entries, see the *Chicago City Directory* for 1903 to 1907, in Chicago Historical Society.

residents of 4538 State Street and the surrounding neighborhood disclose information useful in placing Nellie and Peter Larson during the years 1901 through 1907.

In 1900 the 4500 block of State Street, though not one of the twenty-five Scandinavian settlements scattered throughout the city, had a number of Danish-born residents.[20] The residents of the building in which Peter and Nellie Larson lived provide a sampler of the diversity of people in the block. A Frenchman Albert Durand and his German-born wife lived there with their two adolescent sons; Lizzie Rice and her brother John, who were Irish from Pennsylvania, had a flat; Belle Zigler from Canada shared an apartment with her daughter Laura and son-in-law Franco Pourro; Edward Jennings from Indiana lived there with his English-Canadian wife, Mary, and his son Frank; two Swedes, Ole Anderson and August Hendricks, were lodgers; and three young men, John Lawrence from New York, John Carnsedy from Illinois, and James Fox from Ohio, were all boarders. Their occupations were lithographer, laundress, bookbinder, teamster, electrician, clerk (bazaar and grocery), fireman, milliner, boilermaker, cook, and seamstress. Other residents of the block were mainly from Sweden and Germany, but a few were from Holland, Norway, Denmark, Bohemia, and Italy, and several were American-born. They were employed as sales ladies, shoemaker, tailor, shipping clerk, coachman, life insurance and real estate salesmen, dry cleaners, painter, engineer, laundry men, plumber, music teacher, and milliner.[21]

The various occupations reflected the block's composition as a combination residential and commercial area. The 4500 block of State, like the adjacent blocks, was a less concentrated extension of the business and shopping thoroughfare and major artery that State Street was in the central city Loop. However, the area also had nearby industrial plants, grain elevators, and lumberyards. Stone-front commercial and apartment buildings had been erected along that South Side section of State during the 1880s. The buildings had three stories, with the businesses and stores on the first floor and apartments mainly on the second and third floors. While these buildings were not the older, multiple-family wooden houses and cottages that

20. The Jens Jensen family, for example, lived at 4553, and Nels Holbeck boarded with the John Boscards at 4538, the apartment building to which Peter and Nellie Larson would soon move.

21. *Twelfth Census, 1900: Illinois,* 4538 State Street, Ward 29, Enumeration District 864 (Microfilm reel 285), in Newberry Library; *ibid.,* 4500 block of State Street.

many immigrants inhabited at the turn of the century, particularly nearer the stockyards, they provided an unattractive, noisy residential environment, though one made easily accessible by the Rock Island Railroad and the State Street streetcar line.[22]

Although there were no blacks listed in the 4500 block of State Street, a number of blacks lived in the neighborhood. One block west, in the 4500 block of Dearborn, there were several African-American families, including a coachman, Edward Campbell from Kentucky, and his wife, Rebecca, from Tennessee, and a porter, Charles Robinson from Tennessee, his wife, Belle, from Kentucky, and his sister Betty Kellis. Three blocks south on State was a more substantial African-American community with school-aged children. Susan B. Chase, a caterer and widow of a French-Canadian, headed a household at 4809 that included her two daughters, Bella, a nineteen-year-old printing clerk, and Tulip, born in 1890 and an elementary school student, and one boarder, Joseph Womack, a forty-year-old railroad porter from Tennessee. Perry Wilson, a cook, lived at 4825 with his wife of one year, Lillie, and his sister-in-law May Harris, all in their twenties. Mary Caldwell, a widow with six of her eight children surviving, was also at 4825, but only a daughter (Emma) and three sons (Levi, Henry, and Lawrence) lived with her. At 4827, James Ralston, a railroad porter, lived with Fannie, his wife of thirteen years, and his eight-year-old son, Proctor. A number of the lodgers in the 4800 block of State were railroad porters like James Spurlock, who roomed with Mary Caldwell.[23]

The 4800 block of State would provide Nellie Larson not only with a nearby community of African-American childhood playmates and schoolmates, but also with a long-term friendship with one family. In 1900, the John Mayo family lived at 4811 State; this is the family to whom the adult Nella Larsen would turn after her divorce in 1933.[24] Mayo was thirty-four years old at the turn of the century and had been married for fifteen years. A railroad porter from Texas, he lived in the rented apartment with his wife, Mattie, who was thirty-three and also from Texas, though her parents were from Louisiana, and their only child, Pearl, born February 9, 1892, in Lou-

22. Ibid.; Glen E. Holt and Dominic A. Pacyga, *Chicago: A Historical Guide to the Neighborhoods, the Loop and South Side* (Chicago, 1979), 88.

23. *Twelfth Census, 1900: Illinois*, 4500 Dearborn Street, Ward 32, Enumeration District 1028 (Microfilm reel 285), in Newberry Library; *ibid.*, 4800 State Street.

24. See Nella Larsen to Dorothy Peterson, Wednesday 6th [postmarked September 6, 1933], in JWJ.

isiana. Pearl was Nellie Larson's childhood friend, apparently her closest one, and the Mayos served as her surrogate family.

The Mayos were light-skinned African Americans who were later listed as mulattoes in the 1910 census. They formed a stable family unit that moved into the African-American middle class within a few years. In fact, because railroading was one of the leading occupations for African-American men in turn-of-the-century Chicago, the Mayos were already fairly well placed in terms of social status within the race. They gave Nellie Larson one of her few intimate views of African Americans in what was then considered a middle class. "The head waiters were the top of society," according to a manuscript autobiography of an African-American physician who moved to the city around 1890. "They almost dictated social customs. . . . [N]ext to head waiters were the porters and then came the barbers."[25] Mayo was a porter who worked for the Pullman Company and rented a room in his apartment to another Pullman porter, Hunter Cotton from Louisiana.[26] His first decades with Pullman were those when among Chicago's African Americans, as one porter recalled, "You weren't anybody unless you were a Pullman porter. We handled more money than most of the colored people, and led all of the social life." While porters may have achieved social status in the African-American community, their salaries were not high. When Mayo retired in 1932, his average monthly wage, calculated over 120 months, was $102.34.[27] But in the period just as the new century began, Mayo was better off than many of his neighbors, black or white.

The State Street neighborhood, with its ethnic and racial diversity and its lack of strict class or caste divisions, provided the young Nellie Larson with one basis for her formative years in Chicago. It was a neighborhood in which a mixed-race child could feel at home, and one in which African Americans were no worse or better off than their white immigrant neighbors. In the area where the Larsons lived, there were few deeply entrenched stigmas against people of color and no strict segregation of the races.

A major aspect of Nellie Larson's formative years was the mobility of neighborhood residents. As the immigrant families achieved stability in jobs and their incomes increased, often with the help of rent from lodgers, they

25. Quoted in E. Franklin Frazier, *The Negro Family in Chicago* (Chicago, 1932), 88–89.

26. Mayo started to work for Pullman on July 28, 1892, and remained until his retirement on September 29, 1932 (John H. Mayo, Record of retirement pension, in Pullman Company Records, Special Collections, Newberry Library).

27. Frazier, *The Negro Family in Chicago*, 108.

moved to less commercial areas of the city, particularly to those west of State or south of Fifty-fifth, where they could find apartments on less busy and broad streets than State. The African-American families, too, were not consigned to the area, but exhibited a similar upward mobility. As new opportunities for jobs in Chicago's industries and civil services opened to them, they also moved to more residential streets, generally in an area east of State to Grand Boulevard.

John Mayo is an example. His steady job with a major company provided the means for social mobility. Within eight years, John, Mattie, and Pearl Mayo would move first to the more attractive 3256 LaSalle, and then to a more elegant 3343 Vernon Street, east of Grand Boulevard, in a neighborhood of mulattoes, all railroad and post-office workers, and from there shortly after 1916 to the fashionable 4732 Prairie Avenue apartment previously occupied by Germans and where the adult Nella Larsen would come to visit.[28] Each successive move was to a block or street where the living accommodations and amenities were improvements over the last. In each move, the Mayos were part of the expansion of African Americans into previously all-white areas mainly in the Grand Boulevard section, where blacks had begun to move in the 1890s. They never settled on Grand Boulevard itself (the "Boulevard Denege" as African Americans called it), where the elite black bankers, doctors, merchants, attorneys, and politicians began to live in the 1910s.[29]

By 1910 almost all of those who had lived in the apartments in Nellie Larson's 4500 block of State at the turn of the century were gone. In their place was a new group of immigrants, native-born whites, and, as well, blacks who had moved into the block during the decade. African Americans from Kentucky, Maryland, Virginia, Tennessee, Alabama, Texas, and Missouri, with names such as Dorsey, Huston, King, Jones, Morrison, and Redmon, had arrived in Chicago to work as janitors, washerwomen, and domestics, and as laborers in stockyards and tunnels.[30] The immigrants were

28. See *Lakeside Directory of Chicago*, 1902, in Chicago Historical Society; *Rheas' New Citizen's Directory* (Chicago, 1908), 62; *Thirteenth Census, 1910; Illinois*, 3343 Vernon Avenue, Ward 3, Enumeration District 220, Sheet 13, Line 75 (Microfilm reel 242), in Newberry Library; Chicago telephone directories, 1914–16, 1922–38.

29. Holt and Pacyga, *Chicago*, 88; Lovelyn Evans, in *An Autobiography of Black Chicago*, by Dempsy Travis (Chicago, 1981), 18. See also Alfreda M. Barnett Duster, in *Autobiography of Black Chicago*, by Travis, 212–15.

30. *Thirteenth Census, 1910: Illinois*, 4500 State Street, Ward 32, Enumeration District 353 (Microfilm reel 246), in Newberry Library.

by then primarily from Germany, Sweden, and Russia, though there were also several families from China (the Hongs and the Chins) and Denmark (the Carls and the Jensens). German-born immigrants made up the largest group, but a number of them either had parents who were born in Denmark or who listed Danish as their language.[31] The native- and foreign-born residents worked as drivers, painters, clerks, messengers, elevator starters, and meatcutters, but one of Matilde and Alfred Peterson's daughters was a "writer." A few merchants and tradesmen remained, but the area had already undergone changes.[32]

Peter Larson was, like others in the State Street area, upwardly mobile. After 1907, there is no trace of this Peter Larson in the State Street neighborhood. However, the same individual begins to appear in the 1908 city directory listings as "Peter Larsen, conductor," residing at 143 West 70th Place.[33] He changed the spelling of his surname at some point during the year 1907, the same year that Nellie Larson became Nellie Larsen.

The names "Peter Larson" and "Peter Larsen" are fairly common in Chicago during the first decade of the twentieth century; however, through cross checking addresses, property holdings, occupations, country of origin, age or date of birth, and year of immigration, it is possible to eliminate a number of the Peter Larsons or Larsens and to trace the one who was Nellie Larson's father. For instance, the name occurs most frequently among men from the Swedish population, which was the largest group of Scandinavians in Chicago (48,836 foreign-born in 1900), and it occurs with slightly less frequency among the Norwegian population (22,011 foreign-born in 1900). In the Danish population, the smallest of the Scandinavian groups with only 10,166 foreign-born residents in 1900, the name appears only infrequently.[34] That the Peter Larson who was the father of Nellie/Nella identified with the Danish population reduces immediately the number of men with that same name to trace for possible connections with Nellie Larson/ Nella Larsen.

31. Johanna Peterson, a widow with an independent income who lived at 4555 State, however, combined all these: she was born in Germany, her parents were from Denmark, and she spoke Danish.

32. Nella Larsen's childhood neighborhood, now either deteriorated or cleared for "urban renewal," is overshadowed by the Robert Taylor Homes, a public housing project covering the area west of State between 39th and 54th streets.

33. For Peter *Larsen* entries, see *Chicago City Directory* and *Lakeside Directory of Chicago*, 1908–16, in Chicago Historical Society.

34. *Historic City: The Settlement of Chicago* (Chicago, 1976), 54.

For two years, 1908 and 1909, Peter Larsen's address is *143* West 70th Place; thereafter, his house number becomes simply *43*, because in 1909 the city changed the numbering system for streets.[35] From 1910 to 1916, the city directory lists "Peter Larsen, conductor" at 43 West 70th Place.[36] That Peter *Larsen* is the same Peter *Larson* of 4538 State Street, and the parent of Nellie Larson, is confirmed by the U.S. census of 1910, which enumerated Peter Larsen of 43 West 70th Place as "Conductor (Street ry)" [street railway], married (wife Marie), with one child (daughter Anna).[37] Anna is the name of Nella Larsen Imes's sister, who was located in California in 1964 as heir to her estate.

At the time of the 1910 census, Peter Larsen was forty-three years old. He was purchasing the house at 43 West 70th Place in a neighborhood of single-family dwellings. The house, like the neighborhood, was razed to make way for the Dan Ryan Expressway. Although there was one lodger, Charles Bryman, a twenty-one-year-old who immigrated from Denmark in 1907, the house was occupied by only the Larsen family, which included Peter Larsen, his wife, Marie, a forty-year-old seamstress, and his daughter Anna, seventeen, who was neither employed nor in school. Marie Larsen claimed to have given birth only once and that she had one living child. While the Larsens' daughter Anna is listed as a native of Illinois, the two adult Larsens, along with their boarder, were listed as natives of Denmark. The entire household was enumerated with the racial designation "white."

Peter Larsen had immigrated in 1885, and his wife, Marie, in 1887, which would have placed them in the second wave of Scandinavian immigrants to arrive in the city.[38] In the decades before the October 8, 1871, great fire in Chicago, few natives of Scandinavian countries lived in the city. In 1860, for instance, 1,313 Norwegians, 816 Swedes, and 150 Danes lived in an area along the North Branch of the Chicago River, where they worked in railroad yards, mills, and factories. In 1870, the Swedish community numbered 6,154, nearly surpassing the 6,374 Norwegians and outnumbering by far the 1,243 Danes.[39] The Scandinavian settlement on Chicago's North Side became generally known as Swede Town. When the city began

---

35. See *Lakeside Directory of Chicago,* 1908–1909, in Chicago Historical Society.

36. *Ibid.,* 1910–16. See also *Polk's Directory of Chicago,* 1910–16, in Chicago Historical Society.

37. *Thirteenth Census, 1910: Illinois,* 43 West 70th Place, Ward 32, Sec. 37, Enumeration District 1389, Sheet 1, Line 57 (Microfilm reel 278), in Newberry Library.

38. Their statements, whether accurate or not, are recorded in the *Thirteenth Census, 1910.*

39. *Historic City,* 26, 37.

to rebuild after the fire, the first large wave of Scandinavians began to arrive. The Danes, who were known as artisans and journeymen, worked in the building trades, along with the much larger group of Swedes, already highly respected for their skill in construction.

In the 1880s and 1890s, the Scandinavians, like the Germans and Irish, increased their populations in a second wave of immigration brought on by the building and industrial booms in a Chicago that was transforming the prairie lands surrounding it. They were often directed to Chicago by "runners" who met ships arriving in New York and spread news of Chicago's opportunities. But these groups were beginning to be outnumbered by Poles, Russians, Italians, Bohemians, and Greeks, the newer immigrants who helped to swell the city's population from 298,977 in 1870 to 1,698,575 by 1900.[40] Peter Larsen claimed to have arrived during this period of Chicago's growth, development, and expansion into a major urban center that promised economic, commercial, and cultural prosperity to all those who would work hard.

He and his family were reaping the benefits of their labor, thrift, and industry when in 1907 they moved into a home of their own. As a conductor on the street railway system, Peter Larsen enjoyed a position that, while not white-collar, represented status in an emerging middle class of immigrants. Even before the turn of the century, there was a long waiting list for any job with the city's three railway companies (Chicago City Railway, West Chicago Street Railroad, and North Chicago Street Railroad), but the conductors and the gripmen were the best paid and best treated employees, and they were all white men.[41] Conductors such as Peter Larsen on the Chicago City Railway received twenty-five to thirty cents an hour for an average work day of ten hours and a work week of six days. Although most men took Sundays off, there was no limit to the number of days or hours that an energetic conductor might work, and many worked either longer hours or consecutive days without a break in order to upgrade their living standards. (Horses on the lines, however, only worked a maximum of four hours be-

40. *Ibid.*, 46; St. Clair Drake and Horace E. Cayton, *Black Metropolis: A Study of Negro Life in a Northern City* (New York, 1945), 9–10.

41. Conductors wore uniforms for which they deposited $80, though the deposit also covered the $10 they received daily from the company for making change and as a security for accidents. They and the other railway employees had clubrooms in the carbarns, and they formed literary and athletic clubs, which they maintained with twenty-five cents a month dues. Alan Lind, *Chicago Surface Lines; An Illustrated History* (2nd ed.; Park Forest, Ill., 1974), 368.

fore being relieved.) By 1907, when Peter Larsen relocated to a better neighborhood, work conditions for City Railway employees had improved further because of the advent of labor unions and the replacement of horse and cable lines with electric cars in 1906.[42]

Peter Larsen's block on West 70th Place was essentially a neighborhood of upwardly mobile individuals, like himself, with good jobs that were above those of manual and unskilled laborers. His wife's work as a dressmaker placed her above the lot of most of the Scandinavian women, half of whom were employed as unskilled laborers, as servants and domestics.[43] Neighborhood residents included a railroad brakeman, another conductor, and an electrician, all living in the Larsens' block. The lodger in the Larsens' household was a barber. Others living on West 70th Place were post office employees, nurse, upholsterer, contractor, bookkeeper, and stockyard office worker.[44]

For the most part the lower-middle-class neighborhood was one of native-born whites; few immigrants were listed in the 1910 census. The Larsen family was an exception, along with several families headed by individuals born in England, Scotland, and one family of Italians (at number 15) and another of Germans (at number 26). There were no other Danish immigrants or Danish-descended families in the neighborhood. The neighborhood, part of the E. D. Taylor subdivision, was composed of homeowners, rather than of renters, and it was entirely white. There were no people of color listed as part of the households, either as heads of households or as lodgers or servants. In the entire ward, there had been only 596 blacks out of a total ward population of 56,576 in 1900, and by 1910, there would be only 514 blacks remaining among the ward's total population of 70,408.[45]

The profile of the West 70th Place block indicates that it was not an area in which Nellie Larsen or Nella Larsen, "Colored," would have been easily accepted or have felt comfortable. There were no other persons known to be mulattoes or African Americans living in the first block of West 70th

42. *Ibid.;* James David Johnson, comp., *A Century of Chicago Streetcars, 1858–1958: A Pictorial History of the World's Largest Street Railway* (Wheaton, Ill., 1964), 12.

43. Peter Jones and Melvin Holli, eds., *Ethnic Chicago* (Grand Rapids, 1981), 28. Percentage based upon tables, entitled "Special Reports: Occupations," in *Twelfth Census, 1900,* 516–23.

44. See *Thirteenth Census, 1910: Illinois,* Ward 32, Sec. 47, Enumeration District 1389 (Microfilm reel 278), in Newberry Library. See also Ward 32, Sec. 47, Enumeration District 1386, and Ward 31, Sec. 44, Enumeration District 1387, *ibid.*

45. Information on the West 70th Place neighborhood from the *Thirteenth Census, 1910;* Allan H. Spear, *Black Chicago: The Making of a Ghetto, 1890–1920* (Chicago, 1967), 15.

Place or in the adjacent blocks. West 70th Place then had a racial homogeneity that was distinctly different from the Larsens' old working-class, blue-collar neighborhood on State Street with its diverse immigrant groups and its black and mulatto families. The social and racial configuration of the new neighborhood may have led to the Larsens' denial of Nellie's existence in 1910, but certainly the racial exclusiveness of West 70th Place figured in the secret pain that Nella Larsen carried throughout her adulthood.

Yet there is no basis for romanticizing the racial interactions or exaggerating the climate of racial receptiveness in her former neighborhood on State Street from 1901 through 1907, the years Larsen lived there. State Street may have differed from West 70th Place only in degree. Lovelyn Evans, daughter of a German mother and an African American who owned a storage and moving company founded in 1890, mainly remembered wealth and privilege during this period, but she also admitted that her elite family was isolated in their class and her father sometimes labeled with racial slurs. One working-class African American who arrived in Chicago in 1903 recalled: "I lived on Lincoln Street—there were foreigners there. . . . There was only one other colored family on the block. The white people never used to call my children names."[46]

Incidents of racial hostility may have been infrequent before the Great Migration of the war years, but there is evidence of racial division and resistance to African Americans in mixed communities. One woman in the lower-middle class remembered that "relations between children and adults in such areas were often friendly, [but] the social barriers stiffened during the critical adolescent period. . . . I didn't know much about color until I was about eleven or twelve years old. . . . My playmates were all white. I used to go to their parties and they would come to mine; but after I was old enough to go to high school, that was where the trouble started. I never did have any serious trouble but it wasn't so pleasant as it had been when I was a child."[47] This situation was Nellie Larsen's after she left elementary school. The transformation to young adulthood could have marked the end of an interracial existence that was uncomplicated on the surface.

There was evidently enough racial tension in Chicago for the Manasseh Club to band together in the 1890s and take the motto Equal Rights for All. A fraternal and benevolent society composed of working-class blacks married to whites, the Manasseh Club claimed five hundred members in 1892

---

46. Travis, *Autobiography of Black Chicago*, 218; Drake and Cayton, *Black Metropolis*, 177.

47. Drake and Cayton, *Black Metropolis*, 117.

and remained in existence until the 1920s. It functioned not only as a self-help group in times of financial difficulty and as a social organization holding an annual picnic and dance, but also as a source of "mutual psychological reinforcement."[48]

Peter Larson's move to 143 West 70th Place occurred late in August of 1907.[49] While all of his legal documents for the property are in the name Larson, he became Larsen in his new West Side neighborhood. The relocation, as well as his attitude toward its meaning, may have played a part in his decision to send his daughter to a school for African Americans in the South. Unlike other members of the family, Nellie Larson did not have the appearance of a Dane, even though in social situations she may have been able to pass for a white person from some other ethnic group and in the process of passing to relinquish any social relations or emotional identification with African Americans.[50]

In the Larson family, the presence of a brown-skinned daughter in a white household may have created problems, one of which could have centered on her being a blood relative whose acceptance posed the difficulty of explanation. One explanation could well have been the mother's prior union with a person of color, which would have signaled her violation of a social taboo in a neighborhood of striving native-born whites. But another explanation could have been the denial of Nellie's kinship to the family, which from the child's perspective would have caused confusion and disorientation.

The relocation to a new neighborhood may also have accounted for the change in the spelling of Peter Larson's surname. He assumed Larsen, a spelling that the smallest population of Scandinavians, the Danes, used more frequently than Larson, but that was also more distinctly Scandinavian because both of the other visible Scandinavian groups, the Norwegians and the Swedes, used the -sen spelling as well. By 1900, these three Scandinavian populations numbered 165,901, including the American-born children of immigrants, but the Danish population was only 19,311 of this total.[51] In opting for the different spelling, Peter Larsen reversed the pattern more typically observed in the United States, in which more apparently "foreign" names in sound or spelling are regularized into a more clearly English ver-

---

48. Ibid., 145–46; Spear, Black Chicago, 105.

49. Larson obtained a warranty deed and a trust deed for the property on August 8 and filed them on August 27, 1907 (in Records of Cook County, Title transfers, Chicago Property Records, Book 386-A, p. 261).

50. See Drake and Cayton, Black Metropolis, 164.

51. Historic City, 54.

sion. He took the opposite route. Even given some laxity in adherence to the spellings of foreign surnames, *Larsen* would have linked him more concretely to the large foreign-born community of Scandinavians from Denmark, Sweden, and Norway living in Chicago. If Peter Larson were, in fact, Peter Walker, then the second transformation would begin to account for the peculiarities in Nella Larsen's reconstruction of her childhood.

The less explicable aspect of Peter Larson's transformation into Peter Larsen is that his old State Street neighborhood had a comparatively large number of Scandinavians living in it, whereas the West 70th Place neighborhood had none, with the exception of the Larsens. Emphasizing an ethnic identity in a predominantly Anglo-Saxon neighborhood seems out of character, especially for one attempting to rise in the middle-class world. Peter Larsen's decision to emphasize his ethnicity, nevertheless, was apparently deliberate because *Larson*, as well as the variant *Larrson*, was a common name among the Swedes and Danes in Chicago, but it also appeared in other populations, including the relatively small African-American population in the first decade of the twentieth century.

In 1890, a year before Nellie Larson's birth, Chicago's black population was 14,271, but by 1900, it had more than doubled to a total of 30,150, and in 1910, it was 44,104, which was nevertheless only about 2 percent of the city's total population of 2,185,283. During these three decades African Americans had increased gradually in number and had been absorbed into the "spatial and social order of the city in much the same fashion as the immigrants from Europe, except that the stigma of a recent slavery and the weight of racial prejudice had slowed up the process considerably." In 1900, nineteen of the city's thirty-five wards had less than 1 percent black population, fourteen wards had at least 1 percent, and two wards had more than 10 percent black population. In 1910 two-thirds of the African Americans lived in wards with less than a 50 percent black population, and one-third lived in wards that were less than 2 percent black. Ward 29, which included Nellie Larson's State Street residence at the turn of the century, had a black population of 868, 2.1 percent of the total ward population of 41,214 in 1900, but in 1910, Ward 30, which the area had become after changes in the ward boundaries, had a black population of 6,431, or 12.5 percent of the 51,308 total in the ward.[52] However small these increases may have been

---

52. Frazier, *The Negro Family in Chicago*, 99; St. Clair Drake, *Churches and Voluntary Associations in the Chicago Negro Community* (Chicago, 1940), 119; Spear, *Black Chicago*, 14; Drake and Cayton, *Black Metropolis*, 176; Spear, 15.

in relative terms, between 1905 and 1910 (the period in which Nellie Larson entered junior high school and Peter Larson changed his name), the rapidity of the black population growth began to contribute to racial hostilities.

The period was marked by violence and unrest centered on people of color and their place within Chicago's institutions. In 1904, African Americans had played a major role as scabs and strikebreakers in the meatpacking industry and had been the victims of attacks by union men during that summer when hostility was high because the strike was prolonged and unsuccessful. Eight months later, in April, 1905, the Teamsters Union called a sympathy strike at Montgomery Ward, a decision that triggered the most violent labor disturbance since the Pullman Strike of 1894. This time the hostility went beyond attacks on the black strikebreakers; it spilled over into the general community. Angry whites dragged blacks from streetcars and out of public places. On May 16 they shot an eighteen-year-old African-American youth, and another African-American male was shot on May 21.[53] When African Americans retaliated after the second shooting, a bloody confrontation ensued. It was the worst period of race hysteria in Chicago until the race riot of 1919.

In the aftermath, the city's fairly open racial policies changed dramatically to exclude African Americans from hotels, theaters, stores, hospitals, and neighborhoods. Public schools, in particular, became a main target of discriminatory practices. White children rioted in 1905 when transferred to a predominantly black school, and more than 150 white children boycotted classes when, in 1908, they found themselves in a school attended by blacks. Despite the efforts of Ella Flagg Young, a progressive intellectual and the school superintendent, whites not only persistently lobbied to add a clause to the city charter permitting segregated schools, but were active in unofficial moves to restrict the participation of African-American children in school programs, both educational and social. School-aged children, frequently victims of verbal abuse, were also subject to physical attacks because they were the most visible and vulnerable symbol of the infiltration of African Americans into Chicago's larger social world. Nellie Larson's high school, Wendell Phillips, was "the scene of frequent racial conflicts," one of which was described as a "miniature race war."[54] Whether the racial climate contributed to Peter Larsen's changing his name and sending his brown daughter away from Chicago cannot be ascertained, but it may well have played a role in his decisions.

53. Spear, *Black Chicago*, 39, 40.
54. *Ibid.*, 44, 45.

As a conductor on the city's railway system, Peter Larsen was a firsthand observer to some of the racially motivated attacks. There were numerous minor incidents on streetcars, but only the larger ones were reported by the press. One of the most sensational and least explained occurred on Larsen's State Street line, though some months after he had moved from the neighborhood. The Chicago *Defender* reported in a March 20, 1908, general news item: "Eight persons were hurt in a desperate race riot on a street car between white and colored men, which began at State and 39th Sts. Friday. Razors and revolvers were drawn and fists were freely used. The riot aboard the car continued until the motorman applied the brakes in front of the 50th St. Police Station." [55]

In the midst of the rising racial tensions and struggle of the working classes for parity in the city, Peter Larson moved from State Street in the summer of 1907. When he did, he not only left behind his old name in becoming Peter Larsen, but he also made what now appears to be a conscious effort to disassociate himself from his old identity. He listed himself in the 1908 Chicago telephone directory as "P. Larsen." In using only a first initial in combination with a new spelling of his surname, he virtually disappeared into Chicago's white West Side.

In January, 1912, Peter Larson obtained clear title to the house on West 70th Place, and on July 1, 1916, Peter Larson with his wife transferred the property in a warranty deed. On June 21, Peter Larson with Mary Larson had obtained a warranty deed to 6418 Maryland Avenue. In 1917, Peter *Larsen,* conductor, appears in the City Directory as residing at 6418 Maryland Avenue, which is the house number that Nella Larsen used for Irene Westover Redfield's father in her second novel, *Passing.* His move was farther south to Woodlawn, an area adjacent to the site of the 1893 Columbian Exposition. His new street began at 53rd, continued to 59th where it broke for Midway Plaissance, and then extended only from 63rd to 67th, where it ended at Oak Woods Cemetery. Maryland Avenue had once been named Jackson, a point Gertrude Martin, a minor character in *Passing,* accurately makes in explaining the new location of her husband's meat market ("'Maryland Avenue—used to be Jackson. . . . Near Sixty-third Street.'"). [56] Sixty-third Street was the major business and commercial thoroughfare.

55. Chicago *Defender,* March 20, 1908, p. 1.

56. Records of Cook County, Title transfers, Chicago Property Records, Book 386-A, p. 261, and Book 392-C, p. 174; *Thirteenth Census, 1910: Illinois,* Ward 7, Enumeration District 434, Sheet 14 (Microfilm reel 248), in Newberry Library; *Polk's Directory of Chicago, 1917,* in Chicago Historical Society; Nella Larsen, *Passing,* in *"Quicksand" and "Passing,"* ed. McDowell, 162, 167. Subsequent references to *Passing* will be to this edition.

Although the Great Migration of blacks from the South had already begun with a net in-migration of 61,000 between 1910 and 1920, and with a concomitant strain on housing resources, African Americans had not yet started to settle past 55th Street in any great concentration. However, the Woodlawn area was beginning to attract some members of the African-American upper classes. Situated on the southern periphery of the expanding black community, it was a suburban area with public transportation to the central city. As one African-American professional recalled: "I moved out here because it was sparsely settled . . . not so congested and the air was pure. We formerly lived in the 54th block of Dearborn—most of the better class Negroes were living in that vicinity—but our immediate neighbors were very undesirable, causing disturbances all hours of night. It became so annoying that I was more determined than ever to move further South."[57] While some of the "better class" of African Americans were dispersed in Woodlawn, Peter Larsen's new residence between 64th and 65th streets was in a neighborhood that was still predominantly white.

Located in the Alfred B. McChesney's World's Fair Subdivision, the property at 6420–18 Maryland was a small yellow-brick apartment building occupying nearly three full lots, rather than a single family house. The acquisition moved Peter Larsen into the ranks of the middle-class landlords in the area who rented apartments, four in his case, or single rooms to employees (agents, locomotive engineers, traffic men, clerks, bookkeepers, and lawyers) of the electric railroad and their families. The building was in an excellent location for the railroad workers because at 63rd Street were the Woodlawn Park station of the Illinois Central and the South Side terminal station for the Chicago Surface Lines, which had been formed in 1914 by the merger of the Chicago City Railway, Peter Larsen's employer, with several other city lines.[58] Peter Larsen's purchase of the apartment building gave him a better income than he had had during Nellie's formative years.

The title transfer records for the city indicate that Peter Larson, with his wife, Mary, purchased the property on June 21, 1916, with a warranty deed registered on July 6, 1916.[59] Although Peter Larsen had been using the *-sen* spelling of his name consistently from 1908 to 1917, including his listing for the 1910 census, he used the *-son* spelling for the purchase of the build-

57. Otis Dudley Duncan and Beverly Duncan, *The Negro Population of Chicago: A Study of Residential Succession* (Chicago, 1957), 34; quotation from Frazier, *The Negro Family in Chicago*, 112.

58. Johnson, *A Century of Chicago Streetcars*, 12.

59. Records of Cook County, Title transfers, Chicago Property Records, Book 392-C, p. 174.

ing, and by extension for the legal transaction of business. The *Larsen* spelling does not appear to be his legal name, just as *Mary* appears to be his wife's legal name, rather than the *Marie* she used for the 1910 census.

Between 1917 and 1923 there is a break in publication of the City Directory. When it resumes in 1923, there is no listing for Peter Larsen, conductor, at 6418 Maryland Avenue. Nor is there a listing in the 1928–1929 City Directory, the next one available. Peter Larson apparently died in the 1920s. On September 24, 1920, Peter and Mary Larson completed their mortgage indebtedness for the Maryland Avenue property; the release was registered on November 3, 1920. However, on May 1, 1922, the couple took out a trust deed—a mortgage on the property with a bank and trust company (Greenbaum Sons)—and thereafter the property appears to have been held jointly by the Larsons, Greenbaum Sons, and several other owners until May 31, 1927, when "Peter Larson *et al.*" are released from the 1922 indebtedness. The 1927 release seems to suggest the "estate" or "heirs" of Peter Larson. As nearly as can be determined from available records of property transfers and death certificates (for all deaths recorded for any Peter Larson or Peter Larsen between 1920 and 1930), his death occurred between 1927 and the fall of 1928. His widow Mary/Marie may have remained in Chicago for a time, but by the end of 1928, she seems to have joined her daughter Anna in southern California. In interviews after the appearance of each of her novels, Nella Larsen refers to only a mother and a half-sister living in California, not to a father or stepfather.[60]

A random piece of information from one of those 1920s interviews infers that Larsen's Danish background came by way of her father. She provided Thelma Berlack, a reporter for the *Amsterdam News,* with a summary of her family: "The only relatives she has in this country are her mother, who is white, and a half-sister. They live in California. Her father, a Danish West Indian, died before she was old enough to know much about him. All of his people live in Denmark." Although Larsen repeats the information that her West Indian father died before she knew him, the same information that she had given to Knopf in 1926, she adds a fact that does not appear elsewhere: that all of her father's people lived in Denmark. Late in life, Nella Larsen would describe her father as being "in business in Chicago," and reveal that he was "West Indian, but light-skinned."[61]

60. *Ibid.;* Berlack, "New Author Unearthed"; Mary Rennels, New York *Telegram,* April 13, 1929, in SCF.

61. Berlack, "New Author Unearthed"; Alice L. Carper and Carolyn Lane, interview with author, May 5, 1985.

While the matter of Nella Larsen's family is generally problematical, the matter of her mother is particularly enigmatic. Throughout most of her adult life, she rarely mentioned her mother, except in statements about her Danish heritage. Only one of the public records documenting Larsen's life—her marriage certificate—includes her mother's name, listing her as "Marian Hansen." Her school records and fellowship applications do not identify a mother, not even in reference to a married name. After her own marriage in 1919, Larsen listed only her husband as immediate family in her applications for jobs and passports. The absence of even a naming of her mother is significant because though Larsen publicly claimed her Danish heritage from the maternal side of her family, she never publicly acknowledged her mother's identity or that of the maternal side of her family.

In a private conversation in the 1930s, however, she revealed that her mother was German, though born in Denmark, and that she had once visited with her grandmother in Denmark, who gave her a set of candlesticks. Years later, during the 1950s, she would repeat that her mother was German but from Denmark. Nella Larsen was reluctant to speak directly about her mother. The absence of connection to a mother, then, suggests that Larsen's early development functioned to problematize her defining her identity through relationships of intimacy and care, relationships that have been explained as typical for women.[62]

Marian Hansen, the name Larsen supplied as her mother's in filing for a marriage license, could be a German name. But *Marian* is also comparable to both *Mary* and *Marie*, the names used by Peter Larson's wife and listed on Nellie Walker's birth record. *Marian* seems to be a diminutive of *Mary*, her mother's legal name. In 1907 when Nellie Larson enrolled at Fisk, she used the name Nellie *Marie* Larsen.[63] The middle name, the same as her mother's first name, had not previously appeared in her school records. By 1912 when she entered the Lincoln Hospital School for Nurses, she had become Nella *Marion* Larsen. Not only had a major shift occurred in her stated given name, but one had also occurred in her middle name, which became *Marion*, a masculine form of *Marian*. One explanation may be that the assumption of first *Marie* and then *Marion* as a middle name signaled an attempt to attach herself to her mother, and by extension to her father

62. Frankie Lea Houchins, interviews with author, March 12, December 30, 1984; Carper and Lane interview; Carol Gilligan, *In a Different Voice: Psychological Theory and Women's Development* (Cambridge, Mass., 1982), 17.

63. *Catalogue of the Officers and Students of Fisk University, Nashville, Tennessee, 1907–1908* (Nashville, 1908), 67.

and the family that was becoming increasingly distant. Both of the times she used versions of her mother's name, Larsen was involved in studies leading to work in "care" professions—teaching and nursing. But at those points in her youth, the family that Nellie Larson had known for a brief seven years was moving more exclusively into a white world, while she had been consigned to a black one. Using versions of her mother's name may well have helped anchor her sense of her own identity and position in a world populated not merely by whites but by family as well.

One recent researcher into Nella Larsen's background has formulated another version of her family, one based on an account attributed to her mother, Mary Hanson. According to Charles R. Larson (no relation): "The place of Nella's birth—which she claimed as Chicago—is more problematic. A close friend of the Larsen family for nearly fifty years claimed that Nella's mother, Mary Hanson, told her that Nella had been born in New York and that her father was a Black American chauffeur for the family for whom Nella's mother worked as a domestic. Thus, the question of Nella's biological father remains conjectural."[64] The question of the identity of Nella Larsen's parents is problematic, but not for the reasons Charles Larson provides. Mary Hanson Walker gave birth to Nellie Walker in Chicago, where she had applied for a marriage license with Peter Walker. The story that she allegedly told a longtime family friend is not true. But the question remains, why would Mary Hanson Walker Larson/Larsen fabricate the circumstances of Nellie Walker/Nella Larsen's birth? It is a question at least as puzzling as her denial in 1910 of giving birth to Nella Larsen. Equally puzzling is the account that Charles Larson gives that Anna Larsen, Mary Hanson Larsen's only other child, was reportedly surprised to learn that she had a sister when news of inheriting Nella Larsen's estate reached her in the 1960s.[65] Anna must have known of her sister's existence: from 1901 to 1907, Nella and Anna Larsen, who were only two years apart in age, lived with their parents in the same household. It would appear that there was a conspiracy of silence and deception surrounding Nella Larsen's relationship not only to Anna and Mary Hanson Larsen, but also to Peter Walker and Peter Larsen. And there is the question of how much Nella Larsen actually knew about her parents.

Her version of her family and formative years emerged during her most

---

64. Charles R. Larson, "Whatever Happened to Nella Larsen?," *Belles Lettres*, IV (Spring, 1989), 14. Larson also states, "Census documents and the death certificates of these three people help establish some of the details concerning the Larsen household."

65. *Ibid.*, 15.

public period in Harlem. Alleging the death of a black West Indian father and the alienation from a white mother remarried to a white man provided Nella Larsen with unusual social mobility, and without the baggage of family. The story obviated the necessity of explaining a mother's absence from her life. African Americans would comprehend the racial imperatives that would separate a white mother from her black daughter, and without questioning, they would form a personal bond with the daughter based on a shared understanding of racism. The death of a black father would eliminate questions about her family's social and economic position in Chicago and explain her lack of connection with the black middle class through her father's family. This aspect may have been particularly significant during Larsen's Harlem years when a number of African Americans active in the New Negro Renaissance had Chicago connections; for example, Regina Anderson, librarian during the 1920s at the 135th Street branch of the New York Public Library and roommate of Charles S. Johnson's assistant Ethel Ray, was originally from Wisconsin, but before moving to New York had made her home in Chicago, where her father was a prominent attorney. Larsen's version of her parents and background meant an all-around easier, more acceptable situation for her. Did she, however, have only this version available to her?

In the puzzle that Nella Larsen's background remains even after some of the pieces are in place, there is, in the veiling of Peter Larson as father and the obscuring of Mary Hanson Larson as mother, the possibility that the fictitious family schema she claimed was a symbolical representation of her actual family. One scenario is as plausible as any other that might today be pieced together from the verifiable facts of Nella Larsen's life.

If Peter Larson were in fact a colored Danish Virgin Islander of mixed racial ancestry who had passed for white in Chicago, then Larsen's presentation of a dead father would be a metaphorical rendering of his death as a black person. Because of the mobility among Chicago's various ethnic and racial groups in the 1890s and 1900s, it is not improbable that a light-skinned black man who was also a foreigner might cross the color line for better employment and greater social status. Black men were primarily employed as domestic and personal servants in 1890, but 86.2 percent of the Danish-born immigrants were only slightly better off as manual laborers.[66] An opportunity for a job with the pay of a railway employee and with the

66. Michael F. Funchion, "Irish Chicago: Church, Homeland, Politics, and Class—The Shaping of an Ethnic Group, 1870–1900," in *Ethnic Chicago*, ed. Jones and Holli, 28.

status of a conductor would be incentive enough to pass as white. The presence of a mixed-race child may have become untenable for "white" immigrants rising socially and economically in a Chicago of increasing racial tension. In any case, Nella Larsen's background may well have been even more traumatic than she would claim and more complicated than others could comprehend. In her version of her parentage, Nella Larsen could well have been symbolically addressing an even more grievous alienation from a father who, while passing himself, sent her off to become a completely black person.

There is no need, however, to press speculations about Nella Larsen's beginnings in Chicago.[67] The larger facts are verifiable. Nella Larsen, who throughout her adult life staked a position in the elite upper-middle class of African Americans, was born Nellie Walker and spent her formative years with a "white" father (Peter Larson/Larsen) as her primary parent in a South Side immigrant household composed also of her "white" sister (Anna) and "white" mother (Mary Hanson Walker Larson/Larsen), who denied giving birth to her. The Chicagoans that she knew best were mainly working-class people of ethnic and racial diversity. They were railroad and streetcar workers, store and stockyard workers, clerks and tradespeople whose shops and businesses sprawled along State Street in a teeming urban area that was not yet a slum. The world of the African-American middle class and Chicago's black elite dating from the middle of the nineteenth century, though within her physical view just blocks away on Grand Boulevard, was a world removed. Hemmed in by railroad tracks and streetcar lines, her immediate environment and her family's class precluded her association with African-American society people. Neither did her father, as an ordinary working immigrant, have access to their world.

Yet by means of work, thrift, and opportunity, Peter Larson/Larsen assimilated into the ranks of the lower-middle class of whites, and with him he took his wife, now "Marie" rather than "Mary," and daughter Anna. He did not, however, move his daughter Nellie upward socially with him or affirm her place within the family group. Her skin color precluded assimilation. She entered young adulthood futureless in his world and threatening to it.

In an exercise of authority that, on the one hand, may be viewed as

67. Catherine Drinker Bowen explains that "doubtful and suppositious" is used in the catalogue of the British Museum Reading Room to identify speculative conclusions. Catherine Drinker Bowen, *Biography: The Craft and the Calling* (Boston, 1968), 60.

thoughtful and sympathetic, he enrolled her in the most prestigious African-American school of the time, Fisk University, and in its Normal School that would provide her with the basic training necessary to become both a teacher and a member of the respectable African-American middle class. And he did so despite the fact that Nellie Larson's grades for the school year ending in June, 1907, were not all satisfactory. She received an F in German II, an 87.5 in American history, an 89.5 in English II, and though she had also taken freehand drawing, no grade was recorded for that class. (The F in German is noteworthy because Larsen later claimed German as her mother's first language and one of her own two spoken languages, the other being Danish.) In a sense, then, by disassociation, Peter Larson established an access for Nellie's entry into a solid adulthood as a self-supporting professional at a time when in Chicago there were only 962 African Americans in professions and only 64 of them teachers.[68]

On the other hand, Peter Larson's particular exercising of patriarchal power over his daughter's future can be viewed as rejection and denial of a familial bond. He relegated her to a world that, though in some ways more elevated than his own (that is, college-trained, professional), was much more restricted simply because it was an African-American world subject to the hardships of racial discrimination. And too, as a parent, he was disengaging himself from a daughter and removing her from intimacy with his life. The distance between his home in Chicago and Fisk in Nashville was only a spatial measure of the distance inserted between father and daughter, as well as between mother and daughter. He may have been telling her to enter a world in which she could be comfortable, could find her own place and companions, but he was also telling her to embark upon an independent existence, independent of him and of the world in which he and her mother and sister functioned and in which he could not both include her and maintain his own place and position.

Whether or not all of the reasons were clear to her, Nellie Larsen journeyed away from Chicago in September, 1907. She would not thereafter call that city home. Her doubtful patrimony—skin color, class position, family connection—would become egregious factors affecting her spatial movement, social mobility, and self-perception in the decades ahead.

---

68. Wendell Phillips High School records for June, 1907; Ernestine D. Curry, principal of Wendell Phillips High School, to Thadious M. Davis, September 7, 1984, in possession of Thadious M. Davis; Drake, *Churches and Voluntary Associations*, 121–22.

2

Going Forth into Unknown Regions,
1907–1912

A TRANSFIGURED NELLIE Marie Larsen left Chicago in September of 1907. Her destination was Fisk University in Nashville, Tennessee, where she had been accepted for admission into the Normal Department. The department required the completion of a three-year Normal Preparatory Course or of high school before entrance into the Normal program. At sixteen years of age, Larsen had already completed two years of high school at Wendell Phillips. She was to continue high school in the Normal Department as a third-year student, after which she would enter the junior class of the teacher's training program and in another year graduate from the senior class with the requisites to teach. Her journey to Fisk was movement toward adulthood and preparation for independence in one of the few professions available to women of color. Teaching had become in the decades after the Civil War a haven from racial debasement and a source of social value for African Americans, particularly for females. Despite her separation from her family and a resulting self-polarization, her prospects for a productive future rested in a connection to others through service.

Although only a ten-hour trip from Chicago on the Illinois Central Railroad, Nashville was a world away from the life that young Nellie Larson had known. One way of assessing the impact of the change upon her is by comprehending the physical differences she encountered. Not only was Nashville in the South, but it was a congested city with the beginning of sprawling suburbs that could only marginally qualify as urban in comparison with Chicago. In 1900 Nashville proper covered 10 square miles and had 140 miles of improved streets and 59 miles of sewers for its population of 80,865.[1] In leaving America's second largest city, Nellie Larsen was transported to a spatial environment that was alien.

Less ethnically diverse, Nashville was, unlike Chicago, racially segregated by law as well as by custom. Although in the nineteenth century blacks and whites had lived clustered together in an area close to the commercial center and within three-quarters of a mile of the city's public square, after the turn of the century, whites had moved to more healthful "streetcar suburbs" when the advent of electric streetcars eliminated the need to live near the workplace. They left African Americans behind in tuberculosis-ridden tenements in Black Bottom, a low-lying slum adjacent to downtown and near the river, or in deteriorating neighborhoods such as Hell's Half Acre, an area of shacks sloping up to Capitol Hill. The African-American population, which by 1910 would reach 36,532 out of a total population of 110,362 including the newly incorporated suburbs, was more concentrated and impoverished in the first decade of the twentieth century than Chicago's slightly larger African-American population (44,103 by 1910).[2]

Beyond the physical difference Nashville represented, the Fisk University campus and community presented another unfamiliarity: it was an overwhelmingly African-American environment and prided itself in being such. Founded in 1865 under the auspices of the American Missionary Society of New York and the Western Freedman's Aid Commission of Cincinnati, the school boasted a history of interracial cooperation in educating young people of color. The white founders had designed a Christian education for an emancipated race, and envisioned their mission as "patient, long-continued, exact, and comprehensive work in preparation for high positions and large responsibilities." When the Fisk School opened in January, 1866, its aim was a classical education for both sexes that would expand "to whatever extent the capacity and energy of the race should in the future de-

1. George Rollie Adams and Ralph Jerry Christian, *Nashville: A Pictorial History* (Virginia Beach, 1983), 83. Public facilities and services were more limited in the "Athens of the South," where 72 miles of streetcar lines paled in comparison to the over 1,000 miles of street railways criss-crossing Chicago and carrying 278,832,491 passengers in 1907. See also "Chicago Transportation Facilities," in *Biographical and Industrial: Prominent Citizens and Industries of Chicago*, comp. James Langland (Chicago, 1901), 6, and *Chicago Daily News Almanac Yearbook for 1907*, in Newberry Library, Chicago.

2. Adams and Christian, *Nashville*, 83; Don H. Doyle, *Nashville in the New South, 1880–1930* (Knoxville, 1985), 78–86; T. J. Woofter, Jr., *Negro Problems in Cities* (Garden City, 1928), 32. By 1920 and the beginning of the Great Migration, however, Chicago's African-American population would increase by 148.2 percent to 109,458, while Nashville would lose 890, or 2.4 percent of its African Americans to out-migration (Woofter, *Negro Problems in Cities*, 32).

mand."[3] The qualifiers suggested something of the pervasive notion of a downtrodden race that characterized the Fisk mission. The psychological impact of its race-centeredness on Larsen cannot be underestimated.

Upon her arrival in September, 1907, the lofty race mission had not changed despite the great emphasis at that time on industrial education for African Americans. The school's most famous graduate W. E. B. Du Bois, class of 1888, was at the forefront of an ongoing fight against vocational training as the only viable curriculum for African Americans. Because Fisk's insistence on academic subjects hampered its ability to raise operating funds, the American Missionary Association still paid part of the teachers' salaries and provided much of the administration. The president, the Reverend James Griswold Merrill, D.D., was white, as were a number of the officers and faculty; however, there were no white students, because after 1900, Tennessee law prohibited racial mixing in its schools.

The student body was composed of African Americans from good families. Expected to become race leaders, the students came from across the United States and the West Indies, but the majority of students were from the South. Some were poor and worked to pay school fees; of the three hundred boarding students in 1907, approximately one-half received financial aid from the institution. Other students were the well-off sons and daughters of African-American ministers, teachers, doctors, and lawyers. One student enrolled in the fall of 1907, for example, was the son and namesake of the most famous black man in America, Booker T. Washington of Tuskegee, Alabama, who, though head of a rival institution offering industrial or practical courses, recognized the high quality of a Fisk education and endorsed the college training it provided. Many, like Larsen herself, were the fair-skinned products of interracial unions either in their parents' or grandparents' generation. Counted among these "blue-veined" mulatto students were the children of Nashville's prosperous African Americans, who were descended from the antebellum free-black community and who had emerged in the late nineteenth century as business and professional elites.[4] Joining this privileged group on the basis of her color, Nellie Larsen began the transition from adolescence to adulthood and to an African-American identity.

3. *Catalogue of the Officers and Students of Fisk University, Nashville, Tennessee, 1907–1908* (Nashville, 1908), 7.

4. Charles W. Smith, "First Impressions," *Fisk Herald,* XXV (April, 1908), 18; Joe M. Richardson, *A History of Fisk University, 1865–1946* (University, Ala., 1980), 61; Doyle, *Nashville,* 110.

Located on a sheltered northwest Nashville site formerly occupied by Fort Gillem, Fisk University provided one of the best possible educational environments in which to be a female of color in 1907. African-American females were encouraged to enroll because the school emphasized "the absolute necessity of the *right education* of the girls and young women of the race whose elevation and advancement it was founded to promote." The institution's publicity claimed that the "highest interest of every race and community depends largely upon the intelligence, frugality, virtue, and noble aspirations of its women."[5]

Accordingly, Fisk afforded females the same opportunities for study as males. Young women had "equal advantages with the young men," but they also had the option of the "special provision," a department of their own.[6] At a time when other institutions established for freed blacks, such as Tuskegee Institute, restricted the courses of study open to women, Fisk not only welcomed women students but recruited them.

This practice assisted the institution in a crucial way. A female graduate of Fisk, Margaret Murray, was instrumental in securing financial support for the institution during the period in which Nellie Larsen was enrolled and in helping to ensure support in the subsequent decade. Upon graduating with the class of 1889, Murray went to Tuskegee Institute at the invitation of the principal, Booker T. Washington, who appointed her head of the Ladies' Department. Within two years she was engaged to Washington, whom she married in 1893. As the first lady of Tuskegee, Margaret Murray Washington remained a loyal advocate for her alma mater and used her position to assist Fisk in securing funds from Andrew Carnegie, who contributed $20,000 in 1908 for a new library. In addition, she helped persuade her husband to accept an appointment to the Fisk Board of Trustees in 1909, because in that capacity he could exert his considerable influence with foundations. During his tenure on the board, Washington aided Fisk in raising $300,000 from private organizations and individual philanthropists.[7]

As a female student, Nellie Larsen was not shortchanged in academic pursuits or discriminated against because of her sex, though she may well have resented being thrust into Fisk's black world. Enrolled in the teacher preparation program, which had become increasingly female since the

5. *Fisk University Catalogue, 1907–1908*, 13. The first quotation is from the "General Information" section of the catalogue, circulated among prospective students and their parents.
6. *Ibid.*
7. Richardson, *A History of Fisk*, 67; Doyle, *Nashville*, 206.

founding of the institution, she nonetheless had access to excellent training in traditional academic subjects taught by many of the same professors from the college preparatory and theological departments, and from the college's academic and graduate departments. Two of her instructors, Dora Anna Scribner (rhetoric and English literature) and Mary Elizabeth Spence (French and Greek), both whites with missionary vocations who had spent their careers at Fisk, were among the most respected faculty in the university. In fact, Mary Spence, the daughter of an early Fisk professor and dean, Adam K. Spence, had not only received her undergraduate and master's degree at Fisk (B.A., 1887; M.A., 1892), but also earned a reputation for her insistence upon equality for African Americans.[8]

The year 1907 was a fortuitous time for Fisk students because the school was in the middle of an "era of modernization and readjustment," as one Fisk president later termed the period from 1901 through 1915. It was evolving from what had been mainly "a preparatory normal school and embryo college which placed chief emphasis upon classical education and evangelical religion" into "a liberal arts college of highest standing which emphasiz[ed] both the classical and the practical in education and open-mindedness in a search for the truth in religion." President Merrill, who had assumed his office in 1901 after nearly a year as acting president, took as the school's motto "The development of Christian manhood in an education for service"—which for him meant that the curriculum had to be expanded in order to prepare the students for service. During the first decade and a half of the twentieth century, when illiteracy among African Americans fell from 47 percent to 25 percent, Fisk had begun the effort to increase its offerings in the physical and social sciences, because the white administrators recognized that people of color were better situated to take up the economic and social battles facing the race.[9]

At the same time, the institution upgraded its physical facilities to accommodate the modernized educational programs. The campus, comprising thirty-five acres, had eleven buildings in 1907. With an overall value of buildings and apparatus exceeding $450,000, Fisk was, along with Howard University, Hampton Institute, and Tuskegee Institute, one of the wealthiest institutions for African Americans in the country. Yet unlike the other three,

8. Richardson, *A History of Fisk*, 49.

9. Thomas Elsa Jones, *Inaugural Address, December 7, 1926* (Nashville, 1926), in Special Collections, Fisk University Library; Jones, "Abstract and Argument," in *Inaugural Address;* Richardson, *A History of Fisk*, 63; Jones, "The Second Period," in *Inaugural Address.*

Fisk had a difficult time securing financial support.[10] Development of the college programs and resources to support an expanded curriculum was a primary goal, because after the turn of the century more and better prepared students sought entrance into college rather than normal or theology programs.

Nellie Larsen resided in Jubilee Hall with the other female boarding students. Like all students from outside the Nashville area, she was admitted to the university under the condition that she enter the Boarding Department. Her dormitory was a grand limestone structure that had cost $100,000 to build in 1875. The original company of Jubilee Singers had raised building funds by beginning a concert tour in October, 1871, that took them throughout the United States and to Europe, performing spirituals and hymns. At the dedication of Jubilee Hall on January 1, 1876, the 1873 portrait of the singers, painted by Edmund Havel, Queen Victoria's court artist, decorated the auditorium as a reminder of the school's proud history and of its students' dedication. Each year during the October 6 observation of Jubilee Day, the enormous six-story brick structure became the center of a university-wide celebration. Although the campus was generally known for its beautiful buildings and grounds, Jubilee Hall was its showpiece. One of the largest and best-equipped school buildings in the South, it contained the first elevator in Nashville, though the students complained that its use was mainly for luggage. The modernity of the building was not, however, the most touted feature; that was reserved for its "home life" arrangement.

Overseeing and directing home life in Jubilee Hall was the charge of Eva Louisa Benson, principal of the Women's Department, who gave "special instruction and counsel regarding true womanly conduct and character."[11] She, like the other administrators, fostered the concept of the Fisk family. With the assistance of Sarah Josephine Scott, matron of Jubilee Hall, and Cecile B. Jefferson, head of the dining room, the principal held the female students to the strictest standards of manners, deportment, propriety, and decorum. She conducted the boarding department as a Christian home in which discipline was parental in character and true womanhood its objective.

---

10. *Fisk University Catalogue, 1907–1908,* 9. Two major buildings, however, were completed during Nellie Larsen's enrollment: Chase Hall (1907), to house the Department of Applied Science; and the Carnegie Library (1908), to house a collection of eight thousand bound volumes.

11. *Ibid.,* 14.

While the university claimed that the rules were "few, and in general those of a well-regulated household," the reality was that the young women in Jubilee Hall, like their male counterparts in Livingstone Hall, were treated firmly in matters affecting all personal habits (waking, bathing, eating, studying, sleeping) and were admonished impartially to develop "right habits" by performing on the average of one period a day "some form of labor as directed by the University." The work performed by students helped to keep the monthly tuition and board costs down to thirteen dollars, paid in advance. From the outset, students made a "sacred promise" to observe all regulations concerning conduct, deportment, attendance, and study. Subject to discipline for any "immoral or unworthy" activities whether on or off campus, they were given a list of "strictly forbidden" practices: cursing (or using profanity), gambling, betting, card playing, drinking, smoking (or using tobacco), and dancing. As strict as the regulations were in 1907, they were not nearly as harsh or as petty as they would become in the ten years after 1908, when discipline seemed to become a means and an end in the educational process.[12]

Once Jubilee Hall opened in the third week of September, Nellie Larsen and the other female boarding students were required to wear a uniform on all public occasions. The white shirtwaist blouse of linen or cotton could be made at home but could have no trimming other than tucks; the navy blue suit, a jacket and skirt, had to be purchased in Nashville along with a plain hat. Females were expected to spend only a modest thirteen dollars a year for school clothing, and while they could bring everyday dresses, they were warned that their clothing had to be "becoming, plain and substantial." Neither extravagant finery (silk or satin skirts and shirts) nor elaborate decoration (laces, trimmings, and sashes) was allowed. A work-apron and rain gear, waterproof and rubbers, were mandatory, as were rubber-soled shoes for the gymnasium. The regulations for clothing were intended to level the socioeconomic differences among the students and to stimulate the family-like atmosphere. In later life, perhaps partly in response to her stay at Fisk, Larsen displayed a passion for beautiful clothing and rich fabrics, especially velvet, which she even used as a coat trimming. She loved silk stockings and crepe de Chine sleepwear, particularly in her favorite color, green. She refused to wear anything plain, and admitted publicly to wanting "beautiful and rich things."[13]

12. *Ibid.*, 14, 20; Richardson, *A History of Fisk*, 85; see also 86–90.
13. *Fisk University Catalogue, 1907–1908*, 18; Nella Larsen to Dorothy Peterson, July 12, 1927, in JWJ; Larsen quoted by Mary Rennels, New York *Telegram*, April 13, 1929, in SCF.

An experienced nurse, Grace Althea Page, lived in Jubilee Hall to provide health care for the residents. Her official title was Health Officer. Her charge was both to oversee the health of boarding students, who deposited a fee of one dollar to cover their expenses for medical supplies, and to give "individual advice" to the young women. She particularly encouraged their participation in exercises on the eight acres of land surrounding Jubilee Hall, because the administrators believed that daily wholesome exercise was necessary for good health and that the well-landscaped grounds, "giving retirement to the home life," sheltered the females from unwelcome observation of their exercises.[14]

For the small, one-hundred-pound teenager from Chicago, the protective structure duplicating home and family environment might have been comforting were it not for another aspect of campus life. Fisk, dedicated to making "its students strong, earnest, broadminded Christian men and women, who shall give their lives to the uplifting and benefiting of their people," required attendance at religious services as a means of shaping the characters of African Americans and instilling the proper virtues and attitudes in them. In fact, the religious services were on the same plane with class attendance and regular recitations, and fostered the Christian perspective that many students had toward the school. For example, a college junior displayed the perspective in introducing a *Fisk Herald* essay on supporting the institution:

> No one can visit Fisk University and for the first time look upon its beautiful grounds and magnificent buildings without being . . . impressed. . . . [T]he chapel exercises . . . [with] those pathetic Jubilee songs . . . spontaneously poured forth from the souls of over four hundred sons and daughters of the emancipated slaves . . . completely captivate [a visitor]. . . . [H]e becomes thoroughly convinced . . . that this institution is playing a prominent part in working out this great racial problem; and he is made to believe that God himself is having a hand in the solution.

This introductory assessment concluded with a fervent thanks to God ("our hearts full of joy go out to our heavenly Father in gratitude for this Beacon Light").[15]

---

14. *Fisk University Catalogue, 1907–1908*, 19, 14, 13f.
15. *Ibid.*, 15; Smith, "First Impressions," 18.

Nellie Larsen's background had not prepared her for the missionary zeal of the religious attitudes and activities: mandatory Sunday school followed by church services; social worship on Wednesday nights. Her family life had failed to instill a healthy appreciation for Christian devotion to the uplifting of the Negro race. The Society of Christian Endeavor and the King's Daughters, both established for women students, held no appeal for her. Neither did she empathize with the Mission Study Society's weekly meetings to discuss missionary work in foreign lands. From the perspective of one raised in a big northern city, these activities exaggerated the negative stereotypes of the needy, backward, and downtrodden race that had been used to separate a mixed-race daughter from the white members of her family. As an adult, Larsen maintained that she did not "believe in religion, churches, and the like"; no doubt her formative experiences at Fisk contributed to such views.[16]

Enrollment at Fisk and life in Jubilee Hall underscored the changed status of Nellie Larsen's primary identity. She was "colored," a member of the Negro race, but the transfiguration was not her choice. Her placement in the institution was intended to acclimate her to her racial identity and, perhaps as well, to strip her of claims on her white father, mother, and sister. However, in inculcating the racial heritage of African Americans and in affirming Larsen's relationship to it, Fisk served another purpose as well. It exacerbated Larsen's ambivalence and guilt in basic matters of identity formation. Her conflicting attitudes toward African Americans and her painful separation from her family combined in a period of crisis during which she attempted to resolve for herself the questions of who she was and what she might become.

In an act of self-transformation and self-definition, Nellie Marie Larsen dropped the unusual spelling of her given name (Nellye) when she entered Fisk. Although she had long since abandoned her surname at birth, *Walker* would occasionally surface as her middle name in her official school documents.[17] Among the concentration of rural blacks at Fisk, she discovered that one member of the Normal faculty, Nellie Lillian Rhule, and a number of the students shared her given name. Among them was Nellie Belle Johnson from Eufania, Alabama, a second-year student in Larsen's Normal

16. Nella Larsen quoted in Thelma E. Berlack, "New Author Unearthed Right Here in Harlem," New York *Amsterdam News*, May 23, 1928, p. 16.

17. *Fisk University Catalogue, 1907–1908*, 76 (listing under students in Department of Music for Nelly Walker Larsen).

School program. Bessie Nell Taylor from Athens, Alabama, was also in the second-year Normal School, and Nellie Davis from Nashville was enrolled for first-year studies. There were as well younger grammar school students named Nellie: Nellie Hattie Davis in the eighth grade and Nellie Mary Johnson in the seventh. During the school year, Nellie Larson, who had been *Larsen* for only a matter of months, began to use *Nella* as her given name. The change in name was an insistence upon her difference.

The new first name, in combination with *Larsen*, made her unique even among the Fisk Normal students who were mulattoes. It stressed her ethnic identity over her racial one, and it accentuated her difference from the rural and southern-born blacks named Nellie. *Nella* was not Larsen's creation, though the name was uncommon even among the Scandinavian population of Chicago. Instances of its appearance were rarely recorded before the turn of the century in the United States. Like *Nellie* and *Nell*, *Nella* is a familiar form of *Helen* and *Eleanor*, but unlike the other two, it achieved an independent status later and occurs less frequently.

Embedded in the assertion of *Nella* over *Nellie* is not so much a link to historiography or etymology of derivation but rather a connection with class connotation. *Nella*, as distinct from *Nellie*, addressed not merely aspirations of upward mobility common to the urban, particularly the working-class, populations of Larsen's girlhood environment, but as well a proclivity to disengage from undesirable parameters and an impatience with observed impediments to immediate advancement. As a matter of course, Larsen, like many others in the nation generally and at Fisk in particular, did not want to be poor or connected with the lower classes, but she went a step further: she specifically did not want to be perceived as being poor or lower class. "Like other words, names are symbolic; unlike other words, what they symbolize is unique. A thousand John Does and Jane Does may live and die, but no bearer of those names has the same inheritance, the same history, or the same fears and expectations as any other."[18] *Nella* was a symbol of Larsen's uniqueness, yet it was even more precisely the emblem of her fears and expectations.

The change of name reveals a search for a name that would reconcile an internal perception of self or potentiality with an external reflection of self and positionality. In naming herself, she compensated for the blurred ethnic identity reflected in her physical appearance and for the rejection of her

18. Casey Miller and Kate Swift, *Words and Women: New Language in New Times* (Garden City, 1977), 1–2.

ethnicity by the Larsen family in Chicago, whose primary emphasis was on her race. Nella Larsen made the more foreign version of her already Scandinavian name her own and by means of it grounded herself in an ethnic-specific identity, reordered her definition of herself, and altered her public image. Out of the experience of rejection and denial, as well as from her father's own example, she had learned one means of renewal and rebirth, of recreating and revisioning self through new names.

Over and above ethnicity, she arched the curve of her self-naming to reflect her ambition and her anxiety about class affiliation. Consciousness of class background and family prominence was a salient identifying feature of the Fisk students. Their concerns ultimately helped to isolate the sensitive Larsen from her classmates. Her defense, manifested as haughtiness, was a retreat into herself. She became relatively invisible during her year at Fisk and left little physical evidence of her residency there. Yet her attempt to assert by means of names, the most frequently used aspect for grounding identity, her private conception of herself into the public sphere would not only assuage her fear of being inferior but also become characteristic of her behavior throughout much of her adult life.

In experimenting with renaming herself, Nellie Marie Larsen was not alone. One of her classmates in the third year of the Normal preparatory high school was Grace Virginia Frank, a native of Dundee, New York, who in later years would become Mrs. William Lloyd Imes and Larsen's sister-in-law. Although from a prominent middle-class family, Frank, too, experimented with her name by becoming *Grayce* during the 1907–1908 school year. She, like Larsen, aimed for a more sophisticated self-image that would reiterate her northern origins while separating her from the rural southerners in the school. Unlike Nella Larsen, who used her new name unofficially while in the Normal School, Grayce Virginia Frank entered the different spelling of her name into her official record at Fisk, but she returned to the conventional spelling of her given name upon her graduation.

Although Larsen may have viewed some of her classmates as provincial, she could not ignore the great variety of geographic regions represented among them. For a small school, Fisk had a diverse student body from both urban and rural areas, primarily because the institution had, in sending its graduates out to teach in schools throughout the nation, established an impeccable reputation for the quality of its programs and also because the Fisk Jubilee singers had, in performing around the country and abroad, publicized the school's name and work. As might be expected, the majority of the Normal students came from in-state (thirty-three) and from the southern states Alabama, Louisiana, Kentucky, and Georgia, with a few from Arkansas, Mississippi, Virginia, Florida, and North and South Carolina. One Fisk graduate who attended the kindergarten, training school, and the preparatory school, recalled that "so many of the young women were from Louisiana, Mississippi, and Alabama; their fathers were white and sent them to Fisk."[19] The western states represented were Texas (the second largest enrollment, ten), Nevada, and Colorado, while only New York and Connecticut were represented from the Northeast. In addition to Larsen, there were three students from Chicago—Madelyn Seattle Duncan, Lucy Jane Jackson, and Vivien Marie Peek, the latter two enrolled as special students—but none formed bonds with Larsen. Aside from them, only one other student from Illinois and one from Omaha, Nebraska, represented the Midwest.

Larsen's third-year class, comprising twenty students from thirteen states, was a microcosm of the student population in the Normal Department; and with the exception of its being all-female, it reflected the general diversity of the students enrolled campuswide. Female students were noticeably concentrated in the Normal Department. During the 1907–1908 school year, the Normal Department and its preparatory program had an enrollment of 119 students, 7 of whom were classified as special students and 2 of whom were men. In the ten years before the 1907–1908 term, however, no men had graduated from the teacher-preparation program. Following the turn of the century, male students at Fisk had increasingly elected the collegiate course as preparation for professions other than teaching. Whereas in Chicago Larsen had been exposed to a greater number of ethnic groups, at Fisk she encountered a comparable diversity of African-American people. In later years, she would write of one fictional character's response to an all-black boarding school: "a school for Negroes, where for the first time she could breathe freely, where she discovered that because one was dark, one was not necessarily loathsome, and could, therefore, consider oneself without repulsion."[20] Larsen's consciousness of skin color, though never free from negative connotations, led her to become one of the more accurate recorders of the many different hues visible in African-American people.

The Fisk faculty, too, presented her with a proximity to educated African Americans that she had not enjoyed in her working-class environment in

19. Charlie Mae Singleton, interview with author, March 10, 1987.
20. Nella Larsen, *Quicksand,* in *"Quicksand" and "Passing,"* ed. Deborah E. McDowell (New Brunswick, 1986), 23. Subsequent references to *Quicksand* will be to this edition.

Chicago. Mrs. Minnie Scott Crosthwait, the newly appointed principal of the Normal School, was the first person to be given that official title and the first African-American woman to head the department, which, as of 1907, had graduated 292 students who were teaching in twenty-two states.[21] A graduate of both the Normal and the college courses at Fisk, Mrs. Crosthwait was not only an administrator but also an instructor in mathematics and English. Using *Webster's Composition and Literature* as a textbook, she taught Nella Larsen the grammar review required of all third-year students. Her course, titled "Formal Rhetoric," stressed the use of words, structure of sentences and paragraphs, the making of topical outlines, and knowledge of the five forms of discourse. Although she gave Larsen a grade of 77 for the six-week course, Mrs. Crosthwait gave her a more generous gift of encouragement in her studies, along with a model of a successful African-American woman teacher.

Mrs. Crosthwait's Normal Department was one of the more respected teacher-training programs in the South. From Fisk's beginning, teacher education had been one of its primary missions. A survey conducted in 1900, when graduates of Fisk numbered over 400, revealed 8 college professors; 12 principals and 45 teachers in high or normal schools; 34 principals and 120 instructors in grammar schools; and another 700 teachers who had attended Fisk without graduating.[22] Teachers who had studied at Fisk were highly regarded wherever they went because they were energetic, enterprising, dedicated, and, most important, well trained. Their program included academic subjects as well as practice teaching in the Model School, which by the time of Larsen's enrollment had become the Daniel Hand Training School, comprising elementary grades first through sixth. Circumstance had brought Larsen to Fisk, but given the Normal School's record, she had entered a first-rate institution for teachers.

Fifteen faculty members taught the Normals, as the students in the department were called. The three-year Normal Preparatory Course, in which Larsen was enrolled, was more demanding than many high schools. It required two years of Latin (including one course in Virgil), three courses in algebra and one in mental arithmetic, two courses in plane geometry, one course in solid geometry, two courses in physics, one science course in physi-

21. "The History of the Normal Department at Fisk," *Fisk Herald*, XXV (Thanksgiving, 1907), 8–9.
22. Richardson, *A History of Fisk*, 53.

cal geography and one in botany, four courses in English, seven courses each in vocal music and drawing, four courses in history in addition to two courses in Bible history and one half-term course in the history of education, three courses in elocution, three courses in cooking, one half-term course in penmanship, and two teacher-training courses, which were under the supervision of Belle Ruth Parmenter, principal of the Daniel Hand Training School.[23] The Normal Preparatory Course differed from the College Preparatory Course only in the language requirement, and in the courses in education, cooking, music, and drawing. Within two years, the Normal Department would become part of the college course.

Nella Larsen's program included courses in Latin, plane geometry, advanced algebra, mythology, and rhetoric. Two general reviews were mandatory: the one Principal Crosthwait taught in grammar and another in geography taught by Caroline (Carrie) Bailey Chamberlin, instructor in history and geography. Although a third-year student, Larsen took classes in the first- and second-year curriculum (algebra and Latin) to compensate for work she had missed at Wendell Phillips.

Like other Normal Preparatory students, she experienced a rigorous year. Her class periods were fifty-five minutes long, and she was expected to take five or six classes per term.[24] The school year was divided into three terms: the fall term, which opened in mid-September and ended four days before Christmas; the winter term, which began the day after Christmas and ended in mid-March; and the spring term, which began four to five days after the end of the winter term and concluded with graduation exercises in mid-June. There was little time for anything other than class attendance, preparation, and study, especially because as a boarding student, Larsen also performed required work-service and, along with all other enrolled students, attended mandatory religious services.

As a high school student, Larsen's extracurricular activities were more limited than those of the women students in either the Normal Department or the College Department. At the same time, she had become more of an observer than a participant, partly from choice and partly from necessity. Although she did participate in physical exercises five days a week and in daily religious services, she was not active in the literary societies and clubs for women: the Decagynian, whose objective for the 1907–1908 term was

23. *Fisk University Catalogue, 1907–1908*, 37–38.
24. *Ibid.*, 39.

to study art; D.L.V., which undertook the study of American, English, and Greek literatures for the year; and the Tanner Art Club, which pursued various projects that year, including a study of etiquette in February.[25] Although these clubs met in the reception rooms and parlors of Jubilee Hall, students in the preparatory courses were expected to concentrate mainly on their courses of study, especially if they hoped to be eligible for admission into the Normal or College Course. In addition, as part of her boarding obligation, Larsen worked each day for one hour in Jubilee Hall. She was, however, expected to attend the four faculty-student socials given each year. At these affairs the entire student body of four hundred and faculty of forty-three were invited to Jubilee Hall's parlors for games and dining room for music, singing, and marching. (Dancing was prohibited.) Charlie Mae Singleton, who attended the Normal School, recalls that at the socials "boys and girls paired up just like for dancing, but then they marched instead."[26] When Larsen attended the spring social on Thursday evening, March 24, 1908, she participated in the last school social of the year and her final one as a Fisk student.

Nellie Larsen completed the three terms of her first year at Fisk without achieving distinction in her studies. Yet her grades improved over those of her last year at Wendell Phillips, and she did not fail any of her courses. She finished the first year of Latin (thirty-six weeks) with a grade of 83. In plane geometry, her only other year-long course, she earned a 76, her lowest grade and one point below her grade in grammar review. In advanced algebra (eighteen weeks), however, she earned an 81. Mythology (twenty-three weeks) brought her highest grade, an 87. In rhetoric (twenty-three weeks), she received a 79. For the six-week course geography review she received a grade of 79.[27] Nothing in her grades suggested her later skill and ability in creative writing, though several of the courses (Latin, Greek mythology, rhetoric, and grammar) would prove useful in her career as a writer.

Although she did not excel in any of her classes, Larsen found a measure of happiness in her life at Fisk, because she could apply herself to her studies. However, there may have been a slow dawning of difference between

25. See the *Fisk Herald* issues for November, 1907, Thanksgiving, 1907, Christmas, 1907, and February, 1908.

26. Singleton interview.

27. See list of Larsen's credits, in Fisk registrar to Ernest J. Reece, principal, Library School, May 5, 1922 (Copy courtesy Ann Allen Schockley, Fisk University Library).

herself and her classmates, a recognition that is suggested by her subsequent representation of an autobiographical character in a comparable situation:

> She had been happy there, as happy as a child unused to happiness dared to be. There had been always a feeling of strangeness, of outsideness, and one of holding her breath for fear that it wouldn't last. It hadn't. It had dwindled gradually into eclipse of painful isolation. . . . [S]he became gradually aware of a difference between herself and the girls about her. They had mothers, fathers, brothers, and sisters of whom they spoke frequently, and who sometimes visited them. They went home for vacations which Helga spent in the city where the school was located. They visited each other and knew many of the same people. Discontent for which there was no remedy crept upon her. . . . She had been happier, but still horribly lonely.[28]

The psychological correspondences between Larsen's character Helga and Larsen herself infer that although Fisk constituted an improvement over her life in the preceding year, it was an experience she ultimately chose to suppress because it made her painfully aware of her separateness, her lack of connection to her family and to the race that Fisk emphasized and its students represented. For Larsen, Fisk had initially been an opportunity for connection and belonging, but it had deteriorated into further evidence of her outsider status.

Toward the end of the winter term, Marie Larsen arrived for a visit with her daughter. Her brief stay of a few days, but not its purpose, was recorded in the March edition of the *Fisk Herald,* a monthly publication of the literary societies and clubs.[29] What transpired between the two is not known; however, at the end of the term, Nella Larsen left Fisk.

Why she left is open to conjecture. Her grades were sufficient to continue. Her interest in her school work as preparation for a career in teaching was adequate, yet her training as a teacher was never completed. Perhaps Marie Larsen brought the news that the family could or would no longer support her education at Fisk; perhaps knowing that boarding students could not remain in residence over the summer vacation, she came to ask Nellie not to return to the Larsens in Chicago, but to seek instead to maintain herself.

---

28. Larsen, *Quicksand,* 23–24.
29. See "Personals," *Fisk Herald,* XXV (March, 1908), 22.

What is known is that after the spring of 1908, Nellie Larsen experienced another major disruption. She would not live with her family in Chicago again, and she would retain only minimal contact with them in the years thereafter.

The next four years (1908 to 1912) of her life are a mystery. How she spent the time cannot be precisely determined from her accounts of her life, and no conclusive traces of her for these years have surfaced. In the mid-1920s Larsen would state about this period of her life: "When she was sixteen she went alone to Denmark to visit relatives of her mother in Copenhagen where she remained for three years."[30] During that extended visit, as she also would say in 1926, she studied for two years at the University of Copenhagen in Denmark, not formally, but as an auditor. She gave the years as 1910 to 1912 in her 1929 application for a Guggenheim fellowship. Throughout her public life as a writer, Larsen would refer to her university education in Copenhagen but would rarely mention her year at Fisk, and then only in the context of her college, rather than high school, education. Because she claimed status as an auditor in Denmark, she had no official university records, and the university maintained no records of her enrollment. No documents have surfaced that would indicate that Larsen studied in Copenhagen, and no records support her claim of having lived in Denmark as a teenager.

Had she spent three years in Denmark, she would have accounted for only a part of the period between 1908 and 1912. It is at the end of this period that she dropped two years from her age and began to use 1893 as her date of birth. In fact, she did not travel to Denmark at sixteen, since at that age she entered Fisk's Normal Department. It is, of course, quite possible that she made the journey when she was slightly older than sixteen, at the age of eighteen, for example, even though no passport records exist for her travel to Denmark between 1908 and 1912. While it is difficult to speculate about Larsen's reasons for erasing two years from her life, it is clear that she made a conscious choice to conceal them. It is also clear that these "lost" years initiated her independent and autonomous existence and resulted in the lack of affiliation, community, and relationships that plagued her public years and undermined her self-conception.

Larsen may have married shortly after leaving Fisk and spent at least a

30. Nella Larsen Imes, Author's statement for Alfred A. Knopf, Inc., November 24, 1926, in Alfred A. and Blanche Knopf Collection, Harry Ransom Humanities Center, University of Texas Libraries, Austin.

year in a small southern community. Fisk did not allow the attendance of married or engaged women students, and it disapproved of any serious courtships or dating. In fact, young men were not allowed to walk on the same side of the street as young women. Females who became pregnant while attending Fisk were expelled, and a woman could not marry and remain a student, even if no pregnancy were involved. A liaison with a male student could well have led Larsen to a premature marriage from which she later extricated herself.

Although it is dangerous to read biographical information into imaginative texts, it is fascinating to observe that in Larsen's short stories and novels there are several recurrent ideas about marital relations and other conjugal-type liaisons that suggest a key to her "lost" years. The fictional portrayals also include references to offers of prostitution and to births of children to unmarried women. Julia Hammond, the heroine of Larsen's short story "The Wrong Man," was driven by homelessness and need in her youth to become the mistress of a wealthy man who later sent her to art school. The unnamed mistress of the hero in "Freedom" dies in childbirth on the same day that her lover decides to escape the relationship. Helga Crane in *Quicksand* becomes the sexually sated wife of a country minister and the bedridden mother of a succession of children; she contemplates leaving husband and children as soon as she regains her strength. Clare Kendry in *Passing* marries a man who helps her escape from poverty and drudgery, but she seems intent upon leaving him and their daughter in an effort to regain her identity. Both Helga Crane and Julia Hammond, when they are the most desperate for help, fend off strangers on the street who appear ready to lure them into prostitution.

It is also possible that Larsen returned to Chicago at the end of the 1907–1908 school year and remained there until 1909. She does not appear in the Chicago-area census records for 1910, though her father, mother, and sister do. Larsen may well have departed for Denmark during 1909 and returned before the fall of 1912, when she entered nursing school in New York. Several of her African-American female characters spend a part of their young womanhood living with white relatives. Helga Crane goes to Copenhagen to visit her mother's Danish sister; Clare Kendry lives on Chicago's West Side with her father's white aunts after his death. While it is possible that Larsen could have spent some time with her father's or her mother's "Scandinavian" relatives, it seems unlikely that she spent the entire four-year period in Denmark, because throughout her public life she displayed little intimate or firsthand knowledge of that country, even though she could speak and read Danish. There is simply not enough evidence to say precisely how Nellie Larson/Nella Larsen spent the years between the spring of 1908 and the fall of 1912. It is apparent, however, that the lonely odyssey she began with her departure from Chicago for Nashville would continue to be one of the defining patterns of her adulthood: movement into institutional environments that ultimately could not fulfill her personal needs.

3

Training in New York,
1912–1915

NELLA MARION LARSEN entered New York's Lincoln Hospital and Home Training School for Nurses in 1912, only fourteen years after it opened. Her transformation from the Nellie Marie Walker Larsen who matriculated at Fisk continued. No further references to her birth surname, Walker, would appear in her public or private records, though the name of the heroine of her first novel, Helga *Crane,* contains an associative link to *Walker.* The long legs of a crane, especially when the bird is in motion, may be suggestive of a "walker." With her new name came a new set of objectives and directions indicative of her movement outside of the traditional place of a female within the home.

Her entrance into nursing school also may be read as her refusal to live an existence of expectancy, of waiting for someone or something to rescue her from being consigned to the Negro race. From the point of her emergence in New York, Nella Larsen invented her life. Although her ambivalence about her racial identity did not disappear, she acquiesced to a specific place within the race, which she defined largely as one of service to her people. The service motive was generally complex for women of color, who used the opportunity to care for others as a means of achieving a better quality of life for themselves, but for Larsen it was particularly complex because of the weight of her origins and background. As a provider of health care, she could contribute to improving the condition of African Americans and, thereby, redress some of the odious stereotypes of the race that tainted her within her family. At the same time, as a woman in an emerging profession, she could move into a sphere of wider potential and recognition that was closed to her working-class family.

Larsen began work and study in a combination hospital and home located at East 141st Street between Concord Avenue and Southern Boulevard in the Bronx. She was already twenty-one years old, though her small size and short stature gave her the appearance of one who might be no more than eighteen. She had, however, acquired the maturity for completing a modern three-year program in nursing, which Florence Nightingale had defined for a historic meeting of American nurses in 1893 as "an art requiring an organized, practical, and scientific training." Even earlier, in 1876, Abby Howland Woolsey had described nursing to a committee on New York hospitals as "serious business; it signifies the proper use of fresh air, light, warmth, cleanliness, quiet, the proper selection and administration of food, close observation and report of symptoms, and the most scrupulous fulfillment of medical orders, and all with the greatest economy of the patient's strength." Howland's description and Nightingale's definition were still applicable to the vocation that Nella Larsen chose in 1912. By then, however, nursing was explicitly a way for women to derive a social value outside the domestic sphere. Although subject to exploitation by the male-dominated medical profession, nursing as a woman's profession offered an opportunity for independence, for a livelihood and a home, while also contributing to society.[1]

For Larsen, enrollment in a nursing program meant the opportunity for an education without having to finance it herself, for in exchange for services to the institution, Lincoln's probationers were provided with training, room, board, and a small allowance. At no cost beyond that of travel to the Lincoln Hospital and Home, a young woman, if accepted for admission, could receive training for a respectable profession that was then emerging in importance. Nursing's status was growing at least partially through the efforts of Lincoln's own graduates and of white New Yorkers such as Lillian Wald, who with Mary Brewster had founded visiting nurses in 1893, the

1. Florence Nightingale, "Sick Nursing and Health Nursing," in *Nursing of the Sick, 1893: Papers and Discussions from the International Congress of Charities, Correction and Philanthropy, Chicago, 1893* (New York, 1949), 26; Abby Howland Woolsey, "Hospitals and Training Schools: Report to the Standing Committee on Hospitals of the State Charities Aid Association, New York, May 24, 1876," in *A Century of Nursing* (New York, 1950), 112; Berenice Fisher, "Alice in the Human Services: A Feminist Analysis of Women in the Caring Professions," in *Circles of Care: Work and Identity in Women's Lives*, ed. Emily K. Abel and Margaret K. Nelson (Albany, N.Y., 1990), 112.

Henry Street Settlement, and Public Health Nursing, all the while assisting in drives to have nursing taught as a college curriculum and insisting on the nondiscriminatory hiring of African-American nurses in settlements and public health. By attending Lincoln, a woman of color could achieve both individual dignity and collective value from nursing. She could also become independent and self-supporting, which was particularly important for unmarried females from poor families or, like Larsen, without supportive families. As Lavinia Dock pointed out before the turn of the century, "The promise of an education secures a steady supply of intelligent women" for nurse's training, and African-American women especially found the prospect of education without cost attractive.[2] Even though the work was difficult and the pay minimal, Lincoln's trained nurse had the rare opportunity for social mobility through a variety of professionally related spheres, including postgraduate training, alumnae organizations, national associations, employment registers, teaching positions, and supervisory and administrative posts. Larsen's entrance into Lincoln's program meant, as well, that as an African-American woman of limited means, she could prepare to enter the labor force in a respectable capacity and to become self-sufficient.

How Larsen came to enroll at Lincoln is open to conjecture. The school advertised in African-American newspapers across the country, and its graduates were already serving in segregated hospitals in the East, South, and Midwest. She entered Lincoln as an independent young woman virtually making her own way and responsible for her own course in the world. Whether she chose the school, and a care-giving profession, out of a desire to perform needed work in the public sphere or out of a desire to be needed for her skills is not clear from her statements. What she found upon arrival at Lincoln, however, is significant to understanding her social development in the context of a black-centered world and a community of professional women.

The history of the Lincoln Hospital and Home helps to explain both the positive and the negative value of Larsen's experience as a nursing student. Conceived on October 20, 1839, as the Society for the Relief of Worthy, Aged, Indigent Colored Persons, the Home had begun its mission in two rooms of the city's almshouse, but the directors, Anne Mott and Mary Shotwell, soon found that elderly blacks were in greater need and in larger numbers than originally anticipated. On the eve of the Home's founding,

2. Lavinia L. Dock, "The Relation of Training Schools to Hospitals," in *Nursing of the Sick, 1893,* 19.

approximately sixteen thousand blacks lived in Manhattan and Brooklyn, and eighty-one were in the poorhouse. An expanded charitable undertaking, the Home for the Colored Aged, began in 1842, when a group of eleven white women rented Manhattan property on 51st Street at the North (Hudson) River.[3]

Within a year of locating in the North River home, the society bought, for $5,620, twelve lots with a two-story frame building at 40th Street and Fourth Avenue that had accommodations for a maximum of one hundred people. A sign above the door read: "Thou Shalt No More Be Termed Forsaken" (Isa. 64:15). The motto meant more to the society than merely sheltering and feeding aged, poor blacks, for in 1844 it established an infirmary by adding two large rooms to a new third floor of the 40th Street building. The sick were no longer sent to Bellevue Hospital for treatment. Inmates were charged with the care of the sick in the Colored Home, as it officially became on May 8, 1845, when the Articles of Incorporation changed the name and created a medical council composed of three physicians and three surgeons.[4]

The officers and managers became the Society for the Support of the Colored Home, which raised an endowment of $35,000 designated for overall improvement of conditions for African Americans in New York.[5] By 1848 the shift to medical services necessitated yet another move to more spacious quarters on property at First Avenue and Avenue A between 64th and 65th streets, which the society purchased for $13,000. In each of its relocations, the Colored Home duplicated the northward or uptown movement of New York's black population, which by the middle of the nineteenth century had begun settling in the midtown area as immigrants displaced blacks from lower Manhattan. The Colored Home's new buildings were erected by December, 1848, and these provided increased hospital accommodations for the ailing patients, as well as training workshops for the inmates who assisted in ward work.

3. Seth M. Scheiner, *Negro Mecca: A History of the Negro in New York City, 1865–1920* (New York, 1965), 6; M. A. Harris, *A Negro History Tour of Manhattan* (New York, 1968), 33; "History of Lincoln School for Nurses (Written in 1936)" and "The Lincoln School for Nurses" (Typescripts in Lincoln School for Nurses Collection, SCF), and *Fiftieth Anniversary, 1898–1948* (New York, 1948), in Lincoln School for Nurses Collection.

4. "History of Lincoln School for Nurses"; "The Lincoln School for Nurses"; *Fiftieth Anniversary, 1898–1948;* Act of Incorporation, The Colored Home, May 8, 1945, in Lincoln School for Nurses Collection.

5. Act of Incorporation, The Colored Home, May 8, 1845, *ibid.*

Faced with an ever greater influx of well and sick blacks in 1858 as the Civil War approached and the number of blacks increased to 13,815 in a population of 515,547, the society added a new wing and three stories to the main building on First Avenue. In the aftermath of the draft riots, a week-long outbreak of violent attacks on blacks precipitated on July 11, 1863, by the Conscription Act, the Colored Home's infirmary became a central part of its services. The dual purpose of the Colored Home, room and board combined with medical facilities, was acknowledged in 1882 by the new name: the Colored Home and Hospital. Its mission in the 1880s, still primarily to serve the indigent elderly, became more critical as the black population grew to 19,963 in a general population vastly expanded to 1,206,299 by the influx of Irish and Italian immigrants. Between 1845 and 1884, 30,431 persons received care at the Colored Home, while 20,468 were recorded as admissions.[6]

By the end of the century when the Colored Home and Hospital had two hundred inmates in its care, the focus on medical treatment inspired an expansion of the institution and a change in its direction. The location on First Avenue, much deteriorated after fifty years of use, was no longer considered a healthy environment because of the increased population and a propensity for disease in overcrowded buildings. With the purchase of a thirty-eight-lot parcel of land at East 141st Street between Concord Avenue and Southern Boulevard on July 14, 1897, the society and board of managers began building in a pastoral setting that in 1898 would become part of greater New York with the designation of the Bronx as a city borough. A large, multiwinged, four-story complex situated in the southern end of the borough was the result of their initiative. The modern facility had a tuberculosis building, donated in honor of a black servant, and a maternity building, both of which were connected to the main building by covered corridors. A separate building for contagious diseases was set off from the central complex. A laundry, powerhouse, and morgue also occupied the grounds. On September 7, 1898, the Colored Home and Hospital moved officially to the new site.[7]

Although the Colored Home continued to maintain healthy elderly inmates, a change in direction began with the creation of an outpatient dis-

6. Herman D. Bloch, *The Circle of Discrimination: An Economic and Social Study of the Black Man in New York* (New York, 1969), 31, 39; Adah B. Thoms, *Pathfinders: The Progress of Colored Graduate Nurses* (New York, 1929), 69.

7. "History of Lincoln School for Nurses"; *Fiftieth Anniversary 1898–1948*.

pensary and a School for Colored Females in the Nursing Arts (1898). The medical council and board of managers had envisioned such a school as early as 1845 but could make it a reality only with the acquisition of the 141st Street property, which had the potential for providing living quarters for student nurses. The transition also involved an institutional decision to receive patients of all races, thereby paving the way for the 1902 chartering of the Lincoln Hospital and Home, a name that reflected the major transformation of priorities that had gradually occurred after the introduction of hospital services.[8]

It was to the Lincoln Hospital and Home's Training School for Nurses that Nella Marion Larsen came in 1912. Its relatively long history and considerable endowment made it one of the best-known nursing programs for women of color, but Lincoln was not without racial discord and paternalism. The medical personnel, all white males, did not initially favor the training of African-American women as nurses because they could foresee no work placements for them after the training and beyond the confines of the Colored Hospital.[9]

While a trained nurse of any race was still rare in hospitals of the 1890s, the concept of the black trained nurse was so foreign that the potential for employment could not be determined. A persuasive argument was the assistance that trained nurses would offer both the Colored Hospital and the Home in the form of cheap labor for the wards. An added benefit was that the accepted probationers, African-American women between the ages of twenty-one and thirty-five, would achieve better prospects for remaining virtuous and earning a living than most of their peers in New York whose employment was limited primarily to work as laundresses and servants. Overcoming the physicians' objections, the school eventually provided African-American women with one of their earliest accesses to social mobility and middle-class status through respectable work that eventually led them to supervisory, administrative, and managerial positions in public and private institutions, as well as in federal government service.

In establishing its nursing diploma program, Lincoln followed a pattern inaugurated by a growing number of institutions serving African Americans: Atlanta Baptist Female Seminary (1886), renamed Spelman College in 1924; Chicago's Providence Hospital (1891); Dixie Hospital in Hampton,

8. Annual reports of the Lincoln Hospital and Home, 1901–1902 through 1923–25, in Lincoln School for Nurses Collection.
9. Thoms, *Pathfinders,* 71.

Virginia (1891); Good Samaritan in Charlotte, North Carolina (1891); Tuskegee Institute (1892); Howard University's School of Medicine (1893) and its Freedman's Hospital (1894); and Flint-Goodridge Hospital in New Orleans (1896). These programs, exclusively for training African-American nurses, and approximately eight others across the country were all founded in the decade preceding the beginning of Lincoln's nursing school.[10]

Because of the school's mission of racial uplift and service, Larsen needed only a letter from a doctor, dentist, and minister for admission; a high school diploma was not yet required. At her arrival, eleven classes of graduate nurses, totaling 113 women, had preceded her. Students entered whenever there were vacancies, since fixed times for starting the program had not been set. The training program was fully developed and accredited; indeed, it had already become a model program. Larsen's three-year diploma program had been instituted in 1909, following New York State's 1905 accreditation of the original two-year program that had graduated its first class of six nurses in 1900.[11]

From the inception of the training school, however, all of the administrators, doctors, and superintendents were white, while the inmates, patients, and nurses were black. The organizational structure ensuring authority and public power for whites did not escape notice within or without the institution. In one of her few public statements about her nursing experience, Nella Larsen recalled the racial division of the institution:

> In my nursing days . . . [at] Lincoln Hospital and Home, East 141st Street and Southern Boulevard, New York City . . . during the years from 1912 to 1915 [a]ll the doctors and executives in this institution were white. All the nurses were Negroes. As in any other hospital, all infractions of rules were to be reported to and dealt with by the Su-

10. Mary Elizabeth Carnegie, *The Path We Tread: Blacks in Nursing, 1854–1984* (Philadelphia, 1986), 20–25; Darlene Clark Hine, *Black Women in White: Racial Conflict and Cooperation in the Nursing Profession, 1890–1950* (Bloomington, 1989), 9.

11. That first class, consisting of Grace Gertrude Newman, Nettie Farmer Jarrot (the first student to enroll, in May, 1898), Annie Lotten Marin, Margaret Marie Garner, Gertrude Johnson, and M. Elizabeth Harris, received diplomas from the Board of Managers of the Colored Home and Hospital and the Training School for Nurses in graduation exercises held at the Academy of Medicine, 17 West 43rd Street, on Friday evening, December 7, 1900, though the graduate nurses were not permitted to give a practical demonstration there (1900 Graduation Exercise Program, and Invitation to the graduation, both in Lincoln School for Nurses Collection).

perintendent of Nurses, who was white. It used to distress the old folks . . . that we Negro nurses often had to tell things about each other to the white people.

While Larsen was a student, one 1905 graduate of Lincoln, Adah Belle Samuel Thoms, was assistant superintendent (1906–1922) and assistant director of nurses, and later acting director, but she was never appointed director, because that position was reserved for whites.[12]

Lincoln's separation of the races was one target for criticism that researcher Mary White Ovington did not overlook in her landmark study, *Half A Man: The Status of the Negro in New York,* published in 1911, the year before Larsen's enrollment. Ovington disclosed that African-American graduates of New York medical colleges had to go to Chicago, Philadelphia, or Washington for hospital training, because despite its "training school for colored nurses," Lincoln "neither accepts colored medical graduates as interns, nor allows colored doctors on its staff."[13]

Despite the racial hierarchy and paternalistic racism of the Lincoln Hospital and Home, the first graduation marked the beginning of an illustrious procession of graduate nurses of color trained at what quickly became one of the nation's foremost nursing schools for African-American women.

Although the first group of nursing students lived on Concord Avenue across from the hospital under construction, by Nella Larsen's time nurses were housed for three years in the quarters at Lincoln Hospital. Larsen and the ten members of her class shared, with the other nursing students, a dormitory on the third floor of the hospital that would accommodate the Lincoln students and graduate nurses until 1929 when, following the sale of the hospital, a modern home was built for them. In the austere and cramped

---

12. Nella Larsen, "The Author's Explanation," *Forum,* Supplement 4, LXXXIII (April, 1930), xli–xlii; Mabel Keaton Staupers, *No Time for Prejudice: A Story of the Integration of Negroes in Nursing in the United States* (New York, 1961), 10, 22, 85. It was not until 1941 that Edwina Smyer Hayward was appointed assistant to the white director, Lorraine G. Denhardt, and acting director upon Denhardt's retirement in 1953. In March, 1953, Ivy Nathan Tinkler became the first black appointed director of the school. Lincoln closed in 1961. For a discussion of the long struggle to end discrimination at Lincoln, see Staupers, *No Time for Prejudice,* 83–86.

13. Mary White Ovington, *Half A Man: The Status of the Negro in New York* (New York, 1911), 114. It was not until 1919 that black nurses and doctors were allowed to practice on staff at Harlem Hospital, an institution that, like Lincoln, primarily served blacks. See Harris, *A Negro History Tour,* 109.

quarters where Larsen lived for three years beginning in 1912, there were thirty beds, two bathrooms with three facebowls, two bathtubs, and two toilets, facilities that were in keeping with the ratio of one bathroom for every fifteen students that had been suggested by Katherine L. Lett in 1893.[14] There were no desks for studying. The close quarters, which were stripped of personal adornments, helped to form a dedicated group of students, all of whom received free room and board but little monetary compensation (six dollars a month in their first year) for work performed as part of their education.

Two annual celebrations made the nurses comfortable with their home at Lincoln: Anniversary Day, September 7, when feasting and holiday hours were observed in honor of the relocation to the Bronx; and Christmas, when, beginning on Christmas Eve with a program planned by Mary Wainwright Booth and gifts from the board of managers distributed by the junior students, the nurses created a festive, ceremonial occasion. The Christmas celebration in particular prompted the assistant superintendent to remark, "In this way, we worked together to stimulate a bond of good fellowship, and to give to all a homelike atmosphere."[15] The female-centered environment was akin to that of a girls' school or women's college on the one hand, and to a convent on the other. In fact, one indigent patient during this decade referred to the nurses as "sisters without religion" because she associated their activities with those of nuns in religious orders, which was precisely where organized nursing had begun in the early Middle Ages.[16]

For Larsen, the three years spent in the Lincoln dormitory provided her first sustained interaction with women, and with African-American women in particular, with whom she shared the hard work of tending to patients and inmates, and of learning personal discipline and practical skills. Her intimacy with a community of women dedicated to a common goal and united in a directed effort encouraged simultaneously her sense of belonging and her desire for individuality. Yet, as one of her classmates recalled, she was "not at all at home with those around her," a discomfort her classmates believed was due to "the lack of love and acceptance in her early life."[17] Unfortunately, Larsen's time in the nurses' dormitory was also a missed opportunity for female bonding, for she formed no lasting friendships with

14. Katherine L. Lett, "Nurses' Homes," in *Nursing of the Sick, 1893,* 138.

15. Thoms, *Pathfinders,* 86. See also pp. 75–76 on Anniversary Day, and pp. 85–86 on Christmas activities.

16. Lillian D. Wald, *Windows on Henry Street* (Boston, 1934), 102, 75.

17. Reported by Adelaide Cromwell Hill, Introduction to *Quicksand,* by Nella Larsen (1928; rpr. New York, 1971), 15.

any of her nursing peers, though in the small world of African-American professionals, she periodically encountered Lincoln graduates throughout the rest of her life. In Nashville during the 1930s and long after she had left the field, Larsen renewed her acquaintance with Lucille V. Miller, a member of her class at Lincoln who was then working at Fisk University. In one of her few uses of her health professional experience in the 1930s, she nursed Miller during a major illness.[18]

As a Lincoln student, Larsen was eager to please those in authority. She had already begun the transformation of her background and family that would become more pronounced as she lifted herself into the world of the African-American bourgeoisie. The rigid and spartan nature of communal existence at Lincoln kindled her need for luxury, possessions, and flexibility. Moreover, the intimate contact with destitute, infirmed, and diseased African Americans exacted from her as a working nurse-probationer planted the seeds of her aversion to lower-class, poverty-stricken people of any race and shaped her ambivalent attitude toward work, specifically work performed typically by women. Unlike students in other smaller schools, Larsen and her peers at Lincoln were not required to scrub floors or clean wards; after 1907 maids and orderlies were hired for those duties. Nonetheless, what Larsen would most readily recall about her nursing experiences at Lincoln deemphasized the reality of her association with patients and with other student nurses; instead she stressed her "administrative experience . . . enriched by close association with many well known physicians and surgeons on the staffs."[19] Her experiences at Lincoln taught her to value those in positions of authority and to form what connections she could with them.

Because there were no special classrooms set aside for them, Larsen and the other young nurses worked in the hospital during the day and trained on the wards and received instruction in the evening. "Formal education for nurses was not the primary goal" of most early nursing schools, as Mary Elizabeth Carnegie has pointed out. The major objective of the program at Lincoln and elsewhere was the gaining of clinical experience. Nurses were instructed by doctors primarily at the bedsides of the hospital patients, then considered to be the most effective method of teaching nursing. Those in the senior class at Lincoln, however, also attended afternoon theoretical lectures by physicians and surgeons on the staff, which meant

18. Nella Larsen Imes to Grace Nail Johnson, Thursday [1932], in JWJ.
19. Wald, *Windows on Henry Street*, 80; see Larsen's response to a questionnaire about her activities in Thoms, *Pathfinders*, 113–14.

"that those nurses had to remain on duty late at night to finish up the work of the day, to write reports, and relieve the night nurses for classes." The preliminary course lasted six months, after which those who were retained for the completion of the program signed a promise to remain. Frequently examined by the superintendent of nurses, Alice E. Pierson, who administered both oral and written examinations and, with the board of managers, selected candidates for admission, student nurses were required to pass a final examination with a score of 75 percent or above in order to graduate. Although she had not previously performed well in school, Larsen remained consistently at the top of her class. She responded well to the strictures that demanded duty as the basis for caring.[20]

While the Lincoln Training School did not offer instruction in the arts or humanities, it required an entrance examination in English, writing, and oral reading. Attendance at morning and evening devotions and Sunday evening services, held in the Lincoln Home's Van Santvoord Memorial Chapel, was also required for "spiritual growth."[21] Acquiring the accoutrements of middle-class culture was also an important task. Upon admittance, students were encouraged to read books, visit museums, see plays, and attend concerts. For many of the young women, who were black, mainly poor, rural, and often southern in upbringing, New York City's public libraries, theaters, and museums provided their first experiences of cultural diversity and enrichment. Indeed, many of them chose to remain at Lincoln during their annual two-week vacation in order not only to save the expense of returning to their homes, but also to explore New York City on group excursions chaperoned by the superintendent of nurses.

Although Larsen found herself living and working in a suburban environment, she had access to the city. Public transportation made it possible for her to explore the New York beyond the Lincoln Hospital grounds. The New York Third Avenue elevated railway system, with a station at 143rd Street, connected her section of the borough with the bustling center of Manhattan and with the northern portion of the Bronx where the New York Botanical Gardens and the New York Zoological Park (the Bronx Zoo) were located. Moreover, the subway had, by 1905, extended into the Bronx under 149th Street to Third Avenue and had, at the intersection of

20. Carnegie, The Path We Tread, 22; Thoms, Pathfinders, 77; Susan Reverby, "The Duty or Right to Care? Nursing and Womanhood in Historical Perspective," in Circles of Care, ed. Abel and Nelson, 139.
21. Thoms, Pathfinders, 71.

those two streets, spurred the growth of the "Hub," a shopping area which she and the Lincoln nurses occasionally frequented rather than the older commercial district at 129th Street and Third Avenue in Manhattan.[22]

Larsen also became familiar with Harlem during her student nursing days. It was in this section of the city that the school's alumnae association maintained a home for the graduates; from 1905 to 1912, the nurses' home was located at 61 West 134th Street, but relocated during Larsen's tenure to another rented residence, 188 West 135th Street, where it remained until 1921 when Lincoln's alumnae purchased a permanent Nurses' Alumnae Club at 323 West 138th Street. In the area surrounding the nurses' home, five thousand African-American families had moved between 1903 and 1911 and had begun to create a black city within a city. By 1914, as the Great War began in Europe and prior to the Great Migration in the United States, blacks already resided in 1,100 homes within a twenty-three-block area of Harlem.[23]

Lack of extra money and free time, however, condemned Larsen to many off-duty hours in the nurses' dormitory. One of the main extracurricular activities there was a book discussion group that met once or twice a month and that found encouragement from Mary Wainwright Booth, then president of the board of managers and head of Lincoln Hospital and Home, as well as from Alice Pierson, superintendent of nurses, who first increased the nurses' time for study and recreation. The reading selections were primarily the "great books" of the Western world, which the nurses referred to as "fine books." Already an avid reader, Larsen thrived in the discussion group. Reading had been her favorite pastime since childhood, but in her high school classes at Wendell Phillips, her shyness had inhibited her sharing her knowledge and love of books. Lincoln's family environment was different. In the informal, yet compulsory, book discussion with the small group with whom she lived and worked, Larsen was confident and articulate, though one of her classmates also labeled her "different, even a bit strange."[24]

The discussion group formed one basis of her education in the humanities. It became, in a sense, her general college education. At the same time, it fueled her love for reading and her appetite for books. Had the School for

22. Lloyd Ultan and Gary Hermalyn, *The Bronx in the Innocent Years, 1890–1925* (New York, 1985), xvii–xxx.

23. Thoms, *Pathfinders*, 87–88; Roi Ottley and William J. Weatherby, eds., *The Negro in New York: An Informal History, 1626–1940* (New York, 1969), 183; Gilbert Osofsky, *Harlem: The Making of a Ghetto, Negro New York 1890–1930* (New York, 1968), 122.

24. Reported in Hill, Introduction to *Quicksand*, 15.

Nurses done no more than develop her interest in literature, it would have served her exceedingly well. But, in fact, Lincoln provided Larsen with what was at that point in her life and at that time in history for women of color an even greater opportunity for personal growth.

The Lincoln program gave Larsen an opportunity to become not only self-sufficient but professional. In 1887, after a struggle for control of nurses' training had linked the "nurse question to the woman question," England had granted a royal charter securing the recognition of nursing as a profession. Although the United States census bureau classified "trained nurse" among domestic service workers, the category was becoming in the early years of the century distinctly professional, as well as essentially independent of the male control that was explicit in older terms for nursing: "handmaid of the physician," "official wife of medicine," "younger sister" of the healing arts. In fact, the opening of training schools for nurses in New York (Bellevue Hospital), New Haven (Connecticut State Hospital), and Boston (Massachusetts General Hospital) in 1873, all owing to the work of women physicians, had already instituted nursing as a distinct occupation in the United States.[25]

These early training programs "originated with women, not with governing medical boards." They were organized in accordance with Florence Nightingale's belief that the programs should be considered educational institutions supported by public funds whenever possible, that they should be connected to but administratively separate from hospitals, that their instruction and administration should be the responsibility of professional nurses, and that homes should be established for student nurses. The Nightingale School at St. Thomas' Hospital, London, taught not simply nursing skills, but women's independence within their own liberating structures (the nurses' school and the nurses' home) and women's authority in the workplace. Basically, it taught measures of power and control over women's own labor. "The separate management of the nursing department," Louise Darche maintained in 1893, "first brought about because there seemed no other way of getting the proper control . . . has proved to be the cornerstone of all training-school organization."[26] Essentially, it ensured autono-

25. Wald, *Windows on Henry Street*, 76, 75; Lyndia Flanagan, *One Strong Voice: The Story of the American Nurses' Association* (Kansas City, 1976), 17; Woolsey, "Hospitals and Training Schools," 110.

26. Woolsey, "Hospitals and Training Schools," 110; Flanagan, *One Strong Voice*, 20; Louise Darche, "Proper Organization of Training Schools in America," in *Nursing of the Sick, 1893*, 95.

mous functioning of the all-female nursing management while placing it on an equal, rather than a subordinate, basis with the usually all-male hospital management. Efforts at organizing nursing into a profession, then, stemmed from the dual crusade for women's rights and for women's educational and employment opportunities.

Aside from having a body of specialized knowledge and skills, a profession is also characterized by the development of internal standards and regulations for operation, along with self-governance or organization. Before the end of the nineteenth century, nursing in America evidenced this characteristic. Although Nightingale was not herself an advocate of the professionalization of nursing, she brought modern nursing to the point where organization into a profession was inevitable. In the United States, early nursing leaders such as Lavinia Dock, Isabel Hampton, Irene Sutliffe, Louise Darche, and Edith Draper were firm on the issue of professional organization; their call to action was "To advance we must unite."[27] The majority of the training programs were, in accordance with the Nightingale principles for nursing education, governed independently of hospitals with which they affiliated. The Bellevue Training School, the first of its kind opened in the United States (May 1, 1873) and the New York model for Lincoln, sent a representative to Nightingale in England in order to ascertain her recommended procedures for organizing and administering nurses' training. In addition to taking the control of nurses' training away from male hospital directors and primarily male medical personnel, the independent governance of the training programs paved the way for separate professional organizations, a move that gave nursing public status while providing women with new opportunities for managerial and administrative positions.

The Nurses' Associated Alumnae of the United States and Canada organized in 1896 with support from the American Society of Superintendents of Training Schools for Nurses; its charge in incorporating was the general betterment of the nursing profession. Nurses recognized the need to determine the future of nursing and pioneered the establishing of a code of ethics, the elevating of standards of nursing education, and the promoting of the interests of nurses. It was up to them, because as Darche concluded in 1893, "From its nature nursing is peculiarly a woman's work; a woman originated the training school system in England, women started it in this country, women have brought it to its present stage of development, and it is to women we must look for its future advancement." By 1900, nurses con-

27. Isabel M. Stewart, Introduction to *Nursing of the Sick, 1893*, xvii.

trolled their own national organization and their official journal, the *American Journal of Nursing*. These were the earliest signs of nursing's emergence as a profession.[28]

By 1903, the Nurses' Associated Alumnae, by means of an early form of lobbying, had brought into legislation the Nurse Practice Acts, which regulated licensing laws and credentialing standards for nursing in New York, New Jersey, North Carolina, and Virginia. In 1911 the Associated Alumnae officially became the American Nurses' Association, the representative body of American professional nurses. "Between 1900 and 1911," as Lyndia Flanagan puts it, "the nursing profession 'came of age.'" The negative aspect of this professionalization is that for white women after the turn of the century, "nursing became a type of collective female grasping for an older form of security and power in the face of rapid change. Women who might have been attracted to nursing in the 1880s as a womanly occupation that provided some form of autonomy were, by the turn of the century, increasingly looking elsewhere for work and career."[29]

In 1912, when Larsen began training, few other opportunities for professional careers existed for women of color. The 1900 federal census had shown that 90 percent of employed African-American women were in personal and domestic service. Employment agencies recorded that between 1906 and 1909 in New York, 1,971, or 92.2 percent, of the 2,138 black women they placed earned less than six dollars a week, and that 1,137 of them actually received less than five dollars a week. The 1910 census for New York City had revealed that two-thirds of all black female workers (70.1 percent) were employed in domestic and personal services, and that of the remainder, the majority worked as servants and waitresses, with the rest either laundresses, dressmakers, or seamstresses.[30]

A year later, Mary White Ovington concluded that "despite her efforts and occasional success, the colored girl in New York meets with severer race prejudice than the colored man, and is more persistently kept from attrac-

28. Carnegie, *The Path We Tread*, 69; Darche, "Organization of Training Schools," 103; Flanagan, *One Strong Voice*, 24, 38.

29. Carnegie, *The Path We Tread*, 156; Flanagan, *One Strong Voice*, 41; Reverby, "The Duty or Right to Care?," 141.

30. Ovington, *Half A Man*, 146; *Twelfth Census, 1900: Occupations*, Table 43, p. 638; George E. Haynes, *The Negro at Work in New York City: A Study in Economic Progress* (New York, 1912); Bloch, *The Circle of Discrimination*, 31. The total black population in Manhattan in 1910 was 60,534, and 91,709 for all the boroughs. See James Weldon Johnson, *Black Manhattan* (New York, 1930), 144.

tive work. *She gets the job that the white girl does not want.*" Her plea on behalf of the African-American woman was unequivocal: "Beyond any people in the city she needs all the encouragement that philanthropy, that human courtesy and respect, that the fellowship of the workers can give,— she needs her full status as a woman." Ovington and others recognized that the situation was little changed from the nineteenth century when at the time of Lincoln's founding African-American women mainly held menial occupations such as maids, cooks, scullions, laundresses, and seamstresses.[31]

African-American nurses belonged to a small minority. They not only became part of the American Nurses' Association at its inception, but also organized their own professional association, the National Association of Colored Graduate Nurses, in 1908 after segregationist practices in southern states began to bar them from local membership in the ANA. They recognized that their development was circumscribed by society's discriminatory racial practices and attitudes, but they also knew, as Darlene Clark Hine has concluded, "it was up to black nurses . . . to transform themselves into effective agents for social and professional change."[32]

Important for Larsen and other Lincoln students and graduates, the three-day national organizational meeting of the Colored Graduate Nurses was initiated in New York by Lincoln's Alumnae Association under the leadership of Adah Thoms, who prepared the way for Martha M. Franklin, an 1897 graduate of Women's Hospital in Philadelphia, to present her findings on the status of African-American graduate nurses. Under the auspices of Lincoln Hospital, fifty-two to fifty-eight nurses of color met Tuesday, August 25, 1908, at St. Mark's Methodist Episcopal Church on West 53rd Street to hear the results of Franklin's two-year study.[33] Lincoln's students could take pride in knowing that their Alumnae Association, organized December 1, 1903, expressly "to further the interests of graduates of the Training School . . . by promoting social intercourse among them . . . and advanc[ing] the welfare of the membership in all lawful ways," had

31. Ovington, *Half A Man*, 162 (italics in original), 169; Bloch, *The Circle of Discrimination*, 31.

32. Carnegie, *The Path We Tread*, 70; Mary M. Roberts, *American Nursing: History and Interpretation* (New York, 1954), 78–79, 443–48; Hine, *Black Women in White*, 107.

33. Carnegie, *The Path We Tread*, 93; Roberts, *American Nursing*, 79; Staupers, *No Time for Prejudice*, 16; Thoms, *Pathfinders*, 201–205. Thoms points out that two practical nurses had traveled to the meeting but were rejected because the organization was intended only for graduate nurses, since they were in positions that could enable them to work for higher standards in the profession and for increased requirements for admission to training schools.

been largely responsible for drawing up the goals for the national association and for African-American nurses in general. Those goals expound a clear-sighted activism for racial and professional equality: "to achieve higher professional standards"; "to break down the discriminatory practices facing Negroes in schools of nursing, in jobs, and in nursing organizations"; "to develop leadership among Negro nurses."[34] In developing new career options and organizations for nurses of color, Lincoln's graduates not only fought racial discrimination but also opened a wider stage on which African-American women could operate. They moved themselves upward in social status while uplifting the race.

Nursing students at Lincoln had, then, the immediate model of women in their alumnae association, the first African-American group accepted for membership in the New York State Nurses' Association in 1905. Its ranks included women such as activist Thoms, who not only wrote the first history of African-American graduate nurses but who, along with Ada Jackson Senhouse (class of 1902) and Rosa Williams Brown (class of 1905), represented Lincoln at the 1912 International Graduate Nurses' meeting in Cologne, Germany; Maria A. Clendenin (class of 1909), who was the first hospital social worker to be trained in New York City; and Lula G. Warlick (class of 1910), who served as head nurse in the gynecology department and operating room of Lincoln Hospital and who went on to a comparable position at Providence Hospital in Chicago. All were models giving inspiration and guidance to Larsen and her class during their training. These women attempted to turn the authoritarian and paternalistic model of nursing into something more than discipline, order, and skills. At a time when the nursing profession among white women was experiencing a crisis of definition (an acquiescent "woman's culture of obligation" versus "an activist assault upon the structure and beliefs that oppressed them"[35]), among African-American women it was still an important avenue for movement into the middle class and a major opportunity for self-development and actualization as independent women.

Larsen was well aware that upon completion of her course she would join a relatively elite core of African-American women, all designated "graduate nurse," who, by virtue of that designation and the preparation behind it, were destined to become the leaders, administrators, superintendents,

---

34. Carnegie, *The Path We Tread*, 93–94. In 1951, believing its goals accomplished, the National Association of Colored Graduate Nurses dissolved and merged with the predominantly white American Nurses Association.

35. Reverby, "The Duty or Right to Care?," 139.

supervisors, and teachers in their profession. At the very least, they could anticipate becoming head nurses in charge of other nurses, whether those nurses were trained or not. Despite the overall gloomy picture that Mary White Ovington drew from her research into the status of African Americans in New York, even she observed that "Colored women rank high among the trained nurses of New York."[36] Larsen's desire for achievement, expressed forcefully later in her life, was sparked by the caliber of achievement among Lincoln's graduates and their commitment to lifting their race and bettering themselves. While she may have interpreted her success in completing her training as a signal to her family that she was valued and valuable, she could not escape the broader reality that though nursing liberated her from financial dependence, it did so within rigidly fixed racial parameters. Lincoln was a racially defined school, and her attendance there not only affirmed her racial identity but consigned her to race-specific, gender-defined employment.

On May 13, 1915, just one month after her twenty-fourth birthday, Nella Marion Larsen graduated from the Lincoln Hospital and Home Training School for Nurses. For her class photograph she sat on the front row, eyeing the camera more forthrightly than she would in any of her later pictures. Her expression was solemn; her face dark above the starched white collar and bibbed apron of the new student uniform that had been adopted during her last year. Her school pin, bearing the inscription "*Laetus Sorte Mea,* Lincoln Hospital and Home Training School for Nurses," was visible on her left shoulder.[37] Except for loose strands of hair wisping from beneath her cap, there was nothing to distinguish her from the other graduating nurses: Sarah E. Gantt, Nettie B. Vick, Ruth I. Strickland, Aurelia St.C. Gumbs, Florence E. Johnson, Lucille V. Miller, Muriel F. Fletcher, Annie M. Johnson, Priscilla Bryan, and Olive B. Taylor. Larsen and her classmates had earned their pins and learned the virtues associated with their profession; they had become "self-controlled, unselfish, gentle, compassionate, brave, capable . . . [and] risen from the period of irresponsible girlhood to that of womanhood."[38] In racialized terms, womanhood meant unselfish commitment to the care of others and an elevation of professional duty to racial idealism about the potential of health service to "heal" the race and to actualize the self.

Having scored 94 percent on the state licensing board examination, Lar-

36. Ovington, *Half A Man*, 159.
37. The Latin means "Gladly My Service."
38. Quoted in Reverby, "The Duty or Right to Care?," 139.

sen finished near the top of her class of eleven. During her three years in the training program, she had applied herself and had succeeded to the extent that the director of the program recognized her "great executive ability."[39] As a result of her performance, she was retained as a ward supervisor. The position alleviated the problem of limited options for trained nurses who were African Americans. She took her place on staff just as many of the graduates had before her, but like them she was also prepared to move into the larger world outside of Lincoln Hospital and Home should an employment opportunity arise.

Although the National Association of Colored Graduate Nurses did not begin a central registry service until 1918, it had a volunteer register project that helped to place African-American nursing graduates. Nella Larsen was fortunate that the registry not only operated out of New York but was partly staffed by Lincoln alumnae, because it was through the NACGN and Lincoln's own Graduate Nurses' Home registry that she obtained a position at Tuskegee Institute in Alabama. Her prospects there for creative work seemed brighter than at Lincoln. In 1914, Booker T. Washington had initiated National Negro Health Week at Tuskegee. Washington's progressive plan was intended to unite private and public agencies nationwide in working to improve health care for all black people.[40] Negro Health Week had involved African-American nurses around the country in educational programs and practical demonstrations that functioned directly in calling attention to the needs of African Americans and indirectly in attracting interest in the work of Tuskegee Institute.

After five months on staff at Lincoln, Larsen departed for the South. She was leaving behind the security of a self-contained community, but she had completed her years of public and private training for a career in the outside world. With the idealism and activism instilled by her Lincoln teachers, especially her mentor, Thoms, she saw her future in meaningful service before her in Alabama, where she would become the head nurse at one of the oldest diploma programs for African-American nurses in the country.

39. Alice L. Carper, Eulogy for Nella Larsen, April 6, 1964, typescript in possession of Alice L. Carper.

40. Carnegie, The Path We Tread, 236.

4

Sojourning in the South,
1915–1916

EUROPE WAS AT war in the fall of 1915 when Nella Larsen traveled south to Tuskegee, Alabama. On May 7, one week before her graduation from Lincoln, the *Lusitania* sank. During the rest of the spring and summer there was heated talk of the United States' entry into the war, and the nurses at Lincoln were especially concerned about whether black nurses would be called to serve. By October, when Larsen boarded her train, the rumors had lessened in intensity, though Lincoln's assistant superintendent had already begun to map a strategy to secure the participation of African-American nurses in the American Red Cross. Larsen, however, would not wait for an opportunity to serve. War seemed to her remote, and European combat unrelated to everyday life. There was an immediacy in the challenge represented by Tuskegee. Larsen's train ride took her through the section of the country least disturbed by the threat of war—the rural, agrarian South, which, lacking the great ethnic diversity of New York City, had less immediate concern with the fates of the peoples of warring Europe and a more pressing concern with daily survival.

Her destination was Alabama's Black Belt, where tenant farming was the main source of livelihood. She rode south to Atlanta, where she took the Western Railroad for the 136-mile trip to Tuskegee. When she stepped off the train at Chehew, the junction for Tuskegee, she entered a world that was foreign to her urban upbringing in Chicago and to her formative experiences in New York. At Chehew Station she boarded the Tuskegee Railway. During the last five miles on the connecter line she saw both the scenery that the Tuskegee catalogue had described as "not excelled in the whole South" and the people who had been represented in the catalogue as "cultured and generous."[1] In actuality, the majority of the African-American population still lived much as it had in the nineteenth century, without benefit of primary education, health services, indoor plumbing, or adequate wages.

Larsen arrived at Tuskegee open-minded about Booker T. Washington's great racial experiment. She departed so disillusioned that for the rest of her life she was cynical and contemptuous of all programs for racial uplift and suspicious and condemning of anyone espousing such programs. Upon her arrival, however, Tuskegee offered a chance to refute negative stereotypes of African Americans, and a chance as well to prove to her white family her worth as a person of color. Her work with the best-known African American in the nation would, she believed, elevate her place and demonstrate her value.

Tuskegee Normal and Industrial Institute was located about one mile outside the town of Tuskegee. At the start of the 1915 fall term, the Institute's staff numbered nearly 200, and the students numbered over 2,000. The average was 1,600 students annually, plus 400 in the Summer School for Teachers, 230 in the Children's Training School, and 252 in the Agricultural Short Course. The year that Larsen arrived, the school had listed property of "112 buildings, 2,110 acres of land, about 350 head of live stock, wagons, carriages, farm implements, and other equipment amounting in value to $1,576,062.20." Its permanent endowment fund amounted to $2,195,326.17, which included 19,900 acres of land valued at $250,000.00 and the proceeds from the sale of 5,100 acres of mineral land. By most contemporary yardsticks, the school was in an enviable position of financial security. To Larsen's eyes, it was "a showplace in the Black Belt," but a showplace existing, she said, as "exemplification of the white man's magnanimity, refutation of the black man's inefficiency."[2]

There was no visible sign of inefficiency at Tuskegee. The school adver-

1. *Tuskegee Normal and Industrial Institute Thirty-Fifth Annual Catalog, 1915–1916* (Tuskegee, Ala., 1916), in Booker T. Washington Collection, Hollis Burke Frissell Library, Tuskegee University.

2. Emma Lou Thornbrough, "Booker T. Washington," in *Dictionary of American Negro Biography*, ed. Rayford W. Logan and Michael R. Winston (New York, 1982), 634; Pamphlet for visitors, in WP, Tuskegee Records series, "Lists, Programs, Printed Materials, 1915" file; *Tuskegee Catalog, 1915–1916*, 20; Nella Larsen, *Quicksand*, in *"Quicksand" and "Passing,"* ed. Deborah E. McDowell (New Brunswick, 1986), 4. Subsequent references to *Quicksand* will be to this edition.

tised forty distinct industries, such as brickmaking, tailoring, tinsmithing, sewing, cooking, millinery, printing, shoemaking, and blacksmithing. Students and teachers operated a pumping station, an electric plant, and a steam heating plant, as well as cultivating 900 acres of a truck and fruit farm, though the general farm, including a dairy, occupied 2,000 acres. Its campus of red-brick buildings, many in the colonial style popularized at the turn of the century, was impressive. Nine dormitories, including Rockefeller Hall, the gift of John D. Rockefeller, housed the students. Douglass Hall, named for Frederick Douglass, provided not only dormitory space but a 750-seat assembly hall. Another of the largest buildings, the two-story Andrew Carnegie Library, also contained an assembly room for 225 people and a room used as a historical museum.[3] A beautiful elevated setting and well-tended grounds completed the appearance of a flourishing institution for African Americans.

Although irrevocably urban and conscious of cities as a basis for comparison, Larsen was moved by Tuskegee's natural setting. That setting later prompted one of her few written reactions to natural landscapes, that of the fictional Naxos, a campus based on Tuskegee, in her first novel:

As she went slowly across the empty campus she was conscious of a vague tenderness of the scene spread out before her. It was so incredibly lovely, so appealing, and so facile. The trees in their spring beauty sent through her restive mind a sharp thrill of pleasure. Seductive, charming, and beckoning as cities were, they had not this easy unhuman loveliness. The trees . . . on city avenues and boulevards, in city parks and gardens, were tamed, held prisoners in a surrounding maze of human beings. Here they were free. It was human beings who were prisoners. It was too bad. In the midst of all this radiant life.[4]

The gap between Tuskegee's appearance and its reality of systematic repression shaped Larsen's experiences in Alabama and destroyed the last traces of her youthful idealism.

Scheduled to begin work "on or about November 2nd" at the Tuskegee Institute Training School for Nurses, which had been founded in 1892, Larsen was initially optimistic about her post. Her hiring and that of

3. Pamphlet for visitors, in WP; *Tuskegee Catalog, 1915–1916*, 21–22.
4. Larsen, *Quicksand*, 16.

Dr. A. Maurice Curtis, Jr., suggested an upgrading of the program and services. Curtis' position of house physician was newly created to "bring up the health condition of the student body." His arrival and his medical duties, along with the details of his educational background (graduate of the Howard University Medical School) and family connections (son of the prominent African-American physician Austin M. Curtis of Freedmen Hospital in Washington, D.C.) were announced in the student newspaper on November 13, 1915; the last sentence of the announcement added, "Miss Nellie M. Larsen, of Chicago, Illinois, who has gained wide experience at the Lincoln Hospital in New York City, has been appointed Head Nurse."[5] Larsen's arrival and appointment did not merit a separate notice.

Her official title was head nurse of the John Andrew Memorial Hospital and Nurse Training School. Her salary was $40 per month in cash, plus room, board, and laundry. Because of her lack of long-term experience in nursing and supervision, Larsen received $20 a month less than her predecessor. Her staff consisted of two other women: Mrs. Celia E. Watkins, the matron, from Montgomery, Alabama, and Janie V. Armstead, the assistant head nurse, from Florence, Alabama, who had also been hired for the 1915–1916 school year.[6] The principal, Booker T. Washington, thought it was a mistake to displace Armstead with Larsen, whose appointment had been made after the start of the fall term.[7] Recently hired, Armstead had begun her duties in September, a month before the head nurse's position was filled.

Larsen resided in the head nurse's quarters on the second floor of the hospital. The matter of residence had caused her predecessor, Mrs. Margaret E. Richardson, to resign August 27, 1915, after thirteen years of service as assistant head nurse and later head nurse. Mrs. Richardson, whose home was nearby, said her family, an ailing daughter in particular, needed her with them at night. Although Mrs. Richardson had attempted to explain her situation on July 12 and to receive a waiver of the residency require-

5. John A. Kenney to Booker T. Washington, October 21, 1915, in WP, Tuskegee Records series, "Hospital and Nurse Training School, 1915" file; Adah B. Thoms, *Pathfinders: The Progress of Colored Graduate Nurses* (New York, 1929), 30; *Tuskegee Student*, November 13, 1915, p. 4, in Washington Collection, Hollis Burke Frissell Library. All issues of the *Tuskegee Student* cited hereafter can be found in the Washington Collection.

6. Kenney to Washington, October 21, 1915, in WP; *Tuskegee Catalog, 1915–1916*, 16. See also John A. Kenney to Emmett J. Scott, November 3, 1916, in WP, Tuskegee Records series, "Hospital and Nurse Training School, 1915" file.

7. See Washington's handwritten comment on October 21, 1915, letter from Kenney, in WP.

ment, a committee appointed to look into the matter refused her request on August 2 and concurred with the school's executive council that the head nurse must room in the hospital. The council did not consider that Richardson had been an exemplary employee since September, 1902, or that her request for an exemption from the residency requirement was based on a temporary family crisis. The administration's rigidity cost the hospital not only its head nurse but also the assistant head nurse, Mae Booker, who accepted a position at Southern University in Baton Rouge, Louisiana, for the fall of 1915 when offered a market-value salary of $1,000, which Tuskegee routinely refused to pay its employees.[8]

Larsen took her place on staff with the medical director, Dr. John A. Kenney; the new house physician, Dr. Curtis; a beginning intern from Port of Spain, Trinidad, Dr. Rupert O. Roett; the returning pharmacist from Atlanta, Evelyn G. Houston, Ph.D.; and an experienced stenographer, Edna M. Clanton, who was assigned to the hospital during the summer. Together with the assistant head nurse and the matron, this small staff operated Andrew Memorial Hospital, its nursing program, and the health services for the campus community.[9]

Larsen's multiple responsibilities were in health care and nursing administration. Training student nurses presented the most difficult area of her charges because of an institutional history of overworking and hiring-out the young women in the program. While second-year students provided care for patients in Andrew Memorial, third-year students worked on obstetrical and surgical cases in the town and often spent the entire year assisting white physicians.[10] Fees for their services went directly to Tuskegee, rather than to the student nurses.

Larsen's immediate supervisor, Dr. Kenney, who governed the nursing school and the hospital, had begun his superintendentship in 1905 by suspending several student nurses involved in complaints about "the intermi-

---

8. Margaret E. Richardson to John A. Kenney, August 3, 1915, and Margaret E. Richardson to Booker T. Washington, August 27, 1915, both in WP, Tuskegee Records series, "Hospital, 1915" file; M. E. Richardson to E. Scott, September 8, 1915, and Booker T. Washington to Margaret E. Richardson, September 14, 1915, both in WP; Mae M. Booker to Dr. John A. Kenney, October 24, 1915, in WP, Tuskegee Records series, "Hospital and Nurse Training School, 1915" file.

9. See John A. Kenney to B. T. Washington, November 3, 1915, in WP; *Tuskegee Catalog, 1915–1916*, 16.

10. Darlene Clark Hine, *Black Women in White: Racial Conflict and Cooperation in the Nursing Profession, 1890–1950* (Bloomington, 1989), 54.

nable toil, the long hours, the constant surveillance, and most of all the exploitation inherent in the hiring-out practice." Some of the nurses' poor work conditions were eventually corrected; however, Kenney continued to dismiss serious grievances by attributing "the unrest and instability on the part of the nurses" to their being unprepared "for the serious study" of nursing.[11] Larsen inherited a situation in which her nursing charges were routinely denigrated by a superintendent determined to enhance the image of the hospital with the white physicians of the town and with the principal of Tuskegee Institute.

At the same time, she found that the physical plant was more than comparable to Lincoln's. The facilities were new; the hospital had been completed in 1912 with funding provided by Elizabeth Andrew Mason, a granddaughter of a Massachusetts Civil War governor for whom the hospital was named. Both the medical and nursing facilities benefited from Booker T. Washington's ability to raise funds from northern philanthropists, and the result was a well-planned, fifty-three-bed hospital that also included a lecture room for teaching and demonstrations.[12]

A photograph of the imposing two-story, multiwinged structure with four massive white columns supporting its central portico had helped convince Larsen to take the position. Dedicated February 21, 1913, the E-shaped brick building, situated on one of the highest points of the campus, was visible from every part of the school's central grounds. A fourteen-foot-wide colonial porch, extending eighty-two feet across the front of the structure, provided the entranceway to the first floor, where the medical director and physicians had their offices. Larsen's office, shared with the nursing staff, was also on the first floor, as were twenty-two rooms housing the emergency ward, laboratory, classroom, separate waiting rooms and convalescent and detention wards for girls and boys, bedroom for interns, X-ray room, diet kitchen, pharmacy, kitchen, and dining room. Two wide stairways led to a twenty-six-room second story, which was also served by a passenger elevator and a dumbwaiter. Larsen's private bedroom, along with a sitting room she shared with the assistant head nurse, was on the second floor and within easy reach of the surgical and medical wards. Lighted by electricity and heated by steam, Andrew Memorial was equipped

11. *Ibid.*, 56; John A. Kenney to Executive Council, February 4, 1909, in WP, Box 591, quoted by Hine, *Black Women in White*, 56.

12. Louis R. Harlan, *Booker T. Washington: The Wizard of Tuskegee, 1901–1915* (New York, 1983), 140; Thoms, *Pathfinders*, 30.

with an electric silent call system for the nurses and "modern sanitary plumbing" in the bathrooms and kitchens.[13] The building was intended to be Tuskegee Institute's showplace of modernity.

Dr. George C. Hall, a Chicago surgeon speaking at the hospital's dedication, pointed out that "in the Southland over one million and a half people [are] afflicted with preventable diseases, mostly Hookworms and Malaria, with Tuberculosis and Pneumonia adding to the list," but that Andrew Memorial contributed to the solution "by furnishing a place where the necessary information and efficiency are acquired to protect . . . lives" by "furnish[ing] the young Negro physician positions of internes . . . from which they are rigidly excluded in other institutions." The hospital, Hall concluded, "furnishes laboratory facilities, the need of which would make it impossible for the Negro physician to do up-to-date work. It helps him by increasing his skill, expanding his experiences, and makes him a stronger more useful man in his community."[14] His conclusion, though marred by the assumption that the physician is male, pointed to the added racial significance attached to the hospital and reiterated the kind of publicity statement that brought Larsen to Andrew Memorial.

The facility, however, belied the reality of the nursing program Larsen directed. Her students struggled under oppressive conditions and physical exhaustion. Many of them "required periodic leaves of absence simply to recover from the damage done to their health while working in the hospital." Others were wholly unprepared for even the simple tasks connected with nurse's training, such as answering the telephone and making out daily reports. In assuming the education and training of nurses as her primary responsibility, Larsen had to confront the fact that although Tuskegee's nursing training program had been founded before the turn of the century, it was in 1915 still a small, rudimentary program operated by a minimal instructional staff, with Dr. Kenney as the main supervisor. The objective of the program was "to give instruction to young colored women and men [between the ages of twenty-one and thirty] to learn the art of nursing with its different forms of administration." Candidates from the junior class were accepted on a two-month probation before being admitted to the three-year program, which concentrated on practical nursing in the junior, middle, and senior years. Larsen and Armstead gave the practical nursing demonstrations, while Dr. Kenney and Dr. Curtis, with assistance from the intern,

13. *Tuskegee Student*, March 8, 1913, pp. 1, 6.
14. "An Educational Pilgrimage to Tuskegee," *Tuskegee Student*, March 8, 1913, p. 4.

Dr. Roett, delivered the lectures during the winter months and supervised the practical work. The staff covered physiology, anatomy, dietetics, fever nursing, surgical nursing, massage and hydrotherapy, chemistry, obstetrics, and urinalysis, along with "materi medica." [15]

Because the major emphasis during both terms of the three-year program was practical nursing, Larsen presented teaching demonstrations at the bedsides of patients and supervised the practice of the students working throughout the hospital and infirmary. She discovered, however, that of the seven students who enrolled in the fall of 1915 for courses in nurse training, none met the requirements, so that all seven had to attend the night school to satisfy the minimum expectations of a nursing student. [16] By the end of the term, Larsen singled out two students, Lelia Lay and Dorothy White, who were not making satisfactory progress, and though she could not recommend that they be dropped, she had to advise them and their parents "that their work was not up to standard." [17]

In addition to training nursing students, Larsen worked with Tuskegee's Department of Women's Industries in the child nursing and nurture course. The course, established in 1908 to complete the instruction in home and household duties, involved both the hospital training school and the kindergarten in an effort to provide "peculiar opportunities for young women to become intelligent in the care of children." Larsen, along with the dean of the Women's Department and Georgia K. Smith, the teacher of the kindergarten, gave talks and demonstrations on alternate days of the week, instructing the students in subjects connected with the care and training of children. She delivered her lectures and practical demonstrations in a large room in Dorothy Hall, which was equipped as a nursery. There she addressed both the infant and the older child as topics in her discussions of bathing, care of eyes and mouth, feeding, treatment of physical disorders, care of simple injuries and ordinary childhood diseases, and so on. Occasionally she presented demonstrations at the training school, which was known as the Children's House and which served as a public primary school of seven grades; at other times, she was called to the kindergarten, where

---

15. Hine, *Black Women in White*, 55; *Tuskegee Catalog, 1915–1916*, 111–12.

16. See John A. Kenney to B. T. Washington, October 14, 1915, in WP.

17. Nella Larsen to John Kenney, Medical Director, December 6, 1915, and John Kenney to Executive Council, December 6, 1915, both in WP, Tuskegee Records series, "Executive Council, 1915" file.

thirty children between the ages of three and seven were taught. Both the kindergarten and the Children's House emphasized actual school practice, though educational theories and principles were part of the course in education.[18]

Larsen's work in the child nursing and nurture course brought her into contact with an area of nursing that, while not unfamiliar, would become of special interest to her. The nursery in Dorothy Hall also included the "beginnings of a children's library, where students have an opportunity to become acquainted with some of the best literature for children."[19] One part of the course made use of children's literature and presented amusements for children, including stories, songs, games, pets, toys, and playmates. Although Larsen did not teach this part of the course, she shared in the exchanges and later would build upon them when she recorded Scandinavian games for the *Brownies' Book* and when she worked as a children's librarian.

For a twenty-four-year-old recent graduate of a large nursing program with numerous departments, Nella Larsen faced a challenging job at Tuskegee. She was an administrator, a teacher, and a practicing nurse. She supervised the nursing staff of the hospital, including the workers who prepared meals in dietary kitchens and those who performed cleaning and housekeeping chores under the direction of the matron. She assisted the doctors in the operating and anesthetizing rooms, cared for patients on the wards and in the emergency room, and trained students in the fundamentals of practical nursing. On Saturdays during Health Hour for the Tuskegee community, she demonstrated everything from first aid to bed making and general hygiene. Her position was one of responsibility and required hard work, planning, and stamina. Either she or Armstead, her assistant, was on call in the hospital throughout the day and night, a responsibility that proved especially difficult in December, 1915, when a flu epidemic swelled the hospital roll to ninety-five patients. Not only was Larsen required to attend to the epidemic patients, but she was also expected to supervise their meals, the high cost of which (less than five dollars a day) exacted a reprimand from the executive council. Kenney defended the cost by pointing out: "we are feeding this class of patients higher than we usually feed because they are weaker and we find it best to feed high as they get better more

18. *Tuskegee Catalog, 1915–1916*, 108, 46.
19. *Ibid.*, 108.

quickly."[20] There was, however, little reward for Larsen's low-profile work and less encouragement from the male-dominated administration.

The problem was that Andrew Memorial, as part of Tuskegee Institute, was under the control of Booker T. Washington, who had founded the school in 1881 and fashioned his philosophy of racial uplift by 1895 when, at the Cotton States Exposition, he delivered the Atlanta Compromise Address.[21] Washington's emphasis on industrial education, self-help, and racial cooperation and his notions of thrift, patience, and perseverance, combined with high morals and good manners, earned him the regard of wealthy and influential whites, including industrialists (such as John D. Rockefeller and Andrew Carnegie) and politicians (such as Theodore Roosevelt and William Howard Taft).

When Larsen arrived at the end of October, 1915, the principal was near the end of his life but still at the height of his considerable control over the institution. In fact, though Washington had raised the $55,000 to erect and furnish Andrew Memorial from Bostonian Elizabeth Andrew Mason, he used the building of the facility to reiterate the success of his uplift philosophy during a period when its influence was waning. To reinforce the merits of his industrial programs, Washington made Tuskegee students responsible for the construction of the hospital; they dug the clay, made and laid the bricks, installed the pine walls and birch floors, and completed the electrical wiring, plumbing, and steamfitting. Over three hundred students working under the direction of the teachers in the Mechanical Department contributed to every aspect of the construction, from designing architectural plans and digging the foundation to painting the exterior and slating the roof; students even built the wagons used to haul materials to the site. Students in the wheelwright, blacksmith, paint, harness, and tailor shops all contributed, along with those in the trades of masonry, brickmaking, architectural drawing, sawmilling, carpentry, founding, tinsmithing, engineering, machinery, and plumbing.[22] Their accomplishment in completing so massive a project gestured toward the continued significance of industrial education for African Americans and reiterated the primacy of Washington's educational vision.

20. John A. Kenney to B. T. Washington, October 19, 1915, Kenney to Executive Council, December 6, 1915, J. A. Kenney to Executive Council, December 18, 1915, all in WP.

21. Harlan, *The Wizard of Tuskegee*, ix.

22. *Tuskegee Student*, March 8, 1913, p. 6; "Presenting the Keys of the Hospital," *Tuskegee Student*, March 22, 1913, p. 2.

In 1913 when R. R. Taylor, the director of mechanical industries, presented the keys to Andrew Memorial to Seth Low, chairman of the Tuskegee Board of Trustees and former president of Columbia University, he stated:

> Besides having the building for a Hospital, of the utmost importance has been the opportunity it has given these 326 students to learn trades, serving for them as a laboratory for studying principles and processes and the practical application of them. An illustration of this will be furnished by a letter which I saw only a few days ago, which is typical. An ex-student, who left school before completing his course, wrote that he was earning $12.00 a week working in a neighboring city as a bricklayer. This student laid his first brick on this Hospital. All the knowledge, all the skill of hand, all the experience which he has which enables him to earn $12.00 per week at his trade was gained on this building.[23]

Taylor, the architect responsible for the hospital plans, promoted the success of industrial education and concomitantly the success of Booker T. Washington's practical program and philosophy, which the white dignitaries gathered for the dedication could not miss.

One of them, Julius Rosenwald, had arrived from Chicago on a special train of Pullman's with private cars bearing "men and women whose names [were] a part of the high register of the city of Chicago."[24] Known for philanthropy, Rosenwald counted himself among Washington's supporters. He arrived with his wife and a party of sixty-three distinguished Chicagoans, including Harry Pratt Judson, president of the University of Chicago, and Ella Flagg Young, superintendent of the Chicago public schools, who came to witness firsthand Washington's achievements and the Institute's progress.

Washington's philosophy informed not only the construction of the hospital and nursing school but also the conduct of the all-black staff and student body. Although the teachers were envisioned as being better than the students because of their educational achievement and upward class mobility, they were subject to the same rules and to the strict application of those rules. Larsen compared Tuskegee to "a big knife with cruelly sharp

---

23. "Presenting the Keys of the Hospital," 2. Taylor's entire speech to the trustees is printed in this newspaper article.

24. "An Educational Pilgrimage," *Tuskegee Student,* March 8, 1913, p. 4.

edges cutting all to a pattern, the white man's pattern." As she put it, "Teachers as well as students were subject to the paring process, for it [Tuskegee] tolerated no innovations, no individualisms."[25]

The system of rules and restraints was particularly evident in the devotional services, which occurred not simply on Sunday mornings and evenings when Sunday school and church services were mandatory, but seven days a week, including Friday nights, when all members of the campus community were expected to meet for prayers at different places on the school grounds. In October, 1915, the Committee on Religious Affairs, concerned about evening devotions, determined that "it is desirable to make an effort to secure a larger attendance of both students and teachers," and instituted both a campaign to that end and a third Friday prayer meeting in the assembly room of Tompkins Hall under the direction of a member of the Phelps Bible Training School faculty. Dean of the Bible Training School, G. Lake Imes, wrote the report as secretary for committee; Imes was the first cousin of Elmer S. Imes, who would become Larsen's husband in 1919. The Committee on Religious Affairs had little to worry about. On Tuesdays and Thursdays, teachers and students assembled in a room beneath the dining room for devotional exercises; on Mondays and Wednesdays, they gathered for evening devotional exercises in the dining room. The daily evening exercises followed a set program: the reading of scriptures, a prayer by the principal or a member of the faculty, singing by all of the assembly, and announcements for the following day.[26] No faculty member or student was excused from the exercises, and the effect was a carefully controlled environment.

Nella Larsen created a representation of morning assembly at Tuskegee that captured its militaristic control of lives:

She walked to the window and stood looking down into the great quadrangle below, at the multitude of students streaming from the six big dormitories which, two each, flanked three of its sides, and assembling into neat phalanxes preparatory to marching in military order to the sorry breakfast in Jones Hall on the fourth side. Here and there a male member of the faculty, important and resplendent in the regalia

25. Larsen, *Quicksand*, 4.

26. See Committee on Religious Affairs, Report to the Executive Council, October 15, 1915, in WP, Tuskegee Records series, "Reports of Committees" file; *Tuskegee Catalog, 1915–1916*, 22.

of an army officer, would pause in his prancing or strutting to jerk a negligent or offending student into the proper attitude or place. The massed phalanxes increased in size and number, blotting out pavements, bare earth, and grass. And about it all was a depressing silence, a sullenness almost, until with a horrible abruptness the waiting band blared into "The Star Spangled Banner." The goosestep began. Left, right. Left, right. Forward! March! The automatons moved. The squares disintegrated into fours. Into twos. Disappeared into the gaping doors of Jones Hall. After the last pair of marchers had entered, the huge doors were closed. A few unlucky latecomers, apparently already discouraged, tugged half-heartedly at the knobs, and finding, as they had expected, that they were indeed barred out, turned resignedly away. . . . Seven o'clock it was now. At twelve those children who by some accident had been a little minute or two late would have their first meal after five hours of work and so-called education. Discipline, it was called.[27]

The strict discipline, with the semblance of military life that Larsen delineated, was often synonymous with punishment. She found herself more and more hostile to the controls placed upon every aspect of existence at Tuskegee.

She knew, however, that infractions of the rules and regulations were not tolerated. Teachers and students alike were subject to a demerit system; thirty-three and one-third demerits constituted a warning, and three warnings marked the individual for suspension or expulsion. Students and teachers could receive demerits for failing to have a Bible, for taking "part in any political mass meeting or convention," for playing cards and dice, for using "intoxicating drinks and tobacco," and for a number of other offenses. The violation of some rules merited more severe punishments; for example, "low or profane language" subjected a student to "reprimand, confinement, or other punishment," and made a teacher liable for dismissal. In order to ensure that everyone at Tuskegee was reminded of the rules and had a sense of loyalty to the Institute's discipline, the dean of the Women's Department, Susan Helen Porter, met with the women every Friday afternoon, and the commandant, Major Julius B. Ramsey, met with the men every Saturday evening.[28]

27. Larsen, *Quicksand*, 12–13.
28. *Tuskegee Catalog, 1915–1916*, 28, 29.

Teachers were expected to provide a model of religious, moral, and social decorum, and the majority took their position to be a serious privilege. Historian Louis Harlan reported a complaint from the Institute's famous agricultural scientist, Dr. George Washington Carver, about "loose language by teachers": "The matter of teachers calling each other by their given names—such as 'Hetty,' 'John,' 'Bill,' etc., should be corrected," Carver believed, along with "their addressing each other thus: 'Hello! How are you?' etc."[29] Proper manners, formal decorum, and strict morals were expected in all social or public circumstances and from everyone associated with the institution.

Teachers not only served on various ad hoc committees to investigate the conduct of fellow teachers, but were eager to report the failings of their peers. On March 24, 1915, a committee appointed by Booker T. Washington to talk to a male and a female faculty member who spent too much time together made its report: "In accordance with your instruction we saw Mr. Fugett and Miss Schloss (separately) and advised them that the frequency of their appearance in public together is reason for unfavorable comment. We further advised them, for the sake of every thing to be considered, to abstain from being together so much in the future. They displayed a kindly disposition during the interviews and promised to conform with the advice and suggestions we gave."[30] Had the two offenders not taken the advice kindly, they would have faced dismissal.

Married couples were also subject to scrutiny by faculty committees. In the fall of 1915, one committee investigated two married faculty members who had announced the premature birth of their child. On October 2, the committee reported to Principal Washington that, having obtained the exact date of the marriage from the minister performing the marriage and the exact date of birth of the child from the hospital, it found that "there were only six months and fifteen days between the two," and that it had the assurance of Dr. Kenney that the child had the appearance of a full-term, nine-month baby. The committee recommended that the couple be asked to withdraw from the institution at the earliest possible moment.[31]

In matters of dress and appearance, the codes were equally rigid. Male

29. George Washington Carver to Booker T. Washington, September 13, 1902, quoted in Harlan, *The Wizard of Tuskegee*, 156.

30. Committee report to B. T. Washington, March 24, 1915, in WP, Tuskegee Records series, "Reports of Committees" file.

31. Charles H. Evans, chair of committee, to B. T. Washington, *ibid.*

students, whether in the day or night school, wore a full uniform of dark blue coat, trousers, and military cap, but were required to wear overalls in their agricultural or industrial work. During the summer of 1915, Major Ramsey had attempted to initiate an additional dress requirement: all young men should have white trousers "to be used at proper times and on proper occasions." Women students were required to wear a navy blue uniform and hat and a navy blue woolen coat in winter. They were also expected to have "substantial shirtwaists and school dresses" for their work, but were forbidden from wearing or bringing to the campus any dress or article "made of silk, satin, velvet, and fine laces," and they were discouraged from wearing any colors other than navy, black, and brown. Susan Helen Porter, who had returned from retirement to resume the position of dean of the Women's Department for the 1915–1916 school year, complained in November: "Quite a large number of young women have not as yet provided themselves with the school's uniform. Some . . . seem unconcerned about it. Will it be permissible at this time of the school year to keep from the games young women who cannot give good reasons for not having the school's uniform and to begin in the near future to take them out of line in the Chapel?"[32] Although women faculty and staff were not expected to wear the uniform, they were expected to conform to the same general ideas about proper dress for women, particularly in regard to colors and fabrics.

In reflecting upon the restrictions against color in the women's clothing, Larsen described

drab colors, mostly navy blue, black, brown, unrelieved, save for a scrap of white or tan about the hands or necks. Fragments of a speech made by the dean of women floated through her [the protagonist's] thoughts—"Bright colors are vulgar"—"Black, gray, brown, and navy blue are the most becoming colors for colored people"—"Dark-complected people shouldn't wear yellow, or green or red." The dean was a woman from one of the "first families"—a great "race" woman; she, Helga Crane, a despised mulatto, but something intuitive, some unanalyzed driving spirit of loyalty to the inherent racial need for gorgeousness told her that bright colors *were* fitting and that dark-complexioned people *should* wear yellow, green, and red. Black,

32. *Tuskegee Catalog, 1915–1916,* 27–28; J. B. Ramsey to Executive Council, August 9, 1915, in WP, Tuskegee Records series; S. H. Porter to B. T. Washington, November 12, 1915, in WP, "Women's Department, 1915" file.

brown, and gray were ruinous to them, actually destroyed the luminous tones lurking in their dusky skins. . . . Why she wondered, didn't someone write *A Plea for Color?*[33]

In underscoring the racial repression in the ban on color, Larsen attacked the acceptance of white conceptions about African Americans evident among the exponents of racial uplift: "These people yapped loudly of race, of race consciousness, of race pride, and yet suppressed its most delightful manifestations: love of color, joy of rhythmic motion, naive, spontaneous laughter. Harmony, radiance, and simplicity, all the essentials of spiritual beauty in the race, they had marked for destruction."[34] While Larsen's account may seem harsh, it discerned the implications of such policies.

During Larsen's tenure, Margaret Murray Washington, the director of the Women's Industries Department and Booker T. Washington's third wife, expressed dissatisfaction with a teacher in the training kitchen. The problem was not with her work, Mrs. Washington stated: "I am not making any special criticism upon her training, for I think that perhaps she had had good training, but it is upon the woman, herself." She objected to the woman's appearance and dress: "She is careless and indifferent in her general makeup; not at all orderly and neat in her dress. Her manners are not a bit refined." According to Mrs. Washington, the only solution, if the woman could not be helped to improve herself, was to remove her to some other, less visible line of work in another division. She had already asked the principal to be on the lookout for a replacement.[35]

The work load, racial attitudes, and social environment made life difficult for someone of Larsen's sensibilities. She had an aversion to religious services but an interest in intellectual pursuits, especially reading history and literature, and she had, as well, an attraction to aesthetics in personal appearance, particularly wearing beautiful fabrics and fashionable clothing. As an independent single woman working for her livelihood in a profession representing a relief for African-American women from work as domestics, she disagreed fundamentally with Tuskegee's programs for women.

Sensitized to women's work and political issues by her Lincoln experience, Larsen found the Tuskegee approach particularly repressive. While the

---

33. Larsen, *Quicksand,* 17–18.
34. *Ibid.,* 18.
35. Mrs. B. T. Washington to B. T. Washington, September 30, 1915, in WP, Tuskegee Records series, "Women's Industries" file.

industrial program for males might be considered limiting in terms of academic and intellectual content, it did prepare the students for vocations in trades, such as those enumerated in the work on Andrew Memorial. The programs for females, however, concentrated on domestic duties and child rearing. The Women's Industries Department taught laundering, cooking, plain sewing and dressmaking, ladies' tailoring, millinery, basketry, upholstery, and mattress making. Ten faculty members worked in women's industries; only two nurses worked in Larsen's program with its diverse duties. The myopic assumption that women would not pursue work outside of the home was also reflected in the teaching component in the Normal School's Education Department, which emphasized child care and training on the one hand and vegetable and ornamental gardening on the other. The inequities in the training of women at Tuskegee heightened Larsen's discontent with the institution and its objectives. The Institute routinely denigrated the educational achievements of women faculty. "It was a crime to say 'college,'" a female graduate of Cornell University reported, "or if you happened to mention 'degree' you were termed an egotistic pendant."[36]

These systemic problems went unresolved during Larsen's tenure, despite the death of Booker T. Washington on November 14, 1915, only one day after the *Tuskegee Student* announced Larsen's arrival. Washington died after an extended illness that had worsened during a lecture and fund-raising trip to New York and Connecticut. He entered St. Luke's Hospital in New York on November 5, and three days later wired for Dr. Kenney to travel to New York for advice about the treatment he would need in Tuskegee. On November 10, the seriousness of Washington's condition became public, and two days later, his wife completed arrangements for their travel back to Alabama after the doctors concluded that he had only a few days remaining to live and after he decided that "I was born in the South, I have lived and labored in the South, and I expect to die and be buried in the South."[37]

Washington's death the morning after his arrival in Tuskegee was a shock to the campus community, which had been informed of his grave illness and his scheduled return but not that his death was imminent. That Sunday morning the bells calling the students and staff to regular worship services also called them to mourn their loss. Although the next few days would be

36. "Outside Industries for Girls," in *Tuskegee Catalog, 1915–1916*, 109; Hallie E. Queen to Mary Church Terrell, January 2, 1909, in Mary Church Terrell Papers, Library of Congress.
37. Harlan, *The Wizard of Tuskegee*, 450; Washington quoted by Harlan, 454.

remarkable for the eight thousand prominent and ordinary individuals who would gather for Washington's funeral in the Tuskegee chapel on November 17, as well as for the suicide of a female teacher who jumped from the window of a campus building, the school would quickly return to normalcy and, for the remainder of the term, would follow the routines and dictates that Washington had devised.[38] The appointment of Dr. Robert R. Moton, Washington's friend and disciple from Hampton Institute, ensured an uninterrupted continuity in philosophy, policy, procedure, and practice.

Even after Washington's death, Tuskegee proved to be more oppressive to Larsen than Fisk had been in 1907, and perhaps more perplexing as well, for Fisk had a white president and white members of the faculty, but Tuskegee had a black principal and an all-black faculty. Nearly eight years had gone by since Larsen's first encounter with a black institution in the South, but the passage of time had had very little detectable impact on the restrictions and regimentation at Tuskegee, which, in morals and manners, remained much as it had been in the nineteenth century. While Fisk molded a formidable cadre of African-American middle-class professionals who could close ranks against those who were not members of what Du Bois called the "talented tenth" of the race, Tuskegee encouraged the peonage of African Americans to the land and to industrial education. In the opening section of *Quicksand*, Larsen would fuse Fisk and Tuskegee into Naxos, which became for her the prototypical southern black institution.

Class values and social status permeated outmoded attitudes toward standards of propriety and merit. The Victorian code of proper conduct was complicated by strides for class position. The code was also the basis for a patronizing attitude toward the students, who were called "boys" and "girls," that was expressed by a dean of women: "What the students most need is restraint; they come for the most part from undeveloped homes where there are no standards. This being true we must take an extreme position in order to counteract the tendencies of their lives before coming here."[39] Indeed, the positions taken were extremely prudish.

Larsen satirized such attitudes toward students and class in her portrait of Miss MacGooden, a dormitory matron who admonishes her charges, "And *please* at least try to act like ladies and not savages from the backwoods," without considering that

38. Thornbrough, "Booker T. Washington," in *Dictionary of American Negro Biography,* ed. Logan and Winston, 637; Harlan, *The Wizard of Tuskegee,* 457.

39. Harlan, *The Wizard of Tuskegee,* 155; Josephine B. Bruce to Booker T. Washington, n.d. [*ca.* 1902], quoted by Harlan, 156.

most of her charges had actually come from the backwoods. Quite recently too. Miss MacGooden, humorless, prim, ugly . . . prided herself on being a "lady" from one of the best families—an uncle had been a congressman in the Reconstruction Period. She was therefore . . . perhaps unable to perceive that the inducement to act like a lady, her own acrimonious example, was slight, if not altogether negative. And thinking on Miss MacGooden's "ladyness," . . . she remembered that one's expressed reason for never having married, or intending to marry. There were, so she had been given to understand, things in the matrimonial state that were of necessity entirely too repulsive for a lady of delicate and sensitive nature to submit to.[40]

Although Tuskegee students were principally drawn from the lower, laboring classes in the South, the Institute equated their class position with "a lack of values and morals."[41] The gulf dividing students from the faculty and staff was another target of Larsen's criticism:

Helga Crane had taught in Naxos . . . at first with the keen joy and zest of those immature people who have dreamed dreams of doing good to their fellow men. But gradually this zest was blotted out, giving place to a deep hatred for the trivial hypocrisies and careless cruelties which were, unintentionally perhaps, a part of the Naxos policy of uplift. Yet she had continued to try not only to teach, but to befriend those happy singing children . . . [and] was aware that their smiling submissiveness covered many poignant heartaches and perhaps much secret contempt for their instructors. But she was powerless. In Naxos between teacher and student, between condescending authority and smoldering resentment, the gulf was too great, and too few had tried to cross it.[42]

Larsen was herself in a peculiar position in terms of class. Her education at Lincoln and her profession elevated her into the new black middle class. Her light complexion and straight hair reinforced her perceived status and separated her from the predominantly dark-skinned student body and staff. At the same time, however, she was a woman working far from home and

40. Larsen, *Quicksand*, 12.
41. Harlan, *The Wizard of Tuskegee*, 156.
42. Larsen, *Quicksand*, 5.

without the protection of a father, husband, or family. Women on the campus followed the model of Margaret Murray Washington, who was always referred to as Mrs. Washington in both her public and private lives. Larsen had no evident ties to Tuskegee or to Alabama, as had many on the staff, and moreover she appeared to lack family ties altogether. She could not point to a mother or sister or a single female relative among the sophisticated African-American upper crust. Unlike her colleague Dr. Curtis, for example, she had no connections to anyone in the small world of African Americans in the professions. Curtis was the model for the well-connected James Vayle in *Quicksand;* his father was director of Washington's Freedmen Hospital and a surgeon, and his two brothers were also physicians. His mother, Namahoko Sackoame Curtis, was one of Washington's social and political leaders and a close friend of Mary Church Terrell and Josephine Bruce, who once served as Tuskegee's dean of women. Without necessarily knowing his family intimately, many at Tuskegee did have a personal knowledge of the Curtis family through African-American institutions such as Howard University and its medical school, the medical profession, or the "Black 400," Washington's "colored" aristocracy.[43]

Unlike Larsen, Maurice Curtis belonged. His father had merely telegramed Emmett J. Scott directly to secure his position at the John Andrew Memorial Hospital, and Scott made clear that Maurice had received the appointment because of his "honored family": "Dr. Kenney was just on the eve of . . . employing a young man from another school when your telegram came to hand, and it is because of his desire to consider any recommendation from you that he is letting his month's correspondence with the other young man go by the board to give consideration to your telegram regarding Maurice." In writing to announce Maurice's departure for Tuskegee, Dr. Curtis reminded Scott not only of his son's excellence as an assistant in surgical operations, but also of his family's connections: "The Curtises are making good in this year of our Lord, a son gets an appointment to Tuskegee and a brother gets an appointment to Africa. My brother Jim has been named by the President as Minister to Liberia.[44] Maurice Curtis' privileged background connected him to the African-American upper class and gave

43. See Willard B. Gatewood, *Aristocrats of Color: The Black Elite, 1880–1920* (Bloomington, 1990), 49, 206.

44. Emmett Scott to Dr. A. M. Curtis, October 15, 1915, in WP, Tuskegee Records series, "Applications for Positions, 1915: Medical" file; Dr. A. M. Curtis to Emmett Scott, October 27 [1915], *ibid.*

him access to Tuskegee's inner circle that gathered at the Oaks, Booker T. Washington's official residence.

Larsen's interaction with Curtis, in particular, exacerbated her sense of herself as a nobody. In a fictional sketch full of autobiographical details, she revealed her situation at Tuskegee:

> No family. That was the crux of the whole matter. For Helga, it accounted for everything, her failure here at Naxos, her former loneliness in Nashville. It even accounted for her engagement to James [Vayle]. Negro society . . . was as complicated and as rigid in its ramifications as the highest strata of white society. If you couldn't prove your ancestry and connections, you were tolerated, but you didn't "belong." You could be queer, or even attractive, or bad, or brilliant, or even love beauty and such nonsense if you were a Rankin, or a Leslie, or a Scoville; in other words, if you had a family. But if you were just plain Helga Crane, of whom nobody had ever heard, it was presumptuous of you to be anything but inconspicuous and conformable.[45]

Class privilege and respectability were somewhat incongruously linked with a sense of familiarity with achievement, as well as with a sense of formality about position.

In several ways, then, Nella Larsen was out of place at Tuskegee. Lacking the fluidity of movement and position that characterized urban life, the contained, self-conscious community allowed no space in which she could comfortably fit and no place in which she could develop her interests or her sense of self. In her fiction, she would rail against the restrictive "general atmosphere" and its "air of self-righteous and intolerant dislike of difference." Ultimately neither the responsibility of her job nor the sanctuary of her private quarters was enough to hold her in Alabama and force her adherence to what she termed "the strenuous rigidity of conduct required in this huge educational community of which she was an insignificant part." She resigned in the fall of 1916, and severed forever any naïve notions she had held about racial uplift and southern blacks; or as her character Helga put it: "The South. . . . Negro Education. Suddenly she hated them all. Strange, too, for this was the thing which she had ardently desired to share in, to be a part of this monument to one man's genius and vision."[46]

45. Larsen, *Quicksand*, 8.
46. *Ibid.*, 5, 1, 3.

Ten years later, in rendering her own biography, she commented briefly on her experiences at Tuskegee, but her acerbic statement for the author's information sheet for publisher Alfred A. Knopf was bluntly critical: "[she] accepted a position as Head Nurse of the hospital at Tuskegee Institute—the school founded by Booker T. Washington—but her dislike of conditions there and the school authorities [*sic*] dislike of her appearance and manner were both so intense that after a year they parted with mutual disgust and relief."[47] Not surprisingly, she had little tolerance for propaganda or racial uplift and incorporated her attitude toward a thinly disguised Tuskegee and its unwholesome conditions into a stinging indictment:

> This great community . . . was no longer a school. It had grown into a machine. . . . Life had died out of it. . . . Ideas it rejected, and looked with open hostility on one and all who had the temerity to offer a suggestion or ever so mildly express a disapproval. Enthusiasm, spontaneity, if not actually suppressed, were at least openly regretted as unladylike or ungentlemanly qualities. The place was smug and fat with self-satisfaction.[48]

Anticipating and prefiguring Ralph Ellison and other midcentury respondents to the Tuskegee machine, Larsen made her rebellious protagonist emblematic of her own youthful self escaping this particular southern and racial prison.

47. Nella Larsen Imes, Author's statement for Alfred A. Knopf, Inc., November 24, 1926, in Alfred A. and Blanche Knopf Collection, Harry Ransom Humanities Research Center, University of Texas Libraries, Austin.
48. Larsen, *Quicksand,* 4.

5

Finding a Home,
1916–1919

NELLA LARSEN RETURNED to New York City in 1916, in spite of limitations on the employment of trained nurses. Graduate nurses expected positions and salaries commensurate with their training, but hospitals generally sought to cut costs by hiring untrained aides or nursing students.[1] Graduate nurses of color were even more limited in work options because of their race. With positions in the branches of public health and on the staffs of white hospitals largely closed to them, African-American nurses retained close ties with their hospital schools and overseeing hospitals. Larsen's alma mater, the Lincoln Training School for Nurses, and the Lincoln Hospital were both in need of trained nurses as teachers and supervisors. Out of professional necessity, its top graduates often returned to the school or hospital from other positions, just as they frequently were called away to other teaching or administrative posts that could last for as little as six months. Larsen's stint at Tuskegee was an average term that did not reflect poorly on her professional record. With the assistance of her former teacher, Adah B. Thoms, who was then serving as acting director of the Lincoln School for Nurses, Larsen returned to her alma mater as a supervising nurse.

Her disappointing tenure at Tuskegee lingered as an emotional catalyst for two polarized responses to New York. On the one hand, she determined

---

1. Susan Reverby, "The Duty or Right to Care? Nursing and Womanhood in Historical Perspective," in *Circles of Care: Work and Identity in Women's Lives,* ed. Emily K. Abel and Margaret K. Nelson (Albany, N.Y., 1990), 138.

to distance herself from the pretentious class-consciousness that had alienated her in Alabama; on the other hand, she desired to break through the barriers separating her from middle-class comfort and prominence. Both responses governed her choices and behavior during the next three years, when she began to differentiate her personal needs from racial progress.

Assuming a position at the hospital where she had trained meant going back to the safety and security of a known environment in which her talents were recognized. Her mentor and teacher, Thoms, remained an influential presence at Lincoln and among nursing professionals in New York, and she continued to be supportive of Larsen's abilities and managerial skills. Under Thoms's leadership, Lincoln offered Larsen a haven from the personal frustrations she suffered in Alabama. Caregiving at Lincoln had the mark of professionalism. Although the nurses there, as elsewhere, lacked full autonomy, they had earned a measure of respect for their ability and competency in providing quality health care.[2] The work at Lincoln may have been as rigorous as at Tuskegee, but the New York urban environment offered much that the rural South lacked. And Lincoln itself, which had previously provided Larsen's happiest years as an adult, attracted nursing students and staff from diverse backgrounds and geographical areas. Although some were from small towns in the South or rural regions of the North, the nurses represented a wider range of perspectives and experiences than those she had met in Alabama. She was more comfortable at Lincoln, even though she could not reconcile herself to the conventions of racial uplift.

Several of the Lincoln nurses who welcomed Larsen back had been in her 1915 graduating class; others had begun their programs during her first tenure on the staff. A few, such as Mary R. Tucker, who had assumed the duties of night supervisor when she graduated in 1912, had been employees throughout Larsen's association with Lincoln. Tucker was from Hamilton, Bermuda, where she had been a school teacher before enrolling in Lincoln's nursing course. Olive Taylor Hall, Larsen's classmate from Englewood, New Jersey, had remained at the Lincoln school in the Home Department following graduation and had subsequently been appointed to the hospital's prenatal clinic and maternity ward as a social worker. Louise M. Ross, educated in the Boston public schools, had entered Lincoln the year Larsen graduated and was employed as charge nurse in the Dispensary Department until 1919 when she, like Larsen, went to work for the New York City

2. Emily K. Abel and Margaret K. Nelson, "Circles of Care: An Introductory Essay," in *Circles of Care*, ed. Abel and Nelson, 15.

Department of Health. Larsen initially found Ross formidable but gradually came to enjoy her sense of humor; she would draw upon their relationship to create the minor character Ida Ross in *Quicksand*. Genevieve Haithman McKinney, from Jacksonville, Illinois, also enrolled in 1915, and she too worked at Lincoln in charge of home wards and probationary nurses' ward duties until joining the city health department in 1919.[3] McKinney would become the New York Board of Health's first African-American supervisor of nurses. Ross and McKinney, typical of the Lincoln students in classes immediately following Larsen's, pursued postgraduate education at New York's Hunter College, and at Fordham and Columbia Universities, where they took extension courses while working in health care. During the 1920s, when Larsen would rewrite the facts of her nurse's training, omitting Lincoln in favor of Columbia, she used the combined model of the younger McKinney and Ross, who had more opportunities than she for entering programs at New York's major universities.

Larsen would retain ties with one of her classmates, Lucille V. Miller, throughout the 1920s and early 1930s because of their mutual friendship with Mrs. James Weldon Johnson. Miller, a Newport, Rhode Island, native, had performed social-service work among West Indians in Coconut Grove, Florida, after graduation, but she too returned to work as a school nurse for the New York City Department of Health, a position she kept until 1924 when she resigned to head the health services at Christodora House, the city's oldest settlement house. In 1932, when both Larsen and Miller were living on the Fisk University campus in Nashville, Larsen placed an ailing Miller in the hospital and observed: "One never knows, does one? when one is going to meet and need the people one meets so casually along the road of life." In visiting later to ascertain for Grace Nail Johnson whether Miller's health care was adequate, Larsen commented not only on the quality of the medical facilities and staff, but also on the "comfortable, airy and delightfully situated" room, and the "service—food—is more than excellent. It is very beautiful and dainty—fine china, good silver, real linen, all perfectly arranged. And the food is really good. I tell you this because we both realize that for Lucile [*sic*] these things are essential."[4] Miller, like Larsen and the other Lincoln graduates, fetishized things of quality.

These women, along with Thoms, who, as president of the National As-

---

3. Adah B. Thoms, *Pathfinders: The Progress of Colored Graduate Nurses* (New York, 1929), 117f., 112–13, 105–106, 103–105.

4. *Ibid.*, 111–12; Nella Larsen Imes to Grace Nail Johnson, Thursday [1932], in JWJ.

sociation of Colored Graduate Nurses, was the most senior and politically active of the school's black nursing administrators, were the members of Lincoln's extended "family" who were closest to Larsen upon her return to New York. They represented the progressive element in the African-American health care profession, an association that mitigated some of Larsen's disappointment with her setback in Tuskegee. Equally important, Lincoln fostered the social as well as professional mobility that allowed Larsen to catapult herself from obscurity to visibility among prominent black New Yorkers.

As Lincoln's assistant superintendent of nurses, Larsen thus escaped an unbearably restrictive and isolated position in a provincial community without losing professional status. She received a salary of $800 and maintenance in compensation for her work.[5] At a time when career options for African-American nurses in New York were expanding, she reentered Lincoln with a determination to rise in her profession, to meet new people in the city, and to expand her social life beyond the Bronx hospital and school.

One of her first career opportunities upon her return to New York was the 1916 meeting of the National Association of Colored Graduate Nurses, which, perhaps ironically for Larsen, held an August 16 memorial service for the late Dr. Booker T. Washington, whom James Weldon Johnson, national secretary of the NAACP, eulogized. At that meeting in Mother Zion AME Church on West 136th Street, nurses from around the country elected Thoms president and adopted the motto "Not for ourselves, but for humanity." Larsen's professional opportunities multiplied with the activism of the graduate nurses and with the election, because Thoms had become her closest friend. Not only did Thoms hold Larsen in high esteem, praising her as a "shining example of what the larger possibilities of a nurse may be with the proper educational background and ambitions," but she was also at the center of a series of events that resulted in expanded professional opportunities for African-American nurses in general and for Larsen in particular.[6]

Urban health care had begun a period of enlightenment. Nurses, in particular, were crucial to extending health and social services to schools, settlement houses, baby and maternity clinics, and other private and public facilities. Thoms had recognized the increasing importance of public-health

5. See Nella Larsen Imes, Fellowship application form, 1930–31, John Simon Guggenheim Memorial Foundation, November, 1929, in John Simon Guggenheim Memorial Foundation files, New York.

6. Thoms, *Pathfinders*, 212–13, 114.

nursing, had instituted a course at Lincoln in this new field in 1917, and thereby had enhanced not only the curriculum but the nurses' options for jobs. After the United States entered the war against Germany, Thoms encouraged African-American nurses nationwide to enroll in the American Red Cross, which had previously rejected their applications. During the fall, Thoms succeeded in having African-American nurses accepted into the Red Cross Nursing Service, the agency from which the Army Nurses Corps drew its recruits.[7]

Active in the effort to integrate the Red Cross was someone from Larsen's recent past, Dr. Moton, who, as successor to Booker T. Washington, had attempted to retain Larsen at Andrew Memorial Hospital. Larsen first invited Moton to Lincoln in March, 1917, shortly after her return: "Mrs. Thoms, who is now our 'acting' Superintendent of Nurses is very anxious that you should visit here if it is at all possible, and of course I should like so much to see you." She was drawing upon her personal acquaintance with Moton to enlist his support in the campaign Thoms spearheaded. Although his busy schedule while in New York precluded his visiting Lincoln, Moton became a recruit to the cause of African-American nurses. On May 20, 1918, he wrote to Washington's former secretary, Emmett Scott, denouncing the "exclusion of colored nurses" at a time "when the country needs every ounce of effort."[8] He appealed directly to Scott, who was then working as a special assistant in the War Department.

The Henry Street Settlement House, however, was related more directly than the Red Cross to Larsen's professional growth and upward mobility. Under the leadership of Lillian Wald, the settlement had set a precedent in opportunity and employment with its visiting nurses program. That organization, having hired Elizabeth Tyler as its first African-American nurse in 1906, had actively encouraged the employment and participation of African-American nurses, though mainly in connection with patients of color. The city government had not overlooked the impact that the Henry Street Nursing Service had on the general health of urban residents, particularly its mobilization of nurses during the influenza epidemic of 1918 when Wald chaired the Nurses' Emergency Council under the condition that "all nurs-

7. Mabel Keaton Staupers, No Time for Prejudice: A Story of the Integration of Negroes in Nursing in the United States (New York, 1961), 85, 18.

8. Nella M. Larsen to Dr. R. R. Moton, March 13, 1917, in Robert R. Moton Papers, Hollis Burke Frissell Library, Tuskegee University; letter quoted in Darlene Clark Hine, Black Women in White: Racial Conflict and Cooperation in the Nursing Profession, 1890–1950 (Bloomington, 1989), 103–104.

ing agencies coordinate and all clear through [the Henry Street Nursing Service] as the best organized to meet such an emergency." The American Red Cross had turned over much of the emergency effort to Wald, who under the auspices of the New York County Chapter of the Red Cross issued a call for "coolness and courage and sacrifice on the part of American women" in fighting Spanish influenza: "A stern task confronts our women— not only trained women but untrained women. The housewife, the dietitian, the nurses' aide, the practical nurse, the undergraduate nurse and the trained nurse herself—all are needed."[9]

When the threat of influenza had passed, the Emergency Council disbanded, but not before submitting to the commissioner on health an outlined plan for continuing health care in New York City. The commissioner accepted the plan, which expanded health services and facilities and increased the need for nurses and health professionals in social agencies and public departments. This plan paved the way for Larsen's employment as a district nurse for the New York City Department of Health. (Not until 1930, however, was the first municipal health center established in Harlem.) Larsen and other African-American nurses were thus in an excellent arena for seeking employment outside of the New York hospitals, despite the fact that racism prevented their access to job opportunities in the same degree as their white counterparts. Well-prepared and experienced in positions of responsibility, African-American nurses welcomed new work opportunities. As Thoms had pointed out in her 1917 address to the National Association of Colored Graduate Nurses:

We are all contributing our bit toward making the world a happier and healthier place in which to live and develop. . . . [We] see the progress that has been made by our race in the medical and nursing profession [and] we are filled with pride to know that, despite the handicaps that beset us on every side, we are moving steadily forward. Recently our President [Woodrow Wilson] said . . . that the world must be made safe for democracy. Whether he meant to include us or not makes no difference; we are included and there is no power outside of ourselves that can keep us from sharing with the rest of mankind the liberty and freedom for which democracy stands.[10]

9. Lillian D. Wald, *Windows on Henry Street* (Boston, 1934), 97; Red Cross Flyer for Volunteers, issued by the Nurses' Emergency Council, reprinted in Wald, 98.

10. Staupers, *No Time for Prejudice*, 18, 15–23; Thoms, *Pathfinders*, 215–26.

For Larsen, the impact of Wald's Nurses' Emergency Council and its plan for expanding health care was immediate, because the resulting progressive changes in health services and hiring policies led directly to a career advancement.

In 1918, on Thoms's recommendation, Larsen was appointed a district nurse in the New York Department of Health. The position advanced her career by placing her among a select few African-American nurses, a number of them her Lincoln peers, engaged in public health nursing. While the job did not include maintenance, it paid $1,600, twice her Lincoln salary, for work that was divided among social services, health maintenance, and nursing supervision. Tuskegee became a part of her past that she no longer needed to address, except as part of her professional experience, preparation, and responsibilities in teaching and supervision that she would portray in a positive, advantageous manner: "This administrative experience was enriched by close association with many well known physicians and surgeons on the staff."[11] Beyond that, Larsen offered no other comment about her work at Andrew Memorial Hospital and the nursing school at Tuskegee. On the nature of her friendship with Moton, she remained discreetly silent.

That same year, 1918, Larsen's personal life also changed direction. While she had never been able to repair the breach with her relatives, her social life broadened. She met a newcomer to the New York area, Elmer Samuel Imes, Ph.D., through a service organization of visiting nurses formed by Thoms to work for the Circle for Negro War Relief. Larsen became professionally active in the organization and personally acquainted with its board of directors, which included among its influential members Du Bois, Moton, Grace Nail Johnson, and Arthur B. Spingarn. The work provided Larsen with an access to social functions with some of the city's leading citizens.

The son and brother of ministers, Elmer Imes came from an impressive family. Although not wealthy, the Imes family had the distinction in the early decades of the twentieth century of being college educated and descended from several generations of free blacks who had farmed their own land in Mifflin County, south-central Pennsylvania, and whose men had fought with the Union Army during the Civil War. Elmer's father, Rev. Benjamin Albert Imes, was a Home Missionary who, before assuming missionary posts in the South, had graduated from Oberlin College in 1877 and

11. Larsen Imes, Guggenheim application, November, 1929, in Guggenheim Foundation files; Larsen's statement for the section on Lincoln graduates in Thoms, *Pathfinders*, 114.

from the Oberlin Seminary in 1880. His mother, Elizabeth Rachel Wallace Imes, had been born in slavery in Natchez, Mississippi, and had also attended Oberlin, where she had been brought as a child. His brother, Rev. William Lloyd Imes, had begun in 1915 a pastorate at Bethel Chapel in Plainfield, New Jersey, after having received a B.A. (1910) and an M.A. (1912) from Fisk University and a B.D. from New York's Union Theological Seminary in 1915, the same year that he also received an M.A. in sociology from Columbia University.[12]

Born October 12, 1883, in Memphis, Tennessee, where his father served as pastor of the Second Congregational Church at LeMoyne Institute, Elmer Samuel Imes had been sent to Oberlin for his grammar school education while his father labored in the South. He attended high school in Normal, Alabama, so that he could be closer to his family. Unlike his father and brother, Elmer Imes had chosen a secular vocation, though after his graduation from Fisk University in 1903 he had taught mathematics and science in American Missionary Association schools in Georgia and Alabama.[13]

Upon the death of his father in 1908, Elmer Imes assumed the primary responsibility for his mother. Elmer was the oldest son; his middle brother, Albert Lovejoy Imes, was married and living in Ohio, and the youngest, William Lloyd Imes, was still a college student at Fisk. Light enough in skin color to pass for white, Elizabeth Imes had devoted her life to uplifting the race and performing missionary work with her husband. Her sons believed that she needed their help in adjusting to widowhood, so in 1910 William Lloyd also returned to Alabama after his graduation to teach at the Industrial Missionary Association's school at Beloit and to assist his mother, who was director of the teachers' residence. Elizabeth Imes needed her sons' financial support as well, because the Reverend Benjamin Imes, though much honored during his lifetime for his extensive work in religion and education, had earned a meager living as a missionary and had been denied

12. William Lloyd Imes, "The Black Pastures in Retrospect," in *The Hills Beyond the Hills: 400 Years in the Ministry*, by Paul F. Swarthout *et al.* (Lakemont, N.Y., 1971), 115–16; William Lloyd Imes, *The Black Pastures: An American Pilgrimage in Two Centuries, Essays and Sermons* (Nashville, 1957), 2–3, 145. See also *Who's Who in Colored America*, 1938–40, p. 272, and *Who's Who in America*, 1975–76, p. 317. Imes served in Plainfield from 1915 to 1919. He was also a YMCA chaplain in 1918.

13. Elmer S. Imes, Personnel information sheet, June 7, 1929, in Papers of Thomas Elsa Jones, Fisk University Library; W. F. G. Swann, "Obituary: Elmer Samuel Imes" (Typescript in Special Collections, Fisk Biography file, Fisk University Library).

more lucrative administrative positions within the colleges of the Home Missionary Association because of racial barriers.[14]

Except for a year (1909 to 1910) spent in a graduate sociology program at Fisk, Elmer Imes supported himself and his mother by teaching in an AMA school, Albany Normal, in Albany, Georgia. After completing his M.A. in 1910, Elmer Imes taught at Emerson Institute in Mobile, Alabama.[15] His work was an extension of the dedication to the Home Mission movement that had motivated his father to leave his birthplace in the North to minister to former slaves in the South. Elmer Imes's ambition, however, was to become a scientist, and his efforts were encouraged by his father's younger brother, Dr. Thomas Creigh Imes, a graduate of Hahnemann Medical College and a physician in Philadelphia.[16]

In 1918, Elmer Imes completed a Ph.D. at the University of Michigan and moved to New York to work for the Burrows Magnetic Equipment Corporation in the fields of radiation and electromagnetism. His dissertation, "Measurements on the Near Infra-red Absorption of Some Diatomic Gases," was a pioneering study in infrared spectroscopy that appeared in the *Astrophysical Journal* in 1919.[17] In exploring the means of studying the structure of molecules, Imes verified the applicability of the quantum theory to radiation in all parts of the electromagnetic spectrum.[18] His experimental work on the rotational energy levels of hydrogen fluoride was a turning point in modern scientific thinking that demonstrated the general application of the quantum theory to more than a few limited fields of theoretical or applied physics. A brilliant scientist, Imes was initiated into the national

14. Imes, "The Black Pastures in Retrospect," in *The Hills Beyond the Hills,* by Swarthout et al., 118; Imes, *Black Pastures,* 3–5.

15. See *Catalogue of the Officers, Students and Alumni of Fisk University* for the years 1909–1910, 1910–11, and 1911–12, in Special Collections, Fisk University Library.

16. Imes, "The Black Pastures in Retrospect," in *The Hills Beyond the Hills,* by Swarthout et al., 121.

17. *Astrophysical Journal: An International Review of Spectroscopy and Astronomical Physics,* L (November 1919), 251–76. Information on Elmer S. Imes's work in physics from the papers of Dr. Nelson Fuson, Physics Department, Fisk University.

18. For estimates of Imes's high resolution work in physics, see James G. Spady, "Black Space," in *Blacks in Science: Ancient and Modern,* ed. Ivan Van Sertima (New Brunswick, 1985), 258–65; Nelson Fuson, "Notes on Dr. Earle Plyer's 'The Origins and History of Infrared Spectroscopy,'" presented at the Twenty-Fifth Annual Fisk University Infrared Spectroscopy Institute Symposium, August 16, 1974 (Typescript in Fuson's papers, Physics Department, Fisk University). Ronald E. Mickens is editing a newly discovered, book-length manuscript that Imes wrote in the 1930s and entitled "The Culture of Physics."

honorary scientific fraternity, Sigma Xi, while at Michigan, and later became a member of distinguished physics and engineering societies (the American Society for Testing Materials, the American Institute of Electrical Engineers, and the American Physical Society). In 1931, he was selected as one of the thirteen most gifted African Americans in the United States.[19]

While studying physics at Ann Arbor, Imes had directed a graduate laboratory in physics. His research laboratory, according to W. F. G. Swann, a well-known scientist and engineer, was "a mecca for those who sought an atmosphere of philosophic soundness and levelheaded practicalness." A talented scientific researcher, Imes had multidimensional interests. "Gifted . . . with a poetic disposition, he was widely read in literature, and [was] a discriminating and ardent appreciator of music." His aunt, Mabel Lewis Imes, wife of his father's younger brother Martin, was one of the original Fisk Jubilee Singers who had performed before Queen Victoria in England. His father had tutored his three sons in the classics as part of their preparation for college. Elmer Imes's interest in the humanities was characteristic of the young scientist, who was described as having a "sensitive nature." "He had a delightful sense of humor and a skill in repartee, which he always used, however, with . . . kindliness and consideration."[20] Imes was also methodical and ambitious; after completing a college degree in 1903, he achieved his dream of becoming a physicist over the course of fifteen years.

Named for his paternal grandfather, Samuel, Elmer Samuel Imes was living at 115 Belmont Avenue on Staten Island when he met Nella Larsen. He had already distinguished himself in his highly theoretical and technical field. In his mid-thirties, Imes had completed graduate studies and accepted a position as a research physicist in New York, but he had never married. Until he finished graduate work, he had devoted most of his time to studying and teaching. Once he relocated to New York, however, he sought a fuller personal and social life.

Imes was immediately attracted to the small, pretty Larsen, with whom he shared the experience of a Fisk education and a level-headed, lively intelligence. Serious, yet social, he found in the woman he believed to be ten

19. Fisk *Herald*, October, 1941, p. 3, in Special Collections, Fisk Biography file, "Elmer Imes" folder, Fisk University Library; Imes, Personnel information sheet, June 7, 1929, in Jones Papers, Fisk University Library; Eugene Gordon, Boston *Post*, cited by Ann Allen Shockley, *Afro-American Women Writers, 1746–1933: An Anthology and Critical Guide* (New York, 1989), 438.

20. W. F. G. Swann, "Elmer Samuel Imes," *Science*, XCIV (December, 1941), 600–601; Imes, *Black Pastures*, 25, 5.

years his junior a compatible spirit; in fact, they were mirror images of each other. Both had recently achieved freedom from past restraints; his were from academic studies, and hers were from nursing training and the stint at Tuskegee. With comfortable incomes from new employment, both explored New York's cultural richness.

While the couple had the means to attend music programs and theatrical productions, both were avid readers. Imes especially liked Larsen's interest in books and was intrigued by her habit of reading during his courtship visits to the apartment she shared with other nurses at 984 Morris Avenue, Bronx.[21] He evidently found nothing odd about her reading a book while he sat waiting for her to notice his presence. He thought her a self-sufficient woman who could occupy herself during his long hours in the laboratory and his research trips back to Michigan, and she had a respectable occupation. Although he knew little about her background, he admired her impeccable manners, fashionable attire, and urban worldliness. He himself had spent almost all of his adult life in small towns, on school campuses, and in college communities. He knew that she had changed her name from Nellie to Nella, and he too preferred the more sophisticated version. He may not have known the reason why she had become self-sufficient, or the extent of her trouble with her family and its wounding effects on her sense of herself. Within a year of his arrival in the city, Imes proposed.

For Nella Larsen, the proposal was the beginning of her entry into a privileged African-American world. She had matriculated at Fisk during the tenure of both Elmer's brother William Lloyd (class of 1910) and his wife, Grace Virginia Frank, a native of Dundee, New York, who had, like Larsen, been a student in the Normal School in 1907; however, Larsen had neither graduated from Fisk nor become part of the impressive network of upwardly mobile Fisk alumni. Fisk graduates were among the elite in African-American society; their class position, often based not on wealth but education and a heritage of skin color and other physical features resembling those of whites, gave them access to opportunities ordinary blacks only imagined. Fisk alumni of both sexes were often "race" leaders, the most prominent of whom was Du Bois (class of 1888).

Despite her income and professional standing, Larsen's work limited her to a lower social sphere. While at Tuskegee she had met prominent Fiskites,

---

21. Frankie Lea Houchins, interview with author, March 12, 1984. See Elmer S. Imes and Nella M. Larsen, Certificate of Marriage Registration, No. 1325, May 3, 1919, in Office of the City Clerk, Bronx, New York.

among them Mrs. Booker T. Washington and Elmer Imes's first cousin, George Lake Imes, a Congregational minister, English teacher, and Tuskegee administrator, but her association with them had remained purely professional.[22] Imes appealed to Larsen's desire for social prominence and economic security; moreover, as an older man he satisfied her need for the paternal regard she had lost when Peter Larson/Larsen had positioned himself, his wife, and his daughter Anna entirely within conventional white society. Described both as a "Beau Brummel" and, more frequently, as a father-figure, Imes was an engaging man with old-world charm and courtly manners.[23] Although not demonstrative and affectionate, he was attentive during their courtship and accepted her on her own terms.

On May 3, 1919, Nella Marion Larsen and Elmer Samuel Imes stated their marital vows before the Reverend William Lloyd Imes. The ceremony was held in the chapel of the Union Theological Seminary. The Reverend Imes arranged for the use of the chapel. He and his wife, Grace, had traveled to New York for the wedding from Philadelphia, where he was beginning a new pastorate. Adah Thoms acted as Larsen's attendant and witness, while Charles A. R. McDowell performed those duties for his friend Imes.[24] No members of Nella Larsen's family attended; the small gathering of friends and well-wishers included mainly her Lincoln associates, his family and co-workers, and a few Fiskites. Nella Larsen had shown little interest in religion before her marriage, but she joined a family with strong religious convictions and vocations. From the beginning of the marriage, she was at odds with the Imes family, who, with the exception of William Lloyd Imes, found her unrefined and irreligious.[25]

The newlyweds moved into Imes's Staten Island apartment, which was located in New Brighton near one of the laboratories of the Burrows company and part of a two-mile belt of communities in the northern and eastern section of Richmond County, the least populated borough of New York

22. G. Lake Imes and Elmer S. Imes were the sons of two brothers. G. Lake was the son of Benjamin Imes's older brother George Hezakiah Imes, a Union veteran of the Civil War. See Imes, *Black Pastures,* 2.

23. Shockley, *Afro-American Women Writers,* 437; Frankie Lea Houchins, interview with author, December 30, 1984; John Hope Franklin to Thadious M. Davis, April 4, 1989, in possession of Thadious M. Davis; Youra Qualls, interview with author, January 8, 1989.

24. See Elmer S. Imes and Nella M. Larsen, Certificate of Marriage Registration, May 3, 1919.

25. Adelaide Cromwell Gulliver, interview with author, March 18, 1987.

City.[26] For Nella Larsen Imes, who had celebrated her twenty-eighth birthday just before the wedding, it was the first home of her own outside of residences provided for nurses. After more than a decade of being on her own, and often a lonely outsider, she had both a home and companionship.

During this period of contentment and development, she applied her skills in homemaking and sewing to her household. She had learned sewing and dressmaking from her seamstress mother; whatever else she had learned or internalized from her mother about domesticity is not apparent. She took pride in decorating, in cooking, and in entertaining, though their apartment was far removed from the growing community of African Americans in Manhattan. From the beginning of her marriage, she expended, as she would later admit with regret, a great deal of her energy in housecleaning, especially scrubbing floors, which became her metaphor for the nature of housework.[27]

The marital home must have been a site of ambivalence for Larsen. During the years on her own, Larsen had had to stifle her need for both family and home and to defuse her anger at her deprivation. In assuming the role of wife and homemaker, however, she had to begin the process of activating and responding to those needs long repressed. On the one hand, her own training as a nurse had prepared her for home management, yet the domestic work that she expertly performed in her household was precisely the kind that she had found demeaning in the education of female students at Tuskegee. On the other hand, the making of a home, in the larger sense, caused her to reconsider the family she had lost and, to an extent, to duplicate the model of her mother as homemaker within the Larson/Larsen household. That household and her mother's role within the family setting had been the source of pain for Nella Larsen, so that in assuming the domestic sphere associated with her early trauma, she must have been conflicted and she may have functioned in reaction against her mother, the wife who was complicit in denying her daughter's existence and right to a familial relationship within the home.

Domesticity was never Larsen Imes's sole objective in creating a home. Home was not simply a physical structure that provided a dwelling she at-

26. Staten Island, the Borough of Richmond, had a population of 116,531 in the census of 1920 (Hurbert R. Cornish and Joseph T. Griffin, *Metropolitan New York: Its Geography, History and Civics* [Boston, 1925], 152).

27. Nella Larsen Imes to Carl Van Vechten, Wednesday 1st [October, 1930], in JWJ.

tended; it was a psychological space in which she belonged, was necessary and special. Nursing had trained her not only in hygiene and dietetics but also in leadership and self-development. The profession's strong suit was that, by emphasizing self-governance in its training schools and ward duties and stressing personal amenities in its nurses' homes and living quarters, it taught women that it was possible to exercise greater responsibility in their own lives, especially control over their labor and the benefits derived from it. At the same time that she plunged into domesticity, Larsen Imes continued her job as a district nurse, which gave her a measure of independence and a larger stake in family finances. In many respects, the marriage promised a particular, if conventional, perfection, a rounded shape to her existence.

In the older Imes (thirty-six at the time of the marriage), she found a protective, mentoring, and opinionated partner, though one untraditional enough to acknowledge her earning power and individuality. He was an antidote to her early social deprivation. While she luxuriated in the status of being his wife and became partial to using the phrase "like a princess out of a modern fairy tale" as an emblem of her own situation, she never aspired to the role of an idle Cinderella. She wanted her own limelight and sought personal development of her talents and abilities. She increased the range of her interests in books and the arts. Her husband, cosmopolitan in his tastes, encouraged her to explore new areas in her readings, especially among foreign writers, while she fostered his reading of modern authors. He also introduced her to the newer areas of modern science that were part of his research. She gathered into her realm ideas about ways of living fully in the contemporary world. Henry James's American heroines, in particular, offered models of female self-determination and self-advancement that she found appealing.

This period, at the end of World War I, broadened Larsen Imes's horizons. New York's black population grew during the migration between 1915 and 1919, and Harlem was becoming, as James Weldon Johnson would observe in January, 1920, "the greatest Negro city in the world."[28] On all fronts, there were signs of activity and growth for the emerging city within a city: the major black churches were buying property and building in Harlem; Madame C. J. Walker had moved her hair business there in 1914; Marcus Garvey had founded the Universal Negro Improvement Association there in 1917; the Lincoln and Lafayette theaters had opened to

28. James Weldon Johnson, "The Future of Harlem," New York *Age*, January 10, 1920.

blacks in 1915; fashionable black cabarets, such as the Royal Cafe and the Astoria, replaced the prewar saloons; in 1918 W. C. Handy had moved from Memphis to found the Pace and Handy Music Company on Broadway; and in 1919 Paul Robeson arrived in Harlem. The 369th Infantry, Harlem's Hell Fighters, had been decorated in France and marched up Fifth Avenue on February 17, 1919. Their triumphant return to Harlem had united the community and the blacks of greater New York in a sense of pride and possibility; they symbolized the dreams for a future of achievement and advancement that the African-American newspapers, the *Amsterdam News* and the New York *Age*, chronicled. Even the Red Summer of 1919, with twenty race riots in the United States, did not stop Harlem's progress.

Nella Larsen Imes's own professional organization, the National Association of Colored Graduate Nurses, also enlarged her horizons. Beginning in 1916, the association became active with the National Urban League and the National Association for the Advancement of Colored People, and in 1918 it engaged representatives of the United States Public Health Services in its efforts to improve conditions for black nurses.[29] Larsen Imes had become a district nurse in 1918 largely through the general political activism of the NACGN. By 1921, after the passage of the women's suffrage amendment, the group campaigned to register its members to vote. Its advisory council reached out into the larger New York community of prominent blacks: Lillian Alexander, who would later recommend Larsen Imes for the Harmon Award; George Edmund Haynes, who would be in charge of those awards; Charles S. Johnson, who would head the Urban League and *Opportunity* magazine; Grace Nail Johnson, who along with her husband, James Weldon, would become friends and supporters of Larsen Imes; and Dr. Louis T. Wright, who would develop personal ties with the Imeses.

Anchored firmly in African-American society, Larsen Imes's world became more pronouncedly interracial than it had been during her years at Lincoln or Tuskegee. Elmer Imes moved with ease among whites and blacks. With him, she mingled with whites on Long Island, where Paul D. Cravath, a lawyer and trustee of Fisk whose father had been president of that institution, retreated from Manhattan's summer heat to his parents' estate, and with blacks in Brooklyn and Harlem, where young professionals from good families, such as Dorothy R. Peterson, the daughter of a black diplomat, congregated for bridge parties and social teas.

In 1921, the Imeses moved to Jersey City, New Jersey, where they occu-

---

29. Staupers, *No Time for Prejudice*, 22.

pied a single-family home at 51 Audubon Avenue. Another tenant, Robert S. Hartgrove, rented the top floor of the three-story house, which was located in a predominantly white area of Jersey City. Although Audubon Avenue was tree-lined and wide, the house at 51 had the appearance of a townhouse. It sat close to the street and lacked a front lawn, but it had three large living-room windows from which a small garden and sidewalk tree were visible. The house and the area were comfortable, though not typically suburban.

Larsen and Imes commuted into New York for their jobs: he to Staten Island, she to Manhattan. With better housing at economical prices, Jersey City was actually conveniently located: it was closer to Staten Island than Manhattan, and closer to Manhattan than Staten Island. The Hudson River tunnel to Jersey City had opened in 1908, making it attractive for commuters. Ferries also connected the town to New York City. One of the earliest New Jersey settlements, Jersey City was a center for four railroad lines, through which foodstuff for New York arrived, and a major shipping port, where transatlantic liners docked. The combination of good transportation into greater New York and neighborhood homes with views of the Hudson River made Jersey City a desirable postwar suburb. In 1920, Hudson County (Jersey City) had a population of 298,103; by 1924, the population had grown to 305,911, which was not quite as rapid a growth as that of New York City in the 1920s, but a large increase for a town in New Jersey.[30]

The move coincided with Larsen Imes's dissatisfaction with her work for the Department of Health. As part of her job, she visited the sick, mainly low-income blacks, in their often cramped living spaces in the Columbus Hill or Harlem districts, where African-American nurses were assigned. Many of her patients did not trust modern medicine, preferring instead more familiar home and herbal remedies or superstitious practices. One part of her home visits involved demonstrating how to clean wounds, bathe babies, or disinfect utensils. The work was difficult, the hours long. The employment was neither to her liking nor to her satisfaction. She began to drop in at the 137th Street Branch of the YWCA, where on April 5, 1918, the NACGN headquarters and registry had opened.[31] Although Ruth Sellers, the R.N. who worked as executive secretary of the association, and members of the Y staff, Cecelia Saunders, general secretary, Viola Chapman, membership secretary, and Emma Ransom, chair of the Y, were all helpful,

---

30. Cornish and Griffin, *Metropolitan New York*, 151, 34.
31. Thoms, *Pathfinders*, 217.

they could neither assuage her discontent with her job nor help her find a better one. Larsen Imes would later make use of the YWCA and its secretarial staff in her first novel, though she would relocate the scenes in Chicago.

Her dissatisfaction was, in part, related to her new social environment. Nella Imes, as she was then exclusively known, was the sole wife among those of her husband's friends who, if employed at all, was not a school teacher or librarian. Several of the single women held new types of white-collar jobs for African Americans. Jessie Redmon Fauset, for instance, whom the Imeses met in 1919 when she arrived in New York to become the literary editor of *Crisis*, was a general assistant to Du Bois, who edited the magazine for the NAACP. Although Larsen Imes's personality and inclinations would have eventually fostered displeasure with her work in public health, her marriage to Imes hastened it.

Larsen Imes considered her marriage a move upward in society. Her husband's position as a research physicist was unique for an African-American man, and his connections with what Larsen Imes termed "important" people, mainly professionals, were enviable. Men rather than women were the arbiters of prominence in this social configuration. Imes was a member of the exclusive men's club Sigma Pi Phi, or Boulé, as it was generally called from its formation in 1904. A forerunner of African-American college fraternities, Sigma Pi Phi was founded by medical professionals (two physicians, a dentist, and a pharmacist), members of Philadelphia's "colored aristocracy" who wanted to bring together men who had "demonstrated outstanding ability to compete successfully with whites" and "adhered to a code of unimpeachable personal conduct." One of the founders, Henry M. Minton, defined its purpose: "to bind men of like qualities, tastes, attainments into close sacred union"; "quality not numbers is our aim." With rigorous standards of admission, based on education (a college degree), respectability, and congeniality, Boulé accepted only men of the highest social standing, such as Du Bois and Daniel Hale Williams. A prestigious family background certainly helped. With a nationwide membership of only 177 in 1920, Boulé was "forthrightly elitist," a "model of genteel society," and a brotherhood of cultured men.[32]

Even in terms of church affiliations, Elmer Imes was part of the upper class. He belonged to St. Philip's Protestant Episcopal Church, the wealthi-

32. Willard B. Gatewood, *Aristocrats of Color: The Black Elite, 1880–1920* (Bloomington, 1990), 234, 235.

est African-American congregation in New York. The majority of its members were light-skinned African Americans who in 1910 had purchased church property in Harlem under the auspices of Hutchens C. Bishop, their rector, who looked white and who had the endorsement of well-placed white New Yorkers such as Jacob Schiff, Robert C. Ogden, Seth Low, John J. Delany, George R. Sheldon, and Joseph H. Choate.[33] Once located in the new church building on West 133rd Street, St. Philip's bought in March, 1911, a row of apartment buildings on West 135th Street for over a million dollars; the apartments occupied nearly an entire city block between Lenox and Seventh Avenue. Elmer Imes would remain a member of St. Philip's throughout the remainder of his life. His friends in the congregation included Bishop's son Shelton and John E. Nail, the church's business agent and pioneering Harlem realtor, who was the brother of James Weldon Johnson's wife, Grace.

Larsen Imes's marriage was also a form of social empowerment. Although marriage may often be synonymous with reduction and denial of power for the female, for the African-American female, particularly if she came from the working class, an advantageous marriage was empowering. A publicly sanctioned institution gave her respectability, with a status and a title long denied her by slavery and segregation. The married African-American woman achieved not only an improved place in the larger society but also a transformed self-perception. She was freer to pursue her own interests without challenges to her morals or good name. Marriage to Imes, then, provided Larsen Imes with greater social status and removed some of the obstacles to her social mobility and personal advancement.

Yet, early on in the marriage, Larsen Imes began to feel insecure about her own significance. "Life for both sexes is arduous," as Virginia Woolf observed. "It calls for gigantic courage and strength. More than anything, perhaps, creatures of illusion, as we are, it calls for confidence in oneself. Without self confidence we are as babes in the cradle."[34] Larsen Imes lacked self-confidence, though few would have suspected as much, given her demeanor. She began to emphasize her mixed racial heritage by reminding the Imes family and friends that one part of her family was white, and Scandinavian at that. This racial heritage with its implied superiority provided the basis for her public self-concept, which depended upon attitudes within the

33. See Jervis Anderson, *This Was Harlem: A Cultural Portrait, 1900–1950* (New York, 1982), 254–56.
34. Virginia Woolf, *A Room of One's Own* (New York, 1957), 346.

race toward color as a measure of potentiality or probable achievement. Thus she used her heritage to situate her perceived self within a desirable public context while using that one factor for a trajectory that would close the gap between her perceived self (or "as is" self[35]) and her ideal self (or the self that she believed she should be). Increasingly, she played the snob to mask her own vulnerability. In veiling the crucial details of her mixed-race background, she was furthering rather than repairing the distance between herself and other people.

Mulatto status and light coloring alone could not make her comfortable or secure in this particular grouping of African Americans, many of whom were, like her mother-in-law, much more visibly white than Larsen Imes. Although some, such as John E. Nail, had amassed fortunes, many were professionals of modest means; nevertheless, even A'Lelia Walker, the brown-skinned daughter of the millionaire Madame C. J. Walker, was not fully accepted by this elite because her mother was a former washerwoman. Appearances, profession, and family counted more than money. In response to such strictures, Larsen Imes developed a protective strategy of remaining quiet and aloof at social gatherings. Her public persona was accompanied by a private need to transform herself, a need she soon translated into concrete and ambitious plans.

For the most part, Imes, a man with a highly developed sense of pride in his achievements and sensitivity to his reputation, seemed untroubled by his choice of a marital partner. His wife was intelligent and attractive; that she lacked standing among prominent African Americans, and was what his peers called "a nobody," seemed not to bother him. Like his wife, Imes was somewhat of an iconoclast; nonetheless, he adhered to popular notions among middle-class blacks regarding mates: "lighter and whiter with each generation," and "marry light for the sake of the race." In fact, as researchers such as Edward Reuter have demonstrated, "Within the race, as between the races, color is a physical fact that automatically classifies."[36] Skin color assisted in the demarcation of class for the upper stratum of African Americans. Nella Larsen Imes, only slightly brown, was light enough in complex-

35. Linda Tschirhart Sanford and Mary Ellen Donovan, *Women and Self-Esteem* (New York, 1985), 8–9.

36. Edward B. Reuter, *The American Race Problem: A Study of the Negro* (New York, 1938), 416. See also Melville J. Herskovits, *The American Negro: A Study in Racial Crossing* (New York, 1928), 58, and W. Lloyd Warner, Buford H. Junker, and Walter A. Adams, *Color and Human Nature: Negro Personal Development in a Northern City* (Washington, D.C., 1941), 13–18.

ion to be considered one of the "bright skins" of the race. And she was fairer-skinned than her husband. By playing up her white parentage, she presented an excellent mate for a man who was himself light brown–skinned but darker than his brothers and his mother.

Without diminishing the significance of affection in the choice of marriage partners, color-consciousness within the African-American middle class influenced the formation of relationships. The whiter the individual was in color, the greater his or her chances of transcending class stratification and racial prejudice. The New York *Age,* one of black New York's more conservative newspapers espousing Booker T. Washington's brand of racial uplift, routinely carried ads for skin whiteners and bleaching creams such as Black-No-More, Cocotone Skin Whitener, and Fair-Plex Ointment. African Americans often accepted without question the color evaluations of the dominant culture and the implications about opportunity and class.

In discussing "color lines within the color line," Walter White, himself a fair-skinned, blue-eyed, "passable" African American, observed:

> Living in an atmosphere where swarthiness of skin brings almost automatically denial of opportunity, it is as inevitable as it is regrettable that there should grow up among Negroes themselves distinctions based on skin color and hair texture. . . . Marriages between colored men and women whose skins differ markedly in color, and indeed less intimate relations are frowned upon. Since those of lighter color could more often secure the better jobs an even wider chasm has come between them, as those with economic and cultural opportunity have progressed more rapidly than those whose skin denied them opportunity.
>
> Thus, even among intelligent Negroes there has come into being the fallacious belief that black Negroes are less able to achieve success.[37]

This invidious emphasis on color as a measure of value perhaps contributed to Elmer Imes's initial attraction to the "mulatto" Nella Larsen, who had straight, or "good," hair and features that were more Caucasian than Negroid.

Moreover, the timing of their meeting was right. Imes had not married while at Fisk at least partly because of his greater ambition to become a

---

37. Walter F. White, "Color Lines," *Survey Graphic,* VI (March, 1925), 682.

scientist. He took an exceptionally dim view of marrying before completing an education. More than once he expressed the view that marriage interfered with career, work, and achievement. John Hope Franklin recalls visiting him in 1941: "He asked me if I was married and I proudly told him that I had married the previous year. He frowned and said that this would be the end of me that I would never receive the Ph.D. of which he was aware I was pursuing, and I would not amount to anything. I protested that I had completed *all* of the requirements and would receive the degree at the June Commencement. He expressed disbelief and said that I was merely spouting words that meant nothing."[38]

As Imes's wife, Larsen Imes developed a characteristic that would mark her middle adult years: ambition. Her ambition was an obverse reflection of her husband's. Post–World War I New York offered African Americans new opportunities and directions for careers; the period witnessed "a shift from the myth of inferiority to the idea that Negroes had potentialities for growth and development."[39] African Americans themselves, believing in economic progress as the way to improve their standing with whites, pushed educational preparation for the higher professions and sanctioned the accumulation of personal wealth as necessary for racial uplift. Fueled by the cultural, economic, and social environment of established and emergent African-American professionals in whose circles she was now moving, Larsen Imes was determined to become something more than a nurse. Precisely what she might be remained vague, but her dream of an ideal self and her ambition to achieve began a progress toward coalescence at the end of 1919.

Three clusters of public events scattered throughout the year had already begun to herald a change in the general attitudes of black New Yorkers. The first was the February 17, 1919, return of Harlem's Hell Fighters, the 369th Infantry Regiment, from France. Their return precipitated a hitherto unequaled outpouring of racial pride, solidarity, and accomplishment, because their heroism in combat had come to symbolize a demonstration of black America's potential. The second set of events occurred during the summer when race riots across the nation resulted in the lynching of eighty-three blacks and the injury of scores of others. Out of the violence during the Red Summer of 1919 emerged the birth of the "New Negro," one who would not allow himself, his family, or his race to be victimized without fighting

38. Franklin to Davis, April 4, 1989.

39. Edwin R. Embree and Julia Waxman, *Investments in People: The Story of the Julius Rosenwald Fund* (New York, 1949), 162.

back. The third event was the July, 1919, publication of Claude McKay's valiant sonnet "If We Must Die" in New York's *Liberator,* a socialist magazine of art and literature that later, in 1921, hired McKay as an associate editor. The poem marked the first literary articulation of a bold, aggressive mood among blacks, a spirited refusal to accept oppression: "Like men we'll face the murderous, cowardly pack, / Pressed to the wall, dying, but fighting back!"[40] The reprinting of "If We Must Die" in African-American newspapers and magazines across the country made apparent that literature not only could have mass appeal but could play a significant role in communicating a new racial consciousness. Combined, these events argued for a necessary racial activism.[41]

In November, Du Bois, editor of the *Crisis,* named Jessie Redmon Fauset to the position of literary editor. Almost immediately, the magazine began to provide a forum with a national audience for black writers. Fauset announced in its pages: "The portrayal of black people calls increasingly for black writers." Within a few months, Faucet had conceived the *Brownies' Book* for the

> children, who with eager look
> Scanned vainly library shelf and nook,
> For History or Song or Story
> That told of Colored People's glory.[42]

Published monthly over a two-year period beginning in January, 1920, the *Brownies' Book,* "for the Children of the Sun," included stories, songs, games, poems, biographies, and essays designed for an audience of "all little folk—black and brown and yellow and white," but "especially for Kiddies from Six to Sixteen."[43] Du Bois' column, "As the Crow Flies," informed adults, in addition to children, of world and national events (for instance,

---

40. Claude McKay, "If We Must Die," *Liberator,* II (July, 1919), 21. In September, the poem appeared in the *Messenger,* the official publication of the Brotherhood of Sleeping Car Porters, founded by A. Philip Randolph and Chandler Owen in 1917. See *Messenger,* II (September, 1919), 4. McKay also published the poem in his 1922 volume *Harlem Shadows.*

41. See discussions of 1919 and the emergence of the "New Negro" in Nathan Irvin Huggins, *Harlem Renaissance* (New York, 1971), 52–59, and in David Levering Lewis, *When Harlem Was in Vogue* (New York, 1981), 3–24.

42. Jessie Redmon Fauset, "Dedication," *Brownies' Book,* I (January, 1920).

43. See title pages, *Brownies' Book,* January, 1920–December, 1921.

partitioning and war in Europe, struggles for independence in Egypt, India, and Ireland, progress in the women's rights movement, and maneuvers of the Bolsheviki in Russia) and interpreted their economic, political, and social effects on African Americans.[44] The *Brownies' Book* gave African-American adults, such as the young Langston Hughes, who were inclined toward the literary arts a chance to publish their work. And more important, it gave Nella Larsen Imes, who was searching for an opportunity to actualize her ambition, an impetus for undertaking creative writing and for effecting a change in her individual circumstances.

44. See W. E. B. Du Bois, *Writings in Periodicals Edited by W. E. B. Du Bois: Selections from The Brownies' Book,* ed. Herbert Aptheker (Millwood, N.Y., 1980). For a history of the publication, see Elinor Desverney Sinnette, "'The Brownies' Book': A Pioneer Publication for Children," *Freedomways,* V (First Quarter, 1965), 133–42.

II

A New Negro's Apprenticeship, 1920 – 1927

6

Working for an Education, 1920–1923

IN JUNE, 1920, the *Brownies' Book* carried in its "Playtime" series "Three Scandinavian Games" compiled by Nella Larsen Imes. She introduced "Cat and Rat," "Hawk and Pigeons," and "Travellers": "These are some games which I learned long ago in Denmark, from little Danish children. I hope that you will play them and like them as I did."[1] With this brief statement, Larsen Imes began her transformation into a published author and her transcendence of proscribed social roles. Her appearance in the magazine followed that of James Weldon Johnson and Georgia Douglas Johnson, both of whom were already accomplished creative writers, and that of Langston Hughes, whose several contributions led to the publication of his first major poem, "The Negro Speaks of Rivers" (1921), in *Crisis*. Although Larsen Imes's contribution was slight, it was an auspicious beginning.

Elmer Imes, too, had begun to publish his scientific writings. His work as a research physicist at Burrows Magnetic Equipment Corporation involved scientific applications rather than theoretical formulations, and much of it was based on his research at Michigan in the Physical Laboratory. In 1919, he had published "Measurements on the Near Infra-red Absorption of Some Diatomic Gases," the conclusions of his dissertation research. In 1920, an abstract of his paper, "The Fine-Structure of the Near Infra-red

---

1. Nella Larsen Imes, "Three Scandinavian Games," *Brownies' Book*, I (June, 1920), 191–92.

Absorption Bands of the Gases HCl, HBr, and HF," appeared in the *Physical Review* as part of the proceedings of the American Physical Society meeting in Chicago on November 29, 1919.[2] This second publication, listing Imes and H. M. Randall, his graduate research director, as coauthors, assured Imes of visibility in his field and of invitations from Michigan to continue his experiments there. For him, just as for his wife, the new decade seemed to unfold propitious opportunities.

July, 1920, marked a major transition in Larsen Imes's professional life. Two events occurred that imprinted change. The July, 1920, issue of the *Brownies' Book* carried another "Playtime" piece, "Danish Fun," by Nella Larsen Imes. "Dear Children," she wrote, "These are pleasant memories of my childish days in Denmark."[3] Three games, "The Fox Game," "Hide the Shoe," and "The King is Here," and five "Danish Riddles" made up the one-page contribution, which was shorter than "Three Scandinavian Games," which had appeared in the June issue. Neither length nor audience was significant; what was was that Larsen Imes had completed her second publication in a magazine with a national circulation. Although she had transcribed the games and riddles from memory, she had organized and presented them in her own way. In the process, she discovered the point that Fauset had made in encouraging her to make a submission to the *Brownies' Book:* writing was not difficult.

On July 21, 1920, the second event marking a transition occurred. Mary Wainwright Booth, the director of the board of managers of the Lincoln Hospital Training School for Nurses, died. Her death, after fifty-eight years of service to the Lincoln Hospital and Home, signaled the end of an era for the institution and its graduates; yet the white philanthropists who, like Booth, had been visionary enough to found and support the home, the hospital, and the school for "colored" people, were not progressive enough to appoint an African-American administrator to replace Booth, whose position in her later years had become largely ceremonial.

Their failure to do so made clear to the Lincoln nurses throughout New York City that their opportunities as African-American nurses were still lim-

---

2. Elmer S. Imes, "Measurements on the Near Infra-red Absorption of Some Diatomic Gases," *Astrophysical Journal: An International Review of Spectroscopy and Astronomical Physics,* L (November, 1919), 251–76; H. M. Randall and E. S. Imes, "The Fine-Structure of the Near Infra-red Absorption Bands of the Gases HCl, HBr, and HF," in "The Proceedings of the American Physical Society," *Physical Review: A Journal of Experimental and Theoretical Physics,* 2nd ser., XV (February, 1920), 152–55.

3. Nella Larsen Imes, "Danish Fun," *Brownies' Book,* I (July, 1920), 219.

ited. The profession was not yet willing to give women of color equal access to administrative positions or supervisory jobs in health care and social service, just as the medical profession was unwilling to place African-American physicians on hospital staffs—even those mainly serving African-American patients. (Not until 1925, and only then after an investigation begun in 1923, did Harlem General Hospital appoint African-American doctors to its regular staff.)[4] With a few exceptions, African-American nurses seemed destined to function in "colored-only" clinics, hospitals, or homes located primarily in Harlem or Columbus Hill, and they were to do so under the direction or supervision of whites who were often younger and less experienced.[5] Yet, with the passage of the Nineteenth Amendment to the Constitution in 1920, African-American nurses anticipated some relief through suffrage. Envisioning both redress and empowerment by means of the vote, they mounted voter registration campaigns for women in order to effect a change in New York politics, but their efforts could not bring an immediate end to the politics of race or the practices of discrimination.

On September 15, 1921, Larsen Imes resigned from the New York City Department of Health. The resignation marked a radical shift in her vocation and in her delineation of self. Her disenchantment with career options in health care was complete. Nursing, though respectable and increasingly professional, was not as highly regarded as a white-collar job in a library. Nursing became a topic that she avoided; if she found it necessary to address her nursing course, she would either state or suggest that she trained at Columbia University, where by the early 1920s Lincoln's nursing students in fact took some of their courses.[6] Not only was Columbia a more prestigious educational institution, but it was also outside the usual and expected all-black environment, which Larsen Imes associated with inferiority.

In January, 1922, after working as a volunteer for several months, she started a job as an assistant, grade 1, at the 135th Street branch of the New

4. Dr. Louis T. Wright, however, had been appointed a clinical assistant in the outpatient clinic in 1919. David Levering Lewis, *When Harlem Was in Vogue* (New York, 1981), 216.

5. In 1938 the Commission on the Colored Urban Population asked the director of the Division of Nursing, Department of Hospitals, City of New York, to explain why "there have been absolutely no Negro pupils in Bellevue or Kings County Hospitals training schools, and . . . nothing but Negro pupil nurses in Harlem and Lincoln Hospital training schools." Legislative Document (1939) no. 69, *Second Report of the New York State Commission on the Condition of the Colored Urban Population* (Albany, 1939), 113.

6. See Nella Larsen Imes's nomination form for the 1929 Harmon Foundation Awards, which gives the false impression that she attended Columbia University for nursing (in HFR).

York Public Library. Her salary was $82.66 per month. African-American women were primarily hired to work in Negro branches, one of which was in Harlem, where the black population was rapidly increasing. In Larsen Imes's case, neither the segregated branch nor the lower salary mattered. What mattered was that she was making the transition to a workplace and associations with what she termed "the better class of Negroes." In fact, though the 135th Street branch had not yet become home to Arthur A. Schomburg's collection of historical books on African Americans, it was already, along with the 135th Street YMCA that had housed the African-American nurses' association, one of the active cultural centers in Harlem. The librarian, Ernestine Rose, who had arrived there in 1920 after a post at the Seward Park branch library, instituted poetry readings and lectures along with book discussions. During the next few years, Rose worked to get African Americans into the library system, and with her assistant, Regina Anderson, she established an impressive staff of volunteers, including Fauset, from the NAACP and *Crisis* office, and Ethel Ray, who was Charles S. Johnson's assistant at the Urban League and *Opportunity* and also Anderson's roommate. Together they would create an exciting literary environment in the Harlem library. Through Rose's initiative in 1925, the Carnegie Foundation paid $10,000 to Schomburg for his private collection of rare books on black life.[7]

Larsen Imes's two pieces in the *Brownies' Book* helped to place her in the children's section as a general assistant to the librarians. The Scandinavian games and riddles had served another purpose as well. By carefully wording her introductions to both sets of materials, she had created the impression that she had grown up in Denmark. Larsen Imes does not say specifically that she was a child in Denmark, though she implies as much by using the words "my childish days." In stating that she learned the games "long ago in Denmark" and "from little Danish children," she avoided directly placing herself as a child when she learned them. She was beginning to shape the public fictions of her past that would become the only past with which she could identify.

The short introductory statements established Larsen Imes's public identity as Danish. The mixed racial heritage that she had insisted upon as a

7. *Library School of the New York Public Library Register, 1911–1926* (New York, 1929); File for Mrs. Nella L. Imes, in Employment Records, Personnel Office, New York Public Library; "Miss Rhodes [*sic*] Dies; Integrated Library," New York *Amsterdam News*, April 5, 1961, p. 4; Lewis, *When Harlem Was in Vogue*, 105.

measure of her significance during the first year of her marriage became more pronounced, for she was not merely a "mulatto," but one who had grown up in a white, foreign country.

While many African Americans in the generations immediately following emancipation might have been the offspring of an interracial union, few could assert familial intimacy with and public acknowledgment by the white parent, and even fewer could claim either births or childhoods in Europe, Britain, or Scandinavia. Among the many fair-skinned African Americans who would become part of the Harlem Renaissance, only a few were technically mulattoes, despite the general use of the term. Many of the others (Langston Hughes, Bruce Nugent, Dorothy Peterson, Georgia Douglas Johnson) had some white ancestry, and some, such as Walter White and Fredi Washington, obviously had a great deal. Several of the mulattoes acknowledged having the kind of unusual background that Larsen claimed; for example, Harold Jackman was born in England, and Ethel Ray, a Minnesota native, was the child of a marriage between a Swedish mother and a black father. Curiously, the darker-skinned individuals among the New Negroes, such as Wallace Thurman and Dorothy West, suffered more from a perception of marginal status, though African Americans of all shades certainly suffered the effects of racial discrimination and racist attitudes. Thurman was the more personally tormented by his coloring, but West was frequently called "little black Dorothy" by Jackman, who clarified his meaning in a letter to Countee Cullen: "Did little black Dorothy come to Paris too? . . . Bless her little heart, you know I don't mean a thing by calling her black—she is a lovely child."[8]

In emphasizing a mixed-racial and ethnic background, Larsen Imes was not underscoring marginality. Rather, as a mulatto, Larsen Imes was stressing her place within a particular group of African Americans for whom such backgrounds inferred class position and social prominence. As Danish, she elevated herself even further as unique within this group. For her that elevation was a strategic means of gaining distinction among African Americans who, though celebrating racial achievement, often accepted without question their distinction on the basis of racial mixture. In a sense, she was struggling for self-empowerment by insisting on visibility within the parameters understood by her society. Her route was one that light-skinned African-American women took in order to emancipate themselves from the stereotypical views of women of their race.

8. Harold Jackman to Countee Cullen, Tuesday, June 25, 1929, in CCC.

Coincidentally, during this same period West Indians were becoming more visible politically and more prominent socially in New York. Marcus Garvey, the Jamaican who between 1918 and 1923 headed the Universal Negro Improvement Association and spearheaded a movement of racial pride among the masses of blacks, was the most controversial. Other West Indians, however, included Hubert Harrison, W. A. Domingo, Arthur Schomburg, Eric Walrond, Claude McKay, and Casper Holstein (the king of the numbers racket from the Danish Virgin Islands who has been described as one of the "midwives" of the Harlem Renaissance[9]), and a host of others.

From the time of the appearance of the essays in the *Brownies' Book* through the remainder of her public life, Larsen Imes distanced herself from her Chicago past. For most of her acquaintances during the 1920s and 1930s, it simply did not exist. For example, Bruce Nugent, one of the participants in the Renaissance with an excellent recall of its people and events, would express surprise fifty years later that Nella Larsen was from Chicago. An acquaintance of Larsen Imes's through their mutual close friend Dorothy Peterson, Nugent was not unaware of her "Danish" connections but had always associated her "style" with Philadelphia. Her attitudes, talk, and manners had been so aristocratic that he assumed her to be part of that city's old black elite, since he knew she was not from the only other comparable place, his native city, Washington. Nugent observed that her "manners were something that people who don't have, but admire, resent not having"; her "air" exuded social status.[10]

Nugent's presumption of Larsen Imes's connection to Philadelphia's established black bourgeoisie is understandable. One of her role models during the early 1920s was Jessie Redmon Fauset, whom she met in 1919 through her brother-in-law William Lloyd Imes, who was then prominent in the NAACP and a friend of Du Bois'. Born just outside Philadelphia in Camden County, New Jersey, Fauset had attended public elementary school and the High School for Girls in that city.[11] She was the daughter of an articulate African Methodist Episcopal minister, Redmon Fauset. While her family was never well-off financially, it was educated, cultured, and refined. Fauset herself graduated in 1905 from Cornell University, where she had

9. Lewis, *When Harlem Was in Vogue*, 121, 129–30.

10. Richard Bruce Nugent, interview with author, April 30, 1983.

11. For a discussion of Jessie Redmon Fauset's life and career, see Carolyn Wedin Sylvander, *Jessie Redmon Fauset, Black American Novelist* (Troy, N.Y., 1981).

been elected to Phi Beta Kappa. She returned to Philadelphia to seek employment in the public schools, but her application was denied because of her race. She then taught briefly in the Baltimore school system before moving to Washington, where she taught French at the M Street High School, which Anna Julia Cooper as principal (1901–1906) had successfully defended against a Congressional proposal for a "special colored curriculum."[12]

In 1919, Fauset received an M.A. from the University of Pennsylvania and moved to New York for the job with Du Bois on the *Crisis*. Known for her decorum and her Sunday teas, she was fluent in several languages, had traveled abroad, and wrote graceful prose. She was the epitome of the "new woman" and of the new race consciousness. Her essays and fiction appeared frequently in both the *Crisis* and the *Brownies' Book*. Claude McKay remembered her as "prim, pretty and well dressed, and [she] talked fluently and intelligently. All the radicals liked her, although in her social viewpoint she was away over on the other side of the fence. She belonged to that closed decorous circle of Negro society, which consists of persons who live proudly like the better class of whites, except that they do so on much less money."[13]

Although very much a conventional lady in her demeanor and many of her attitudes, Fauset was a modern sophisticate who wore fashionable frocks purchased during her trips to France and smoked fancy cigarettes wrapped in colored papers to match her outfits. In a playful mood, she once remarked, "Men don't give me candy, they give me cigarettes," and indeed she had a collection of different types and brands. She would strike an elegant pose and smoke in public, even at the Civic Club in the company of the staid Du Bois.[14]

Fauset's background, credentials, achievement, and style impressed Nella Larsen Imes, who saw in Fauset a reflection of the accomplished woman that she herself wanted, and intended, to be. Nine years older than Larsen Imes, Fauset not only had a heightened political consciousness of the African-American world but also a keen feminist understanding of the conditions of women. She represented the African-American women's sorority,

12. See Thadious M. Davis, "Anna Julia Cooper," in *American Women Authors*, ed. Lina E. Mainiero (4 vols.; New York, 1979), I, 401–404, and Louise Daniel Hutchinson, *Anna Julia Cooper: A Voice from the South* (Washington, D.C., 1981).

13. Claude McKay, *A Long Way from Home* (1937; rpr. New York, 1970), 112.

14. Ethel Ray Nance, interview with Ann Allen Shockley, November 18, 1970 (San Francisco) and December 23, 1970 (Nashville), transcript in Special Collections, Fisk Oral History Project, Fisk University Library.

Delta Sigma Theta, as a delegate to the Second Pan-African Congress in London (1921). There she spoke out on women's rights and told her audience how "colored women were everywhere branching out into new fields of activity in the professions and business." [15] Such sentiments particularly endeared her to Larsen Imes, who was at a transitional point at which a new vocation and a rewriting of her self were possible. For Larsen Imes, Fauset functioned as a mirror reflecting a different female image, and her own potential. Fauset's image is in the background of Larsen Imes's transformations of self in the 1920s, and it would reappear as psychological transference in her disintegration during the 1930s.

As an assistant in the 135th Street branch of the New York Public Library, Larsen Imes was pleased with the change in her career, and the staff was impressed with her. Welford Wilson recalls that as a boy visiting the library, he thought she was "so beautiful, always wearing her hair in a bun and being friendly with us children." Her maturity and air of confidence quickly marked her as a potential candidate for the Library School of the New York Public Library. The Library School, founded in 1911, had not thus far admitted African Americans into the certificate and the diploma programs, though African-American employees of the New York Public Library were eligible to attend some of the classes, lectures, and demonstrations. Larsen Imes's obvious poise and intelligence, along with her love of books and reading, made her an attractive applicant. Beyond that, her desire to better herself and to improve her class position gave her the will and determination to beat the odds against a woman of color being admitted. Encouraged by her colleagues and supervisors at the 135th Street branch, she investigated the possibility of becoming a certified librarian, because that particular kind of white-collar work was more suited to her interests, abilities, and self-perception. Whether she was conscious of it or not, Larsen Imes was in the process of falling "out of the marriage plot that demands not only that a woman marry but that the marriage and its progeny be her life's absolute and only center." [16] She was moving beyond the structures of dependency that a marriage of social unequals had produced.

Gaining admission to the Library School was not easy. The students accepted were mainly women from prestigious colleges and universities. Lar-

15. *Crisis*, XXII (December, 1921) reprinted an account of Fauset's London speech from the Glasgow *Herald*. See Sylvander, *Jessie Redmon Fauset*, 67–68.

16. Welford Wilson, interview with author, March 18, 1988; Carolyn Heilbrun, *Writing a Woman's Life* (New York, 1988), 51.

sen Imes had no university training. Applicants had to be at least twenty years of age and had to submit a doctor's statement "certifying the individual's ability to do continuous mental and physical work"; anyone over the age of thirty-five was advised against undertaking the program. The school's faculty reviewed all applicants who were graduates of approved colleges for admission. Applicants lacking college degrees had first to meet the minimum requirement of graduation from high school, or the equivalent, and then to take an entrance examination. The final candidates for admission were selected on the basis of the examination or college grades, their personalities, education, and experience. The Normal School at Fisk submitted Larsen Imes's record at the request of Ernest J. Reece, Library School principal, but lacking a degree, she was required to take the entrance examination, which was divided into five parts: history, current events, general information, literature, and foreign languages (French and German).[17]

The Library School recommended that applicants prepare for the examination by gaining familiarity with general histories and histories of literature, and by regularly reading a local newspaper, a metropolitan newspaper, and one or more weekly and monthly periodicals devoted to current events.[18] The 1921–1922 circular provided a section entitled "Specimen Entrance Examination Questions," which potential applicants might review. The questions were rigorous. The history section, for example, containing seven questions out of which five had to be answered, asked the applicant to "describe briefly some of the movements which were prominent in Europe between 1750 and 1850," and to "write about 200 words on one of the following topics: Social life in ancient Rome, Monasticism in Europe, The influence of Greece upon Rome, Guilds." The literature section also asked for the answers to five out of seven questions that included "Discuss the differences between the poetry of the present time and that of the Victorian period, illustrating your points by some specific titles," "Characterize in from two hundred to three hundred words the work of one of the following authors: John Galsworthy, Henry James, George Meredith, Anthony Trollope," and "Name some measures of social reform which have been furthered by works of fiction, and the novels which have had a part in them." The languages section required translations of two substantial

17. *Library School of the New York Public Library Circular of Information, 1921–22* (New York, 1922), 14; Fisk registrar to Ernest J. Reece, principal, Library School, May 5, 1922, (copy courtesy Ann Allen Shockley, Fisk University Library).

18. *Library School Circular, 1921–22*, 15.

French and German passages—*without* the help of a dictionary. The 1921–1922 samples were from "Le Livre de Mon Ami" by Anatole France and from "Deutsche Marchen, gesammelt durch die Bruder Grimm. Die Boten des Todes."[19] Interestingly, all of the authors cited in the Library School's sample questions reappeared in various versions of Larsen Imes's list of her favorite authors, and several of the authors appeared in her writing. Anatole France, for example, would figure in the conclusion of her first novel, and Galsworthy would become a reference point in her letter to *Opportunity* magazine regarding Walter White's novel *Flight*.

More important, her preparation for the examination disciplined and directed her reading. She expanded her range of interests and, quite possibly, her interpretive abilities. This experience of intense reading became one of her most valuable preparations for becoming a novelist, and it helps to explain the rich literary texture of her writing, which was different from the reticence of her speech. "Reading is a silent, private activity," Elizabeth Flynn has observed, "and so perhaps affords women a degree of protection not present when they speak. Quite possibly the hedging and tentativeness of women's speech are transformed into useful interpretative strategies— receptivity and yet critical assessment of the text—in the act of reading. A willingness to listen, a sensitivity to emotional nuance, an ability to empathize with and yet judge, may be disadvantages in speech but advantages in reading."[20] These qualities are also advantages in writing, and would prove useful to Larsen Imes's fiction.

In addition to reading and studying literature and history, Larsen Imes taught herself French for the entrance examination. She had studied German at Wendell Phillips High School but had performed poorly, though she was familiar with the spoken language from her mother and her immigrant neighbors in Chicago. However, she now had a reason for gaining reading proficiency. Her husband, who read French and German for his scientific work, helped her prepare. Also eager to help was a young Brooklyn resident, Dorothy Peterson, whom she had met at the library. Peterson was fluent in Spanish, which she had learned as a child during her father's tenure as a U.S. consul to Venezuela and later Puerto Rico. She knew French as well, having studied it at New York University.

19. *Ibid.*; see samples of questions from all four categories, pp. 26–30.
20. Elizabeth A. Flynn, "Gender and Reading," in *Gender and Reading: Essays on Readers, Texts, and Contexts*, ed. Elizabeth A. Flynn and Patrocino P. Schweickart (Baltimore, 1986), 286.

Besides studying and working at the library, Larsen Imes, with her husband, commuted often from New Jersey for social activities. They attended social functions at the homes of the James Weldon Johnsons, the Charles S. Johnsons, and the Walter Whites. White, who had moved from Atlanta in 1918, became their close friend. With the arrival of the black musical comedy *Shuffle Along* on May 22, 1921, they had also become avid theatergoers, as had most of those who saw Florence Mills, Josephine Baker, and the rest of the Broadway cast perform songs written by Noble Sissle and Eubie Blake in a show written by Flournoy Miller and Aubrey Lyles. Langston Hughes later marked the beginning of the black renaissance with the long-running *Shuffle Along*, as well as its successor, *Runnin' Wild* (a 1923 show by Miller and Lyles).[21] For the Imeses in 1921, however, *Shuffle Along* was merely the start of a long social season.

On Saturday, June 10, 1922, Larsen Imes arrived for the 9 A.M. administering of the Library School entrance examination for the 1922–1923 year. She had reviewed, studied, and prepared for more than six months. The hard work paid off; she passed the exam, but admission was not assured. Both her race and her education were liabilities. During the summer, after the faculty had evaluated her scores along with her transcript from the Fisk Normal School and her work with the Department of Health, she was accepted into the program for the fall. Later she would insist that her acceptance was "an experiment it being entirely contrary to the policy of the school [to] admit Negroes." But in 1922, she gladly requested a year's leave from her job at the Harlem branch library in order to enter the program of study. On September 9, 1922, her official leave began.[22]

Although the job in the library had been a means of achieving status, it was also a way of gaining access to further education. The New York Public Library's policy was to encourage its employees to seek admission to its library school. For Larsen Imes, the program of study was, like nurses' training, an education directed toward practical training for work, toward immediate preparation for joining a specified labor force. Although she had the intellectual capacity for the "higher" professions, her educational endeavors were those which would, within a relatively short period of time

---

21. Langston Hughes, *The Big Sea* (1940; rpr. New York, 1986), 223.

22. Nella Larsen Imes, Author's statement for Alfred A. Knopf, Inc., November 24, 1926, in Alfred A. and Blanche Knopf Collection, Harry Ransom Humanities Research Center, University of Texas Libraries, Austin; File for Mrs. Imes, in Employment Records, Personnel Office, New York Public Library.

and with a minimum of cash outlay, enable her to become employable and self-supporting.

She also believed, as did other African Americans in the period between the wars, that education was a major key to upward mobility for the race and that education would secure for individual African Americans a foothold in the political, cultural, social, and economic world of the United States. Her gender compounded the difficulty posed by her race in breaking the cycle of undereducation and relegation to undesirable jobs. She would portray, in *Quicksand*, the difficulties faced by a middle-class African-American female seeking employment.

Larsen Imes desired college education, comparable to that of Fauset, Anderson, or Peterson, but her personal situation had never fully afforded her an opportunity to achieve that desire. Her race and sex limited her options for a college education in the humanities for which she was temperamentally and intellectually suited, and her independence, which she might have valued under other circumstances, meant in practical terms an absence of financial support and familial encouragement to pursue an academic program at the college level. Her tastes were artistic and humanistic, but unfortunately she did not have the chance to study formally in the areas that most directly appealed to her.

As a self-made woman seeking access to education, Larsen Imes stands out, along with Zora Neale Hurston, from the best-known women of the Harlem Renaissance. Fauset had the support of her family, even though its financial resources were not great; poet Georgia Douglas Johnson came from a Georgia family that sent her to Atlanta University and Oberlin College to study art; artist and writer Gwendolyn Bennett pursued studies in art at the Pratt Institute and Columbia University, though her family would have preferred her taking up a more conventional program. And others, such as Dorothy Peterson, Angelina Grimké, and Clarissa Scott Delaney, had the assistance of their families in attending college or university. Hurston, Larsen Imes's closest counterpart, created her own educational opportunities, which she financed without the help of family.

Both Larsen Imes and Hurston were born in 1891 and both adopted later dates of birth, though Hurston would lose an entire decade from her age rather than a few years. In changing her age by ten years, however, Hurston could avail herself of opportunities for a college education in the 1920s when Larsen Imes, even with the omission of two years from her age, could not. Hurston had made her way up from the South to enroll at Morgan Academy in Baltimore, Howard University in Washington, D.C., Barnard College and Columbia University in New York. By means of her own labor and ingenuity, she managed to receive not only a college education but a degree in anthropology, a field that interested her and that she studied on the graduate level with a major authority in the social sciences, Franz Boas of Columbia. She found a way to combine freedom of movement from place to place in search of opportunity and satisfaction—an activity usually restricted to men—with respectability and purpose, which for women was typically associated with remaining at or close to home.

Lacking Hurston's way with wealthy patrons, Larsen Imes never had the luxury of a college program leading to a degree. Her personal need for security had not permitted her the risk of taking so openly to the road as did Hurston. She was very much the self-educated woman in terms of what interested her most: arts and letters. Unlike Hurston, who took pride in her self-made status, in her service-oriented jobs, and in her individual accomplishments when most of the odds were against her, Larsen Imes never indicated at what personal costs she managed to receive her training as a nurse or, in a step up, as a librarian. But like Hurston's, her independent progress through a variety of training programs and employments suggests something of the ordinary African-American female's gradual progress out of domestic service between the two world wars.

From September 5 through September 16, the preliminary instruction and practical work started at the Library School's quarters in the central building of the New York Public Library on Fifth Avenue and Forty-second Street. Students normally paid $75 in tuition for the first year, but as a first-year student using a New York City address, Larsen Imes paid $45. Her tenure at the 135th Street branch had not been long enough to exempt her from the fee. During the two-semester program, she would also need another $75 for textbooks, supplies, and tours of libraries in the New York area, which were required for certification.

On Monday, September 18, instruction began. Larsen Imes found herself in classes with students who came from fifteen states, including Georgia and Alabama in the South, Michigan and Ohio in the Midwest, and California in the West, and from four foreign countries—Canada, France, Holland, and Norway. The October, 1922, issue of *Library School Notes* carried the announcement of the new class of junior registrants; listed among the forty-two mainly single white females was "Mrs. Nella *Larson* Imes, New York City." [23] The Library School used the spelling of her name that had appeared in her official school records.

Only one of her classmates, Mary Althea Skinner of New York City,

23. *Library School Notes*, X (October, 1922), 1 (italics added).

formed a friendship with her. Larsen Imes described Skinner as "good-looking, rich and intelligent [and] knows the secret of being friendly without being patronizing." Their friendship would last throughout the 1920s. After receiving her library certificate, Skinner worked at the Fordham branch of the New York Public Library (from 1923 to 1924) and for a time in Cairo, Egypt, as a YMCA librarian (from 1924 to 1926) before marrying Alden W. Boyd and moving to Chicago. Her last visit with Larsen Imes was in 1927 when, on her way from Chicago to Europe, she attended a tea at the Imeses' 135th Street apartment.[24]

During the two 17-week semesters, Larsen Imes took fourteen courses leading to a certificate. In the first semester, from September 5, 1922, to February 2, 1923, she had cataloguing and subject headings, reference work, book selection, library administration, classification, and American libraries. For the next semester, from February 5 to June 4, 1923, she took the second part of cataloguing and subject headings, reference work, book selection, and library administration, along with new courses in bibliography, current events, printing and indexing, and practical work.[25] The course in practical work was actually an internship, lasting for four weeks at the start of the second semester. Larsen Imes completed her practice at the Seward Park branch of the New York Public Library, where she later worked for two months (November and December, 1923) after her formal program ended.

Larsen Imes's course work during the second term led to her first published essay, a review of Kathleen Norris' novel *Certain People of Importance* (1922). She had read the author's other novels but considered the most recent her best, so that for a book description in the book selection course she selected *Certain People of Importance*. Expanding the description, she submitted it to the *Messenger,* though Norris' story of two San Francisco families, the Crabtrees and the Brewers, was not concerned with people of color or racial issues. Other than finding the title inappropriate ("The material is certainly ordinary, both in people and in their environment"), Larsen Imes praised the text: "Mrs. Norris has peopled her stage with characters that are powerfully human and satisfyingly authentic." The authenticity she linked to "the writer's put[ting] into [her characters] the richness of her

24. Nella Larsen Imes to Carl Van Vechten, n.d. [postmarked June 29, 1927], in JWJ; *Library School Register, 1911–1926,* 23.

25. *Library School of the New York Public Library Circular of Information, 1922–23* (New York, 1923), 16–17, 18–19.

own personality." As a result, she pointed out: "The charm is remarkable. It surrounds Victoria Brewer like an aura so that one loves her. It enmeshes Aunt Fan so that one likes her and stands in somewhat childlike awe of her, despite one's perception of her very human limitations. It gives a mellowness even to the parental officiousness of Pa and Ma Brewer so that one sympathizes with them." Emphasizing characters, "their atmosphere, their interests, what makes them," as Larsen Imes put it, the brief review anticipates her own concern with character in fiction.[26]

Shortly after the book review appeared, Larsen Imes received a certificate at the Library School's presentation ceremony on Friday morning, June 8, 1923. Although a few of her classmates receiving certificates in the junior class would continue for another year as senior registrants in the diploma program, she would not. The diploma program was intended primarily for experienced librarians and for those trained librarians entering administration. Whether or not Larsen Imes desired to continue in the senior program, she clearly resented the school's racial policies.[27] In 1926 when the Library School became a part of Columbia University, she was glad to see the end of the program as she had experienced it. Decoded, her negative comments about the school may well have been signals that she had been discouraged by the officials from applying for the diploma program. Her certificate, nonetheless, made her eligible for a grade 2 position with the library; that level of employment raised her salary to $109.75 per month.[28] She ended her official leave on July 1, 1923, and ended her formal education, as well.

Other opportunities were, however, opening for her, and several of her friends were already pointing toward them. James Weldon Johnson had begun to sound the way in his preface to *The Book of American Negro Poetry* (1922):

> A people may become great through many means, but there is only one measure by which its greatness is recognized and acknowledged. The final measure of the greatness of all peoples is the amount and standard of the literature and art they have produced. . . . No people that has produced great literature and art has ever been looked upon by the world as distinctly inferior.

26. Mrs. Nella Larsen Imes, "*Certain People of Importance* by Mrs. Kathleen Norris," *Messenger*, V (May, 1923), 713.

27. See Larsen Imes's author's statement for Knopf.

28. File for Mrs. Imes, in Employment Records, Personnel Office, New York Public Library.

> The status of the Negro in the United States is more a question of national mental attitude toward race than of actual conditions. And nothing will do more to change that mental attitude and raise his status than a demonstration of intellectual parity by the Negro through the production of literature and art.[29]

As one of the senior black men of letters in New York and the head of the NAACP, Johnson wrote with authority about the bright prospects for the work ahead in the decade.

That same year, 1922, two others with whom Larsen Imes had formed friendships reinforced the notion that producing literature and art was crucial for changing prevalent attitudes toward blacks. Fauset, in the NAACP's *Crisis* office, and White, the NAACP's assistant secretary, began to write novels, and they encouraged Larsen Imes to do so as well. As James Weldon Johnson's assistant, the affable White met a number of people in the New York literary world. In a spring, 1922, meeting with H. L. Mencken, editor of the *Smart Set*, White talked about his response to T. S. Stribling's new novel, *Birthright*, about a Harvard-educated mulatto's return to the South. Stribling, a native of Tennessee, had written a sympathetic novel about the tragedy of racism. Although White applauded the author's central focus on Peter Siner, the protagonist, he believed that a southern-born black trained in the North would not have acted as naïvely as Siner. Mencken was interested in White's opinions concerning the white novelist's failure to portray accurately the hero's plight and urged White to write his own portrayal.

Fauset, too, had responded to *Birthright*'s "realistic" treatment of black life. She understood that Stribling had presented a black hero who believed in the superiority of whites and in the primitivism of blacks. She, White, and Larsen Imes discussed the novel's shortcomings. "Nella Larsen and Walter White were affected just as I was," Fauset said. "We could do it better." She later recalled their conclusion: "We reasoned, 'Here is an audience waiting to hear the truth about us. Let us who are better qualified to present that truth than any white writer, try to do so.'"[30]

The three all took up Fauset's challenge, but lacking the resources and the experience of Fauset and White, Larsen Imes would make the slowest

---

29. James Weldon Johnson, Preface to *The Book of American Negro Poetry*, ed. James Weldon Johnson (1922; rev. ed. New York, 1931), 9.

30. Jessie Fauset, quoted in Marion L. Starkey, "Jessie Fauset," *Southern Workman*, LXI (May, 1932), 218–19.

start. Yet she immediately recognized writing as a new opportunity for her future. She had been more affected than the others by Stribling's statement, "No people can become civilized until the woman has the power of choice among the males. . . . The History of the white race shows the gradual increase of the woman's power of choice."[31] In it was perhaps a notion comparable to James Weldon Johnson's exhortations about race, greatness, and literature. She had enough confidence in her potential to begin planning a novel, and, once again, new directions.

31. T. S. Stribling, *Birthright* (Garden City, 1922), 277.

7

Becoming a Writer,
1923–1926

RECEIVING A CERTIFICATE from the Library School in June was almost anticlimactic for Nella Larsen Imes. She spent November and December, 1923, at the downtown Seward Park branch, and in January she returned to the 135th Street branch. Her official position was assistant, grade 2, for which her salary increased to $1,300, still $300 less than her pay as a district nurse.[1] Scarcely had she settled into her work as an assistant children's librarian when she began to envision another possibility for her talents. Already her horizons had expanded; the idea of becoming a novelist had taken hold.

She, Fauset, and White were not alone in anticipating the work to be done in fiction. In August, two months after Larsen Imes received her certificate, she and the others read Boni and Liveright's announcement of Jean Toomer's *Cane*. They had not been unaware of the young poet from Washington. In the spring of 1922, his "Song of a Son" had appeared in the April issue of *Crisis*, which Fauset had edited. One of the popular young New York poets, Countee Cullen, had met Toomer in Washington, where Alain Locke and Georgia Douglas Johnson were encouraging his work.[2] Claude

---

1. *Library School of the New York Public Library Register, 1911–1926* (New York, 1929), and Nella Larsen Imes, Fellowship application form, 1930–31, John Simon Guggenheim Foundation, November, 1929, in John Simon Guggenheim Memorial Foundation files, New York.

2. Cynthia Earl Kerman and Richard Eldridge, *The Lives of Jean Toomer: A Hunger for Wholeness* (Baton Rouge, 1987), 92, 94.

McKay at the *Liberator* had published three of his pieces from *Cane*, "Carma," "Reapers," and "Becky" (August and September, 1922). Dorothy Peterson had been introduced to Toomer after his May, 1923, arrival in New York. Still, the beauty of his lyrical book, mixing poetry and fiction, caught them by surprise. Although Du Bois' *Darkwater* had appeared in 1920 and Claude McKay's volume of poems *Harlem Dancer* in 1922, *Cane* was the first work of fiction by a young African-American writer to be published by a major New York house in over a decade.

Walter White had expected his novel *The Fire in the Flint* to appear that summer.[3] He had written it not long after taking up the challenge of portraying African Americans truthfully in fiction, during an amazingly productive twelve-day retreat in the Berkshires summer house of Mary White Ovington, then chair of the NAACP Board of Directors. His publisher, Doran and Company, was hesitant to proceed because a book about a noble black doctor lynched by hostile whites in the South might offend white southern readers. None of the endorsements from sympathetic white southerners such as Will Alexander or T. J. Woofter persuaded Doran to bring out the novel. It would appear over a year later in September, 1924, when Alfred A. Knopf, a publisher suggested by Mencken, who was by then the editor of *American Mercury*, accepted the manuscript without reservations about alienating white readers.

While Toomer did not welcome being singled out as a racial milestone, White was more than eager to promote the race. Formerly an insurance salesman and cashier for Standard Life in Atlanta, he was excellent at promotion. A great talker, White had an enormous amount of energy. He wanted to meet everyone and remembered everyone's first name.[4] He also immediately called everyone by his or her first name, including the formidable Eleanor Roosevelt.[5] Committed to the work of racial progress, he became a major cultural entrepreneur, using every resource available through his connection with the NAACP to foster literary production among African-American writers. He believed in the "talented tenth" (though he did not actually adopt Du Bois' term) as the hope of the race

3. See Walter White, *A Man Called White* (New York, 1948), for an account of the writing and publication of *The Fire in the Flint*.

4. Ethel Ray Nance, interview with Ann Allen Shockley, November 18, 1970 (San Francisco), and December 23, 1970 (Nashville), transcript in Special Collections, Fisk Oral History Project, Fisk University Library.

5. Bruce Kellner, *Carl Van Vechten and the Irreverent Decades* (Norman, Okla., 1968), 197.

and in the ability of artists to make a major contribution in combatting racism.

By inviting influential whites from downtown to social gatherings at his apartment, White expected to change stereotypical images, win friends for African Americans in general, and gain support for African-American artists in particular. His "Sugar Hill" apartment at 409 Edgecombe Avenue, the fourteen-story Roger Morris Apartments near the southeast corner of 139th Street and overlooking the Hudson River, became what Langston Hughes called "quite a party center."[6] On the thirteenth floor of Harlem's tallest building, White's apartment had five enormous rooms, hardwood floors, moldings and panels on the walls, a grand piano, and was "full of wonderful art work."[7] There he hosted some of the most prominent blacks and whites in the city. And there shortly after his novel appeared, he introduced Nella Larsen and Elmer Imes to Carl Van Vechten, who had begun his career in New York as a dance and music critic but had begun to write novels in the 1920s.[8]

For Larsen Imes, meeting Van Vechten and becoming a regular at White's gatherings marked another turning point. No longer solely dependent upon her husband for social contacts, she cemented friendships with two of the most outgoing men in the cultural awakening during the 1920s. Both men thrived on social activities, and both thought highly enough of Larsen Imes to involve her in much of their doings. Unlike the more aloof Du Bois and the more restrained James Weldon Johnson who endorsed her work, White and Van Vechten actively promoted her as one of the accomplished African-American women of the day. For Larsen Imes the attention meant an inclusion that she had seldom enjoyed; it bolstered her self-confidence and alleviated the sense of rejection that was one of the scars from her youth.

In 1924 she was promoted to children's librarian. Placed in charge of the children's room at the 135th Street branch, she received a pay increase, bringing her salary to $1,500. The nature of the work, however, compensated for the loss of the nurse's salary, which she would never make up. The

6. Langston Hughes, *The Big Sea* (1940; rpr. New York, 1986), 248.

7. See White's daughter Jane's account of the apartment in Jervis Anderson, "That Was New York Harlem: IV—Hard Times and Beyond," *New Yorker,* July 20, 1981, p. 74.

8. Larsen Imes met Van Vechten during 1924. See Nella Imes to Carl Van Vechten, Friday [*ca.* 1925–26], in CVV. Larsen Imes mentions Van Vechten's first NAACP dance: "Happy Rhone's. 1924. Fania too." Arthur "Happy" Rhone's nightclub at 143rd and Lenox was the site of the NAACP's annual dance in 1924. See also Kellner, *Carl Van Vechten and the Irreverent Decades,* 198.

world of books and reading brought her into direct contact with more than African-American children, for it situated her in Harlem, one center of what Alain Locke called "a fresh spiritual and cultural focusing," where "Negro life [was] seizing upon its first chances of group expression and self-determination." The library itself was becoming even more community-oriented and attracting many different African-American New Yorkers to the numerous programs it sponsored. Popular programs in literary topics and current events provided a platform for prominent public figures to discuss the changing position of African-American life and thought. Regina Anderson, who had started to work as circulation librarian at the 135th Street branch after her arrival in 1922 from Chicago, would often digest seven or eight new books at night in order to present a review of them at the library the next day. Readings by young writers such as Countee Cullen and Eric Walrond generated enthusiastic excitement because their "unusual outburst of creative expression" was read as a "heralding sign" of a New Negro who reflected the potential of the entire race. Harlem was becoming not only a mecca for migrating African Americans, some 87,415 of whom would arrive there during the decade, it was also being transformed into a haven for African-American artists, and a "culture capital," as James Weldon Johnson dubbed Harlem in predicting that it would become "the intellectual, the cultural and the financial center for Negroes in the United States."[9]

In fact, Larsen Imes's friend Jessie Fauset, rather than Walter White, should receive credit for much of the early cultural and literary activity. Fauset had from the beginning of her work at *Crisis* in 1919 sought out and published many of the writers who would achieve fame: Langston Hughes, Jean Toomer, Countee Cullen, and Claude McKay. She had overcome Du Bois' reservations about using the arts in uplifting the race and worked diligently at building bridges with the young people whose talents and potential she astutely recognized. As an older friend of Regina Anderson and a volunteer at the 135th Street branch, she had channeled news of young writers to the library staff. At the start of the new decade, she was already having Sunday afternoon teas to discuss literature and the arts. These Sunday socials at the apartment she shared with her sister Helen Lanning became so

9. *Library School Register, 1911–1926,* and Larsen Imes, Guggenheim application, November, 1929, in Guggenheim Foundation files; Alain Locke, "Harlem," *Survey Graphic,* VI (March, 1925), 630; Nance, interview with Shockley; Alain Locke, Foreword to *The New Negro,* ed. Locke (New York, 1925), xvii; James Weldon Johnson, "Harlem: The Culture Capital," in *The New Negro,* ed. Locke, 311.

regular that everyone knew to drop by during certain hours, to bring along a guest if desired, and to expect to see friends or meet interesting people.[10]

Fauset's novel *There Is Confusion* was the first to be published in response to *Birthright*. She had not written it as fast as White had *The Fire in the Flint,* but she had more quickly found a committed publisher in Boni and Liveright, who, after bringing out Toomer's novel in the summer of 1923, had Fauset's in print the following spring. In March, Boni and Liveright launched *There Is Confusion* with an ad campaign, in part because Toomer's book had not sold well.[11] To celebrate the publication of Fauset's novel, over a hundred guests gathered on March 21, 1924, for a dinner at the Civic Club, a private club with open membership policies regarding race and sex, located in lower Manhattan at 14 West Twelfth Street just off Fifth Avenue.

Organized by Charles S. Johnson, the social scientist who edited *Opportunity* for the Urban League, the gala affair had honoring Fauset as a secondary motive. Johnson had invited Langston Hughes, Jean Toomer, Walter White, Eric Walrond, Gwendolyn Bennett, and all of the emerging younger writers to the Writers' Guild dinner in order to have them meet and mingle with the older generation of writers—Du Bois, James Weldon Johnson, Georgia Douglas Johnson, Alice Dunbar-Nelson, and so on. Toomer would not attend; Hughes could not, for he was out of the country. Johnson had invited as well a number of the major white "literary personages of the city," as he put it in drawing up a list that included "Carl Van Doren, editor of the *Century,* Frederick Allen of *Harper's,* Walter Bartlett of *Scribner's,* Devere Allen of the *World Tomorrow,* Freda Kirchwey of the *Nation,* Paul Kellogg of the *Survey,* Horace Liveright of Boni, Liveright Publishers."[12]

Johnson's plan was to provide an occasion for whites in the publishing world to meet the new black writers. Alain Locke arrived from Washington, where he taught philosophy at Howard University, to act as master of ceremonies. Locke delivered his remarks dismissing "the older school of Negro writers," in which he included Du Bois, and acknowledging James Weldon Johnson's encouragement of the younger group. Carl Van Doran then presented a talk entitled "The Younger Generation of Negro Writers." Finally,

10. Nance, interview with Shockley.

11. Carolyn Wedin Sylvander, *Jessie Redmon Fauset: Black American Novelist* (Troy, N.Y., 1981), 70–71.

12. See Charles S. Johnson to Ethel Ray, March 24, 1924, quoted in *The Harlem Renaissance Remembered,* by Arna Bontemps (New York, 1972), 11.

after a host of others spoke, Jessie Fauset had a chance to address the audience.[13]

The occasion was not to honor Fauset; it was intended to promote *Opportunity*, founded only the previous year, and to announce the work of the younger writers, two of whom, Countee Cullen and Gwendolyn Bennett, read from their poetry. The extraordinarily successful evening has often been credited with launching the New Negro Renaissance because on this occasion Paul Kellogg of *Survey Graphic* approached Johnson about devoting an entire issue to the work of the new generation. The result was Alain Locke's editing the March, 1925, issue, "Harlem, the Mecca of the New Negro," and subsequently the book form *The New Negro*, published by Albert and Charles Boni in December.[14]

Although Nella Larsen Imes, along with her husband, was in the audience for the Civic Club dinner, she was not a focus of attention. With no creative writing in print, she was not considered one of the New Negro writers. The occasion nevertheless had a major impact on her career as a writer, just as it had upon that of Jessie Fauset. More was at stake than Fauset's pride, for the dinner had several hidden agendas. Charles S. Johnson's maneuver was a coup by which he effectively deflated Fauset's position among the new writers, many of whom she had mentored, and deflated as well the position of *Crisis* and, by extension, Du Bois. By presenting the suave and intelligent, but at that point sorely uninformed, Locke as a leader of the new movement, Johnson dismissed Fauset, a woman who was instinctively feminist and unquestionably committed to African Americans, despite her primness and her insistence on respectability.

For Fauset, and for Larsen Imes as well, this dismissal meant that during the next three dynamic years the leading figures and the most influential ones in the literary movement were all males, some of whom, like Locke in particular, were not only chauvinists but misogynists. When Charles S. Johnson blocked Fauset's further development as a leader by elevating Locke, the unspoken antagonism toward women and the latent sexual rivalry triumphed. Women were largely excluded from decision-making circles, particularly after 1926 when Fauset, seemingly disillusioned both

---

13. "The Debut of the Younger School of Negro Writers," *Opportunity*, II (May, 1924), 143–44; see also David Levering Lewis, *When Harlem Was in Vogue* (New York, 1981), 93–94.

14. See Amritjit Singh, *The Novels of the Harlem Renaissance: Twelve Black Writers, 1923–1933* (University Park, Pa., 1976), 15–20.

with the turn of events and with her mentor Du Bois, resigned from her position on *Crisis*. While Johnson's larger objectives were, as David Levering Lewis correctly states, "markets, exposure, education, intercultural exchange," all "to redeem, through art, the standing of his people," his anti-feminist, behind-the-scenes work was calculated and manipulative.[15] While Fauset possessed the vision to help young artists, she lacked Johnson's organizational skills and could not have achieved for the young movement what Johnson did. Fauset may have realized as much, because in the fall of 1924, just as the New Negro movement took shape, she left for a year of study in France.

In the aftermath of the *Opportunity* dinner, Larsen Imes's relation to the men and the women in the cultural movement became more complicated. For her, Johnson's emphasis on an art "free of propaganda and protest," articulated in his essay "An Opportunity for Negro Writers," would cause a reassessment of the work that she might achieve as a writer.[16] His influence placed her in a peculiar position that was comparable to Fauset's though even less secure, because Larsen Imes's need for success was far more acute. Moreover, she envied Fauset's achievements and *savoir faire*. Yet Fauset was a female role model and a more direct link than Charles Johnson to the community of writers.

Estrangement from Fauset would leave Larsen Imes in relative isolation. Nella Larsen Imes was roughly ten years older than Dorothy Peterson, Gwendolyn Bennett, and (so everyone believed at the time) Zora Hurston, and nearly twenty years older than Dorothy West and Helene Johnson. Alice Dunbar-Nelson was nearly fifty, almost twenty years older than Larsen Imes. And Georgia Douglas Johnson was at least ten years older than Larsen Imes. Both Dunbar-Nelson and Johnson were removed from New York, the one in Delaware and the other in Washington; moreover, Dunbar-Nelson, concentrating on her career as a journalist, wrote little creative work in the 1920s, and Johnson, unsuccessful in gaining a publisher for her poetry, turned toward writing plays during the Renaissance. Fauset was ten years older than Larsen Imes; neither had actual peers among the women writers, but each came closest to representing a peer for the other.

Although age difference cannot explain other motives that were no doubt at work, the relative chronological isolation of Larsen Imes from other

15. Lewis, *When Harlem Was in Vogue*, 97, 90.

16. Charles S. Johnson, "An Opportunity for Negro Writers," *Opportunity*, II (September, 1924), 199.

women writers, combined with Fauset's departure first for France and then from *Crisis*, moved her increasingly toward male writers (Walter White and Carl Van Vechten) as colleagues, models, and mentors. Her adoption of the objectives and the view of art espoused by Johnson and Locke moved her gradually away from the racially conscious White, who soon turned from fiction to exposés of American racism. Eventually she had left only the white male Van Vechten, who though generous in spirit and unfailingly interested in African Americans, never fully comprehended Nella Larsen Imes as a woman of color.

The Civic Club affair, however, was only one act in the drama of black New York in 1924. The aspiring writer Arna Bontemps reflected what was a general opinion of a Harlem changed into a dynamic aesthetic landscape: "In some places, the autumn of 1924 may have been an unremarkable season. In Harlem it was like a foretaste of paradise. A blue haze descended at night and with it strings of fairy lights on the broad avenues. From the window of a small room in an apartment on Fifth and 129th Street I looked over the rooftops of Negrodom and tried to believe my eyes. What [a] city! What a world!" It was a world "full of golden hopes and romantic dreams" that drew not only a Nella Imes from New Jersey, but an Arna Bontemps all the way from California "to find the job [he] wanted, to hear the music of [his] taste, to see serious plays and, God willing, to become a writer." [17]

If the fall of 1924 seemed part of "a remarkable season," then 1925 was a remarkable year. The vision of Harlem was contagious. Opportunity and potential seemed unlimited; New York, too busy to indulge racial hatred, seemed "as nearly ideal a place for colored people as exists in America." The first stop for many was the 135th Street library, as was the case with Bontemps, who set out on his first day in Harlem "looking for the Public Library" because someone had told him it was the place to go. [18] In the right place at the right time, Larsen Imes began to function with new groups of "the *best* people," as she labeled those who seemed to be achievers of any sort.

She cemented her friendship with Dorothy Peterson during this time. Peterson, born June 21, 1897, came from a well-established New York family. Fluent in Spanish, which she taught at a Brooklyn high school, Peterson had

<hr />

17. Arna Bontemps, Preface to *Personals*, by Bontemps (1963; London, 1973), 4.

18. Walter White, "Color Lines," *Survey Graphic*, VI (March, 1925), 681; Arna Bontemps, interview with Ann Allen Shockley, July 14, 1972, transcript in Special Collections, Fisk Oral History Project, Fisk University Library.

spent the summer of 1923 studying French at New York University. Her interest in languages was a reflection of her cosmopolitan tastes. Not only did she move easily among African Americans in New York, she functioned comfortably in international and interracial settings. Langston Hughes described her as "a charming colored girl who had grown up mostly in Puerto Rico, and who moved with such poise among . . . colorful celebrities that I thought when I first met her she was a white girl of the grande monde, slightly sun-tanned."[19] Lively, fun-loving, and adventuresome, Peterson was grounded in family, yet independent. She attracted a large following of friends with diverse interests.

On February 8, 1925, Larsen Imes went over to Brooklyn for one of Peterson's literary gatherings. Dorothy's brother, Sidney, helped to enliven the evening. An elegant, witty youth who later became a physician, he became almost immediately the brother Larsen Imes never had. Harold Jackman, Peterson's close friend and sometimes escort who was rarely at a loss for words, was there, and so was Eric Walrond, who was a favorite of the Petersons because, having grown up in Central America, he too was fluent in Spanish and was, like Dorothy's father, a journalist. Jerome Bowers Peterson had worked for the New York *Globe* and had been one of the founders of the New York *Age* before going into foreign service. He continued his editorial work for the *Age* after his return to Brooklyn from Venezuela and Puerto Rico, though by the 1920s he was more liberal than the paper had become under a conservative member of Booker T. Washington's Tuskegee machine, Fred R. Moore. Interested in literature and art, Peterson encouraged the modest interracial literary salon in his Monroe Street home over which his daughter presided. From his first meeting with Larsen Imes, he adopted a parental attitude that would develop into genuine affection for her and concern for her welfare, especially for her writing, which he championed throughout the decade.

Formerly an editor for Marcus Garvey's *Negro World*, Walrond was *Opportunity*'s business manager. Having studied at City College and Columbia, in addition to operating a weekly newspaper, he was already well known and well liked in the black community. He had the ability to make friends easily. He was, as Ethel Ray said, "always bringing someone to Harlem, or if people wanted to come, they would get in touch with Walrond

19. Dorothy Peterson to Grace Nail Johnson, July 30, 1923, in JWJ; Hughes, *The Big Sea*, 252.

and he [would] see that [they met] interesting people."[20] Walrond brought Donald Angus and Carl Van Vechten to the Petersons' that night, and for many years thereafter the group would celebrate the anniversary of that meeting.[21]

Although it was not Larsen Imes's first introduction to Van Vechten, the smaller group setting, and without Walter White's overshadowing presence, gave her a moment in the spotlight. One idea linked to the new burst of literary activity particularly intrigued Van Vechten; it concerned the need for a bookshop in Harlem. That discussion would continue during the next year.[22]

Conversation was the staple at the dinners and parties that followed throughout the winter and spring of 1925. Nella and Elmer Imes became part of an expanding interracial circuit, exchanging invitations and ideas. Even dinners to which they were not guests could later in the evening become informal stop-in parties. On May 9, for instance, when Van Vechten invited Du Bois and Bernadine Szold for dinner, Elmer and Nella Imes, Dorothy Peterson, Jean Toomer, Dorothy and Jimmie Harris, Rita Romilly, Lawrence Langner, and Donald Angus all stopped in for after-dinner drinks. The lively group talked well into the night, but Toomer and Romilly continued their conversation with Van Vechten until 4:30 in the morning. A few days later, Nella and Elmer Imes reciprocated by hosting Van Vechten in Jersey City.[23] The invitations kept many from the same small group involved in rounds of talk, much of which circled back to literary and artistic topics.

By all accounts, Larsen Imes was extremely well read. Charles S. Johnson thought so. He was not hard-pressed to praise her for possessing "a most extraordinarily wide acquaintance with past and current literature." On the basis of her knowledge of books and her experience as a librarian, Walter White recommended her to Samuel Craig, president of the Book League of America, for a possible position. Visitors to the Imeses' apartment noticed immediately that their living room was literally lined with "books and more

20. Nance, interview with Shockley.
21. See Carl Van Vechten to Harold Jackman, on the sixteenth anniversary of their meeting, February 8, 1941, in *The Letters of Carl Van Vechten,* ed. Bruce Kellner (New York, 1987), 176.
22. See Nella Imes to Carl Van Vechten, Wednesday, September 29, 1926, in JWJ, and Nella Imes to Carl Van Vechten, Wednesday, 6th [1926], in CVV.
23. Carl Van Vechten, Daybook, May 9 and 16, 1925, in CVV.

books." Similar to her heroine in *Quicksand* in the pleasure she took in books, Larsen Imes used reading as a primary way of relaxing and entertaining herself. And in the college-educated company she kept, reading was her way of asserting her intellectual capacity. Shortly after she returned from Europe in 1932, she expressed regret that she had been without her books: "I am away from my books and have been so long denied the pleasure of looking into them when and where I wished—or just anywhere." An avid reader interested in all periods and genres, she was especially fond of adventure stories and mysteries. Whatever volumes she could not afford to buy, she borrowed from friends or the public library. Occasionally, she asked that friends traveling abroad bring her particular books, such as James Joyce's *Ulysses*, which she requested from Dorothy Peterson in 1927.[24]

Larsen Imes was preoccupied with reading. The activity was satisfying partly because in an existence dependent upon reshaping lived experience, stories serve as models. As Carolyn Heilbrun has suggested: "It is a hard thing to make up stories to live by. We can only retell and live by the stories we have read and heard. We live our lives through texts. They may be read, or chanted, or expressed electronically, or come to us, like murmurings of our mothers, telling us what conventions demand. Whatever their form or medium, these stories have formed us all; they are what we must use to make new fictions, new narratives."[25] In Larsen Imes's recurrent efforts to transform and engender self, reading life writings, fictional or autobiographical, empowered her, alleviated her isolation by conflating her narrative of self with those of others and by situating her realities within a larger collectivity.

Elmer Imes supported her interest in reading by recommending authors and purchasing books, which the couple later discussed. His Christmas gifts usually included books, particularly while Larsen Imes was in Spain.[26] He first introduced his wife to Carl Van Vechten's works, when, after completing *Peter Whiffle: His Life and Works* (1922), he urged her to read Van

---

24. Charles S. Johnson to Walter White, August 5, 1926, in WW, NAACP; Walter F. White to Samuel Craig, September 25, 1928, *ibid.;* Thelma E. Berlack, "New Author Unearthed Right Here in Harlem," New York *Amsterdam News*, May 23, 1928, p. 16; Nella Larsen Imes to Carl Van Vechten, Saturday 2nd [postmarked April 2, 1932], in CVV; Andrew G. Meyer, interview with author, May 25, 1982; Nella Larsen to Dorothy Peterson, July 12, 1927, in JWJ.

25. Carolyn Heilbrun, *Writing a Woman's Life* (New York, 1988), 37.

26. Elmer Imes to Carl Van Vechten, December 3, 1930, in JWJ. Imes expresses concern about whether Nella's Christmas books would reach her in time for the holiday.

Vechten's novel, or as she put it, "worried me and Walter [White] to death until one summer we read it." By 1929, her enthusiasm for Van Vechten's books far exceeded her husband's; that year she identified Van Vechten and Galsworthy as her favorite authors, both of whom, along with a veritable legion of other authors, influenced her writing.[27]

Both older and contemporary works of literature engaged her, so much so that from the beginning of her acquaintance with Carl Van Vechten a mutual appetite for reading defined their friendship. With Van Vechten initially taking the lead by sending her two books, but with Larsen Imes quickly reciprocating, they shared books by American, British, and Continental authors and exchanged reactions to them.[28] On September 29, 1926, for instance, she acknowledged receipt of a book by Carlo Goldoni: "I was particularly glad for it as I mean eventually to acquire most of the Blue Jade series. This makes seven. I am curious about the period too, although I know little of it except through Casanova's memoirs which I read some four years ago . . . —and of course Elinor Wylie."[29] Goldoni (1707–1793), a playwright who reformed the Italian theater and wrote for the French, was one of fourteen foreign authors published by 1926 in Alfred A. Knopf's Blue Jade Library. *The Memoirs of Carlo Goldoni, Written by Himself,* was, like other volumes in the series, a work in translation, and one that Larsen Imes enjoyed because of Goldoni's clashes with eighteenth-century conventions, as well as with jealous rival authors.

Although she admired Goldoni's treatment of social injustices in his comedies, her esteem for two other books in the Blue Jade Library was greater: Marmaduke Pickthall's *Saïd the Fisherman* (1903; Blue Jade Library, 1925) she ranked highly for its "keen insight"; and Francisco de Quevedo-Villegas' *Pablo de Segovia* (1595; Blue Jade Library, 1926) she thought "marvelous" and contemplated its effect in "a tale of a Negro ruf-

27. Nella Imes to Carl Van Vechten, Wednesday, eleventh [postmarked August 12, 1926], in CVV; Mary Rennels, New York *Telegram,* April 13, 1929, in SCF. After *Peter Whiffle,* Imes's enthusiasm for Van Vechten's books remained high; he even read the French version of *Nigger Heaven.* See Elmer S. Imes to Carl Van Vechten, n.d. [postmarked March 3, 1928], in JWJ.

28. See, for example, Nella Imes to Carl Van Vechten, n.d. [1924], in CVV, on Van Vechten's *Tatooed Countess;* Nella Imes to Carl Van Vechten, Wednesday, seventeenth [postmarked September 18, 1925], in JWJ, Larsen Imes to Van Vechten, Saturday 2nd [postmarked April 2, 1932], in CVV, and Imes to Van Vechten, Wednesday 6th [1926], in CVV, on Osbert Sitwell's *Triple Fugue* and Van Vechten's *Nigger Heaven;* Nella Imes to Carl Van Vechten, Monday 6th [1926], in CVV, on Marmaduke Pickthall's *Valley of the Kings.*

29. Imes to Van Vechten, Wednesday, September 29, 1926, in JWJ.

fian told in this naive manner." (This idea about "blackening" the work of another writer would eventually cause her to be challenged for plagiarism.) She also admired Pickthall's *Valley of the Kings* (1926) for "its effective gentle irony." [30]

Her other books from the Blue Jade Library included *The Letters of Abelard and Heloise*, *The Adventures of Hajji Baba of Ispana*, Stendhal's *The Life of Henri Brulard*, Theophile Gautier's *Romantic in Spain*, and Heldane Macfall's *Wooings of Jezebel Pettyfer*. These and other titles from the 1925 and 1926 series would be joined by new editions throughout the rest of the 1920s. James Weldon Johnson's *Autobiography of an Ex-Coloured Man*, published in the Blue Jade Library in 1927, was the only book by an African American in the series. The eclectic collection of world literature reflects not only her wide range of readings but also her insatiable curiosity about life beyond the United States—a curiosity that the cosmopolitan but whimsical intellectual Van Vechten stimulated and helped satisfy. This shared interest in books, as much as Van Vechten's influence in literary New York, anchored their friendship over the next decade and prompted Larsen Imes to declare: "I think you are the grandest friend that I've ever had, and I hope I will never do anything to merit the withdrawal of your friendship." [31] In the 1930s, it would be she, however, who would withdraw from the friendship.

From January, 1924, to October, 1925, Larsen Imes worked at the 135th Street branch, a grandstand seat from which to observe all of the latest milestones in New Negro doings. In the spring of 1925, Walter White enthusiastically listed them for Claude McKay, who was in France: "Things are certainly moving with rapidity now as far as the Negro artist is concerned. Countee Cullen has had a book of verse accepted by Harper. . . . Knopf accepted a volume by Langston Hughes. Rudolph Fisher . . . has had two excellent short stories in *The Atlantic Monthly*. . . . James Weldon Johnson is at work on a book of Negro Spirituals and the field of creative writers seems to be growing daily." After telling of a Roland Hayes tour, Paul Robeson and Lawrence Brown recitals, and Julius Bledso's promise, White concluded: "The Negro artist is really in the ascendancy just now. There is unlimited opportunity. . . . [Y]ou will be amazed at the eagerness of magazine editors and book publishers to get hold of promising writers."

30. See Imes to Van Vechten, Wednesday, eleventh [postmarked August 12, 1926], on *Saïd the Fisherman*, in CVV, and Nella Imes to Carl Van Vechten, November 12, 1926, on *Pablo de Segovia*, in JWJ; Imes to Van Vechten, Monday 6th [1926], in CVV.

31. Nella Larsen Imes to Carl Van Vechten, Saturday [postmarked February 18, 1928], in JWJ.

He urged McKay to get some of his work ready at once, so as not to miss out on what the group was achieving. The activity was indeed taking another turn, as Arna Bontemps also saw it: "We began to recognize ourselves as a 'group' and to become a little self-conscious about our 'significance.' When we were not too busy having fun, we were shown off and exhibited . . . in scores of places to all kinds of people. And we heard the sighs of wonder, amazement and sometimes admiration . . . that here was one of the 'New Negroes.'"[32] Group identity was in.

Late in the spring of 1925, Larsen Imes became part of a mainly literary group of blacks that Jean Toomer organized for lectures and demonstrations in Gurdjieffian philosophy. Dorothy Peterson, attracted to the handsome Toomer and no doubt also to his "admixture of physical and spiritual drives," was one of the principal students. Some observers believed that the "intense devotion he generated in individuals as disparate as Margaret Naumburg [wife of author Waldo Frank], Dorothy Peterson, and Mabel Dodge Luhan was the result of his intellectual and emotional fervor combined with his physical attractiveness." Peterson encouraged Larsen Imes's attendance, because she agreed with Toomer's belief that "those who were most likely to become absorbed . . . would be educated, relatively successful people who were seeking a remedy for their 'incompleteness.'"[33] In recruiting Larsen Imes, along with Wallace Thurman, Harold Jackman, and Aaron Douglas, Peterson identified those she considered most open to self-exploration.

A number of the Harlem literati, or "niggerati" as Zora Hurston was by then calling them, did attend to discover more about the Russian mystic philosopher Gurdjieff, or perhaps about Toomer; but most, like Arna Bontemps, came to one meeting and did not return. They were too busy enjoying being New Negroes to adopt the nonracial philosophy Toomer presented. Toomer's timing was off; that same spring, on May 1, *Opportunity* held its first annual banquet to announce the winners of its first literary contest. Those receiving the awards comprised a virtual "who's who" of the Renaissance: Langston Hughes, Countee Cullen, Eric Walrond, Zora Hurston, Marita Bonner, Clarissa Scott, Frank Horne, Sterling Brown, and so on.[34] A little money and a lot of publicity made the Harlem writers difficult conquests for Toomer.

32. Walter F. White to Claude McKay, May 20, 1925, in WW, NAACP; Bontemps, Preface to *Personals*, 4.
33. Kerman and Eldridge, *The Lives of Jean Toomer*, 172.
34. *Ibid.*; "Contest Awards," *Opportunity*, III (May, 1925), 142–43.

The fledgling artists were in another bind, as Langston Hughes observed:

The trouble with such a life-pattern in Harlem was that practically everybody had to work all day to make a living, and the cult of Gurdjieff demanded not only study and application, but a large amount of inner observation and silent concentration as well. So while some of Mr. Toomer's best disciples were sitting long hours concentrating, unaware of time, unfortunately they lost their jobs, and could no longer pay the handsome young teacher for his instructions. Others had so little time to concentrate, if they wanted to live and eat, that their advance toward cosmic consciousness was slow and their hope of achieving awareness distant indeed. So Jean Toomer left his Harlem group and went downtown to drop the seeds of Gurdjieff in less dark and poverty-stricken fields.[35]

The core group lasted only a year, though when Toomer gave up on Harlem, Dorothy Peterson transferred to a downtown group led by A. R. Orage, an experienced Gurdjieff disciple and Toomer's own teacher. Peterson and Dorothy Hunt Harris, an African American who lived in Greenwich Village but participated in Toomer's Harlem meetings, were the most committed to finding and regenerating themselves through Gurdjieff's Fourth Way. Both were from the privileged class of African Americans who had the money to enjoy good educations, foreign travel, and leisured lives, and interestingly, both would become attracted to the theater. Harris, then married to the artist Jimmie Harris, had attended Atlanta University, the alma mater of James Weldon Johnson and Walter White. The daughter of the principal of the Fort Valley Institute, she was from one of "the best families in Georgia," as White put it in endorsing her attempt to get a role in a Paul Robeson play. To a greater extent than Peterson, Harris became converted to Gurdjieff's philosophy. In 1927, confessing to having become overly absorbed in her personal search, she reportedly said that "maybe next year she would have time to look after her friends having spent so much time in her soul this year."[36]

35. Hughes, *The Big Sea*, 241–42. See also the discussion of Hughes's contact with Gurdjieff's followers in Greenwich Village in Arnold Rampersad, *The Life of Langston Hughes* (2 vols.; New York, 1986), I, 120–23.

36. Kerman and Eldridge, *The Lives of Jean Toomer*, 145; Walter White to Horace Liveright, June 7, 1926, in WW, NAACP; Larsen to Peterson, July 12, 1927, in JWJ.

Like her two friends, Nella Larsen Imes was attracted to Toomer's teachings. She was searching for something, and the group validated the legitimacy of her search. The idea of self-regeneration had a special appeal to her, given the self-fashioning that she had accomplished. Unlike the two Dorothys, however, she was too practical-minded and materialistic to give herself over to the spiritual base of the philosophy or to Toomer's mysticism. She was also unmoved by his sexual appeal, because though she would portray women's sexuality frankly in her fiction, she apparently suppressed, for the most part, sexual drives in her own life. Whether she repressed physical manifestations of sex with her husband because of her "daughterly," and thus incestual, regard for him is difficult to ascertain; however, there is indication that some frigidity on her part led to sexual dissatisfaction in the marriage, as well as to his extramarital affairs and to her attraction to younger white males.

Her two friends were another matter. She found their involvement with the Gurdjieffs unreasonable and frequently joked about Dorothy Harris' being "pseudo-religious," though she found Harris "charming" and a good bridge partner. She also humorously conveyed to Dorothy Peterson, who was in Europe and on the way to Gurdjieff's institute at Fontainebleau, Elmer Imes's message: "Remember Katherine Mansfield." [37] (Mansfield had died at Fontainebleau in 1923.) The warning was intended to caution Peterson against putting too much faith in the healing potential of Gurdjieff's philosophy.

Perhaps the Gurdjieffs lacked appeal, too, because Larsen Imes was unwilling to give up her personal goal of attaining significance through writing before she had a chance to become a writer. For her, the cultural movement had combined at an optimum moment with her ambition to create in fiction and in life the identity she wanted for herself. While Gurdjieff's philosophy might earlier have provided a basis for redirecting an internally aimless life, it could not compete by the mid-1920s with the individuation Larsen Imes desired through the expression of her creativity. In coming to terms with the opposing factors within her self and in attaining her fullest potential, she was indeed seeking an internal development that would integrate parts of her self, but only those parts that she determined necessary to actualize and sustain the self she desired in her interpersonal relationships. Of necessity,

37. Nella Larsen Imes to Carl Van Vechten, n.d. [postmarked June 29, 1927], Larsen to Peterson, July 12, 1927, and Nella Larsen to Dorothy Peterson, Tuesday 19th [July, 1927], all in JWJ.

she was already experienced at directing her life and creating an identity. What she consciously sought was control over how others responded to her, over her identity in the larger world; Gurdjieff did not offer a mechanism for such control, but writing did.

She had been honing her craft throughout the year. In mid-February, she had reduced her library position to half-time in order to allow more time for writing. She wrote short fiction, which she attempted to place in magazines. In September, when she accompanied Elmer Imes to Montreal for a physics meeting, she formulated plans for her career.[38] Elmer Imes had just left his job as a research physicist at Burrows Magnetic Equipment Corporation for employment as a research engineer with Edward A. Everett. The manufacturing company offered a salary plus the prospect of extra income from inventions connected with signal lights for railroads. With the assurance of more money in the household, Larsen Imes took a three-month leave of absence from the public library. From October through December, 1925, she devoted her attention to writing.

During these three months, she suffered colds and influenza, the illnesses that, along with pneumonia, plagued her adulthood. Poor health often required that she suspend her normal activities, both social and domestic.[39] Her recuperations typically included long periods in bed, periods that she spent reading. Illness and recovery played a major part in her unconscious strategy for psychical survival, by ensuring a periodic renewal of her energies to protect her personal space. The requisite recovery allowed for the solitary reflection that fueled her fiction and for uninterrupted time to write.

On January 1, 1926, she terminated her full-time employment with the public library on the basis of "poor health." Perhaps not coincidentally, the first of Larsen Imes's creative works appeared in print in the same month as her resignation from the library. Only briefly, from March to July, 1929, and from October to December, 1929, would she return to the library system as a general assistant when her husband's job loss and increased financial pressures made her employment mandatory. "On the 1st of July," she

38. File for Mrs. Nella L. Imes, in Employment Records, Personnel Office, New York Public Library; Imes to Van Vechten, Wednesday, seventeenth [postmarked September 18, 1925], in JWJ.

39. See, for example, Elmer Imes to Van Vechten, n.d. [postmarked March 3, 1928], Nella Larsen Imes to Carl Van Vechten, Saturday, July 28 [postmarked July 31, 1929], and Nella Larsen Imes to Carl Van Vechten, n.d. [postmarked March 19, 1928], all in JWJ. See also Berlack, "New Author Unearthed," 16; and New York Amsterdam News, February 26, 1929, p. 4.

wrote, "I stop working and certainly no [one] could be more elated over a thing than I am about this, unless it's Elmer."[40] But necessity caused her to return to work during the last three months of the year. However, from the point in the mid-twenties when she resigned from the library, through the publication of her novels in the late twenties, to the end of her visibility in New York in the mid-thirties, she held no permanent salaried job.

Larsen Imes's reading and work experiences formed the general preparation for her career as a writer. Her multiple training programs and jobs had accentuated, on the one hand, a sense of the freedom possible for women and, on the other, an awareness of the limitations placed on the individual female by the environment in which she existed. Larsen Imes's movement through various institutions, places, and jobs in a relatively short period prevented her from becoming fully an insider in any one of her settings. Her position as outsider, or often as newcomer, who had neither remained in one place for long nor retained binding familial or communal ties to any place, sharpened her observations of life around her.

Although dispersed throughout the North and the South, the African-American middle class in which she functioned was a very small community interconnected through churches and church-related organizations and conventions; schools and their clubs, sororities, fraternities, and alumni groups; and news publications. The African-American press, in particular, served not only as a source of information but also as a medium of connection. Newspapers such as the New York *Age,* the *Amsterdam News,* the Chicago *Defender,* and the Baltimore *Afro-American* paid equal attention to political and economic occurrences, social and literary trends, educational and religious affairs, and entertainment and sports events. The rise of numerous African-American magazines and journals after World War I strengthened the functions of the black press and especially brought the African-American literary community even closer together.[41] At the forefront were the NAACP's *Crisis,* the Urban League's *Opportunity,* and the Brotherhood of Sleeping Car Porters' *Messenger,* all of which originated in New York and enjoyed national circulation. Walter White sent a list of black publications to the George Doran Company, which was considering the publication

---

40. File for Mrs. Imes, in Employment Records, Personnel Office, New York Public Library; Nella Larsen Imes to Carl Van Vechten, Friday, fourteenth [postmarked June 15, 1929], in JWJ.

41. See Abby Arthur Johnson and Ronald Maberry Johnson, *Propaganda and Aesthetics: The Literary Politics of African-American Magazines in the Twentieth Century* (1979; Amherst, 1991), 31–96.

of *The Fire in the Flint,* and remarked: "Through these seven publications you can reach practically all reading and thinking Negroes."[42]

Although Larsen Imes lived in the New York area and was active in the emerging cultural movement of the 1920s, she remained on the fringes. She had no African-American school ties or family connections; she viewed uplift and racial organizations skeptically, particularly after her experience at Tuskegee Institute; and she dismissed religion and the African-American church, more so after her marriage into the Imes family, which she dubbed "tiresome" and "ultra religious."[43] Although she neither identified nor fraternized with the growing community of West Indians in New York, she was known in that community for her claim to Virgin Islands ancestry. Several "Virgin Islanders thought that she capitalized on her mixed Danish-African heritage and held aloof from people who were not well-connected."[44] An outsider's perspective made her more objective in viewing situations and people and also more subjective in her analyses or interpretations of them. "The Nella Larsen who emerges from her letters," William Bedford Clark rightly has concluded, "is first and foremost an *observer* who views the oftentimes absurd world around her from the detached perspective of the perennial outsider." Nevertheless, it is no mere division between insider and outsider that distinguishes Larsen Imes, but instead a multiplicity of stances and a plurality of perspectives, freely assumed and articulated. More than the role-playing that even close friends recognized in her postures and gestures, Larsen Imes had the ability to envelope herself in distinct, and mutually exclusive, personae that complicated her responses to her surroundings and other people.[45] Her complex perspectives combined well with her ongoing absorption in reading and her tenure as a librarian to provide her with a clear conception of how to direct and develop her writing.

The shifts of emphasis in her professional life underscore an impulsiveness and a restlessness in her nature, or as she put it, that her "greatest weakness" was "dissatisfaction." More significant, in her career choices

---

42. Walter White to Alan Rinehart, George H. Doran Co., August 27, 1925, in WW, NAACP.

43. Imes to Van Vechten, November 12, 1926, in JWJ.

44. Lewis, *When Harlem Was in Vogue,* 231. His informant, G. James Fleming, however, only knew Larsen by reputation (G. James Fleming to Thadious Davis, October 2, October 16, 1983, in possession of Thadious M. Davis).

45. William Bedford Clark, "The Letters of Nella Larsen to Carl Van Vechten: A Survey," *Resources for American Literary Study,* VIII (Fall, 1978), 195; Alice L. Carper and Carolyn Lane, interview with author, May 5, 1985.

Larsen Imes searched for an occupation that was compatible with her interests, needs, and ambitions. Her work as a librarian reflected a life-long love for books, which, she remarked, were satisfying "materially." Her work with books, along with the cultural activity in Harlem, helped propel her toward a career as a writer. As a writer, she could make tangible use of her experiences, yet at the same time intensify, clarify, and interpret them. She could draw from her wealth of readings to stimulate her imagination and to challenge her creativity. "The realm of art is," as Irvin Edman maintains, "identical with the realm of man's deliberate control of that world of materials and movements among which he must make his home, of that inner world of random impulses and automatic processes which constitute his inner being."[46] Intellectually and emotionally, Larsen Imes would find a satisfactory outlet for her talents and ambitions, desires and needs, public persona and private self in writing.

In January and April of 1926, she published two stories in *Young's Realistic Stories Magazine* under the pseudonym Allen Semi—Nella Imes in reverse. Embedded within the pseudonym was the identity that she had created years earlier (Nella) and a mask that reversed her gender identity. The choice of a masculine pseudonym may have been a matter of expediency and strategy, a way of striking the more familiar posture of the author-artist as male, thereby increasing the chances of a publisher's acceptance.

This choice seemingly freed her from some of the held-over Victorian notions about the proper subjects for women to consider intellectually or imaginatively. The freedom clearly was not uncontemplated, because the subject of one of her pseudonymous stories is freedom, the stepping outside of place, position, and identity in order to observe the impact of the transformation, not on self, but on others. Thus as Allen Semi, Nella Larsen Imes was uninhibited. She could broach the subjects of sexual barter, prostitution, mistresses, children born out of wedlock, or of women other than as daughters, wives, mothers, and outside the traditional domestic sphere. With the male façade, she claimed an authority of experience in these subject areas usually denied to the female, especially to one who surveyed them without moral commentary.

Although she navigated a course around patriarchal prescriptions for the female writer, she also patterned her narratives after the male-defined formula *Young's Magazine* expected. *Young's*, directed toward an audience of

---

46. Larsen quoted by Rennels, New York *Telegram*, April, 13, 1929; Irvin Edman, *Arts and the Man: A Short Introduction to Aesthetics* (1928; rpr. New York, 1939), 14.

women, was a monthly publication of the C. H. Young Publishing Company, located at 709 Sixth Avenue, New York. It provided Larsen Imes with a training ground for her fiction that appealed to women, but from the perspective of male fantasies. The magazine covers usually featured drawings of beautiful young women in poses suggestive of seduction, romance, and intrigue. The illustration for the January, 1926, issue, which contained Larsen Imes's first published story, "The Wrong Man," was a sketch of a bare-shouldered woman surrounded by balloons and the sign "Kisses for Sale." The April, 1926, issue, with her second story, "Freedom," had a cover illustration of a dreamy-eyed woman in a thin-strapped dress, cradling a feather fan to her face. *Young's* carried short stories and novelettes with such provocative titles as "Wisdom of the Serpent" (advertised on the January, 1926, cover), "The Hootch Dancer," "Pearls for Purity," "Cold Lips," and "White Man's Land" (the lead story in the April, 1926, issue). Compared to these titles and their appeals to female sexuality, Larsen Imes's "The Wrong Man" and "Freedom" are staid, but her narratives, like most of these others, reveal an internalization of male-constructed images of women as sexual objects.

The pseudonym Allen Semi served another purpose. In 1926, Nella Larsen had been married to Elmer Imes for seven years, and throughout those years she had assumed her marital name, Imes, both as an expected part of the marriage contract and as a clear signal of firm class position. She had dropped *Larsen* from her name from 1919 through the late 1920s. *Semi* veiled the *Imes* identity, a measure perhaps necessitated by the unusual name *Imes,* which would be easily recognizable. Not only was Elmer Imes well known in New York circles, particularly among the Fisk alumni and the congregation at St. Philip's Protestant Episcopal, the most exclusive black church in New York, but his brother William Lloyd was even more eminent. In 1925 the Reverend Imes had moved from Philadelphia to New York as pastor of St. James Presbyterian Church, one of the major Harlem congregations, and that same year he was appointed to the NAACP Board of Directors. The Imes name would have been recognized and adversely so, given the subject of the publication: the wife of a prominent New Yorker who, having once been the mistress of a wealthy man who saved her from the streets and educated her, faces the possible public exposure of her past.

In addition to protecting her family and gender identities, *Semi,* a prefix meaning half or partly, not fully or imperfectly, also disguised her racial identity. The unusual name lacked a clear ethnic or racial association. Although *Young's* published some fiction treating racial themes, neither of

Larsen Imes's stories concerned African-American characters or racial issues; yet both were preparatory for her novels. Announcing the arrival of
the beginning apprentice writer, but masking her race and gender, the name
was the kind of play on words and meaning that Larsen Imes thoroughly
enjoyed.

"The Wrong Man," the last story in the January issue, was printed in
double-columns and was three and one-half pages long. It was very short
compared with *Young's* typical entries. The plot line is simple. The scene is
an exclusive Long Island dance party at which an orchestra breaks into
"something wild and impressionistic with a primitive staccato understrain
of jazz."[47] With the advent of "savage strains" into the music, an exotic
man suddenly appears among the sophisticated partygoers, one of whom is
Julia Romley, the heroine. Julia, married to Jim Romley, is a gray-eyed, red-
haired beauty and a successful interior decorator who observes that she has
"love, wealth and position" (244).

However, she also has a past as Julia Hammond, a San Francisco girl
who became the mistress of Ralph Tyler when she found herself hungry and
homeless. Tyler's money had allowed her to attend an art school in Chicago,
where she studied interior decorating. From that start she had been able to
reach New York, establish a studio, and achieve success. Her marriage to
the wealthy Jim Romley had assured her of a place in one of Long Island's
"most exclusive sets," but with the appearance of the "tall, thin man" with
a "lean face yellowed and hardened as if by years in the tropics" (244),
Julia's secure life and five years of marital happiness seem threatened. Ralph
Tyler, Julia's former lover, is the stranger. He also happens to be a college
friend of Jim Romley, and famous and wealthy enough from his years of
adventures as an explorer in Asia to attract Jim's attention.

Desperate to prevent her husband from finding out about her past, Julia
sends a note to Tyler requesting that he meet her in the summer house.
Minutes later, she confesses her predicament to a man hidden in the darkness and begs him to refrain from destroying her marriage by revealing that
she had been a starving girl whom he had taken in off the streets. She confides: "'You think that even now I should tell him [her husband, Jim] that I
was your mistress once. You don't know Jim. He'd never understand that,
when a girl has been sick and starving on the streets, anything can happen
to her; that she's grateful for food and shelter at any price. You won't tell

---

47. Nella Imes [Allen Semi], "The Wrong Man," *Young's Realistic Stories Magazine,* L
(January, 1926), 244 (hereafter cited parenthetically in the text).

him, will you?'" (246). The man promises that her secret is safe with him; but as he lights a match for his cigarette, he becomes clearly visible as "the wrong man," not Ralph Tyler. Her note had been delivered to someone else. The story ends with Julia's discovery.

"The Wrong Man" reveals several important concerns of Larsen Imes's. First, the dance setting, elaborately described in the opening paragraph, shows her concern with specific details, bright colors, and the trappings of wealth. Her women wear "gorgeous things" that keep the room ablaze "with color," while her men wear "the inevitable black and white," which "lent just enough preciseness to add interest to the riotously hued scene" (243). Julia describes the scene as being "'wonderful . . . the people, the music, the color, and these lovely rooms; like a princess's ball in a fairy tale'" (244). The analogy is the same one Larsen Imes used in reference to Van Vechten's wife, Fania Marinoff, when they first met. Although the narrative perspective is that of an insider, the central character sees the party as an outsider; surely, for example, if Julia were as successful and Jim as wealthy as the narrator claims, then such affairs should be ordinary after five years of married life. She is, instead, awestruck by the people and her surroundings.

Another of the concerns that becomes characteristic of Larsen Imes's later fiction is with capturing the dialogue of the rich set that is central to her depictions. In "The Wrong Man," she is not very successful, even though not all of the conversations are as stilted as the one George Hill initiates with his "'Some show, what?'" (244).

Perhaps the most significant concern shown in this first story is the one for the surprise ending. Both "The Wrong Man" and "Freedom" rely upon a sudden turn of events for resolution. They are similar to the endings made popular by O. Henry's short stories. In the short story form, the device seems appropriate; however, Larsen Imes inadequately transfers the unexpected ending to both of her novels, primarily to her second novel, *Passing,* in which more preparation for the final events is necessary. Her dependence upon such endings may be a manifestation of self-doubt about the resolution of those self-revelatory aspects of her fictions.

Despite its embryonic form, the tension or competition between two women, ostensibly friends, is worth observing as one of her concerns. Julia Romley eyes Myra Redmon, the hostess, and notices that "Myra always had a lion in tow" (243). Later, Julia "felt a flash of resentful anger against Myra. Why was she always carting about impossible people?" (244). Her reaction to Myra is a mixture of approval, regard, envy, and pique. Although undeveloped in this story, Julia's attitude toward Myra is similar to that of Helga Crane toward Anne Grey in *Quicksand* and Irene Redfield toward Clare Kendry in *Passing*. The undertow of the latent rivalry has little to do with competition for men. Julia may remark upon Myra Redmon's appearance or entourage of males, but what she apparently resents and is bothered by the most is Myra's ease with her class position, with money and wealth, with privilege and place, and above all with her self. Julia's response to Myra is a resentment corresponding to Max Scheler's definition of envy: "a feeling of impotence which vitiates our attempt to acquire something because it belongs to another. . . . *Envy* occurs only when our efforts to acquire [what belongs to another] fail and we are left with a feeling of impotence." [48] Within Larsen Imes's text, then, Julia is envious of Myra, and that envy may also be representative of Larsen Imes's own response to Jessie Fauset. Myra's surname, *Redmon,* links her to Jessie *Redmon* Fauset and implies Larsen Imes's consciousness of her ambivalence toward Fauset.

Myra is born to the pedestal; Julia has managed to have men elevate her to it. The result is an ill-defined jealously combined with fear, the fear of exposure for being an inadequate person or having an unsatisfactory background. Julia does not recognize that she has achieved a remarkable success in the terms that mean the most to her. She wants to belong to the socially and culturally elite, and she has indeed become part of that group by virtue of using her talents and opportunities, no matter whether they were inspired or assisted by men. In her response to Myra, Julia fails to appreciate her own distinctiveness as a career woman and to value her work as being as worthwhile as social stature. She signals that Larsen Imes as apprentice author presented a social reality in women's relationships that denied gender-bonding and female interdependence.

The strongest aspect of Larsen Imes's apprenticeship fiction is, nevertheless, her characterization of women. Julia Hammond Romley suggests a fascinating personality. She is, like all of Larsen Imes's heroines to some extent, a self-made woman. The psychology of that particular type is never fully revealed in any of the fiction, but in each novel, Larsen Imes attempts to portray some aspect of the inner life of such women. For the most part, she infers a richly complex interior, and as with Julia, she does not completely delineate the external story of the woman's background that impinges directly upon her psychological and emotional life. She merely paints with brief strokes that which deserves stronger development.

All of her women have secrets, and the particular characterization of the

48. Quoted in René Girard, *Deceit, Desire, and the Novel: Self and Other in Literary Structure* (1961; rpr. Baltimore, 1976), 12–13.

woman with the secret or the hidden past becomes a stock feature in Larsen Imes's small output of fiction. Fiction, Virginia Woolf remarked, "is like a spider's web, attached ever so lightly perhaps, but still attached to life at all four corners." Larsen Imes's use of the woman with a secret or with a hidden life in her fiction may well be self-presentation. In the fictional context of Julia Romley, she may have been refracting her own experience, particularly her past and the four years between her departure from the Fisk Normal Department and her enrollment in the Lincoln Training School for Nurses. Judith Kegan Gardiner has observed that "women writers often use their texts, particularly those focused on female heroes, as part of a self-defining process involving empathetic identifications with those characters."[49] Even if the situational contexts between Julia and Nella were not identical, the emotional nexus was strikingly similar.

The triad of men in the text validates the core of secrecy. Ralph Tyler, the former lover and man-in-the-shadows of Julia's past, contrasts with Jim Romley, the husband and man-in-the-spotlight central to Julia's present existence. Although connected by schools and heritage, the two are separated by Julia's secret. Jim must not gain access to Julia's past if he, as much as she, is to remain in "good standing" in a public, elite societal space. Ralph must suppress his intimate knowledge of Julia if he is to retain his status as public "hero." However, the anonymous "wrong man" who listens to Julia's plea is the linchpin in the text. He is an outsider who, like Julia herself, crosses the boundaries separating insider and outsider, powerful and powerless. His fascination in continuing to listen to a story not meant for him actualizes what Julia fears: that someone other than herself will be able to control her life. In gender-specific terms, he actualizes the difficulty that Julia has experienced in seizing her female identity away from the domination of males. Sissela Bok has suggested that there are "powerful motives behind the attraction of secrets": "the desire to gain control, to feel superior to those not in possession of the secrets, and the longing for the sheer enjoyment and intimacy that learning secrets can bring." Thus, the man's promise to keep Julia's secret safe suggests another transference of her power over self; but because the man remains an unknown quantity that could be good, bad, or indifferent, he is connected to Julia in that "the sense of the mysterious and the unfathomable in human beings bespeaks the recognition that

49. Virginia Woolf, *A Room of One's Own* (New York, 1957), 350; Judith Kegan Gardiner, "Mind mother: psychoanalysis and feminism," in *Making a Difference: Feminist Literary Criticism*, ed. Gayle Greene and Coppélia Kahn (London, 1985), 137.

no one can be known in entirety, neither from within or from without. Some aspects will remain forever in the dark; others will be glimpsed briefly, and with all the distortions that we know, only to sink out of sight as attention moves elsewhere or is forced aside."[50]

"Freedom," the second of the stories to appear in *Young's*, further explores "the mysterious and the unfathomable in human beings," but unlike her other published works, it has a male protagonist. Moreover, it is a text suggestive of the author's self-motivation some ten years later when she dropped out of her life in New York and disappeared from any active contact with her acquaintances and friends. The three-page, double-columned story moves rapidly. A nameless protagonist simply decides one day as he is walking down "the Avenue" that he will withdraw from the life he is leading with his mistress. He makes the decision to travel and not return to the world that he has known. He interprets his decision as freedom from the woman, freedom to be himself without the influence of any woman: "he had stepped from a warm, scented place into a cold, brisk breeze. He was happy. The world had turned to silver and gold, and life again became a magical adventure. Even the placards in the shops shone with the light of paradise upon them. One caught and held his eye. Travel. . . . Yes, he would travel; lose himself in India, China, the South Seas. . . . Radiance from the most battered vehicle and the meanest pedestrian. Gladness flooded him. He was free."[51] Despite the reversal of the expected female gender identity, the situation may be read as freedom from traditional love and marriage, and the text read as a discourse on one's coming to power over convention, though the price of stepping out of the marriage plot is self-destruction.

After two years, he becomes curious about how his mistress reacted to his disappearance. She had not responded to his first telegram announcing a "prolonged business trip and an indefinite return," a fact that had annoyed him (242). When he finally decides to contact her, he discovers that she had died in childbirth on the very day that he chose to disappear. "He hated the fact that she had finished with him, rather than he with her" (242). Angry at her ability to spoil his life, first by living and then by dying, he becomes more and more deranged, until gradually "his anger and resentment retreated, leaving in their wake a gentle stir of regret and remorse"

50. Sissela Bok, *Secrets: On the Ethics of Concealment and Revelation* (New York, 1982), 34, 35.

51. Nella Imes [Allen Semi], "Freedom," *Young's Realistic Stories Magazine,* LI (April, 1926), 242 (hereafter cited parenthetically in the text).

(243). By then, however, he is completely mad. A number of images render his mental deterioration: "his mind became puppet to a disturbing tension" (242); "burrs pricking at his breaking faculties"; "heavy mental dejection . . . weighted him down"; "dragging him down into black depression"; "mental fog, thick as soot, . . . trapped him"; "the rising tide of . . . mental chaos . . . engulfing him"; "increasing mental haziness"; "thought fired his disintegrating brain" (243). He believes that she is alive and will come to him. He waits, but she does not come. Realizing that she will not come, he resolves to go to her. He opens a French door and steps out to her "—and down to the pavement a hundred feet below" (243).

While "Freedom" differs from the other Larsen Imes works in its male protagonist, it is nonetheless similar to them in its exploration of the sub-consciousness and consciousness of a troubled individual unable to identify correctly the cause of the troubles. The nameless protagonist is himself responsible for his misery and for his fate. He accepts responsibility for what he has done with his life and to the life of another, but at that very moment, he loses all touch with reality. Like Helga Crane in *Quicksand,* he assumes that a change of location, a spatial relocation, will somehow solve the unrest within him. Like Irene Redfield in *Passing,* he transfers the cause of his unhappiness and distress to another person, whom he blames for his disappointment with himself and his life.

In "Freedom," Larsen Imes uses the seasons, just as she does in *Quicksand,* to suggest the impact of time upon the individual's interior self. Spring is the moment of freedom and the fateful decision; autumn is the time for awaiting the arrival of the dead mistress. Her techniques in the story are those of a modern writer: interior and narrated monologues. Her concern is with mental states and thought processes, especially as they become disturbed. The story takes place entirely within the mind of the man; there is no dialogue at all. Similarly, in *Passing* most of the significant sections take place within the consciousness of Irene Redfield, whose thoughts project the action forward. Larsen Imes reconstituted the imagery used to describe the protagonist's mental deterioration in the "quicksand" motif that charts Helga Crane's downward spiral. The window as a solution to the man's plight anticipates the open window at the end of *Passing,* which is also a convenient solution to Clare Kendry's problem, as well as to Irene's. Death becomes a way out for the man, just as it is a way out of the narrative complications for Irene and Clare. "Freedom" even more than "The Wrong Man" previews the metaphorical and psychological dimensions that would appear in the novels. Larsen Imes seems to have known intuitively that "the truth of metaphysical desire is death," as René Girard has said: "This is the inevitable end of the contradiction on which that desire is based."[52]

The aspect of the story that is the most suggestive, however, does not have to do with the treatment of death or with Larsen Imes's later fictional characters, but rather with the author herself. That she could conceive of an individual's so arbitrarily and easily walking away from a dissatisfying life and taking up a new one without anyone's interfering or discovering may suggest an analogue to her own life, particularly to her individual past immediately preceding her entrance into Lincoln and her familial past centering on her father, Peter Larson. Larsen Imes's attraction to the idea is clear. The same theme is apparent in her first story, "The Wrong Man," in which the main character also walks away from a former life. She reiterates it during the 1930s in her literal duplication of the fiction's central act.

The basic situation is one appearing often in literature, and it has tantalized American authors in particular: the person who simply chooses to disappear without a trace, yet is obsessed with the impact of his or her disappearance on those left behind.[53] Nathaniel Hawthorne uses the idea in "Wakefield," which Larsen Imes knew from his *Twice-Told Tales* (1837). In this story of a man who for twenty years lives one block away from home and daily observes his wife and house, Hawthorne focuses on human egotism, but he also includes the themes of secrecy and mystery in human motivation. "Wakefield" concludes, "Amid the seeming confusion of our mysterious world, individuals are so nicely adjusted to a system, and systems to one another, and to a whole, that by stepping aside for a moment, a man exposes himself to a fearful risk of loosing his place forever."[54]

Although neither Larsen Imes nor any other author using this theme has suggested that the life of the enigmatic person, alone and alienated from the past, is happy or easy, she represents the decision to step outside of systems, to lead an isolated life, as a spontaneous one that brings with it a certain sense of freedom and, perhaps more important, of absolute control over one's own life and sphere. The empowerment may be negative in the end,

52. Girard, *Deceit, Desire, and the Novel,* 282.

53. With the assistance of generous colleagues at the University of North Carolina, Chapel Hill, I compiled a list of about forty instances of this theme in British and American literatures. The texts included those by authors such as Chaucer, Shakespeare, Milton, Dickens, Hardy, Joyce, Washington Irving, Hawthorne, Mark Twain, Raymond Chandler, Faulkner, Hemingway, Cather, Ralph Ellison, and Richard Wright.

54. Nathaniel Hawthorne, *Twice-Told Tales,* Centenary Edition of the Works of Nathaniel Hawthorne, IX (Columbus, 1974), 140.

but it is a clearly stated personal or individual good in this text. However, as she reveals in her two short texts, the past has a way of reasserting itself into the present—either in the form of memories ("Freedom") that can lead to psychosis or in the form of a person ("The Wrong Man") who reappears with knowledge of the past and as an embodiment of that abandoned past.

Perhaps equally as suggestive is the correlation between this theme and the idea of passing that engaged African-American people both in their creative fiction and in their actual lives during the Renaissance. James Weldon Johnson's *Autobiography of an Ex-Coloured Man* presents the life of a black man who passes for white and who ultimately contemplates with some regret the race and heritage he has left behind. Although he does not return to his race, Johnson's protagonist is comparable to others, such as Walter White's Mimi (*Flight*), in the literature of passing; these "passers" continue to view the African-American world from their vantage point in the white one. For the most part, the passing character in the fiction returns to the black race in the end. However, in real life, African Americans who crossed the color line most often did not return. At the end of the 1920s, one headline in the Pittsburgh *Courier* informed readers, "There are 20,000 Persons 'Passing' Says Noted Author." White himself relates in the opening chapter of his autobiography how "every year approximately twelve thousand white-skinned Negroes disappear."[55] While there is probably no way to document such claims, it seems certain that the vast majority of those who crossed into the white world remained there.

This theme may have been fascinating to Larsen because her father quite possibly had been passing. But beyond the possible speculations, the verifiable facts in his case are suggestive. Like the character in "Freedom," Peter Larson did walk away from the multiracial, multi-ethnic world of his State Street neighborhood, and immediately upon moving into an all-white, mainly Anglo-Saxon neighborhood, he changed the spelling of his name, listed himself by his first initial in the telephone directory, and sent his brown daughter away to a black school in the South. Larsen Imes may well have been projecting her own secret wish for Peter Larson/Larsen when she has her character long for the woman he has abandoned and die as he tries to join her again, but only after he has already been thoroughly destroyed by guilt. Alternatively, if the protagonist is a representation of Larsen Imes herself, then the fictional events suggest that she may have wanted to disappear into the white world, as did her family, but that she could find no viable route to do so. The situational contexts suggest that, though sub-merged, the central figures from Larsen Imes's familial past were not erased from her memory.

Larsen Imes's two stories in *Young's,* read intertextually with her other published fiction, reveal the integral relationship between landscapes and mental processes, between physical shapes and boundaries and human man-ners and styles, between racial and economic structures. The texts are dis-courses on the attempt to comprehend the agony felt by a victim of irra-tional fears that, while irrational, nonetheless emanate from a secret reality harbored by the individual. The actual or threatened disclosure of that se-cret, or of the attitudes necessitating it, results in a fragmentation of the personality and an assault on the identity created or assumed by the indi-vidual. Secrecy and silence or the failure to communicate block all avenues of exchange and escape in the stories and consequently frustrate all possibil-ity for meaning and control.

Implicit in both stories, too, is the domination that men have or seek over women. The victimization of women is indicated by the protagonist's aban-doning his mistress in "Freedom," just as it is by the power that Ralph Tyler, Jim Romley, and the unnamed man have over Julia in "The Wrong Man." In the two texts, there is the recognition of male privilege, especially in the treatment in "The Wrong Man," with its portrayal of the class and educa-tion of the men and their shared experience of privileged lives. In both sto-ries, the female is precariously at the mercy of such men, who seem unaware of the harmful extent of their power. For Julia it is not merely Ralph (lover) or Jim (husband), but also the unnamed stranger (any man or everyman) in the shadows to whom she confesses her secret. For the unidentified mistress in "Freedom," it is not only her impulsive lover who abandons her just as she is about to give birth, but it is also the larger patriarchal society that would, had she lived, excise her from the bonds of respectability.

Perhaps most telling is the absence in the fiction of parental attention to the child. Julia's parents and family life are part of the hidden past. Their role in contributing to or preventing her being left homeless and on the streets is missing from the narrative. Similarly, in "Freedom," the death of the mistress in childbirth occurs with no prior indication that the woman was pregnant at the time of the narrator's disappearance. His concern, once he makes the discovery of her death, is with himself and his dead mistress, but not at all with the child, whose fate remains unknown. Both stories are silent on the mother's role in the nurturing of the child. There is no repre-sentation of the expected ties between mother and offspring.

Larsen Imes's novels follow the same strategy. *Quicksand* expresses anger toward the mother and to a lesser extent the father, who becomes part of Helga's reconciliation with self and race when she chooses to leave Denmark for Harlem. *Passing* attends briefly to fathers, both Irene's and Clare's, as a way of contrasting their childhoods, but mothers do not figure in their development, except by inference; that is, neither mother exerts a shaping influence or model for the daughter, and both disappear from the narrative without any suggestion of female or maternal bonding. In writing the script of the absent mother, Larsen Imes embedded her personal history and her unresolved responses to that history. Her texts conform to an aspect of women's fiction in the 1920s that, as Marianne Hirsch has observed, "is as though the narrative of the mother-daughter attachment can only be extrapolated from the later father-daughter bond, even though its impact is at least equally powerful."[56]

"The Wrong Man" and "Freedom" were not the only short stories Larsen Imes wrote during her apprenticeship. She wrote at least two others, "Tea" and "Charity." "Tea," whose title probably alluded to a poem by Wallace Stevens that Van Vechten used in *Nigger Heaven*, may have been published in 1926, as Dorothy Peterson mentioned in supporting Larsen Imes's 1929 Harmon nomination. If "Tea" appeared in print in 1926, then it did so pseudonymously, though not in *Young's*. Larsen Imes herself later cited only the two stories in *Young's* among her published works, but she listed the writing of short stories and book reviews among her current activities.[57] "Charity" was unpublished as of 1929, and probably remained so. Neither text has surfaced. During her lifetime, few ever knew that she had written or published short stories. She wanted to be known as a serious writer, as a *novelist*.

Between the January and April, 1926, publication of "The Wrong Man" and "Freedom," Larsen Imes had been busy with more than additional short stories. She had begun to work on her first novel. While the preliminary work may actually have started as early as 1922, when Fauset and White began their novels, it did not begin to occupy most of her attention until January, 1926, when she took a leave of absence from her job. By then the

56. Marianne Hirsch, *The Mother/Daughter Plot: Narrative, Psychoanalysis, Feminism* (Bloomington, 1989), 100.

57. Dorothy R. Peterson, Confidential statement, August 10, 1929, in HFR, Recommendations folder—1929 Literature Awards; Larsen Imes, Guggenheim application, November, 1929, in Guggenheim Foundation files.

book most likely had already taken shape. Literary gossip was a main topic of conversation in her circle, especially after the May 1 Urban League dinner announcing the winners of *Opportunity*'s second literary contest. Larsen Imes had not entered the competition, but Zora Hurston, Wallace Thurman, Arna Bontemps, Frank Horne, Gwendolyn Bennett and Claude McKay (both sending submissions from France), Jessie Fauset's brother Arthur Huff, and Rudolph Fisher's sister Pearl all had won prizes or honorable mentions. Even Dorothy Peterson had appeared in the April issue of *Opportunity* with a book review of Alberto Insua's *El Negro Que Tenía la Alma Blanca (The Black Man Who Had a White Soul)*.[58] Larsen Imes may have felt left out of the literary chitchat and leaked the news of her novel. By summer, word of the novel was out.

Van Vechten, who had not been informed and thought he ought to be, inquired in June about the rumor and offered his assistance. Larsen Imes's response was somewhat coy: "How do these things get about? It is the awful Truth. But, who knows if I'll ever get through with the damned thing. Certainly not I." As a protective measure, she assumed a nonchalant poise: "the thing might turn out to be utter rot. . . . When I first started, I honestly thought it was really good; now, something more than halfway, I'm afraid it's frightfully bad." As a way of protecting herself from criticism should the work indeed turn out to be "bad," she added: "I'm getting rather bored with it. I wonder how many half finished novels there are knocking about the world."[59]

While claiming that she was only halfway through, she showed that she had obviously given the publication of the novel serious thought, so much so that she presented Van Vechten with her options for publishing it. Albert and Charles Boni had a contest going to attract manuscripts from African-American writers, but the rumor was that they were getting nothing worth publishing. Even their thousand-dollar prize did not tempt her to become "merely the best of a bad lot," especially since "anything literate is sure to be awarded the honor."[60] In fact, half of literate Harlem seemed to be writing novels, even the poets. Bontemps, who had just won *Opportunity*'s Alexander Pushkin Prize for "Golgotha Is a Mountain," was at work on his

---

58. "Contest Awards," *Opportunity*, IV (May, 1926), 156–57; Dorothy R. Peterson, Review of *El Negro Que Tenía La Alma Blanca*, by Alberto Insua, in *Opportunity*, IV (April, 1926), 132–33.

59. Nella Imes to Carl Van Vechten, Wednesday [postmarked July 1, 1926], in JWJ.

60. *Ibid*. See also Nella Imes to Carl Van Vechten, Wednesday 21st [postmarked July 21, 1926], in JWJ.

first novel, "Chariot in the Clouds." Langston Hughes was planning his first book of prose already entitled "Scarlet Flowers: The Autobiography of a Young Poet." Dorothy Peterson was also writing a novel while teaching high school, but she would not complete and begin to show it for another two years.[61]

Larsen Imes liked the quality of Knopf's books much better than Boni's, but his reputation for having turned down Fauset's *There Is Confusion* made her wary. He was, she said, "very hard to please, (see Mr. Llewelyn Powys and hear Miss Jessie Fauset)." Knopf, who was determined to build a reputable, and important, publishing house, had also rejected Powys' manuscript. Larsen Imes bolstered her confidence by reminding herself that "good makeups deserve good books." Three weeks later she would close the matter of a publisher: "I have definitely decided against the Bonis, even if Knopf wont have me. In that case, I think I'll try The Viking Press." She had returned to the measured optimism about her chances expressed in her initial response to Van Vechten. "Perhaps, it may be good enough for Knopf," she concluded. "Certainly you would know, if anybody."[62] With that, she ended her debate with herself, and having sufficiently raised Van Vechten's curiosity about her work, she accepted his offer to read her novel in progress. At the same time, by flattering "a trusting soul," as she labeled Van Vechten in their exchanges about the manuscript, she successfully manipulated him into a determination to help her. Larsen Imes understood well the power of white males in the New York literary establishment, and she knew that as a female and a woman of color in search of a major publisher, she needed support from within their ranks.

61. Bontemps, interview with Shockley; Langston Hughes to Walter White, October 29, 1925, Walter White to Langston Hughes, December 15, 1925, and Langston Hughes to Walter White, December 17, 1925, all in WW, NAACP;. on Peterson's novel, see Harold Jackman to Countee Cullen, Thursday, December 13, 1928, in CCC, and also Kerman and Eldridge, *The Lives of Jean Toomer*, 366.

62. Imes to Van Vechten, Wednesday [postmarked July 1, 1926], and Nella Imes to Carl Van Vechten, December 7, 1926, both in JWJ; Imes to Van Vechten, Wednesday 21st [postmarked July 21, 1926], *ibid.*; Imes to Van Vechten, Wednesday [postmarked July 1, 1926], *ibid.*

An early photograph of Nellie Larsen, taken during her high school
studies at the Fisk Normal School, 1908.
Courtesy Moorland-Spingarn Research Center, Howard University

Lincoln School of Nurses graduating class of 1915. Nella Larsen
is second from the left on the front row.
*Courtesy Photographs and Prints Division, Schomburg Center for Research in Black Culture,
The New York Public Library, Astor, Lenox and Tilden Foundations*

This 1928 photograph of Nella Larsen was taken by James Allen for publicity for
Quicksand and was submitted with her 1928 Harmon Awards nomination.
Library of Congress

Nella Larsen Imes, *ca.* 1930, after winning a Guggenheim travel and study grant.
*Photograph by Pinchot Studio. Courtesy Yale Collection of American Literature, Beinecke
Rare Book and Manuscript Library, Yale University*

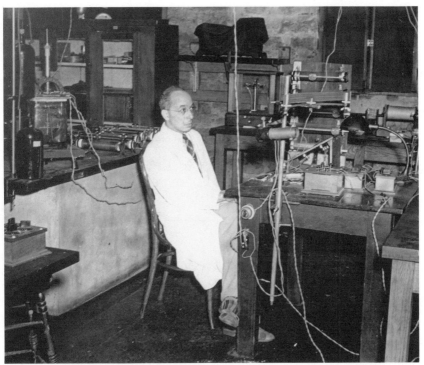

Elmer S. Imes in his physics laboratory at Fisk University, *ca.* 1935.
Courtesy Special Collections, Fisk University Library

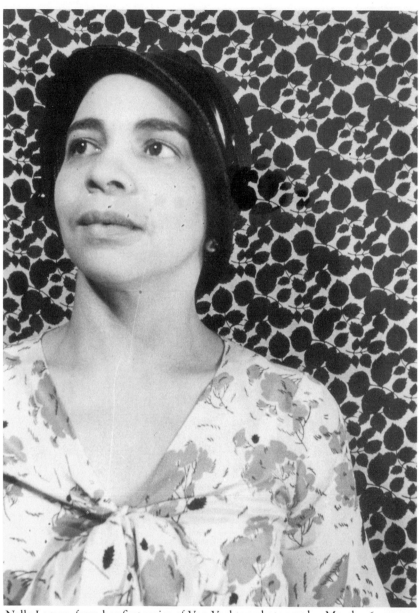

Nella Larsen, from her first series of Van Vechten photographs, March 26, 1932. *Photograph by Carl Van Vechten. Courtesy Estate of Carl Van Vechten, Joseph Solomon, Executor, and Yale Collection of American Literature, Beinecke Rare Book and Manuscript Library, Yale University*

Nella Larsen, August 17, 1932, prior to her departure for Nashville.
Photograph by Carl Van Vechten. Courtesy Estate of Carl Van Vechten, Joseph Solomon, Executor, and Yale Collection of American Literature, Beinecke Rare Book and Manuscript Library, Yale University

Dorothy Peterson, Nella Larsen, and Sidney Peterson, August 17, 1932.
*Photograph by Carl Van Vechten. Courtesy Estate of Carl Van Vechten, Joseph Solomon,
Executor, and Yale Collection of American Literature, Beinecke Rare Book and Manuscript
Library, Yale University*

Sidney and Dorothy Peterson, July 11, 1937.
Photograph by Carl Van Vechten. Courtesy Estate of Carl Van Vechten, Joseph Solomon,
Executor, and Yale Collection of American Literature, Beinecke Rare Book and Manuscript
Library, Yale University

Front and back views of Nella Larsen's 1928 Harmon Awards
Bronze Medal in Literature.
*Photographs by Keith E. Jacobson. Copyright 1993 by Keith E. Jacobson.
Used with permission*

Nella Larsen, November 23, 1934, after her divorce, in her last
Van Vechten photography session.
*Photograph by Carl Van Vechten. Courtesy Estate of Carl Van Vechten, Joseph Solomon,
Executor, and Yale Collection of American Literature, Beinecke Rare Book and Manuscript
Library, Yale University*

8

Moving to the Renaissance,
1926–1927

THE SUMMER OF 1926 was the beginning of the most remarkable period of Nella Larsen Imes's public life. After leaving her job with the public library, she began tentatively to prepare a place for herself among the African-American artists who had seen her initially as little more than a socially respectable, well-read matron with literary inclinations. The major publications of the first wave of the Renaissance, the Harlem issue of *Survey Graphic* and the *New Negro* anthology (both 1925), had contained no mention of her. Nor had her name appeared in the pages of *Opportunity* or *Crisis*. But her interest in literature had not gone unnoticed, especially by Jessie Fauset before her departure for Europe. Walter White in Harlem and Carl Van Vechten downtown became her mentors, while Dorothy Peterson became her best personal supporter. In different ways, all three encouraged her and understood her determination to become a novelist.

At the same time, White, Van Vechten, and Peterson began to consider her a fixture in the burgeoning social life on both sides of 110th Street that accompanied the literary renaissance. While the three had distinctly different personalities and styles, all shared an outgoing temperament that complemented Larsen Imes's reserve. White had established himself as a novelist along with his responsibilities at the NAACP, and that combination, abetted by his thorough enjoyment of power-brokering, quickly made him a leader in promoting African-American artists and their work. Van Vechten, a popular journalist whose career as a novelist had skyrocketed, immersed himself in black music, theater, and literature, as well as in Harlem's night life, so much so that his own residence at 150 West Fifty-fifth Street had become an outpost in white Manhattan for black artists and their down-town supporters. Peterson, who generated boundless energy and friendships across class and racial lines, had kept the interracial salon going in her upper-class Brooklyn home and fostered, through her involvement with Gurdjieff, extensive connections with the dance, theater, and arts people who lived in the Greenwich Village area. These three fed Larsen Imes's ambition to become a novelist and increased her circle of acquaintances among black and white writers, publishers, journalists, singers, and diverse other practitioners and patrons of the arts. They provided a degree of intimacy in friendship that she had not previously enjoyed.

Female friendship with Peterson allowed expression not only of her hopes and dreams, but also of her fears, reservations, and emotions that the males might misinterpret as failings. Their bond, inspired by Peterson's zest for life and her attentive personality, loosened Larsen Imes's reserve. Her reticence, habitual in social gatherings, disappeared in Peterson's company.[1] As much sister as friend, Peterson evoked the desire for familial bonds that the Larsens had denied Nella.

With the self-affirmation of friendships, Larsen Imes began to thrive on activity. She and Elmer Imes still resided in Jersey City but gravitated toward New York, where Harlem, invaded by blacks from the South and whites from downtown, was becoming a cultural center for African-American life. They would drive into the city in their fashionable car, collect their nondriving urban friends, and spend evenings at Lillian and Ernest Alexander's soirées, Grace and James Weldon Johnson's gumbo suppers, Gladys and Walter White's mixers, Dorothy and Jimmie Harris' parties, the new Savoy Ballroom, or popular clubs and shows. Or they would entertain at home and have one of their city friends pick up their guests for the drive over to New Jersey. While Elmer seemed to take their comings and goings in stride, Nella savored every nuance. "This is to say," she wrote to Van Vechten, who had been invited for one of their dinners, "that Dr. Smith, (Alonzo De G. Smith—isn't that gorgeous?) will call for you Sunday at about six o'clock—of Standard time,—to bring you over. I believe you have met him, at the first N. A. A. C. P. Dance you attended." Logistics, however, prevented the Imeses from entertaining regularly, and finances limited their efforts to a small scale. Notwithstanding these minor irritations, Larsen Imes was thrilled about her role in these gay times, as she observed of her life during an especially busy season: "for the past month it has seemed always

1. Richard Bruce Nugent, interview with author, April 30, 1983; see also Adelaide Cromwell Hill, Introduction to *Quicksand*, by Nella Larsen (1928; rpr. New York, 1971), 15.

to be tea time, as the immortal Alice remarked, with never time to wash the dishes between whiles."[2]

During the summer of 1926, she ensured the assistance not only of Van Vechten with her novel, but also of Walter White, whose second novel, *Flight* (1926), had not received the expected superlative review in the pages of *Opportunity*. Larsen would soon be drawn into the controversy over the merits of White's novel because of her friendship with White and her interest in his subject. *Flight* told the story of a New Orleans Creole of color, Mimi Daquin, attempting to find a place for herself in a racially segregated society. Her search takes her into Atlanta's black bourgeoisie and Harlem's social scene, as well as into the white world when she passes across the color line before eventually returning to her race.

Frank Horne, in reviewing the novel, focused on the "glaring fault," the inadequate development and motivation of the heroine, who "never becomes activated by the warm breath of life," and on the unconvincing ending, which "strikes a hollow, blatant note": "She leaves a white world, with all its advantages of body and spirit, a position of eminence which she has developed out of the soul-sweat of her spirit, to go back to 'her people.' How then to be received?—how to adjust to a lower, cramped scale of life that had become so full?—how to compensate for the intense freedom of 'being white?' Truly, has Mimi been left in the lurch." Horne also found White's style generally wanting in "clarity" and in "sentence structure" and his writing "inept" and "blighted by inadequate expressions and purile vocabulary," as well as by "ludicrously overdrawn and quaintly inapt" similes.[3]

White was furious. He had become a friend of Sinclair Lewis, and had received Lewis' help in refining *Flight* and his endorsement of the final product. Convinced, then, that the novel was stronger than *Fire in the Flint*, White resented the audacity of the young writer who had failed to appreciate its merits:

> Mr. Horne is a likeable and intelligent young man but his review . . .
> indicates clearly that he has no conception of the broad aspects of my
> novel. I confess it is a bit discouraging when one of the few reputable
> journals published by Negroes permits a story which has taken many

2. Nella Imes to Carl Van Vechten, Friday [*ca.* 1925–26], in CVV; Nella Imes to Carl Van Vechten, Monday [*ca.* 1925–26], *ibid.*

3. Frank Horne, "Our Book Shelf," *Opportunity*, IV (July, 1926), 227. See also Edward E. Waldron, *Walter White and the Harlem Renaissance* (Port Washington, N.Y., 1978), 100–107.

months of hard work to create to be reviewed by one who fails to understand it. There is an unfortunate tendency among some of those who call themselves new Negroes to use criticism as a means of demonstrating how "brave" and "unfettered" they are.

His protest to Charles S. Johnson, the editor of *Opportunity*, concluded pointedly: "It would be an unfortunate thing . . . if criticism by colored critics of stories written by colored writers should descend into a mere exposition of smartness." Johnson's response was cordial, but not sympathetic. "Really, we have so few novels and novelists, that one wishes to be most careful in getting honest, as well as stimulating appraisals."[4]

After prompting from an insistent White, who wrote a second letter and most likely exerted the influence of his position at the NAACP, Johnson arranged for Larsen Imes to answer the negative criticism. Attempting to be conciliatory, he informed White of the decision on August 5. "Contrary to the feeling expressed in your letter of July 28th, there is more that can be done about your novel, FLIGHT, the review of which you felt missed the important aspects of the theme." He particularly wanted to avoid any appearance of rivalry between the NAACP and its *Crisis* magazine and the Urban League and its *Opportunity*. Recognizing both that White as an NAACP official was one of the most visible men of color in the United States and that the literary movement that *Opportunity* had helped spur was still in its infancy, he tried to dispel any hint of bias: "Really, I am inclined to go to the extreme in this instance—to be certain of being fair in a situation which could so easily be misunderstood." His solution was, in effect, a victory for White: "I have solicited already from one person a rather full expression of the point of view which I think you would regard as being fully in sympathy with the spirit of the book, and I intend to publish this as a letter apropos of the review and in our Book Section. The person is Mrs. Nella Imes, who writes well and has a most extraordinarily wide acquaintance with past and current literature."[5] Although he touted Larsen Imes's qualifications, Johnson knew of her friendship with White. He may even have been given her name by someone acting behind the scenes and at White's suggestion.

On August 11, 1926, Larsen Imes sent White a carbon of her letter in

4. Walter White to Charles S. Johnson, July 6, 1926, in WW, NAACP; Charles S. Johnson to Walter White, July 22, 1926, *ibid.*

5. Charles S. Johnson to Walter White, August 5, 1926, *ibid.*; see also Walter White to Charles S. Johnson, July 28, 1926, *ibid.*

response to the review. Dating the accompanying note "Tuesday, Twelfth," she observed, "I see I've got the date wrong, but no matter. A little fast." She had quickly responded to what must have been a personal request not merely from Johnson but from White: "Here it is. The carbon is awfully messy, but I'm not a typist. I hope you can read it. I have not said all that I wanted to, nor what I have said as effectively as I would like."[6] The enclosed carbon was in fact very "messy."

In formulating the response and in typing it herself, she set the stage for two phases of White's assistance with her own manuscript-in-progress: his reading her work and his securing a secretary to type it. On August 16, White acknowledged receipt of the copy of Larsen Imes's letter in a short note of appreciation: "I am eternally grateful to you. It is a magnificent answer and you understood 'Mimi' even better than I did. I shan't soon forget this generous act of yours."[7]

At the time of its composition, Larsen Imes's letter to the editor of *Opportunity* was one of the longest and most self-revelatory pieces she had written for a reading public. Her pseudonymous stories in *Young's Magazine* had not introduced her as a writer to the African-American community; in addition, her review of *Certain People of Importance* in the *Messenger* had been quite brief. Although she had taken on a better-known young writer in the foremost African-American literary organization, she indicated something of her anxiety about the letter by signing her carbon "Allen L. Semi" (the reverse spelling of Nella L. Imes), which was her pen name for the publication of her stories.

The letter appeared in the Correspondence section of the September issue. Two of her introductory paragraphs were dropped; in these she situated herself in the critical discourse:

> I pass over your reviewer's main reason for exasperation with "Flight," the fact that he had hoped some day to write a novel on this subject, because it is not at all pertinent to the review. A bit naive, of course, and usually "not done," but still unimportant, and certainly no business of your readers.
>
> It is the blindness, not the abuse which annoys me. Though I doubt if even Mr. Stuart Sherman or Mr. Carl Van Doran, supposing they had shared your reviewer's feelings, would have treated "Flight" so

6. Nella Larsen Imes to Walter White, Tuesday, Twelfth [March, 1926], *ibid.*
7. Walter White to Nella L. Imes, August 16, 1926, *ibid.*

roughly. My quarrel with this very interesting piece of literary criticism is that seemingly your reviewer lacked the ability or the range of reading to understand the book which he attacked with so much assurance.[8]

Her defense of *Flight,* however, was an extended commentary upon the merits of White's novel, upon its relationship to modern literature, and upon Larsen Imes's own aesthetic preferences. She wondered, for instance, why Horne had chosen Louis Hémon's "passive French-Canadian girl [Maria Chapdelaine]," Edith Wharton's "trapped Mattie [Frome]," and Gustave Flaubert's "Salammbo of ancient Carthage, with whom to disparage the sensitive, rebellious, modern Mimi": "Certainly, these are for their own environment and times, excellent characters. But so is Mimi for hers. And would not Galsworthy's unsurpassable Irene Forsyte, or Jacobsen's Maria [*sic*] Grubbe have been more effective for purposes of comparison as well as for disparagement? They, like Mimi Daquin, threw away material things for the fulfillment of their spiritual destinies."[9] Larsen Imes was insisting upon the modernity of Mimi and her place among other modern heroines whose complexities she believed resulted at least in part from the environment and milieu in which they existed.

In singling out the Danish author Jens Peter Jacobsen (1847–1885), she specifically pointed not only to his novel *Marie Grubbe* (1876), a celebrated instance of an aristocratic seventeenth-century heroine who defies societal expectations of class and comfort by marrying one of her young servants when she is past forty and already divorced from three disappointing husbands, but also to the modern, scientific spirit of the novel. Jacobsen, a natural scientist who translated Darwin's *On the Origin of Species* into Danish, attended to the evolution of personality in *Marie Grubbe* and to the study of human decay in his only other novel, *Niels Lyhne* (1880). Despite his small output in fiction, Jacobsen was one of the major modernists in Denmark. "He found new methods of approach to truth and even a new manner of seeing human nature. In an age that had wearied of generalities, he emphasized the unique and the characteristic. To a generation that had ceased to accept anything because it was accepted before, he brought

8. Nella L. Imes [Allen L. Semi] to Charles S. Johnson, n.d. [August 11 or 12, 1926], *ibid.*

9. Nella Imes, "Correspondence," *Opportunity,* IV (September, 1926), 295. Subsequent quotations from Larsen Imes about *Flight* are taken from this source, unless otherwise indicated.

the new power of scientific observation in the domain of the mind and spirit." [10]

In her observations, Larsen Imes was not forwarding a deterministic view, but instead utilizing her reading of Jacobsen and her understanding of Max Planck's quantum theory (1900) and Albert Einstein's relativity theories (1905, 1916), which were essential to Elmer Imes's research on the rotational energy levels of hydrogen fluoride and on infrared spectrum bands. Her husband's work and the "new science" contributed to her interest in the randomness of human experience. No doubt her own personal and social history, which contributed to her emphasis on the present and the future, also caused her to privilege social evolutionism, thereby allowing for change, mobility, and transmutation. She was aware of the changing nature of human relationships and of the contemporary efforts in literature and science to understand human psychology and personality, especially theoretical conceptions about the relative value of both experience and events. Contesting Horne's implications in Mimi's regard, Larsen Imes denied the existence of a single spatial and chronological frame of reference.

Larsen Imes concluded that Horne's critique of the ending of *Flight* missed the "dominant note": "it is the white race, which is lost, doomed to destruction by its own mechanical gods. . . . It was this that made Mimi turn from it. Surely, the thesis of 'Flight' is 'what shall it profit a man if he gain the whole world and lose his own soul?'" In emphasizing the appropriate working out of this thesis, she observed that for Mimi "there were no advantages of the spirit in the white world, and so, spiritual things being essential to her full existence she gave up voluntarily the material advantages."

Larsen Imes also incorporated references to modern literature to support her opinion of the ending: "Judging by present day standards of fiction, the ending of 'Flight' is the perfect one, perfect in its aesthetic coloring, perfect in its subtle simplicity. For others of this type, I refer your reviewer to Sherwood Anderson's 'Dark Laughter,' to Carl Van Vechten's 'Firecrackers,' to Joseph Hergesheimer's 'Tubal Cane' [*sic*]." These references led to the final point in the printed letter: "To my mind, warped as I have confessed by the European and the American moderns, 'Flight' is a far better piece of work than 'the Fire in the Flint.' Less dramatic, it is more fastidious and required

10. Hanna A. Larsen, Introduction to *Marie Grubbe: A Lady of the Seventeenth Century*, by J. P. Jacobsen, trans. Hanna A. Larsen (New York, 1917), v.

more understanding, keener insight. Actions and words count less and the poetic conception of the character, the psychology of the scene more, than in the earlier work. 'Flight' shows a more mature artistry." Placing White's novel squarely within the modernist camp, Larsen Imes confessed that her thinking had been influenced by modern writers.

The main paragraph of her confession, however, had not found its way into the printed version. There she had written:

"How," asks your reviewer will [Mimi] "adjust on a lower cramped scale of life that had become so full, how compensate for the intense freedom of being white?" Again, I point out that her life had *not* been full, it had, perhaps been novel, but not full. And I resent that word "lower", and in a lesser degree the word "cramped". I maintain that neither is applicable to Negro life, especially among people of Mimi's class. Inner peace compensated her for the "intense freedom of being white". Some people "feel" their race [lines of corrected carbon illegible]. . . . Mr. White evidently does, and so has given us Mimi Da-quin. [lines of corrected carbon illegible] . . . now to your reviewer's complaints about the author's style. He grumbles about the lack of "clarity", "confusion of characters", "faulty sentence structure". These sins escape me in my two readings, and even after they had been so publicly pointed out, I failed to find them. Even the opening sentence, so particularly cited, still seems to me all right. But then, I have been recently reading Huysmans, Conrad, Proust, and Thomas Mann. Naturally these things would not irritate me as they would an admirer of Louis Hemon and Mrs. [Edith] Wharton. Too, there's Galsworthy, who opens his latest novel [*The White Monkey*] with a sentence of some thirty-odd words.[11]

Larsen Imes made clear in the unpublished section of her letter that her views were based upon her readings of a broad spectrum of modern works, as well as upon two readings of *Flight*. Whereas she did not praise the novel as being of the highest order in style or content (it had received, after all, mixed reviews in the New York *Times*, the London *Times*, and the *Saturday Review of Literature*), she found little grounds for the attack upon the work and the author. In fact, she suggested that Horne had "read the book hastily,

11. Imes [Allen L. Semi] to Johnson, n.d. [August 11 or 12, 1926], in WW, NAACP.

superficially, and so missed both its meaning and its charm." Her suggestion might well be a veiled reference to Flaubert's defense of *Salammbô* against the charges of historical inaccuracy and problematic fictional representations, especially his application of the methods of the modern novel to antiquity. Flaubert not only answered his major critic, the influential Charles Augustin Sainte-Beuve, with a spirited and detailed refutation but also attacked others with the observation, "You have read me so carelessly that you nearly always misquote me." [12] Larsen Imes takes a similar strategy at the end of her letter.

While Johnson may have extended himself in order to be fair to White and *Flight,* he did not let the matter end with Larsen Imes's letter. The next month he published Frank Horne's rebuttal, which was longer than either the original review or Larsen Imes's response. The piece was an attack not only on the novel, but on Larsen Imes's "brilliantly illogical" answer: "She falls headlong into a similar pathetic fallacy with the novel she so zealously defends, in that she, too, mistakes the *intention* for the accomplishment, the *conception* for the expression." Horne took Larsen Imes to task for her conception of "modern." "Is not Hamlet 'modern'?" he railed before concluding: "Mrs. Imes is surely aware that there is no such thing in the kingdom of art as 'times' and 'environment.' Not only is a thing of beauty a joy forever, but a character simply, powerfully and beautifully alive is forever modern." Horne was arguing at cross purposes. Unaware that Larsen Imes was evoking the new relativity theory from contemporary science and attempting to apply it to fiction, he could not concede her point about modernity and, therefore, insisted upon what he called "neither . . . chronology nor pigmentation, but . . . the eternal verity of art" in whose "intense and glaring light, *Flight* is a poor book." He remained "quite incorrigible," as he stated in concluding: "I firmly attest that Mr. White is a jolly fine fellow, but I as vehemently insist that he had not written a jolly fine book." [13]

Although Larsen Imes had nothing more to offer in public about the critical controversy, White was furious enough to write his own letter for publication in *Opportunity.* It was December before his combative piece appeared, stretching the controversy out over a six-month period and *Flight* into four issues of *Opportunity* (the latter Johnson duly noted in his letter of October 16 acknowledging his intention to publish White's letter). While

12. Gustave Flaubert to M. Froehner, January 21, 1862, quoted in Appendix to *Salammbô,* by Flaubert (1862; rpr. New York, 1919), 387.
13. Frank Horne, "Correspondence," *Opportunity,* IV (October, 1926), 326.

the entire exchange had been unprecedented in the African-American press, White's response as an author was unheard of, a point about which he was well aware:

> I think it is a swell idea to have Mrs. Imes and Mr. Horne disagreeing *in print* over the merits or lack of them in my novel. Most human beings buy a particular brand of soap or garters or cheese because they constantly see advertisements of that brand and not so much because other brands are inferior. The same rule applies largely to books. That is the reason why most authors (including the author of "Flight") prefer treatments of their work in this order: first favorable reviews; second, unfavorable notices; third and most distasteful of all, a damning silence. To help avoid the latter is partly the reason for this letter.

What he actually wanted to do, however, was to chastise Horne for his grammatical errors, his misreading, and his immaturity, the point on which he ended his letter: "Perhaps in a few years from now, Mr. Horne will not speak with quite the assured air of a combination Anatole France and H. L. Mencken."[14]

For her part, Larsen Imes had achieved what she set out to do for *Flight* and for her own reputation. Her letter had alerted a wide audience that she was knowledgeable and articulate about contemporary literature. She was now preoccupied with her novel, not with White's. Immediately after her defense of *Flight,* she turned to White for a favor in kind. She wanted him to read her manuscript. By October 1, he had barely had time to begin reading it that week, for not only was he still embroiled in the literary quarrel, but he was "burdened . . . with household duties and the role of both father and mother":

> I have only had a chance to read a part of the MS. There are one or two minor things which I think can be improved but I like the story immensely. In the one incident where your heroine talks with the school principal, you bring her sharply to life. At the same time, I think you have handled beautifully the principal. I vaguely feared that you would make him a wholly unsympathetic character and I was glad

14. Charles S. Johnson to Walter White, October 16, 1926, in WW, NAACP; Walter White to Editor of *Opportunity,* October 9, 1926, *ibid.*

that you didn't for you showed understanding and sympathy with both his and the heroine's [sic]. More later when I have had a chance to finish reading the script and to digest it.[15]

As the scene with the principal occurs in the early section of the novel, White probably had looked at the manuscript only after being prodded by Larsen Imes. Busy with his job and family, he was also planning a new book, a biographical study of famous blacks, which he had entitled "Etchings in Black" and for which he had written a two-page proposal.[16] His suggestions for minor improvements were not what Larsen Imes sought. She wanted a substantial critique of her fiction, but White was not the person for that job, at least not while he was engrossed in his defense of *Flight*.

Larsen Imes soon saw that he could be more helpful to her in other ways. Her manuscript needed typing and she clearly was not a typist. "The thing is 35,000 words," she wrote in entreating his help: "Walter, do you remember telling me that Miss Overton *might* be persuaded into doing my mss for me. You said I believe that she did such excellent work, and has had the proper experience in doing such things. (Lord knows I wish I had.) If I asked her very nicely, do you think she would do mine, which will be finished next week? I'm very anxious about this. You might tell her that I'm a *very* nice person and very helpless—excite her pity."[17]

White enlisted Carrie B. Overton, who was his secretary from December 4, 1925, to March 1, 1927, when she resigned because of her health. She agreed to type the manuscript after he played up Larsen Imes's "helplessness": "When I finished painting the picture to Mrs. Overton of you as a poor, pathetic soul, she almost burst into tears and promised me that she would write you today regarding the MSS."[18] Throughout the early fall, the manuscript was in the competent hands of an expert typist.

Larsen Imes had been busy, though less visible, on another literary front during the summer, and this one proved to be the more critical to her career aspirations. Van Vechten's novel on African-American life in Harlem, *Nigger Heaven,* came out at the end of July and immediately became the talk of all of literary Harlem. The announcement of the book in the *Mercury* as a forthcoming Knopf title earlier in the summer had already aroused dismay

15. Walter White to Nella L. Imes, October 1, 1926, *ibid.*
16. See "Proposed Book by Walter White" [1926], *ibid.*
17. Nella Imes to Walter White, Monday [November, 1926], *ibid.*
18. Walter White to Nella Imes, November 16, 1926, *ibid.*

and outrage among some African Americans, such as Du Bois and Fauset, who felt vindicated in their suspicion that Van Vechten was no friend but was instead using the gullible to exploit the race. "Go inspectin' like Van Vechten," a line in Andy Razaf's revue song "Go Harlem," contained one popular opinion of Van Vechten's excursions to Harlem. Although some, aware that his respect for people of color dated back to his childhood in Cedar Rapids, insisted that his purpose was to reduce barriers between the races, they ignored the element of voyeurism in his fascination with African Americans. For instance, he had been amazed, upon first meeting Walter White, by an African American who "speaks French and talks of Debussy and Marcel Proust in an off-hand way. An entirely new kind of Negro to me. I shall, I hope, see something of these cultured circles."[19]

No one could judge from his title what he had made of his recent observations of African-American life. Even the sardonic Elmer Imes had remarked to Nella, "'Your people' don't buy books, but that's one they are all going to buy." Larsen Imes herself admitted that "everyone [was] on tiptoe," wondering what to expect from Van Vechten after such an inflammatory title. For her part, she was convinced of Van Vechten's sincerity and altruism in the racial cause. Three of her fellow New Negro writers, Walter White, James Weldon Johnson, and Rudolph Fisher, had read the work before publication. She herself had read enough to know that the title owed something to *Prancing Nigger* (1925), the flippant American title of *Sorrow in Sunlight* (1924), a novel by the British aesthete Ronald Firbank, whose writings Van Vechten promoted in the United States.[20]

When she received a signed copy from Van Vechten at the beginning of August, she was at home anticipating "a very dreary week-end" alone because Elmer had gone to the country. Having just had a haircut that she thought make her "look like the 'wrath of god,'" Larsen Imes remained at home. She acknowledged the arrival of the book by giving Van Vechten a glimpse into her private world, a domestic environment transformed by romance fiction:

"Nigger Heaven" arrived a few minutes ago, two-thirty, to be exact. Therefore I shall have a wonderful time. I'm terribly excited. Too, almost incited to forgo the ritual which the reading of particular books

19. Carl Van Vechten to Edna Keaton, n.d. [August, 1924], in *The Letters of Carl Van Vechten*, ed. Bruce Kellner (New Haven, 1987), 69.
20. Nella Imes to Carl Van Vechten, Wednesday 21st [postmarked July 21, 1926], in JWJ.

always demands of me, a Houbigant scented bath, the donning of my best green crepe de chine pyjamas, fresh flowers on the bed side table, piles of freshly covered pillows and my nicest bed cover,—and sit right down to it. But no, impatient as I am, I shall make it a ceremony. Not to do so would be blasphemous.

. . . Thanks and other things will follow after the pleasures. Just now, everything waits but that pleasure.[21]

She was becoming a heroine of fiction, perhaps fashioned out of her own stories of a wealthy Myra Redmon or Julia Hammond Romley from "The Wrong Man" or Helga Crane in the opening of *Quicksand*. In analyzing the romance genre, Janice Radway has pointed out: "If the story's setting is contemporary, brand-name appliances, popular furniture styles, and trendy accesories . . . typically populate the heroine's apartment. . . . [The] descriptions assert tacitly that the imaginary world of the novel is as real as the reader's world because it is filled with the same, solid, teeming profusion of commodities."[22] Larsen Imes recreated the practice of romance fiction in describing her preparation for reading *Nigger Heaven*. Staged with details of commodification to spark Van Vechten's identification with the familiar yet exotic scene and with Larsen Imes as a kindred spirit in her appetite for pleasure in sumptuous surroundings in life and in fiction, Larsen Imes's scenario also invites a voyeuristic gaze into an intimate moment in a middle-class African-American woman's life. By describing the ceremony she concocted for reading, Larsen Imes emphasized not merely her sense of aesthetic pleasure and identification with romantic fiction, but also a measure of her affectations and the degree of her removal from ordinary African-American life. All this was meant to endear her to aesthete Van Vechten. In differentiating herself from racially defined others, specifically stereotyped lower-class blacks, Larsen Imes exercised her creative myth-making power over herself and over Van Vechten's image of African Americans.

Her positive response to *Nigger Heaven*, however, was not simply intended to curry favor with the author, despite the flattery of some of her remarks: "Was it you or another who told me of the shock of one of your friends because 'Carl Van Vechten knows a Negro?' Well! What will she say when she reads this sly story, with its air of deceptive simplicity and discov-

21. Nella Imes to Carl Van Vechten, Friday, Sixth [August, 1926], in CVV.

22. Janice A. Radway, *Reading the Romance: Women, Patriarchy, and Popular Literature* (Chapel Hill, 1984), 194.

ers that Carl Van Vechten knows the Negro?" The novel provoked a genuine outpouring of feelings: "I dont think that, just now, I can tell you all that I feel about this book, because I really dont know myself. . . . You see its too close, too true, as if you had undressed the lot of us and turned on a strong light. Too, I feel a kind of despair. Why, oh why, couldn't we have done something as big as this for ourselves? Fear, I suppose. It is big, big in its pity, big in its cruelties."[23]

Yet in less than a week after receiving a copy, she was able to write a thoughtful three-page letter about *Nigger Heaven:*

> It is a fine tale, this story of the deterioration and subsequent ruin of a weakling who blames all his troubles on that old scapegoat, the race problem. Dangerous too. But with what exquisite balance you have avoided the propaganda pitfall. But of course, you would. Like your Lasca Sartoris, who so superbly breasts the flood of racial prejudice (black and white).
>
> I like that. I mean your dispassionate way of simply proceeding with the tale, getting on to the tragic denouement, merely stating thus and so is the case, and leaving it at that, —in effect, if the reader is a doubting Thomas, let him draw back and be damned to hell. And yet, how forceful it is.[24]

Because she did not trust one reading, Larsen Imes had actually read the novel three times within the first week of receiving it. "The first time, I tore through it breathlessly. The second time I read it ever so carefully tasting the full savor of its fastidious styles and subtleties. . . . The last time, yesterday, I amused myself, picking out the characters and picking apart the composites." She believed that the book captured "the spirit inherent" in African Americans; nevertheless, she was "crazy to see the reviews," as she was "not so much interested in what 'your people' [whites] will say" as she was in "what the other folks [blacks] will make of it." She wondered, as well, whether they would believe Van Vechten's portraits and enjoy his story as much as she had the "marvelous . . . result of [his] imagination and instructive perception working together. The scenes, the descriptions, the conver-

23. Nella Imes to Carl Van Vechten, Wednesday, eleventh [postmarked August 12, 1926], in CVV.
24. *Ibid.*

sations are as spontaneous as life. The whole thing moves easily and surely." Her appreciation for the novel would remain firm; in the years of her own success as a novelist she counted "*Nigger Heaven* as one of the big influences on Harlem and its artistic life during the last five years."[25]

Elmer Imes, too, had read the novel quickly upon his return. He was also "very enthusiastic about it," because he thought it showed "the same understanding and keen insight as *Saïd the Fisherman*," a novel by Marmaduke Pickthall that he and his wife admired. His response surprised Larsen Imes, who had not expected him to like *Nigger Heaven*. His opinion of the novel would remain high, especially because of its moral; he praised the book anew in 1928, after reading the French edition.[26] Neither Elmer nor Nella remarked that the novel's central female character, the librarian Mary Love, was modeled on a composite of Dorothy Peterson, Jessie Fauset, and Nella Larsen Imes herself.

Larsen Imes returned to work on her own writing after completing *Nigger Heaven*. "I have gone back to my novel," she informed Van Vechten at the end of one of her long commentaries on his book. "Celebrated the return by destroying a good half of what was completed. It was awful." Her reading of his novel and the reviews of it influenced her assessment. She set to work trying to achieve both the spontaneity of *Nigger Heaven* and what she called "the mixedness of things, the savagery under the sophistication," that Van Vechten captured. In an effort to make her characters and language more authentic and evocative of the contemporary scene, she rewrote the section that dealt with Harlem. Concentrating, too, on an undogmatic approach to the scenes, she kept *Nigger Heaven* as a stylistic model.[27] Although Van Vechten had not yet seen any of the manuscript and was off to Europe in September, he had already indirectly influenced a portion of its content.

Within a few months of the publication of *Nigger Heaven*, Larsen Imes had become intimate enough with Van Vechten to use the term *niggers* freely in corresponding with him. After a visit from Rudolph and Jane Fisher, she had no qualms about repeating an in-joke: "'Bud' [Rudolph] told us that he blew in on you unexpectedly one day last week and thought that he had gotten into a house in the wrong neighborhood because 'the

25. *Ibid.*; Nella Larsen Imes to Carl Van Vechten, July 15, 1930 [postcard], in CVV.

26. Larsen Imes to Van Vechten, July 15, 1930 [postcard], in CVV; Elmer Imes to Carl Van Vechten, n.d. [postmarked March 3, 1928], in JWJ.

27. Nella Imes to Carl Van Vechten, Wednesday, 6th [1926], in CVV.

place was full of niggers.'" That Van Vechten, too, treated Larsen Imes as a confidante is suggested by her concern about concealing his letters: "Almost I had nervous prostration because in the move I thought I had lost your letters—and that possibly Elmer had found them—."[28]

Their closeness was partly in response to her steadfast loyalty to him and *Nigger Heaven,* which many African Americans, including Du Bois, had attacked for its representation of primitivism and sensationalism in Harlem. Larsen Imes had collected the reviews and saved them for Dorothy Peterson's return from Europe; in the process she had begun what was to be a hobby throughout the rest of the 1920s—"collecting Van Vechteniana," as she labeled it.[29] "Surely Nigger Heaven is the most reviewed book of this season. I've got an even dozen actual reviews and six comments. Of course, I missed some. Two, I know of. The more I think of it, the more I believe that it would make a corking good play, and be well received too. Why don't you?"[30] Her enthusiasm was boundless: "Miss Butcher should have a dinner of peacock tongues served in a plate of silver lapis"; "Hubert Harrison. Ugh! More on him another time"; "I liked Burton Rascoe's review. He did you much better than the Blind-Bow Boy in 1923. I was just re-reading his review of that."[31] "The 'Times' one *is* the best of all. Evidently a very perceptive man Mr. Clark. I must go to the library and read him up."[32] In a sense, her close following of the reviews signaled a vicarious experience of authorship and of public response to authorship.

In answer to Van Vechten's query about her response to Eric Walrond's review, she said: "Yes, I saw Eric in the S.R. [*Saturday Review*]. What was intelligible to me was awfully good and should, I think, be printed where C.P. [Colored People] will read it. But, parts of it I didn't 'get' at all; just words I thought. The same for Mr. Niles in the New Republic. In spots he seemed actually incoherent. I for one, didn't know what he was talking

---

28. Nella Imes to Carl Van Vechten, November 12, 1926, in JWJ; Nella Imes to Carl Van Vechten, Wednesday [postmarked April 6, 1927], *ibid.*

29. Nella Imes to Carl Van Vechten, Wednesday [continuation of letter, dated Monday 6th, from September, 1926], in CVV; see also Nella Larsen Imes, Author's statement for Alfred A. Knopf, Inc., November 24, 1926, in Alfred A. and Blanche Knopf Collection, Harry Ransom Humanities Research Center, University of Texas Libraries, Austin.

30. Imes to Van Vechten, Wednesday, 6th [1926], in CVV.

31. Imes to Van Vechten, Friday [*ca.* 1925–26], *ibid.* See also Bruce Kellner, *Carl Van Vechten and the Irreverent Decades* (Norman, Okla., 1968), 206–23.

32. Imes to Van Vechten, Wednesday [continuation of Monday 6th, from September, 1926], in CVV.

about and wondered if he did." In this same letter, she revealed the extent to which Elmer Imes, too, was involved in following the debate over the novel:

> Miss Ovington's review is exactly what's needed. She hit the nail pretty squarely on the head when she told us to read a bit further. (Elmer and I laughed together over her statements that she was unfamiliar with some of the words in the glossary. How shocking, if she were not.)
>
> And your letter was the first intimation that Elmer had, that Heebie Jeebies wasn't some kind of itch. After my explanation and description of the rag he said, "Well, I was right. It is an eruption." [33]

Not surprisingly, given their flattery, both Nella and Elmer Imes were counted among Van Vechten's favored African-American friends by fall. Elmer even instructed his wife, who did most of the corresponding, to mail Van Vechten some of his writings: "A week ago Elmer went off to an engineering conference leaving instructions to send you some of his things. Well, interesting as it is, I put it off until I could find Eneas Africanus, which I think is even more interesting than my husband's writings. What I am sending is the most understandable thing we have in the house. Perhaps there are more in the laboratory. I enclose the letters because they give a clearer idea of what his work really is." [34]

While Larsen Imes was cementing her friendship with Van Vechten downtown, she was aware of a collaboration uptown that resulted in the November appearance of *Fire!!: A Quarterly Devoted to the Younger Negro Artists*. The little magazine seemed an auspicious beginning of new literary endeavors that would provide even more opportunities for the growing number of black writers. Edited by Wallace Thurman and named after a composition by Langston Hughes, *Fire!!* took issue with the rather staid and conservative bent of the older generation of black literati. The magazine was intended, Hughes later recalled, to "burn up a lot of the old, dead conventional Negro-white ideas of the past, *épater le bourgeois* into a realization of the existence of the younger Negro writers and artists, and provide . . . an outlet for publication not available in the limited pages of . . .

33. Imes to Van Vechten, Wednesday, 6th [1926], *ibid.*
34. Nella Imes to Carl Van Vechten, Monday 6th [1926], *ibid.*

the *Crisis, Opportunity,* and the *Messenger*—the first two being house organs of inter-racial organizations, and the latter being God knows what." [35]

In a sense, Hughes, Thurman, and their associates in the production and editing—Gwendolyn Bennett, Richard Bruce (Nugent), Zora Neale Hurston, Aaron Douglas, and John Davis—were attempting to actualize Hughes's declaration in "The Negro Artist and the Racial Mountain," printed in June by the *Nation:* "we younger Negro artists who create now intend to express our individual dark-skinned selves without fear or shame. If white people are pleased we are glad. If they are not, it doesn't matter. We know we are beautiful. And ugly too. The tom-tom cries and the tom-tom laughs. If colored people are pleased we are glad. If they are not, their displeasure doesn't matter either. We build our temples for tomorrow, strong as we know how, and we stand on top of the mountain, free within ourselves." Hughes's insistence on the autonomy of a racial art took into account the realities for the black writer. As he wrote, "The road for the serious black artist, then, who would produce a racial art is almost certainly rocky and the mountain high. Until recently he received almost no encouragement for his work from either white or colored people." [36]

Among the nine patrons for the first issue were three of Larsen Imes's then-close associates: Dorothy Hunt Harris, Dorothy Peterson, and Van Vechten. While Larsen Imes was sympathetic to the quarterly's objectives, she had been out of work since January and lacked the money to act as a patron. She and her husband lived always slightly on the edge of being financially overextended.

Although she knew all of those involved with the actual writing and editorial work, she was not particularly close to any of them. In fact, the young writers, Thurman, Hughes, Bennett, Hurston, and Nugent in particular, were all not only very much younger than Larsen, but also much more bohemian than she. Even Arthur Huff Fauset, Jessie's brother, issued in *Fire!!* a scathing commentary on the "Intelligentsia," which he accused of "sophisticated bigotry," "snobbish sycophantish high-brown hero-worshipp[ing]," and "reading H. L. M. [Mencken] and George Jean Nathan, know[ing] . . . Freud from cover to cover," but being "more adept at discovering pig pens than they are at digging for pearls." Without specific reference to anyone by name, Fauset's attack was clearly linked to the same African Americans

35. Langston Hughes, *The Big Sea* (1940; rpr. New York, 1986), 385–86.
36. Langston Hughes, "The Negro Artist and the Racial Mountain," *Nation,* CXXII (June 28, 1926), 694.

whom Thurman, in "Fire Burns a Department of Comments," lambasted for their reactions to *Nigger Heaven:* "This so-called intelligentsia of Harlem has exposed its inherent stupidity."[37] While Larsen Imes saw herself as a "modern," irreverent and unconventional, she had not yet established herself as a writer and would not take the risks of a Thurman or Fauset.

Her identity was still largely tied to that of her older husband and the more conservative, striving black middle class, even though she frequently made her Imes in-laws and the middle class the targets of her wit. A few weeks before *Fire!!* appeared, she had remarked her return from "a tiresome visit in Philadelphia among the ultra-religious," by which she referred to her husband's family and the friends of his brother the Reverend William Lloyd Imes, and she had commented on the "pathetically amusing" attitudes of the racial uplift workers, such as those of the NAACP.[38]

Despite her insouciance (expressed privately to the white Van Vechten), Larsen Imes sought a social acceptance and prominence among African Americans that the new breed at *Fire!!* could not forward but might well impede. Besides, she was not comfortable with the masses of black people, especially lower, working-class folk whom the *Fire!!* editors tended to celebrate. Her reluctance to have the name that she had worked hard to achieve associated with the brave little magazine ironically accounts in part for her failure to emerge, during the heightened Renaissance activities of 1926 and 1927, as one of the better-known new literary talents. Although the staff members of *Fire!!* produced only a single issue before the journal folded from lack of funds, they made a name for themselves. Even those who had previously published little, such as Bennett and Nugent, would go on to achieve modest reputations as artists. (Bennett would write the "Ebony Flute" columns for *Opportunity,* and Nugent would work as an actor in *Porgy* and other plays.)

The November appearance of *Fire!!,* nonetheless, strengthened Larsen Imes's sense of promise for African-American writers as 1926 came toward an end. It gave her further proof of the reality of a New Negro Renaissance in the making. The publication also may well have inspired her sophisticated self-fashioning that same month in her author's statement for Knopf, which had expressed an interest in her manuscript. In two brief strokes, she separated herself and her ideology from the Booker T. Washington Tuskegee School of conservative racial thought and from the New York

37. Arthur Huff Fauset, "Intelligentsia," *Fire!!,* I (November, 1926), 45–46; Wallace Thurman, "Fire Burns a Department of Comments," *ibid.,* 47.
38. Imes to Van Vechten, November 12, 1926, in JWJ.

Public Library School of paternalistic attitudes toward African Americans.

Larsen Imes had class aspirations embedded in her determination to become a novelist. Her objective was to have a career in the world of art and letters. She had already rejected the ordinary world of work for the leisure to write. Her dream did not carry with it a place for herself in a bohemian world of artists; rather, it was an updated version of the dream of a middle-class woman to achieve status, position, and money within the upper social echelons and, in her case, in both the black and the white worlds. Larsen Imes's version of the dream included making money, which she perceived to be the key to the kind of life she wanted for herself. "I *must* make some money," she confided to Dorothy Peterson; however, she did not wish any one to view her as having to work.[39]

Inspired by the interest in literature among African Americans and the near completion of her first novel, she began to envision operating a bookstore in Harlem. It was not to be at all an ordinary place, but instead a smart shop where the fashionable could browse and buy, and authors could read their work. Larsen Imes discussed the possibility with Van Vechten, who shared the idea, with James Weldon Johnson, who was "favorably impressed," and with Walter White, who claimed he had "been bitten by the same idea almost" and "had thought of consulting Doubleday about it."[40] White had found her idea for a bookshop "so fascinating" that he said he had "been able to think of little else" since she told him about it, and he began to have grand plans for it:

> In addition to the book evenings and other such methods of inveigling folks into the shop, it occurred to me that, being really the only Negro book shop in the country, it might well become a national thing, drawing its customers from every part of the country. One of the ways by which this can be done is to swipe the idea of the recently organized Book-of-the-Month Club. . . .
>
> I do not think that the present Book-of-the-Month Club would reach very many colored people nor would many of them just now be interested in the books that Canby, Broune, Morley, Canfield, and White select. On the other hand, there are a lot of people who would . . . be interested in keeping abreast of books by and about Negroes. You could play upon that distinctly racial interest and in time you could get them . . . to buy books by Willa Cather, Sherwood

39. Nella Larsen to Dorothy Peterson, Thursday 21st [July, 1927], *ibid.*
40. Nella Imes to Carl Van Vechten, Wednesday, September 29, 1926, *ibid.*

Anderson and others who are not distinctly racial. I am sure, too, that we could get up a very good mailing list from lists secured from people like Charles S. Johnson, James Weldon Johnson, and others who know the illiterate [*sic*] Negroes in all parts of the country. I, of course, would be glad to help. What do you think of the idea?

Carl has just telephoned me and asked me to come by and see him this afternoon. I suspect he wants to tell me about the book shop.[41]

White's enthusiasm was encouraging; so was his business savvy, because Larsen Imes was quite serious about pursuing the venture. She consulted James Weldon Johnson, who told her that "on occasion [he] talked with various publishers about the distribution of books (certain books I think he said) in Harlem, and that they all deplored the absence of a shop up there *and* would be very glad to cooperate with any reliable and competent agency or person." She discovered that many others had thought of the need for a bookstore but that no one had developed it. Perceiving herself as that "competent person" who could develop and implement a plan for the business, she had already considered the people and groups who would buy books: "Secretaries at the Y.M.C.A. and Y.W.C.A. would both welcome and help advertise the shop, and order few books which they buy through it. . . . [V]isiting summer school students purchase a great many books. The branch libraries too would help with the advertising and place a few orders. . . . Elmer's brother [William Lloyd Imes], I know recommends books to his congregation [St. James Presbyterian] and they have a small incipient [?] library in the church, to which they add now and then. And Bibles!"[42]

Larsen Imes had excellent ideas for the bookshop, but she did not have the finances. Her hope was that Van Vechten would be the investor and secure funds for the business. Unfortunately, she had overestimated his fortune in 1926; not until 1928 when he inherited a share of his rich brother's estate would Van Vechten become wealthy. Despite his appearance of affluence, he could neither supply the capital then nor commit himself for later. Disheartened, Larsen Imes wrote to him: "Oh, I do understand that the bookshop is only a vision. But, it's an exciting one. Inciting too."[43]

Her disappointment must have been great when a year later Douglas Howe opened the Hobby Horse Bookshop at 205 West 136th Street, which

41. White to Imes, October 1, 1926, in WW, NAACP.
42. Imes to Van Vechten, Wednesday, September 29, 1926, in JWJ.
43. Imes to Van Vechten, Wednesday, 6th [1926], in CVV.

was, just as Larsen Imes had envisioned, a tea room and bookstore where African-American writers congregated and sometimes read from their books on display. That disappointment underscored the sarcasm in her report to Dorothy Peterson: "You know too that we'd been around to Mr. Howes [*sic*] bookshop. Had tea . . . there one afternoon, but did not meet Mr. Howe. The Chicago Defender in speaking of the charm of Mr. Howe's bookshop & the tea room says, 'Miss Dorothy Peterson Brooklyn society maid and Mrs Elmer Imes, Harlem matron *and novelist* find our lunches very superior.' (to what)." Howe's success with Hobby Horse must have been even more galling four years later when he relocated to a new shop opposite A'Lelia Walker's studio, while Larsen Imes had been forced by financial difficulties to return temporarily to work at the public library.[44]

While the bookshop was only a vision Larsen Imes could not materialize, her manuscript was typed and ready for Van Vechten's promised reading. Early in December he completed the job and offered suggestions for strengthening the manuscript. Although he had taken it to Knopf, he thought that it was much too short, a point with which Larsen Imes agreed: "Yes, I do think the thing is perhaps not so much *too short,* as *too thin.* The truth is that I got awfully tired of it about the middle of the Copenhagen episode. That and the last chapter ought to be longer. I should hate terribly to have to write even one more word for the damned thing, but I suppose I could if I absolutely had to. I don't think the title is so good either."[45] She had worked diligently on crafting the novel, but she remained cavalier about it. Because she had presented herself as having spent part of her childhood and adulthood in Denmark, she had to explain the lapses in her creation of the Copenhagen segment. She was prepared to rewrite the manuscript, for she had already invested a year of work in it and it held the promise of success, recognition, and money—if accepted for publication.

Larsen Imes was also prepared for Knopf's rejecting the novel, as she pointed out to Van Vechten:

If the Knopfs don't take the thing, I will, of course be disappointed, but, nothing more. Not surprised, or shocked, or cross. And, I am more grateful to you than I know how to say, for reading it and taking

44. See "The Hobby Horse" entry in *The Harlem Renaissance: A Historical Dictionary of the Era,* ed. Bruce Kellner (New York, 1987), 170; Nella Larsen to Dorothy Peterson, Tuesday 2nd [August, 1927, Larsen's emphasis], in JWJ; Harold Jackman to Countee Cullen, January 27, 1930, in CCC.
45. Nella Imes to Carl Van Vechten, December 7, 1926, in JWJ.

it to them, regardless of the outcome. I realize very well that any aspiring author, black, white, or green, would thank his stars for such favor from such source. And, certainly, had I been told, in the not so distant past, that I was to fall into such good fortune, I should have considered the prophet a little mad, to put it mildly.[46]

Van Vechten, too, had done some preparations. He had cautioned Larsen Imes against building her hopes up prematurely, and he had apologized—in advance—for any seeming violation of her hospitality should the manuscript, for any reason, not fare well with Knopf. Although Larsen Imes had been unable to tell him so in person, because as she put it she was "not good at saying these things," she understood both his warning and his effort on her behalf: "So, even if, because of the thing's lack of merit, or publishing conditions, they don't take it, I wont [sic] feel that you have 'violated my hospitality',—which incidentally had been returned seventy time [sic] seven—, but that you have gone out of your way to do me a great kindness, which leaves me eternally in your debt."[47]

Van Vechten's sponsorship, as she well knew, could only smooth her way with the publisher; it did not assure her an acceptance. Neither he nor White, who also endorsed the manuscript, was in a position to convince Knopf to take a poorly written work. The publisher's decision on *Quicksand* would, finally, be based on the manuscript's own merit, and that decision had not yet been made. Nevertheless, the end of the year brought her a feeling of accomplishment: she had completed a novel. She could be counted in the ranks of "aspiring authors" in the New Negro Renaissance.

Although she had completed the manuscript that would become *Quicksand* before the end of 1926, Larsen Imes had to revise. She spent the first few months of the new year working on the novel and determined to avoid interference with her writing. In hiatus from much of the social activity that was going on in New York, she explained to her friends: "I have decided not to have a social life . . . because I have to work like a nigger."[48]

In February she took time out to attend several parties, including one of her favorites, an unusual Van Vechten party on the occasion of George Washington's birthday. "We had a delightful time at your house on the truthful George's birthday," she wrote in appreciation. "We are both agreed that it was quite the most pleasant and interesting party we have been to for

46. *Ibid.*
47. *Ibid.*
48. Larsen to Peterson, Thursday 21st [July, 1927], in JWJ.

a long time. Comfortable and congenial too." A month later Elmer Imes was still raving about that "wonderful party," which Langston Hughes described as "a gossip party, where everybody was at liberty to go around the room repeating the worst things they could make up or recall about each other to their friends on opposite sides of the room—who were sure to go right over and tell them all about it."[49] Such diversions were rare; Larsen Imes was determined to complete her book.

At the beginning of March, she finished the revisions and returned the manuscript to Knopf. She had developed the manuscript by 21,000 words, increasing it from 35,000 to 56,000 words, but she was not satisfied: "It's pretty rotten—in more ways than one." She was not confident that she had done all that she might have to produce a good novel. "I wanted very much to ask you to read it first again," she told Van Vechten, "but I feared that would be imposing too much on your good nature. Besides, the manuscript was in such a terrible condition that I was actually ashamed to have you see it. It had, however, to be that way or not at all."[50] She was responding to a sense of urgency stemming from her personal desire to actualize her ambition and from Walter White's assessment of the literary climate as opportune for African-American writers if they acted quickly.

Her fears about the quality of her manuscript were ill-founded. Within a week, Knopf called to inform her that the company would publish *Quicksand*. The firm's head reader, Harry Block, was assigned as her editor. Larsen Imes was elated. She had succeeded not only in writing a novel but in having it accepted by her first choice, a major New York publisher.

Elmer Imes, too, was pleased. He had joked about her prospects for publication while she was revising the novel. As she told it: "Elmer says that if I do get the present one [novel] published that 'your people' will run me out of these United States. (He didn't use the words 'your people' either, in referring to them.)" Despite his feigned concern about the responses of African Americans, Elmer Imes had been steadfast in his encouragement of his wife's efforts to complete the book. He was the first to express gratitude to Van Vechten for his assistance: "Thank you, too, for getting her settled about the book. Knopfs' called up Thursday to say that they were returning it to be put into shape for the printer."[51]

With the publication of her novel ensured, Larsen Imes turned her atten-

49. Nella Imes to Carl Van Vechten, Monday, Seventh [March, 1927], *ibid.;* Elmer Imes to Carl Van Vechten, n.d. [postmarked March 18, 1927], *ibid.;* Hughes, *The Big Sea,* 253.

50. N. Imes to Van Vechten, Monday, Seventh [March, 1927], in JWJ.

51. *Ibid.;* E. Imes to Van Vechten, n.d. [postmarked March 18, 1927], *ibid.*

tion to another of her objectives: moving to New York City. She had begun to see the comfortable house on Audubon Street in Jersey City as an inconvenience. It was too far removed from the city and the center of her social, and soon to be professional, life. Dorothy Peterson, whose large house in Brooklyn was the scene for many literary gatherings, had already taken an apartment downtown on Second Avenue so that she could be closer to the activity in the city, particularly to the Gurdjieff meetings in Greenwich Village. Larsen Imes intended to have a similarly convenient location, but she wanted to move to one of the prestigious apartment complexes in Harlem.

The luxury Paul Laurance Dunbar Apartments were under construction on five acres at Seventh and Eighth avenues between 149th and 150th streets. The complex was her ideal. It would have over five hundred apartments in six buildings situated around a courtyard and flower gardens. Tenants were already signing up for the units. The Imeses' friend Rudolph Fisher moved into the Dunbar Apartments as soon as they were completed, as did Du Bois, Robeson, and other famous African Americans along with white-collar workers. But with only one wage-earner, the Imeses could not afford the rent of $64.50 for a four-room apartment, or $84 to $99 for a six-room apartment with two baths.[52] Although in 1927 Imes was one of only thirty-nine African Americans holding doctorates in the United States, his salary at Edward A. Everett's was not large, and the average rent in Harlem that year was $41.77, or $10 more than New York rents for four-room apartments.[53] Although rent parties (called parlor socials and social whist parties) were an accepted part of life in Harlem, people of the Imeses' class did not hold them.[54] Neither did Nella Larsen Imes wish to wait for an apartment. Despite the fact that housing in Harlem was not easy to find, before the end of March the Imeses located a place on 135th Street, which they saw as "a relief to all friends of ours. A convenience, too, to them, as well as to us."[55]

52. See David Levering Lewis, *When Harlem Was in Vogue* (New York, 1981), 217–18, and Kellner, ed., *The Harlem Renaissance*, 107–108.

53. Lewis gives the number of black doctorates, along with that of college graduates (13,580). Lewis, *When Harlem Was in Vogue*, 15. See also Gilbert Osofsky, *Harlem: The Making of a Ghetto, Negro New York 1890–1930* (New York, 1968), 136.

54. Ethel Ray Nance, interview with Ann Allen Shockley, November 18, 1970 (San Francisco) and December 23, 1970 (Nashville), transcript in Special Collections, Fisk Oral History Project, Fisk University Library.

55. Nella Imes to Carl Van Vechten, Monday, fourteenth [postmarked March 14, 1927], in JWJ.

At the beginning of April, when Nella Larsen and Elmer Imes left Jersey City for their apartment in Harlem's West 135th Street, they arrived during the height of some of the most exciting times black New York would ever know. The "New Negro" was in vogue, and Harlem, "the Negro Metropolis" as James Weldon Johnson pronounced, was leading the way to a new age in African-American life. One of the popular sayings of the day among blacks was "I'd rather be a lamp post in Harlem than the mayor of Atlanta." Whites had, of course, discovered Harlem, especially its night life and places such as the Cotton Club, where Duke Ellington's band played for white patrons, or Connie's Inn and Small's Paradise, where revues occurred nightly. Rudolph Fisher described the phenomenon as the "Caucasian Invasion" in "The Caucasian Storms Harlem," an article for *American Mercury* that Larsen Imes termed only "fairish" because it was "mostly about cabarets." Van Vechten described the "invasion" another way when informing Gertrude Stein, then entertaining the brown-skinned blond vamp Nora Holt Ray at tea in France, "New York has gone almost completely native and soon we'll all be mixed up." Nella and Elmer Imes, like 87,417 other African Americans between 1920 and 1930, joined the migration to the center of their America.[56] They saw their fifth-floor walk-up apartment at 236 West 135th Street as an improvement over their house in Jersey City mainly because it *was* in Harlem.

Larsen Imes's new home was number 5-A, a spacious five-room apartment. It had "the air of a Greenwich Village studio," as one visitor observed. Everything was carefully arranged to create an informal air. The living room, with a long sofa in the center, was filled with "vari-colored pillows, paintings, books and more books, flowers, large and small vases."[57] An immaculate housekeeper, Larsen Imes was also a tasteful decorator with a developed sense of modern style, which she used in sewing furbishings. The apartment was a showpiece for the entertaining that she planned to do now that she was more conveniently located.

Exhilarated by the activity in Harlem and her increased visibility among literary people, she saw herself as part of a special world. She shared the vision of a number of serious observers of the racial scene in America, including Walter White, who concluded in his 1925 essay, "Color Lines," that

---

56. Larsen to Peterson, Thursday 21st [1927], *ibid.*, Carl Van Vechten to Gertrude Stein, December 10, 1926, in *Letters of Carl Van Vechten*, ed. Kellner, 90; Osofsky, *Harlem*, 130.

57. Thelma E. Berlack, "New Author Unearthed Right Here in Harlem," New York *Amsterdam News*, May 23, 1928, p. 16.

New York City had more to offer blacks than any other place in the nation because "most people in New York are so busy that they haven't time to spend hating other people." She also agreed with the optimistic view of Charles S. Johnson and Alain Locke that the Negro Renaissance would "infuse a new essence into the general stream of culture."[58]

Larsen Imes's move to the city marked the convergence of her social and literary interests. Her corrected manuscript had been submitted to Knopf in March before she left Jersey City. Already a partygoer and -giver on a minor scale, she welcomed the opportunity to be closer to her friends and to the social life in New York, and expressed relief at the elimination of the inconvenience of commuting to and from New Jersey. She was delighted, for instance, in May when Van Vechten agreed to go to the third annual *Opportunity* dinner with her, Elmer Imes, and Dorothy Peterson, to whom Van Vechten wrote: "If you can get Elmer and Nella to stop for me with their beautiful buggy I shall be delighted to join you for cocktails before." To make an entrance at the star-studded affair with the celebrity Van Vechten, who had survived the furor over his exploitation of black life in *Nigger Heaven,* was a major coup, despite the fact that the "principal excitement at the Dinner was our late arrival, slightly soused, about which there was much unfavorable comment." The little band of latecomers to the May 7 affair included Dorothy's brother Sidney Peterson, who received an honorable mention for his essay "What's in a Name?" in the "Personal Experience Sketches" competition, the category in which Larsen Imes's antagonist in the *Flight* controversy, Frank Horne, won the $10 third prize.[59] Their entrance had almost upstaged the presence of Paul Green, who had won the 1927 Pulitzer Prize for his play *In Abraham's Bosom.*

By 1927, Larsen Imes was also already a published author. Few of her acquaintances knew of her stories in *Young's,* yet many, including Charles S. Johnson, had accepted her as an author. She had read stories in March for the 1927 *Opportunity* literary contest, even though her name did not appear among the list of distinguished judges: "Theodore Dreiser, Novelist; Wilbure Daniel Steele, Short Story Writer; Eric Walrond, Author and Journalist; Zona Gale, Novelist and Playwright; Irita Van Doren, Editor of

58. Walter White, "Color Lines," *Survey Graphic,* VI (March, 1925), 681; Alain Locke, "Our Little Renaissance," in *Ebony and Topaz: A Collectanea,* ed. Charles S. Johnson (New York, 1927), 117.

59. Carl Van Vechten to Dorothy Peterson, May 2, 1927, in JWJ; Carl Van Vechten to Langston Hughes, May 11 [1927], in *Letters of Carl Van Vechten,* ed. Kellner, 95; "Contest Awards," *Opportunity,* V (June, 1927), 179.

Books of the *New York Herald-Tribune;* and Harry Hansen, Critic." She found the stories amusing but mediocre: "Shifting. Very diverting. One contains this prize, 'I have decided to cast my Rubikorn with you.'"[60] Her low opinion of the fiction was in keeping with Johnson's assessment of the overall quality of work submitted; he discontinued the contests after that year.

All of Larsen Imes's associates knew about her novel, and they were beginning to know her as Nella or Nella Larsen, rather than as Mrs. Imes. The transition to New York brought another transformation of her identity.

During the spring and summer following the move to Harlem, Elmer Imes appeared less central to his wife's social life. There may have been a breach in their relationship at the end of May, when she did not give details about an accident and noticeably omitted mention of her husband: "Yesterday I had a rather painful accident in which I got my face and neck pretty well splattered up with hot grease. The result being that all tied up and bandaged as I am I'm really not presentable. The good God only knows how long I'll be confined to the house. However, I can bear that if finally I am to emerge unspotted." As though Imes were not there, she concluded: "Maybe, I will take myself to the country for some weeks, when the doctors decide that I'll heal all right without further attention. I'm not sure yet."[61] Tinged with uncertainty and loneliness, her consideration of a stay in the country is her first statement of any extended activities without her husband. Imes, however, was frequently away, not only in Ann Arbor for research, but also on Long Island or in Bordentown (New Jersey) visiting with friends and at Oak Bluffs (Massachusetts) vacationing with his family, who were convinced, by then, that his wife lacked a proper respect for their values.[62]

At the beginning of June, she first began routinely to insert *Larsen* into her signature, whereas previously she had used *Nella Imes* exclusively, except in her 1920 *Brownies' Book* pieces, her 1923 book review in the *Messenger,* and her 1926 signed author's statement for Knopf, when she used *Nella Larsen Imes.* (She had placed her married name in parentheses on the publisher's form, thus signaling her intention to publish under *Larsen.*) The exceptions all related to public appearances as a writer, and in them she asserted a self not exclusively linked to being Mrs. Elmer Imes.

60. "Contest Awards," 179; Imes to Van Vechten, Monday, fourteenth [postmarked March 14, 1927], in JWJ.

61. Nella Larsen Imes to Carl Van Vechten, n.d. [postmarked June 2, 1927], in JWJ.

62. Adelaide Cromwell Gulliver, interview with author, March 18, 1987.

The use of *Larsen* in her signature for personal correspondence in 1927 was deliberate. As her marriage became less important as a means of stabilizing her identity and as her writing developed from a dream into a reality, she established an identity different from that of Mrs. Nella Imes. She signaled this shift in self-image in her letters to Carl Van Vechten, to whom she had written friendly letters from 1924 to spring, 1927, all signed *Nella Imes;* however, in a letter postmarked June 2, 1927, she became *Nella Larsen Imes.* While she would remain a Harlem matron, she was less dependent upon her husband and his achievements for her primary identity. The change of name may have also been intended as a vindication of herself to her mother, Marie, and her sister, Anna, with whom she was no longer in close contact, but to whom she would occasionally refer. In less than a year, with the publication of her first novel, she would become *Nella Larsen,* novelist and socialite, known primarily from that point on by her maiden name. Many of her associates from the early years of her marriage and from the early 1920s, however, continued to refer to her as Nella Imes, and a few, like Grace Nail Johnson, would insist on calling her Nellie Imes.

During June and the rest of the summer of 1927, Larsen took the acceptance of her book manuscript as an indication of her potential as a novelist. With a surge of energy following her accident and book contract, she wrote steadily on a new novel, which Knopf had informally asked to publish. The working title was "Nig," a clear nod to Van Vechten's provocative title. "I *have* been working," she said at the end of June. "Finished a kind of short story about 6000 words which I think of sending to Harper's though I'm not at all sure it's quite the type." Investing an idea in a story that might have become a novel bothered her ("I'm inclined to believe that I've squandered an idea that would have made a novel"), because though *Quicksand* was not yet in print, she considered herself a novelist—not merely a writer of fiction.[63] That story may have been the now-lost "Tea," inspired by Van Vechten's use in *Nigger Heaven* of Wallace Stevens' poem of that title.

She grew more confident about her writing, her identity, and her popularity. Harry Block asked her to read a book in Danish for Knopf. The book, unidentified by title, may have been under review for the Blue Jade series. For her effort, Larsen received $5 and a testament to her multicultural background.[64] Block's request and her compliance are the only extant evidence of her knowledge of Danish; none of her associates seemed aware of her ability to speak or read Danish. In reading the text, she may have drawn

63. Nella Larsen Imes to Carl Van Vechten, n.d. [postmarked June 29, 1927], in JWJ.
64. Nella Larsen to Dorothy Peterson, Tuesday 19th [July, 1927], *ibid.*

upon her knowledge of the language spoken in her childhood home in Chicago, where she may have learned enough Danish from her parents to become fluent. If during the period between 1908 and 1912 she actually traveled to Denmark, then she could have acquired fluency at that time. Or, as with French, she could have taught herself Danish. Reading the book cemented her ethnic identity with her publisher and with Van Vechten, whom she promptly informed of her assignment.[65]

Larsen had become a mainstay at the gatherings of Van Vechten, White, Fauset, and Lillian Alexander, as well as at those of African-American professionals such as Dr. Alonzo De G. Smith, whose medical practice was across the street from the Imeses' apartment. In fact, her invitations to Lillian and Ernest "Scolly" Alexander's confirmed her arrival in black society. The Alexanders' annual picnic at Greenwood Lake, New York, their country home forty-seven miles outside of the city (later named Green Pastures after the successful black play in 1930), was one of the events that indicated the social prominence of black New Yorkers. While she went to A'Lelia Walker's on occasion, she did not seek out the heiress to the Madame C. J. Walker hair preparation fortune, who, though known for her lavish weekends at her half-million-dollar estate, Villa Lewaro, in Irvington-on-Hudson and crowded parties at her 136th Street limestone mansion, was not one of the "higher" social class that Larsen courted. Had Walker been the white daughter of a washerwoman, turned businesswoman and self-made millionaire, she would have been more greatly admired by Larsen, who did not discriminate class position as distinct from wealth so keenly among the whites she met. Larsen was becoming even more of a snob; besides, when she, Elmer, and Rita Romilly gave a party for A'Lelia Walker on August 7, 1925, Walker arrived forty-five minutes late, "soused and promptly passed out."[66]

It did not take an increasingly class-conscious Nella Larsen long to become dissatisfied with her Harlem neighbors. "It's hellish noisey here, but the view interesting," she had said upon first relocating to the apartment. Outside, the street was given over to strolling and socializing, both of which James Weldon Johnson depicted favorably:

The masses of Harlem get a good deal of pleasure out of things far too simple for most other folks. In the evenings of summer and on Sundays they get lots of enjoyment out of strolling. . . . Strolling in Harlem does

65. *Ibid.*
66. Carl Van Vechten, Daybook, August 7, 1925, in CVV.

not mean merely walking along Lenox or upper Seventh Avenue or One Hundred and Thirty-fifth Street; it means that these streets are places for socializing. One puts on one's best clothes and fares forth to pass the time pleasantly with the friends and acquaintances and, most important of all, the strangers he is sure of meeting. One saunters along, he hails this one, exchanges a word or two with that one, stops for a short chat with the other one. He comes up to a laughing, chattering group, in which he may have only one friend or acquaintance, but that gives him the privilege of joining in. He does join in and takes part in the joking, the small talk and gossip, and makes new acquaintances. . . . This is not simply going out for a walk; it is more like going out for adventure.[67]

For Larsen, the seeming pleasantry of Harlem's socializing on the streets wore thin. Soon both the noise and the view were sources of complaint.

She had wanted to live in Washington Heights, the most prestigious, and primarily white, residential area in upper Manhattan, but she and Imes lacked the money to obtain an apartment in its imposing buildings replete with doormen and elevator operators. She had known of another elegant area, the brownstones designed by Stanford White on West 138th and 139th streets in Harlem. Labeled "Strivers' Row" and owned, not rented, by wealthy African Americans such as the Alexanders and the Nails, the buildings represented the good location and quiet neighborhood that she desired, but they, too, were beyond her means. She settled with some reluctance on 135th Street in a less elegant but certainly respectable block. In fact, both James Weldon Johnson and Rev. Shelton Hale Bishop, the pastor at St. Philip's, lived one block away at 187 West 135th Street.

Hardly had she had a chance to establish herself in the apartment when she began to search in earnest for another: "I'm still looking for a place to move," she told Dorothy Peterson just three months after her move to 135th Street. "It's really rather ridiculous I suppose. but_____. Right now when I look out into the Harlem Streets I feel just like Helga Crane in my novel. Furious at being connected with all these niggers." She enlisted an acquaintance, Marion Beasley, to help in the search. Several weeks later, when no other prospects had surfaced, she considered taking a different five-room apartment on the second floor, rear, in her same building, which had

67. Imes to Van Vechten, Wednesday, n.d. [postmarked April 6, 1927], in JWJ; James Weldon Johnson, *Black Manhattan* (New York, 1930), 162–63.

the advantages of "Not so many steps. Not so noisey [sic]—but—more accessible."[68]

The graciousness of her apartment's interior was not enough to make her forget that she was trapped in an external environment populated by lower-class blacks and southern émigrés. In becoming "the greatest Negro City in the world," Harlem had reached a population density of more than 336 people per acre, creating congestion to the point of "indecency."[69] At the same time, the twenty-five-block area was distinctly divided along class lines. Lofty Sugar Hill looked down upon the streets where the poorer, less-educated, more vulnerable lived crowded together. Upward mobility into the professional classes had enabled some African Americans to distance themselves psychologically, if not always spatially, from the struggling masses of the race. Larsen, without being monied herself, claimed that segment of the race living in material ease and relative security; as for the rest of the race, she resented its proximity and its visibility. Ordinary African Americans were at best a curiosity and at worst a liability to be avoided as much as possible, given the reality of Harlem's geography.

Her views reflected the paradoxical thinking evident in the New Negro Renaissance. On the one hand, the social expression or manifestation of human creativity and the psychological basis of perception or judgments of taste and beauty were expressions of a concern with black culture—its African origins and its folk survivals. Alain Locke had applauded the "nascent" center of "folk-expression and self-determination" in his 1925 essay "Harlem": "A railroad ticket and a suitcase, like a Bagdad carpet, transport the Negro peasant from the cotton-field and farm to the heart of the most complex urban civilization. Here, in the mass, he must and does survive a jump of two generations in social economy and of a century and more in civilization. Meanwhile the Negro poet, student, artist, thinker, by the very move that normally would take him off at a tangent from the masses, finds himself in their midst, in a situation concentrating the racial side of his experience and heightening his race-consciousness."[70] Theoretically, the intermingling of the different groups, peasants and artists in Locke's formulation, would inspire heightened racial expression.

But on the other hand, the statements and aspects of judgment during the

68. Larsen to Peterson, Tuesday 19th [July, 1927], in JWJ; Larsen to Peterson, Tuesday 2nd [August, 1927], ibid.

69. Osofsky, Harlem, 140.

70. Alain Locke, "Harlem," Survey Graphic, VI (March, 1925), 630.

Renaissance revealed both class bias against the reality of lower-class folk and high-culture predilections constraining perception of acceptable blacks. A rather presumptuous Van Vechten had indicated as much when he said to Langston Hughes, "You and I are the only colored people who really love *niggers.*"[71]

In addition to beginning the search for a better apartment, Larsen spent the summer seeing friends off for Europe, attending teas, parties, shows, and stadium concerts, playing bridge (one of her few passions), and basking in newfound popularity. Van Vechten and Fania Marinoff, his Russian-born wife, returned to New York; Van Vechten had been in California at the start of the year and Marinoff in Europe. The party given by banker Edward Wasserman on February 11 to celebrate their return also marked Larsen's place among Van Vechten's intimate, though numerous, friends. At the welcome, she and Elmer Imes had joined a host of whites (including the artists Florine Stettheimer and Covarrubias and the opera diva Marguerite D'Alvarez) and other black guests: Grace and James Weldon Johnson, whom Van Vechten counted as his closest friends among the many African Americans he knew; Alain Locke, who traveled from Washington; A'Lelia Walker, whose own parties Van Vechten rarely missed; Dorothy Peterson, who would grow closer to Van Vechten in later years; Dorothy and Jimmie Harris, who knew everyone in the artistic Village set that Van Vechten also cultivated; Langston Hughes, who had dedicated his second book of poetry, *Fine Clothes to the Jew* (1927), to Van Vechten; and Nora Holt Ray, whom Van Vechten had used as the model for Lasca Sartoris in *Nigger Heaven* and had dubbed "the Sheka of Harlem," for "her trail [was] strewn with bones, many of them no longer hard."[72]

Marinoff's gift to Larsen was a brass box for cigarettes, which Larsen interpreted as a sign of her acceptance as a close friend. She admired Marinoff and was more awed by her than by Van Vechten. Marinoff's career as an actress on stage and in motion pictures represented the glamorous life of Larsen's fantasies. She praised Marinoff as "delightful, in appearance and manner—like a princess out of a modern fairy tale."[73] Little did she realize that the petite, delicate-looking Marinoff had known poverty during her

71. Carl Van Vechten to Langston Hughes, March 25 [1927], in *Letters of Carl Van Vechten*, ed. Kellner, 95.

72. Carl Van Vechten to H. L. Mencken, n.d. [*ca.* 1925], *ibid.*, 87.

73. Nella Larsen to Dorothy Peterson, July 12, 1927, in JWJ; Imes to Van Vechten, Monday 6th [1926], in CVV.

youth and hard times in the early years of her marriage to Van Vechten, but had elevated her status by means of grueling work in the theater. Larsen believed—paradoxically, given her own background—that surfaces told the whole story of a person's life.

Throughout the summer Marinoff and Van Vechten routinely invited Nella and Elmer Imes to their Fifty-fifth Street apartment for intimate dinners or large parties. Their white friends downtown had begun to do so as well. When Wasserman gave a "night party" for Marinoff, he included the Imeses along with the Walter Whites, James Weldon Johnson, Blanche Knopf, Gene Markey, Samuel Hoffenstein, Rita Romilly, Harry Block, and Muriel Draper, who in turn asked the Imeses to tea with six others including the playwright Robert Littlejohn. "Eddie" Wasserman had inherited part of the Seligman banking fortune from his mother. He became a close friend of the Imeses, inviting them to his elegant dinners such as the one for Ethel Waters, at which they dined with Van Vechten, Donald Angus, Langston Hughes, and the newlyweds Zora Neale Hurston and Dr. Herbert Sheen. From among the others, the Imeses so liked Harry Block that they chose visiting him over hearing blues singer and recording artist Clara Smith perform, and they thought he might be interested in Dorothy Peterson, to whose affairs of the heart they paid particular attention. Both Block and Wasserman were part of the mainly white group, brought together and animated by Van Vechten, with which Nella and Elmer Imes socialized during the summer. The others were Draper, Witter Bynner, and Isa Glenn, in addition to Marinoff; it was that group, minus Bynner, that after attending the opening of Ethel Waters' "excruciatingly funny" revue *Africana* at the Daly 63rd Street Theatre on July 11, began a round of gaiety that would last all summer.[74]

This new grouping of friends would so occupy Larsen that she never quite managed to visit Dorothy's father, Jerome Peterson, who had befriended her as a second daughter. Throughout July, she wrote to Dorothy Peterson in France of her intention to go over to Brooklyn for a visit. But by August, she would confess: "I feel *very* much ashamed to say that I have not seen your father since you left. And, Sidney tells Elmer, today he leaves for his vacation. He is well, so Sidney says—I shall write him though while he is away. And worst of all, I've got a book that I wanted to get to him before

74. Larsen to Peterson, July 12, 1927, in JWJ; Larsen to Peterson, Tuesday 2nd [August, 1927], in JWJ; Arnold Rampersad, *The Life of Langston Hughes* (2 vols.; New York, 1986), I, 154; Imes to White, Monday [November, 1926], in WW, NAACP.

he got off. However, sending's better I guess."[75] Her pangs of conscience about ignoring the elder Peterson were somewhat relieved by visits from Sidney, who often dropped in on the Imeses and appeared at Van Vechten's in town.

An assimilationist and a social climber, Larsen took more pride in her inclusion in interracial gatherings than she did in all-black affairs. Although she reveled in being in the company of whites who were worlds apart from the working-class immigrants she had known in Chicago, she was completely comfortable only with Van Vechten. Elmer Imes, on the other hand, moved with absolute ease and assurance among them. He was especially fond of Marinoff, whom he treated with courtly gallantry (conveying his utter devastation by her absences from their group excursions) and with gentlemanly flirtation (sending her valentines depicting "shines" [blacks], which Larsen objected to because they were not "pretty.")[76]

The summer's heat, however, made life miserable. Larsen's low tolerance for hot weather meant that she was frequently incapacitated. She missed the July 3 opening of a new Miller and Lyles show, *Rang-Tang*, and the party afterward, because she was "utterly prostrated by the heat." Lamenting that she had to cancel her plans for an amusing night out, she revealed, "I haven't had on clothes for days." She often remained in the apartment in various stages of undress during the daytime in order to escape the heat and its effects on her health, which deteriorated during July and August from colds that frequently confined her to bed.[77]

At the same time, she rarely missed the evening rounds of dinners, cocktails, and parties, because so much was still new and fascinating to her. When she met the visiting British writer Osbert Sitwell at Van Vechten's, for example, she was so excited that she immediately obtained his book *Triple Fugue* from the public library to immerse herself in his work. Her meeting with Du Bose Heyward, who was in New York from his native Charleston, South Carolina, for the 1927 dramatization of his novel *Porgy* (1925), brought another star-struck response: "Isn't Mr. Heyward interesting to meet?—and natural? You know, theoretically, I hate all Southerners as 'a matter of principle,' but actually, I have never met one I didn't like." With

---

75. Larsen to Peterson, Tuesday 2nd [August, 1927], in JWJ.

76. Imes to Van Vechten, Monday, Seventh [March, 1927], *ibid.*; Nella Larsen Imes to Carl Van Vechten, Saturday [postmarked February 18, 1928], *ibid.*

77. Larsen to Peterson, Tuesday 19th [July, 1927], *ibid.*; Larsen to Peterson, Tuesday 2nd [August, 1927], *ibid.*

Elmer, Isa Glenn, and Witter Bynner, she attended a dinner Van Vechten gave to entertain his visiting sister Emma Van Vechten Shaffer and niece Elizabeth. On that occasion she met "Julian Langer [*sic*]" who, she thought, was "by way of being a *real* person. . . . He's been everywhere and seen everything." However, she reserved her most unabashed enthusiasm for Hunter Stagg, editor at *Review,* a little magazine in Richmond: "I had a very exciting time while Hunter Stagg was here. I think he's perfectly grand, etc., etc. But alas! thinking back, I'm afraid I failed to take advantage of my opportunities, and as everyone knows it can never happen again, —never the exact mood, that delightful feeling of, —oh—er—pleasure."[78] In a year's time, she had adopted the mannerisms and affectations of the personalities that appeared in Van Vechten's novels.

Larsen realized that she was not invited to all the parties that she considered important. Regina Anderson, Ethel Ray, and Louella Tucker, the trio of young women whose apartment at 580 St. Nicholas Avenue was an informal salon and refuge for New Negro artists, rarely invited Larsen to their gatherings. And when Dorothy Hunt Harris had a bon voyage party before she left for Europe in July, she failed to include Larsen, with whom she had played bridge the week before she sailed. As Larsen reported it: "None of us, Carl, Harry, Nella, Elmer, were invited to her party. I don't know who was except Hap, Lelia, Earl & Anna. Anyway, all the amusing people were at Eddie's [Wasserman]. I was the same night." A week later, she observed, "There are no parties—to which I have been invited." While she added "Thank God!" to indicate her relief in having some time to herself, she flourished in the social limelight and in being able to recount her experiences, especially those with celebrities: "I'm asked to go to Carl's to drink a cocktail on Friday afternoon. I don't know if it's in honor of the [Walter] Whites sailing or not." Or with people who were fashionable in African-American circles, such as the tennis tournaments at Hampton, and in white circles, such as the Jack Dempsey boxing matches: "Tonight we're going to the prize fight. Dempsey–Sharkey. It's at the Polo Grounds. Tickets 11.00 up. Elmer got two $27.50 from his chief. They had been given to him. I'm quite enthusiastic about it—the crowds they say are marvelous."[79]

78. Imes to Van Vechten, Wednesday, 6th [1926], in CVV; Imes to Van Vechten, November 12, 1926, Larsen to Peterson, Tuesday 2nd [August, 1927], and Imes to Van Vechten, Saturday [postmarked February 18, 1928], all in JWJ.

79. Larsen to Peterson, July 12, 1927, Larsen to Peterson, Tuesday 19th [July, 1927], and Larsen to Peterson, Thursday 21st [July, 1927], all in JWJ.

Throughout the season of popularity, Larsen remained very much a satiric observer of those around her. "Last night we went in to call on the Whites who are packing," she wrote Peterson, who was in France, where Walter White was heading on a Guggenheim fellowship to write his third novel. "They intend to look you up—and you have my *very* deepest sympathy."[80] Actually, she would miss Gladys and Walter White, who would be away for the year, because despite their personal foibles both accepted Larsen without question. Much like Peterson, whom she also missed during the summer months she spent in Europe, the Whites could be counted on for their expressions of friendship. Walter White placed her name on the lists of those to be invited to literary affairs, such as Langston Hughes's poetry reading after the publication of his book of poems *The Weary Blues* (1926), and the lists of those to be sent copies or notices of new books by blacks, such as Countee Cullen's *Copper Sun* (1927). Gladys White, whom many, like Hughes, considered one of the most beautiful women in Harlem, especially initiated invitations to the Imeses for evenings together without the rich and famous from downtown: "Gladys asked me to ask if you and Elmer couldn't come over to dinner one night this week—Thursday, Friday, or Saturday will suit us splendidly. Unfortunately, we cannot easily make it on Sunday for that is the maid's day off and we do want you to have a good meal."[81] It may well have been a misdirected latent jealously of the Whites' scale of living that rankled Larsen enough to ridicule them.

Larsen herself was not as successful a hostess as she wanted to be. She was bothered by her inability to entertain Ethel Waters, who was fast emerging as the most popular of the black singers and actresses in New York shows. Waters, who for a time lived in a fashionable apartment building at 508 St. Nicholas Avenue, seemed social and agreeable enough to accept an invitation to tea, but on the appointed afternoon she never appeared. Larsen had invited Dorothy Peterson and Mary Skinner from her class at the Library School; another friend, Gussie Booth, dropped in for an unexpected visit. "We sat about and waited and waited, got hungrier and hungrier," Larsen said. All waited until 7:00 before eating the sandwiches and cakes

---

80. Larsen to Peterson, Tuesday 19th [July, 1927, Larsen's emphasis], *ibid.*

81. See Walter White, "List of Persons to Whom Were Sent Announcements of Langston Hughes' Reading," January 31st [1926], "Persons to be Written Concerning 'Flight'" [1926], "Persons to Whom It Would be Advantageous to Send Copies of 'Copper Sun'" [1927], all in WW, NAACP; Hughes, *The Big Sea,* 248; White to Imes, November 16, 1926, in WW, NAACP.

she had carefully prepared for the guests: "I was very disappointed because I felt sure it was going to be a success. Everything was just right."[82]

Larsen had hoped to make a social conquest by becoming a friend of the popular Waters. Dorothy Peterson had intended "if things fell out that way, to ask her to go out to Brooklyn with [Nella] and Elmer on Friday night"; Gussie Booth, married to a friend of Sidney and Dorothy Peterson, was not especially concerned about meeting Waters: "Gussie knows nothing about her—and doesn't care, so she would have been perfectly natural."[83]

Larsen tried repeatedly to discover why Waters had not shown up. Several days after the ruined tea, she asked Van Vechten to find out what might have happened: "Did she get stage fright at the last minute? Was she disconcerted because she had been asked to come alone without friend husband? Why didn't she 'phone if she was tied up?" Larsen also blamed herself for not confirming the date and time. "Probably I should have phoned when she didn't arrive by five-thirty.—Still that seems a little unusual. Not done. We parted quite pleasantly after leaving your [Van Vechten's] house last week. Our last words were 'Monday then, about five.' It's all very mysterious."[84] She never seemed to realize that Ethel Waters had no way of knowing the afternoon was an occasion planned for *her*.

Larsen was amused enough by a newspaper item several weeks after the tea to inform Peterson: "You *do* remember the tea for Ethel Waters—?—. Well, the Pittsburgh Courier says 'Among those who have entertained Miss Waters are Mr. & Mrs. Carl Van Vechten, at dinner. Mr. Edward Wasserman, millionaire banker, at a formal evening party. Mrs. Nella Larsen Imes *at tea*.'" The piece of information went without comment on the *Courier's* reporting, most likely because she had placed it herself in advance of the occasion. A year later, in September, 1928, Larsen made other attempts to befriend Waters, who was by then extraordinarily successful and living next door to Elmer's brother, Rev. William Lloyd Imes. "I went to see Ethel, but she wasn't expected that day to be in to evening." And in June, 1929, she was still trying: "I don't know what to do about Ethel. I have called on her——out. I have written her——no answer. I shall, however keep trying."[85] Her persistence in the face of obvious rebuffs is one way of gauging her determination to achieve social recognition and celebrity status.

82. Imes to Van Vechten, n.d. [postmarked June 29, 1927], in JWJ.

83. *Ibid.*

84. *Ibid.*

85. Larsen to Peterson, Tuesday 2nd [August, 1927], Nella Larsen Imes to Carl Van Vech-

The failure to entertain Waters in the 1920s was one of the stories Larsen would continue to tell, slightly differently and more dramatically, until well into the 1930s, when she used it as a way of casting a humorous light on herself and her activities during Harlem's heyday. In the 1930s, she told the story, adding that Van Vechten had persuaded her to give a tea for Waters and that she had invited all of Harlem society, from A'Lelia Walker down, but that the only people who came were Dorothy Peterson and her father. Larsen expanded the later version even further for white friends; she said that a few years after her tea and after her divorce, someone in Harlem society gave a party for Waters, but did not invite Larsen.[86] By the 1930s, the tea stood for the capriciousness of Harlem's elite and Larsen's failure to be accepted into that closed society. But even in the late 1920s, the incident dramatized what remained a sore point for Larsen: she never felt fully accepted by either the theater and entertainment segment of Harlem or the socially prominent upper classes of African Americans.

Anxious always to be "Nella" rather than "Nellie" from an indeterminate family in Chicago, she could not let go of an unfounded feeling of inferiority that displayed itself in a condescending attitude toward others, particularly African Americans of whatever class. Although intelligent and witty, she seemed remote. She envied the verbal flash of a Rudolph Fisher, who was known for his incisive, nonstop repartee. While in private an astute social critic, she would not offer her opinions in public. Neither would she stoop to the entertaining but outrageous antics of a Zora Neale Hurston playing the darky or the dozens and of a Bruce Nugent leaving tie, socks, and sometimes shoes at home during his evenings out. Although different from the others, Larsen's was similarly a carefully cultivated persona. She, however, was on the verge of making herself visible and upstaging them all. *Quicksand* was nearly ready for publication.

---

ten, Monday [postmarked September 3, 1928], and Nella Larsen Imes to Carl Van Vechten, n.d. [postmarked June 14, 1929], all in JWJ.

86. Andrew G. Meyer to Thadious Davis, January 17, 1982, in possession of Thadious M. Davis.

III

A Novelist's Achievement,
1927 – 1930

9

Arriving with *Quicksand*,
1927–1928

NELLA LARSEN MOVED to Harlem in anticipation of the publication of *Quicksand* and the launching of her career as a novelist. Keenly aware of the opportunities that African-American writers suddenly had, she intended to be well-positioned to seize whatever came her way. "Dorothy, you'd better write some poetry, or something," she told Peterson in July, 1927. "I've met a man from Macmillan's who's asked me to look out for any Negro stuff and send them [*sic*] to him. (Rather mixed grounds but you get the implication.)"[1] She understood that publishers were searching for "Negro materials" in response to the wave of white interest in the exotic and the primitive. But at the same time, she reasoned that African Americans should take advantage of the situation and reap whatever they could from the demand for race materials. She believed that her intelligent, lively friends would certainly want to produce "poetry, or something" in order to cash in on the opportunity for recognition and prestige that publishing, particularly with a white firm, would bring.

Larsen did not express the clear vision of Claude McKay who, though often volatile and quixotic, was level-headed about the implications of both white patronage and sudden interest in things "Negro": "I am so happy about the increased interest in the creative life of the Negro. It is for the Negro aspirants to the creative life themselves to make the best of it—to discipline themselves and do the work that will hold ground firmly [to] the

1. Nella Larsen to Dorothy Peterson, Thursday 21st [July, 1927], in JWJ.

very highest white standards. Nothing less will help Negro art forward; a boom is a splendid thing but if the masses are not up to standard people turn aside from them after the novelty has worn off."[2] Early on in an era of conscious marketing of race, McKay attempted to shift the emphasis away from quantity and publication to "the creative life" and quality.

Even while holding to white standards as the aesthetic measure, McKay understood the danger of assuming that creative expression could be used as a social and political commodity to sell as a sign of racial advancement and achievement. He sought financial support for his work from whichever quarters he could find sympathy, because as he put it, "my position is tragic. I am always working under the shadow of insecurity and it paralyses me." At the same time, however, McKay warned black artists: "We are made impotent by the fears and misgivings of minorities and by the harsh judgment of majority opinion, and thus we become emasculated in ideas and the expression of them. I know what I am talking about. Every work of art is in reality personal propaganda. It is the way in which the artist sees life and wants to represent it."[3]

McKay's views were similar to those of Langston Hughes in "The Negro Artist and the Racial Mountain." Hughes, though at the time attached to a white patron, Charlotte Osgood Mason, had speculated that "the present vogue in things Negro . . . may do as much harm as good for the budding colored artist," because "the Negro artist works against an undertow of sharp criticism and misunderstanding from his own group and unintentional bribes from the whites."[4] Although still in college at Lincoln University, Hughes was well aware that attention from white publishers, patrons, and literati enhanced the standing of black artists within their own racial group. He understood that the attention had the potential of influencing not only the artists' work but their conceptions of themselves as African Americans.

Du Bois held similar views. In "Criteria of Negro Art," he observed that "there are today a surprising number of white people who are getting a great satisfaction out of these younger Negro writers, because they think it is going to stop agitation of the Negro question. . . . And many colored people are all too eager to follow this advice; especially those who are weary of the

2. Claude McKay to Walter White, June 25, 1925, in WW, NAACP.

3. Claude McKay to Walter White, September, 1925, *ibid.*

4. Langston Hughes, "The Negro Artist and the Racial Mountain," *Nation,* CCXXII (June 28, 1926), 693.

eternal struggle along the color line, who are afraid to fight and to whom the money of philanthropists and the alluring publicity are subtle and deadly bribes." During his long struggle for African-American rights, Du Bois would add to his perception of white patronage and philanthropy as deterrents to black activism. Reflecting upon his 1901 statement that "the problem of the Twentieth Century is the problem of the color-line," he added another dimension to the discourse on the position of African-American artists: "An art expression is normally evoked by the conscious and unconscious demand of people for portrayal of their own emotion and experience. But in the case of the American Negroes, the audience, which embodies the demand and which pays sometimes enormous price for satisfaction, is not the Negro group, but the white group. And the pattern of what the white group wants does not necessarily agree with the natural desire of Negroes. The whole of Negro literature is therefore curiously divided."[5]

Both Du Bois for the older generation and Hughes for the younger were responding to what James Weldon Johnson called "a newer approach" to the race problem:

It requires a minimum of pleas, or propaganda, or philanthropy. It depends more upon what the Negro himself does than upon what someone does for him. It is the approach along the line of intellectual and artistic achievement of Negroes, and may be called the art approach to the Negro problem. This method of approaching a solution to the race question has the advantage of affording great and rapid progress with the least friction and of providing a common platform upon which most people are willing to stand. The results of this method seem to carry a high degree of finality, to be the thing itself that was to be demonstrated.[6]

Johnson expressed the notion that the art produced by African Americans could of itself alleviate race prejudice, and that it could do so without either

5. W. E. B. Du Bois, "Criteria of Negro Art," *Crisis*, XXXII (October, 1926), 294; W. E. B. Du Bois, "The Problem of the Twentieth Century Is the Problem of the Color Line," Pittsburgh *Courier*, January 14, 1950, rpr. in *W. E. B. Du Bois on Sociology and the Black Community*, ed. Dan S. Green and Edwin D. Driver (Chicago, 1978), 281–89 (see 286).

6. James Weldon Johnson, "Race Prejudice and the Negro Artist," *Harper's*, CLVII (November, 1928), 769–70.

overt propaganda on the part of the artists or pacifying philanthropy on the part of whites. Yet the climate of the 1920s in New York made it difficult for the racial artist to mediate the two poles.

Nella Larsen understood her milieu and the position of the African-American artist within it. In an atmosphere of almost reverse racial acculturation for whites, her own motives for writing were mixed. She welcomed the intense white interest in things Negro as an opportunity for herself and others to achieve more than they would even have dared dream previously. She had listened during the past few years as Walter White promoted the Negro cultural awakening, extolled the rewards of participation, and reminded the writers not only of the "three or four first rate publishers" who had asked him "to keep an eye open for likely material," but also of "personal contacts," which he considered "one of the best means of getting people interested to the point of buying a writer's books."[7]

The literary climate that White personified and the other black and white purveyors of culture endorsed was one that created two prongs of inspiration for Larsen: public acclaim and social status, in particular interracial social activity, which was assumed to be a primary method of alleviating American racism. For Larsen, who had been denied public acknowledgment by her own family, public acclaim was a special prize that could command the acceptance that had not been granted during her formative years. It could also validate both her existence and her worth.

A conscious retention of her experience as a stigmatized female child of color in a narrow white world underscored her notion of the tangible rewards of writing. For one who had keenly felt isolation and disconnection throughout much of her youth, social activity was a balm that could place her in the center of life and produce the security of belonging. If that activity were concentrated in the circles of the "famous," the rich, and the powerful, then it would accentuate her value and elevate her position. The forging of a racial identity was a general objective of the New Negro Renaissance, but for Larsen, the validating of a personal identity, conjoining gender and race, was even more essential. While she indeed displayed an "assertive intelligence" and a "quick-witted opportunism," as David Levering Lewis has claimed, she also had the temperamental and emotional proclivity for writing.[8] Beyond that, she had talent and ability. Her turning to writing was a

---

7. Walter White to Claude McKay, May 20, 1925, in WW, NAACP; Walter White to Langston Hughes, May, 1922, *ibid.*

8. David Levering Lewis, *When Harlem Was in Vogue* (New York, 1981), 231.

process of reciprocal enrichment between the New Negro literary movement and her own female self.

Larsen's inspiration to write may have been sparked by the reception accorded the African-American writers ("sighs of wonder, amazement and sometimes admiration"); however, it was fueled by an innate love for literature. She had spent much of her youth and womanhood reading books and finding pleasure and satisfaction in being transported to worlds inside their pages. Although she admitted not knowing what would satisfy her spiritually, she said that books would satisfy her materially (along with money and travel).[9]

Books were essential to Larsen's material well-being, but they represented more than physical objects. She knew the power of words to heal and subdue and create. She relied upon books for companionship, for direction, and for affirmation. Thus, she brought to her writing a desire beyond tangible rewards and practical results, the celebrity status and public recognition emphasized in the cultural milieu of the New Negro awakening. Her desire was to create art that would courageously function to control the self and nature, that would simultaneously express herself and transcend self.

Larsen's first novel, then, would encompass what she so aptly called "the mixedness of things." While she never published a statement about her motivations for writing or her attitudes about the meaning of writing in her life, she seemingly agreed with the statement Washington poet Georgia Douglas Johnson provided for the 1927 *Opportunity* "Contest Spotlight," a series of personal statements by the contest winners: "I sing because I love to sing—runs the lines of a popular song; even so, I might say, I write because I love to write, for this is indeed true. If I might ask of some fairy godmother special favors, one would sure to be for a clearing space, elbow room in which to think and write and live beyond the reach of the Wolf's fingers. However, much that we do and write about comes just because of this daily struggle for bread and breath—, so, perhaps it's just as well."[10] Johnson recognized that a love for writing and the leisure to write are essential to the creative person, but that the absence of material

9. Arna Bontemps, *Personals* (1963; London, 1973), 4; Larsen quoted by Mary Rennels, New York *Telegram*, April 13, 1929, in SCF.

10. Nella Imes to Carl Van Vechten, Wednesday, eleventh [postmarked August 12, 1926], in CVV; Georgia Douglas Johnson, "The Contest Spotlight," *Opportunity*, V (June, 1927), 204.

security might be viewed as an incentive for writing. Success and acclaim, though not trivial concerns, were not then the whole of the motivation to create.

Once Larsen attained a measure of "clearing space" and "elbow room," she attempted to intensify and to verify the larger racial mandates of the Renaissance in her fiction, yet she also tried to clarify and to interpret her own gender experiences, including those that reflected "that inner world of random impulses and automatic processes which constitute [the] inner being." She stated publicly that "recognition and liberation will come to the negro [sic] only through individual effort." She echoed in a less eloquent way the position that Alain Locke had first elaborated in the Harlem issue of Survey Graphic: "What stirs inarticulately in the masses is already vocal upon the lips of the talented few, and the future listens . . . forecasting in the mirror of art what we must see and recognize in the streets of reality tomorrow." Locke maintained that black artists exist in a symbiotic relationship with the black masses. In this relationship, as Michael Lomax has pointed out, "what helps Locke's 'talented few' helps the black majority as well. This sanguine analysis is based upon Locke's perception of the functional relevancy of the new artistic productions to the broader social world and, more specifically, his perception of the importance not only of the artistic creations of 'Negro Youth' to his *own* social status and advancement, but to the general status and advancement of the black group as a whole." In addressing this same aspect of Locke's beliefs, David Levering Lewis has concluded more generally that "the architects of the Renaissance believed in ultimate victory through the maximizing of the exception. They deceived themselves into thinking that race relations in the United States were amenable to the assimilationist patterns of a Latin country."[11]

In situating herself as one of the exceptions, or "talented few," Larsen identified herself as a member of the new African-American elite, composed largely of artists and intellectuals, and linked her personal aspirations to those of the larger African-American population, whose aspirations she articulated as "recognition and liberation." By demonstrating the cultural and artistic gifts of the race through her own creative writing, she placed herself,

---

11. Irvin Edman, *Arts and the Man: A Short Introduction to Aesthetics* (1928; rpr. New York, 1939), 14; Larsen quoted by Rennels, New York *Telegram*, April 13, 1929; Alain Locke, "Negro Youth Speaks," in *The New Negro*, by Locke (New York, 1925), 47; Michael Lomax, "Fantasies of Affirmation: The 1920's Novel," *CLA Journal*, XVI (December, 1972), 236; Lewis, *When Harlem Was in Vogue*, 305–306.

and other African Americans by extension, in a position to receive what Lewis has termed "slight humane and material consideration." [12] Basically, Larsen expressed views commonly held in racial discourse during the Renaissance.

As early in the cultural movement as 1924, one white critic, Carl Van Doren, had suggested that the younger generation of black writers would be "artists while being critics," because they would discover that the "facts about Negroes in the United States are themselves propaganda—devastating and unanswerable." In 1927, Locke had already begun to defend the movement against Mencken's charges that it had "kindled no great art" by stressing that "Negro artists are just the by-product of the Negro Renaissance; its main accomplishment will be to infuse a new essence into the general stream of culture." Locke's main emphasis was that "we must divorce it [the Renaissance] from propaganda and politics," because "overt propaganda now is as exceptional as it used to be typical. The acceptance of race is steadily becoming less rhetorical, and more instinctively taken for granted." His insistence on separating art and propaganda was grounded in the belief that the race was "at the interesting moment when the prophet becomes the poet and when prophecy becomes the expressive song, the chant of fulfillment." [13]

Locke's assessment appealed to Larsen. She saw herself as an artist, not a propagandist for the race. She was quick to point out not only that Knopf had "made her promise to do two more manuscripts . . . neither is to be of the propaganda type," but also that "people of the artistic type have a definite chance to help solve the race problem." Her remarks prompted Elmer Imes to accuse her of "trying to pose as a silly uplifter of the race" in bringing up the propaganda issue. [14]

Although the Art versus Propaganda battle had been waged in the pages of *Crisis* in 1926, debate about the portrayal of African Americans in literature was ongoing as the Renaissance progressed. [15] It could not easily be

12. Lewis, *When Harlem Was in Vogue*, 305.

13. Carl Van Doren, "The Younger Generation of Negro Writers," *Opportunity*, II (May, 1924), 144–45; Alain Locke, "Our Little Renaissance," in *Ebony and Topaz: A Collectanea*, ed. Charles S. Johnson (New York, 1927), 117; Alain Locke, "Art or Propaganda?," *Harlem*, I (November, 1928), 12.

14. Thelma E. Berlack, "New Author Unearthed Right Here in Harlem," New York *Amsterdam News*, May 23, 1928, p. 16; Elmer Imes quoted in Nella Larsen Imes to Carl Van Vechten, n.d. [postmarked April 15, 1929], in JWJ.

15. See "The Negro in Art: How Shall He Be Portrayed? A Symposium," *Crisis*, XXXI

settled because some defenders of the race refused to accept the disassociation of art from propaganda. Du Bois, for instance, insisted: "All art is propaganda . . . ; the apostle of Beauty . . . becomes the apostle of Truth and Right not by choice but by inner and outer compulsion." Several decades later, Sterling Brown, a poet who began his writing career during the Renaissance, would echo Du Bois by stating that "the truth of Negro experience in America is strong enough propaganda."[16]

Both Brown and Du Bois raised the issue that few during the Renaissance would willingly admit: the agenda for many African Americans—intellectuals and artists alike—was for the advancement of the race in a culture dominated by whites. In this admission, Du Bois and Brown differed from Larsen and from Locke, who said, "After Beauty, let Truth come into the Renaissance picture,—a later cue, but a welcome one."[17] Nevertheless, on a subliminal level, artists and theoreticians in the cultural awakening knew that whatever validity individual African Americans could give to the "truth" of their racial experience and to the reality that some African Americans could create poems, plays, and stories (published by the white press and reviewed by white critics) meant forwarding their cause of racial progress and of racial assimilation.

James Weldon Johnson, whose collection of Negro folk sermons, *God's Trombones* (1927), had just been published, provided another reason why the controversy over Art versus Propaganda was so crucial to the Renaissance between 1926 and 1929:

The colored people of the United States . . . are a segregated and antagonized minority . . . unremittingly on the defensive. Their faults and failings are exploited to produce exaggerated effects. Consequently, they have a strong feeling against exhibiting to the world any but their best points. They feel that other groups may afford to do otherwise but, as yet, the Negro cannot. This is not to say that they refuse to listen to criticism of themselves, for they often listen to Negro speakers excoriating the race for its faults and foibles and vices. But

---

(June, 1926), and Edward E. Waldron, *Walter White and the Harlem Renaissance* (Port Washington, N.Y., 1978), 33–39.

16. W. E. B. Du Bois, "Criteria for Negro Art," *Crisis,* XXXII (October, 1926), 297; Sterling Brown, "The Negro Author and His Publisher," *Negro Quarterly,* IX (Spring, 1942), 14–15.

17. Locke, "Art or Propaganda?," 12.

these criticisms are not for the printed page. They are not for the ears and eyes of white America.[18]

Johnson perceived that the problem was larger than the issue of propaganda; he believed, along with others such as Countee Cullen, that African-American artists could not yet afford to represent the race in negative terms, despite their obligation to explore racial subjects.

Larsen, who sought acceptance in the most sophisticated circles of white artists and celebrities, was unwilling to make such an admission. She prided herself on being different from the masses of African Americans, and consequently distanced herself and her fictional portrayals from them. In part, her attitude stemmed from a fear of being absorbed into the masses, which she viewed as having the potential to extinguish a concrete, autonomous, and productive self. She publicized her status as a mulatto and called attention to her "Nordic" side, despite the fact that her "white" relatives had caused her enormous personal pain by disparaging her blackness.[19] She preferred identification with whites, which she believed could prevent her being subsumed into the stereotyped lower rungs of the African-American race. Yet, she was not immune to issues of racial portrayal, racial art and propaganda, because the disparate ideological positions on these issues slanted the public reception and critical readings of her fiction. By the time her fiction appeared at the end of the 1920s, the question was no longer whether African Americans could write novels, but rather what they would say in them.

Much of the heady intellectual debate about art subsided in November when Harlem plunged into mourning. Florence Mills, the singer who had first captivated audiences with her performance in *Shuffle Along* (1921) and who had taken *Blackbirds of 1926* from Broadway to London, died of appendicitis on November 1. All of Harlem grieved for her because no other stage star had so represented the coming of age of African-American entertainment. Langston Hughes even used Mills's 1921 rise to stardom to date the beginning of the New Negro Renaissance, though he credited the writers and entire cast of *Shuffle Along* with giving "just the proper push—a pre-

18. James Weldon Johnson, "Dilemma of the Negro Author," *American Mercury*, XV (December, 1928), 480; see also James Weldon Johnson, "Negro Authors and White Publishers," *Crisis*, XXXVI (July, 1929), 228–29.

19. See Rennels, New York *Telegram*, April 13, 1929.

Charleston kick—to that Negro vogue of the 20's, that spread to books, African sculpture, music, and dancing."[20]

Five thousand mourners attended Mills's funeral services at Mother Zion Church, and 100,000 people lined the streets outside. Thousands more had already viewed the body during the five days it lay in state. The impressive funeral procession to Woodlawn Cemetery included eleven cars carrying flowers, thirty gray-clad chorus girls escorting the hearse, and flocks of blackbirds descending from an airplane.[21] The homage to Mills was one of Harlem's most spectacular occasions. At the same time, it was a sobering reminder of vulnerability.

Larsen settled into a somber mood of work on her second novel. Almost inexplicably she was troubled by Mills's death. Whereas normally she was exhilarated by fall because it meant an emergence from the stifling heat of summer, now she had little enthusiasm for plays or parties or people. The holidays and new year, however, reawakened her social side. By February, she began to reflect on the rounds of gaiety as interruptions. "I am going into retreat," she told Van Vechten after his party for Hunter Stagg, who was visiting from Richmond. "I do want to finish my book in the next two months."[22] She had driven herself during the previous two years to produce fiction while widening her social circle, a fact that pleased her almost as much as did the impending publication of her first novel.

Van Vechten remained her steadfast friend and mentor. His continuing interest in her work and his inclusion of her and Elmer Imes in his large and small gatherings prompted her to express her gratitude on more than one occasion during the winter. In one such expression, she observed of their friendship: "It has been a nice three years. . . . [Y]ou're the grandest friend. . . . I don't, of course, see now, any immediate way to get myself off the red ink side of your ledger, but I'm not really worrying about that because you do understand."[23] Larsen had begun to depend increasingly on Van Vechten's friendship. The Walter Whites had departed for Europe in July, 1927, and their descriptions of high life in Paris, the Riviera, Nice, Villefranche-sur-Mer, and their eight-room villa with a maid were more

20. Langston Hughes, *The Big Sea* (1940; rpr. New York, 1986), 223–24.

21. James Weldon Johnson, *Black Manhattan* (New York, 1930), 201; U. S. Thompson, "Florence Mills," in *Negro: An Anthology,* ed. Nancy Cunard (1934; rpr. New York, 1970), 201.

22. Nella Larsen Imes to Carl Van Vechten, Saturday [postmarked February 18, 1928], in JWJ.

23. *Ibid.*

than Larsen could bear.[24] Dorothy Peterson, though as active and as reliable a friend as ever, had returned from the summer in Europe to her job teaching Spanish in Brooklyn, and she was busily writing a novel that she shared with her former Gurdjieff teacher, Jean Toomer, but not with Larsen.[25] While Jessie Fauset was back in New York, she had begun a teaching job and was at work on another novel of her own. Fauset's Sunday afternoon teas, though still functioning, were no longer as fashionable as they had been in the early 1920s. The problem was compounded by Harlem's "growing and changing," as Harold Jackman reported. "Why every dance I go to these days. I see more people I *don't* know than those I do know. At one time I used to know almost everybody at a party, and strange to say these new people one doesn't seem to have seen around here at any time either."[26] Van Vechten's trip to California to work a new book, *Spider Boy,* left a void that Larsen filled with her two passions, bridge and writing.

She pushed herself hard during the winter to complete her second novel, but she suffered from another series of colds. During the months between December and March, she had five different episodes of ill health, each forcing her into bed rest. Elmer Imes believed she has lost all tolerance for winter weather, but he tried to make light of the situation in writing to Van Vechten, who was in Los Angeles: "You must help me get her to California when you come back. It would never do for you both to be there at the same time!" Larsen herself admitted that the colds were becoming too frequent and that the relapses interfered with her writing. "Down with my old friend, the grip [*sic*] again," she revealed while lamenting, "I am having the most hellish time with my novel. I've torn it all up and now face the prospect of starting all over again—if at all."[27]

She was in bad spirits, the sort that made her snipe at old friends. The absent Walter and Gladys White were favorite targets because of their unconcealed pleasure in their children, Jane and Walter, their infant son whom Larsen dubbed "the heir apparent," "the poor infant" of "so many names."

24. The Whites ultimately moved to a modest apartment in Avignon when, during tourist season, prices soared in Villefranche. See Lewis, *When Harlem Was in Vogue,* 204.

25. See Dorothy Peterson to Jean Toomer, November 10, 1928, quoted in *The Lives of Jean Toomer: A Hunger for Wholeness,* by Cynthia Earl Kerman and Richard Eldridge (Baton Rouge, 1987), 366. See also Harold Jackman to Countee Cullen, Thursday, December 13, 1928, in CCC. Jackman reports that Peterson had just completed her novel.

26. Harold Jackman to Countee Cullen, November 19, 1928, in CCC.

27. Elmer Imes to Carl Van Vechten, n.d. [postmarked March 3, 1928], in JWJ; Nella Larsen Imes to Carl Van Vechten, n.d. [postmarked March 19, 1928], *ibid.*

A letter from Gladys White with a photograph, labeled "Brother at six months," made her inexplicably angry, though she recovered enough to observe: "now he is simply Brother. When he is about six and starting school and they are compelled to call him something else, you'll see that it will be Walter." Although she was quite accurate, because the boy's name was Walter Carl Darrow White, her antagonism toward the Whites seemed out of proportion to their rather simple joy in the child. For over a year, she had persistently directed her wit against the Whites. After the birth of their son, she remarked: "Gladys called up to inquire why I hadn't called to gaze upon the son and heir (?) I congratulated her effusiously [sic] on its being a boy. 'Yes,' she said triumphantly 'Walter wanted a boy to *carry on his name.'"* Her punch line, which she did not deliver to Gladys White, was "There are only five pages of Whites in the New York telephone directory alone. And two in the Brooklyn one. Now if it had been Van Vechten, or Imes————."[28] Her jokes eventually caused Walter White to become "piqued," as she put it, and to distance himself from her.[29]

Du Bois also raised her ire when, on the occasion of his sixtieth birthday, a committee sought to raise $2,500 as a birthday gift: "Some nerve I say. I'm about to celebrate a birthday too and I feel like writing and telling them that. I could use $2500 myself. In fact I think it will do me more good at thirty-five than him at sixty."[30] Her spirits were such that Du Bois' support of her work meant little.

The publication of her novel later that same month improved her mood. The advance copies arrived on March 17. Attractively bound in orange cloth with a border trim, *Quicksand* was, as Larsen had hoped, another of Knopf's beautiful books. Knopf's attention to detail that she had observed when considering possible publishers was evident. The title page was printed with two ink colors; the title and Knopf symbol were in a rich brown, which was the color used for the titles in the "Negro in Unusual

28. Larsen Imes to Van Vechten, n.d. [postmarked March 19, 1928], *ibid.;* Nella Larsen Imes to Carl Van Vechten, n.d. [postmarked June 29, 1927], *ibid.* The Whites' son, Walter Carl Darrow, was named "Carl" to honor both Van Vechten and a Chicago physician, while "Darrow" was for attorney Clarence Darrow.

29. Nella Larsen Imes to Carl Van Vechten, n.d. [postmarked June 14, 1929], in JWJ. Dorothy Peterson repeated to White exactly what Larsen had said: "He dedicated his first book to Gladys, his second to Jane his daughter, but . . . he feared to dedicate the third to his son, because we would discover what the infant's name really is."

30. Larsen Imes to Van Vechten, n.d. [postmarked March 19, 1928], in JWJ. Larsen was actually about to celebrate her thirty-seventh birthday.

Fiction" list on the facing page. Printed in a typeface called Caslon, the text was both handsome and readable. Larsen's spirits soared. She immediately began to inscribe her author's copies for her closest friends. Each message was personal. The one for Edward Wasserman, for example, read: "For Eddie/in memory of his parties/Nella/March 17, 1928."[31]

Larsen had already sent one of the advance copies to Gertrude Stein in Paris with a note: "Carl [Van Vechten] asked me to send you my poor first book, and I am doing so. Please don't think me too presumptuous. I hope some day to have that great good fortune of seeing and talking with you." In labeling *Quicksand* her "poor first book," she linked it by implication to Stein's *Three Lives,* and to "Melanctha" in particular, which, she revealed, she had "read many times. And always I get from it some new thing—a truly great story." Inscribed within the text of her letter to Stein was her hope for the greatness of *Quicksand* in capturing, as "Melanctha" had, the interior spirit of an African-American woman: "I never cease to wonder how you came to write it ["Melanctha"] and just why you and not one of us should so accurately have caught the spirit of this race of mine."[32] Even before *Quicksand* was officially released, Larsen envisioned her novel and its protagonist, Helga, in the fullest range of possibilities for capturing the emotional, psychological, and sexual internality and spirit of the race.

Released on March 30, 1928, *Quicksand* appeared exactly a year to the month after Knopf had accepted the manuscript. Dedicated to "E. S. I." (Elmer Samuel Imes), the novel carried an epigraph from Langston Hughes's poem "Cross":

> My old man died in a fine big house,
> My ma died in a shack.
> I wonder where I'm going to die,
> Being neither white nor black?

The epigraph served two introductory purposes. First, it established the connection between *Quicksand* and the Harlem Renaissance by evoking Hughes, the best known of the younger writers because of his two volumes

31. Nella Larsen Imes to Edward Wasserman, Home Thursday [postmarked April 5, 1928], in Serendipity Books Catalog 43 (1985), item 331A. The letter is now in the Schomburg Center for Research in Black Culture.

32. Nella Larsen Imes to Gertrude Stein, February 1, 1928, in *The Flowers of Friendship: Letters Written to Gertrude Stein,* ed. Donald Gallup (New York, 1979), 216.

of poetry, *The Weary Blues* and *Fine Clothes to the Jew*. Second, the selected lines immediately announced the cross-cultural and interracial thematic core, along with the underlying ideas of conflict with heritage and quest for place or identity. Although the last line ("Being neither white nor black") is the most specifically related to the heroine, Helga Crane, who is of mixed-racial heritage, it was popularly linked to Larsen herself, whose author's statement accompanying the press releases reiterated her status as a mulatto. Nella Larsen had enveloped her own life story in *Quicksand*, but her exaggeration of the autobiographical connections would, in the year ahead, overcast her imaginative, psychological creation of character.

The major New York publications (the *Amsterdam News*, New York *Herald Tribune*, New York *Times*, *Saturday Review of Literature*, *Crisis*, *Opportunity*) ran reviews that, along with a host of others in newspapers and periodicals around the country, praised Larsen's achievement in her first novel, but linked it to her own story as a mulatto. In all, more than twenty-five reviews and numerous announcements appeared between April 8, 1928, when the *New York Times Book Review* featured the book in "Latest Works of Fiction," and January, 1929, when *Opportunity* carried Alain Locke's "1928: A Retrospective." These contemporary reviewers failed to apprehend the psychological drama reproduced in *Quicksand;* the novel was a text of a daughter's coming to terms with her mother, an act of an enraged child's displacing a mother's intuited story with her own necessary one.

Most noticeable in *Quicksand* is Larsen's portrayal of mixed-race existence. Helga Crane's physical appearance immediately positions her in the world of mulattoes and reduces her to an object for speculation:

> An observer would have thought her well fitted to that framing of light and shade. A slight girl of twenty-two years, with narrow, sloping shoulders and delicate, but well-turned, arms and legs, she had, none the less, an air of radiant, careless health. In vivid green and gold negligee and glistening brocaded mules, deep sunk in the big high-backed chair, against whose dark tapestry her sharply cut face, with skin like yellow satin, was distinctly outlined, she was—to use a hackneyed word—attractive. Black, very broad brows over soft, yet penetrating, dark eyes, and a pretty mouth, whose sensitive and sensuous lips had a slight questioning petulance and a tiny dissatisfied droop, were the features on which the observer's attention would fasten; though her nose was good, her ears delicately chiseled, and her curly blue-black

hair plentiful and always straying in a little wayward, delightful way. Just then it tumbled, falling unrestrained about her face and on to her shoulders.[33]

Helga's two visible heredities become the sign of her dual cultural allegiances and her often contradictory impulses. Her "mulatto condition is," Mary V. Dearborn suggests, "a metaphor for a divided self." Larsen avoids the stereotypical depiction of the "tragic mulatto," the passive victim of two different bloods warring in her veins. Nevertheless, as Hortense E. Thornton has shown by examining critical assessments, the familiar, but limiting, tragic-mulatto motif preconditions some readers into oversimplifying Helga. Larsen attributes the mulatto's "tragic sense of nonbelonging to individual and family problems," as Amritjit Singh points out, "rather than to the biological fact of miscegenation." However, Larsen places pressure on any uncomplicated reading of the mulatto because, as Hazel Carby observes, "the mulatto figure is a device of mediation; it allows for a fictional exploration of the relationship between the races while being at the same time an imaginary expression of the relationship between the races."[34]

In addition to establishing Helga as a mulatto, the decorative framing of the female body in the opening of the novel initiates a controlling discourse on gender. The study poses for observation a self-conscious young woman of elegant and exotic beauty, according to white standards. Framed in light, her yellow skin and green and gold negligee objectify her female body, and the play of shade emphasizes her exotic sexuality. The focus on Helga's femaleness, combined with her race, in the privacy of her bedroom sets the stage for her seeking to define a space for self-actualization and to redefine herself as subject.

Vital and spirited, Helga is a restless, complex personality who changes her external environment whenever she feels entrapped. Educated and intelligent, she is more than a static, beautiful object. She seeks synthesis of self, direction, and work that would integrate her private needs and ambitions

33. Nella Larsen, *Quicksand*, in *"Quicksand" and "Passing,"* ed. Deborah E. McDowell (New Brunswick, 1986), 2 (hereafter cited parenthetically in the text).

34. Mary V. Dearborn, *Pocahontas's Daughters: Gender and Ethnicity in American Culture* (New York, 1986), 59; Hortense E. Thornton, "Sexism as Quagmire: Nella Larsen's *Quicksand*," *CLA Journal*, XVI (March, 1973), 290–92; Amritjit Singh, *The Novels of the Harlem Renaissance: Twelve Black Writers, 1923–1933* (University Park, Pa., 1976), 103; Hazel Carby, *Reconstructing Womanhood: The Emergence of the Afro-American Woman Novelist* (New York, 1987), 171.

with public roles and responsibilities. Her quest is for a viable identity as an adult female of color in a modern multifaceted world. The episodic construction follows her search for changes in and control over her emotional and psychological states by moving to different geographic locations: "She began to make plans to dream delightful dreams of changes, of life somewhere else. Some place where at last she would be permanently satisfied . . . where she would be appreciated, and understood" (56–57). No single place measures up to her expectations and needs. Resolutely independent, she resists marriage and concubinage as forms of entrapment and subservience, which she reads in her mother's life and in the social relations of all sexually active women. Although she finds employment as a teacher, a companion, and a secretary, few opportunities for work utilizing her full range of abili- ties are available to her because of her race.

In rendering Helga's active quest for agency and empowerment, Larsen infuses the text with a realistic treatment of the complexities of cultural experiences. She raises issues of privilege, otherness, marginality, and identity to provide a substantive conceptual core to the life of a woman who is socially constructed as black in a world in which the majority culture is white and in which the dominant representations of blacks issue from whites. But she also uses those same issues to challenge the social roles available to the female in a patriarchal culture. Jens Peter Jacobsen's early realistic text, *Marie Grubbe,* with its rendering of a woman's geographical mobility and her insistence on the right to choose her own brand of existence across class lines and economic status, figures in the background. In *Quicksand,* the details are the environmental and material trappings of a mainly middle-class commodity culture in small southern communities, large northern cities, and a foreign capital. Harlem of the 1920s is the major physical landscape for the graphic explorations of Helga Crane's search for an identity within an African-American world. The Harlem segments contain a richly detailed portrait of place within a specific cultural context, the emergence of modern black New York. Clearly identified, but less fully realized, Copenhagen provides the foreign backdrop for Helga's quest within a white world. The interlude in Denmark embodies old-world wealth and class privilege. The texture and diversity of the physical settings combine with the intensity and necessity of Helga's gendered and racial search to mark one of the major achievements in *Quicksand.*

The power of the novel, however, does not rest on the narrative surface. It emanates from the core of Helga's existence and from the interpolation of her mother's story into Helga's own. Her mother, Karen Nilssen, long dead when the narrative opens, was Danish, and her father, whom she has never known, was a person of color whose legacy to his daughter is entanglement in a male, racialized story. Because Helga inherits her father's race, and with it the culture's racial restrictions, her restless quest seems superficially to conform to the race-defined and gender-specific story of a black male's search for recognition and place. Certainly, early in life Helga had been scarred by the desertion of her father, a "gay suave scoundrel" (23) and by the remoteness of her "sad, cold" mother, who had been "flung into poverty, sordidness, and dissipation" (23). Nonetheless, Karen Nilssen, not the unnamed father, is the central figure in textual relation to Helga and the one held accountable for Helga's adult condition. Anger, the usually controlled but always controlling emotion, is part of the connective tissue between the two females: "A peculiar characteristic trait, cold, slowly accumulated unreason in which all values were distorted or else ceased to exist, had with surprising ferociousness shaken the bulwarks of that self-restraint which was also, curiously, a part of her nature. And now that it had waned as quickly as it had risen, she smiled again . . . which wiped away the little hardness which had congealed her lovely face. Nevertheless she was soothed by the impetuous discharge of violence, and a sigh of relief came over her" (4–5).

Quicksand is comparable to a "discharge of violence," an expression of anger usually suppressed and restrained. It is a reflection of Helga's inner knowledge of her response to her mother, who figures in Helga's consciousness as "a little pathetic, a little hard, and a little unapproachable" (23). Helga's "cold" trait and "the little hardness" sometimes visible in her face link her to her mother, who is part of the daughter's "uneasy sense of being engaged with some formidable antagonist, nameless and un-understood" (10). Karen Nilssen is, in a sense, that nameless and veiled antagonist. Helga observes that she "detested cool, perfectly controlled people" (22–23), but she fails to connect her emotion to Karen Nilssen, whom she repeatedly describes in those same terms. Throughout most of the text, Helga has difficulty understanding her responses to her mother's life: "She had outraged her own pride, and she had terribly wronged her mother by her insidious implication. Why? Her thoughts lingered with her mother. . . . A fair Scandinavian girl in love with life, with love, passion, dreaming, and risking all in one blind surrender. A cruel sacrifice. In forgetting all but love she had forgotten, or had perhaps never known, that some things the world never forgives. But as Helga knew, she had remembered, or had learned in suffering and longing all the rest of her life" (23).

The implication seems to be that Helga's mother had risked all in violating racial taboos and marrying Helga's father. But another reading is that the mother sacrifices her child for the sake of a man and her own happiness. This interpretation is reinforced by the repetition of the mother's sacrifice in marrying a second time: "That second marriage, to a man of her own race, but not of her own kind—so passionate, so instinctively resented by Helga even at the trivial age of six—she now understood as a grievous necessity. Even foolish, despised women must have food and clothing; even unloved little Negro girls must be somehow provided for. Memory, flown back to those years following the marriage, dealt her torturing stabs" (23). Although Helga claims to understand her mother's action as "a grievous necessity," she has never forgiven her mother for choosing a man over her child. Because of her mother's choices, Helga's childhood, "one long, changeless stretch of aching misery of soul" (23), was marked by "ugly scarifying quarrels," "her own childish self-effacement," and "her mother's careful management" (23), their mutual attempt to mediate the "spiritual wounds" and "ugly scarifying quarrels" of their daily lives. As an adult, Helga has suppressed her anger toward her mother, particularly for her complicity in her child's suffering and her acquiescence to patriarchal power over females.

It is her anger, nonetheless, that fuels much of the narrative tension and of Helga's inner life. In Naxos, for instance, she labels her furious decision to leave a "new revolt . . . [a] lack of Acquiescence" (7). Anger, often diffused and misdirected, erupts inexplicably and uncontrolled. In reflecting upon her revelations about her mother, however, she does question her own motives: "Why, if she had said so much, hadn't she said more about herself and her mother? . . . Why had she lost her temper and given way to angry half-truths?—Angry half-truths—Angry half—" (26). In leaving unfinished and unexplored these questions she raises early in the narrative, Helga gestures toward locating her story within the parameters of her relationship to her mother.

That relationship and Helga's attitude toward it function in the background of the race and gender themes in the novel. These two aspects link Helga to Maureen Murdock's observation of "some daughters . . . taught a subtle form of compromise and self-hatred by their mothers," who attempt to repair the damage: "A young girl looks to her mother for clues as to what it means to be a woman, and if her mother is powerless, the daughter feels humiliated about being female. In her desire not to be anything like her mother, she may strive for power at the expense of other needs. 'Many daughters live in rage at their mother for having accepted, too readily and passively, "whatever comes."' Until she makes this unconscious reaction conscious, the daughter will continue to function *in reaction* to her mother."[35]

The adult Helga recognizes that her "inherent aloneness," an essential "part of her very being" (45), stems from her childhood isolation within a destructive family. Nevertheless, because she cannot consciously come to terms with her mother's role in her "aloneness," Helga can neither reconstitute a supportive family nor relinquish her need for one. She cannot adequately break the cultural proscription against anger in the female or the social prescription against a child's anger toward a mother, and thus forbidden healthy expressions of anger, she is unable to resolve her ambivalences regarding her desire for empowerment and control over her life. Deflecting her anger from her mother and toward her white relatives or the black bourgeoisie, Helga assumes various guises for spiritual, psychical, and racial acceptance. Although she believes that only family can provide love, security, acceptance, and place for her, she cannot reconstitute what was lost in her formative years, at least partly because she fears overt expression will result in further rejection and failure. Therefore, Helga is silenced; she can neither voice her innermost reality to others nor express that reality in her own story. She reenacts her mother's story, but without the maturity to interpret its meaning. Her emotional development, arrested at a critical stage, is so incomplete that Helga, though twenty-three, is still childlike.

In the final sequence of *Quicksand*, "there was her mother, whom she had loved from a distance and finally so scornfully blamed, who appeared as she always remembered her, unbelievably beautiful, young, and remote" (128).

There is no single representation of Helga's scornfully blaming her mother; assumed but unarticulated, it is the unseen and unvoiced that makes *Quicksand* a powerful first novel. It is, as well, the emotional autobiographical impetus that charged Nella Larsen's writing of fiction. Given the specific details of Larsen's early life, the text brings to the surface the unseen antagonist confounding and compelling the author. Her absent and often nameless mother, Marie Larson/Larsen, functioned as a catalyst for Larsen's self-exploration and self-revelation in *Quicksand*, but what her

35. Maureen Murdock, *The Heroine's Journey: Woman's Quest for Wholeness* (Boston, 1990), 19. Murdock quotes from Adrienne Rich, *Of Woman Born: Motherhood as Experience and Institution* (New York, 1976), 246–47.

readers saw was largely the physical correspondences between Nella Larsen and Helga Crane and the resemblances in their personal trajectories.

The resemblances are striking. Initially, Helga has a position teaching English at Naxos, a small black college in the South that is modeled largely on the Tuskegee Institute that Larsen knew during her brief tenure there. The fictional school, however, also incorporates Larsen's earlier experience of Fisk University. Derived from Larsen's reading of Greek mythology begun as a student at Fisk, the name Naxos is evocative of abandonment, exile, longing, and despair. Larsen figures her own emotional responses to having been sent away from Peter and Marie Larsen and their "white" world to Fisk, the small college synonymous with a "black" world. The largest of the Greek Cycladic islands, Naxos was the place where Theseus abandoned Ariadne. Although the myth of Theseus and Ariadne appropriately provides a name for Larsen's fictional college, Naxos also is the island dedicated to Dionysius; as Missy Dehn Kubitschek has observed, Dionysius is a "figure of female desire removed from the female and mediated through the sexuality of the male. Female sexuality at Naxos will be defined by men and then closely constrained." Yet another source is, as Deborah McDowell has suggested, the word *Saxon*.[36] Larsen coined the name as a play on words, in order to make an ironical statement about the worship of the white, Anglo-Saxon world dominating the black institution and its "race" leaders. Larsen loved word games almost as much as she loved to point out the contradictions in the racial ideology of African Americans.

Set in Naxos, the first five chapters establish the tensions of the novel and the secrets of the heroine's existence. Helga at Naxos is a study in contradiction and displacement. Alone in her dormitory room in the opening scene, she sits "in soft gloom," in opulence and austerity: "Only a single reading lamp, dimmed by a great black and red shade, made a pool of light on the blue Chinese carpet, on the bright covers of the books which she had taken down from their long shelves, on the white pages of the opened one selected, on the shining brass bowl covered with many-colored nasturtiums beside her on the low table, and on the oriental silk which covered the stool at the slim feet" (1). Unlike any of the other rooms, Helga's is carefully appointed to provide "tranquillity" and "quiet" (1); it is composed conspicuously as an "intentional" retreat from classroom and campus. As a

---

36. Missy Dehn Kubitschek, *Claiming the Heritage: African-American Women Novelists and History* (Jackson, Miss., 1990), 102–103; Deborah E. McDowell, Introduction to *"Quicksand" and "Passing,"* by Nella Larsen, ed. McDowell (New Brunswick, 1986), xvii.

personalized environment within a context of conformity, "the room which held her" (6) is both a reflection of and an extension of Helga's isolated self. Furnishings and fabrics define her alienated personality as well as her values: "All her life Helga Crane had loved and longed for nice things. Indeed, it was this craving, this urge for beauty which had helped to bring her into disfavor" (6). Jewel colors, exotic patterns, rare fabrics, and antique objects all constitute her aesthetic preference for beauty over utility and function as markers of her participation in a commodity culture. In a sense, Helga's desire to surround herself with expensive and beautiful consumer goods, almost to make luxury a synonym for herself, is a statement that her misguided mother made a poor trade in distancing herself from her daughter for life's essentials. Helga as daughter is more precious and rarer than ordinary food on the table, but Karen Nilssen, sealed in remoteness, was unable to decipher this.

Comfortable with "things" because they compensate for her lack of family or friends, Helga also loves books because they provide escape from her habit of analyzing her position and offer her alternative ways of interpreting her life. While books with "bright covers" contribute to the depiction of Helga's aesthetic sense, they extend the larger portrait of her psychological state and intellectual disposition. Moreover, as objects covalent with other possessions yet valued above them, they immediately dispel any suspicion that the heroine is a mindless creature seeking merely material comfort. Marmaduke Pickthall's *Saïd the Fisherman* is Helga's reading in the opening scene. Although selected because she "wanted forgetfulness, complete mental relaxation" (2), the book is not "light" reading. Set in Egypt, the novel traces the life of a simple, spiritual man from 1871 to 1882 and culminates in his death in the aftermath of a British attack on Alexandria, when Egyptian troops left the city to a plundering mob. An orientalist and spiritualist born in Britain, Pickthall wrote *Saïd the Fisherman,* his first novel, at the turn of the century, but not until its appearance in Knopf's Blue Jade Library in 1925 did it find an audience in the United States. Comparable to Helga's selection, at the end of the novel, of Anatole France's story "The Procurator of Judea" for diversion from "the sounds of joyous religious abandon" (131), the use of Pickthall's novel accentuates Helga's fashionable, wide-ranging tastes and her discerning intelligence about the relationship between subjects in books and concerns in mundane life.

At every stage in the narrative, the disjunction or the harmony between public and personal space becomes the gauge of Helga's internal state. For example, the home in New York where she lives as a guest is "in complete accord with what she designated as her 'aesthetic sense'" because the large, cream-colored rooms are tastefully and richly appointed with "historic things mingl[ing] harmoniously and comfortably with brass-bound Chinese tea-chests, luxurious deep chairs and davenports, tiny tables of gay colors, a lacquered jade-green settee with gleaming black satin cushions, lustrous Eastern rugs, ancient copper, Japanese prints, some fine etchings, profusion of precious bric-a-brac, and endless shelves filled with books" (44). Such detailed descriptions of beautiful objects suggest the leisurely attention to setting of a nineteenth-century British novel or, as Mary Lay suggests, a Henry James novel; however, in *Quicksand* they function to convey Helga's artistic sensibility while masking her private dissatisfactions with herself.[37] Was her mother's bargain the better? Helga's signature throughout the narrative stages remains her ability to surround herself with rare, expensive things in an attempt to forestall the "formidable antagonist," which was a "ruthless force, a quality within herself, . . . frustrating her" (10–11).

Not surprisingly, Helga rejects Naxos, its students, and its teachers because she feels at odds with the restrictive environment. Seeing herself as different not merely in her appreciation of beauty and color in clothing and furnishings, but also in ideology and outlook, she wants the opportunity to live a fuller life than the racialized institution will allow. While desiring approval and recognition of her value and worth as an individual, Helga is incapable of actually revealing herself to her colleagues, particularly her need to retain connection to the white race. "'You never tell anybody anything about yourself,'" her fellow English teacher, Margaret Creighton, observes in attempting to discover the source of Helga's discontent (13). Although they remark on her secrecy, her associates notice most of all Helga's taste for colorful, exquisite objects and her difference from others at Naxos. Margaret sees this difference as an asset for the campus community: "'It's nice having you here, Helga. We all think so. Even the dead ones. We need a few decorations to brighten our sad lives'" (14). As "decoration," Helga is trivialized, yet as "need" she is crucial. Margaret reiterates a central tension in Helga's living out a response to her mother. Neither her love of beauty nor her need for appreciation allows her to accept offers of friendship. Secrecy about her past necessitates a guarding of her self in the present.

Family, both the individual members related by marriage and blood who make up a domestic community and the social group through which human

37. Mary M. Lay, "Parallels: Henry James's *Portrait of a Lady* and Nella Larsen's *Quicksand*," *CLA Journal*, XX (June, 1977), 475–86.

beings first derive a shared identity, becomes one obsession shaping her life and limiting her possibilities for constructive action. "No family. That was the crux of the whole matter. For Helga it accounted for everything, her failure in Naxos, her former loneliness in Nashville [where she had attended boarding school]" (8). Her fixation on family is behind her attraction to James Vayle, a teacher to whom she was engaged. Based on the physician A. Maurice Curtis, with whom Larsen worked at Tuskegee, Vayle's character is never fully realized. Given Tuskegee's prohibition against fraternization between male and female employees, there is no record of Larsen's involvement with Curtis. Vayle's name, suggestive of the veil within which people of color functioned, according to Du Bois, is at once a lure and a repulse. His were "people of consequence" with the "social background" (8) she craved, yet she dislikes their rigidity. "Negro society, she had learned, was as complicated in its ramifications as the highest strata of white society. If you couldn't prove your ancestry and connections, you were tolerated, but you didn't 'belong.' You could be queer, or even attractive, or bad, or brilliant, or even love beauty and such nonsense if you were a Rankin, or Leslie, or Scoville; in other words, if you had family. But if you were just plain Helga Crane, of whom nobody had ever heard, it was presumptuous of you to be anything but inconspicuous and conformable" (8). In part, Larsen also attacked the Imes family in her portrayal of "Negro society." Because of the oppressive destruction of the African-American family and the sexual exploitation of the African-American woman during slavery, the Vayles and much of the black bourgeoisie place an inordinate emphasis on proper, legitimate family status.

Although she seeks a personal freedom of expression and individuality that is unacceptable to the Vayles, Helga longs nonetheless for the kind of African-American family connections they represent. An "illegitimate" child and a social orphan, she accepts their designation of proper lineage as racial ancestry and cultural heritage out of which an individual establishes and measures her historical place in the larger society. At the same time, Helga considers whites, especially her relatives, "sinister folk . . . who had stolen her birthright. Their past contribution to her life, which had been but shame and grief, she had hidden away from brown folk in a locked closet, 'never,' she told herself, 'to be reopened'" (45). Cultural disinheritance and economic marginality replace her birthright stolen by her white relatives. Thus, both the sense of loss and the burden of denial motivate her silence and aloofness, as well as her accumulation of things and her emphasis on beauty used to mask her deprivations.

These personal characteristics, developed as a defense against low self-esteem, interfere with her acceptance of alternative communities that could substitute for family. Creighton and other minor women characters throughout the narrative extend offers of friendship and acceptance outside the sphere of patriarchal control. Female teachers, secretaries, socialites, and church members all attempt to draw her into their communities of women and out of her personal isolation. As African-American women, they have accepted their race and their gender; however, for Helga, race in the absence of family is too impersonal and abstract to satisfy her immediate familial needs, while gender exaggerates her vulnerability in a society still defining women primarily in terms of wives, mothers, and daughters. None of the other women has the answers to the complex problem facing Helga, but each has something to teach her about living constructively and interdependently with self and female others. Unable to recover from an irrevocable sense of maternal deprivation, she dismisses their overtures, does not learn from them, and remains trapped in an inflated, harmful sense of her uniqueness. Her destructive nostalgia for a childhood she did not have makes it impossible for her to accept adult alternative communities or to express her anger fully against whites, the embodiment of her childhood misery.

Despite a final interview with the school's principal, Dr. Robert Anderson, that nearly witnesses her acknowledgment of anger and almost causes a reversal of her decision, Helga departs from Naxos and the South, which is associated with all the limitations of the school. Larsen modeled Anderson upon Dr. Robert R. Moton, Booker T. Washington's successor as principal of Tuskegee, with whom she retained a friendly relationship. In *Quicksand*, Anderson is slightly enigmatic but not unattractive. He intuitively understands Helga and questions her motives for leaving in such a way as to encourage her reconsideration, yet he also appears hemmed in by the school's philosophy of racial uplift and propriety. Although he recognizes the hypocrisy in the institution's racial stance, he is unable to act to free himself from it. As a result, he is represented as a man holding himself in check. His repression mirrors Helga's inability to unleash feelings or emotions. Yet whenever she is in Anderson's presence, Helga feels a "vague sense of yearning, that longing for sympathy and understanding" and as well a "thousand indefinite longings" (50–51). Only belatedly does she recognize as sexual attraction the "aching delirium" she experiences when remembering Anderson.

Failing to reconcile her differences with Naxos and Anderson, Helga travels to Chicago, her former home and the antithesis of sleepy, repressive Naxos. "Gray Chicago seethed, surged, and scurried about her" (27), but it is less hospitable than she had expected. There she sought to reclaim her lost childhood by seeking out her maternal uncle, Peter Nilssen, a representative of security because of his financial assistance during her girlhood. Modeled upon Larsen's own father, Uncle Peter is a relatively sympathetic, though absent and arbitrary, individual who figures patriarchal bonds, especially duty, responsibility, and financial support, in his relation to Helga. She goes to him as a niece, daughter of his favorite sister, in need of not only money but affection and direction; however, he is away from home, and whatever desired effect his presence might have filled is voided. His new wife, a haughty white woman, rejects any familial association with a person of color and disavows Helga's claim as a relative. The portrait of the disapproving white aunt is suggestive of Nella Larsen's own mother, who could not or would not publicly claim kinship with her "colored" daughter.

Without the expected financial support of her relative, Helga seeks another job. She is especially concerned with obtaining work that, ideally, would duplicate her private space, represented by her dormitory room in Naxos, in the public world. Failing to have the necessary credentials for a position with the library that would have enabled her to satisfy her knowledge and love of books and unable to find what she considers "acceptable" work in Chicago, Helga secures a job as a travel companion and speech editor that takes her to New York and to the center of life among the upper circles of Harlem in its heyday. Her benefactress, Mrs. Jeanette Hayes-Rore, a minister's widow and a prominent "race" woman, is a fictional portrait of Mrs. Eva Jenifer-Rice, a Chicago matron, widow of a minister, and founder of the Southside YWCA, at 3424 Rhodes Avenue, in 1914. Mrs. Jenifer-Rice managed to have that African-American branch of the Y for women accepted as an incorporated and affiliated branch of the national organization in 1915; thereafter, as its first president, she shepherded it into more spacious quarters at 3451 Indiana Avenue in 1919, and remained the guiding spirit behind the Y's 1927 move to a brand new building at 4555–59 South Parkway, one of the finest YWCA facilities in the West at that time. The secretaries at the YWCA in Chicago where Helga Crane stays put her in touch with Mrs. Jeanette Hayes-Rore when they discover her desperate need for a job. One of the primary missions of the early Y founded by Mrs. Jenifer-Rice and a committee of clergymen's wives was the assistance of young girls arriving in Chicago seeking housing and employment.[38]

For a short time, Helga's life in New York appears satisfactory, though she recognizes that it is "bounded by Central Park, Fifth Avenue, St. Nicholas Park, and One Hundred and Forty-fifth Street. Not at all a narrow life, as Negroes lived it, as Helga Crane knew it. Everything was there" (46). Yet, because her position in Harlem life is based upon the suppression and erasure of actual family history, Helga has little chance of having her desires actualized in New York. Mrs. Hayes-Rore, though insisting that "if you didn't have people, you wouldn't be living. Everybody has people" (38), extends the web of secrecy in Helga's life by advising, "I wouldn't mention that my people were white, if I were you. Colored people don't understand it" (41).

With Mrs. Hayes-Rore's intercession, Helga secures a secretarial job at a Harlem insurance company. She especially enjoys living with Anne Grey, a well-to-do, cultured widow and the niece of Mrs. Hayes-Rore. Anne provides her with elegant accommodations, access to Harlem society, and "a sense of freedom" (46). Through Anne's status and space, and the lie Helga perpetrates to attain them, Helga achieves her need to reinvent herself. Anne Grey shares some characteristics of Larsen's socialite friend, Dorothy Peterson, though Peterson never married: "She carried herself as queens are reputed to bear themselves, and probably do not. . . . She possessed an impeccably fastidious taste in clothes, knowing what suited her and wearing it with an air of unconscious assurance. The unusual thing, a native New Yorker, she was also a person of distinction, financially independent, well connected and much sought after. And she was interesting, an odd confusion of wit and intense earnestness; a vivid and remarkable person. . . . She was almost perfect" (45).

But soon after settling into a stylish existence of secretarial work by day and "books, the theater, parties" (45) at night, Helga begins to recoil from her physical space and from the African Americans surrounding her. Her secretive excursions outside of Harlem are defiant responses to the injunction against revealing the miscegenation that produced her; Mrs. Hayes-Rore "felt that [Helga's story] dealing as it did with race intermingling and possible adultery, was beyond definite discussion. For among black people,

---

38. See *The Book of Achievement—The World Over Featuring the Negro in Chicago, 1779–1929* (Chicago, 1929), 121, 134–35, Vol. I of Frederic H. H. Robb, ed., *The Wonder Book,* 2 vols.

as among white people, it is tacitly understood that these things are not mentioned—and therefore they do not exist" (39). Helga's very existence, then, is at stake in her residence in Harlem; the substance of that existence can only be affirmed by her excursions into white New York.

She tires especially of Grey's inconsistent attitudes toward race: "She hated white people with a deep and burning hatred. . . . But she aped their clothes, their manners, and their gracious ways of living. While proclaiming loudly the undiluted good of all things Negro, she yet disliked the songs, the dances, and the softly blurred speech of the race" (48). In preferring "Pavlova to Florence Mills, John McCormack to Taylor Gordon, Walter Hampden to Paul Robeson" (49), Grey is imprisoned in the hegemony of white males whose hierarchical, paternalistic attitudes toward females and blacks she accepts unexamined. She is no different from Helga's other friends in Harlem who prattle on against the viciousness of whites but imitate their culture and their preferences. As members of an emerging African-American middle class, they are self-consciously aware of their position between the world of whites, the purveyors of values for emulation, and the world of lower-class blacks, the stereotype of behavior for rejection.

A chance meeting with Dr. Anderson ignites Helga's exasperation with her Harlem associates. Anderson, employed as a welfare worker in New York after proving to be "too liberal, too lenient, for education as it was inflicted in Naxos" (52), has an emotional effect upon Helga: "A peculiar, not wholly disagreeable, quiver ran down her spine. She felt an odd little faintness. The blood rushed to her face" (49). Her sexual excitement is once more misread, so that she feels the same "anger and defiant desire to hurt" him that she experienced in Naxos. Harlem, now personified in Anderson's sexual magnetism and Helga's inexplicable anger, becomes intolerable.

A five thousand dollar check from her Uncle Peter, along with a letter encouraging her to visit her mother's sister in Copenhagen, solves Helga's dilemma. She leaves the United States with the intention of settling permanently in Denmark. Her affluent Aunt Katrina and uncle, Poul Dahl, represent family and kin from a brief happy interlude in Helga's childhood. Denmark means freedom from the racism of the United States, but it also means a retracing of her maternal heritage, as well as economic dependency and a renunciation of autonomy. Once in Copenhagen she soon discovers that she is an exotic foreigner who is attractive to Danes ultimately because of her "primitive" African heritage. Although her aunt and uncle love her and are not racists, they emphasize her difference and her dependency by carefully dressing her in brilliant colors, décolleté gowns, and outlandish finery, some of which their maid Marie refashions for her—an ironical allusion to Larsen's dressmaker mother, Marie.

Helga becomes an object; her body is objectified, commodified, and placed on the marriage market. Her relatives' great ambition is to marry her off to one of Denmark's most famous artists and, in the process, increase their own social standing. Ibsen's character Nora is figured in Helga's plight, and the Dahls, as Missy Dehn Kubitschek points out, evoke *A Doll's House,* his play in which she appears.[39] The measures the Dahls use to establish their niece in their society force Helga to acknowledge the complexity of her situation and the manipulation of her body. She understands that her relatives are transforming her into both a pampered doll and a sexual commodity. While she yearns to move backward in time and reclaim her youth, she desires to do so as an adult and as an agent. She realizes that she cannot accomplish her purpose in Denmark among Scandinavians who have no understanding of what it means to be a woman of color and specifically an African American.

When Axel Olsen, a prominent Danish painter, propositions her rather than proposes, he prompts her twofold discovery: she is a sensual being with something of the primitive hidden beneath her controlled exterior, and she misses the companionship of blacks. Although Olsen cares enough for her to propose marriage after recognizing his mistake, he is undeterred in his opinion of her: "'You know, Helga, you are a contradiction. . . . You have the warm impulsive nature of the women of Africa, but, my lovely, you have, I fear, the soul of a prostitute. You sell yourself to the highest buyer'" (87). Helga's response surprises Olsen and herself: "'I'm not for sale. Not to you. *Not to any white man.* I don't care at all to be owned. Even by you'" (87; my emphasis). Although her explanation stresses female autonomy and independence, it underscores racial memory and acceptance. There remains, however, an element of recognition of her salability in the marriage marketplace, but Helga insists on defining that market as an African-American one. "'I couldn't marry a white man. . . . It isn't just you, not just personal. . . . It's deeper, broader than that. It's racial. . . . [I]f we were married you might come to be ashamed of me, to hate me, to hate all dark people. My mother did that'" (88). She focuses not on her own potential response to an interracial marriage but on Olsen's, because the painful model available to her is her mother's reaction both to her father and to Helga herself.

Repulsed in addition by Olsen's painting ("some disgusting sensual crea-

39. Kubitschek, *Claiming the Heritage,* 99.

ture with her features" [89]), which refigures the "dissipation" (23) she names in her mother's relation to her father, Helga knows she can never marry him, not even to repay the Dahls. Not only is the sexual nature of his attraction repugnant, but the representation of it is unrecognizable as Helga Crane. Although she is offended by his sexual attraction and is unprepared for his overt desire, she and the Dahls have, perhaps not unwittingly, used her obsession with clothes to attract men. On the one hand, in posturing and in dressing, Helga consciously and naïvely, if not innocently, seeks to mask her many insecurities and her self-perceived inadequacies. On the other hand, with the eyes of a painter manipulating a canvas, Olsen has stripped away the clothing and laid aside the mask to see what his masculine passion has projected onto Helga's body. Rejecting his proposal and, with it, a secure, contained life in Copenhagen, she resolves to return to New York, though not before she has an apotheosis, a vision of her father and his motives:

> For the first time, Helga Crane felt sympathy rather than contempt and hatred for that father, who so often and so angrily she had blamed for his desertion of her mother. She understood, now, his rejection, his repudiation, of the formal claim her mother had represented. She understood his yearning, his intolerable need for the inexhaustible humor and the incessant hope of his own kind, his need for those things, not material, indigenous to all Negro environments. She understood and could sympathize with his facile surrender to the irresistible ties of race, now that they dragged at her own heart. (92)

Satisfied by a black cultural identity that includes an awareness of her physicality separate from an object-state, she becomes more aggressive in fulfilling her sexual drives. At peace with her father, she consciously enters a different spatial relation to her mother. In distinguishing her self as subject from her self as object, she forges action against the grain of her previous passivity. Failing in an attempt to motivate Anderson to a comparable state of action, she retreats from the man she has suddenly recognized as a potential lover in spite of his marriage to Anne Grey. In the aftermath, she has a shattering religious experience in a storefront church, marries the preacher conducting the service, and returns with him to his native Alabama. She succumbs to the "Bacchic vehemence" (113) of the church service and to her own desires projected onto the religiosity of the primitive congregation.

Helga's impulsive conversion, whether real and properly motivated or not, frees her of the inhibitions and anxieties retarding self-expression. But with her surrender to religious and sexual ecstasy, she no longer attempts to bridge the division between her emotions, arrested in childhood, and her intellect, matured and analytical.

She starts yet another new life in a rural African-American community, "a scattered and primitive flock" (118), pastored by her husband, the Reverend Pleasant Green, who represents God and father-figure. Her rush into a marriage after Anderson's rejection fulfills the logic of her search for family and of her repression of sexuality, because her emotional freedom, recovered in a religious frenzy akin to a sexual climax (115–17), quickly translates into the traditional female roles as wife and mother. Only twice in the narrative is Helga reduced to a tearful, emotional outpouring: once when she tells her family history to Mrs. Hayes-Rore ("the torment which she had gone through loomed before her as something brutal and undeserved. Passionately, tearfully, incoherently, the final words tumbled from her quivering petulant lips" [39]); and again when she wanders into the storefront church ("Maddened, she grasped at the railing, and with no previous intention began to yell like one insane . . . while torrents of tears streamed down her face. She was unconscious of the words she uttered, or their meaning" [113–14]).

The two instances of incoherent testifying are linked not only in their reductive impact on the controlled articulate Helga, but also in their underlying allusions to her desire for familial succor. In both cases, she separates words from meaning, and voice becomes the primary signifier of her experience. While Mrs. Hayes-Rore is audience-listener in the first instance, in the second, "a nameless" people function not only as audience-observer but also as active participants in the drama of conversion.

On a rational level, Helga's marriage means the creation of a new family unit for the adult and the cementing of familial bonds with offspring. She considers the decision to marry "a chance at stability, at permanent happiness. . . . [S]he clutched the hope, the desire to believe that now at last she had found some One, some Power, who was interested in her. Would help her" (117). The marriage is a reenactment of her mother's solution to being deserted by her first husband. Just as her mother's second husband is a stern representative of a patriarch, so the simple, conventional Green is a refiguring of the patriarchy. Green offers Helga an uncomplicated life as a minister's wife and as a member of a religion that subordinates human responsibility to God's will: "Actually and metaphorically she bowed her head before God, trusting in Him to see her through. Secretly she was glad that she had not to worry about herself or anything. It was a relief . . . to put the entire responsibility on someone else" (126). As Colette Dowling observes, in choosing husbands and marriage, women often look for a prince who will "rescue them from responsibility": "Give them a pedestal high enough above the dangers of authentic living and they'll be happy just sitting there." [40] It was the choice Helga's mother had made, though her choice was represented as necessity, and it is also the choice Helga makes.

On an emotional level, the marriage satisfies Helga's longing to return to childhood and to correct its unhappy state. It is a concealment and repression of her adult female self. She idealizes the simplicity of existing in a childlike state ("a supreme aspiration toward the regaining of simple happiness, a happiness unburdened by the complexities of the lives she had known" [114]) while being sexually satisfied as an adult woman ("Emotional, palpitating, amorous, all that was living in her sprang like rank weeds at the tingling thought of night, with a vitality so strong that it devoured all shoots of reason" [122]). Initially "proud and gratified that he belonged to her" (122), ultimately Helga is unfulfilled in a union with the pompous, unkempt Green, who becomes synonymous with the triple threat Helga had feared would engulf and destroy her: southerness (as seen in rural, unglorified black folk); submission (in particular to paternal and spiritual authorities); and sexuality (in primitive abandon to desire).

Life with Green in the poor Alabama community allows Helga little expression for her particular aesthetic values, for her sensibility asserting beauty over utility. She intends to transform the women in the congregation by instructing them "according to her ideas of beauty" (119), but she detects disinterest despite their agreeable smiles and promises. The women appreciate much more her fashion-conscious double within the community, Clementine Richards, "a strapping black beauty of magnificent Amazon proportions and bold shining eyes of jet-like hardness. A person of awesome appearance. All chains, strings of beads, jingling bracelets, flying ribbons, feathery neckpieces, and flowery hats" (119). Clementine is African not only in her physical appearance but also in her tastes, which mirror those imposed upon Helga in Denmark. Even more than the other women, "Clementine was inclined to treat Helga with only partially concealed contemptuousness, considering her a poor thing without style" (119). For Helga,

---

40. Colette Dowling, *The Cinderella Complex: Women's Hidden Fears of Independence* (New York, 1982), 140.

whose notions of aesthetics and beauty are Eurocentric and white, Clementine is an expression of her own repressed otherness, though in acknowledging Clementine's "magnificent, . . . awesome appearance," Helga does not modify her sense of mission or of herself.

Once the reality of her own household work—gardening, "cooking, dishwashing, sweeping, dusting, mending, and darning" (120) and conjugal duties—sets in, she sadly admits, "There was no time for the pursuit of beauty, or for the uplifting of other harassed and teeming women, or for the instruction of their neglected children" (124). Her roles as helpmeet and mother channel her creativity into narrow outlets unsuited to her individual temperament and sensibilities. Southern "folk" culture and rural subsistence do not empower Helga or liberate her from anxiety; instead, they lead to a more pronounced psychic rage and to a recognition of her own victimization.

Helga's vitality does not last. The poverty of the community and her own deprivation are so alien that she can neither be happy nor "subdue the cleanly scrubbed ugliness of her own surroundings into soft inoffensive beauty" (121). The production of art or texts is, in a pattern familiar in conventional female maturation within the marriage plot, displaced by the reproduction of children. Procreation substitutes for textual creation, and Helga the potential creative artist is lost, just as Helga the artist creating her self has already been obscured by the more vividly real and vital Clementine Richards. Two pregnancies within twenty months deplete her energy and leave her virtually incapable of caring for her twin boys, her daughter, or herself. With the birth of her fourth child, she becomes too weak to fulfill her social roles as wife and mother.

Powerless to control her body or her environment, she retreats further within herself. She surrenders to the care and authority of Miss Hartley, a nurse from Mobile and "a brusquely efficient woman who produced order out of chaos and quiet out of bedlam" (128) and in whom Larsen invested some of her own experiences as a nurse. Although Helga remains convinced that she will leave her husband and return to the material comforts of the smart set in New York, she cannot abandon her children, because much of the misery of her own life stemmed from her treatment by her parents. Her emancipatory strategies of the past are no longer viable, because the desertion by her black father and the indifference of her white mother combine with all her lost opportunities for happiness to create an oppressive sense of powerlessness and emptiness within her, a condition even her children cannot displace. Even reading, her refuge at the beginning of the narrative, is denied her, though Nurse Hartley consents to read to her and in so doing reiterates Helga's loss of self and control.

Despite her debilitated state, Helga clearly sees her mother in herself. Despite remoteness, her mother neither abandoned her nor denied connection to her, so that Helga experiences her resemblance to her mother without rejecting the family. But it is by design that Helga returns in the end to a vision of her mother that had been submerged after the opening sequence of the novel and veiled in Helga's own beginnings. In reliving her mother's story without comprehension, Helga's own is muted, silenced. "The mother's discourse, *when it can be voiced at all,* is always repetitive, literal, hopeless representation," according to Marianne Hirsch. "It is rooted in the body that shivers, hurts, bleeds, suffers, burns, rather than in the eyes, or in the voice, which can utter its cries of pain." In repeating the matrilineal tie even while rejecting it, Helga feels, however, engulfed in a "quagmire" of her own making, and understands the implications: "It seemed hundreds of years since she had been strong. And she would need strength. For in some way she was determined to get herself out of this bog into which she had strayed. Or—she would have to die" (134). Helga's choice, like her mother's before her, is to assume either the burden of motherhood or the quest for selfhood. As Hirsch suggests, "For women who reject unconditionally the lives and stories of their mothers, there is nowhere to go."[41] Helga dooms herself to erasure because she cannot read the message of her mother's decision and becomes immobilized by the thought of relinquishing either her children or her separate self.

Quicksand ends neither with Helga's physical escape nor with her literal death; it concludes with her becoming pregnant with a fifth child before she has recovered from the birth of the fourth. Her loss of autonomy and self-determination is signed by her inability to control her body and by the debilitating effects of reproduction and motherhood: "In that period of racking pain and calamitous fright Helga had learned what passion and credulity could do to one. In her was born angry bitterness and an enormous disgust. The cruel, unrelieved suffering had beaten down her protective wall" (130). In this sense, the Helga Crane who had dominated the narrative is symbolically dead.

41. Nancy Chodorow, *The Reproduction of Mothering: Psychoanalysis and the Sociology of Gender* (Berkeley, 1978), 92–104; Marianne Hirsch, "Maternal Narratives: 'Cruel Enough to Stop the Blood,'" in *Reading Black, Reading Feminist: A Critical Anthology,* ed. Henry Louis Gates, Jr. (New York, 1990), 426, Hirsch's emphasis.

Helga ends, much as she begins in Naxos, isolated within a small room and in bed where "she could think, would have a certain amount of quiet. Of aloneness" (130). The bed, however, has become womblike and dangerous. A change of environment as relief from her condition is practically impossible; her children deprive her of other creative expressions because she remains restricted by her personal understanding of family: "she wanted to leave them. . . . The recollection of her own childhood, lonely, unloved rose too poignantly before her for her to consider calmly such a solution. . . . [T]o leave them would be a tearing agony, a rending of deepest fibers" (135). Emotional and intellectual connectedness escape her; her existence is as fragmented as it was at the beginning of the novel.

Lacking the means to repair her life, she slips into fantasy, a "serene haven" in which she envisions the figures from her past: her mother, Robert Anderson, James Vayle, Axel Olsen, Audrey Denny, Mrs. Hayes-Rore, and the Dahls, all of whom symbolize her lost opportunities for connection and expression (128–29). Of these, Audrey Denny, the only character with whom Helga never directly interacts, represents an element of Helga's own self that she does not allow herself to become.

First seen at a Harlem cabaret in the company of Robert Anderson, Audrey resembles Helga in appearance and taste, but she expresses her personality differently. She is "placid, taking quietly and without a fuss the things she wanted" (129). Helga views her as a "beautiful, calm cool girl who had the assurance, the courage, so placidly to ignore racial barriers and give her attention to people" (62). Helga regards her with "envious admiration" (62) because Audrey is bound neither by conventional models for African-American women nor by traditional roles for women. Recognizing what she wants, Audrey has the courage to define her own life in keeping with her objectives and her knowledge of herself. By merging the fragmented world that traps Helga, Audrey seems to live not only fully but creatively.

Larsen based Audrey Denny on Blanche Dunn, the exquisitely dressed, alabaster-skinned beauty known in the 1920s for her unique ability to do nothing and to do it better than anyone else. She was, as David Levering Lewis puts it, "tall, slender, ambiguously beige, with the cool, sculptured, haughty beauty of an Andalusian courtesan. . . . She was what whites and many Harlemites thought the Negro would become in the Golden Age, totally untouched by race prejudice and free of all racial concerns." Van Vechten and Harold Jackman adored her. She had a parade of sponsors, including diplomats and noblemen, one of whom she married and settled with in Capri. But during Harlem's heyday, she went from elegant restaurants, to

Broadway openings and exclusive speakeasies (such as the Hot Cha, where she had a permanent table), to shopping trips in Paris, races at Saratoga, and the shore at Atlantic City.[42]

Blanche Dunn left an impression on all who knew her. Bruce Nugent remembered her uniqueness: "This life, which came so easily and unfought for . . . became in reality her career. Her ability to accept the fact that the world was a pleasant place in which to live had never diminished." As Bruce Kellner points out, "Although this serenely beautiful Jamaican girl appeared with Paul Robeson in the film version of *The Emperor Jones,* she was a widely recognizable figure in the social life of the Harlem Renaissance. . . . Unconcerned with racial matters, Blanche Dunn did nothing, apparently, but attend first night parties . . . and floor shows. Her startling glamour . . . was enhanced by a massive calm."[43]

Larsen's admiring portrait of Dunn in the character of Audrey Denny conforms to the consensus, particularly in the matters of languid beauty, social sophistication, and racial impartiality.[44] While she would explore this unusual type of African-American woman more extensively in Clare Kendry Bellew in *Passing,* she uses the character suggestively in *Quicksand* as Helga's sexually confident and race-free psychological double.

That Helga cannot fuse the parts of herself that Audrey Denny represents signals that healthy survival in racial and sexual contexts is impossible. The dramatic ending, with Helga Crane ironically aware of her disintegrating self, is graphic realism that may seem too drastic a shift of fortune for the search for self-affirmation she undertakes, but it is thematically and symbolically in keeping with her downward spiral into despair and destruction. From the beginning, she is a divided person who wants a full, rich life, one marked by achievement and recognition; yet she is also an ambivalent individual incapable of adhering to any one set path in life, primarily because she does not know what she wants to be or what her potential is. Her own restless nature and her latent sexual desires combine with her conflicting attitudes toward race and gender to cause her downfall. "With the obscuring curtain of religion rent, she was able to look about her and see with shocked eyes this thing that she had done to herself" (130). Even in her weakened state, she sees the "terrible reality" of her position: "At first she

42. Lewis, *When Harlem Was in Vogue,* 244.

43. Nugent quoted by Lewis, 244; Bruce Kellner, *The Harlem Renaissance: A Historical Dictionary of the Era* (New York, 1987), 108.

44. See Larsen, *Quicksand,* 60–62.

had felt only an astonished anger at the quagmire in which she had engulfed herself. She had ruined her life. Made it impossible ever again to do the things that she wanted, have the things that she loved, mingle with the people she liked. She had, to put it as brutally as anyone could, been a fool. The damnedest kind of a fool. And she had paid for it. Enough. More than enough" (133). In assessing her responsibility for her life, Helga settles on the word *fool* and, in doing so, echoes the label she had applied to her mother (23).

Helga's tragedy is personal but far-reaching in its implications. Her female perspective intensifies the psychological dualism inherent in her obsessive awareness that she is a product of both white and black cultures. As a mulatto in environments clearly defined by race, Helga has reservations about the world of whites and that of blacks; as a modern woman without the protection of family and money, she has questions about a society with fixed roles for men and women. Unfortunately, she does not have the personal resources and strength necessary for extricating herself from her dilemma or for formulating a positive definition of herself. Without birth control, she has little hope of escaping from the cycle of sex, pregnancy, and illness. Ultimately, there is in her position "a quality of passivity, of resignation, of suppressed anger that results," Mary Helen Washington says, "from the stifling of desire and energy." [45]

Read as symbolic metafiction, as a novel about the creation of art or the artist's struggle to create art, *Quicksand* offers an allegory of the African-American woman artist. Helga is a female artist figure in search of her art and of a medium for expressing it. The character follows the kind of search that Van Vechten presented in *Peter Whiffle* and James Joyce in *A Portrait of the Artist as a Young Man* and that marked much of the modern fiction that Larsen most admired. Helga is, in a sense, a portrait of the failed artist as a young woman of color, comparable to James Weldon Johnson's *Autobiography of An Ex-Coloured Man* in conjoining race and failed artistic expression. Because of the influence of Joseph Hergesheimer, Van Vechten, Ronald Firbank, and others who treated the frustration and inability of the artist ever to come directly to art, the portrait is not as clear-cut to readers of today as it would have been to Larsen's contemporaries familiar with this sophisticated 1920s genre and subject matter. Written expression is the form of art most closely identified with Helga, an English teacher who loves

45. Mary Helen Washington, *Invented Lives: Narratives of Black Women, 1860–1960* (Garden City, 1987), 166.

books and chooses topics for writing, such as "A Plea for Color" (18). Larsen adds the factors of race and gender to her artist figure, so that the foreground of the novel obscures to a degree the background odyssey that is the portrayal of the female artist's failed search for self and subject. Her embedding of Stein's "Melanctha" into the narrative gestures toward a gendered search for voice and actualization. In a different context, Houston Baker, Jr., labels *Quicksand*, along with *Passing* and Jessie Fauset's *Plum Bun*, "'what if . . . ' texts—provocative dancings at the very borders of social and sexual taboo."[46] The "what if" of Larsen's narrative, however, is not conflated to sexual desire alone; it is expanded to include a desire, dominant yet obfuscated, for a textual production of self in art as much as in life. In seeking a personal emancipation that would allow her to write, Helga recreates her mother's story, but too late does she realize the implications of what she has set out to do. Despite her artistic inclinations and sensibility, Helga never writes; the reason her life, complicated by both gender and race, does not come fully to art is, in one sense, the subject worked out in the entire text.

The novel becomes a cautionary tale of the creative process, with the life of the female struggling to become an artist expressive of her matrilineal heritage as the central idea. The artist is clearly visible in Helga Crane, even though she can find no viable outlet for her aesthetic concerns. She has her need and capacity to create aborted by motherhood, by bearing children in an endless cycle that parodies the condition of women whose artistic emergence is blocked, whose creative energies are diverted into family life. Childbirth and childrearing, depicted in the contexts of sickness and death, are not only unsatisfactory but also destructive. Helga is more burdened by the presence of a family of her own than she had been by the absence of one; under its pressures she sinks into a waste that smothers her artistic life before it can come to fruition. Since she could find only blockages in the black and white worlds, Helga mistakenly anticipates finding her inspiration among the common, ordinary folk of the rural South, as some in the Harlem Renaissance clearly believed. Although she struggles to maintain a sense of herself that is different from that of her neighbors in the small town, eventually she becomes like them, as the ironical reference to France's "Procurator of Judea" suggests. The forgetfulness that Pilate claims regarding his condemning Christ to death is indicative of Helga's own potential course. If

46. Houston A. Baker, Jr., *Workings of the Spirit: The Poetics of Afro-American Women's Writings* (Chicago, 1991), 36.

she could lose all historical consciousness and forget her former life, the claims of art and self-fulfillment, then she would be a mother to her children and a wife to her husband.

The problem is critical for female artists, as Sylvia Plath recognized while still a graduate student: "a woman has to sacrific all claims of femininity and family to be a writer."[47] The psyche Larsen explores is female, one aware of sexuality and of race, but also one self-consciously concerned with values of the individual that have to do with art and the life of the imagination. Always her refuge and sustenance, Helga's imagination provides the sole place where she is consistently gratified and fully realized.

Larsen treats the life of imagination and possibility in her second novel. Clare Kendry, who passes for white, makes up her life entirely from her own imagination. She perceives who she might be and then she creates that person, but she is not imaginatively tied to any one concept of self, particularly because she has accurately read the meaning of her mother's life. She risks re-creating herself as her own sense of need and ideality shifts.

Helga Crane, too, is a self-made woman, self-made in the sense that she has invented herself. Her exterior belies what she believes herself to be. When Robert Anderson calls her "a lady" of "dignity and breeding," "inherited from good stock," she hurls back, "'I was born in a Chicago slum'" (21), and "'My father was a gambler who deserted my mother, a white immigrant. It is even uncertain that they were married'" (21). When Anne Grey welcomes her to the fashionable brownstone after Jeanette Hayes-Rore fabricates Helga's background, she begins "to feel like a criminal" (42), at least partly because she is isolated within the story of the male, in her father's racialized story, and because in claiming only her father's race, she denies her mother's. Within an inventive search for wholeness and truth, Helga demands her own story without its imprisonment in a male guise, as is, she believes, her mother's story. She has, however, acquired an education and cultivated her tastes so that she can be the person she wants to be. She is not always successful, primarily because she is not certain whether she can be satisfied with the ordinary life that most in society ultimately accept. She feels an enormous need for greatness, for distinction, but her imagination fails to produce a process for fulfilling her need. Much of the energy and the imagination required for writing or self-expression goes into self-creation, self-generation. Instead of finding a means of artistic expression, Helga finds marriage and motherhood, which have not actually been the

47. Sylvia Plath, quoted in Tillie Olsen, *Silences* (New York, 1979), 30.

goals of her energy, independence, and intelligence. True to her understanding that the individual need of a woman may be greater than that allowed by men and marriage, Larsen invariably depicts marriage as problematical and as vulnerable to threats from the outside (jealous women) and from the inside (self-disillusion). Neither husband nor wife is able to understand all of the dynamics of the union, but the wife is acutely sensitive to the power the husband has in the union. He is, after all, free to choose her, to leave her, and to choose another, which is the hidden threat in *Quicksand* as well as in *Passing*. In Helga Crane's case, romantic love and bodily surrender to the power and sexuality of the male, or more aptly the negative capacities of male privilege, suffocate her drive toward creative self-fulfillment or art.

Throughout *Quicksand*, Larsen is most effective in using symbolism to enhance characterization and to underscore theme. Images of entrapment, suffocation, and asphyxiation become more prominent and integral toward the end of the novel, where they skillfully evoke Helga's mental and physical condition, but from the outset of the novel, they complement the journey, a major structural device. The literal journey functions symbolically as well, because *Quicksand* is not only a *Künstlerromane* but also a *Bildungsroman,* interrelating psychological and social forces in Helga Crane's search for definition and development. Each phase of the spatial journey, Naxos, Chicago, Harlem, Denmark, Alabama, accompanied by corresponding seasons of the year, marks a symbolic stage in her developing consciousness.[48] The episodic narrative structure, linked to Larsen's apprenticeship as a reader and contributor to popular romance and women's magazines, depends upon scene changes to converge action and meaning in Helga's spiritual quest for growth, emergence, and identity. Throughout there is an integral relationship between environmental landscapes and mental processes, between physical shapes and boundaries and human manners and styles, between racial and economic structures. Despite Helga's failure, which may be linked structurally to a quest for sexuality in the novel of eros as Annis Pratt has defined it, the novel is moving and successful.[49] Its messages extend from the focus on an individual mulatto heroine by making her restless energy and relentless search endemic to modern identity in general and to female identity in particular.

Although its complexity was not perceived, *Quicksand* was far from being an ignored first novel. The positive assessment in *Saturday Review of*

---

48. Thornton, "Sexism as Quagmire," 294.
49. Annis Pratt, *Archetypal Patterns in Women's Fiction* (Bloomington, 1981), 168.

Literature presented the note recurrent in reviews by whites. "The style of the book is well-mannered and touched here and there with beauty. But the chief interest lies in the fact that its principal character is a person of a quite unusual mixture of blood rather than in what she does or says or what happens to her." Southerner Roark Bradford, whose book of black folk stories, *Ol' Man Adam an' His Chillun,* had just been released, wrote in a qualified appraisal for the New York *Herald Tribune* that "in spite of its failure to hold up to the end, the book is good," and praised the "real charm" of "Larsen's delicate achievement in maintaining for a long time an indefinable, wistful feeling." That and the "saneness" of Larsen's writing about race, he said, would cause *Quicksand* to be "widely read and discussed." In "What Gods! What Gongs!" for the *New Republic,* T. S. Matthews exclaimed, "You have met the Negro."[50]

E. Merrill Root, however, was the most poetic in phrasing his appreciation for the "Negro" aspects and their symbolic meanings: "But the book, in so far as it is Miss Larsen herself, is excellent. She has, in so far as she has simply bared a modern Negro soul, race-divided and disillusioned by our current misosophy, done us a service. . . . The book is a noteworthy hour-hand of ebony, pointing to midnight in the Negro soul, in the modern soul. But it is for us to realize that midnight is the beginning of morning."[51] Although Root equated the "Negro" metaphorically with modernity, white reviewers, fascinated in the 1920s by voyeuristic encounters with primitivistic "Negrodom," were typically concerned with the treatment of race and the depiction of black life in the urban settings sensationalized in Van Vechten's *Nigger Heaven.*

African-American reviewers also observed Larsen's handling of racial themes; however, their primary concern was with Larsen's stand on miscegenation and propaganda. Gwendolyn Bennett anticipated the tenor of the responses when she announced the arrival of *Quicksand* in her May "Ebony Flute" column for *Opportunity:* "Many folks will be interested to hear that this book does not set as its tempo that of the Harlem cabaret—this is the story of the struggle of an interesting cultured Negro woman against her environment. Negroes who are squeamish about writers exposing our worst

50. "New Books: Fiction," *Saturday Review of Literature,* May 19, 1928, p. 896; Roark Bradford, "Books," New York *Herald Tribune,* May 13, 1928, p. 522; T. S. Matthews, "What Gods! What Gongs!," *New Republic,* LV (May 30, 1928), 50.

51. E. Merrill Root, "Ebony Hour-Hand, Pointing to Midnight," *Christian Century* (October 18, 1928), 1262.

side will be relieved that Harlem night-life is more or less submerged by this author in the psychological struggle of the heroine." Arthur Huff Fauset in the last issue of *Black Opals,* a little magazine published in Philadelphia, agreed with Bennett and pronounced a major breakthrough, "a step forward": "For the first time, perhaps, a Negro author has succeeded in writing a novel about colored characters in which the propaganda motive is decidedly absent." In "Miscegenation? Bah!" the *Amsterdam News* reviewer was pleased that Larsen had written "neither a plea to be taken into the white race nor a long scream of hatred for everything Caucasian." Similarly, in assuaging misgivings, Barefield Gordon of the Chicago *Defender* called *Quicksand* a "fine[ly] written" and "artistically sound" novel, for the "use of the Negro as a theme is neither for exhibition nor propaganda, but for the author's idea of telling a story." The review in the Baltimore *Afro-American* amounted to little more than a statement of relief that after "super-sexed stories like 'Rainbow Round My Shoulder' and 'Home to Harlem,' 'Quicksand' is a refreshing story, built on the proposition there is something else in Negro life besides jazz and cabarets."[52]

Larsen was elated that black and white reviewers took her book seriously and were enthusiastic about her debut. She had rightly anticipated that the most important review from the black press would appear in *Opportunity.* She was more anxious about it than any of the others because the reviewers selected were more knowledgeable about African-American literary history and more sophisticated about recent literature. Her anxiety was somewhat allayed when Eda Lou Walton's review appeared in July. Less enthusiastic than critics in the white press, Walton nevertheless understood Larsen's purpose, particularly her delineation of a modern female, but she was not entirely satisfied: "To tell the story of a cultivated and sensitive woman's defeat through her own sex-desire is a difficult task. When the woman is a mulatto and beset by hereditary, social and racial forces over which she has little control and into which she cannot fit, her character is so complex that any analysis takes a mature imagination. This, I believe, Miss Larsen is too young to have."[53]

52. Gwendolyn Bennett, "The Ebony Flute," *Opportunity,* VI (May, 1928), 153; Arthur Huff Fauset, Review of Nella Larsen's *Quicksand,* in *Black Opals,* I (June, 1928), 19; "Miscegenation? Bah!," New York *Amsterdam News,* May 16, 1928, in SCF; Barefield Gordon, "Quest for Life," Chicago *Defender,* August 25, 1928, in SCF; "Book a Week," Baltimore *Afro-American,* May 15, 1928, in SCF.

53. Eda Lou Walton, Review of *Quicksand,* by Nella Larsen, in *Opportunity,* VI (July, 1928), 212.

Reading literally, Walton complained that the young Helga at the beginning of the book "cannot be the older woman of the latter half." She especially singled out "the fault of fine-writing" for criticism because she found that "the elaborateness of uninteresting detail" functioned merely "to assure us that her Helga is cultured and modern": "Miss Larsen writes a little too carefully of the objective evidences of culture and too carelessly of the refinement within the woman herself." In only one paragraph of the long review did she come close to praising Larsen: "*Quicksand* is, for all this comment, a good tale, and a good first novel. Miss Larsen's prettiness of style may, with more writing, become power. She will undoubtedly learn more effectual working out of laws of cause and event within characters. She has already the ability to interest us in her people and their problems."[54] While the review was both fair and perceptive, it was the most disappointing Larsen received because of the status and influence of *Opportunity* among African Americans, particularly writers.

Criticism of Larsen's characterizations, however, was not confined to printed reviews. While Walton focused attention on the development of Helga, others in the African-American community targeted the portrait of the unwashed minister and his primitive Alabama congregation. Religious African Americans saw it as an affront to the church; Larsens' in-laws took it as an insult to the Imes family, which for two generations had been prominent in the black church and in the missionary field of Alabama. Her father-in-law had spent his life ministering in the South, and even her husband had taught in American Missionary Association schools in Alabama and Georgia. Larsen's irreverence in light of her connection to the Imes family was shocking.

Du Bois, however, was not offended by Larsen's treatment, and hailed the text as "fine, thoughtful and courageous. It is, on the whole, the best piece of fiction that Negro America has produced since the heyday of [Charles] Chesnutt, and stands easily with Jessie Fauset's 'There is Confusion,' in its subtle comprehension of the curious cross currents that swirl about the black American." Using *Quicksand* as an instructive counterpoint to Claude McKay's new novel (*Home to Harlem* "nauseates me, and after the dirtier parts of its filth I feel distinctly like taking a bath"), Du Bois painted an admiring portrait of Helga as "master of her whimsical, unsatisfied soul," and as one "typical of the new, honest, young fighting Negro

54. *Ibid.*, 213.

woman," who "beaten down even to death . . . never will surrender to hypocrisy and convention."[55]

Like Du Bois, Alain Locke was impressed by Larsen's ability to render contemporary issues in a fresh perspective. He properly termed *Quicksand* "a social document of importance, and as well, a living, moving picture of a type not often in the foreground of Negro fiction, and here treated for the first time with adequacy." Unlike Du Bois, he made no reference to the female protagonist or the gender-related issues, but he applauded the new directions charted in the novel. "Indeed this whole side of the problem which was once handled exclusively as a grim tragedy of blood and fateful heredity now shows a tendency to shift to another plane of discussion, as the problem of divided social loyalties and the issues of the conflict of cultures."[56]

Despite the attention of Locke, Du Bois, and other luminaries, *Quicksand* was published late in the Harlem Renaissance. Larsen's claim that the novel took her "five months in her head and six weeks on the typewriter" notwithstanding, it had actually taken from January to October, 1926, to complete the first readable version, and from October, 1926, to March, 1927, to rewrite the final manuscript.[57] Knopf then took from the spring of 1927 to the spring of 1928 to produce the novel. By the time *Quicksand* left the presses in 1928, most of the fire and verve of the Renaissance were over, and much of its attendant significance, the opportunities for publishing, had actually decreased even while the number of new writers had increased.

In 1927, *Opportunity* had suspended its literary contests because of the poor quality of the entries. Larsen barely had a chance to establish a name as a writer before one of the major organs for spreading that name was lost. And in 1928, Charles S. Johnson, recognizing the inability of *Opportunity* to support itself, left New York for the academic life at Fisk University. His move foreshadowed the gradual exodus of most of the prominent Renaissance figures. Johnson's parting tribute to the literary and cultural movement that he had helped foster was the anthology of writings, *Ebony and Topaz* (1927). Larsen made no contribution; at press time, she had not yet been taken seriously as a writer.

55. W. E. B. Du Bois, "Two Novels," *Crisis*, XXXV (June, 1928), 202.
56. Alain Locke, "1928: A Retrospective Review," *Opportunity*, VII (January, 1929), 9.
57. Berlack, "New Author Unearthed," 16.

Included in the collection, however, was Locke's apology for the lack of achievement in the works and writers, "Our Little Renaissance," which came just two years after his enthusiastic heralding of a new age in black culture and literature in *The New Negro* (1925). His essay is almost a swan song for what might have been. Thus, Larsen, whose novel was in production when the opening strains of a farewell began, arrived at the precise moment when the movement had passed its peak.

Her writing in progress, then, took a turn away from the New Negro Renaissance and toward the white artists, publishers, and audiences who had seemingly welcomed the appearance of her work without reservations about her race. When *Quicksand* appeared, Larsen was already nearly finished with her second novel, *Passing,* and within the year would be at work on her third, "Crowning Mercy," which became her "white book." In it she turned away from African Americans and matters of race and toward a treatment of the white world that had been her training ground for fiction in her short stories for *Young's Magazine.* Astute enough to realize that some of the momentum was gone from the Renaissance movement, she was also cognizant of the lessening of interest in works by New Negro writers. Her solution was a novel about whites. She envisioned herself a novelist, and a novelist without a racial designation before it. What she did not fully realize was that one aspect of her acceptance as a novelist was based on her racial affiliation.

The most important commentary related to the directions Larsen would take after *Quicksand* appeared in January, 1929, when Locke, still *the* spokesman for the Renaissance, gave *Opportunity* readers his cautionary assessment of the year's output by African-American writers. Accompanying his "1928: A Retrospective Review" with a quarter-page photograph of Nella Larsen, Locke called the year "the floodtide of the present Negrophile movement" because of the number of books published on African-American life, but the expected optimism about how the numbers might project the future was missing.

> More books have been published . . . by both white and Negro authors than was the normal output of more than a decade in the past. More aspects of Negro life have been treated than were ever even dreamed of. The proportions show the typical curve of a major American fad, and to a certain extent, this indeed it is. We shall not fully realize it until the inevitable reaction comes; when as the popular interest flags, the movement will lose thousands of supporters who are now under

its spell, but who tomorrow would be equally hypnotized by the next craze.[58]

Locke warned that a downswing of interest was bound to occur, almost as the logical extension of a fad that must necessarily peak and then wane. Yet his view was not without hope for a better period ahead: "To my mind the movement for the vital expression of Negro life can only truly begin as the fad breaks off. There is an inevitable distortion under the hectic interest and forcing of the present vogue for Negro idioms. An introspective calm, a spiritually poised approach, a deeply matured understanding are finally necessary." Locke was taking stock not merely of the year's output in literature but of the entire movement and its short history of just over three years. "To get above ground, more forcing has had to be endured; to win a hearing, much exploitation has had to be tolerated. There is as much spiritual bondage in these things as there ever was material bondage in slavery. Certainly the Negro artist must point the way when this significant movement comes, and establish the values by which Negro literature and art are to be permanently gauged after the fluctuating experimentalism of the last few years."[59]

He could well have been echoing Langston Hughes's words in "The Negro Artist and the Racial Mountain," but the context was different. Locke refused to relinquish the dream of what a Negro Renaissance might eventually mean, but he was willing, though reluctant, to give up the very means that he had courted for himself and for others. Perhaps no other major promoter of the new writers had been so overt in seeking white patronage. His almost sycophantic relationship with the wealthy white matron Charlotte Osgood Mason in attempting to direct the output and the talents of Zora Neale Hurston and Langston Hughes was, by January, 1929, well known.

While Larsen did not solicit such financial patronage, she did court the endorsement of prominent whites and blacks for her literary career and her social life. In the first few weeks after the publication of *Quicksand* and before any reviews appeared, she wrote to Edward Wasserman, who was at work on a review even though he was not in the literary business: "I do want to see your review. Will you have a copy? I'm too poor to subscribe to a clipping bureau. Besides, what's the use? It seems that your review will be

---

58. Locke, "1928: A Retrospective Review," 8.
59. *Ibid.*

the only notice I'll have. I would like to see that."[60] Larsen's anxiety, whether real or feigned, was soon allieviated, because within the next few months reviews of *Quicksand* appeared in the white and black presses across the United States and in England. While she could not afford a clipping service, she scrupulously collected, saved, and bound all of the printed reviews, just as she had done for Van Vechten's *Nigger Heaven*. These, her personal record of accomplishment, became the main asset in her professional portfolio accompanying all of her applications for awards or fellowships.[61]

April and May, the months after the publication of *Quicksand*, were filled with the kinds of activities Larsen relished—teas, receptions, formal dinners, and parties—and with a strengthening of her resolve to move to a more suitable apartment. In April, the month of Du Bois' daughter Yolande's marriage to Countee Cullen, she planned cocktails for a number of the wedding guests: "I am asking a few of the thousand and one invited guests to come by here for a cocktail before proceeding to the solemnities." She wrote to Eddie Wasserman, "Please come if you can. Come even if you are not expected at the wedding. . . . Any time between four and five-thirty you can wet your whistle at 236 West 135th Street." The gala wedding, scheduled for six o'clock on Monday, April 9, was the major social event in Harlem that spring, but Larsen and Elmer Imes never arrived at the Reverend Frederick Cullen's Salem Methodist Episcopal Church for the ceremony. Their guests for afternoon drinks made an evening of it: "People kept coming in and then deciding not to go on to the wedding. So we were here until eight o'clock. Then we went out to dinner." Larsen was delighted as always with her success as a hostess, but she showed her sense of humor in describing the evening to Wasserman, who had not appeared. "It was very amusing . . . because the sandwiches kept getting fewer and fewer and I kept rescuing them from hungry guests and saying firmly 'you'll have to leave some for Eddie Wasserman and someone else.' Then when you didn't appear they accused me of trying to save the food."[62]

By early May, Larsen's quest for place and position seemed achieved. She

60. Nella Larsen Imes to Edward Wasserman, Home Sunday [postmarked April 16, 1928], in Serendipity Books Catalogue 43 (1985), item 331B. The letter is now in the Schomburg Center for Research in Black Culture.

61. See Nominee's cards for Nella Larsen Imes, dated August 23, 1928, and April 3, 1929, in HFR; see also Nella Larsen Imes to George E. Haynes, Monday, April first [1929], *ibid.*

62. Imes to Wasserman, Home Thursday [postmarked April 5, 1928], in Serendipity Books Catalogue 43; Imes to Wasserman, Home Sunday [postmarked April 16, 1928], *ibid.*

secured an apartment farther uptown, 2588 Seventh Avenue, Apartment 6N, in the Dunbar Apartments, the fashionable address she had desired upon first moving from New Jersey. The top floor apartment provided just the right residential setting, yet she facetiously nicknamed it "Uncle Tom's Cabin," because the income from *Quicksand* enabled her to become a tenant/owner. Larsen had finally arrived in style, for the award-winning garden complex, with its restriction against "boisterousness and horseplay" and its owner's purchase plan, catered to Harlem's elite.[63]

The high point was a tea planned in her honor on Sunday, May 13. It recognized her literary accomplishment and her social standing. She could not contain her excitement: "the Woman's Auxiliary [triple underscore] of the N. A. A. C. P. is going to give a tea for me [multiple underscore for *me*]!!"[64] Harlem society had nodded in her direction, and with Lillian Alexander, wife of a wealthy physician, spearheading the arrangements, the tea was tantamount to a debutante's party.

For Larsen, this event was a victory of sorts, because apparently she had previously suffered some snub by the Woman's Auxiliary. In announcing the invitation to Van Vechten, she pondered the social politics of the occasion: "The good God only knows why [she was being honored at the tea]. I hope you will get an invitation because this will be a time when I will need all of my friends. . . . I acted as if nothing had happened, and declared myself very flattered. I dread breaking the news to Elmer, because I'm sure he'll be so furious that he'll have a convulsion of some sort. I hope I did the wise thing to accept." Whatever had occurred in the past did not prevent her or her husband from attending the Sunday afternoon affair, or from basking in the afterglow from a well-placed account in the *Amsterdam News* ("Nella Larsen, Author of 'Quicksand,' Honor Guest at NAACP Tea").[65]

The one sticking point during these several months of popularity and attention was her second novel. Using the model of Van Vechten's publication of a novel a year between 1922 and 1926, she wanted to finish the book for Knopf while interest in her work was high enough to ensure good sales. The critical reception of *Quicksand* had convinced her that she could earn a living as a novelist. Yet despite her pleasure in the personal notes of appreciation for her published novel, she was unhappy with herself for failing to

63. See the *Dunbar News*, May 14, 1929, p. 4, in SCF.
64. Nella Larsen Imes to Carl Van Vechten, n.d. [postmarked May 1, 1928], in JWJ.
65. *Ibid.*; "Nella Larsen, Author of 'Quicksand,' Honor Guest at NAACP Tea," New York *Amsterdam News*, May 23, 1928, p. 5.

complete the new book. "It is impossible for me," she admitted to Van Vechten in April, "to tell how much your letters [regarding *Quicksand*] cheered a poor coloured child who for some reason or another has been feeling blue over that same old book [the novel-in-progress entitled 'Nig']."[66] Not even the first glimmer of success would waylay her long-range objective to become, as she said, a "famous" novelist.

66. Nella Larsen Imes to Carl Van Vechten, "Home," n.d. [*ca.* April, 1928], in JWJ.

10

Succeeding with *Passing,*
1928–1929

AT THE END of August, 1928, Nella Larsen completed "Nig," the 45,000-word manuscript of her second novel. Her announcement was triumphant: "I have had a very hellish week, but have finished my manuscript. This in spite of having been locked out for a day and a half, and sudden death."[1] As always she took pride in beating the odds, but with Elmer Imes away at Michigan and with the summer heat oppressing her, she experienced more difficulty than usual in concentrating on the last stages of her writing. She worked under a self-imposed deadline to produce a final version.

Larsen had intended to have Van Vechten read it before his departure for Europe, but the manuscript appeared too "very badly done—even to me," she admitted. Because Walter White, who had secured a typist for *Quicksand,* was just returning from France when "Nig" was ready for typing, Larsen had not troubled him for assistance. She had typed the manuscript herself, and without a carbon. "I did try," she said, "but just couldn't do it." Yet she wanted a reading, Van Vechten's in particular: "I don't suppose, or expect that at this eleventh hour you will have time to read it. And I realize that it's my fault entirely. This C.P.T. will be the destruction of us all." Although comfortable enough with Van Vechten to joke about the legendary lateness of "Colored People's Time" and to entitle her work "Nig" after his controversial *Nigger Heaven,* Larsen was still uneasy about

1. Nella Larsen Imes to Carl Van Vechten, Monday [postmarked September 3, 1928], in JWJ.

asking him directly to read her work. Claiming to be "sorry and disappointed" with herself for not having finished it sooner, she inveigled his assistance: "I may type it again. . . . Perhaps after another going over, the typing will look better. In that case I could send you a copy, if you'd not mind too much being bothered on a Saturday. Do let me know exactly how you feel."[2]

Part of her urgency to secure Van Vechten's help and her reluctance to impose on him was due to his highs and lows that summer. In June, Avery Hopwood, his longtime friend and the author of popular comedies, died of a heart attack while wading in the Mediterranean Sea. Hopwood's death stunned Van Vechten: "It is my first experience with death of an intimate contemporary and it is frightening." Larsen lamented Hopwood's loss as a "wide, deep and personal" tragedy for Van Vechten, though she, too, was saddened by the suddenness of the death. She had seen Hopwood the night before he sailed for Europe. Van Vechten had been planning a motor tour of Europe with Hopwood, Nora Holt, and Fania Marinoff when news of the death reached him. In addition to recovering from the shock of Hopwood's death, he was basking in the attention brought by his new book, *Spider Boy: A Scenario for a Moving Picture,* which appeared late in July. Ambrose Deacon, the hero of the comic novel satirizing Hollywood and the movie industry, was partly based on Avery Hopwood, whose personality had also contributed to Peter Whiffle, Van Vechten's best-known fictional character.[3]

Early in August, Larsen had written to cheer and congratulate Van Vechten:

> You've done it again! Spider-boy is delightful. How beautifully nasty you are about the movies and how amusing you say that they are manufactured like "clo'kes and suits" by the manufacturers of "clo'kes and suits."
>
> And I do think that your relation of the annoyances of fame is delightful—and barbed.

2. *Ibid.*

3. Carl Van Vechten to Joseph Hergesheimer, July 3 [1928], in *The Letters of Carl Van Vechten,* ed. Bruce Kellner (New York, 1987), 103–104; Nella Larsen Imes to Carl Van Vechten, n.d. [postmarked July 3, 1928], in JWJ; Carl Van Vechten to Fania Marinoff, n.d. [June 20, 1928], and Carl Van Vechten to Avery Hopwood, n.d. [June, 1928], both in *Letters of Carl Van Vechten,* ed. Kellner, 102–103; Edward Lueders, *Carl Van Vechten* (New York, 1965), 111.

My reaction to the blurb however is something like this:

X   A gay book
me Yes but—
X   Certainly a gay book
me Yes but—
X   Anybody can see it's a gay book.
me But ——
X   You're an idiot
me Yes I know, but ——[4]

The note was the most playful of those she wrote to Van Vechten about his books, no doubt because *Spider Boy* was the most fanciful work of a novelist who, at that moment, needed levity.

By the end of August, Van Vechten's departure for Paris was imminent. Larsen was running out of time for getting the manuscript to him for a reading. On Monday, September 3, she had promised a completed typescript by Saturday, and she kept her word. After spending five days laboring over the retyping, she wrote Van Vechten: "I have this day completed your novel 'Nig.' That is, it has only to be copied. Thank God, glory Hallelluia [*sic*] Amen!" Still flattering Van Vechten, she emphasized the personal toll that the work on the book had taken. "Though years have flown by since last we met, I still have a place in [my] memory for you and often wonder if you still look the same. Life, disease and hard labor have laid their heavy hands on me however——." Her motive was more than cajoling Van Vechten into reading the manuscript: she had set her sights upon a literary prize for her first novel.

> I want to tell you that I am asking for the Harmon Award and am taking the liberty of using your name as "a responsible person who knows by contact the work and ability of the applicant." A little ambiguous but I hope it's all right. Looking back on the year's out put of Negro literature, I don't see why I shouldn't have a book in. There's only Claude McKay besides. —Rudolph [Fisher] is just too late—— and the Harmon Foundation is in some way tied up with the same up lift so maybe "Home to Harlem" won't get a very warm welcome.[5]

4. Nella Larsen Imes to Carl Van Vechten, Monday, n.d. [postmarked August 6, 1928], in CVV.

5. Nella Larsen Imes to Carl Van Vechten, Saturday [September, 1928], in JWJ.

Late in August, Larsen had begun considering her chance for one of the new William E. Harmon Foundation Awards for Distinguished Achievement Among Negroes, which had been established "to focus public attention on notable accomplishments of the Negro race in the U. S. and, by bringing this work to the notice of a wider public, to assist in the development of a greater economic security for the race."[6] Inspired by the reception accorded *Quicksand*, she had written to Dr. George E. Haynes on August 25, asking for the "necessary application forms . . . and any additional information that I need to have to compete." A graduate of Fisk, Haynes had been in Elmer Imes's class of 1903 and had remained a friend of both Elmer and his brother William Lloyd, who had been an undergraduate at Fisk when Haynes was in a graduate program there. Haynes also knew William Lloyd Imes from the Federal Council of the Churches of Christ in America. Beginning in 1925, Imes had been active on the council's commissions on race relations, worship, and international peace and good will.[7]

As secretary of the Commission on the Church and Race Relations for the Federal Council of Churches, which administered the Harmon Awards, Haynes sent Larsen an application blank and a Harmon Foundation leaflet by return mail; moreover, he or someone in the office changed the date on Larsen's letter from August to July and noted sending out the requested materials on July 26. The reason for the change was clear: the deadline for the nomination or application blank was August 15. Larsen's request had arrived eleven days after the completed form was due in the commission's office, but the strong Fisk alumni network smoothed her way. As it turned out, Haynes's efforts on her behalf were made moot when, because of a lack of applications, the deadline was officially moved to September 10.[8]

By that time, Van Vechten had sailed on the RMS *Mauretania* after the most raucous of his departure parties. "Hundreds, including the fascinating Nora Holt, came to do me hommage [*sic*] and to lap up as much champagne as they could decently imbibe." Nella Larsen was in the interracial throng crowding Van Vechten's royal suite and prompting him to observe, "I am sure the personnel of the ship must have decided that Booker T. Washington

6. Hannah Moriarta to James Weldon Johnson, July 25, 1928, *ibid*. Moriarta was the assistant for the Harmon Awards.

7. Nella Larsen Imes to George E. Haynes, July 25, 1928, in HFR; William Lloyd Imes, *The Black Pastures: An American Pilgrimage in Two Centuries, Essays and Sermons* (Nashville, 1957), 146.

8. Larsen Imes to Haynes, July 25, 1928, in HFR (information typed onto the letter); "Harmon Awards Contest Closes on September 10th," New York *Amsterdam News*, September 5, 1928, p. 16.

was sailing. Nora Holt sang 'My Daddy Rocks Me [With a Steady Roll]' in the last moments." Supposedly, as the glamorous African American with blond hair finished the risqué blues, a white woman gushed, "How well you sing spirituals, my dear."[9]

Larsen sought a Harmon Award in literature, one of the eight fields in which prizes were to be given.[10] In completing the nomination form, she used Mrs. E. R. Alexander, one of the civic and social leaders in Harlem, as the person to propose her for the award. Phi Beta Kappa from the University of Minnesota, Lillian Alexander was an excellent choice. Married to physician "Scolly" Alexander and appearing frequently in the society pages, she was actively involved with women's issues and organizations. She chaired the education department at the 137th Street YWCA, was a member of the national board of the Y, secretary of the Columbus Hill Day Nursery, and an organizer of Club Caroline, a home for young working women.[11] Alexander's nomination ensured the viability of Larsen's application.

Larsen listed James Weldon Johnson, Jerome Peterson, and Edward Wasserman as "three responsible persons" who could attest to her achievements.[12] Van Vechten, whom she had initially approached about a recommendation, was not among the three; however, as he was scheduled to leave for France when the nomination blank was due, he may have suggested Wasserman as an alternative. Both Wasserman and Peterson, Dorothy's father, listed Van Vechten as someone who could give further information about the candidate's achievements, and both noted that he was currently abroad.

Johnson, Peterson, and Wasserman received recommendation forms from the Commission on the Church and Race Relations in mid-September. Haynes instructed them to keep their responses confidential but to supply enough material on "Nella *Larson* Imes," as he spelled her name, so that the Harmon Award judges could make an informed decision.[13] The three responded immediately. James Weldon Johnson knew Larsen personally

9. Carl Van Vechten to Carrie, Ettie, and Florine Stettheimer, September 6 [1928], in *Letters of Carl Van Vechten*, ed. Kellner, 105; Carl Van Vechten to Emily Clark, quoted in *Carl Van Vechten and the Twenties*, by Edward Lueders (Albuquerque, 1955), 130; Bruce Kellner, *Carl Van Vechten and the Irreverent Decades* (Norman, Okla., 1968), 237.

10. The other fields were music, fine arts, business (including industry), science (including invention), education, religious service, and race relations.

11. New York *Amsterdam News*, November 7, 1928, p. 4.

12. Nella Larsen Imes, Harmon Awards nomination form, August 10, 1928, in HFR.

13. George E. Haynes, 1928 Harmon Awards form letter for recommendations, September 17, 1928, *ibid.*

through Walter White, his assistant at the NAACP, and through William Lloyd Imes, her brother-in-law and a member of the NAACP Board of Directors. His comments on her novel, though positive, were terse, perhaps because he was one of the few African-American dignitaries who praised McKay's *Home to Harlem* and supported McKay in the Harmon Awards.[14] He called *Quicksand* a "well-written novel . . . that gives promise of finer accomplishment" and that "is a social and sincere piece of literary work."[15]

Unlike Johnson, Peterson did not have a reputation as a creative writer, yet his recommendation was more attentive to the specifics of Larsen's achievement in her first novel: "I consider her achievement distinguished not merely because she wrote a work of fiction, but because of the manner in which it was done. The insight into feminine character displayed and the psychological instinct that dismissed the easy solution of a happy ending and left the logic of events to run its course. The question raised as to the effect of emotional religion upon unbalanced temperaments is deserving of study, though the treatment of the ministry in the book is rather in the nature of an indictment." Peterson recognized Larsen's ability in probing feminine psychology and honesty in confronting difficult issues. Moreover, he acknowledged her modernity as an achievement for an African-American writer: "The book stimulates curiosity and provokes not a few questions of a psychological and ethnological trend. It could be called 'a human document,' with more aptness than is usually given that hackneyed term. The author's style has distinction because of its simplicity and directness. She treats some delicate situations without lapsing into suggestiveness or grossness of diction, a remarkable feat for most modern writers."[16] In referring to the fusion of racial, psychological, and sexual issues, Peterson revealed his own astuteness in reading *Quicksand*, because he was one of the few African-American males to observe Larsen's handling of these topics.

Edward Wasserman, the only white among the three, also noted that *Quicksand* was "a truly remarkable document, both as a story and as a psychological study"; however, his praise for the work was reserved for its racial aspects. Noting "its interest and importance, racially," he remarked: "It is the one negro [*sic*] novel that has style, and I have read them all." His

---

14. See Wayne F. Cooper, *Claude McKay: Rebel Sojourner in the Harlem Renaissance* (Baton Rouge, 1987), 348.

15. James Weldon Johnson, 1928 Harmon Awards recommendation form, September 22, 1928, in HFR.

16. Jerome B. Peterson, 1928 Harmon Awards recommendation form, September 19, 1928, *ibid.*

assertion of knowledge about "Negro novels" is almost akin to the humorous account Langston Hughes provided of Salvador Dali's knowledge of the Negro when Dorothy Peterson asked if he knew anything about Negroes: "'Everything!' Dali answered. 'I've met Nancy Cunard!'" Wasserman, of course, had met Carl Van Vechten, and his recommendation reflects as much:

> Having read practically every negro [*sic*] novel, I consider Mrs. Imes has written a brilliant story of great racial interest. She has touched upon the problem of a mulatto—surely a great one. Her novel is brilliantly written, is a good story, and for the first time in literature, shows that a negro [*sic*] can be cultured, refined and literary. She has done much to elevate her race from the bars and brothels of other negro [*sic*] writers, to show that they are capable of fine thinking and fine living. Besides, the psychological study of the heroine is an extremely penetrating study of a racial phenomenon. Though I know other negro [*sic*] writers personally, I consider Mrs. Imes to be almost unique in her refinement and skill.[17]

Wasserman obviously had not read Jessie Fauset or the writers who predated the "Harlem School," but his enthusiastic pronouncements of Larsen's uniqueness in racial fiction probably served her well, especially with the white judges for the literary awards.

Having completed her part for the Harmon competition, Larsen did not remain idle while waiting for the results. In mid-October, she was back into the social activities of Harlem and happily announcing that Knopf would publish "Nig" on April 19, 1929. Her spirits soared because Harry Block, her Knopf editor, championed the novel as being "at least four times better than *Quicksand*"; nonetheless, she doubted that estimation because, as she said, "it was done too quickly[,] two months—not counting the time it took me to type it." Despite claiming to have written both of her novels rapidly, she considered her writing laboriously slow. She would be surprised to learn the opinion of a reviewer of *Passing:* "I wish with all my heart that instead of bringing forth another novel next year, Mrs. Imes would, after a decade

---

17. Edward Wasserman, 1928 Harmon Awards recommendation form, September 19, 1928, *ibid.;* Langston Hughes, *The Big Sea* (1940; rpr. New York, 1986), 253. Cunard, the shipping heiress, had taken up the "Negro" cause and was collecting materials for her massive anthology, *Negro* (1934).

of brooding, give the world its needed epic of the American social order belonging to both African and European stocks."[18]

When *Harlem* magazine started operation that fall, Larsen received an invitation to contribute. Edited by Wallace Thurman, the publication was the successor of *Fire!!*, and like that earlier ill-fated venture, *Harlem* began on very little capital. Thurman's inability to pay contributors was one deciding factor in Larsen's declining the invitation in spite of being named on the November inaugural issue's back cover among the future contributors— Claude McKay, Countee Cullen, Rudolph Fisher, Arthur Fauset, Eva Jessye (author of *My Spirituals*), Heyward Broun (columnist for the New York *Telegram* and the *Nation*), and Dorothy Peterson (listed as a drama critic and translator).[19] Larsen was also aware that Thurman linked her novel unfavorably to Du Bois and the conservative element of the Renaissance, perhaps in part because she had also declined to make a financial contribution to Thurman's other magazine, *Fire!!*.[20] After weighing the possibility of having her name in *Harlem* with other better-known Harlem writers, she concluded: "Since money is my ultimate goal, I am afraid I wont [sic] be able to do it." Her decision was a sound one; before the end of November, Thurman was in Chicago and Salt Lake City, and as many had predicted, *Harlem* was no more.[21]

Although they were reluctant to admit it, the Imeses were facing a financial crisis because Elmer Imes had been ill that fall and was so in "need of a long vacation" that Larsen began looking for work: "I am thinking of returning to the library, if I can't get a job that suits and pays me better." One of the potential jobs was with the Book League of America. In September, Walter White had recommended her as an excellent candidate for a position with the league. In addition to mentioning her training and work as a librarian, particularly her expertise "in cataloguing and manuscript reading," White cited her achievement as a writer: "Mrs. Imes' novel is in my opinion

18. Nella Larsen Imes to Carl Van Vechten, Monday, October fifteenth [postmarked October 19, 1928], in JWJ; Mary Fleming Labaree, Review of *Passing*, by Nella Larsen, in *Opportunity*, VII (August, 1929), 255.

19. See *Harlem: A Forum of Negro Life*, I (November, 1928), in Claude Barnett Collection, Chicago Historical Society.

20. See Wallace Thurman, "High, Low, Past and Present," *ibid.*, 32.

21. Larsen Imes to Van Vechten, Monday, October fifteenth [postmarked October 19, 1928], in JWJ; Harold Jackman to Countee Cullen, December 6, 1928, in CCC. See also Abby Arthur Johnson and Ronald Maberry Johnson, *Propaganda and Aesthetics: The Literary Politics of African-American Magazines in the Twentieth Century* (1979; Amherst, 1991), 86–88.

one of the best written by any Negro author and one of the most distinguished first novels by an American author written within recent years." Always practical in his work in race relations, he added: "Aside from her general experiences and ability I feel that it would be a very real advantage to the Book League of America to have a young colored person of ability attached to its staff. There is a large and constantly growing number of book reading and book buying Negroes in the United States and Mrs. Imes is very well known among them. Her connection with the Book League would I am sure commend the Book League instantly and favorably to these persons." [22]

On the basis of the recommendation, Larsen went for an informal meeting with Samuel Craig, the president of the Book League, and David Roderick, the vice-president. She discussed with Roderick her ideas about the league. Failing to hear from her again by mid-October, Roderick contacted White, who wrote immediately to Larsen: "I suggest you telephone Mr. Roderick as soon as possible. I hope something comes of this." [23] Nothing, however, came of the discussions; the Book League did not offer her a position.

Neither Larsen nor White was daunted. Before the end of the year, she would, at his encouragement, apply for a Guggenheim fellowship, and he would recommend her with even more enthusiasm than he displayed in the letter to the Book League.

> It seems to me that she has a gift for prose writing and an objectivity in approaching her material such as no other person possesses who now is writing fiction regarding the Negro. . . . I was most pleased at the revelation of the technical development shown in her handling of the two stories [her two novels]. She is possessed of an uncanny instinct for divining and depicting those emotions which govern the words and acts of her characters. She writes with an economy and with a lack of verbosity which is characteristic of another woman writer—Willa Cather—whom I admire greatly.

Having "watched very carefully and with great interest and admiration, her development as a writer," White wanted to see Larsen free of financial wor-

22. Larsen Imes to Van Vechten, Monday, October fifteenth [postmarked October 19, 1928], in JWJ; Walter F. White to Samuel Craig, September 25, 1928, in WW, NAACP.

23. David Roderick to Walter White, October 18, 1928, in WW, NAACP; Walter White to Nella Larsen Imes, October 19, 1928, *ibid.*

ries so that she might advance and become "an even finer artist than she is today."[24]

Although she needed money, Larsen had not immediately pursued the contact with the Book League, because she was planning a party. The affair was in honor of her book, and was, as she said, "*very very* dicty" with Edward Wasserman, Blanche Knopf, and Van Vechten's niece, Elizabeth Shaffer, among the guests from downtown.[25] In addition to spending time playing bridge in Harlem and socializing in Greenwich Village, where she had become a regular at Muriel Draper's teas, she had also been preparing "Nig" for the printer. While a job on Fifth Avenue at the Book League was attractive, it was not nearly as appealing as the possibility of earning a living as a writer.

Magazine writing, at least for the struggling black publications, could not meet her need for money; additionally, Larsen did not write easily, even though she had produced her books in relatively short periods. The invitation from *Harlem* magazine had prompted the admission, "I write so slowly and with such great reluctance that it seems a waste of time."[26]

The speed with which she completed her novels and the admission of writing slowly and reluctantly are not incongruous. Larsen wrote much of her psychological life into her novels. Her first drafts came quickly, but revising them was agonizing for several reasons. The most straightforward have to do with the process of reinventing fact. Like many other novelists, Larsen based much of her characterizations upon actual people, whom she rewrote to disguise their identities. Similarly, she initially drew events from her own life experiences, and then recreated them in less recognizable ways.

Other factors, however, made revising more painstaking for her. First, she wanted her fiction to engage the modern scene, in particular Harlem, not merely because interest on the part of white publishers and critics in such material was high but primarily because she herself valued the literary flowering in the New Negro Awakening to the extent that she desired identification with it. In revising, she devised anchors for her stories in the familiar Harlem world and linked her fiction and herself as author to the cultural renaissance. Second, Larsen had read widely in popular magazines and had carefully studied numerous novels from earlier and contemporary

24. Walter F. White to Henry Allen Moe, n.d. [November, 1929], *ibid.*
25. Larsen Imes to Van Vechten, Monday, October fifteenth [postmarked October 19, 1928], in JWJ.
26. *Ibid.*

periods written by British, European, and American authors. She had a storehouse of connotations and allusions from the variety of fictional forms she enjoyed: romances, mysteries, adventure stories, *Bildungsroman, Künstlerromane,* and so on. She also had her own short stories, particularly the two published in *Young's,* to draw upon. For instance, she transposed an entire scene from "The Wrong Man" to *Passing.* In the short story, Julia Hammond Romley looks over an all-white crowd at a fashionable dance: "Young men, old men, young women, older women, slim girls, fat women, stout men, glided by." In the novel, Irene Redfield surveys a mixed crowd at the Negro Welfare Dance: "Young men, old men, white men, youthful women, older women, pink women, golden women; fat men, thin men, tall men, short men, stout women, slim women, stately women, small women moved by." [27] With few changes in wording, Larsen duplicates the scene, which in both texts turns on the heroine's reciting of a nursery rhyme ("Rich man, poor man, / Beggar man, thief, / Doctor, lawyer, / Indian chief.") and her observing a female antagonist dancing with a tall dark man (Myra Redmon with Ralph Tyler in "The Wrong Man," and Clare Kendry with Ralph Hazleton in *Passing*). [28]

In the revisions of her novels, Larsen took her previous compositions and her readings into account in an effort to produce the most effective fiction she could. Her practice was to layer physical details and psychological motivations into her stories after she had first sketched her plot and characters. Thus, when she counted five weeks for writing *Quicksand* and two months for *Passing,* she allowed only the time to conceive and draft the novels. Actually, she had spent nearly two years on *Quicksand* and a year on *Passing.*

November brought a chance to do the kind of writing that she had first attempted in 1923. The editors of *Opportunity* asked her to review *Black Sadie,* a first novel by the white author Thomas Bowyer Campbell. Eager for books about African Americans, all of the Harlem in-crowd was reading the narrative of Sadie's rise from obscurity in the South to notoriety as an artist's model and later cabaret dancer in New York. Although Julia Peterkin's *Scarlet Sister Mary* supplanted *Black Sadie* as a Literary Guild selection, there was considerable interest in Campbell's unlettered heroine and

27. Nella Imes [Allen Semi], "The Wrong Man," *Young's Realistic Stories Magazine,* L (January, 1926), 244; Nella Larsen, *Passing,* in *"Quicksand" and "Passing,"* ed. Deborah E. McDowell (New Brunswick, 1986), 204. Subsequent references to *Passing* will be to this edition.

28. Imes [Semi], "The Wrong Man," 244; Larsen, *Passing,* 204–205.

her promotion and exploitation by whites as a cult figure at the center of a "New Negro" fad. Jackman, who kept up with popular literary tastes, tried unsuccessfully to purchase Campbell's novel for Countee Cullen, who was in France; even the large stores like Macy's and Gimbel's were out.[29] Larsen accepted the offer to review *Black Sadie* without hesitating, for her only previous appearance in the journal most closely associated with the Renaissance had been her correspondence concerning Walter White's *Flight* in 1926. The prominent writers in the Renaissance had all published in *Opportunity,* and even aspiring writers such as her friend Dorothy Peterson had contributed articles or reviews. The publicity would be a boost to her new novel; but moreover, writing the review would preoccupy her during November and December when, as she knew, the Harmon judges were making their decisions.

Larsen did not know that her competition for the award included more than the several authors who had completed novels in 1928 (Du Bois, McKay, and Rudolph Fisher). Neither was she aware that the five literature judges—Dorothy Scarborough, William Stanley Braithwaite, W. D. Howe, James Melvin Lee, and John C. Farrar—were having a difficult time reaching a consensus. Their difficulty underscored the problem of white critics who held fixed expectations of African-American texts and preconceived notions of African-American writers. The judges had begun to read materials for the twenty-seven candidates in October. By the middle of December, they had agreed on the merits of seven candidates: W. E. B. Du Bois, Arthur Huff Fauset, Jessie Redmon Fauset, Leslie Pinckney Hill, Nella Larsen Imes, Georgia Douglas Johnson, and Claude McKay. But the agreement ended there. Scarborough, a novelist and professor at Columbia, ranked Claude McKay first because she believed he "had more literary genius than any of the other candidates." The others she ranked in the following order: Du Bois, Jessie Fauset, Larsen Imes, Arthur Fauset, Hill, and Johnson. Larsen was fourth on the list despite Scarborough's comment: "Her novel, QUICKSAND, has much that is interesting both in material and treatment. The changes of scene and type of life show that she has had a rather wide and varied experience. The characterization of the young woman with her restless nature and changing desire is a good piece of work. The end has ironic keenness."[30]

Both Lee, director of New York University's Journalism Department, and

29. Harold Jackman to Countee Cullen, November 19, 1928, in CCC.
30. Dorothy Scarborough to George E. Haynes, December 14, 1928, in HFR.

Farrar, a publisher at Doubleday, Doran and Company, agreed with Scarborough that McKay deserved the first-place award. Lee considered McKay's poems in *Harlem Shadows* as strengthening the case for the novel *Home to Harlem*, which he defended as "legitimate art" portraying "some of the scarlet sides of life." Although Lee voted for Arthur Fauset as the second-place winner and commended Du Bois as a close contender for the Bronze Award, he observed of Larsen's novel: "In some respects—and these are the most essential—I regard 'Quicksand' by Nella Larsen (Imes) as the most important novel of the year to be written by a Negro. It had a sincerity and an artistic ending that would justify the award of the bronze medal to her if that honor were limited to a single piece of creative work."[31] Lee understood the Harmon Awards to be based upon an assessment of the authors' entire canon.

Farrar, too, voted for McKay on the basis of the poetry and prose, which had "shown fire, power and originality, also a talent peculiarly and definitely racial." He ranked Du Bois second for his "highest attainment" as a "scholar, thinker and prose writer," but not on the merits of *Dark Princess*, which he considered "an inferior performance." Farrar ranked Larsen third, though he stated: "This novel is first class. While it has not the fire of Claude McKay's work, it has fine sympathy and persuasiveness." The two Fausets came fourth and fifth on his list, with Jessie as fourth because her "work is competent but it seems to me not outstanding."[32]

The other two judges voted for Larsen as the first-place winner. Critic and anthologist William S. Braithwaite, the only African American among the judges, relegated McKay to an honorable mention, while Howe, editor at Charles Scribner's Sons, did not include McKay at all on his list of six (Larsen, Du Bois, Arthur Fauset, Jessie Fauset, Johnson, and Hill). Braithwaite voted for Jessie Fauset for the bronze, and included only Du Bois and Hill with McKay in his list of honorable mentions.[33]

After Haynes tabulated the results, he informed the judges on December 21 that McKay had the majority vote. He called for "a more decisive opinion" on McKay, and observed: "It seems that Nella Larsen Imes is the choice for the Bronze Award as she has two votes for the Gold Award and

---

31. J. Melvin Lee, Memorandum concerning the Harmon Award in Literature, December 5, 1928, *ibid.*

32. John Farrar to George E. Haynes, October 29, 1928, *ibid.*

33. See "Opinion of William Stanley Braithwaite—Literature" and "Rankings of Mr. W. D. Howe—Literature," in HFR, 1928 Harmon Awards—Judges Folder.

two other judges enter her name, which places her far in the lead of any other candidate except McKay." Haynes asked that the judges make a final decision and inform him by special delivery. His request drew unexpected responses. The first to respond, Scarborough still believed that the Bronze Medal should go to Du Bois. Lee had no objections to the results and was "glad that the decision is not unanimous. I am afraid of things that are." Howe deferred to the judgment of the committee, but added: "I appreciate the quality of Claude McKay's work, but I do not think that I would have given it first place." The second response from Braithwaite essentially challenged the procedure and maintained that Larsen should receive the Gold Award because her two first-place votes were on the basis of the one work, *Quicksand*, whereas McKay's three votes were for *Home to Harlem* and his previous work.[34]

Braithwaite believed *Quicksand* to be "in all respects a better piece of literature than 'Home to Harlem.'" His objection to awarding the Gold Medal to McKay was not linked solely, as some have claimed, to the conservatism of the older African-American establishment or to a hostility toward McKay and his subject matter.[35] Larsen's book, after all, was highly critical of the African-American elite, unflattering toward the black church, and fairly explicit in sexual matters. Braithwaite reasoned that since one of the judges, Lee, had not voted for Larsen but had clearly stated that her novel was the finest of the year, the 3–2 vote in favor of McKay could easily have been shifted to Larsen, particularly because others of the judges, Scarborough in particular, seemed to vote for McKay more for his past work than for *Home to Harlem*. "My method," he concluded, "was to judge the material submitted and not the general and potential character of the authors' ability. An impartial judgment convinces me that of all the material entered as candidates Mrs. Imes' 'Quicksand' is the best and should be given the first award."[36] Braithwaite rightly concluded that Larsen, as a new author, was at a disadvantage in the selection process.

Both Lee and Scarborough defended their positions immediately. Lee insisted that, according to the printed literature, the Harmon Awards were

34. George E. Haynes to the Judges of the Harmon Award Candidates in the Field of Literature, December 21, 1928, in HFR; Dorothy Scarborough to George E. Haynes, December 21st [1928], *ibid.*; J. Melvin Lee to George E. Haynes, December 22, 1928, *ibid.*; W. D. Howe to George E. Haynes, December 24, 1928, *ibid.*; William Stanley Braithwaite to George E. Haynes, December 26, 1928, *ibid.*

35. Cooper, *Claude McKay*, 348.

36. Braithwaite to Haynes, December 26, 1928, in HFR.

"not prize contests" and that all the data submitted in support of a candidate had to be considered. He saw no inconsistency in his voting for McKay but praising Larsen. "I see no reason why I should change my opinion concerning the award of the Gold Medal," he claimed. "In the case of the award of the Bronze Medal extra credit has been given to a single piece [*Quicksand*] for sincerity of purpose and for skilled craftsmanship. That is the only concession that can be made."[37]

Scarborough, on the other hand, defended in general terms her choice of McKay, who, in her opinion, had "shown versatility and a range of work in prose and verse that exhibit marked ability. I do think that he has potential power that will enable him to go on and do still better work." However, she presented in great detail her reservations about Larsen's work:

"Quicksand" is also a good book, and . . . Mrs. Imes has pronounced talent in fiction writing. I felt that the latter part of the story was less convincing than the earlier chapters, where they were excellent. I was pleased that the story was not strained to provide the illogical cheerful ending. . . . But I felt that the character of the young woman as the author had shown her earlier, would not have been one to relax permanently to the life of the wife of a crude country preacher, and to bearing his innumerable children. That young woman would have found a way to escape, even though she left the preacher and the babies behind, I felt. She had shown such restlessness in unsatisfactory situations before, had moved on, even when she had bright prospects of success to be achieved by staying on, that I cannot think she would have stayed on in a situation that was surely more repellent to her than any she had known.[38]

Her reading of Larsen's final segment was fair, and it echoed reviewers' criticism of the novel. But neither Scarborough nor Lee was willing to admit that the scrutiny given *Quicksand* was more intense than the cursory reading of *Home to Harlem*. Scarborough was particularly adamant because she had been the judge favoring McKay even before reading the awards materials; she, in fact, had taken the initiative to have McKay's pub-

37. J. Melvin Lee to George Haynes, December 28, 1928, *ibid*.
38. Dorothy Scarborough, Memorandum concerning the Harmon Award for 1928, December 27, 1928, *ibid*.

lisher send copies of his novel to the selection committee.[39] Since none of the judges would accept Braithwaite's position or reconsider the vote, McKay remained the Gold Award winner, but his selection could not be made unanimous.

At the end of December, Larsen received notification of her Bronze Award for Distinguished Achievement Among Negroes in Literature. The award consisted of a $100 honorarium and a medal cast in bronze. Because the Harmon Foundation planned a public awards ceremony for February 12, 1929, a date selected for the symbolism associated with Lincoln's birthday, the foundation requested her to keep the information confidential until January 3, when the newspapers would receive official notices. Haynes, writing for the foundation and the Commission on Race Relations, congratulated Larsen for her achievement, and added a personal note, "[I] sincerely trust that the public recognition which is now coming to you may encourage you in your work."[40]

Nonetheless, by mid-December, Larsen was already hinting at the recognition she might receive. She was glowing at a party of celebrities given by Alta and Aaron Douglas, though one report painted it as less than entertaining: "Alta and Aaron Douglas gave one of those 'lovely' evenings to meet a Miss G. A. Gollock, an English missionary who has written a book called 'Sons of Africa,' for which Aaron drew things. Miss Gollock spoke about *the group* and 'your African cousins' as she pleases to call them. . . . We all smiled and smiled and breathed freely again when the dear lady left."[41] Larsen, Walter and Gladys White, Rudolph Fisher, Lloyd Thomas, Louise Thomas, Lillian and Scolly Alexander, Dorothy and Sidney Peterson, Harold Jackman, and others in the group must have had a difficult time containing themselves, but, sans Miss Gollock, Larsen thrived on having a place among Harlem's smart set.

Nella Larsen, novelist, indeed received her second wave of public recognition throughout the beginning months of 1929. In January, news on the Harmon Awards was released to the press. The *Amsterdam News* not only carried the announcement but also included a picture of Mrs. Nella Larsen Imes, which the Harlem arts photographer James Allen had made in 1928 and which she had submitted with her Harmon application.[42] The honor of

39. Dorothy Scarborough to George E. Haynes, December 12, 1928, *ibid.*
40. George E. Haynes to Nella Larsen, December 31, 1928, *ibid.*
41. Harold Jackman to Countee Cullen, Thursday, December 13, 1928, in CCC.
42. "Three Harmon Foundation Awards for Achievement Go to Persons Here," New York

being selected for the Bronze Award by a jury of authors, critics, and editors and of placing second to an established writer caused the African-American community to treat her respectfully as a serious writer. Within days of the news story, the West 135th Street branch of the New York Public Library invited her to speak. After years of functioning on the fringe of Harlem's literary community, Larsen was finally included as one of the major writers.

Yet support for her work was not unanimous among the players in the Harlem literary scene. Several of the men, seemingly piqued at the intrepidity of an emerging female author, were unappreciative of her novel and irritated as well by the flattering attention in the white press, as in the opening sentence of Margery Latimer's review for *Book World:* "This book makes you want to read everything that Nella Larsen will ever write." [43] Wallace Thurman, at work on his own novel with an African-American female protagonist confronting race and color in the search for identity, had dismissed *Quicksand* as a book that would please the genteel black bourgeoisie, particularly Du Bois. Jackman veiled his criticism of Larsen's novel by comparatively stating his preference for Esther Hyman's *Study in Bronze* (1928) because it was "better done and more clearly thought out, and in spite of the fact that it doesn't end on a happy note, it hasn't that defeatist ring." Jackman, however, was obviously disappointed that Larsen and McKay had received Harmon Awards instead of his friend Countee Cullen, whom he tried to cheer: "Keep your brave spirit and don't do too much regretting." Even in his veiled antagonism toward Larsen, Jackman could find fewer ways to denigrate her work than he could Jessie Fauset's new novel: "'Plum Bun' is lousy, absolutely terrible. Really, I don't see how the publishers could take it. Jessie doesn't know men, she doesn't write prose well; it is bad, bad, bad. . . . [I]t is one of the worst books I have read in a long time." [44]

During January, *Opportunity* appeared with Larsen's review of *Black Sadie.* The short piece, signed "Nella Larsen," conveyed the breezy style that

Amsterdam News, January 9, 1929, p. 3. See also Mary Bennett, "The Harmon Awards," *Opportunity*, VII (February, 1929), 48.

43. Margery Latimer, "The Book World," New York *World*, July 22, 1928, in SCF. Latimer does go on to say that *Quicksand* "is neither distinguished nor excellent and it is not 'a modern masterpiece' but it wakes you up, makes you aware that there are other races besides the white race."

44. Wallace Thurman, "High, Low, Past and Present," 31–32; Harold Jackman to Countee Cullen, Thursday, January 3, 1929, and Harold Jackman to Countee Cullen, Thursday, January 3, 1929, both in CCC.

was becoming more pronounced in her work. "BLACK SADIE—What a title! Great, isn't it? Unfortunately the book, which is the story of a Negro dancing girl's rise to popularity, isn't." Larsen panned Campbell for incorporating every "strangeness, every crudity, every laxity" imagined about African Americans, as well as for his awkward writing and disorderly arrangement of materials. "Nevertheless," she concluded, "in spite of its twaddle concerning the inherent qualities of the Negro, in spite of its affectations of style, the book is worth reading. Sadie, a handsome black wench, is an interesting and forceful character, which no one interested in modern Negro fiction can afford to ignore." Larsen was taken with the heroine's success in gaining what she wanted and in impressing the other characters, and the reader, with her "delightful sunny" personality in a stark, brutal universe. She admired women like Sadie who, though rude or ill-mannered, overcame the odds: "But she [Sadie] *is* successful."[45] For Larsen, success, not the means of obtaining it, was the yardstick for measuring an individual.

Before the end of January, her own success was clouded by illness. Larsen contracted influenza and was bedridden for several weeks. Her case of flu was serious enough to be treated by a physician, Dr. Vernon Ayer, and to cause her cancellation of her speaking engagement at the 135th Street branch of the public library. The lecture, entitled "What present-day negro [sic] writers are saying, and how" and scheduled for Thursday evening, January 31, had been well publicized, including a notice in the New York Public Library's *Staff News* for January 24, which "cordially invited" members of the staff, "many of whom knew Mrs. Imes when she was in the Library," to attend.[46] The general publicity for the lecture and the report of her illness, accompanied by a photograph, in the *Amsterdam News* attested to her increased stature as an author in Harlem.

Larsen's bout with influenza eased in time for the awards ceremony on Tuesday, February 12, at Mother AME Zion Church. Larsen and Dr. Channing H. Tobias, national secretary of the YMCA and winner of the Bronze Award in religious service, were the only Harmon recipients present. James Weldon Johnson accepted the $400 and Gold Medal for McKay in absentia. The church was filled, however, with prominent guests, all celebrating the

---

45. Nella Larsen, Review of *Black Sadie,* by T. Bowyer Campbell, in *Opportunity,* VII (January, 1929), 24.

46. "Improving," New York *Amsterdam News,* February 6, 1929, p. 4; New York Public Library *Staff News,* January 24, 1929, p. 10. The caption under the photograph of Mrs. Nella Larsen Imes in the *Amsterdam News* states that the canceled talk had been scheduled for Friday night, February 1, 1929. *Staff News* publicized the talk for Thursday, January 31.

third annual presentation ceremony as well as the spirit of interracial cooperation. Stephen S. Wise, rabbi of the Free Synagogue, gave the main address, and Helen G. Harmon, vice-president of the Harmon Foundation, also spoke. Mayor James J. Walker presented the awards. Larsen accepted the 2½-inch medal. On one side, "Harmon Foundation Award" encircled a ship at sea; on the other, "Inspiration" and "Achievement" encircled "Literature/1928/Nella Larsen Imes." Her husband and closest friends applauded from the audience. The evening marked the highest point of her public reception as a novelist, and she seemed to be disproving Alain Locke's reported assessment of the "younger Negro artists": "Locke takes his position as 'godfather' or 'grandfather,' whichever you wish, of the 'movement' very seriously. He thinks that the Negroes haven't used the opportunities to the best possible advantage. You know how vaguely he talks. Well, I couldn't get all he implied; it was a little abstract for me."[47]

Larsen's moment in the spotlight was shortlived. She was upstaged by her former mentor, Jessie Fauset, who dominated Harlem's social calendar during the rest of February and March. In February the occasion was the appearance in the United States of Fauset's second novel, *Plum Bun*, first published in Britain, which treated two educated sisters, one dark and tranquil about race and the other light and discontent enough to pass for white. At one tea honoring Fauset, Larsen arrived to find Dorothy Peterson, Richmond Barthé, the sculptor recently arrived from Chicago, and Harold Jackman already there and pronouncing it "very boring," though Jackman subsequently remarked: "Later when more people began coming it livened up but there was never any real *abandon*. . . . Papa Du Bois said a few fitting remarks and all in all everyone seemed to have a good time."[48] The accompanying round of teas and receptions had barely subsided when dinners, dances, bridge parties, luncheons, and showers for Fauset's April wedding began.

At forty-seven, Fauset had surprised even those attuned to celebrities by announcing her engagement to Herbert E. Harris, a veteran of World War I and an official of the Victory Life Insurance Company, who like Fauset had never married. Her former associates at the *Crisis* and the NAACP and other friends in Harlem hosted prenuptial events that may have been as much to meet the bridegroom as to entertain Fauset. Regina Anderson, from

47. Description from Harmon Bronze Medal, Nella Larsen Imes, 1928; Harold Jackman to Countee Cullen, February 14, 1929, in CCC.

48. Harold Jackman to Countee Cullen, February 19, 1929, in CCC.

the Harlem branch of the public library, herself recently married to W. T. Andrews, held a bridge shower, and William Lloyd Imes gave a dinner party, both of which Nella Larsen attended but failed to remark upon in her extant correspondence. On April 3, Fauset was married in her Seventh Avenue home before seventy-five witnesses. She wore white satin, and her four attendants wore rainbow-colored taffeta. More than two hundred guests attended the formal reception at Utopia Neighborhood House. Attracting more attention than the February high-society wedding of the Imeses' friend Dr. Alonzo De G. Smith to a social worker from New Haven, Fauset's fashionable wedding made the front page of the *Amsterdam News* and prompted even the sardonic Jackman to laud its "grand style" and Fauset's appearance ("She made a beautiful bride, as the old folks say, and she looked very young").[49]

After the marriage, Fauset and Larsen became even more distant than they had been in the years following Fauset's departure from *Crisis* and return to teaching. The distance was due not only to Fauset's total engrossment with being Mrs. Harris and a homemaker for her "dear little Herbie," her "dear Husband," but also to Larsen's increased absorption with becoming successful and staving off competition.[50] While competitive enough to resist comparisons between her own fiction and Fauset's and to desire accolades for its superior style, Larsen did not disparage the other writer's work, unlike Zora Neale Hurston, who, recognizing that Langston Hughes's folk material was comparable to her own, complained: "Hughes ought to stop publishing all those secular folk songs as his poetry. Now when he got off 'Weary Blues' (most of it a song I and most southerners have known all our lives) I said nothing for I knew I'd never be forgiven by certain people for 'crying down' what the 'white folks had exalted,' but when he gets off another 'Me and mah honey got two mo' days tuh do de buck' I dont [*sic*] see how I can refrain from speaking."[51]

In mid-April, Larsen recaptured public attention. Her second novel, *Passing*, appeared. Someone at Knopf had suggested the change of its title because "Nig" might be too inflammatory for a novel by an unproven

49. "Jessie Redmon Fauset, French Teacher and Author, Now Bride of H. E. Harris," New York *Amsterdam News*, April 10, 1929, p. 1; Harold Jackman to Countee Cullen, Thursday, April 4, 1929, in CCC.

50. Jackman reports that Fauset took the "marriage business very heavily," from fixing meals to wanting to write a book about sex. Harold Jackman to Countee Cullen, Friday, May 10, 1929, in CCC.

51. Zora Neale Hurston to Countee Cullen, March 11 [1926], *ibid*.

writer, while "Passing," and the phenomenon's connection to miscegenation, would incite interest without giving offense. Larsen did not object; even without the allusion to *Nigger Heaven*, her new book, handsomely bound in black cloth with a trim stamped in orange, was for her mentor Carl Van Vechten and his wife, Fania Marinoff. The dedication to the Van Vechtens signaled her literary arrival. On April 17, Dorothy Peterson hosted a tea "for Nella Larsen-Imes in honor of the publication of her second novel," as the society news account read. The affair had a guest list that must have pleased Larsen, because it included Walter White, Aaron and Alta Douglas, Grace Nail Johnson, Muriel Draper, Max Ewing, Ellery Larsson, Harry Block, Dorothy and Jimmie Harris, Edward Wasserman, John Hunt, Ernest Alexander, Inez Wilson, Marion Beasley, Harold Jackman, Crystal Byrd, and quite a few of the recognizable socialites in Harlem.[52] Peterson's tea followed another pre-publication tea given by Alfred and Blanche Knopf at the Sherry-Netherland Hotel for their author and her guests. These elegant affairs were followed by a lavish "dansart" hosted by Wasserman the day before the official publication, and they all gave Larsen a visibility she had not enjoyed a year earlier when *Quicksand* appeared.[53]

Officially released on April 26, 1929, *Passing* confirmed Larsen's promise and place among New Negro authors. In fact, with the publication of two novels within thirteen months, the thirty-eight-year-old author had become as prolific as Fauset. The epigraph from "Heritage" by Countee Cullen reiterated her connection with the Harlem Renaissance:

> One three centuries removed
> From the scenes his fathers loved,
> Spicy grove, cinnamon tree
> What is Africa to me?

The long poem had appeared in Cullen's first and best-known book, *Color* (1925), a collection Larsen had not exactly praised. Yet the four lines from "Heritage" were evocative of the role of culture in shaping one's identity and, specifically, of Africa and primitivism in the "civilized" African American's existence in the European-influenced Western world. Like Gwendolyn

52. See Dorothy Peterson Papers, Folder 27, in JWJ.
53. See Announcement card, Thursday, the twenty-fifth of April [1929], in Carl Van Vechten, 1928–29 folder, JWJ.

Bennett's poem also entitled "Heritage," Cullen's evoked the difference between the often romantic image of historical connections with Africa char-
acterizing the Renaissance and the stark reality of the American black
writer's cultural distance from an African past. The juxtaposition of past
and present sets the stage for Larsen's bringing together long-separated
childhood friends and their two different cultures, neither of which draws
directly or allusively upon Africa as an environmental place.

Larsen answered the question posed by "Heritage" in a tense narrative that
explored racial identity, its arbitrary social construction, and its distinct,
devastating impact on the individual. *Passing* treats two light-skinned
women from Chicago who had been friends during their childhood and who
are intricately connected in responding to boundaries and boundlessness in
their existence. One, Irene Westover, is from a secure middle-class African-
American family. Married to Brian Redfield, a successful physician, and the
mother of two sons, she is part of the privileged class in Harlem, where she
enjoys social prominence and material comforts, all within the boundaries
of racially designated spaces for African Americans. She is also an embodiment of Larsen's own social self. The other woman, Clare Kendry, is the
daughter of a janitor who drank too much and died in a barroom fight.
Raised by her father's white aunts, she has escaped a life of drudgery and
entered a fluid, seemingly boundless state by marrying a wealthy white man,
John Bellew, who assumes that she too is white. She is a figure of an ideal
self that Larsen desired. Much of the narrative is devoted to establishing the
levels of complicity and the differences between the personalities of the two
women, the one who "passes" and the one aware of the deception, though
the perspective is primarily that of Irene, who reflects on and reacts to the
reappearance of her once-black friend. The internal worlds of the two characters are inextricably interconnected with their external worlds, and their
physical appearances are reflections of their attitudes toward individuality,
race, and women of color, as well as projections of their bifurcated inner
selves. What emerges in the process is Larsen's subtext, her obsessive return
to the dynamic interaction of personalities, her own and her parents' and
sister's, with race, an interaction that contributed to the woman she was
and to the novelist she had become.

Less skillfully developed than *Quicksand*, *Passing* reads like a novel operating in codes, whose meanings the author is thinking through in the process of writing.[54] *Passing* is, nonetheless, a more carefully structured study

54. My thanks to John Turner for this insight.

of the psychology of an African-American woman committed to middle-class values and ideals. Like *Quicksand, Passing* situates the female at the center of discourses on race and individuality, but in its demystification of the woman of color, *Passing* insists that not everything about her can or should be known, and the known may initially appear contradictory to the process of demystifying the racialized female. The novel depends upon an acceptance of diversity and complexity as the textures of African-American female life and rejects any totalizing gender or race view, even though it explores the cultural conditions and proscriptions that shape, but do not determine, the life of a female of color. In "The Cat Came Back," a contemporary review of *Passing* for the *Amsterdam News,* Aubrey Bowser made a similar observation of the complexity of race, though not of gender, in Larsen's text: "The ethnological distinction of race, though accurate enough in a physical sense and serviceable as a generalization, is a poor guide in dealing with questions of race as they are. Race is a matter of mind rather than body, of background rather than foreground."[55]

Divided into three parts, "Encounter," "Re-encounter," and "Finale," introducing the structure of replications and ritual returns, the novel begins in the narrative present but immediately proceeds with the retrieval of memory that is one of its main concerns. In the opening scene, Irene Redfield receives a letter, "a thin sly thing which bore no return address to betray the sender. And there was, too, something mysterious and slightly furtive about it."[56] Because she had received a similar letter two years earlier, Irene recognizes not only "the long envelope of thin Italian paper," the "purple ink," and the "foreign paper of extraordinary size," but also the "almost illegible scrawl" as belonging to Clare Kendry, whose handwriting is "out of place and alien," "furtive, but yet . . . a little flaunting" against the distinctive stationery (143). The letter sets the stage for Clare's own mysterious and furtive yet, simultaneously, bold and flaunting personality. A written text is the access to personal memory and to the construction of character. Irene's receipt of the letter immediately provokes her memory of Clare as a girl in Chicago and evokes her recollection of the woman two years before: "'That time in Chicago.' The words stood out from among the many paragraphs of other words, bringing with them a clear, sharp remembrance, in which even now, after two years, humiliation, resentment, and rage were mingled"

55. Aubrey Bowser, "The Cat Came Back," New York *Amsterdam News,* June 5, 1929, p. 20.
56. Larsen, *Passing,* 143. Subsequent references to *Passing* are cited parenthetically in the text.

(145). The remainder of "Encounter," chapters 2 through 4, is a prolonged memory of those past events, which begins with a signal of Irene as an interpreter of past experience: "This is what Irene Redfield remembered" (146). The other two parts, "Re-encounter" and "Finale," are the working out of Irene's personal memory and flawed interpretation in order to achieve meaning in the present.

Passing, though opening with reflection on a letter that might suggest epistolary modes of nineteenth-century fiction, integrates more of Larsen's reading in modern literature than did *Quicksand,* in which she depended more mechanically upon Helga Crane's reading of books to gesture toward the modernity of her novel. In *Passing,* the characters convey the effects of reading rather than display their reading of specific texts, and suffused throughout are the "new" ideas about human psychology that Larsen had absorbed from her reading of popularized Sigmund Freud and Otto Rank. Rank's extended stay in America during the 1920s had generated an interest in his ideas among those in Van Vechten's circle; in particular, his placing the artist in the act of creation at the center of his theories of psychoanalysis had called attention to the will to create one's personality as more basic than sexual instinct. His linking of the neurotic and the artist as "similarly driven by an intense longing for immortality, a desire to transcend the anxiety of the human condition," presented the neurotic character as "shaped from misguided strength and inventiveness."[57] But in addition, Larsen was taken with the then-popular notions of inferiority complexes, doubles, and phallic symbols, as well as in psychological interpretations of childhood and its impact on the adult. These and other ideas from the "new science" on the randomness of human behavior and the relativism of environment, which had influenced her husband's work on Einstein's and Planck's theories, contributed to her different use of reading in *Passing.* Her modern usages and readings were not lost on the reviewer of *Passing* for the New York *Times,* who concluded that "what she is after in 'Passing' is the presentation of two psychological conflicts": "Miss Larsen is quite adroit at tracing the involved processes of a mind that is divided against itself, that fights between the dictates of reason and desire. She follows the windings of Irene Redfield's thought without chasing the fleeting shades of cerebral processes into blind alleys: hence she is not a good stream-of-consciousness writer, but rather a good recorder of essentials."[58]

57. See Michael Vincent Miller, "An Urge More Vital than Sex," *New York Times Book Review,* March 24, 1984, p. 3.
58. *New York Times Book Review,* April 28, 1929, p. 14.

Whether or not the distinction between Larsen as a "stream-of-consciousness writer" and a "recorder of essentials" is accurate, the novel evidenced her sophisticated readings and the permeation of popularized psychoanalytic thought. Clare Kendry, for instance, owes her passive nature in part to Gertrude Stein's Melanctha in *Three Lives,* and the conflict between the parts of a divided self, realized in the opposition between Melanctha Herbert and Jeff Campbell, becomes one basis for the bipolar relationship between Clare and Irene Redfield, but another basis is the psychological concept of the double. The treatment of the environment and its impact in shaping the lives of individuals owes much to Theodore Dreiser's *Sister Carrie* and Sinclair Lewis' *Main Street* but also to the processes of the inventive contest of the will to transcend limiting conditions. Irene's narrated monologues and stream of consciousness reflect Larsen's reading of Joyce's *Ulysses* and her understanding of William James's explanations of the human thought process, though Larsen depended, too, on the modernist concept of the unreliable observer as represented by Joseph Conrad in *Heart of Darkness.*

Because Larsen was still under the spell of Van Vechten ("the best thing that ever happened to the Negro race"), she shifted from writing what was intended to be her "Chicago" novel and a working out of the interpolated story of Julia Hammond Romley's secret Chicago background from "The Wrong Man." [59] She completed instead a text in which Harlem of 1927 is not only central but comparable to the sophisticated white Manhattan depicted in Van Vechten's novels. Not only are there references to Josephine Baker, Ethel Waters, and *Shuffle Along* (219) in "Re-encounter," but the NAACP and the Urban League appear as the Negro Welfare League, and Fania Marinoff and Van Vechten figure as Bianca and Hugh Wentworth, a celebrity writer of "awfully good" but "contemptuous" novels (198). Chicago, however, is the setting for "Encounter," the first and longest part, and for the powerful memories that dominate the other two parts, and it allows Larsen to explore her own shadowy psychohistory veiled in her familial background.

In the action line of *Passing,* Clare and Irene meet in the bright afternoon world of a Chicago rooftop cafe. Their meeting place, the fashionable Drayton Hotel, is modeled on the Drake and the Morrison hotels in Chicago. The Drake Hotel, located on the Gold Coast end of Michigan Avenue and Walton Place at Lakeshore Drive, and the Morrison Hotel, then in the Loop at Madison and Clark streets and known for its Terrace Garden Restaurant,

59. Nella Imes to Van Vechten, Monday, Seventh [March, 1927], in JWJ.

were among Chicago's most elegant and exclusive dining and dancing places. In the outdoor world of Chicago's white smart set, the two "passing" women of color from the South Side do not initially recognize each other because they have both escaped the spatial boundaries imposed by the racial segregation in the city. But when they place each other within the context of race, they travel backward into the morning world of their youths in Chicago, where though of different socioeconomic and class backgrounds, they shared the experience of what it means to grow up urban, female, and black. When they resume their friendship in New York, it is in the evening world of their separate maturities: gala affairs, parties, dinners, costume balls, and after-hours cabarets. Both are partially obscured from scrutiny in the Harlem darkness, which negates the social boundaries hemming in a racialized part of the city and which produces an illusion of limitlessness and boundlessness. The three different periods contribute to the fusion of past (largely defined in terms of Chicago) and present (represented by Harlem) that Larsen uses in constructing her text and characters.

Light-skinned Irene Westover Redfield grew up middle-class and comfortable in Chicago. She is modeled upon Larsen's girlhood friend Pearl Mayo and also upon Irene McCoy, a prominent Chicagoan active in the YWCA and a graduate of the Fisk Normal Department (1909). Irene recognizes that she wants security more than anything else in life and that her greatest satisfaction lies in her husband, Brian, and her sons, Ted and Junior. She sacrifices her own self for complacent absorption in family: "security was the most important and desired thing in life. . . . She wanted only to be tranquil . . . to be allowed to direct for their own good the lives of her sons and husband" (235). In her own way, Irene is selfish and determined, but she is motivated by her conception of the ideal family and her own self-importance in actualizing the ideal. She admits that she is unwilling to take risks, either with her own future or that of her sons. Irene will not consider a move to Brazil, which Brian desires; she believes that their lives are secure and that they are too well established in Harlem to seek intangible freedoms in a foreign country. Feeling safe in her life of class privilege, servants, bridge parties, charity balls, and smart fashions, she views change of any sort as threatening. Her fears, however, reflect her absorption of patriarchal culture. Her attention to her father, husband, and sons shapes and displaces her sense of self, her possibilities and potential, her values and worth.

Her discontented husband longs for a different life in Brazil, and her pampered sons want a knowledge of life beyond the narrow restrictions she imposes on them. Brian, based largely on Larsen's husband, is dissatisfied with life in the United States because he desires freedom from the racism that impinges upon his existence despite his relatively insulated profession and his status in the black community. His placid exterior has begun to wear thin, and this gives Irene cause to fear: "That old fear, with strength increased, the fear of the future. . . . And, try as she might, she could not shake it off. It was as if she had admitted to herself that against that easy surface of her husband's concordance with her wishes, which had . . . covered an increasing inclination to tear himself and his possessions from their proper setting, she was helpless" (193). Irene assuages her fears by reminding herself that Brian "was fond of her, loved her in his slightly undemonstrative way" (190).

Junior and Ted are unhappy with being sheltered and try to discover more about the larger world, represented by their seeking knowledge of sex. While Junior has Brian's coloring, he has Irene's temperament, "practical and determined" (192). Ted, however, is like his father: "speculative and withdrawn . . . less positive in his ideas and desires. About him there was a deceiving air of candour [*sic*] that was . . . like his father's show of reasonable acquiescence. If, for the time being, and with a charming appearance of artlessness, he submitted to the force of superior strength, or some other immovable condition or circumstance, it was because of his intense dislike of scenes and unpleasant argument. Brian over again" (192). From the beginning of the narrative, it is Ted, the embodiment of his father, who is responsible for Irene's frustration in the Chicago heat. She had been searching for a particular book for him when out of fatigue she had sought refuge at the Drayton Hotel. "Why was it almost invariably he wanted something that was difficult or impossible to get? Like his father. For ever wanting something that he couldn't have" (148). Her husband's and sons' passive objection to her determining their existences causes Irene to doubt her ability to control their joint destinies.

In the representation of Irene within a conventional construction of the female, Larsen turns again to the pervasive and compelling psychology of family, particularly as it was deviously configured in her own social history. "The notion of family romance," as Marianne Hirsch points out, "extrapolated from Freudian definitions and extended beyond them, can account for the ambivalences and duplicities contained in the fantasies of difference and singularity, the pull toward complicity, and the difficulties of dissent. It accounts for the process of 'becoming-woman,' of en-genderment, which is intimately tied to the process of transmission and the relationship to previous generations of women." [60] In Irene, Larsen found a vehicle for deconstructing her responses to herself as a woman of color, to her mother as a white woman, and to the family as an institutional and emotional structure.

Clare Kendry, passing for white as Mrs. John Bellew, enters Irene's life and reveals that she has been, and still is, willing to risk anything in order to have whatever she wants. Although seemingly even-tempered and pleasant, she has a "having" nature, evident though her face is an "ivory mask" (157). She seems to want most the company of African Americans, whom she misses in her life with a man who despises blacks and uses racial slurs freely. Although the mother of a daughter, she thinks nothing of jeopardizing her marriage by renewing her friendship with Irene, visiting at the Redfields' home, and socializing in Harlem. She seems on the verge of renouncing her position as a wealthy white matron, accepting life as a person of color, and possibly taking her friend's husband as a mate.

Like Audrey Denny, Helga's alter ego in *Quicksand,* Clare moves with confidence and courage in two worlds and has "retained her ability to secure the things that she wanted in the face of any opposition. . . . About her there was some quality, hard and persistent, with strength and endurance of rock, that could not be beaten or ignored." Clare is an aggressive individual who seeks self-satisfaction without the timidity society instills in females. Despite the existence of Margery, her ten-year-old daughter, she does not elevate the needs of her family above her own. "'Children aren't everything,'" she declares. "'There are other things in the world'" (210). Neither does she allow the deprivations of her childhood to damage her adult life. She accepts her unhappy formative years but does not allow the past to determine her chances for individual happiness and fulfillment. She has daring, nerve, and self-absorption; there is "nothing sacrificial in Clare Kendry's idea of life, no allegiance beyond her immediate desire . . . selfish, and cold, and hard. . . . [Y]et she had, too, a strange capacity of transforming warmth and passion, verging sometimes almost on theatrical heroics" (144). In passing for white, she has escaped deprivation and dependence upon her unsympathetic white aunts, who are unaware that she has married into the white world of wealth and security. After recognizing that she requires more than money and security for happiness, Clare returns secretly to the African-American community through her connection with her childhood friend, Irene Redfield.

In Clare, Larsen images a woman who has completely broken with her

60. Marianne Hirsch, *The Mother/Daughter Plot: Narrative, Psychoanalysis, Feminism* (Bloomington, 1989), 11.

past, has refashioned herself, and feels no guilt about her decisions and actions. She represents the desirable and also the dreaded in the female: the desirable, in that Clare separates herself from the untenable in her existence; and the dreaded, in that no social strictures can hold her in.

Unlike Clare, Irene fills the traditional and dutiful role of woman as wife and mother. She admits, "'I take being a mother seriously. I *am* wrapped up in my boys and the running of my house. I can't help it'" (210). Her creativity is diverted into developing the abilities of others and nurturing the family. The cost is great: "she couldn't now be sure that she had ever truly known love. Not even for Brian. He was her husband and the father of her sons. But was he anything more? Had she ever wanted or tried for more? . . . [S]he thought not" (235). By limiting herself to total absorption in family, she neither lives fully nor feels deeply, but she does enact an ethics of care that Larsen associated not only with Irene as a conventional female within the text but with the "female" profession of nursing, external to the text.

Irene's relationship to Clare is a much more developed version of Helga Crane's to Audrey Denny in *Quicksand*. Clare represents the personal and psychological characteristics that Irene needs to become a complete person. Race loyalty veils the contours of their symbiotic relationship: "The instinctive loyalty to race. Why couldn't she [Irene] get free of it? Why should it include Clare? . . . What she felt was not so much resentment as a dull despair because she could not change herself in this respect, could not separate individuals, herself from Clare Kendry" (227). Irene's interest in her long-lost friend does not stem from Clare's passing for white, but from Clare's courage to be herself, her attempt to live as fully as possible, both emotionally and materially. "Safety and closure," Carolyn Heilbrun points out, "are not places of adventure, or experience, or life"; the two make for enclosure, and they "forbid life to be experienced directly." Clare's presence disturbs Irene's values and exposes the limitations of her conceptions, but at the same time, Clare's verve in living, especially as white, is a projection of Irene's own wish-fulfillment, her suppressed desire to experience life fully and beyond the limitations imposed by race. Du Bois labeled Clare a "lonesome hedonist" in contrast to Irene, "the race-conscious Puritan." Although he may have been less than accurate in his reference to Irene, Du Bois is on to something about the connection to hedonistic impulse in Clare's attitude toward living.[61]

61. Carolyn Heilbrun, *Writing a Woman's Life* (New York, 1988), 20; W. E. B. Du Bois, "The Browsing Reader," *Crisis*, XXXVI (July, 1929), 248.

The soul-searching that preoccupies Irene throughout much of the novel begins immediately after her reunion with her friend. Clare is the text of Irene's meditations on self and other. During their second meeting in the Bellews' Chicago hotel suite, and the only one that takes places in Clare's white world, Irene formulates the crisis of self that dominates the narrative; she experiences an acute sense of alienation from others and from something within her: "a sense of aloneness, in her adherence to her own class and kind; not merely in the great thing of marriage, but in the whole pattern of her life" (166). Her fate in marriage as a union is the disappointment of feeling particularly unjoined and alone. Marriage as an institution of secrets and separation becomes one of the dominant themes accompanying Irene's sense of her predicament. But within the text, issues of race, as socially constructed in the United States, are inextricably embedded in the issue of marriage for the female.

The scene in the Morgan Hotel, also modeled upon the Morrison, reunites Clare, Irene, and Gertrude Martin, another childhood friend, now married to a white butcher who is aware of his wife's race. Their interaction depends upon their memories of childhood, but their discourse turns on their adulthoods as reproductive females. While childbearing is part of each woman's concept of her gendered self, it is problematized by her configuration of her racial self. Like Helga Crane, Gertrude has twin boys, but she has decided against having other children because she, not her white husband, fears their skin might be dark. The dialogue between Clare and Gertrude on the "hellish" fear of giving birth to a dark-skinned child (Irene's husband and one of her sons are dark-skinned) is a response to a secret fear of the passing individual, whose detection depends not upon uncovering links to "colored" ancestors but upon reproducing live issue resembling those ancestors. The result is that the body of the passer is the repository of evidence negating itself as a refigured "white" person. In establishing this particular aspect of passing, Larsen was addressing a general problem of assimilation for the passer, but she may well have been alluding to the specific problem that traumatized her parents and stigmatized her own self at birth.

The reunion of the three women is marred not only by the discourse on skin color as a determining factor in bearing children, but also by Irene's observance of class differences between herself and Gertrude, and by the appearance of Clare's bigoted husband who calls his wife "Nig," makes racist remarks, and angers Irene and Gertrude, neither of whom he has detected as black (159–70). The suggestion is that the sisterhood of the three childhood friends cannot sustain itself given the reality of class and race prejudices, as well as the reality that different women have different aspects of self at stake in marriage and procreation.

Each subsequent meeting with Clare becomes an occasion for Irene's self-examination, inspired by a mirror image of her self or her suppressed desires. Not infrequently, the accompanying emotion is anger that she cannot suppress: "Rage boiled up in her" (221). Angered by Clare's ability to fashion herself and her insistence on having what she desires, Irene cannot control the self-imaging it produces. In fleeting moments, she acknowledges aspects of the other woman as her own: "in the look she gave Irene, there was something groping, hopeless, and yet so absolutely determined that it was like an image of the futile searching and the firm resolution in Irene's own soul" (200). Although their expressions rely upon different conceptions of reality, their inner selves are linked by searches for meaning in the social arena and by determination to claim whatever sacrifices they have made as "worth it," as Clare observes in her note to Irene after their meeting at the Morgan Hotel. Increasingly, Irene grows aware of her fragmentation and dissatisfaction as she observes the other woman and her self. The dialogic relationship of the two depends upon diametrically opposed conceptions of being female.

The moment in the narrative that perhaps most clearly reveals the oppositional values but sympathetic psychology of the two occurs when Irene cautions that the daughter will suffer the consequences of the mother's secret trips to Harlem. Clare responds, "'I think . . . that being a mother is the cruellest [*sic*] thing in the world'" (197). Here, just as in *Quicksand*, Larsen presents the negative, entrapping aspects of motherhood. The statement strikes a responsive chord in Irene: "'Yes,' Irene softly agreed. For a moment she was unable to say more, so accurately had Clare put into words that which not so defined, was often in her own heart" (197). Irene's affirmative answer is not surprising, because Clare's behavior and words have already provoked an examination of her motivations and beliefs. However, she redirects the truth of the statement to her own concerns by adding, "'And the most responsible, Clare. We mothers are all responsible for the security and happiness of our children'" (197). The meaning of the mother's own needs is lost and obscured by Irene's shift of emphasis to the children, but the dialogue lifts to the surface one of the major tensions of the text.

In this scene, Larsen grapples with the meaning of motherhood, recognizes its complexities, but concludes with an affirmation of maternal responsibilities to the child. Despite the surface of her narrative, she could not condone, even by implication, a mother's abandonment of her child. The specter of Marie Larsen figures in her backing away from the implications of the perception she assigns to Clare. Larsen reckoned from her own personal history that the consequences for the child were too great to adopt Clare's perspective, that the discourse was, not too subversive, but too close to a justification for a mother's abnegation of maternal responsibility. Mothers are noticeably absent from the formative years of Clare and Irene. Although the mothers of both are mentioned, they do not figure as models for their daughters' perceptions of motherhood. Indeed, it appears that in an unspecified way, each daughter is responding to a lack of intimacy with a distant mother by inventing for herself a way to be maternal.

Irene's faith in the safe, acceptable role she has chosen deteriorates as Clare's presence magnifies the insubstantial nature of her marriage and the core of her existence. Irene remains ostensibly rational and controlled, but her mental breakdown is almost inevitable. In a rapid and sketchy process, Clare's aggression is transfered to Irene, whose depth of feeling and strength of will are prefigured near the beginning of the narrative when, in tearing up a letter from Clare and throwing it from a moving train, she acts out symbolic aggression against Clare that anticipates the novel's ending: "With an unusual methodicalness she tore the offending letter into tiny ragged squares that fluttered down and made a small heap in her black *crepe de Chine* lap. The destruction completed, she gathered them up, rose and moved to the train's end. Standing there, she dropped them over the railing and watched them scatter, on tracks, on cinders, on forlorn grass, in rills of dirty water" (196).

In holding to her views, Irene is not so much morally responsible as she is frightened of life without restraints. Her friend precipitates the crisis by asking openly: "'What does it matter? One risk more or less, if we're not safe anyway . . . can't make all the difference in the world. It can't to me. . . . I'm used to risks'" (117). Clare prizes risk-taking precisely because existence itself is unsafe for the female. Literally, the risk for which she prepares Irene and herself is a complete return to the world of African Americans, which includes Brian, according to Irene's formulation of her friend's intent and objective. Whether or not Clare desires her friend's husband, she warns, "'I haven't any proper morals or sense of duty, as you have . . . to get the things I want badly enough, I'd do anything, hurt anybody, throw anything away. Really 'Rene, I'm not safe'" (210). On another level, she exposes the assertiveness following self-definition needed by the female to live fully or by the female artist to pursue her work. The ensuing struggle between these two women takes place inside Irene as a struggle between freedom and restraint, innovation and conventionality.

Much of the surface tension in the narrative stems from Irene's perception that Clare is a threat to her marriage and to her security. She senses that Brian is attracted to the beautiful, blond, and daring Clare; she fears that he might leave her for the other woman, particularly should she return to her race. Little of Clare's thinking about Brian is central to the narrative; she is somehow as elusive as she is beautiful. Gradually, it is Irene who unfolds Clare's character, and exposes her own: "a suspicion . . . surprised and shocked her . . . that in spite of her determined selfishness the woman before her was yet capable of heights and depths of feeling that she, Irene Redfield, had never known." "She was aware, too, of a dim premonition of some impending disaster. It was as if Clare Kendry had said to her, for whom safety, security, were all-important: 'Safe! Damn being safe!' and meant it" (195). Irene becomes a woman who is more and more distracted and disturbed as she either discovers or imagines the threat posed by her friend.

A suggestive aspect of the text is that Clare apparently could not return to her race. Once Larsen develops the story line of a woman who misses her race enough to risk the detection of her blackness, she has few options for resolving the tangled plot. Larsen cannot sufficiently motivate Clare to return, yet she cannot logically dismiss Clare's attraction to people of color and to Harlem. At the same time, Larsen cannot wholly approve of Irene's narrow materialism, nor can she punish or condemn her for it. Her solution, unrealistic and somewhat ambivalent, is to have Clare fall, jump, or be pushed from an open apartment window at a Harlem party just as her irate husband appears to denounce her. Death by going out an open window had also been the solution Larsen used in "Freedom," the second of her published short stories, and as in that earlier fiction, death completes the ritual of return to the rejected object of affection and desire. In the final scenes, Irene is made to look suspiciously like a woman who has committed murder, whether accidentally or intentionally. The narrative concludes with Irene still concerned about appearances and about salvaging as much of her comfortable married life as possible, particularly with the threat of Clare removed.

Clare, as the woman assuming maximum responsibility for her own life and finding a measure of freedom of expression—though without the certainty of happiness or security—is killed by Irene, who had been brought to a dangerous exploration of her own possibilities for creative self-expression. Clare's death is ruled "Death by misadventure."[62] Margaret Cheney Dawson, reviewing the novel for the New York *Herald Tribune,* quotes the statement to emphasize the difference between the policeman's "official" view of the death and Irene's perception of it.[63] Irene's response to the death is spontaneous:

> Gone! The soft white face, the bright hair, the disturbing scarlet mouth, the dreaming eyes, the caressing smile, the whole torturing loveliness that had been Clare Kendry. That beauty that had torn at Irene's placid life. Gone! The mocking daring, the gallantry of her pose, the ringing bells of her laughter.
>
> Irene wasn't sorry. She was amazed, incredulous almost. (239)

Yet her response is also veiled: "If she could only be as free of mental as she was of bodily vigor; could only put from her memory the vision of her hand on Clare's arm. 'It was an accident, a terrible accident,' she muttered fiercely. '*It was*'" (239). As is the case with much of the narrative, Irene insists upon her own perception of reality, which in this instance coincides with that of the police inspector.

The fusion of Irene with that other part of herself is impossible given her social world, her espoused values, and her survival instincts. Although Claudia Tate argues that Clare is a possible suicide, it is symbolically appropriate that Irene kills Clare, who embodies the dangerous, subversive, and willful characteristics of an individual who would risk everything for her own potential well-being, who would try on one way of being and discard it if

62. The sentence is included in Alfred A. Knopf's first printing of *Passing* (New York, 1929), 209. Contrary to the ending presented in *"Quicksand" and "Passing,"* ed. Deborah E. McDowell (New Brunswick, 1986), 246, and to McDowell's statement regarding it (246), the original first edition did include a short final paragraph in which Irene hears "the strange man [a police officer] saying: 'Death by misadventure,' I'm inclined to believe. Let's go up and have another look at the window." See also Mark J. Madigan, "'Then everything was Dark'?: The Two Endings of Nella Larsen's *Passing*," *Papers of the Bibliographical Society of America,* LXXXIII (December, 1989), 521–23.

63. Margaret Cheney Dawson, "The Color Line," New York *Herald Tribune,* April 28, 1929, p. 6. Dawson, like other contemporary reviewers, used Knopf's first edition, first printing, which includes the statement in a final paragraph dropped from the third printing of *Passing.*

it were found wanting.[64] These characteristics Larsen seemingly associated with self-exploration in writing, for in creative writing the personality of the writer is not only defined and asserted but also exposed to constant threat, particularly the sort that uses the author's creation as a self-referential text.

In killing a rival part of her self, Irene chooses security at the expense of a threatening, but perhaps more meaningful, existence. "Security. Was it just a word? If not, then was it only by the sacrifice of other things, happiness, love, or some wild ecstasy . . . that it could be obtained? And did too much striving, too much faith in safety and permanence, unfit one for these other things?" (235). Irene's striving for safety and permanence is no more laudable than Clare's risk-taking; each route, isolated without the tempering force of the other, is destructive, and neither arrives at creative self-expression. However, Irene's questions are not merely philosophical musings for rhetorical effect. They are explorations of Clare's alterity, as well as serious attempts to express the troubling conflicts of a woman's values and ambitions, the disturbing ambivalences in a woman's psyche and desires.

Yet the novel ends without having Irene actually confront the problem of what to do with her own life, beyond that of her marriage and her roles as wife and mother. It resolves none of the issues it raises.[65] Irene avoids "the problem that has no name," to use Betty Freidan's label for women's social roles, and leaves unresolved the issues raised by the reapparition of her past and all of its latent possibilities. Like *Quicksand,* then, *Passing* concludes in ambivalence. While there may be no viable alternative offered to the identity provided in Larsen's novel by family, there is especially for Irene, and comparably for Helga Crane, an inescapable sense of personal limitation imposed by the meaning of family, whether that meaning is shaped by society or by the individual herself. Neither Irene nor Clare effectively solves the problem of familial responsibilities in a woman's life, of externally imposed roles that do not adequately fulfill a woman's desires and needs.

Larsen blamed fatigue for the thinness of *Quicksand* after the Copenhagen episode, but the similar brevity at the end of *Passing* proved that weariness was not the only cause.[66] She fails to explore the meaning of her imagi-

---

64. Claudia Tate, "Nella Larsen's *Passing:* A Problem of Interpretation," *Black American Literature Forum,* XIV (Winter 1980), 145.

65. See Sister Mary Ellen Doyle, S.C.N., "The Heroines of Black Novels," in *Perspectives on Afro-American Women,* ed. Willa Johnson and Thomas Green (Washington, D.C., 1975), 114.

66. Nella Imes to Carl Van Vechten, December 7, 1926, in JWJ.

native sequences despite adhering to the logic, and she fails to understand the dynamics of two different attitudes toward her female characters. While Larsen's ending disrupts the expectations of both the romance and the quest plot often used by women writers, she does not appear to be "writing beyond the ending," as Rachel Blau DuPlessis terms the "invention of strategies that sever the narrative from formerly conventional structures of fiction and consciousness about women."[67]

Larsen herself was not satisfied with the ending of her novel. After having what she called "the most hellish time" trying to finish *Passing*, she still remarked "feeling blue over that same old book," once she had a completed manuscript for Knopf.[68] Although she does not say so, she may well have been responsible for dropping the final paragraph of the novel after the second printing in order to suspend the action before a verdict is reached on Clare's death and Irene's fate. She concludes the text of the revised third printing of *Passing* with a sentence doubly evocative of female unconsciousness: "Then everything was dark" (242).

Despite what the title suggests, racial passing is only one of the issues that Larsen treats in the novel.[69] Irene's attitudes toward passing are complex. On the one hand, she resents those individuals, like Clare, who would pass and leave the race, even though she herself casually crosses the color line whenever it is convenient to do so. In fact, when she first encounters Clare, Irene is passing in order to be served in a Chicago café. On the other hand, she admires the nerve that it takes to pass for white and feels obligated to protect the individual who is passing. Since Irene knows that Clare's reasons for passing are clearly tied to economic pressures exacerbated by her femaleness, which would have handicapped her efforts to become self-supportive, rather than to an avoidance of racial oppression, she finds it difficult to fault her friend's decision to marry into the white race. It is one indication that Irene acknowledges that the female's body is a commodity in marriage. In fact, after seeing Clare in smart clothes and in expensive places, others of their friends in Chicago believed that she had become a commodity without a marriage license, that she was a prostitute.

67. Rachel Blau DuPlessis, *Writing Beyond the Ending: Narrative Strategies of Twentieth-Century Women Writers* (Bloomington, 1985), x.

68. Nella Larsen Imes to Carl Van Vechten, n.d. [postmarked March 19, 1928], in JWJ; Nella Larsen Imes to Carl Van Vechten, "Home," n.d. [*ca.* April, 1928], *ibid.*

69. See Mary Mabel Youman, "Nella Larsen's *Passing*: A Study in Irony," *CLA Journal*, XVIII (December, 1974), 235–41.

What is never clear, however, is precisely how Clare feels about crossing over or about African Americans. She apparently has great respect for Irene's father and mother, who treated her well when she was a neglected child, and for Irene, who accepted her as a friend despite her poverty, but she does not seem to feel deeply about African Americans as a group or about individual African Americans whom she meets in the course of the narrative. Certainly, she does not appear responsive enough to them to want to leave her present life in order to join them permanently in Harlem; yet a deep-seated but indefinable racial attraction seemingly draws her back to a black world. In this attraction, Clare is comparable to Mimi Daquin, the heroine of Walter White's *Flight*. However, Clare is largely unknowable. Larsen provides Clare with a social history, but Clare has no life, no motivation, and no emotion beyond that which Irene projects onto her. Clare remains a screen upon which Irene's psyche is made visible.

Just as in *Quicksand*, Larsen uses the protagonist's fear of cultural disinheritance to mask her own anxiety. In both novels, Larsen masks a rage against the black bourgeoisie and the white elite, and she directs her anger against herself, personified by Helga Crane, Irene Redfield, and Clare Kendry. Attacking both groups for their subtle cruelties and intended slights, Larsen exposes their hypocrisies. Simultaneously, however, she evidences a longing to be part of both groups and a desire to find acceptance within them. Because her own anger is partly irrational, Larsen cannot adequately explain its presence within her women characters; neither can she sufficiently manipulate their motivations to make sense to a reader. Each of the heroines engages in destructive behavior, just as Larsen did. Each heroine is also distanced from the culture of black America, particularly the rural and folk culture of southern-born or southern-influenced blacks.

Irene suggests much of what is apparently the case with Larsen herself: that she had been incompletely socialized by women in the developmental stages, in the process of maturation. Instead of experiencing the attachment and connection that identifies and defines maturation for the female, Larsen and her character Irene, as well as Clare, have only shadowy representations of mothers or maternal women in their lives. They are deprived of a matrilineal heritage that nurtures and nourishes. They have instead developed much as Carol Gilligan has described male development: they move into maturity by accepting and seeking separation, competition, and individuation as a way of succeeding in the adult world. Irene, however, masks her competitive and aggressive side by seeming to defer to others and to seek female community, particularly in the Negro Welfare League, which Larsen uses ironically to undercut Irene's seeming altruism.[70]

Larsen's theme of jealousy and rivalry for the affections of a husband, however, are based on a more immediate situation in her life. Her own husband was seeing another woman who was, in fact, white. Larsen made the discovery while she was at work on *Passing,* but she did not confront Imes, who had seemed to be an ideal husband for her. Despite her personal surprise and hurt, she chose, instead, to conceal her knowledge of the affair and, following Van Vechten's counsel, to pretend that nothing was wrong.[71] During the summer and fall of 1928, she had labored over the completion of her novel while agonizing over her marital crisis. This personal situation of a wife secretly fearful of the disintegration of her marriage and obsessively jealous of the "white" beauty displacing her husband's affections pervades the novel, particularly the last part, "Finale," which, as critics have observed, seems to run counter to the initial themes of passing across the color line and of racial solidarity.

Passing, even more than *Quicksand,* depends upon silence, concealment, and secrecy. The relationship between the concealed and the revealed, announced by Clare's letter to Irene in the opening chapter, is more complex because the central consciousness, though not rendered by means of a first-person narrator, is unreliable. Irene is incapable of being honest with herself. While affirming middle-class life in Harlem, she seems to despise African Americans. Her denial takes shape within her responses to Clare's emerging affirmation of her race. Although Clare is the character publicly masking her actual identity, she does not divorce herself from her identity privately. Within enclosed spaces, whether outdoors or in, Clare freely acknowledges who she is. Irene, however, appears transparent in public, yet in the scenes set in her private spaces, she seems to hide aspects of her identity even from herself.

Interestingly, in both *Passing* and *Quicksand* a woman of color, a woman of mixed-racial ancestry, associates with a white male and ultimately rejects him. In *Passing,* John Bellew has married Clare, and in *Quicksand,* Axel Olsen proposes to Helga. The females' self-consciousness of racial oppres-

---

70. Carol Gilligan, *In a Different Voice: Psychological Theory and Women's Development* (Cambridge, Mass., 1982), 151–66; see Deborah E. McDowell, "'That nameless . . . shameful impulse': Sexuality in Nella Larsen's *Quicksand* and *Passing,*" in *Black Feminist Criticism and Critical Theory,* ed. Joe Weixlmann and Houston A. Baker, Jr. (Greenwood, Fla., 1988), 155, Vol. III of Weixlmann, ed., *Studies in Black American Literature.*

71. Larsen Imes to Van Vechten, Monday [postmarked September 3, 1928], in JWJ.

sion and prejudice permeates these relationships. In the one, Clare tolerates the marriage by masking her emotions; in the other, Helga rejects marriage because she is too readily angered by racial injustice and prejudice. The duplication of the situation suggests a connection with Larsen's own family background.

Larsen's characters are incapable of liberating themselves from their secrets. Helga Crane can never completely bare the truth of her life to any of the women or men she meets; she is trapped in hiding the truth of her unhappy childhood from those who might understand it, and therefore her, better. Irene almost entirely conceals her perceptions of her world and herself from her family and her friend Clare, who is involved as well in the major extended deception of the novel. Before her reunion with Irene, Clare had not divulged her secret to anyone and lived comfortably in a world of wealth and bigotry. Although Clare confides in Irene, neither woman will admit that she harbors some resentment toward the other. Irene seems always to have been jealous of Clare's "beauty," her fragile, golden blondness, and of her verve and self-confidence. Clare seems jealous of Irene's security within a stable family, both in Chicago with her loving, responsible, and respectable parents and in New York with her husband and sons. Larsen seems highly sensitive to the impossibility of truth between characters; she designs their few attempts so that they end in confusion and lack of communication.

Deborah McDowell has pointed to the lesbian undertone in Irene's attraction to Clare and to the eroticism in Larsen's descriptions of the two characters' interaction.[72] That reading of the undercurrent symbolism is viable. Moreover, Larsen frequently associated with a literary and theater crowd that included lesbians, homosexuals, and bisexuals who were open in their sexual preferences. Bruce Nugent, for example, considered his homosexuality part of his bohemianism. Van Vechten, too, had a loving but "open" marriage with Fania Marinoff, leaving him free to share the company of other males. And among the females, Edna Thomas and Olivia Wyndham lived together, at times with Edna's husband, Lloyd. Some, such as Wallace Thurman, veiled their sex lives. Still others, like Larsen's friend Dorothy Peterson, were apparently not yet consciously aware of their own sexual preferences, but not prudish about those of their friends and associates.

When Larsen was writing *Passing*, she witnessed the police raids on three

---

72. McDowell, Introduction to *"Quicksand" and "Passing,"* ed. McDowell, xxiii–xxvi.

Broadway plays, *The Captive*, by Edouard Bourdet, *Sex*, by Mae West, and *The Virgin Man*, by William Francis Durgan and H. F. Maltby. Forty-one authors, producers, and actors, including Mae West and Basil Rathbone, were arrested for violating public morality. *The Captive*, featuring Helen Menken and Rathbone, was a treatment of lesbianism, and it had been performed 160 times before the February 9, 1927, raid. Sensitive and serious, the play reportedly had intellectuals weeping over the conclusion, though Mae West told a reporter, "'You may think I'm kidding, but plays like *The Captive* make me blush.'"[73] Lesbianism as a theme in a popular work, then, was neither unfamiliar nor shocking in Larsen's sophisticated milieu.

While latent lesbianism may well be inscribed in Irene's attraction to Clare, it does not entirely account for it. Several attractions are at work; one of them is Irene's own aesthetic attraction to whiteness: white values, white standards of beauty, behavior. The logical extension of her black bourgeoisie life-style and ideology, which Larsen does not entirely condemn though she satirizes it, concludes in an elevation of Clare's whiteness—blond, pale, ivory—to the level of icon. As icon, Clare functions as object rather than subject, a factor that accounts for some dissatisfaction with her passiveness and illusiveness in the text.

The iconography, however, also issues from Irene's insistence on finding a visible flaw in Clare's whiteness. She locates it in Clare's eyes, which function as a mirror reflecting Irene's own speculative "Negro" eyes. As Cheryl Wall suggests, "Irene invents for Clare a complex inner life. But she is not responding to the person before her so much as to her own notions of Otherness. Clare's 'Negro eyes' symbolize the unconscious, the unknowable, the erotic, and the passive. In other words, they symbolize those aspects of the psyche Irene denies within herself."[74] Clare's eyes are the focal point of Irene's self-objectification; however, they are also Irene's own eyes, which she superimposes upon Clare's white body and through which she attacks both her racial self and her white object of desire.

On the other hand, Clare may be viewed as a metaphorical representation of Larsen's own mother, the distant and obscured parent whose reality cannot be entirely or completely imagined, while Irene represents Larsen herself, the abandoned child who in adulthood still has a need for a mother. Clare's desertion of Irene for the white race may figuratively present Marie

73. Allen Churchill, *The Theatrical 20's* (New York, 1975), 232, 233, 235.

74. Cheryl A. Wall, "Passing for What? Aspects of Identity in Nella Larsen's Novels," *Black American Literature Forum*, XX (Spring–Summer, 1986), 108–109.

Larsen's desertion of Nella. In this case, desertion can either be willful or circumstantial; however, from the child's perspective, the end result, that is, the absent mother, is the same. Because Marie Larsen chose material security and social comfort over her daughter's well-being, she cannot be rehabilitated unless she repudiates her notions of race.

One fascinating psychological dimension in the relationship between Clare and Irene is that if Clare is read as parent and if the maternal/paternal roles are reversed, as Larsen frequently reversed roles and names, then Clare becomes a representation of Peter Larsen with the racist Bellew as spouse standing in for Marie/Mary Larsen, the mother who resented the presence of her own black daughter in her reconfigured family. Margery, the absent daughter dispelled to a boarding school, becomes the youthful embodiment of Larsen's girlhood self. The situation is much the same in *Quicksand* when Peter Nilssen's unnamed wife rejects all claims of kinship for herself and her husband with his black niece. In *Passing,* Clare's remarkable strength of will, and her equally apparent weakness of character, becomes a way of understanding Peter Larsen, his inability to protect his daughter, and his crossing the color line. Irene, then, in her need for Clare's friendship and affection, becomes the child who continues the search for the lost parent. Irene apparently comes from a happy family, but upon closer examination, her mother is absent, and her father is caring but subservient to the vagaries of race and class. Her adult interaction with him cannot take place in the foreground of the novel because Clare has come to embody that father and the attraction for family and its whiteness, which, in becoming excessive, leads to self-doubt, feelings of inadequacy, and fears of additional or renewed loss.

The novel is a story of loss and retribution. In one sense it is an explanation and expiation of the child/daughter's desire at once to reclaim the affection of the parent and intimacy and the frustration of that desire into a rage to murder, to kill, and to destroy in order finally to protect self against the psychological threat and damage that the attainment of the parent would ultimately mean. Upon Clare's death, Irene reverts to a childlike helplessness, and her release of emotion is compared to a child's: "Irene struggled against the sob of thankfulness that rose in her throat. Choked down, it turned to a whimper, like a hurt child's" (241). The struggle of the female child with her father for power, for control over her life, is metaphorically, then, another dimension of the relationship existing between Irene and Clare.

Ironically, however, lost or removed parents are beyond the reach of the murderous rage, but the child, the self, is not. Clare, as a projection of that self, is forever young and unchanged; "she had remained almost what she had always been, an attractive, somewhat lonely child—selfish, wilful, and disturbing" (202). She is vulnerable to the attack of the enraged subconscious. Irene then becomes the adult responding to her childhood self through another medium, another body.

If Irene's sons, Brian Junior and Ted, and Clare's daughter, Margery, have no real grounding in the story, it may be because these children are projections of Larsen's ambivalent attitudes toward children. Irene wants to be a parent who does all for the benefit of her sons; Clare does all for the benefit of herself. The child Margery, like a young version of Larsen herself, is isolated from parents, committed to an institutional life in a boarding school, and is the least of her mother's or her father's concerns. Her birth, synonymous with fear of exposure as black and the resolution not to reproduce again, precipitates Clare's anxiety over both her individual future and conjugal relations.

Reading the relationship between the two women as a paradigm of female friendship and competitiveness also accounts for the attraction and repulsion principle embedded in the novel. Larsen chose as models for her fiction British and American writers in whose works women's friendships and the conventions of intimacy among women are significantly defined. Although she treats the emergence of a woman's sexuality in both of the novels, she does so partially with the attitudes toward sex and sexuality that are more in keeping with Victorian mores and manners and that are at odds, rather than compatible, with the new, Freudian ideas of the world of the 1920s that also influenced her thinking about sexuality and psychology.

The older conventions encompassing intimacy and touch as displays of friendship also depend upon almost ritualized demonstrations of affection between female friends. Larsen structured the ways in which women interact and interrelate according to models available in women's magazines and in the fiction of Edith Wharton and Henry James, despite recognizing their stylistic antithesis to some of her concerns. One reviewer, in fact, observed a "certain artificiality" in the style: "She [Larsen] has gone to Mrs. Wharton and the elegant sophisticates for her lessons in writing. She insinuates, she interpolates, she relucts."[75] At the same time, however, Larsen, as well as Van Vechten and others among her white avant-garde associates, was con-

---

75. "Books of the Day—The Dilemma of Mixed Race: Another Study of the Color-Line in New York," New York *Sun*, May 1, 1929, in SCF.

cerned with portraying sexuality, but more compulsively and obsessively than other women writers of the Harlem Renaissance. She was very much aware of Freud, Jung, and their works, and searched for a picture postcard with what she termed the "most phallic-like" building, in order to reference symbols and send a coded message to a sophisticated male friend.

While *Quicksand* displayed Larsen's agnosticism and Helga Crane's loss of faith in politics (the racial uplift doctrine of Naxos), in philosophy (the aesthetics of beauty), in romantic love (Robert Anderson), in religion (Pleasant Green), and ultimately in art, *Passing* reveals a loss of faith in the past, in friendship, in family, particularly a matrilineal heritage. In both fictions, the loss of personal and psychological freedom is at work. In *Passing*, unlike *Quicksand*, inhospitable external environments and fundamental conflicts with others are not the cause or the symptom; instead, the diminishing of self and the narrowing of options for living fully emanate from within the individual who is trapped in a metaphysical dilemma, aggravated by the psychological-historical legacies of slavery in America: the unofficial color caste.

Reviews in contemporary white and black publications, such as *Crisis, Opportunity, Bookman, Saturday Review,* the New York *Herald Tribune,* the *New York Times Book Review,* and the London *Times Literary Supplement,* emphasized the exotic theme of passing across the color line, identified the author as "partly of negro [*sic*] blood," and stressed what the New York *Sun* reviewer called "that double consciousness which torments the half-caste the world over." The twelve major reviews of the novel were largely favorable, particularly in terms of the lack of sentimentality in the portraiture, as W. B. Seabrook observed: "The sharpness and definition of the author's mind (even when her characters are awash in indecision) are qualities for which any novel reader should be grateful." Nonetheless, the reviews were not as flattering as those Larsen received for *Quicksand.* Clare's "opaqueness" and beauty posed problems for some, as did her failure to remain at the center of the narrative and her lack of motivation for returning to the race, which prompted several complaints about the ending. Esther Hyman, writing for *Bookman,* noticed that the novel lacked "sufficient depth": "Even in these days of tolerance and broad-mindedness towards artistic forms, a mere forty thousand words are not sufficient to develop a theme of importance against a firm and satisfying background. . . . [T]he dramatic climax lacks conviction, not so much because of the insufficiency of the preparation—it needs a very decided push, such as could scarcely escape the attention of a crowd of people with gaze concentrated upon the victim, to send a woman hurtling through a window." Larsen's style bothered a few readers, one of whom fumed: "'Passing' falls into the modern affectation of broken sentences with deleted verbs. It stutters. The author has taken less pains with her work."[76] That conclusion seemed to pervade the reviews, but it did not prevent a genuine celebration of Larsen's text as a "coming of age" of the "Negro" novel. Seabrook was especially flattering to Larsen in this regard: "She has produced a work so fine, sensitive, and distinguished that it rises above race categories and becomes that rare object, a good novel." The dropping of the racial category of the novel was considered the mark of the "Negro" novelist's success. As Du Bois put it for the readers of *Crisis*, "If the American Negro renaissance gives us many more books like this, with its sincerity, its simplicity and charm, we can soon with equanimity drop the word 'Negro.'"[77]

Although she was not as elated over her reviews as she had been a year earlier, Larsen must have found the conclusions reached by Seabrook and Du Bois vindication and justification of what she hoped to achieve on a literal and symbolic level with her novel. She attempted to both attach herself to the race and detach herself from it in her second novel. Her oblique uncovering of more of her permanent scars from her psycho-social history was a process that resulted, not in healing, however slow, but in ambivalence about race, deeper and more pronounced than ever before.

76. *Ibid.*; W. B. Seabrook, "Touch of the Tar-brush," *Saturday Review of Literature*, May 18, 1929, p. 1017; Esther Hyman, Review of *Passing*, by Nella Larsen, in *Bookman*, LXIX (June, 1929), 428; Bowser, "The Cat Came Back," 20.

77. Seabrook, "Touch of the Tar-brush," 1018; Du Bois, "The Browsing Reader," 248.

11

Catching a "Flying Glimpse of the Panorama,"
1929–1930

A HEAT WAVE in June and July, 1929, brought Harlemites into the streets. Larsen, observing their efforts to find relief, displayed an increasing disdain for her neighbors: "It is just a little hotter than hell here these days and the ghetto is literally teeming with women wearing one garment through which can be seen various protuberances, men wearing not much more than suspenders, but fortunately always these. As for the children—well 'The innocent voyage' has very little on them."[1] But her attempt at humor could not disguise her inability to cope with the heat, which brought on headaches and summer colds and kept her feeling listless.[2]

She was having trouble writing. "Nor am I writing anything. I can't." Larsen had returned to work at the New York Public Library, and between her job there and her social engagements downtown, "getting around to places like the Ritz, the Roosevelt and the Pensylvania [*sic*] and Biltmore roofs," she had little free time for writing. Braving the heat at the end of June, she attended a party at A'Lelia Walker's studio, but as another guest observed, "It was as crowded as most of her parties are and with the heat it was unbearable."[3]

1. Nella Larsen Imes to Carl Van Vechten, Friday, fourteenth [postmarked June 15, 1929], in JWJ.
2. Nella Larsen Imes to Carl Van Vechten, Saturday, July 28 [postmarked July 31, 1929], *ibid.*
3. *Ibid.*; Harold Jackman to Countee Cullen, June 29, 1929, in CCC.

Larsen's social activity was a way of diverting her frustration at being unable to move ahead quickly on a new novel that had not had a sufficient process of incubation. Although she may not have been suffering from a writer's creative block, she was clearly suffering anxiety about her work, which had come to embody much of her sense of identity. When, as Anthony Storr has observed, the success or failure of creative writing is "substituted for personal success or failure in interpersonal relations," it becomes extremely difficult to pursue the work; this difficulty often occurs "in people who have given up hope of being loved in the way they would like to be; usually because they did not feel themselves loved as children."[4]

Throughout the 1920s, Larsen had effectively displaced her sense of being unloved as a child. Her marriage, combined with her evolution as a writer, had generated the sense of belonging she missed as a child. But her sense of well-being was suddenly threatened. Personal and financial problems in her marriage were beginning to cause the stress manifested in her inability to write. During the summer, Larsen and Imes grew increasingly distant. He went about his research as usual and planned to attend a meeting of physicists in Canada before continuing to Ann Arbor for a stretch of work. She, still basking in the public reception of her second novel, wanted to continue her social life. "I shall be, as always, at home this summer, mostly alone I think," she informed Van Vechten. "Elmer is planning to go to Canada and later to Ann Arbor I believe."[5]

No longer certain of Imes's plans, but certain of her exclusion from them, she needed an escort and found one in Colin Hackforth-Jones, an Englishman on holiday in the States whom she had met at a party given by Lawrence Langner. Introduced to Hackforth-Jones by the artist Florine Stettheimer, Larsen thought of him as "a nice person to take one around, dances well, is amusing and seems not to have any race consciousness at all." After spending most of June and July in his company, Larsen explained her actions by saying that her husband was "out of town most weekends, as usual in the summer," and that he would be "away for the month of September," which meant: "I shall be here . . . most beastly lonesome." Her highly visible excursions with Hackforth-Jones reflected a shift in her attention—away from Imes and her marriage. Ronald de Sousa has explained that "a change in patterns of attention . . . entail[s] a change in emotion."[6] By diverting

4. Anthony Storr, *The Dynamics of Creation* (New York, 1985), 221.
5. Larsen Imes to Van Vechten, Friday, fourteenth [postmarked June 15, 1929], in JWJ.
6. *Ibid.;* Nella Larsen Imes to Carl Van Vechten, July 31, 1929, *ibid.;* Ronald de Sousa,

herself from Imes's seeming neglect, Larsen tried to deflect her anger and her suspicion that she had been replaced in Imes's affection. Given the precariousness of her husband's personal situation, Larsen's anxiety was justified.

Elmer Imes was preoccupied during that summer. He had begun a transition to an academic position as a way out of financial and marital difficulties. Initially, his efforts concentrated on the University of Michigan, where he had an excellent reputation for his research in spectroscopy, and on Fisk University, which was expanding its academic departments under a new president. Always reticent about his work, Imes had become disillusioned with his prospects in private industry. Academic scientists had access to equipment and to research collaboratives missing in most companies, where money for laboratories and research was tied to sales. An added factor, which he had been slow to admit, was his race. While not barring him from all opportunity, it limited his potential for advancement.

His wife's phenomenal success had exacerbated his sense of being stifled. Although he had encouraged her work, he was unprepared for the publicity it generated and for the attention she received. Nella Larsen, novelist, had become a conspicuous reality, while Elmer Imes, physicist, had somehow faded into the background. He remarked that she enjoyed having what he called "the whip hand" in the marriage. And indeed almost as compensation for inequities in backgrounds, Larsen was becoming more overbearing with her success. Elmer Imes was a proud man, as his friends recalled. "He was very haughty, so sure of himself, but he had a caustic personality," Mrs. John Work remembered. Imes's pride in his achievement was being tested. His only two professional publications had appeared in 1919 and 1920, shortly after he had completed his doctorate at Ann Arbor. He was sensitive to the implication of his failure to publish; he tried to account for the lapse by calling attention to "three years of work resulting in several patents. . . . Because of the hope to commercialize the processes and apparatus involved it was not possible to publish, in the purely scientific sense." His industrial patents for work on railroad and signal appliances had brought few rewards during his nearly three years with the manufacturer Edward A. Everett, and as he put it, he "lack[ed] the financial backing to go further."[7] At forty-five, Imes was anxious about his own career.

"The Rationality of Emotions," in *Explaining Emotions,* ed. Amelie Oksenberg Rorty (Berkeley, 1980), 141.

7. Elmer Imes to Carl Van Vechten, June 21, 1932, in JWJ; Mrs. John (Edith) Work, inter-

For nearly a year, he had been engaged in discussions with the Fisk University president, Thomas E. Jones. In September of 1928, he had sent a night letter to Jones about possible employment at Fisk, but the telegrammed response was discouraging: "Budget and personalities make probably impossible this year." Undaunted, Imes wrote a lengthy response in which he explained his inquiry and his decision to approach Fisk:

> I realized, of course, that it is a very inopportune time at which to discuss possible school work for this year, but the circumstances make me feel that it should be done. Very suddenly I am in the position of changing employment. My present connection is as Research Engineer. . . . The laboratory has developments to its credit far beyond the factory production schedule and in view of the drastic lowering of railroad purchasing we are cutting overhead to the lowest possible amount. This may seem to necessitate an entire cessation of research work unless, as now seems improbable, buying on the part of the railroads should suddenly increase.
>
> Other possible connections are developing, but I find myself thinking very seriously of the hope which I have always had of someday returning to school work. Because I dislike change and because a new connection at this time would most probably very greatly postpone another change, I decided to approach Fisk.[8]

Although he suggested that his research laboratory might soon be cut and his job lost, Imes painted an attractive picture of his potential value to the university:

> In the course of ten years of commercial research I have gathered familiarity with a few problems which could with great profit be taken into a university laboratory. . . . At present there is the possibility that I shall go into the consulting field along this particular line.
>
> I have heard that Fisk has, or is about to have, certain subsidies for scientific research and my thought was that it might be possible within

---

view with author, March 8, 1987; E. S. Imes to Thomas E. Jones, September 25, 1928, in Papers of Thomas Elsa Jones, Fisk University Library.

8. Thomas E. Jones to E. S. Imes, September 24, 1928, in Jones Papers; Imes to Jones, September 25, 1928, *ibid.*

two years to do two things—First, the physics department might be put on the map by one or more publications having real scientific and technical value, and second, it could be established whether or not I could fit definitely into the scheme of things there as head of the physics department.[9]

Imes was after his own laboratory, which he estimated would require an expenditure of $5,000 to $7,500 for startup costs, aside from his salary. The sum was great, yet his plan was reasonable, he said, because "a small amount of success might lead to substantial subsidies for the research laboratory." He pointed to the possibility either of his arranging his time so that his consulting work would cover the total expense, or of his conducting a large part of the research elsewhere, thereby reducing by 25 percent to 50 percent the initial projected expense. Jones's reply remained firm: "I regret to say that it is impossible for Fisk to begin developing this most desirable department of research and instruction in Physics until we can have cash in hand with which to begin the project."[10]

Imes, however, read the reply as encouragement for further discussions and asked for a personal interview whenever Jones had time during a New York trip. His tactic worked. At the end of January, 1929, Jones asked for a conference on February 1, when he expected to be in the Fisk New York office on Fifth Avenue.[11] At that meeting, he offered Imes a position, and suggested that Nella Larsen would have the possibility of work in the Fisk library. When Imes responded on February 12 to the offer, he was pleased but not overjoyed. He took a practical view of his own affairs, his research at Michigan, his financial needs, and his wife's reactions. In effect, he asked to postpone his moving to Fisk until the fall of 1930, which would give him a year and a half to arrange the change in his affairs and would give the school ample time to complete a new science building. "But most important of all," Imes added, "it would leave me free to go for a year to the Department of Engineering Research (in the Physics Department) at Ann Arbor. A year in a real Physics Department with the latitude I would have if I should go to Ann Arbor would mean a great deal to Fisk through me."[12]

9. Imes to Jones, September 25, 1928, *ibid.*

10. *Ibid.;* Thomas E. Jones to E. S. Imes, October 6, 1928, in Jones Papers.

11. E. S. Imes to Thomas E. Jones, November 30, 1928, *ibid.;* Thomas E. Jones to E. S. Imes, January 31, 1929, *ibid.*

12. E. S. Imes to Thomas E. Jones, February 12, 1929, *ibid.*

Imes made his hope of working at his undergraduate alma mater plain: "I want to come to Fisk. . . . I am trying to arrange things so that there will be every chance for my work to be successful and happy if I do come. My attitude will be that such a connection if consumated [*sic*] is to be the last and most important of my life." At the same time, however, he raised the issue of salary and conveyed the difficulty that the offer might present:

> In my talk with you I made no comment on the proposed salary since I knew that the figure mentioned represented a very large increase over what Fisk has been able to pay in the past. It would help the purely personal side of the change of work if the figure were put at $5000 with the understanding that in the first year 10% of this would go into the Department.
>
> Mrs. Imes appreciated the possibility of Library work should we come to Fisk, but does not quite reconcile herself to a 25% drop in my contribution to the budget. This is not vital, but I mention it as part of my policy of absolute frankness with you.[13]

While he wanted the job, and perhaps believed that it presented his best opportunity for development of his interests and career, he intended not only to explore all of his options before making a commitment, but also to negotiate a lucrative financial arrangement in the process. What he could not adequately convey, given Jones's emphasis on Fisk as a "family," was that Larsen had little interest in leaving New York and that he wanted the move as much to distance himself from her as to further his scientific research.

At the end of February, 1929, Jones suggested that Imes accept the position at Michigan for one year, during which he would be listed as a professor of physics at Fisk on leave of absence. The suggestion was intended to allow Imes an opportunity to supervise the purchase of laboratory equipment for the new department. In addition to asking that Imes occasionally visit to oversee the installation of the lab, Jones also proposed that Nella Larsen could, if she desired, move a year in advance of her husband and begin work in the library, so that Imes could find housing near the campus and move their belongings before he completed his obligations in the North. Jones was less forthcoming in regard to salary: "I believe we can make a

13. *Ibid.*

satisfactory adjustment . . . unless the requirement of both you and Mrs. Imes is simply out of proportion to the salaries that we pay persons of your training and experience, and in that case, of course, there is nothing more we can do." [14]

Imes did not respond until the beginning of April, when he explained why he could not accept a resident connection with Fisk until the fall of 1930. He had investigated his chances at Michigan, only to discover that the Department of Research Engineering connected with the physics program was not in favor of a one-year regular appointment, but could offer him a special fellowship with a stipend of $2,500. Imes found the allowance insufficient, so decided against pursuing the fellowship. Meanwhile, his employer had, according to Imes, insisted that he honor his contract, as the company could not afford a change in personnel for the fall of 1929; moreover, Imes had renewed hope that he might regain possession of several patents that he had lost when the corporation formed to develop them had been forced into bankruptcy and receivership. He had, then, several different reasons for deferring a resident appointment at Fisk, not the least of which was the publication in April of Larsen's second novel, which held some promise of monetary rewards, or as Imes assessed it, "There are numerous amenities being offered her so that she feels that she needs me here." [15] In fact, Larsen was taking a circuitous route to saving her marriage by keeping her husband in New York. While amenities may have been in the offing, she was prepared to return to work if employment meant assuring Imes's residency in New York. She had spent too much of her life alone to relinquish his companionship easily.

Imes and Larsen were in need of money. She had not worked outside the home since the beginning of 1926, and nearly three years later with Imes's research job in jeopardy and the serious negotiations with Fisk under way, Larsen resumed work with the New York Public Library as a general assistant. From March until July, 1929, she held the library position, which helped pay their bills but consumed the time that she wanted to spend writing. Because both Larsen and Imes spent money freely on luxuries and had no independent incomes, they frequently lived well beyond their means, as evidenced, for example, by their tenant-purchase arrangement for their apartment in the Dunbar Apartments. His salary might have supported a more modest lifestyle while his job with Everett was being phased out, but

14. Thomas E. Jones to E. S. Imes, February 27, 1929, in Jones Papers.
15. E. S. Imes to Thomas E. Jones, April 4, 1929, *ibid.*

neither Imes nor Larsen would economize. Both had grown accustomed to living well, and neither had attempted to save. In July, 1929, she was able to end her work at the library, because that month Imes had finally concluded an amenable contract with Fisk, which would not pay a salary until the fall of 1930 but would pay his expenses for organizing a physics department and finance his campus visits and professional obligations.[16] By August 15, 1929, Imes had come to regret the delay in the contract with Fisk, since he had been forced into tending his resignation at Edward Everett effective on the first of September; however, he was unable to change the agreement with Fisk because the budget for the 1929–1930 academic year had already been appropriated and the best readjustment that he could receive was part-time status granting a "minimum figure" to cover his "personal and family obligations."[17]

Larsen had begun to express some anxiety over financial problems during the winter and spring of 1928, but her financial situation had begun to worsen the previous summer. In her correspondence with Dorothy Peterson, Larsen often brought up the subject of money, especially by the summer of 1927, when she had been out of work for more than a year. In a series of letters to Peterson in France, she wrote about her finances in the context of a coat for which Peterson was to purchase fabric. In the last of the series, she asked Peterson to disregard everything that she had written about the fabric, the coat, and money for it, because she revealed, "I *must* make some money. Almost I have decided to sell my house and spend a couple of years abroad."[18] Although she did not mention her house again and it is not clear to which house she referred, she would continue to stress her need for money, but rarely would she consider finding a job.

At the same time, Larsen's recognition as a writer brought offers for journalistic assignments from *Harlem, Liberty,* and *Forum* magazines. Although pressed for money, she could see the absurdity of an offer from *Forbes.* A representative of the magazine asked her "about making a trip through the South, and gathering materials on the Negro (plantation) for him to use in articles. All expenses paid and a whole hundred dollars for the work. The South in the summer on Negro Plantations (what ever they are)

16. See Thomas E. Jones to E. S. Imes, May 4, 1929, and E. S. Imes to Thomas E. Jones, May 10, 1929, both *ibid.*

17. Thomas E. Jones to E. S. Imes, August 21, 1929, and E. S. Imes to Thomas E. Jones, August 15, 1929, both *ibid.*

18. Nella Larsen to Dorothy Peterson, Thursday 21st [July, 1927], in JWJ. See also Nella Larsen to Dorothy Peterson, July 12, 1927, *ibid.*

and in Jim Crow cars all for a hundred dollars. I felt it was a shame to take the money." Despite Larsen's use of humor to deflate the offer and her condition, financial pressures perhaps account for her submission in mid-1929 of the ill-fated short story "Sanctuary" to *Forum* for $200, when she was back at the public library but not yet solvent. She, like other published authors, was not making money from her novels; while *Quicksand* initially sold for $2.50 a copy and *Passing* for $2.00 she expected that both would shortly be reduced in price. At the beginning of 1929, Cullen's *Copper Sun* was marked down to $.35, Hughes's *Weary Blues* to $.25, and Joyce's *Dublin Days* to only $.10.[19]

In November the appearance of Taylor Gordon's *Born to Be* (1929) revitalized Larsen's writing. Reading the autobiography of the African-American singer and entertainer from Montana a second time, she was convinced that it was "a very amazing book—as well as a very amusing one—in many ways," and she wrote Gordon to tell him so. Jackman, who had an advance copy at the end of October, had already pronounced it "a bitch. . . . [I]t is terrible." Before the publication of *Born to Be*, Larsen had thought that the book was bound to be a "howling success" because Van Vechten was writting the foreword and Muriel Draper the introduction, and Miguel Covarrubias was drawing the illustrations; however, she had also been skeptical about its reception because she believed white audiences and reviewers were becoming bored with books about blacks. But when the New York *Times*, like the *Herald Tribune* and other New York papers, pronounced it "highly amusing," Larsen found encouragement for her own writing. She began work on a piece about Van Vechten that she intended to entitle "Toward Nigger Heaven." [20] Although she indicated that she would clarify a few points for her essay with Van Vechten in the next week or so, Larsen apparently did not complete the essay. Invigorated and putting aside emotional insecurity about the fate of her writing, she resumed work on her third novel.

Larsen's focus on her writing was also a way of dealing with the death of a helpful friend in her Harlem crowd. Marion Beasley died in mid-

19. Nella Larsen Imes to Carl Van Vechten, July 28, 1929, *ibid.*; Larsen Imes to Van Vechten, Friday, fourteenth [postmarked June 15, 1929], *ibid.*; Harold Jackman to Countee Cullen, Thursday, January 31, 1929, in CCC.

20. Nella Larsen Imes to Carl Van Vechten, Tuesday [postmarked November 12, 1929], in JWJ; Harold Jackman to Countee Cullen, October 31, 1929, in CCC; Larsen Imes to Van Vechten, Saturday, July 28 [postmarked July 31, 1929], in JWJ; Larsen Imes to Van Vechten, Tuesday [postmarked November 12, 1929], in JWJ.

November. Beasley had put considerable effort into locating an apartment for the Imeses when they wanted to leave New Jersey. Larsen said little in response to Beasley's death, because expressions of loss were difficult for her. She could, however, make light of another death that November: "I see by the papers that Nicholas J. Nelson Jr. really was bumped off. If it had happened the night he was up here [in Harlem] think what a grand time you [Van Vechten] and I would have had as witnesses. Poor dear, I suppose his tremendous inferiority complex was what finished him."[21]

On December 8, 1929, the NAACP hosted an all-star benefit at the Forrest Theater. The Sunday affair was "downtown—think of it—downtown," as Jackman noted the irony: "I couldn't go—couldn't afford it." Although she could not "afford" it either, Larsen attended the dance. An excerpt from *Quicksand* appeared in the program book, which had a cover drawing by Aaron Douglas. The selection, entitled "Moving Mosaic or N. A. A. C. P. Dance, 1929," showed her now characteristic élan:

> There was the sooty black, shiny black, taupe, mahogany, bronze, copper, gold, orange, yellow, peach, ivory, white. There was white hair, gray hair, yellow hair, red hair, brown hair, black hair, indefinite hair, straight hair, curly hair, straightened hair, crinkly hair, wooly hair. Black eyes in white faces, brown eyes in black faces, green eyes in yellow faces, blue eyes in tan faces, gray eyes in brown faces. Young men, old men, black men, white men, flapper women, older women, pink women, golden women, fat men, thin men, tall men, short men, stately women, small women, slim women, stout women, ambling lazily to a crooning melody or twisting their bodies to a sudden steaming rhythm or shaking themselves to the thump of unseen tom-toms. Africa, Europe, and a pinch of Asia in a fantastic motley of ugliness and beauty.

Larsen's use of "ugliness and beauty" in the final statement makes her attitude toward such dances clear; attraction and repulsion had become more pronounced in her view of African Americans. But whoever had selected her piece for the program was careful to break the passage off in the middle of a sentence and omit the end of the paragraph: "in a fantastic motley of

21. Nella Larsen to Dorothy Peterson, Tuesday 19th [July, 1927], in JWJ; Imes to Van Vechten, Tuesday [postmarked November 12, 1929], *ibid*.

ugliness and beauty, semibarbaric, sophisticated, exotic, were here. But she was blind to its charm, purposely aloof and a little contemptuous, and soon her interest in the moving mosaic waned."[22]

After the posh dance, Larsen and a large group, including James Weldon Johnson and Charles S. Johnson, headed uptown for A'Lelia Walker's Dark Tower, where they were in for another kind of excitement. Walker was charging $.50 for admission, but Mac Stinnett, her social secretary, refused to pay: "Lelia struck Stinnett and he wanted to fight her. . . . [I]t was a riot. Your people, hm hm!"[23] The near brawl was for Larsen another evidence of the mixing of the "semibarbaric" and "sophisticated" mentioned in her piece for the dance booklet.

Although "Moving Mosaic" gave her further publicity as a writer, the month of December would bring a major career disappointment. George E. Haynes, secretary of the Federal Council of Churches of Christ and coordinator of the Harmon Awards, had earlier in the year informed her that she was eligible for consideration for the new round of Harmon Awards. He suggested that she leave the supporting materials already in her file from the previous year with the Commission on the Church and Race Relations, which was the overseer for the awards. Haynes had written Larsen in response to her April 1, 1929, query about the return of the bound reviews of *Quicksand*, which she wanted to use for the publication of *Passing* later in April. On August 1, Lillian Alexander nominated Larsen for the second time, though Larsen filled in the personal information and supplied the list of people who would recommend her.[24]

Du Bois, Dorothy Peterson, and Van Vechten completed the confidential statement on the author's achievement for Larsen's second entry in the Harmon Awards. Du Bois submitted the briefest of the three on *Crisis* letterhead rather than on the official form: "I have known Mrs. Nella L. Imes for 10 years. I regard her work as important and outstanding." Van Vechten's statement was concise in praising Larsen as "probably the most interesting

22. Harold Jackman to Countee Cullen, December 12, 1929, in CCC; Nella Larsen Imes, "Moving Mosaic or N.A.A.C.P. Dance, 1929," in *All-Star Benefit Concert for the National Association for the Advancement of Colored People* (program book), December 8, 1929, p. 10, in CVV; Nella Larsen, *Quicksand*, in *"Quicksand" and "Passing,"* ed. Deborah E. McDowell (New Brunswick, 1986), 59–60.

23. Jackman to Cullen, December 12, 1929, in CCC.

24. George Haynes to Nella Larsen Imes, April 3, 1929, in HFR; Nella Larsen Imes to George E. Haynes, Monday, April first [1929], *ibid.*; Nella Larsen Imes, Nomination blank, William E. Harmon Awards for Distinguished Achievement Among Negroes, 1929, *ibid.*

and the most promising of the young writers of her race": "Both . . . novels are written with an insight into character, an intensive development, and in a fine English style which proclaims the true novelist. Both objectively and subjectively they are a psychological advance over any previous work by a Negro novelist." Peterson presented the fullest description of Larsen's work, listing not only the two novels but five short stories: "Freedom," "Tea," "The Wrong Man" (all given as published in 1926), "Sanctuary" (not yet published), and "Charity" (the latest and unpublished).[25]

In attesting to the outstanding character of her friend's work, Peterson wrote: "her education and life in Europe and America, her travel, her work in different fields—as nurse, librarian, teacher etc., her broad contact with many different classes of native and foreign races with an ability to understand and portray all these, sympathetically." In giving her reasons for endorsing Larsen for the award, she stated: "I feel that her honest and logical presentation of modern problems, her keen insight into human motives, particularly her gift for interpreting feminine psychology combined with her gift for clear and beautiful writing, all form a definite force for better understanding in race relations and raise the artistic standards of Negro writers."[26] Peterson, the only woman among those recommending Larsen, identified the lasting strength of the novels—"interpreting feminine psychology"—which ironically may have undercut Larsen's potential for winning a first-place award in race relations.

During September, Haynes had compiled a list of the 1929 nominees in literature. *Nellie* L. Imes was one of the fourteen nominees, who also included Walter White, Georgia Douglas Johnson, and Leslie Pinckney Hill among the better known authors. Wallace Thurman, whose novel *The Blacker the Berry* had appeared, was noticeably absent from the list. Haynes, like other New Yorkers who had come to know Larsen well after her marriage to Imes, used her given name along with her married name, despite the publication of her novels under the name Nella Larsen. Despite Haynes's encouragement of Larsen's entry into the competition, the 1929 Harmon Awards had a political undercurrent that worked against Larsen for the second year in a row. During October, November, and early December, the packets of candidates' materials made the round of judges, from

25. W. E. B. Du Bois to George E. Haynes, August 12, 1929, *ibid.;* Carl Van Vechten, 1929 Harmon Awards recommendation form, August 23, 1929, *ibid.;* Dorothy R. Peterson, 1929 Harmon Awards recommendation form, August 10, 1929, *ibid.*

26. Peterson, 1929 Harmon Awards recommendation form, *ibid.*

Joel E. Spingarn to Lewis Mumford to John G. Farrar to Alain Locke, and finally to Dorothy Scarborough. Although each judge voted as he or she completed the reading of materials, it was not until December 10, 1929, that Haynes could tally the results and send copies of the judges' comments and rankings to the selection committee.[27]

Larsen and White emerged as the two major contenders for the 1929 awards. White had received two votes for first place (Scarborough and Farrar); one qualified vote for first place (Mumford); one qualified vote for second place (Spingarn); and one vote for third place (Locke). Larsen received one vote for first place (Locke); two votes for second place (Farrar and Mumford); one qualified vote for second place (Spingarn); and one vote for third place (Scarborough). Only five of the other candidates received votes: Georgia Douglas Johnson, Elizabeth Ross Haynes, Leslie Pinckney Hill, James Alpheus Butler, and George Reginald Margetson. Scarborough voted a sixth place for Butler and a seventh place for Margetson. Hill received two fourth-place votes from Locke and Mumford, one fifth-place vote from Scarborough, and an honorable mention from Spingarn. Elizabeth Ross Haynes received one vote for second place from Scarborough, one for third place from Farrar, and one comment, "worth watching," from Mumford.

While White and Larsen were clearly the front-runners, neither was an overwhelming favorite. Haynes concluded that the votes gave White the second-place Bronze Award, because two judges (Mumford and Spingarn) did not favor awarding a first-place Gold Award, and he pointed out that as "Mrs. Imes is not eligible for the Bronze Award a second time, we conclude you will give only one award." Locke, who had voted for Larsen in first place, did not contest the decision. Perhaps he knew of Braithwaite's solitary, and losing, stance in her favor over Claude McKay in the previous year's ballot, or perhaps he recognized that Scarborough, who had refused to rank Larsen's work highly in both competitions, was unlikely to change her vote. Locke did tactfully remind Haynes "that if the same principle of not repeating applies to honorable mention, Mrs. Georgia Douglas Johnson should not receive this citation again this year." The suggestion for honorable mentions stemmed from Spingarn's initial ranking on November 22: "In order that the standards of the Harmon Awards be maintained at a

27. Candidates folder, 1929 Harmon Awards for Literature, *ibid.* See Judges: Literature—forwarding of materials folder, 1929 Harmon Awards, *ibid.;* Dr. George E. Haynes to Judges in Literature, 1929 Harmon Awards, December 10, 1929, *ibid.*

high level, I recommend that no first prize in Literature be awarded for 1929, that the second prize be divided between Nella Larsen Imes and Walter White, and that honorable mention be accorded to Georgia Douglas and Leslie Pinckney Hill." Spingarn had reiterated his point after the tabulations were in: "it would be wiser to give no first prize, to give Mr. White second prize, and to award honorable mention to Nella Larsen Imes, Georgia Douglas Johnson, Leslie Pinckney Hill, and Elizabeth Ross Haynes, all of whom have received commendation from one or more judges. I assume that Mrs. Imes could receive honorable mention even though she may not be eligible again to a second place."[28] Despite Spingarn's persistence, no honorable mentions were given.

Larsen had not fared as well as she, and others, had hoped. The rule against repeat winners in a category worked against her, but more important was that the male judges, with the exception of Locke, held a more favorable view of White, apparently agreeing with Mumford that "his novels, like those of Mr. Upton Sinclair, do not lack a certain power and intensity, and, taken with his study in 'Rope and Faggot,' his work is a serious contribution to present-day thought. Miss Larsen . . . is *a far better novelist;* and she has a more subtle, a more individual approach to the difficulties of race-relationship: her art, her command of language, are both a little too close to journalism."[29] The assumption was that, despite her being a better novelist, Larsen's subject matter was merely her own life's experiences. The self-fashioning she had worked so hard to achieve ultimately called the imaginative content of her art into question. The irony of the situation was lost on the judges, but not on Larsen, who turned her attention to another aspect of her career.

Larsen's disappointment with the results, and the politics, of the Harmon Awards was soon offset by the recognition of her work by the Guggenheim Foundation. Her application went into the foundation's office one day before the November 15, 1929, deadline. She had done her own typing of the four-page form, and after adding one sheet with her accomplishments and plans for study, she hand-delivered the application to the office at 551 Fifth

28. Haynes to Judges in Literature, 1929 Harmon Awards, December 10, 1929, *ibid.;* Alain Locke to George Haynes, December 11, 1929, in Judges Decision: Literature folder, 1929 Harmon Awards, *ibid.;* Joel E. Spingarn to George E. Haynes, November 22, 1929, Judges Decision folder, *ibid.;* Joel E. Spingarn to George E. Haynes, December 13, 1929, Judges Decision folder, *ibid.*

29. Lewis Mumford to George E. Haynes, October 23, 1929, Judges Decision folder, *ibid.* (emphasis added).

Avenue. Larsen listed her field as creative writing and her project as a novel set in the United States and Europe. She sought support in gathering first-hand information about the "intellectual and physical freedom for the Negro" in Europe, an idea she had used in *Quicksand* as part of Helga Crane's analysis of her condition: "This knowledge, this certainty of the division of her life into two parts in two lands, into physical freedom in Europe and spiritual freedom in America, was unfortunate, inconvenient, expensive. It was . . . even a trifle ridiculous, and mentally she caricatured herself moving shuttlelike from continent to continent. From the prejudiced restrictions of the New World to the easy formality of the Old, from the pale calm of Copenhagen to the colorful lure of Harlem." Specifically during a year abroad, Larsen intended to contrast France and Spain with the United States: "I have never been to these countries and therefore feel that I am not prepared without visiting them to judge attitudes and reactions of my hero in a foreign and favorable or more unfavorable environment. My plan is, travel and residence in Europe, principally the South of France and Spain, while completing the novel." [30]

In stating her plans, Larsen had followed the lead of Walter White, who had presented a comparable proposal for the 1926 Guggenheim fellowships and had spent his fellowship year in the south of France working on a novel treating three generations of a black family. Having encouraged her to apply, White, along with Van Vechten, James Weldon Johnson, Muriel Draper, and Blanche Knopf, wrote in support of the application. White had not completed his fellowship project, but he had written instead *Rope and Faggot: A Biography of Judge Lynch* (1929), a study of lynching that was the basis of his entry in the 1929 Harmon Awards in Literature. Although he did not envision himself in competition with Larsen, White's receiving the Harmon Bronze Award was balanced by Larsen's receiving a Guggenheim grant. When the announcement arrived in March, she immediately wrote Henry Allen Moe, secretary of the Guggenheim Foundation, to thank him, the trustees, and the selection committee for "the exciting news": "I very much hope that through it [the fellowship] I will be able to do something really good." [31] The award was one of the few high points for Larsen during 1930,

---

30. Nella Larsen Imes, Fellowship application form, 1930–31, John Simon Guggenheim Memorial Foundation, November, 1929, in John Simon Guggenheim Memorial Foundation files, New York; Larsen, *Quicksand*, in *"Quicksand" and "Passing,"* ed. McDowell, 96.

31. Nella Larsen Imes to Henry Allen Moe, March 16, 1930, in Guggenheim Foundation files.

but unfortunately, she was already complicating her work on the proposed novel by attaching too many personal identifications to it. She thought that the new novel would have to prove her value as a writer and validate her as a person.

Others of the New Negro authors were also having difficulty achieving and maintaining success. Wallace Thurman's play *Harlem* was back on Broadway for a short run at the end of October, but Thurman was ill: "he drinks so much and such bad stuff it is a wonder that the lining of his stomach hasn't been eaten away—and now he's going away on one of his 'seclusion' stints." But in addition to personal problems affecting their work, some of the New Negroes were becoming hostile to their fellow artists. Despite his health, Thurman was no exception, as he revealed in writing to Langston Hughes:

> Found *Banjo* turgid and tiresome. *Passing* possessed some of the same faults as *Quicksand*. *Rope and Faggot* good for Library Reference. Nella Larsen can write, but oh my god she knows so little how to invest her characters with any life like possibilities. They always outrage the reader, not naturally as people have a way of doing in real life, but artificially like ill managed putppetts [*sic*]. Claude [McKay] I believe has shot his bolt. Jessie Fauset should be taken to Philadelphia and creamated [*sic*]. You should write a book. Countee should be castrated and taken to Paris as the Shah's enuch [*sic*]. Jean Toomer should be enshrined as a genius and immortal and he should also publish his new book about which gossipp [*sic*] is raving. Bud Fisher should stick to short stories. Zora should learn craftsmanship and surprise the world and outstrip her contemporaries as well. Bruce [Nugent] should be spanked, put in a monastery and made to concentrate on writing. Gwennie [Bennett] should stick to what she is doing. Aaron [Douglas] needs a change of scenery and a psychic shock. Eric [Walrond] ought to finish The Big Ditch or destroy it. I should commit suicide. Don't mind such ravings.[32]

In this increasingly judgmental climate, Larsen's short story "Sanctuary" appeared in the January issue of *Forum* magazine. Winold Reiss, the artist

---

32. Jackman to Cullen, October 31, 1929, in CCC; Wallace Thurman to Langston Hughes, n.d., in Langston Hughes Papers, Beinecke Rare Book and Manuscript Library, Yale University.

who painted the portraits and book decorations for Locke's anthology *The New Negro,* provided four illustrations and sketched the decorative lettering of the title and the author's name. The story was her first with a southern setting and regional dialect, both of which contributed to the development of character and of plot. There is no way of determining whether it was her first story with African-American characters; however, it was the first published under her own name, which had become fairly well known in New York following the favorable reviews of her two novels. Name recognition may have assisted in having the text accepted.

Divided into four parts, "Sanctuary" treats one evening in the life of a black woman in an isolated, forsaken area on the southern coast:

Between Merton and Shawboro, there is a strip of desolation some half a mile wide and nearly ten miles long between the sea and old fields of ruined plantations. Skirting the edge of this narrow jungle is a partly grown-over road which still shows traces of furrows made by the wheels of wagons that have long since rotted away or been cut into firewood. This road is little used, now that the state has built its new highway a bit to the west and wagons are less numerous than automobiles.[33]

Annie Poole, the mother of a grown son who lives with her, is "a tiny, withered woman—fifty perhaps—with a wrinkled face the color of old copper, framed by a crinkly mass of white hair" (15). Alone in her cottage, she is making biscuits for supper when Jim Hammer, "a big, black man with pale brown eyes" (15), enters her kitchen without knocking. First seen hiding outside the cottage and looking into a window, Jim is a friend of Mrs. Poole's son Obadiah, but he stands in low esteem in her eyes. She cannot understand her son's friendship with "'youall no'count trash,'" for she "'shuah don' see nuffin' in you but a heap o' dirt'" (16). As she suspected, Jim is on the run from "white folks" for having shot someone. For her son's sake, she hides Jim Hammer in her feather bed. When the white sheriff and his men appear, they bring the bad news that it is Obadiah who has been shot and killed. The men carry Obadiah's body into the house and leave to continue their search for Jim Hammer. Annie Poole does not reveal

<hr>

33. Nella Larsen, "Sanctuary," *Forum,* LXXXIII (January, 1930), 15. Subsequent references cited parenthetically in the text.

that she is harboring the fugitive, not even after she knows that he has killed her son. Instead, she goes into the room where he is hiding. "It seemed like a long time before Obadiah's mother spoke. When she did there were no tears, no reproaches; but there was a raging fury in her voice as she lashed out. 'Git outen mah feather baid, Jim Hammer, an' don' nevah stop thankin' yo' Jesus he don gib you dat black face'" (18).

Although Larsen's rendition of Negro dialect is more faithful to literary models than actual speech, her text depends on two underlying conceptions for meaning: racial solidarity among oppressed blacks, and racial brutality against blacks by whites, including law officers. Mrs. Poole gives Jim Hammer sanctuary because she understands the threat of mob action and the fear of lynching. Implicitly she knows that her own son, despite his apparently fine qualities, could easily by chance have been in Jim's predicament. She acts partly out of a mother's love for her own child, and partly out of a sense of racial kinship with Jim, who may not amount to much but who nonetheless is a human being. As she allows, "'Obadiah's right fon' o' you, an' . . . white folks is white folks'" (16). The text relies mainly on atmosphere with little attention to human psychology, which had become a hallmark of Larsen's fiction.

Shortly after "Sanctuary" appeared, rumors began to circulate about Larsen's having stolen the story. On January 27, Harold Jackman, who like Bruce Nugent rarely missed any gossip, alerted Countee Cullen:

> Literary dirt: Nella Larsen Imes has a story in the *Forum* for this month called *Sanctuary*. It has been found out—at least Sidney Peterson was the first to my knowledge to discover this—that it is an exact blue print of a story by Sheila Kaye-Smith called *Mrs. Adis* which is in a book called *Joanna Gooden Marries and Other Stories*. The only difference is that Nella has made a racial story out of hers, but the procedure is the same as Kaye-Smith's, and Anne and Sidney have found out that the dialogue in some places is almost identical. If you can get ahold of the *Forum* and the Smith book do so and compare them. But isn't that a terrible thing. It remains to be seen whether the *Forum* people will find this out.[34]

Jackman took special note of any social gossip, because using his grandfather's name, Basil Winter, he wrote pieces for Geraldyn Dismond's *Interstate-Tattler*.

34. Harold Jackman to Countee Cullen, January 27, 1930, in CCC.

News of the publication and the suspicion about it traveled quickly. During the next few weeks, more of the literati in Harlem heard about Larsen's "steal." "No one," Jackman confided in February, "who has heard about Nella Larsen's steal has quite gotten over it. . . . Do . . . compare the two. . . . '[D]ear' Nella is still in New York."[35] In writing to an intimate friend, Jackman was frank and unhesitant in his accusation.

Larsen was in town saying very little about the charges, but revealing that "very few people . . . are nice to me." The few who rallied to her support were, as she put it, "grand and worth so much more than all the others." Peterson, whose brother Sidney had helped to spread the suspicion, stood by her friend, as did Van Vechten. He sent her a set of glasses to lift her spirits, and succeeded enough to evoke an outpouring of gratitude: "After all I do believe that some people love me."[36]

Countee Cullen also exhibited support by writing Jackman: "don't be too hasty in your judgment against poor Nell," but his letter irked Jackman:

> Boy, that gal has used some of the identical words Miss Smith uses in her *Mrs. Adis*, and as for the dialogue, little Nell, I'll call her this time, has just changed it to make it colored. The technique and method is identical—description, dialogue, denouement—are incontestably congruent. . . . you see when you get Kaye-Smith's work. Is it known? I'll say it is. All literary Harlem knows about it, and I hear that the *Forum* has gotten wind of it and has written Nella about it. Nella's benefactor, Carl Van Vechten, is trying to justify his protégée but his arguments are so weak and in this case so stupid.[37]

Jackman, who had never been one of Larsen's close friends, refused to exercise either sympathy or doubt, but he was correct in insisting upon the similarities between Kaye-Smith's "Mrs. Adis" and Larsen's work. Kaye-Smith's story had first appeared in *Century* magazine in January of 1922. Set in England, it followed the same pattern of development as "Sanctuary," beginning with a similar attention to description:

> In northeastern Sussex a great tongue of land runs into Kent by Scotney Castle. It is a land of woods, the old hammer-woods of the Sussex

35. Harold Jackman to Countee Cullen, February 10, 1930, *ibid.*
36. Nella Larsen Imes to Carl Van Vechten, Tuesday [postmarked March 5, 1930], in JWJ.
37. Harold Jackman to Countee Cullen, March, 13, 1930, in CCC.

iron industry, and among the woods gleam the hammer-ponds, holding in their mirrors the sunsets and sunrises. Owing to the thickness of the woods, great masses of oak and beech in a dense undergrowth of hazel and chestnut and frail sallow, the road that passes Mrs. Adis's cottage is dark before twilight has crept away from the fields beyond.[38]

In both stories, the opening description of a "cottage" in an isolated setting later leads to a focus on a man moving "stealthily" outside, looking into a window and seeing a lone woman preparing food. Peter Crouch in "Mrs. Adis" enters the cottage without knocking, just as Jim Hammer does in "Sanctuary." From that point on, Peter's encounter with Mrs. Adis is similar to Jim's with Mrs. Poole. He has shot a man and is running from the authorities. Peter, too, wants the woman to hide him for the sake of his friendship with her son Tom, so that he can make good his escape. Mrs. Adis is much like Mrs. Poole in appearance and attitude; she is "a small, frail-looking woman, with a brown hard face on which the skin had dried in innumerable small hair-like wrinkles" (322). She disapproves of Peter: "You have n't been an over-good friend to Tom. . . . Tom always thought better of you than you deserved" (322). She hides Peter in a lean-to behind her kitchen. When the men arrive from Scotney Castle, they bring the "bad news" of Tom's death and of Peter's responsibility for the killing. Like Annie Poole, Mrs. Adis does not disclose the hiding place of her son's killer. Instead, she waits until the men leave, goes to the lean-to, unlocks the door, and returns to the room where her son's body lies. The story ends with a focus on Peter Crouch: "[He] knew what he must do, the only thing she wanted him to do, the only thing he could possibly do: he opened the door and silently went out" (326).

Kaye-Smith's story depends upon class rather than race. Peter had been "snaring rabbits" on the castle grounds when the keeper, several men from Scotney Castle, and Tom Adis approached. Peter had fired his gun into the group to avoid detection for poaching, and had been unaware of the identity of his victim. The men from the castle plan a swift justice once they capture the guilty party: "he shall swing" (324). Peter's danger is comparable to Jim Hammer's in "Sanctuary," and Mrs. Adis is, like Mrs. Poole, linked more closely to her son's killer than she is to those who search for him.

The similarities of the two stories in language, description, setting, at-

---

38. Sheila Kaye-Smith, "Mrs. Adis," *Century*, CIII (January, 1922), 321. Subsequent references cited parenthetically in the text.

mosphere, characterization, action, plot, and theme, all are too exact to be merely parallel story lines. Larsen apparently followed Kaye-Smith's work in both overall pattern and specific detail. Even a cursory reading reveals as much. Had she heard an oral version of "Mrs. Adis" either from an elderly patient at Lincoln Hospital, as she claimed, or from "literary banter at Van Vechten's," as Bruce Nugent believed, the similarities would not have been so exact.[39] Larsen's contemporary supporters, both personal friends and the editors of *Forum,* gave her the benefit of doubt and accepted her explanation of coincidence, an explanation that has also been favored by recent historians of the Harlem Renaissance. David Levering Lewis, for example, concludes: "Larsen herself seemed much too intelligent (though not, perhaps, too principled) to have stolen another's work. It appeared far more likely to have been coincidence . . . or . . . something subconsciously filed away."[40] Such explanations, nevertheless, become less plausible when the two stories are side by side for comparison.

Larsen may well have gambled on no one's recognizing the similarities between her story and the earlier one, especially because of her use of black characters and dialect. Or, she actually may *not* have considered that using the idea and format would constitute plagiarism. During her apprenticeship she had contemplated how certain works treating white characters might be translated into "Negro" material. Her 1926 response to one book in Knopf's Blue Jade Library is suggestive: "Pablo de Segovia is marvelous. A tale of a Negro ruffian told in this naive manner would be interesting. I think somebody, Mencken perhaps, has made this suggestion somewhere."[41] Francisco de Quevedo-Villegas' Spanish text had appeared first in 1596, but Knopf had reprinted *Pablo de Segovia* in translation in 1926. Larsen's enthusiastic comment about the story may carry an implication for "Sanctuary." She may well have believed that there was nothing deceptive about using "Mrs. Adis" as a storyboard for her work about black characters told in the same manner; the decade was, after all, one that accepted black adaptations of works by whites, particularly in the public world of the New York stage. With the charge of plagiarism against her, however, Larsen may well have decided that to reveal her naïveté in using Kaye-Smith's work would be more damaging than to conceal any knowledge of the story.

Her explanation to the editors of *Forum* depended on the acceptance of

39. Nugent quoted in David Levering Lewis, *When Harlem Was in Vogue* (New York, 1981), 250.

40. *Ibid.*

41. Nella Imes to Carl Van Vechten, November 12, 1926, in JWJ.

coincidence. Larsen had to respond to the "striking resemblance" noticed by a reader, Marion Boyd of Oxford, Ohio, who informed *Forum* that with the exception of dialect and setting "the stories are identical. The structure, situation, characters, and plot are the same. One finds in Miss Larsen's story the same words and expressions used by Sheila Kaye-Smith." Larsen prefaced her explanation with a direct statement: "I haven't as yet seen the *Century* story, but it seems to me that anyone who intended to lift a story would have avoided doing it as obviously as this appears to have been done—judging from the excerpts which you have sent me." In explaining how she had come by the material, she revealed that an elderly woman inmate of the Lincoln Hospital and Home, a Mrs. Christopher, had told her a factual account of the death of her husband at the hands of "a young Negro" who had "come to her for hiding without knowing whom he had killed." Mrs. Christopher shielded the killer even after the officers of the law arrived to notify her of her husband's death, because "she intended to deal with him herself afterwards without any interference from 'white folks.'" According to Larsen, Mrs. Christopher told the story because she was distressed that Lincoln's "Negro nurses often had to tell things about each other to the white people," as all the doctors, executives, and the superintendent of nurses at the institution were white, but all the nurses black. Mrs. Christopher's "oft-repeated convictions were that if the Negro race would only stick together, we might get somewhere some day, and that what the white folks didn't know about us wouldn't hurt us."[42]

Larsen claimed that she "believed the story absolutely," but that "lately, in talking it over with Negroes, I find that the tale is so old and so well known that it is almost folklore." She went on to provide more details on the tale: "It has many variations: sometimes it is the woman's brother, husband, son, lover, preacher, beloved master, or even her father, mother, sister, or daughter who is killed. A Negro sociologist tells me that there are literally hundreds of these stories. Anyone could have written it up at any time." In her own version of the tale, she had initially planned "to use Harlem with its particular tempo and atmosphere as a setting, as well as the Harlemese language." She decided against the urban setting ultimately because "that little old Negro countrywoman was so vivid before me that I wanted to get her down just as I remembered her." Larsen concluded her explanation in a curious way: "Had I any idea that there was already a story with a similar

---

42. Marion Boyd, Letter in "Our Rostrum," *Forum*, Supplement 4, LXXXIII (April, 1930), xli; Nella Larsen, "The Author's Explanation," *ibid.*, xli, xlii.

plot in existence, I don't think I would have made use of the material at all; or, if I had, I should certainly have taken the city for the background and would have told the story exactly as it was told to me, or much more differently than I have done."[43] Finally, she suggests that she might well have used the material—only differently. The statement may be a veiled revelation that she had been so naïve as to use Kaye-Smith's material, only "differently"— but not differently enough.

Forum's editors supported Larsen by adding that she had sent the magazine four rough drafts of the story along with her letter of explanation. The drafts showed "just how she worked it out from the plot stage to its final form. . . . A careful examination of this material has convinced us that the story, 'Sanctuary,' was written by Nella Larsen in the manner she describes. The coincidence is, indeed, extraordinary, but there are many well-authenticated cases of similar coincidences in history."[44] They cited as examples the cases of Edison and an Englishman simultaneously inventing the incandescent lamp and of Darwin and A. R. Wallace independently formulating the theory of natural selection at the same time. Their support helped to clear the air, but it could not completely restore Larsen's credibility. Her Guggenheim fellowship for researching and writing a new novel took on added significance, for it meant a further opportunity to repair her reputation as a writer.

Elmer Imes's full-time position at Fisk for the 1930–1931 academic year coincided with the start of his wife's grant. His salary as professor and head of the Department of Physics was $4,500 for the first year, with an increase of $500 for the second.[45] In leaving New York, he joined several prominent New York residents in relocating to Nashville; Charles S. Johnson had departed the Urban League and *Opportunity* magazine in 1928 for the Sociology Department, and James Weldon Johnson, after fifteen years as secretary of the NAACP, would accept a Fisk chair in creative writing in 1931.

Imes had spent much of the fall of 1929 in Nashville, but in February, 1930, he prepared for an extended stay to plan the physics facilities in the new science complex. He was not accompanied by his wife, but shortly after his arrival, he sent Van Vechten a note: "Conditions here have warranted my coming and I am busy hurling monkey wrenches. Incidentally I need the money. . . . Please cheer Nella up if occasionally she seems to be a little blue

43. Larsen, "The Author's Explanation," *ibid.*, xlii.
44. Editor's Note, *Forum*, Supplement 4, LXXXIII (April, 1930), xli.
45. Jones to Imes, May 4, 1929, in Jones Papers.

about my leaving."[46] In telling Van Vechten about his departure, Imes tried to signal a reason for his wife's depression. While he knew that Van Vechten would recognize Larsen's need for companionship in the city, he might also have understood that Van Vechten could already have been aware of his motive for not including her in his plans: Elmer Imes was having an affair. Larsen would not visit her husband in Nashville until May. The separation during the winter deepened their estrangement and intensified her anxiety.

The winter was especially difficult for Larsen because of the plagiarism accusation. Although she had the buffer of planning a fall departure for her research in Europe, she went through the ordeal of explaining to the editors of *Forum* and formulating a published response alone. Her spirits were so low that she confided in Van Vechten, "sometimes I feel entirely alone," yet at the same time, the opening of the play *The Green Pastures*, in which her friend Dorothy Peterson had a role, caused a drastic mood swing: "This poor coloured child has done very little work during the past week. But then 'Green Pastures,' only happens once (or twice perhaps) in a life time. I have felt like dancing in the streets." She added, perhaps as much to lift her own spirits as for Van Vechten's benefit, "Don't you think we ought to have a play out of 'Nigger Heaven'?"[47]

On opening night, Wednesday, February 26, 1930, Peterson, who appeared, under the name Dorothy Randolph, as Cain's Girl, threw a party for the all-black cast of *The Green Pastures* and for her friends. Larsen, of course, attended both the opening at the Mansfield Theater on West 47th Street and the party, but her reception by some was not what she would have wanted, though in her enthusiasm for the play, she may not have noticed. "I went down to Dorothy's place," Jackman reported to Cullen, who was still in France, "and you should have heard painful Nella Imes tell about a cocktail party on Park Avenue, and a luncheon date here; she thinks she is so much hell—I could have strangled her that night." But on March 16, when Jackman and Larsen were Peterson's guests at an exclusive party at the nightclub Small's for the *Green Pastures* company, they were too absorbed in the merrymaking, and the renovations bringing the club up to the standards of the Cotton Club and Connie's Inn, to talk about Park Avenue or its white residents, though "Sanctuary" shadowed their interaction. Two

46. Elmer Imes to Carl Van Vechten, February 11, 1930, in JWJ.

47. Nella Larsen Imes to Carl Van Vechten, Tuesday [postmarked March 5, 1930], *ibid.* Marc Connelly's *Green Pastures* was an adaptation of Bradford's *Ol' Man Adam an' His Chillun*, a series of sketches about southern blacks and their religion.

nights after the opening, Larsen was indeed off to a dinner party on Park Avenue. She, Nora Holt, Hal Bynner, and Lewis Cole had been invited to Van Vechten's apartment for an evening of basking in the success of *The Green Pastures*.[48]

Larsen's high spirits continued through March. The Baltimore *Afro-American* carried a reprint of the New York papers' announcement of her Guggenheim grant. Accompanied by a James Allen photograph of Larsen, the brief notice gave the dollar amount of her award, $2,000, and mentioned that *Passing* "was one of the sensational books last year."[49] But favorable publicity in the African-American press was not enough to allay her mounting self-doubt.

Immediately after the "Author's Explanation," clarifying the origins of her story, appeared in the April issue of *Forum*, Larsen prepared for a trip to Nashville, but without enthusiasm. On the eve of her May 12 departure, she tinged her farewells with protective sarcasm: "Tomorrow I am leaving for Nashville, a dutiful wife going down to visit her husband. It will only be for about two weeks or so." Still in Tennessee at the end of May, she no longer disguised her marital troubles: "I will probably be starting home some day in the later part of next week. Elmer wanted me to come down and I rather thought it was the diplomatic thing to do. Now that I've been nice and everything I think that's all that can be expected."[50] The estrangement was not to be repaired by Larsen's halfhearted assumption of the role of a "summer wife," the name given to the wives of Fisk professors who worked elsewhere during the academic year but spent the summer on campus with their "nine-month bachelor" husbands.

The trip to Nashville was a major event for reasons other than those connected with wifely duties. Larsen had, during her marriage, rarely acknowledged the brief period that she had spent in the Fisk Normal Department. Her visit in May of 1930 was the first return she had made to Nashville and Fisk since her departure nearly twenty-two years earlier. Much had changed in her life and her fortune; she had established a very different identity for herself. Fisk was a reminder of the person she had once been. She chose to ignore any prior connection with the institution and couched

48. Harold Jackman to Countee Cullen, February 28, 1930, in CCC; Carl Van Vechten to Fania Marinoff, February 28, 1930, in *The Letters of Carl Van Vechten,* ed. Bruce Kellner (New York, 1987), 112.

49. Baltimore *Afro-American,* March 29, 1930, in SCF.

50. Nella Larsen Imes to Carl Van Vechten, May 11, 1930, in JWJ; Nella Larsen Imes to Carl Van Vechten, May 22, 1930, *ibid.*

all of her reactions to the campus in terms that would imply a first-time visitor. For instance, she wrote to Fania Marinoff and Van Vechten: "Carl would adore the Negro streets. They look like stage settings. And the Negroes themselves! I've never seen anything quite so true to what's expected. Mostly black and good natured and apparently quite shiftless, frightfully clean and decked out in the most appalling colours; but some how just right. Terribly poor. The poor whites are also exactly as expected but not so amusing. Rather, tragic and depressing."[51]

Although one critic, William Bedford Clark, has emphasized Larsen's objectivity in this particular description of poor blacks and has concluded that "it would be easy enough to accuse Larsen of a certain smugness here, but a close reading . . . indicates that poor blacks, however economically deprived, somehow possess a vitality and strength lacking in their white counterparts," he misses the dishonesty in Larsen's observations, because he erroneously assumes that she is rendering her impression of seeing African Americans in Nashville for the very first time. Others have made the same mistake: S. P. Fullinwinder, for example, states that Larsen's "real understanding of her race was small. She seems to have seen her first southern Negro on a visit to Nashville in 1930."[52] The truth is that Larsen was no stranger to the appearance of the streets or of the black residents. While she may have wanted to impress Marinoff and Van Vechten with her reportage and her implicit sophistication in contrast to her southern surroundings, she delivered her remarks about the black masses as though she herself were not black, which may be labeled objectivity, but which more accurately appears to be distance and disassociation.

Her general responses were not negative: "It is really quite delightful here. Beautiful country and handsome men. I am staying in a fascinating old house with lovely old furniture and delicate faded chintzes and lots of books." The grace and comfort of the Fiskites satisfied her appetite for class position and culture. Nevertheless, the distance she assumed toward Fisk, Nashville, and the South functioned to ensure her alienation from the place and the people. In separating herself from any vestiges of familiarity, she cut off much of the potential for accepting and being accepted by the close-knit Fisk community: "Fisk is very delightful with a rather interesting faculty.

---

51. Larsen Imes to Van Vechten, May 22, 1930, *ibid.*

52. William Bedford Clark, "The Letters of Nella Larsen to Carl Van Vechten: A Survey," *Resources for American Literary Study*, VIII (Fall, 1978), 196; S. P. Fullinwinder, *The Mind and Mood of Black America: Twentieth-Century Thought* (Homewood, Ill., 1969), 151.

Mixed. The nicest ones are two handsome Southerners and an Austrian and a rather remarkable Negro chemist [St. Elmo Brady, editor of the *Fisk Herald* when Larsen was at the Normal School]. Grounds and buildings are quite lovely." [53] There is evidence of measured appreciation for what she saw at Fisk. Her decision, however, to act as a condescending outsider removed any future possibility of belonging or of making a home on the campus. This error in judgment would prove to be costly.

Her casual observations about poor blacks reiterate her conception of money and wealth as a major factor determining the value of individuals of any race. There is an element in her response both to poor people and to expensive things that is reminiscent of Daisy Buchanan in F. Scott Fitzgerald's *Great Gatsby* (1925), who cried at the sight of Jay Gatsby's beautiful shirts but who could run over a human being with a car and show no remorse at all. Larsen, much like Daisy, views poverty as drastically reducing a person's worth. The highly visible poverty of an entire group, especially the mass of blacks in the streets of Nashville or Harlem, made the group offensive, particularly to the part of Larsen's self that loved and desired, as she said, "things—beautiful and rich things." [54] She reserved her sensitivity for such "things" rather than for people.

Larsen's social life diminished after her return to New York that summer. Some of her friends were away; some were busy working, and others she avoided. A few, like Jackman, used the "Sanctuary" affair to avoid her. Jackman considered it her comeuppance: "Poor Nell is right; it is poor, pas Nell." As he put it, "It is known all over Harlem that Nella Larsen stole Sheila Kaye-Smith's story, and now that Nella has been awarded a Guggenheim fellowship, everyone is quite sorry, especially when such people like Langston Hughes and Bud Fisher are on the horizon and are more deserving of the award." [55] While thinly veiling the gender competitiveness that underlay much of the Harlem Renaissance, Jackman voiced what he believed to be the popular estimate of Larsen's talent, to which the "Sanctuary" incident gave credence.

One of Larsen's typical complaints that summer was "I can't seem to learn a word about Nora Ray." Nora Holt Ray, a singer with a *joie de vivre* and a devil-may-care attitude about her reputation or scandal, was one of

53. Larsen Imes to Van Vechten, May 22, 1930, in JWJ.

54. Mary Rennels, New York *Telegram*, April 13, 1929, in SCF.

55. Jackman to Cullen, March 13, 1930, in CCC; Harold Jackman to Countee Cullen, March 17, 1930, *ibid.*

Larsen's social acquaintances from Van Vechten's circle, but not someone she had usually sought out. With few options for social outlets, Larsen was desperate. Not until late in the summer did she hear from Nora Ray, but an anticipated reunion ended in disappointment, according to Larsen: "I asked her to lunch, but she never arrived. That is, she hadn't after I'd waited in the McAlpine lobby for an hour and a few minutes."[56] She even tried to get Jackman to determine Ray's whereabouts, mainly because she was searching for friends who might amuse her with their doings and stories while ignoring her predicament.

June and July were, she said, difficult months of "nothing. no new plays, no parties. no amusing people," relieved only by her readings, especially Gilmore Millen's *Sweet Man* (1930), which she considered "one of the most extraordinary books" she had read and so "fascinating" that she went "about doing a lot of publicity for it."[57] The protagonist of *Sweet Man*, a light-skinned southern black named John Henry, goes from being a proud sharecropper to being the kept man of a Memphis prostitute. Although he learns to hate whites for their treatment of blacks, John Henry becomes the lover of a white woman whom he eventually decides to leave in order to return to a simpler life in the country with the wife he had abandoned along with the farm. Before he can act on his decision, his white lover dies accidentally. Realizing he will be accused of murdering her, John Henry kills himself. Larsen was struck by the comparison between rural and urban life and by the force of the naturalistic view of characters in Millen's novel, perhaps because she had taken to admitting to being a fatalist, as she told Mary Rennels in an April 13, 1929, interview for the New York *Telegram*: "I don't have any way of approaching life. . . . [I]t does things to me instead."[58] Millen's plot incorporated the theme of shedding one life for another that Larsen herself wrote into all of her fiction. Moreover, the textual treatment of the black male–white female plot, the same plot that was threatening her marriage, asserted in no uncertain terms the destructiveness of any such liaisons.

Several other books offered some distraction. James Weldon Johnson's *Black Manhattan* (1930) she enjoyed but found one fault: "he failed to

---

56. Nella Larsen Imes to Carl Van Vechten, Monday 25th [postmarked August 26, 1930], in CVV; Nella Larsen Imes to Carl Van Vechten, n.d. [September, 1930], in JWJ.

57. Nella Larsen Imes to Carl Van Vechten, July 21, 1930, and July 15, 1930 [postcard], in JWJ; see also Nella Larsen Imes to Carl Van Vechten, June 10, 1930, *ibid.*

58. Nella Larsen quoted by Rennels, New York *Telegram*, April 13, 1929, in SCF.

include Nigger Heaven as one of the big influences on Harlem and its artistic life during the last five years." In writing her congratulations to Johnson, she delivered her appreciation for the work in greater detail:

> I am one of the ninety-nine and nine tenths percent to whom information of any kind must be painlessly administered. But I went straight through Black Manhattan one afternoon without one weary second. I especially like the chapters which deal with Florence Mills and the Negro Church and Dr. Du Bois. And the Garvey chapter—oh, most especially the Garvey chapter. And—but I like them all. And the last [on Harlem as still in the making]!
> You have done a good job, written a big book. For the form too is very delightful. Its unusual restraint, no whining, and no bragging give it great dignity and grace. To me it has a rare quality—of breadth, and yet fineness—that reminds me of Walter Pater in his less tired moments. The Renaissance essays. And curiously enough this holds for the matter as well as the method.[59]

Despite her own troubles, Larsen still had an infinite appreciation for Harlem as a cultural phenomenon, in which she was a participant, as Johnson mentioned in his next-to-last chapter. His book appealed to her, as well as to other insiders in Harlem's artistic community, because he had not tried to write a strict history; as he said in the preface: "I have attempted only to etch in the background of the Negro in latter-day New York, to give a cutback in projecting a picture of Negro Harlem; I have avoided statistical data and included only as much documentation as seemed to me necessary for my main purpose."[60]

Johnson's emphasis on the Harlem Renaissance, which Larsen knew best, and his optimistic prognosis for the future, in which she believed most, made Black Manhattan an antidote for her failing spirits. With Van Vechten vacationing in Paris and Dorothy Peterson performing in The Green Pastures, Larsen missed the reassurances of her two strongest supporters. The fiction that had come rather easily before was now painstakingly slow. Her fluctuating fortune and spirits, along with the summer's heat, interfered

59. Nella Larsen Imes to Carl Van Vechten, Sunday, 13th [postmarked July 15, 1930], in CVV; Nella Imes to James Weldon Johnson, Tuesday, July 22nd [1930], in JWJ.
60. James Weldon Johnson, Black Manhattan (New York, 1930), xvii.

with work, despite her determination to complete her third novel before leaving for Europe. "It's hot as hell in town," she observed in July, "99 degrees in the shade. . . . I can't go anywhere because I haven't finished that damned book."[61]

Elmer Imes returned from Fisk for a short time in July before leaving for his research in Ann Arbor; however, he had his own circle of friends, and so he did little to change Larsen's situation. In fact, she observed on July 21, "Elmer is out to Mr. Cravath's place on Long Island. I wasn't invited."[62] Elmer was spending more time in the circle of Fiskites who gathered at the home of Paul Cravath, chair of the Fisk University Board of Trustees. While his engagements with Cravath involved the business of developing a physics department, they were social as well, especially during this period when Imes was seeing a woman who also was a frequent guest.

At the end of July, Larsen was invited with Imes to spend a few days in Bordentown, New Jersey, with a party organized by Sidney Peterson, who wanted not only company from the city, but also a copy of Van Vechten's latest novel, *Parties* (1930), which portrayed the social decadence of the 1920s and was a farewell to that era and its excesses. Larsen sent Van Vechten clippings about the novel, but she did not write him what had become customary, a long praise song for his work. Instead, she deferred to Harry Hansen's review, which she said "was so exactly almost what my own comment was and is." Dorothy Peterson, on the other hand, wrote immediately to Van Vechten after the weekend of reading *Parties* at Bordentown: "I am crazed about Parties!! Bruce [Nugent] came down and lived with me so he could read it—because I wouldn't let it go out of the house. . . . Bruce swears that he was in a state of continued intoxication all the time he was reading Parties, due to nothing but Parties of course. We're all waiting breathlessly for the reviews."[63] The publication of *Parties* and the brief excursion with the Petersons were not enough to change either Larsen's estimation that "it was a rotten summer—from my point of view," or her estrangement from her husband.[64]

What had occurred between Imes and Larsen would not emerge from her accounts of the summer, yet in July she rescheduled her anticipated October

61. Larsen Imes to Van Vechten, July 21, 1930, in JWJ.
62. *Ibid.*
63. Dorothy Peterson to Carl Van Vechten, August 1, 1930, in CVV; Larsen Imes to Van Vechten, Monday 25th [postmarked August 26, 1930], *ibid.;* Dorothy Peterson to Carl Van Vechten, August 13th [1930], *ibid.*
64. Larsen Imes to Van Vechten, Monday 25th [postmarked August 26, 1930], *ibid.*

departure for Spain and attempted to leave on August 9 on the *Rocham-beau*.[65] Because her Guggenheim fellowship commenced on the first of September, the foundation would not allow an August departure; as a result, she booked passage on the first available ship after the first, the *Patria,* which sailed on September 19.[66] After making the travel arrangements, she promptly became ill, and was just recovering by the sixteenth of August. Although she was reticent about the traumatic events that precipitated her early departure, she discussed them privately with Van Vechten and Peterson. Later in the fall, she would send her thanks to Van Vechten from Lisbon for, as she put it, "letting me cry on you the day I left. I mean to take your advice and do and say nothing about it. In fact I hadn't—expect for Dorothy. And she understands that its [*sic*] all rather indefinite and somewhat precarious."[67]

While Larsen's statement is discreet, Elmer Imes's explanation, written the day before his wife sailed, is explicit. "Nella has so wanted to see you," he confided in Van Vechten, who had just returned from France. "If she does see you and ask your advice about a very delicate matter . . . I wish you to read the enclosed note before you decide what to say to her. I do not believe that this is taking any unfair advantage, and I do wish you to hear her first. The question is with regard to our future. . . . I think that her and my interests are the same in the matter and am only taking this method so that you may know certain phases which she may omit in talking to you."[68]

He sent an accompanying letter, sealed in an envelope labeled "Please destroy if not necessary to use." Yet, he must have suspected that the curious Van Vechten would read its contents, which explained Imes's problem: "Early in the year and quite by accident Nella became possessed of information which pointed decidedly to the fact that I was at the time very much interested in another girl. Like the sweet little sport she is she decided to keep along and not say anything about it, feeling that no matter what happened nothing could change our relationship. Of course, this created a situation beyond even her ability to carry off." Imes made no statement that would suggest his intention to end his extramarital affair; instead, without trepidation, he clarified his position. "It is not necessary for her [Nella] to

65. Nella Larsen Imes, Passport application, July 25, 1930, in State Department Records. See also Larsen Imes to Van Vechten, July 21, 1930, in JWJ.

66. Larsen Imes to Van Vechten, Monday 25th [postmarked August 26, 1930], in CVV. See also Nella Larsen Imes to Henry Allen Moe, August 16, 1930, in Guggenheim Foundation files.

67. Nella Larsen Imes to Carl Van Vechten, Wednesday 1st [October, 1930], in JWJ.

68. Elmer Imes to Carl Van Vechten, n.d. [postmarked September 18, 1930], *ibid.*

feel that there is any question of her 'going it alone' or of being under ne-cessity [*sic*] of taking steps of any sort to guarantee support," he concluded, because "I want to do all for her that I can and be everything to her that she will let me be. I am not denying that I am very much in love with the other girl—very much indeed, but she does not expect or wish me to forget to love Nella. A quite unresolved situation—but possible if we can be clear headed." [69] Larsen had not only considered her options outside of marriage but had threatened legal action to guarantee financial support in the event of a divorce. Both she and Imes knew that his affair with a white female would cast Larsen in the role of racial victim and Imes in the role of social transgressor.

Imes's attempt to evoke understanding, if not sympathy, emphasized rea-son and caution. He tried to diffuse any impulsiveness on his wife's part that might lead to a public disclosure of his affair. His primary concern was not his wife but his job: "If I am to work out these things I must do so for myself. There can be not [*sic*] publicity—my job would be gone in ten min-utes and I wouldn't be able to do anything for anybody—I have asked that Nella not do anything or make any hard and fast decisions until I see her next summer." [70] In seeking Van Vechten's confidence, Imes sought assist-ance in controlling his wife so that she would neither embarrass him nor affect his position at Fisk. He regarded Van Vechten as a trusted ally who would not only understand but also accept the male's version of the triangle. He did not, however, reveal to Van Vechten the racial identity of the woman. Imes's need to control Larsen is clear from his convoluted reasoning and his unrepentant attitude. "He *liked* white women," several of his friends stated, using identical words and tone to explain Imes's behavior. [71]

Imes's rendition of the affair suggests not that Larsen was "a sweet little sport" but that she was a disturbed woman who tried initially to avoid an unpleasant situation by her silence and the pretense of not knowing. How she survived the hurt or managed to act with any degree of normalcy while keeping silent seemed immaterial to Imes. Had the threat of disruption of their marriage occurred before her self-actualization as a writer, Larsen might have perceived it as "not just the loss of a relationship but as some-

---

69. Undated letter, enclosed with Imes to Van Vechten, n.d. [postmarked September 18, 1930], in JWJ.

70. *Ibid.*

71. Axel Hansen, interview with author, March 8, 1987; Pearl Creswell, interview with author, March 10, 1987; Edith Work interview; Mrs. Minerva Johnson Hawkins, interview with author, March 11, 1987.

thing closer to a total loss of self."[72] Instead, she suffered anxiety and depression, but she did not lose the self she had engendered. After at least six months of ignoring an unchanging reality, she decided at the end of August to "talk it over," as Imes revealed, but when conversation did not result in the termination of the extramarital relationship, she determined to "eliminate herself—that it is the best all around," by leaving immediately for Spain. Imes believed that during the months of deception, of knowing and not letting on that she knew, Larsen had "made herself thoroughly miserable," yet he ignored his part in her misery and shouldered no blame. By insisting that both she and her husband face the truth, Larsen braved the dissolution of the marriage, even though Imes offered the weak reassurance "that no matter what new things may come into my life, Nella has her own place."[73] Imes, however, would not assure her of the same kind of marriage that they had once shared, and she, at least temporarily, rejected anything less. Whereas she was pained and surprised by the events, he was bewildered and conciliatory. The reconciliation he proposed was not, however, one that she would accept.

Imes insinuated that she would seek a divorce but that the final decision would be put off until after her sojourn in Spain. What he did not seem to comprehend was the extraordinary psychological burden Larsen assumed just as she was preparing to explore the theme of "difference in intellectual and physical freedom for the Negro—and the effect on him—between Europe" and the United States, the theme which she had proposed for her Guggenheim project. Throughout her "research" in Europe, she would be restricted by the limbo state of her marriage and by the knowledge that divorce among her class of African-American peers was unthinkable. Ironically, by electing to postpone the major decision about her marriage, Larsen accepted Imes's marriage of convenience. This capitulation solved her own anxieties about appearance and status but ultimately exacted a toll from both her marriage and her career.

The year following the publication of *Passing* had been climactic for the swiftness of the reversals in Larsen's fortunes. As a writer and as a wife, she experienced unexpected oscillation. Plagiarism and gossip undermined her writing while infidelity and insensitivity weakened her marriage. She began to lose the control that she had exercised over herself, her identity, and her

72. Jean Baker Miller, *Toward a New Psychology of Women* (Boston, 1976), 83.

73. Undated letter enclosed with Imes to Van Vechten, n.d. [postmarked September 18, 1930], in JWJ.

IV

A WOMAN'S HARVEST,
1930 – 1964

12

Struggling Against Drought,
1930–1932

When the *Patria* cleared New York harbor on September 19, 1930, Nella Larsen welcomed leaving the city skyline along with her unfaithful husband and gossiping associates. The months since the appearance of "Sanctuary," and with it the public charges of plagiarism, had been difficult enough, but the more recent weeks with the private discussions of infidelity had been genuinely traumatic. She sought escape in Europe, and she hoped others might see her fellowship year more as a triumph. She realized that her carefully composed life was beginning to disintegrate, and she wondered whether she was somehow responsible. She was, in a sense, moving toward an awareness about her female self that Jean Wyatt has articulated: "Because each of us is simultaneously a subject constructed by social discourse and the locus of an 'other scene' where different desires play and different cognitive possibilities arise, there is in everyone a source of contradictory energy capable of challenging social formations—including the social formation of one's own conscious self." [1]

Larsen's confrontation with the change in her marriage, or her perception of it, brought her to a hard assessment of her work as a writer. Once in Spain, she resolved "to work like a nigger," because "thinking it over, I've come to the conclusion that I've never expended any real honest-to-goodness labour on anything in my life (except floors and woodwork)." Her

1. Jean Wyatt, *Reconstructing Desire: The Role of the Unconscious in Women's Reading and Writing* (Chapel Hill, 1990), 2.

admission may not be "quite fair" to herself, as she readily pointed out, but it was an important recognition of the fact that as a wife, she had spent, and took pride in spending, a great deal of her time doing housework. The results were tangible, but not lasting. Even in applying for the Guggenheim, she had listed her present occupation as: "Hack writing. *Housework. Sewing.*" And prior to the application, she had informed a reporter for the *Amsterdam News* that her "hobbies" were "doing her own housework . . . sewing and playing bridge."[2] Larsen wanted to actualize a part of her own self as visible and praiseworthy in household chores, yet despite her laudable efforts, she discovered that she was vulnerable to rejection and the house subject to dismantling. Her resolve to put her energy into writing was a denial neither of the significance of domestic chores (and performing them well) nor of the labor in her previous fiction, but it was a resolution to face more honestly the reality of her own motivations and expectations.

Her resolution reflected her shift away from the love-marriage-domesticity plot available to women, and her understanding that, as Carolyn Heilbrun has observed, "there will be narratives of female lives only when women no longer live their lives isolated in the houses and the stories of men."[3] Rather than seeing a reflection of herself in a beautifully appointed and maintained living space, Larsen turned forcefully to expending her creative energy on a more lasting representation of her female self. At the apogee of her life as a writer, she understood her writing to be her best form of control over her identity and understood the depth of her commitment to literary work.

Unfortunately, the years of Larsen's greatest resolve to write coincided with the most stressful years of her marriage. There was an apparent causal sequence. She set out in 1930 to achieve fame and the resulting status in her own right just as her marriage deteriorated irreparably. Her time abroad, from September, 1930, to January, 1932, offered respite from her marriage and an affirmation of her writerly self. It was not a "try at rejecting her Blackness," as one critic has claimed, though in Europe she did seek a particular kind of freedom from a specified racial constraint.[4] On an elementary

2. Nella Larsen Imes to Carl Van Vechten, Wednesday 1st [October, 1930], in JWJ; Nella Larsen Imes, Fellowship application form, John Simon Guggenheim Memorial Foundation, November, 1929, in John Simon Guggenheim Memorial Foundation files, New York; Thelma E. Berlack, "New Author Unearthed Right Here in Harlem," New York *Amsterdam News*, May 23, 1928, p. 16.

3. Carolyn Heilbrun, *Writing a Woman's Life* (New York, 1988), 47.

4. Quotation from Hoyt Fuller, Introduction to *Passing*, by Nella Larsen (New York, 1971), 12.

level perhaps, she sought to redefine herself, as she once had with her assertion of "mulatto" status in a race-conscious society, but in Europe she would make herself on the basis of her own effort.

Europe, with all of its attendant meanings for Americans concerned with "culture," was to foster the transformation of the housewife-turned-novelist into the novelist with fame. It was also to mark the survival and transcendency of the rejected wife. Yet environments alone, as Larsen well understood in her fiction, cannot sustain such weighty expectations. What she established was a different set of constraints—partly attitudinal, partly emotional—within the context of different spaces, Spain and France. Predicated upon her individual preferences, standards, and tastes, she found that changes in external environment, and in the ground from which one relates to it, do not predetermine personal contentment or satisfaction, but they do provide a different plane for an accumulation of new experiences that might lead to contentment.

Given the contexts of her sojourn, Larsen's motives regarding her work were somewhat transparent, though admittedly complex, so that even under the most conducive circumstances in Spain and France she was still bound by an internal pressure to achieve. Because achievement by her own standards meant public or external acknowledgment attending the production of work, its pursuit in a new setting intensified a split between her work as a creative process and her work as a product, a split that revealed her European setting as an extension and continuation of the one she had experienced in New York.

Larsen's characteristic behavior and responses duplicated themselves in Europe. She worked in Spain, privately on her novel and publicly on her social standing. Essentially, she became dependent upon what she termed a "gay" social life with "amusing" people for measuring herself, and upon money for expanding the parameters of her world. She took the kind of perspective that Virginia Woolf espoused, "Intellectual freedom depends upon material things," to an unexpected level of literal meaning and interpretation.[5]

From the beginning of her confrontation with Imes about his affair, Nella Larsen threatened to force him to support her financially, though according to Imes, "there was never any question of deserting her or of shirking any responsibility towards her."[6] Larsen believed otherwise, and asserted her claim for money to support her writing career and her style of living. She

5. Virginia Woolf, *A Room of One's Own* (New York, 1957), 354.
6. Elmer Imes to Carl Van Vechten, n.d. [postmarked September 18, 1930], in JWJ.

recognized Imes's need for the respectability of a conventional marriage to deflect attention in the South away from his affair with a white woman, and she exploited the situation to her advantage. Larsen's fixation upon money in her relationship with her husband may have been a way of reinforcing the ties between them, despite the fact that she did not record her desire to hold on to him. Money was her preoccupation in her references to Imes while she was in Europe.

Whereas Imes claimed: "I am rather holding my breath and also my pocketbook for Nella's needs. She has seemed to need a great deal so far [in her first two months in Spain]," Larsen observed: "I heard from Elmer the other day for the 1st time in 4 mo. And only then to berate me for having spent as much money as I have." At the same time that he announced watching his money for his wife's needs, Imes made a request of Van Vechten regarding his friend: "Our director of publicity and a very good friend, Ethel Gilbert, will be in New York at the Woodstock for a few days after the 10th [December, 1930]. I wish very much you could know her. She has more enthusiasm to the square inch than any one I know and fits her work better."[7] His own enthusiasm for Gilbert had increased considerably in his wife's absence, and he sought tentative approval of her from his friends. He ignored the possibility that his wife might have informed their mutual friends that the obvious strain in their marriage was caused by his affair with Gilbert.

Ethel Bedient Gilbert had gone to Fisk in 1928 as director of publicity and finance. Her duties included coordinating the fund-raising tours of the Fisk Jubilee Singers, who almost from the inception of the college provided one of the institution's major sources of money. A Quaker and a friend of the Cravath family long associated with Fisk, Gilbert had formerly lived in Chambersburg, Pennsylvania, where she began service as president of the Girls' Club in 1923. Before marrying a newspaper editor and moving to Pennsylvania, she had been connected with the National Child Labor Committee and later with the Harmon Foundation as director. "I used to go each year to speak at the YWCA for colored girls in Harlem, at the request of Mrs. Cecilia Saunders," Gilbert reminded Walter White in the fall of 1926 when she contacted him at the NAACP about her positive effort in converting racial views in Chambersburg, which she called "a conservative town

7. Elmer Imes to Carl Van Vechten, December 3, 1930, *ibid.*; Nella Larsen Imes to Carl Van Vechten, Thursday, June fourth, 1931, *ibid.*; E. Imes to Van Vechten, December 3, 1930, *ibid.*

near the Mason and Dixon lines." She had invited "a colored friend . . . well-educated, beautiful, charming" to teach handcrafts at the club, and managed to have her hired by emphasizing her ability rather than her color. Gilbert believed that the woman's hiring and teaching "the course so successfully, as to be asked to return for a second year," showed how racial attitudes might be changed if "we didn't continually make issues of things—just *live* without Prejudice."[8]

White's *Fire in the Flint* was the impetus for Gilbert's letter. After reading about the novel in her husband's newspaper, she wanted to encourage White with the positive signs of her recent experience and to let him know that some whites were without racial prejudice: "I've had some bitter experiences being a 'nigger-lover.' I lived in the South three years. I was brought to womanhood—miraculously—without a grain of prejudice against any class or nation or race."[9] During the next year, Gilbert corresponded several times with White about her race efforts. Following her divorce, she had returned to New York and arranged the job at Fisk through her friendship with Paul Cravath, who served as trustee. Her liberal racial attitudes endeared her to the Fisk community, especially students, who often benefited from her personal generosity, and her views on race may well have attracted Imes to her and she to him.

Nella Larsen knew of the woman's place in her husband's life and of the time the two spent together: "Before I started [the trip to Europe] he promised to come over when school closed. Now, I do not know. It seems doubtful. I have a suspicion that he will do as he did most of last summer—that is—spend his vacation with Mrs. Gilbert. I don't care about that. But I do object to being left short of money."[10] Imes did indeed manage a trip to Europe during the summer of 1930, a trip he subsequently regretted because it solved nothing and instead kept him from his work and from his relationship with Gilbert.[11] For her part, Larsen consistently underplayed any concern about his private affairs, all the while expressing her strong concern about money, which objectified but did not embody the conflict with Imes and created a neutral ground for possibly resolving the conflict. Her objection to being left without sufficient resources was especially relevant to her situation in Europe.

8. Ethel Bedient Gilbert to Walter White, October 18, 1926, in WW, NAACP.
9. *Ibid.*
10. Larsen Imes to Van Vechten, Thursday, June fourth, 1931, in JWJ.
11. See Elmer Imes to Carl Van Vechten, June 21, 1931, *ibid.*

The life that she assumed in Spain and France was one requiring money or resourceful management. Lacking any substantial cash reserve, she was extremely resourceful, moving from costly hotels to inexpensive ones to houses or flats, accepting invitations for extended visits with acquaintances or others for whom she had secured letters of introduction before her departure from the States. Because she chose to live among people to whom money, as well as time, she remarked, "means nothing," for they presume it, her finances were taxed, but her notions of what her husband should provide remained exaggerated. She often observed concerning costly excursions: "I think I shall go, if my finances hold out! Or if I can prevail upon my husband to supplement them." Her repeated requests for silk stockings resulted in his sending her "a whole trunk" of them, according to his secretary at that time.[12]

Quite straightforwardly, Larsen had planned an itinerary that would allow her to enjoy Spain and France as social enclaves. "I am sailing . . . for Lisbon, from there across Spain to Mallorca, where I mean to stay until I get my work done, and then go to France (Paris) by way of Marsailles [sic] and Toulen [sic]." Her excursions would take her to Monte Carlo, where she won "gangs of money," to Nice and the Riviera, where she stayed with the parents of a friend, who had "a sufficient portion of this world's goods, a big house in a good neighborhood with counts, lords, and American millionaires for neighbors."[13]

The actual crossing took one week. When Larsen arrived in Lisbon, she took a room at the Avenida Palace Hotel, which was close to the central train station. One of her first postcards home announced: "Arrived! Very amusing trip. . . . Millions of churches in this place. Also millions of men ready for——anything."[14] Almost immediately she recognized the sexual vulnerability of a woman traveling alone, but she was in high spirits, and refused to be intimidated by unwelcome overtures from Portuguese men, though she was disappointed that Lisbon was "rather expensive . . . $1.75 for a mere manicure and not such a good one at that and taxis! About $1.50 for something like twenty minutes. . . . Clothes are impossible." The city

12. Nella Larsen Imes to Carl Van Vechten, January 25, 1931, *ibid.*; Larsen Imes to Van Vechten, Thursday, June fourth, 1931, *ibid.*; Frankie Lea Houchins, interview with author, March 12, 1984.

13. Nella Larsen Imes to Carl Van Vechten, Monday 25th [postmarked August 26, 1930], in CVV; Nella Larsen Imes to Mr. & Mrs. Carl Van Vechten, 27 IV 31 [postcard, April 27, 1931], in JWJ; Nella Larsen Imes to Carl Van Vechten, May 3, 1931, in JWJ.

14. Nella Larsen Imes to Carl Van Vechten, n.d. [*ca.* September 28, 1930], in JWJ.

fared better in other areas: "I don't think the hotels are so bad. This is the best room with bath and meals $10.00 a day. Trolleys—and they are much, much better than any I've ever ridden in. [Cost] 2½c." [15] Although the notice of trolleys, Lisbon's electric tramways, may seem uncharacteristic, she had, in fact, ridden and been fascinated by trolleys, streetcars, and elevated trains from the time of her childhood in Chicago when her father worked as a street railway operator and later conductor.

Although she claimed disinterest in the historical sites ("I'm not awfully keen on monuments historical or other wise. . . . [S]ad to say I haven't visited the museums or picture galleries and don't intend to"), Larsen was struck by the Moorish palaces and fortresses. Built high up in the hills, they were "simply amazing. How they did it in those days the good god only knows. . . . Curious African trait that to build in such inaccessible places." [16] She referred to a section where the cathedral Se Patriarchal, the oldest ecclesiastical edifice in the city, founded in 1150, was situated halfway up the castle hill. Se Patriarchal was once a Moorish mosque. Nearby was Castello de Sao Jorge, the old Moorish citadel and the former Moorish alcazar, which had been used as Alphonso III's royal residence in the thirteenth century.

The presence of Africa in Portugal fascinated her in terms of race as well as of class. "The Moors have certainly left their seed here. About 50 per cent of the population are as dark or darker than I am. And a large majority have distinctly Negroid features. There are too, a few Negroes, pure black. They seem, however, to arouse no comment or curiosity (except in me)." [17] That evidence of racial mixture was common and unheeded surprised her. Even though she had read about the Moors' arrival in Portugal and Spain from Africa, she had not expected to see such a visible legacy of their presence in the faces of the people.

Perhaps what surprised her most was that class positions were unrelated to the skin color or features. She observed that the "dark and heavy African traits" are not confined to the lower classes, that "some of the well born people" have these traits while "many of the servants and peasants have the distinctly Roman patrician face." [18] This situation was almost a reverse of what Larsen knew in the States, where the darker and more African the

15. Larsen Imes to Van Vechten, Wednesday 1st [October, 1930], *ibid.*
16. *Ibid.*
17. *Ibid.*
18. *Ibid.*

features of a person, the more likely he or she would be lower-class, while lighter and more Caucasian features indicated higher standing. Her observations on race in Portugal were the only ones during her year and a half abroad that related directly to her project for the Guggenheim fellowship.

Portugal was not her final destination. At the end of the first week in November, 1930, she set out for Spain, stopping briefly in Madrid, which drew an enthusiastic response: she "simply adored" everything about that city.[19] Her destination was Palma de Mallorca in the Balearic Islands, where she spent the major part of her fellowship tenure. In Huerta de Palma, she settled into the village of El Terreno at the Reina Victoria Hotel, a small dependence of Palma's Grand Hotel. Located on the sea, opposite Castillo de Bellver, a royal residence from the second half of the thirteenth century, the Victoria was a pension suitable for a long stay. From there she assessed the "gorgeous country," its inhabitants of Spaniards and foreigners ("decaying Englishmen and spreading German ladies"), and quickly decided to find a house in Terreno, which she considered "quite the nicest part of the city," with "famous" residents and guests: John Galsworthy (one of her favorite authors), Somerset Maugham, Robert Graves, Laura Riding, Liam O'Flaherty, and others ranging from French painters to the British governor of Nigeria.[20] Aside from the prevalence of English, Terreno's basic appeal was that it was a writer's vacation retreat, one in which she expected to locate a receptive community. But before she could settle in, Larsen developed pneumonia. As she put it, "Like an idiot I came here and promptly proceeded to get very sick."[21] The illness delayed her finding a house until mid-November.

She leased a house with a servant at José Villalonga 32 for $55 a month, with food costing another $30, and prepared for "a long siege of work" from the start of her occupancy in November, 1930, to the first of May, 1931.[22] She negotiated one month off the six-month lease because, she asked, "how do I know what I'll want to do next May?" The question was

19. Nella Larsen Imes to Carl Van Vechten, Wednesday 12th [postmarked November, 1930], in JWJ.

20. See Larsen Imes to Carl Van Vechten, Wednesday 12th [postmarked November, 1930], and Nella Larsen Imes to Carl Van Vechten, Thursday 12th November 1930, and January 25, 1931, all *ibid.*, and Nella Larsen Imes to Henry Allen Moe, January 11, 1931, in Guggenheim Foundation files.

21. Larsen Imes to Van Vechten, Wednesday 12th [postmarked November, 1930], in JWJ.

22. *Ibid.*, and Larsen Imes to Van Vechten, Thursday 12th November 1930, in JWJ. The two letters are dated "12th" but with different days of the week.

prescient. She discovered almost immediately that her expectations of a receptive community were false, and that Terreno was lonely for a single female, even one with a purpose and a vocation. Yet, she persevered with plans for the novel-in-progress she had brought from the States: "I think my white book is really good. Perhaps being a bit lonely is doing me good, or rather doing what I'm trying to do, good."[23] Her shock at Sinclair Lewis' being the first American to receive the Nobel Prize in literature ("How come?" she queried from Spain) subsided into an extra incentive for her work.[24]

Writing occupied her in December, though she took time out for solitary literary excursions to Valldemosa, where at the Carthusian convent, Cariuja de Valldemosa, she saw the room George Sand occupied in 1838: "Yesterday I went to Valledemosa [sic] and looked at the place where George Sand and Chopin spent so many unhappy months. It is quite beautiful and the rooms are said to be preserved as they were then. If I hadn't been afraid of landing in a Spanish jail I certainly would have stolen some original manuscripts for you. They were only sketches and studies I suppose but it was really criminal the way they were lying loose."[25] Her spirits were high and her resolve to complete her manuscript was strong. In girding herself for loneliness, Larsen was unaware that on Mallorca the season for visitors began late in winter, and that during winter and spring, the quaint and quiet community changed dramatically.

Once the season began, its intense activities acclimated her to different expectations. The influx of foreigners seeking diversion and amusement quickly transformed her existence in Terreno. By January she reported: "life here is so hectic that its [sic] almost impossible to find time to sleep. I haven't been to Capri, but I doubt if it could have been even in its greatest days more amusing than this," and immediately, she applied for an extension of her fellowship.[26] Throughout this "gay" season on Mallorca, Larsen enjoyed first-hand the parties, the arrivals, the departures, and vicariously the antics of the wealthy and their friends. She cavorted with them, took sightseeing trips, and learned to ride. She also absorbed their gossip and stored away at least one of the more melodramatic stories that she later used as a

23. Larsen Imes to Van Vechten, Wednesday 12th [postmarked November, 1930], *ibid.;* Larsen Imes to Van Vechten, Thursday 12th November 1930, *ibid.*
24. Larsen Imes to Van Vechten, Wednesday 12th [postmarked November, 1930], *ibid.*
25. *Ibid.*
26. Larsen Imes to Van Vechten, January 25, 1931, in JWJ; Larsen Imes to Moe, January 11, 1931, in Guggenheim Foundation files.

model, not in her fiction, but in her real life. Poet Laura Riding had, on April 27, 1929, drunk Lysol and jumped from the fourth-floor window of a house in London, while her married paramour, the poet and novelist Robert Graves, followed her from the third floor, but neither was injured seriously. All in all, Larsen decided, "It's comfortable and I like it. You go dashing about all night from one place on the island to another."[27] It was an ideal social environment for someone needing amusement, but less so for an aspiring writer.

Her race was not an issue, but in two instances, at least, her race attracted unattached men who gravitated to the unaccompanied American woman of color. In the first, a young southerner from Richmond, Virginia, who, though "suffering from acute intellectualism," according to Larsen, came to visit her frequently, because, she explained, "the only people Southerners spoke to away from home were Negroes."[28] He was one of the few Americans with whom she associated, preferring to see little of the others, perhaps because of their limited capacity for interracial associations.

In the second, a "delightful young English-Scots man" who was "rather important. Terribly good-looking, filthy rich, and rather famous polo-player and all that," and "very convenient for opening doors, picking up handkerchiefs—and such things," may have been attracted by her race, as she casually noted: "he thinks we look awfully well together because he's so tall and blond and I'm so little and brown." In observing his convenience for her, she overlooked his positioning her as exotic other, and she intimated that unattended females were not the norm and that her access to company was not through other females, but through males who may have been seeking romantic or sexual diversion. The man, whom she did not identify by name, had first seen Larsen in the American Bar and appeared at her house shortly thereafter under the pretext that she had left her cigarette lighter there. The man, she said, "appeared suddenly at my house one evening offering me a gold and green enamel cigarette lighter which he informed me I'd forgotten in the American Bar. Well, . . . I'd never seen the lighter before. We both knew this. But I took it and thanked him for bothering, returning it some days later because as I told him I'd noticed he'd been using matches ever since he'd brought me the lighter."[29]

Although several critics have suggested that Larsen considered marrying

27. Larsen Imes to Van Vechten, January 25, 1931, in JWJ.
28. *Ibid.*
29. *Ibid.*

an Englishman while she was in Europe, there is no indication that the relationship with the "famous polo-player" was anything other than a very brief, casual affair, though Larsen intimated that she planned to spend June and July in Scotland, presumably with the English-Scotsman. Her description of his being merely "convenient" may have veiled the importance he, a wealthy white male, assumed in offsetting her husband's attention to a white woman. Her encounters with him and with the southerner are her only two references to the matter of her race during her stay in Spain; both represent race as a positive factor in her interactions with strangers, exclusively men. Perhaps a more noticeable omission in Larsen's observations of her difference is the matter of gender; she does not remark on reactions to her being a woman traveling and living alone in a traditional society unaccustomed to the presence of a visiting female without an accompanying relative, companion, local host, or sponsor.

The attention from the two young men would not last. The young southerner departed suddenly; she repeated the suspicion "that he was asked to leave. It's a little way they have here if one is too gay or gets too tight too often." At the end of the winter season, the polo player and most of the other vacationers in Palma were gone as well. By the end of March, Larsen was distressed. "Life goes on here as it has for hundreds of years placid and monotonous. . . . The Spanish fleet is in the bay. Its officers are very nice but not exciting or amusing." [30] She had calculated neither the intensity nor the brevity of the social life: "I don't see how I'm going to stand it for the next three weeks [until her departure for Paris], but I've got to. All the amusing people have gone, and really I've never been so lonely in my life. I could almost weep from boredom. I do hope I'm not going to be so forlorn in Paris." [31] Although a man could well have found himself in a similar state, Larsen's situation was gendered female; her experience of freedom from racial restrictions was circumvented by her female gender identity, which was subject to social restrictions that she had not anticipated. There was little for her to do as a woman alone; too-frequent appearances at the American Bar would have labeled her as a sexually loose woman, for her smoking and drinking in public had already marked her as modern and unconventional.

Voiced in familiar terms—personal loneliness, longing for amusing people, travel as escape—her observation suggests the extent to which she

---

30. Nella Larsen Imes to Carl Van Vechten, March 22nd, 1931, in JWJ; Nella Larsen Imes to Carl Van Vechten, n.d. [postmarked March 31, 1931], *ibid.*

31. Larsen Imes to Van Vechten, March 22nd, 1931, *ibid.*

had made writing a minor activity during the season, perhaps in part because her social life in Palma had satisfied her desire for recognition, recognition that she had expected to receive only as the result of her writing. In
January, she had indicated that she was attending to her novel in spite of her
new interests: "I am doing positively my last job of typing on my book
Crowning Mercy. It's very difficult because I'm learning to ride these days
and after hours in the saddle its [sic] hard to sit on a chair—for a beginner—
I never knew before what a tender part of the anatomy the kenetta is."[32]

Although she had worked intermittently on her book "Crowning Mercy,"
she had come to realize that "this is the land of tomorrow, and with my
Negro blood and everything I took the disease very easily." It was not until
she found herself alone and bored that she returned to what she termed "the
blood sweating" of rewriting the novel, which a playwright whom she met
on the island had evaluated as "rotten," but which Larsen concluded had
"good stuff," though she agreed with his conclusion. Perhaps the unidentified white playwright had recognized that she was not on her strongest,
most familiar ground. A novel about white people may not have appeared
to be Larsen's métier, but it was a work that she had chosen to undertake
well before she left the United States. Nonetheless, as Langston Hughes had
observed, "An artist must be free to choose what he does, certainly, but he
must also never be afraid to do what he might choose."[33]

In the absence of diverting activity and a positive opinion of her novel,
she wrote diligently throughout April. Revising, she said, had "taken ten
years off [her life] span. It's a dog's life, all right."[34] Paris could wait until
May, but the novel could not. Her sense of urgency stemmed from a denial
of her request for a three- or six-month extension of her fellowship. The
extension was denied because of a shortage of funds for renewals; during
the Depression, the foundation attempted to support as many first-time applicants as in previous years. She received Henry Allen Moe's response for
the Guggenheim Foundation on the same day that she resolved to revise her
novel.[35] In replying to Moe on March 31, she made one of her two extended,
though relatively brief, statements to him about her novel: "I am something
more than about half-finished, what with going over and over again and

32. Larsen Imes to Van Vechten, January 25, 1931, *ibid.*

33. Nella Larsen Imes to Carl Van Vechten, April 7th [1931], *ibid.;* Langston Hughes, "The
Negro Artist and the Racial Mountain," *Nation,* CXXII (June 28, 1926), 694.

34. Larsen Imes to Van Vechten, April 7th [1931], in JWJ.

35. Larsen See Imes to Van Vechten, March 22nd, 1931, *ibid.,* and Nella Larsen Imes to
Henry Allen Moe, March 31, 1931, in Guggenheim Foundation files.

revising and casting away and adding. Doing the thing has been quite fascinating, and will be, I hope ever so." Confronted with the reality of her fellowship's end, she "sweated blood over it [her novel]," and consoled herself with Van Vechten's maxim: "easy writing makes bad reading."[36] Disciplined to work as always during times of distress, she completed the revisions before leaving Palma.

As usual, interspersed was her reading of Spanish books in translation and American novels. Alin Laubreaux's *Mulatto Johnny* (1931), translated by Coley Taylor, she "liked very much though it isn't quite done." Laubreaux's novel clearly had an appeal for Larsen; it traced twelve years of adventures in the life of Yan, a mixed-race youth from New Caledonia. After traveling from his village into the Europeanized world of Mallicolo, Dixieland, and Brisbane and becoming Mulatto Johnny, Yan recognizes that "he was alone, friendless, without family, nameless. His existence, which could have been that of a civilized man, was over; it finished here on the beach where twelve years ago he thought it was beginning anew."[37] In a final renewal that is a return to his roots, Yan strips himself of his European clothing, ties a string of coconut leaves around his waist, and walks back to his mother's village. Laubreaux's heavy emphasis of Yan as an exotic primitive at the expense of developing his psychology, however, may have caused Larsen to see *Mulatto Johnny* as flawed.

Of American novels, she especially relished George Schuyler's satire *Black No More* (1931), which she had received from Van Vechten. "I spent all day Sunday, when I should have been doing other things, reading it," she commented. "I was crazy about it—the material I mean—especially Garvey and our friends of the N.A.A.C.P. (Don't tell them) and the ending! I didn't however, think it was as well done as it might be."[38] Her assessment suggests that she was reading critically and annotating the shortcomings of others as a way of improving her own manuscript.

However, Larsen was unable to use her experiences in Palma as a basis for changing her perceptions of her work or her beliefs about social popularity. Instead of learning from her experiences in Spain, Larsen continued the cycle established there during much of the remainder of her stay in Eu-

36. Larsen Imes to Moe, March 31, 1931, in Guggenheim Foundation files; Larsen Imes to Van Vechten, April 7th [1931], in JWJ.

37. Larsen Imes to Van Vechten, April 7th [1931], in JWJ; Alin Laubreaux, *Mulatto Johnny*, trans. Coley Taylor (New York, 1931), 234.

38. Nella Larsen Imes to Carl Van Vechten, March 3, 1931, in JWJ.

rope: a flurry of social activity followed by a span of writing. This habitual response, though understandable given both her isolation from friends and her estrangement from Imes, affected her work, because she could not achieve a degree of consistency toward it. Spurts of work allowed just enough time to make a beginning, but not enough to develop her project.

The six letters sent over the course of her stay in Europe to Moe as secretary of the Guggenheim Foundation contained few reports of her work. Upon her arrival in October, she reported: "I have already put pen to paper, or rather paper into the typewriter." Her second letter, dated January 11, 1931, like the March 31 one after the denial of an extension, contained her longest, most explicit paragraph about her work: "The work goes fairly well. A little slower than is usual with me. But—I like it. Of course that means nothing because I really can't tell if it's good or not. But the way I hope and pray that it is is like a physical pain almost. I do so want to be famous." This truthful expression of doubt, desire, and need perhaps best reveals Larsen's assessment of both her work and her identity. With her marital life in limbo, and with it her sense of public significance, she invested her hopes for future social position in her work. In April, she did not mention her work at all, and in May only to say from Paris, "I shall probably remain here for some time, trying to get my work finished." In her final letter, an expression of gratitude to the foundation, she revealed, "I have not finished my work, but . . . I mean to go back to Spain . . . and get on with it."[39]

More often, the letters focused appreciatively on her surroundings: from "a very beautiful spot. Comfortable room, good food, lovely weather—and quiet" in the first, from October 20, 1930, through "it is very beautiful . . . very quiet . . . but terribly warm, and getting hotter day by day" in the third, dated March 31, 1931, to "the weather is pleasanter and the living cheaper" in the last, dated September 26, 1931.[40]

On the one hand, it should be expected that during her first trip to Europe she would not concentrate solely on her work. As she put it, "I'm sick

39. Nella Larsen Imes to Henry Allen Moe, Wednesday 20th [October, 1930], in Guggenheim Foundation files; Larsen Imes to Moe, January 11, 1931, *ibid.*; Nella Larsen Imes to Henry Allen Moe, April 21, 1931, and Sunday, May 25th [1931], both *ibid.*; Nella Larsen Imes to Henry Allen Moe, September 26, 1931, *ibid.*

40. Larsen Imes to Moe, Wednesday 20th [October, 1930], March 31, 1931, and September 26, 1931, all *ibid.* See also Larsen Imes to Moe, January 11, 1931, April 21, 1931, and Sunday, May 25th [1931], all *ibid.*

as a cat and ought to be in bed—but one doesn't go to bed on one's first visit to Paris—so—."[41] And if one adds her sense of wonder and excitement about her surroundings to her apprehensions and disappointment about her marriage, then her responses are quite appropriate. On the other hand, it appears that the tension between the individual work and social interaction, which is confined neither to her particular circumstances nor to her specific kind of work, was exacerbated by her underlying conception of writing: writing was a "product" that could, upon reception, confirm self-identity as well as verify self-worth. In the midst of public attention, Larsen could not engage in solitary work, though she knew that only the completion of another novel would sustain her status as a celebrity and reconfirm her sense of self-worth.

In referring to her writing in terms of effort expended and production achieved, she obscured writing as a creative act or process. While her lack of commentary about writing as a creative process may simply stem from the nature of the correspondence, her commentaries on writing as a product suggest otherwise. The problem seems to have been that Larsen presupposed that the result of her private, though declared, undertaking of writing determined who and what she was. This belief undermined the actual process of the writing, but the activity, however burdensome, remained a proof of her identification as writer.

Larsen labeled herself "novelist," and in the production of "novels" sought affirmation, esteem, and later vindication as well. The creative process itself did not, then, become central to her goals or ends, but was instead diminished to the effort necessary to reach a tangible result. It would be simple to attribute her attitudes, conceptions, and motives to the shallowness of her character, especially because in reading her comments and observations one may be struck by her superficial language and concerns. Nonetheless her attitudes and conceptions about writing in and of themselves assume a deeper meaning.

She did not define art as a social function; she presented no such larger generalizations or definitions. Her attitude toward writing as a product-oriented career can be seen in the context of the Harlem Renaissance as a special historical and cultural configuration emphasizing, in terms of plateaus of expression reached, a racial awakening and new consciousness of the contributions African Americans had made and could make to Ameri-

41. Nella Larsen Imes to Carl Van Vechten, n.d. [postmarked May 11, 1931], in JWJ.

can culture. Larsen had a precedent for understanding writing in the contexts of upward mobility, status, and achievement, as well as for using her fiction to affirm identity and significance.

The prevailing model during the Harlem Renaissance validated the power of the African-American writer to define self in the larger world, yet it validated, too, the power of the larger world to determine and arbitrate the conditions of that validation. The process or the act of writing brought a measure of satisfaction or partial fulfillment and the ability to conceive ideas and transform them into words mattered. Defining self and achieving acceptance of identity in the creative process were both difficult, however, when a primary measure used against African Americans in denying or undermining "black" identity was neither creative potential nor artistic capacity but rather the visibly "black" appearance separating African Americans from others. There were few possible escapes from the entrapment of negative views of African-American racial identity; the Harlem Renaissance as a conscious cultural movement offered redefinition of both racial identity and perceptions of race.

Creative work thus served social and political functions, though its artistic or aesthetic purpose was not forgotten. Tangible production was the most viable means of asserting the existence of the "New Negro" and of measuring racial achievement. Achievement for Nella Larsen and other racially defined writers, then, was construed as public or external acknowledgment, without which the creative act was incomplete. Achievement rested on the fact of publication and reception by an audience, often a "white" audience. The trap was not immediately evident. African-American authors such as Larsen who wanted or needed, for whatever cluster of reasons, validation of self in the external world of majority culture resorted to what that culture accepted as usable, to what that culture used as measurement, and to what that culture named as worthy of measurement. When gender constraints were added to racial proscriptions, the situation was further complicated for female "New Negro" writers.

For Larsen in the sparkling social world of the Harlem Renaissance, with its interracial conclaves and its hopes for uplift, the product (the novel, the play, the poem, the story, the song in print, on stage or record) offered evidence of the "New Negro's" reality, being, and meaning. Each group of published works was carefully added to the list of verifiable products, of achievements of self and race; each writer's productivity was dutifully proclaimed in the records for the year. It is not surprising that the tally-sheet approach could not last, that the writers could not endure, so that in retrospect, one can marvel not at the lists of works produced during a relatively brief period, but at the toll of casualties—those African-American writers who, for whatever conjunction of personal factors and external causes, simply did not make it into the next decade or, if into it, not out of it.

Given the exigencies of her social world and the traits of her personal makeup—insecurities, ambivalences, predilections, ambitions—Larsen could scarcely have thought of her work as anything other than a product. Her resolve to become famous in 1930 reaffirmed her conception of a writer, and that affirmation itself, abetted by its particular divisive contexts, contributed ultimately to her subsequent withdrawal from public life. Larsen in Palma, but already anticipating Paris as an escape from both the public threat of war and the private threat of disintegration, may not have been able at that moment to examine the tenets of the Harlem Renaissance or her relationship to those tenets.

The political situation in Spain worsened as Larsen was preparing to leave Palma. Spain was in a revolution that would lead to a republic. On April 14, King Alphonso XIII was forced to leave the country. When Spain was proclaimed a republic, Larsen realized that it was "very critical, though one reads in the papers that it is perfectly peaceful." All modes of transportation had halted, except for a few boats. During the week that she waited for the next French boat, she and the other islanders were running low on food and other supplies: "we have been living on what we had in the house or what we could get from the peasants round about, since all or most of the shops are closed." [42]

She felt personally inconvenienced by the revolution: "The populace seem to think that republic means an eternal holiday." Subsequently, from the safe vantage point of France, she came to understand the implications of the situation and to "feel that [she] was lucky to get away as comfortably as [she] did." Later in the spring, she would admit: "I was simply terrified. I don't care if I never see Spain again." [43]

When Larsen arrived in Paris in May of 1931, she found a social sphere that extended and magnified what she had experienced in Harlem during the heyday of the Renaissance in the 1920s, for not only did African-American artists and celebrities travel frequently to Europe, but average middle-class African Americans managed to get there too. She had traveled

42. Larsen Imes to Moe, April 21, 1931, in Guggenheim Foundation files.
43. *Ibid.*; Larsen Imes to Moe, Sunday, May 25th [1931], in Guggenheim Foundation files; Larsen Imes to Van Vechten, n.d. [postmarked May 11, 1931], in JWJ.

to Paris by way of Monte Carlo and Nice, where she stayed with a couple she had met on her trip from the States. She had visited briefly in Toulon, but her intended host W. B. ("Willie") Seabrook, who had reviewed *Passing* for the *Saturday Review of Literature*, was already in Paris; on the Riviera she had been the guest of Jack Carter's wealthy and fair-skinned mother and stepfather, where they may have been passing. ("I can't make out whether they pass or not, or simply say nothing about it."[44]) The visit to the Riviera impressed her the most because the unnamed couple lived lavishly: "They entertain all sorts of people including the aforesaid kind [counts, lords, and millionaires], as well as people like Sid Chaplin and Rex Ingram, and seem always to be in the Paris Herald, Riviera society section. Their garden is lovely and their cars very swell. They took me everywhere and introduced me to everyone who was left—it was a bit after the season. The whole thing was very interesting and amusing."[45]

In Paris, Larsen found a decent room at the Hotel Rovaro, 44 Rue Brunel, and felt lucky that she had, because the city was full of tourists for the Colonial Exposition. Centrally located and near her bank and mail, the Rovaro was expensive, so she soon found a cheaper room at the Hotel Paris-Dinard, 29 Rue Cassette. She visited Harold Jackman, who was vacationing in France; lunched with Seabrook, whom she located upon her arrival; attended concerts by two African Americans gaining recognition in Europe, the singer Roland Hayes and the violinist and composer Clarence Cameron White; saw a performance of Van Vechten's *Nigger Heaven*, adapted by Josephine Baker, already the exotic toast of Paris; drank at the famous cabaret run by Bricktop, a red-haired African American from West Virginia by way of Chicago; gathered gossip about Eric Walrond and Claude McKay, then living abroad after their literary successes in New York; and was the guest of honor, along with Roland Hayes and others, at a posh Paris tea.[46] The catalogue of people and events could easily be shifted to the Harlem that she knew well. Even in France, the "New Negro" was in vogue.

The high point of her first two weeks in Paris, however, was being a guest of honor at a tea given by Rose Wheeler. Seabrook, Marjorie Worthington,

44. Larsen Imes to Van Vechten, May 3, 1931, *ibid.* Larsen met Jack Carter through Dorothy Peterson. Active in the New York theater world, Carter appeared in *Stevedore* (1934) and in several other plays in the 1920s and 1930s.

45. Larsen Imes to Van Vechten, May 3, 1931, in JWJ.

46. See Larsen Imes to Van Vechten, May 3, 1931, Larsen Imes to Van Vechten, n.d. [postmarked May 11, 1931], Larsen Imes to Van Vechten, Thursday, June fourth, 1931, and Nella Larsen Imes to Carl Van Vechten, 8/30/31 [postcard], all in JWJ.

and Hayes were the other honorees. Larsen knew Hayes from New York, and though she cared little for his singing of spirituals ("terrible"), she found his German songs "inexpressibly wonderful." Worthington and Sea-brook, who married in 1935, had recently published books and were known for their adventures in traveling through the Sahara to Timbuktu. Seabrook admired Larsen's writing, especially her form, "classically pure in outline, single in theme and in impression, and . . . powerful in catastrophe," and he was intrigued by her delineation of "the tar-brush" of race.[47] His own texts were often tales of the exotic, primitive, or supernatural; *Jungle Ways* (1931), treating cannibals and primitives, had just appeared, and he had already published *Adventures in Arabia* (1927) and *The Magic Island* (1929), stories of voodoo set in Haiti. Worthington's *Spider Web* (1930) established her as one of the promising American writers in France, where she lived from 1926 to 1934. In 1931, she was already writing *Mrs. Taylor* (1932), the first in a succession of popular 1930s novels, *Scarlet Josephine* (1933), *Come, My Coach!* (1935), and *Manhattan Solo* (1937).

Larsen was thrilled by the association with Worthington and Seabrook, though she did not remark on their curiosity about her racial "otherness." "I did like both of them tremendously," she conceded in anticipating the tea. "I look forward to that with—well everything," she wrote to Van Vechten as the Friday afternoon affair approached. Her anticipation was great be-cause the tea was in the Wheelers' new, "lovely" flat, decorated by the artist Man Ray, who had also promised to do pictures of Larsen.[48] Larsen's exotic look and her writing career must have attracted the Dadaist and surrealist Man Ray, because he was then in a phase of photographing women. He was especially interested in representations of "the new woman," the kind of emancipated female that Larsen clearly was, but he apparently never man-aged to do a sitting with her. Yet even without a photo session with Man Ray, Larsen had arrived, and her initial uncertainty about Paris, "I don't just know what I'm going to do here," had been laid to rest.[49]

Wheeler's tea meant that Larsen had been taken up by a level of society that she had never been intimate with in the States. Larsen met Seabrook, Worthington, and the Wheelers, for instance, only after her arrival in France. Others whom she felt honored to meet were the William Aspenwall

---

47. Larsen Imes to Van Vechten, n.d. [postmarked May 11, 1931], *ibid.;* W. B. Seabrook, "Touch of the Tar-brush," *Saturday Review of Literature,* May 18, 1929, p. 1017.

48. Larsen Imes to Van Vechten, n.d. [postmarked May 11, 1931], in JWJ.

49. Quotation from Larsen Imes to Van Vechten, May 3, 1931, *ibid.*

Bradleys, whose name or occupation she did not even recognize when she was first invited to their home but "knew he was—or is—a very important person," and Mrs. Arthur Garfield Hayes, who was a friend of Tom Rutherford's and who, Larsen said, "almost fell into my arms telling me how she felt as if she'd known me all my life because Tom had talked so much about me."[50] Receiving invitations from these individuals, and others of their class, convinced Larsen that her arrival in Paris was a success.

In preparation for Dorothy and Sidney Peterson's arrival in June, she had sublet an apartment for three months from Paul Brulin, whose first wife was the ethnomusicologist Natalie Curtis. The apartment, at 31 bis Rue Campagne Premiere in Montparnasse, added to Larsen's enjoyment of the city and the Petersons to her pleasure in its social circles. They were not only close friends but seasoned travelers. She shared with them her first-hand accounts of the latest happenings: news of Eric Walrond in Toulon; Claude McKay and Anita Thompson together in Tangier writing books; Texas Guinan barred from France; Louis [Lewis] Cole and his following interested in his dancing; Paris hangouts of café society; and the "very dull" Colonial Exposition. The "in" place was Bricktop's Monico, the elegant club that had just opened in 1931; it was her second club and larger than the original Bricktop's on Rue Pigalle, which had earned her fame as a nightclub hostess. Everyone from European royalty to out-of-work musicians congregated at Bricktop's, which many used for "a combination maildrop, bank, rehearsal hall, club house—and even a neighborhood bar."[51] Although she did not tell the Petersons, Larsen had missed seeing Bricktop at the club and pronounced "the whole thing . . . pretty dull. An off-night perhaps."[52]

When Elmer Imes, who had foregone his annual research in Michigan, arrived in July, he found his wife and the Petersons already well-established in the Rue Campagne Premiere and chic café society. "We're having a wild time," Larsen happily concluded for her friends at home, though her hus-

---

50. *Ibid.* William Aspenwall Bradley was the most successful of the American literary agents in France and was responsible for securing Claude McKay's publishing contract for *Banjo* and *Home to Harlem.*

51. "Bricktop: Nightclub Queen Tells Story of Cafe Society in Paris and Rome," *Ebony,* XXXVIII (December, 1983), 65. Bricktop, Ada Beatrice Queen Victoria Louise Virginia Smith (1894–1984), operated clubs in Paris until 1940 when the Germans arrived. The year before her death, she completed an autobiography, *Bricktop by Bricktop,* by Ada Smith Duconge with Jim Haskins (New York, 1983).

52. Larsen Imes to Van Vechten, n.d. [postmarked May 11, 1931], JWJ.

band, who spent part of his time in Germany visiting with a fellow scientist, was not included in the "we."[53]

Elmer Imes traveled to Bavaria, Austria, and Italy. "The girls [Nella and Dorothy Peterson] did not go," he reported, "although I arranged a house for three weeks in Munich." They were not interested in leaving France, where Paris provided even more excitement than they had imagined, and they were reluctant to travel with Imes, whose relationship with his wife was becoming more explosive. Imes had met a number of physicists in France, and toward the end of his vacation, he spent two weeks in September at the School of Physics, University of Paris, which he described as "more theoretical than experimental but every contact helps." He would rather have been in attendance at the meeting of the British association of physicists, where his friend W. F. G. Swann from the Bartol Laboratory in Philadelphia was headed after his visit in Paris, but he had "neither the time nor the money" to do so. He was expected back at Fisk for the beginning of the academic year. He later was disappointed with his trip, but on a personal rather than professional level, perhaps because it did not achieve a satisfactory reconciliation with his wife. He resented, as he put it, "chasing off to Europe just because it seemed the thing to do."[54]

Despite her husband's disappointments, Nella Larsen was in exuberant spirits throughout the summer. With Dorothy Peterson and another friend, she posted a card from the Tower of St. Jacques to Van Vechten with the inscription: "3 nice girls out together, Nella. This is the most phallic picture we could find, Katie [Warriner]. And tight, tight, tight, tight—Dorothy." The three signed the postcard on the posts of the tower. Peterson's indication of their drinking ("tight") was in jest, but she and Larsen drank quantities of French wine through the afternoons and evenings. They were busy hosting visiting friends, such as Countee Cullen, who stopped into their Montparnasse apartment to read from Arna Bontemps' novel *God Sends Sunday* (1931), and they were making a round of parties, including luncheons with Miguel Covarrubias and other artists.[55] They were determined to absorb as much of the ambience of the French as possible during their holiday.

53. Larsen Imes to Van Vechten, 8/30/31 [postcard], Elmer Imes to Carl Van Vechten, 8/25/31 [postcard], both in JWJ.

54. E. Imes to Van Vechten, 8/25/31 [postcard], *ibid.;* Elmer Imes to Thomas E. Jones, September 8, 1931, in papers of Thomas Elsa Jones, Fisk University Library; Elmer Imes to Carl Van Vechten, 6/31/32, in JWJ.

55. Nella Larsen Imes, Katie Warriner, and Dorothy Peterson to Carl Van Vechten, July 12, 1931 [postcard] *ibid.;* Dorothy Peterson to Carl Van Vechten, July 19, 1931, *ibid.*

The dramatic Dorothy, who had taken a leave of absence from her teaching position to appear in *The Green Pastures,* was even livelier than ever. She had just completed the long Broadway run that had kept her close to New York, and she would be returning midyear to the more mundane job of high school teaching. Fluent in both French and Spanish, Dorothy enabled Larsen, whose French and Spanish were inadequate for conversation, to experience Europe differently. Dorothy's presence as guide, translator, and companion brought a measure of comfort and structure to the remainder of Larsen's stay abroad.

September, 1931, brought cold weather to Paris, departures for the States, and quiet to Larsen's flat. Coincidental to Imes's scheduled leaving for Nashville, Larsen became ill, so he postponed his departure. On September 8, he wrote to Jones at Fisk about his delay in starting back for the fall quarter:

> I have just cancelled my passage for New York on the [name of ship omitted] sailing tomorrow and have tentatively booked passage for the 23rd reaching NY on the 30th. This is done on account of Mrs. Imes' health which is causing us both a great deal of anxiety. As the result of her illness last winter her chest is in a very bad condition and the last few weeks of unseasonable wet cold weather is responsible for a cold that is regarded as serious. She is quite frightened and discouraged by minor hemorrhages and it seems best for me to stay with her until she is definitely better. We have arranged a companion for her and the present thought is to establish her for the next few months at Malaga (Spain) where the mild climate will likely help her get back to normal. At least her Paris physician thinks this is best and she rather agrees.[56]

Larsen had prepared to return to Spain in September but was forced to convalesce until the first of October. Paris' attractions had vanished with the onset of cold weather: "Cold as hades here. We are all wearing red flannels and woolen stockings."[57] Peterson, the companion Imes mentioned, remained in Paris with the intention, as she announced to their departing friends, of having adventures all the way from France to Africa. In October

56. E. Imes to Jones, September 8, 1931, in Jones Papers.
57. Nella Larsen Imes to Carl Van Vechten, n.d. [*ca.* mid-September, 1931], in JWJ.

when Larsen recovered from her bout with pneumonia, she was a ready companion for the three months of excursions Peterson had planned. Unlike Larsen, Peterson was no stranger to Europe, having spent many summers there. Moreover, she had known romantic disappointment with Jean Toomer, who had courted her in the early 1920s but in 1931 had "married white," as the saying goes. Toomer's bride, Margery Latimer, was a novelist in her own right and, in a small irony of connection, had reviewed *Quicksand* for Harry Hansen's *Book World*, remarking on "the great space between black and white, the elaborate mental barrier, and . . . the reason for it and the inhumanity of it."[58] Peterson planned to entertain Larsen, and clearly herself as well, on a grand tour that would divert her friend from recurring poor health and them both from troubles with men.

The two women left Paris for "Spain and West Africa where [they] hope[d] to get warm again." They traveled to Toulon, on to the Spanish Riviera, Malaga, to Gibraltar, on to Tangier and Tetuan, Morocco, and back to Spain for the Christmas holidays in Granada.[59] Their longest stay was in the Costa del Sol capital city, Malaga, which became their home base during October and most of November. It allowed easy access to Gibraltar from Le Lina and into Tangier across the Strait of Gibraltar, as well as to Granada, Seville, and Costa del Sol. There Larsen attempted once again to concentrate on her neglected writing, especially when Peterson ventured away on sidetrips with other friends. "Today I am having (Thank god!!) a day to myself," she remarked when Peterson departed for a day's trip to Gibraltar. With gun emplacements in the upper galleries of the Rock, caves along the base, and ruins of a Moorish castle, the British colony of Gibraltar was a popular excursion site. But Larsen was intent upon starting a new book, a novel entitled "Mirage." "Crowning Mercy," as she had observed in late September while still in Paris, remained "not quite finished," yet for the most part she immersed herself in travel adventures with the spirited

58. Margery Latimer, Review of *Quicksand*, by Nella Larsen, in "Book World," New York *World*, July 22, 1928, in SCF.

59. Nella Larsen Imes to Carl Van Vechten, 9/27/31 [postcard], in JWJ; Nella Larsen Imes to Carl Van Vechten, n.d. [postcard from Malaga, 1931], *ibid.;* Nella Larsen Imes to Carl Van Vechten, November 24, 1931 [postcard from Malaga], *ibid.;* Nella Larsen Imes to Mr. and Mrs. Carl Van Vechten, November 26, 1931 [postcard from Gibraltar], *ibid.;* Nella Larsen Imes to Carl Van Vechten, n.d. [postcard from Tetuan, Morocco], *ibid.;* Nella Larsen Imes to Carl Van Vechten, n.d. [postcard from Alhambra Salus de las Dos Hermanas, Granada, Spain], *ibid.* See also Dorothy Peterson and Nella Larsen Imes to Grace Nail Johnson, December, 1931 [postcard from Granada], *ibid.*

Peterson, who had an unlimited capacity for discovering things to do and people to do them with and to remain quite socially proper in the process. Thirty years later, Peterson would leave the United States to settle permanently in this part of Spain, where finally she chose the Andalusian capital of Seville as her home.[60]

On the twenty-fourth of November, Peterson and Larsen began to plan their return to the States, but their route would take them first to Africa by way of Gibraltar. After a day of excursions on the Rock, they headed for Africa on the twenty-seventh. They arrived in the port city Tangier and after a few days continued on to Tetuan; Morocco was "simply fascinating," but it was colder than they had anticipated: "The deeper we go into Africa the colder it gets. We came on here from Tangiers [sic] Sunday and have already bought good old fashioned woolen b.v.d.s."[61] The weather diminished Larsen's enthusiasm for traveling in Morocco because she dreaded another bout with pneumonia, so they began the journey back to Spain, where they would celebrate the Nativity and the New Year in the mountain setting of the Moorish city Granada.

In January, 1932, a reluctant Larsen and a tired Peterson headed for New York, where there was no winter hibernation. One friend entertaining them observed: "Dorothy looks fine, she has let her hair go gray and is very handsome indeed. Nella is lovely."[62] The stunning photographs that Van Vechten took of them on March 26 corroborated the observation; both women presented self-composed, beautiful, and mature faces to his camera. While living with Peterson's father on Monroe Street in Brooklyn, they resumed a round of parties, visits, concerts—such as the one for Paul Robeson at Town Hall—and meetings—an interracial one in Harlem, for instance, where Larsen and Rudolph Fisher "represented the arts and spoke quite delightfully," according to Peterson's account.[63] Although Peterson regretted "the

60. Nella Larsen Imes to Carl Van Vechten, n.d. [postcard from Malaga, ca. mid-November, 1931], ibid.; Larsen Imes to Moe, September 26, 1931, in Guggenheim Foundation files; Carla L. Peterson to Thadious M. Davis, December 2, 1982, in possession of Thadious M. Davis. See also Dorothy Peterson to Carl Van Vechten, October 30, 1959, and Carl Van Vechten to Dorothy Peterson, April 21, 1959, both in JWJ.

61. Larsen Imes to Van Vechten, November 24, 1931 [postcard from Malaga], in JWJ; Larsen Imes to Mr. and Mrs. Van Vechten, November 26, 1931 [postcard from Gibraltar], ibid.; Nella Larsen Imes to Carl Van Vechten, n.d. [ca. early December, 1931], ibid.

62. Elizabeth Shaffer Hull to Grace Nail Johnson, February 2nd [1932], ibid.

63. Dorothy Peterson to Grace Nail Johnson, March 8, 1932, ibid.; see also Hull to Johnson, February 2nd [1932], ibid.

passing of some interesting phase of my life . . . the ending of my 'globe trotting,'" she busied herself with "remaking acquaintances" in a New York not, she said, "devoid of all interest." She was also teaching and preparing to return to her Second Avenue apartment by the end of May, where she anticipated spending the summer "unless a new adventure turns up."[64]

Larsen had soon found a place to live, "her own charming little apartment on West 11th St. just off Fifth Avenue—very swank and everything," as Peterson described it. Yet she had difficulty deciding what to do next. She moved into the apartment at 53 West Eleventh Street in a downtown neighborhood on the first of March, 1932. It had been two months since she had returned from Europe, and she had made no effort to join her husband in Nashville. He had anticipated her return to the States in January and had begun arrangements with the Fisk administrators for a house during the fall.[65]

Jobless and uninterested in work, Larsen tried to find a way of organizing her life, particularly with Elmer Imes permanently relocated in the South. She attended a few parties, played bridge, and kept up her friendship with Van Vechten, who entertained Larsen and Dorothy and Sidney Peterson on March 26, 1932, when he photographed them together and individually. "I am really proud of your photographs and hope you like them," Van Vechten informed Dorothy Peterson. "I have sent Sidney his ten (which are superb) and Nella hers, and the group picture. To see them all you will have to MEET." Larsen was delighted with her photographs, as she indicated to Van Vechten: "I think they are very unusual and extraordinarily interesting. And they are so like me. The group pictures are charming. And Sidney's are quite wonderful. But I am afraid that—though they are more beautiful—I don't like Dorothy's as much as I do my own."[66] Such diversions were rare, for she neither renewed her interests in Harlem nor left for Nashville, where she was expected to appear in order to present some semblance of a marriage for the Fisk community.

The stress of her suspended position brought on another illness. In March, just after moving into her new apartment, she came down with pleurisy. The case was so severe that she no longer had to entertain the thought of going to Nashville. When she had not recovered enough by mid-

64. Peterson to Johnson, March 8, 1932, *ibid.*
65. *Ibid.*; E. Imes to Jones, September 8, 1931, in Jones Papers.
66. Carl Van Vechten to Dorothy Peterson, April 5, 1932, in JWJ; Nella Larsen Imes to Carl Van Vechten, n.d. [postmarked April 11, 1932], *ibid.*

April to travel south, she caused concern among her friends. Peterson, especially, recognized that Larsen was not only reluctant but fearful of joining her husband; she wrote to their friend Grace Nail Johnson, who had already moved to Nashville with her husband James Weldon:

> Nella has been far from well. . . . She had intended leaving for Fisk immediately after getting her apartment to rights but a touch of pleurisy kept her in bed for a week—then getting up inopportunely for various parties that she had no business attending, put her back in bed again and again. However, she really plans leaving for Nashville next week [the third week of April]. . . . Do drop her a line in the mean time for her illness has left her quite depressed. Perhaps if you let her know that you, at least, were looking forward to her visit, it would provide the impetus for a definite date for her departure, as in her present state she seems inclined to put it off from day to day until she regains her strength.[67]

In seeking Johnson's assistance with her friend, Peterson only thinly veiled her worry over Larsen's mental and physical well-being. As tactfully as possible, she called Johnson's attention to Larsen's anxiety and depression and to their implied cause—Elmer Imes in Nashville, who was no longer interested in a reconciliation—a cause that was bound to have a major and deleterious impact on Larsen's life and style.

Peterson noticed the signs of depression, because even though Larsen ventured out to some evening affairs, she was less sociable and scarcely invited anyone to visit her. Her excuse was that the apartment on West Eleventh was "so bleak and small and depressing, I hate having people see it—However—if winter comes—and all the rest." The description is contrary to Peterson's of the "swank" and "charming," though also "little" apartment, yet for Larsen the reality was that her own place was not a seven-room, spacious apartment of the sort she had shared with Imes. It was, however, her own, but that was not enough to compensate for the comedown in status that she perceived it to be. She insisted that she continued to feel "a bit woozy in the head" from her illness, so that she remained at home reading D. H. Lawrence's *Lorenzo at Taos*.[68]

---

67. Dorothy Peterson to Grace Nail Johnson, April 15th [1932], *ibid.*
68. Nella Larsen Imes to Carl Van Vechten and Fania Marinoff, n.d. [postmarked April 20, 1932], *ibid.*

Although her illness may have been the result of a variety of physical ailments that could prolong recovery, it was not the only reason she remained largely secluded on West Eleventh Street. Larsen was sensitive to appearances on two counts. The first she pointed out: she felt reluctant to have close social ties aware of her "bleak," "depressing" surroundings. The second she must have been aware of, if only on a subconscious and unarticulated level: she felt deprived of her social partner and husband. And on the second count, she feared the worst, that Imes no longer wanted her as his wife.

At the end of April, after celebrating a "delightful" birthday with the Van Vechtens, Larsen sent "Thousands of thanks" to her hosts who, like Peterson, remained caring and attentive friends, and then left for Nashville. Not only had Grace Nail Johnson encouraged her to leave New York, but Thomas E. Jones, president of Fisk, had urged her to join her husband. She followed Van Vechten's suggestion of taking a train to Cleveland and from there a plane to Nashville. The mode of travel provided a diversion. Rather than focusing her attention on her destination and the unknown that lay before her, she placed her modern mode of travel at the center of her concerns, which included the reduced travel time of eighteen hours, rather than an anticipated thirty-six by train, and the comparable costs—"only five dollars more, which is after all what one would spend for meals on the long land ride."[69]

In Nashville, Larsen and Imes lived in an apartment near the James Weldon Johnsons' large house on Seventeenth Street, North, just off the Fisk campus. They did not yet have their own house. As old friends from New York, the Johnsons invited them over frequently as guests. Grace Johnson, in particular, made life "comfortable" for Larsen, who thought it "marvelous" having them for neighbors, because James Weldon's prestigious place in the community and in the African-American world made his home a lively social center with black and white visitors from across the nation.[70] It was the kind of atmosphere Larsen enjoyed most. Not until much later would she admit that the Johnsons' presence nearby had helped reduce the tensions in her own household.

Initially, Larsen believed that being in Nashville was "rather exciting,

69. *Ibid.*

70. Nella Larsen Imes to Carl Van Vechten, n.d. [postmarked May 14, 1932], in JWJ. See also Nella Larsen Imes to Carl Van Vechten and Fania Marinoff, n.d. [postmarked June 27, 1933], *ibid.*

weather, people, and country," and the urbane Johnson's creative writing class confirmed her sense that Fisk was "interesting and very much alive." She visited the class several times and on one occasion made a speech to the students, which on reflection she considered "pretty bad."[71] Nonetheless, the writing course lifted her level of enthusiasm for campus life. She wrote to friends in New York that the course was "great and inspiring"; she had Van Vechten's niece Elizabeth Shaffer Hull longing to hear the lectures and to visit Fisk because, from Larsen's accounts, "it sounds like such an exciting place."[72]

Fisk in the 1930s was a dynamic place. Samuel Allen recalled:

Even in the thirties, the school attracted a wide array of fascinating people. Jimmie Lunceford led his band for one of the college dances. Duke Ellington regaled the students by playing the piano in the lobby of historic Jubilee Hall, with such exuberance—we've long remembered—he broke off one of the keys. Du Bois delivered the commencement address for our graduating class; his subject was The Revelation of St. Orgne, the Damned, a seemingly allegorical tale of the efforts of an heroic figure to bring goodness, truth and beauty, as well as justice, to his people. As soon as the ceremonies were over, a small band of youthful scholars rushed to the library to discover how they had missed St. Orgne. Nobody knew who he was! What century? What country, what kingdom, mythical or otherwise? Only sometime later did the full revelation come. Orgne was Negro spelled backward. At one point in the mid thirties, Franklin Delano Roosevelt and his retinue drove up the oval before Jubilee Hall.

In addition to distinguished visitors, Fisk's faculty was outstanding: St. Elmo Brady in chemistry, James Weldon Johnson and Sterling Brown in literature, John Work in music, Aaron Douglas in art, and Charles S. Johnson in sociology. Johnson's departure for Nashville had surprised Larsen when she was in Europe: "I can't understand why but it will be very good for him to get away from the uplift and to have a good deal more leisure to do the things he wants and ought to do." She did not realize then that, as Allen remem-

---

71. Larsen Imes to Van Vechten, n.d. [postmarked May 14, 1932], *ibid.* See also Elizabeth Shaffer Hull to Grace Nail Johnson, May 27, 1932, *ibid.*

72. Hull to Johnson, May 27, 1932, *ibid.*

bered, "the Fisk community was largely sheltered from the racial patterns prevailing beyond; and in the thirties, the University was an unusually rich educational and cultural center."[73]

The campus not only prided itself on "a leisurely and indulgent atmosphere wreathed with the rich fragrance of magnolia and wild plum and crab apple," but also on its academic standing: "It seemed difficult [in the 1930s] not to think of it as the summit of black institutions of higher learning. Some students amused themselves in insisting that at football games, Fisk students would chant: One Two Three Four, *Whom* are we for. We were less amused, of course, when students from the opposing schools would approach the Fisk cheering section and in mock support shout over their shoulders in our direction the University initials."[74]

During the first trip to Nashville after her return from Europe, Larsen ignored what was obvious to the Fisk community: there was something wrong with her marriage. Even when Jones approached her about moving permanently to Nashville, his implication went unheeded. "Dr. Jones . . . seems to feel that I might come here to live for at least a portion of the year and offers to build the kind of house I want." Although she could admit that she had not made up her mind, she could not admit that her relocation to Nashville did not depend entirely upon her. Imes remained noncommittal. Larsen created the impression that her career as a novelist kept her in New York, but her explanations did not stop the rumors of marital troubles, which she herself had heard: "There seems to be a lot of gossip floating about. But then, there's always gossip anywhere."[75]

The situation, however, went beyond mere gossip. Youra Qualls, a student who worked for Imes, recalled his "romancing Mrs. Gilbert": "one of my secretarial duties was to send her books and candy and address envelopes; he wrote to her every day." Other students also knew that "Dr. Imes had a steady companion . . . in Mrs. Ethel B. Gilbert," as John Hope Franklin, Fisk Class of 1935, remembered:

> In my freshman and sophomore years, I worked as a typist in Mrs. Gilbert's office, and we became fast friends by the time I reached the ripe age of seventeen. During that time she became ill and was in

73. Samuel Allen to Thadious M. Davis, March 7, 1989, in possession of Thadious M. Davis; Larsen Imes to Van Vechten, April 7th [1931], in JWJ.

74. Allen to Davis, March 7, 1989.

75. Larsen Imes to Van Vechten, n.d. [postmarked May 14, 1932], in JWJ.

the Vanderbilt hospital for a week or two. I went to see her there, which was itself something of an adventure since I had never before been in a hospital, and since this was "across town" where, at best, I felt insecure. I sat with her for at least a half-hour carrying on an animated conversation as we laughed about various incidents. . . . At one point she mentioned something that puzzled me. Feeling perfectly at ease with her, I pressed her for clarification. It was then that a voice came from the shadows in another part of the room. "Just wait for her to tell you. If she wishes to she will tell you. If not, she will not." Had I been near a door *or* a window I would have departed forthwith!! It was Dr. Imes whose presence I had not known until he spoke. After that, I kept my distance from him.[76]

Larsen was unable to conceal her marital problems from friends in New York. At the same time that Larsen was assuring them of how pleasant things were in Nashville, Imes was making frantic phone calls about her behavior and his fears that she would actually stay in Nashville: "I don't know how wise it is to have her here. She has the most ungodly ability to keep me in an unpleasant stew, which can only end in further estrangement—However she considers that she has the whip hand and thinks that this is what she wants."[77] Larsen was determined to make her husband pay for his transgressions, even at the expense of her own happiness. She seemed to feel the most vindicated when he was disconcerted out of his typically placid, self-contained manner. While she may having been trying to get his attention, she appeared oblivious to his increasing withdrawal from her; yet she must have been hurt by it. Imes proceeded with his usual plans for summer work at Ann Arbor on a new research project that would keep him there from June to September. Michigan had always been his private retreat. He made no provisions for his wife.

While Imes may have referred to his wife's "whip hand," he was equally aggressive in obtaining what he wanted for himself, his laboratory, and his students, "who not only respected Dr. Imes but feared him as well. We thought he would 'do us in' at the slightest provocation." Axel Hansen remembered Imes as "formal, very objective and very reserved, but he loved

76. Youra Qualls, interview with author, January 8, 1989; John Hope Franklin to Thadious M. Davis, April 4, 1989, in possession of Thadious M. Davis.

77. Elmer Imes to Carl Van Vechten, June 21, 1932, in JWJ; see also Elmer Imes to Carl Van Vechten, May 19, 1932 [telegram], *ibid.*

ladies; he would go to concerts in the Fisk chapel with a tuxedo on and in the company of a white woman." But Imes was also "a wonderful fatherly figure, sophisticated, worldly-wise, and [possessed] a tenderness for young people," Youra Qualls concluded of Imes during her undergraduate days at Fisk, when she saw him as "a very kind, romantic figure."[78] Like his wife, Imes was not an uncomplicated person; he, too, exhibited contradictory personality traits.

Larsen concealed as best she could the distance that was unmistakable between herself and Imes. She reflected an uncertainty about her future, however, by planning simultaneously to move to Nashville and to return to Spain and Morocco. She left for New York at the first of June, three weeks before Imes departed for Michigan. By July, she still considered both of her options for September viable and applied for a renewal of her passport on July 25, 1932.[79] Escape to a foreign country might provide relief from an increasingly complicated situation, and there she might begin her life anew. The dream of escape, though seductive, competed with that of reigning over home and husband in relative comfort and ease. Although her vacillations are apparent, her motives are not. On the one hand, she obviously found the social life and material comforts of Fisk, including her own maid, superior to what she had experienced in New York City upon her return from Europe. Her tiny apartment on West Eleventh made the offer of a house in Nashville too important to ignore. But even a custom-built house was not enough to temper her reservations, because, on the other hand, she knew the reality of her marital problems, and that they were far from simple. Her husband's affection and concern had shifted almost entirely to someone else who was, after all, also a member of the Fisk community. By September, Larsen had decided she could not afford a move to Spain, as she had no income aside from that Imes would provide. She knew that she would not live in reduced circumstances in New York. Following her material self-interest, she returned to Nashville and to a husband who, as she had previously observed in a flash of her old wit, continued to look "very unwell, poor dear; but I don't know what I can do about it."[80]

78. Franklin to Davis, April 4, 1989; Axel Hansen, interview with author, March 8, 1987; Qualls interview, January 8, 1989.

79. Nella Larsen Imes, Application for renewal of U.S. passport, July 25, 1932, in State Department Records.

80. Larsen Imes to Van Vechten, n.d. [postmarked May 14, 1932], in JWJ.

13

Sowing Dreams,
1933–1941

DURING THE EARLY months of 1933, Larsen remained in Nashville. She and Imes moved into a new house at 1806 Morena Street, which had been one condition of her relocation. It was a dream house, unique even for the Fisk campus, which took pride in the beauty of its faculty residences. The two-story structure with a red tile roof was soundly built of double brick walls, stuccoed and painted white, as were most of the houses on the campus.[1] Designed by McKissack and McKissack, an African-American architectural firm founded in 1901, the house had exquisite details, which Elmer Imes helped plan. In the spring of 1930, he had submitted his "requirements" to Mr. McKissack, who worked on "a plan which [would] come within the university budget." It was expensive, though President Jones had insisted that the trustees of Fisk did not feel "justified in putting more than $7,500 into a faculty home for [Imes] and Mrs. Imes."[2]

Although not among the largest houses on the campus, it was one of the most modern in design and convenience. Leatrice Taylor McKissack, an officer of the firm that built the house, remembered it as her childhood home where her father, Dr. A. A. Taylor, who was a dean at Fisk during the 1930s,

---

1. Marian Roberts and Leatrice Taylor McKissack, interview with author, March 10, 1987. The house, still in excellent condition, has remained the property of Fisk University and is occupied by a faculty member.

2. Elmer Imes to Thomas E. Jones, April 18, 1930, in Papers of Thomas Elsa Jones, Fisk University Library; Thomas E. Jones to Elmer Imes, June—eleventh—1932, *ibid.*

moved the family when Imes vacated it. She recalled that trees lined the walkway to the front entry and its decorative screened door. A mahogany bench extended across the slate-floored vestibule, which was separated from the living room by a French door with mahogany casings. The spacious living room had a large fireplace and three windows overlooking the front yard. A library, recessed in one area of the living room, was lined with mahogany bookcases with two windows high over the shelves. Double French doors led to the dining room.[3]

Marian Roberts, a longtime resident of the house, can still draw its layout from memory. The large kitchen, situated off a landing with three steps leading to stairs up to the second floor or down to the basement, and three steps leading down to the living room, featured a breakfast room with built-in dark mahogany Dutch seats and a window with glass shelves enclosed in mahogany. Over the kitchen sink was another window overlooking the yard. Glass-doored cabinets lined the wall leading to the back porch, and the pantry contained more cabinets and shelves. Given the financial constraints of the 1930s, the house was particularly elegant.[4]

Larsen had a more limited input into the interior specifications and finishings than her husband; however, Jones had sought to "accommodate [her] desires" before her departure for Europe. She had been given the standard choices for faculty residences—English cottage, colonial, or bungalow—and, with her husband, agreed on the Tudor style. Of all the gracious rooms on the first floor, she seemed the most proud of the kitchen, for which she had requested tomato-red paint with black trim. A Fisk student who worked in the house in exchange for meals recalled how unusual red paint was for a kitchen at that time, and how much Larsen loved bright colors, even though she complained about "niggers" wearing loud colors.[5]

While she wanted a kitchen that was uniquely her own, she had also insisted on a maid and a cook, so that she herself spent little time in the kitchen preparing meals. She had enlisted Grace Johnson in finding help, though by the end of her stay in Nashville, she was eager to pass one maid, Ora, on to the Johnsons: "About Ora. I am quite certain I will not be here next year. And I know that you will be pleased with her. I shall pay her—say for a little vacation—when I go; so that she will not feel that she must set

3. McKissack interview, March 10, 1987.
4. Roberts interview, March 10, 1987.
5. Thomas E. Jones to Elmer Imes, April Third, 1930, in Jones Papers; Frankie Lea Houchins, interview with author, March 12, 1984.

about making arrangements at once, but can wait to talk with you when you return."[6]

Although she was solicitous regarding Ora, Larsen exhibited a peculiar trait in dealing with domestics. She renamed each of her domestic helpers and called them versions of names that whites stereotypically associated with rural or working-class blacks, just as she had chosen "Zulena" and "Sadie" as names for the maids in her novel *Passing*. In retaliation, Frankie Lea Houchins and others working in the household called her "Nellie" behind her back, taking their cue from Grace Johnson, who had always used Larsen's given name. Like Houchins, Isaiah and Pearl Creswell remembered that Imes knew his wife's real name was "Nellie," but he never called her that, though they always did.[7]

Workers in and visitors to the house remarked that the second floor had been "especially designed for a couple not getting along," and Marian Roberts believed that Imes planned the second floor to have privacy from his wife.[8] The entire master suite, with its own study and bathroom, could be shut off from the two bedrooms and bath on the other side of the stairwell. The layout of the upstairs had, in fact, been specifically planned by Elmer Imes, who was intent upon keeping a distance between himself and his wife.

Under happier circumstances, the spacious, comfortable place, only a block above the Fisk campus at Eighteenth Avenue North, would have been a congenial workplace for the writer. However, because tensions were mounting between Larsen and Imes, she found it even more difficult than usual to concentrate on her work without exaggerating the mechanics of writing. She refused to use pens or pencils, choosing to write only with long strips of lead. She was turning into her conception of the eccentric literary artist, different from any of the academic writers on the campus. It was a way of calling attention to her public significance as a novelist and disguising her pain in an untenable situation. She continued to work on "Fall Fever," a novel that focused on a woman's deception by her husband and a sexually aggressive, menopausal woman's efforts to attract the other woman's husband to her bed. The antagonist was a thinly disguised portrait of Ethel Gilbert who, though no longer on campus, maintained an affiliation

---

6. Nella Larsen Imes to Grace Nail Johnson, Thursday [1932], in JWJ.

7. Houchins interview, March 12, 1984; see also Nella Larsen, *Passing*, in *"Quicksand" and "Passing,"* ed. Deborah E. McDowell (New Brunswick, 1986), 164, 230; Isaiah and Pearl Creswell, interview with author, March 11, 1987.

8. Roberts interview, March 10, 1987.

with the school while in the North. Larsen completed the novel in a manuscript typed by Houchins, who described it as "disgusting."[9] It was never published, and no version seems to have survived.

In spite of her handsome physical surroundings, Larsen was struggling against breakdown and disintegration. She may also have been suffering from a thyroid condition, because her eyes had begun to bulge and her hair to thin to the point of barely covering her scalp. Whatever were her physical ailments, she did not seek medical treatment. "She popped aspirins almost constantly," and she, as well as Imes, were chain smokers. She was often tense, and her behavior was very uncharacteristic of the Nella Larsen who lived in New York. According to Houchins: "Her nerves were frazzled; she would pace the floor and pull out her hair by the handfuls. Afterwards, she refused to go out or be seen." On the rare occasions when she had to leave the house, she wore a hat. Once she asked Houchins to drive her to town, but when "the car hit a bump crossing a railroad track, she claimed I was trying to kill her, and insisted I take her back. She was a strange person."[10]

Minerva Johnson Hawkins, who was married to the Fisk football coach during the early 1930s, admitted more sympathetically that "no one knew her [Larsen] well. . . . Dr. Jones was sold on family and created the aura of Fisk family. He insisted on Nella's coming for reconciling. She probably felt alienated after being brought to campus under those circumstances . . . when everyone knew that Imes and Gilbert were very involved."[11] Clearly, Larsen was in a thinly veiled state of agony from which there was no clearcut remedy.

The gay social life that she had reported in Nashville during 1932 no longer existed for her at the beginning of 1933. She would not visit or socialize with anyone, not even the James Weldon Johnsons, who were her neighbors and old friends. At least one close-hand observer remarked her dislike for both Johnsons, though she pretended otherwise in their presence. She had become a reluctant correspondent; in February, her loyal friend Van Vechten wrote to Grace Johnson in Nashville: "I haven't heard one word from Nella Larsen Imes since she left New York. Does she want me to forget her?"[12]

9. Houchins interview, March 12, 1984.

10. *Ibid.*, and Frankie Lea Houchins, interview with author, December 30, 1984.

11. Mrs. Minerva Johnson Hawkins, interview with author, March 11, 1987.

12. Houchins interview, March 12, 1984; Carl Van Vechten to Grace N. Johnson, February 11, 1933, in JWJ.

Larsen had virtually stopped corresponding with friends in New York. After receiving birthday greetings in April, she felt obliged to respond: "It was sweet of you to remember me. I do mean to write but life is pretty terrible these days. However, I can't say I wasn't warned."[13] This was a rare admission. Three years earlier, Imes had characterized his wife as a "good little sport" who tried to go things alone. During what were perhaps the most difficult times, both publicly and privately, that Larsen would experience as an adult, she made every effort to conceal from her friends, and perhaps from herself, the state of things and "to go it alone."

In arguing for a woman's right to selfhood, Elizabeth Cady Stanton pointed out in 1892: "In discussing the rights of a woman, we are to consider first what belongs to her as an individual, in a world of her own, the arbiter of her own destiny, an imaginary Robinson Crusoe with her woman Friday on a solitary island. Her rights under such circumstances are to use all her faculties for her own safety and happiness." Larsen was, in a sense, on an isolated island, for she was cut off from her valued and trusted system of support, and she was surrounded by individuals who appeared hostile to her very existence. Yet even her tough-minded determination could not entirely conceal her difficult situation. As she finally wrote to Van Vechten and Marinoff, "Do forgive me dears, but life is so damned complicated, and there was no reason writing to say that."[14] Although the reality beneath the surface of the "good life" in Nashville was unpleasant, it was one that she persistently attempted to hide.

Why did she subject herself to so complicated a situation? On the surface, it seems that she wanted the financial security and material comfort that life with Imes offered. The self-destructiveness manifested while she was in the house with Imes, however, suggests that she was able to enjoy neither security nor comfort. Her inability to remove herself or to change the dynamics of the marriage suggests that she was not only deluding herself but repressing her need for Imes, who had demonstrated, during the early years of their marriage, attention, care, and affection that she had missed throughout much of her life. Their bonding provided an emotional safe harbor and their union a connectedness. Larsen may have been terrified of losing Imes.

By summer, she turned her attention away from the difficulty of her situa-

---

13. Nella Larsen Imes to Carl Van Vechten, May 12, 1933, in JWJ.

14. Elizabeth Cady Stanton, "Solitude of Self," in *Feminism: The Essential Historical Writings*, ed. Miriam Schneir (New York, 1972), 157; Nella Larsen Imes to Carl Van Vechten and Fania Marinoff, n.d. [postmarked June 27, 1933], in JWJ.

tion and toward connection with others. She represented a fresh picture of "gay times" with her neighbors, the Johnsons, and of the comforts of her "rather nice" house, as well as of her new work, a novel written with a young man, who did the men and she the women, which she thought made it "rather fun to do."[15] Larsen had begun a new, joint project with Edward Donahoe, a white Oklahoman introduced to the Fisk community by his friend Tom Mabry, who had moved south to teach at Vanderbilt upon graduating from Harvard. Donahoe, along with Mabry, had worked briefly at Alfred A. Knopf's in the 1920s and while there had formed friendships with Harry Block, Larsen's editor, and John Becker, an art dealer. Donahoe and Mabry were not only racial liberals but actively sought opportunities for socializing with African Americans. Mabry became James Weldon Johnson's assistant in classes at Fisk after getting into trouble at Vanderbilt. He had invited Langston Hughes and Johnson, who had recently arrived for his new position in Nashville, to his home for a party. Mabry and Donahoe had naïvely planned the interracial party for January 23, 1932, without considering the strict social separation of the races in Nashville, particularly among the academics at Vanderbilt. Allen Tate was so enraged by the invitation that he responded with a discourse on race relations in which he stated, "My theory of the racial relations is this: there should be no social intercourse between the races unless we are willing for that to lead to marriage," and which he signed "Yours for realism and a proper respect for the colored race."[16]

At thirty-three, Donahoe was an aspiring writer at work on his first novel, *Madness in the Heart,* which was not published until 1937. He was from a wealthy family and spent much of his time sojourning in Europe, Mexico, New York, and Connecticut, where in the late thirties he bought a house outside of Stamford. For a time in the early thirties, however, he spent a large portion of the year in Nashville with Mabry, and he considered building a house outside of town. It was during this period that he met Larsen and showered her with attention at a time when she felt isolated from other close friendships.

15. Larsen Imes to Van Vechten and Marinoff, n.d. [postmarked June 27, 1933], in JWJ. Larsen does not reveal in this letter that the man is Edward Donahoe, but she does inform Dorothy Peterson of his identity. See Nella Larsen to Dorothy Peterson, n.d. [postmarked July 29, 1933], in JWJ.

16. Allen Tate to Tom Mabry, January 20, 1932, *ibid.* See also Arnold Rampersad's account of this incident and its effect upon Johnson in *The Life of Langston Hughes* (2 vols.; New York, 1986), I, 231.

Donahoe and Larsen immediately became compatible friends, though he was nine years younger than she. They encouraged each other to write, and they read each other's drafts. She was revising "Mirage," a novel begun during her fellowship year in Europe. Donahoe read it in May and reported in June that "it was *terrible*." After the accusation of plagiarism in 1930, Larsen often sought evaluations of her manuscripts. She agreed with Donahoe's estimate: "Early this month [July], I took a look at it, and I give you my word it was worse than that. It was appalling (2 l's?). The stuff was good. But the *writing!* So I've done it all over, except that chapter that made you [Dorothy Peterson] so ill, and the last. And I've changed the name to Fall Fever."[17] By Larsen's own account, the manuscript needed a major overhaul.

Together she and Donahoe began a collaborative novel, "Adrian and Evadne." She worked on developing the female characters while Donahoe developed the males. The manuscript apparently was completed, for Larsen states that it "went through Brandt and Brandt," literary agents. It may well have served primarily as a diversion for the two authors. Larsen described the novel as "a perfectly silly thing, and there are no characters in the book who have these names."[18] The novel may have been a sophisticated reworking of the Evadne story from Virgil's *Aeneid,* which presents Evadne the wife of Capaneus, one of the seven against Thebes whom Zeus struck dead with a thunderbolt for boasting that even Zeus could not prevent him from entering Thebes. Evadne threw herself onto her husband's funeral pyre and died, a model of fidelity. The collaborative novel could have been a modern satire of the myth, intended to explore Larsen's marital situation.

As life became difficult, Larsen turned her attention to her writing, just as she had in the past, particularly in 1930 when she first discovered her husband's infidelity. The revision of "Mirage" into "Fall Fever" and the writing of the women for "Adrian and Evadne" were not enough to occupy her time. She began writing in July a cathartic novel for which she used the working title "The Wingless Hour," which came from a line in Swinburne's poem "Felise":

> Can ye beat off one wave with prayer
> Can ye move mountains? bid the flower
> Take flight and turn a bird in air?

17. Nella Larsen to Dorothy Peterson, July 29, 1933, in JWJ.
18. *Ibid.*

Can ye hold fast for shine and shower
One wingless hour?

She quoted this lone stanza to Dorothy Peterson, without either identifying the poem or discussing her novel's relationship to it. It seems appropriate that Swinburne's long poem, which questions the future and bids the past "Good night, good-bye," would lend a title to one of Larsen's projected works. It was most likely the last new novel that she undertook, but there is no indication that she went beyond the initial stages of planning it. Yet she was already thinking about submitting it, along with "Fall Fever," to Brandt and Brandt, but admitting that she had promised Harry Block, her editor at Knopf, "a year or so ago to let him see them." I could of course," she decided, "send a letter with them asking Brandt and Brandt to show them to him first." [19] She made no reference to her novel "Crowning Mercy," the "white novel" that had occupied her prior to her departure for Europe in 1930.

Carl D. Brandt, son of the founder of Brandt and Brandt Literary Agents, reviewed the firm's records and concluded, "It is clear that we never actually handled [Larsen's] work, and all correspondence files from those years have long since been destroyed." A partner in the founding of the agency, Zelma Corning Brandt, though failing to remember Larsen, recalled that she "never handled her work as a literary agent." [20] Nothing, therefore, seems to have become of Larsen's approach to the Brandt literary agency.

Larsen exhibited the greatest enthusiasm during the summer for her writing and for Donahoe's friendship. She had begun to depend upon him both for companionship and for reassurance about her writing. When she pulled out a novel that she had started writing while in Malaga during 1931, she looked at it as another possible joint writing project. "We'll probably do it together. Edward the men and I the women. How do you like 'The Gilded Palm Tree' for a title?" Her mood was happier than it had been for most of the year. She was even able to laugh at herself: "You will notice that I'm getting good on titles all of a sudden." And judging her writing in "The Gilded Palm Tree" as "mostly pretty good," she refused to let the heat, an

19. Larsen to Peterson, n.d. [postmarked July 29, 1933], in JWJ.
20. Carl D. Brandt to Thadious M. Davis, December 15, 1983, and Zelma Corning Brandt to Thadious M. Davis, n.d. [postmarked December 30, 1983], both in possession of Thadious M. Davis.

old enemy of her spirits, bother her: "It's hot as hell here. Good writing weather."[21]

For an entire year, between the spring of 1932 and the summer of 1933, she lived in a world of half-truths and self-deception. Her efforts were not only for others but for herself. She was struggling to sow new dreams and to redirect her life toward the work that had brought her success and satisfaction. Her method involved an intentional obscuring of her domestic reality. The pattern of concealment had been established much earlier in her life, when she found it easier to avoid being completely honest or straightforward about herself—who she was and what affected her. She attempted to carry through in the same way once again. She projected onto her work all of her energy, and possibly her frustration, during most of the summer, but the spurt of energetic enthusiasm for writing would not last.

Her domestic situation in Nashville finally began to unravel and become untenable. As the fact that she had been supplanted in her husband's affections by a woman of the other race became public knowledge, it undermined one of her claims to individual meaning and public significance: that she was half-white. When one of the major premises for self-distinction and divination collapsed and she faced public exposure for being somehow less than the all-white woman then in her husband's life, Larsen's behavior became erratic and her insistence that *she* was a *novelist* increased. Pearl Creswell, who graduated from Fisk in 1932 and married a Fisk administrator that same year, was under the "impression that she was not as important as the other writers" at Fisk. Creswell played bridge with the Imeses and remembered how Larsen nervously touched her books at bridge. She also remembered Imes from the bridge parties: "He was a sophisticated, debonair man and seemed to like the attention of ladies or even depended on it for his image." Isaiah Creswell also recalled the bridge foursomes during 1932 and 1933, when Imes was a "reckless player," but a good one.[22]

Larsen's appraisal of her marriage alternated as it had since 1930—between acceptance of the inevitability of dissolution and anticipation that the marriage could somehow survive. It was not always apparent to others that she dreaded an end. Negative patterns of behavior, appropriate to ensuring that the inevitable would occur, dominated her actions. Her temper was furious and unpredictable. Imes's mother, though ailing, refused to

21. Larsen to Peterson, July 29, 1933, in JWJ.

22. Pearl Creswell, interview with author, March 10, 1987; Isaiah Creswell interview, March 11, 1987.

move into the house with Larsen; one visit to the household was "too ghastly a time," she said, for her to consider another stay.[23]

The portrait that emerges of Larsen during 1933 is one of a frantic woman who, though making a deliberate effort to be different and eccentric, was actually crying out for affection and sympathy. She took drastic measures, feigned suicide by cutting her wrists and smearing blood over the house.[24] But she made no effort to seek help or leave Nashville.

Wild and damaging stories circulated around Nashville and Fisk about her reactions to her husband's friendship with the other woman. One rumor was so widespread and persistent that it appeared in the headlines of a national African-American newspaper: "Recall 'Jump' From Window." Reportedly, Larsen had "jumped or had fallen out of a window and done herself bodily harm," though the official version from the Fisk administration was that "Mrs. Imes had fallen down the steps and broken her leg."[25] In fact, Larsen had fallen out of a first-story window, and according to Houchins, who believed the fall was intentional to build a case against Imes, the ground below was soft from the landscaping being done on the premises.[26] Whatever the motivations, Larsen's fall from a window is suggestive of Laura Riding's jump from a window in London when she and Robert Graves were involved in complicated marital relations. Larsen knew of the Riding-Graves incident from her stay in Majorca, but whether she was consciously or deviously duplicating it is not apparent. In a more bizarre twist of coincidence, Larsen's fall also replicates those of two of her fictional characters: Clare Kendry in *Passing* and the unnamed male in "Freedom," for whom an open window provided an escape from their personal entrapments.

The sensationalized "news" report of the dramatic events went to explain the alleged background of the incident: "Professor Imes . . . for a long time lived alone at Fisk while his wife was in New York or abroad. During that time he was seen frequently with a white member of Fisk university's administrative staff at social affairs and off the campus." The situation resulted in action being taken by university officials, "when gossiping tongues wagged," to have Mrs. Imes on the campus and to provide a home for the

23. Elizabeth Imes quoted in Elmer Imes to Thomas E. Jones, July 22, 1933, in Jones Papers.

24. Houchins interview, March 12, 1984.

25. "Fisk Professor Divorced by N. Y. Novelist," Baltimore *Afro-American*, October 7, 1933, p. 1. "Recall 'Jump' from Window" was one of three subheadlines appearing with the story. In a separate column on the front page, the newspaper carried a photograph of Larsen with the caption "Broke Leg Now She's Divorced."

26. Houchins interview, March 12, 1984.

couple. But, the explosive newspaper account concluded, after Larsen's jump or fall, "the white member of the university staff with whom Professor Imes had been friendly, offered her resignation," which was accepted.[27]

While the Baltimore *Afro-American*'s account may have been more gossip than news, it had kernels of truth: Elmer Imes had, in fact, developed a friendship with Ethel Gilbert, the Fisk director of public relations, and their relationship had become quite public during his wife's absence. What few knew was that the two had become friends in New York before either moved to Fisk, and that their relationship had already begun to threaten the Imes marriage in 1930. At Fisk, Imes became Gilbert's frequent escort for campus events and chapel programs. Although Fisk, then isolated from Nashville proper, had a racially integrated faculty and promoted an image of family among the employees and students, it was still a southern black institution. The white president, active in raising funds for the school's survival during the Depression and already having cut salaries by 10 percent on July 1, 1932, feared the whole affair would ruin the school in the eyes of white philanthropists.[28] Larsen's volatile response was added fuel for the scandal.

Gilbert submitted her resignation in a letter of December 15, 1932: "It is increasingly apparent to me, as it must be to you, that I cannot remain at Fisk. It was very unwise of me to allow myself to be persuaded to stay this year. I knew last spring that I shouldn't do it. But I do feel a deep obligation to Fisk in the matter of the choir [Fisk Jubilee Singers] tour and also . . . that I should do what I could to keep up what those supposedly wiser than I called 'appearances.' Personally, I've always liked honesty and frankness better than appearances unaccompanied by them." Actually, throughout the spring and summer of 1932, she had been actively negotiating for a campus house to be built for her and had enlisted the help of her old friend Paul Cravath, head of the trustees, in her efforts. Cravath offered to provide furnishings for the house, as Gilbert, a divorcée, intended to use it as an unofficial center for students; President Jones, nevertheless, was reluctant, for he objected to providing a home for "divided families," and he had been advised by the trustees that "in view of the present depression," a larger portion of both his and Gilbert's time should be devoted to "money raising."[29]

27. "Fisk Professor Divorced by N. Y. Novelist," 1.

28. Thomas E. Jones to Ethel B. Gilbert, June—Twenty-fourth—1932, in Jones Papers.

29. Ethel B. Gilbert to Thomas E. Jones, Sunday, December 15 [1932], *ibid.;* Ethel B. Gilbert to Thomas E. Jones, March 25, 1932, *ibid.;* Thomas E. Jones to Ethel B. Gilbert, April—Twenty Sixth—1932, *ibid.*

In tendering the resignation, which she wanted effective March 1, Gilbert suggested that Jones use the trustees' decision about the increase in time for fund raising as a reason for her leaving the job: "I am not asking any special favors but I do think my service to the University and my willingness to leave . . . and save the University further embarrassment, earns that consideration. . . . The reason for my leaving as far as the general public is concerned can be that I cannot do road work and you must have some one who can. The less said by anyone the better. I want no defense of me from anybody, no apology for me. Making a living will be difficult at best." [30]

Jones, who from his inauguration in 1926 had worked diligently to strengthen the school's image, did not respond officially to the resignation until February, 1933, when he accepted it for the end of the fiscal year and skirted the issue of scandal by stressing his understanding that the "action is being taken because of your [Gilbert's] distaste for road work in the solicitation of funds. Since the finances of the University will not permit us to engage both a field man and an office secretary in charge of publicity and finance, and since it seems that during these times a field secretary is most essential, I have no other course left than to accept your resignation." [31] In following Gilbert's suggestion, he indicated how valuable her work had been to the institution. Further, he extended her employment through the fiscal year, so that the termination of her work on campus did not end her fund-raising duties for the university. Gilbert moved to New York City, where she enlisted support for Fisk's endowment drive, opened an office for that purpose at 150 Nassau Street, and received her salary for her efforts. [32] Her removal from Nashville in 1933, however, ended neither the relationship with Imes nor the spread of gossip.

The front-page account in a nationally circulated newspaper and the publicity about domestic discord aggravated Larsen's embarrassment in Nashville. The situation with Imes, who maintained silence and reserve, clearly caused her great consternation and motivated impetuous behavior, though some members of the community believed that her actions were calculated to build a public case against Imes to effect a large divorce settlement. Yet she apparently was genuinely hurt by the situation and confused about

---

30. Gilbert to Jones, Sunday, December 15 [1932], *ibid.*
31. Thomas E. Jones to Ethel B. Gilbert, February Sixth, Nineteen Thirty Three, *ibid.*
32. See Thomas E. Jones to Ethel B. Gilbert, n.d. [week of March 11, 1933], and Ethel B. Gilbert to Thomas E. Jones and Members of the Fisk Endowment Committee, June 29, 1933, both *ibid.*

how to proceed. Her ambivalent behavior perhaps stemmed from a self-conscious awareness of herself as the object of public observation, but it was manifested in exaggerated, theatrical forms. And it was entirely possible that, as she insisted years later, she loved her husband.[33]

In July, 1933, Nella Larsen Imes finally made a decision to divorce Elmer Imes in Nashville, where, as she reported to her confidante, Dorothy Peterson, "it can be done discretly [*sic*] in *ten* days for a hundred dollars or so. Can you imagine that?" She cited eight grounds for divorce in Tennessee, including "Desertion for two years" and "Failure of a wife to return to the state if husband is living and working in Tennessee," to which she called Peterson's attention: "Note these last two: It explains a lot, especially why I am here still after coming for a mere visit." Her wording suggests that she was calculating her culpability should Imes seek to divorce her. The marriage had deteriorated to the extent that she feared Imes would ignore possible damage to his career at Fisk and file for divorce on the grounds of her deserting him. But Imes apparently had no intention of taking action himself, not because he thought the marriage could be saved, but because he believed that the gentlemanly course was to let the woman divorce the man. He would that July, however, admit to having gone through a "year of agony . . . catering to Mrs. Imes' notions," to being determined to meet her conditions, so that he "would not have to endure another such year."[34]

Larsen's own assessment was not without mixed humor and cynicism: "As I see it you pays your money and you takes your choice. And that's that. . . . Much simpler, don't you think, to get it here quietly, quickly, and cheaply, and be done with it? No waiting around to establish residence. No hanging about to have a decree made final. A session with a good lawyer, a morning in court. And then finis!"[35] A month later, she chose "cruelty" as the grounds for her divorce on August 30, 1933.

The divorce hearing took place in the First Circuit Court of Davidson County, Nashville, with Judge A. G. Rutherford presiding. Larsen's attorney, W. H. G. Caldwell, had prepared a detailed bill, which charged Imes with "such cruel and inhuman conduct towards complainant [Larsen] as renders it unsafe and improper for her to cohabit with him and be under his

33. Houchins interviews, March 12 and December 30, 1984; Carolyn Lane and Alice L. Carper, interview with author, May 5, 1985.

34. Larsen to Peterson, n.d. [postmarked July 29, 1933], in JWJ; Houchins interview, December 30, 1984; E. Imes to Jones, July 22, 1933, in Jones Papers.

35. Larsen to Peterson, n.d. [postmarked July 28, 1933], in JWJ.

dominion and control." Judge Rutherford ruled that the proof was sufficient and that Imes "has offered such indignities to [Larsen's] person as to render her condition intolerable and thereby forced her to withdraw and that he has abandoned the complainant and turned her out of doors and refused and neglected to provide for her." Even for a time during which fault and grounds had to be established for divorce, the complaints against Imes seemed more severe than usually necessary in such cases. Caldwell had served his client well, because the severity of the charges meant that Larsen was not only granted the divorce but also given a generous settlement, for a Depression-era proceeding. In fact, so generous were the financial terms that the Baltimore *Afro-American,* in reporting the divorce, used "Imes Must Pay" as a subheadline for the story. A student in the class Imes was teaching when a newsboy came around calling out the headline "Imes Must Pay" recalled that Imes "turned and left the class without saying a word." [36]

Rutherford's decree ordered Imes to pay an initial sum of $375.00 before the first of September and monthly alimony: "on or before the 5th of each month thereafter beginning with the month of October, 1933, and including August 1934 the defendant will pay . . . the sum of $175.00 per month, and on or before the 5th of September, 1934, and on or before the 5th of each month thereafter until further orders of this court, the defendant will pay . . . the sum of $150.00." Although there was no other cash settlement, Larsen was allowed to select whatever furniture she desired from their house, and Imes was directed to have it crated and stored until she wanted it shipped to her new residence. At that point he would be obligated to pay for the shipment. Imes also was directed to pay for all costs involved in the divorce proceedings. [37] He never recovered from the dire financial strain the divorce placed upon him.

One week later, Larsen was in Chicago writing casually to Dorothy Peterson and Grace Johnson about the people she had seen socially there. In the middle of one letter, she shifted abruptly to her purpose in writing: "I divorced Elmer last Wednesday very quickly and quietly. He is getting married tomorrow in Wellington Ohio. The new Mrs. Imes (or shall I say the second) will live in the North while he works in the South. It wont [sic] be

36. First Circuit Court of Davidson County, Tennessee, Minute Book 76, p. 207, August 30, 1933, in Circuit Court Clerk's Office, Davidson County, Nashville; Baltimore *Afro-American,* October 21, 1933, p. 1; Louis Roberts, telephone conversation with author, March 29, 1988.

37. First Circuit Court Minute Book 76, p. 207.

much different from last year. She was on [the] road a great deal and he was always away meeting her places. So much for that!"[38] Her air of unconcern was a mask to hide her emotional state, which showed through in the appearance and form of the letter. The handwriting is scrawled, though the letter is not a hasty note; it is one of her longer and more extended pieces of correspondence. It ends several times, but each time resumes with a new subject that invariably returns to Elmer Imes and the divorce. She could not bring herself to admit, even to a close friend, how disturbed she actually was about the official dissolution of her marriage. Two levels of discourse collide in the letter.

On the surface, Larsen's preoccupation is with practical matters, particularly planning her financial affairs. "When I get my business affairs settled here I will have a few pennies which I shall probably put into an annuity for safety's sake."[39] Her "few pennies" would amount to more income annually than any of her past salaries as a nurse or a librarian. The money would provide her with financial independence and security, which she had never had.

Her practicality about finances, however, did not disguise a second level of discourse, represented in the disclosure: "There is nothing else to tell. Oh! yes! Elmer expects to be a father along in February or March of next year. I put that swell." A degree of bitterness lies imbedded at the center of the seemingly offhanded remark. Although there does not appear to be any evidence to support Larsen's statement about the expected child, that she believed Elmer and his intended bride would become parents was an added sore point for forty-two-year-old Larsen, who had never had children but had once remarked that she had hopes for the "luxury of ten children." Neither bitterness nor anger would surface directly in her statements. Shortly after the divorce, she told a reporter that she "held no rancor against either party."[40]

Larsen did not address directly the important issue of her feelings about Imes and the breakup of her marriage. During the 1920s she had operated under the presumption of her husband's affection and had enjoyed status as his wife. When she had remarked on his absences, she registered both a

---

38. Nella Larsen to Dorothy Peterson, Wednesday 6th [postmarked September 6, 1933], in JWJ.

39. *Ibid.*

40. *Ibid.*; Mary Rennels, New York *Telegram*, April 13, 1929, in SCF; "Love Triangle Behind Fisk Univ. Divorce," Baltimore *Afro-American*, October 21, 1933, p. 2.

complaint about his inattention, particularly his leaving her without an escort, and an announcement of his social prestige, which reflected and magnified her own. She had acknowledged, in effect, the special place in the black community that Imes held, because so few African Americans had Ph.D. degrees, and even fewer were scientists. In the twenties, too, she had sought a measure of independence from her husband by establishing her own interests and career. During those years, she had chosen her own name rather than his for the publication of her novels. But her efforts were intended initially to assert a part of her own separate identity while still enjoying the public identity created by her marriage. Whether she loved Imes or felt great affection for him was something that remained private. Some of her acquaintances maintained that she did not love him, but others insisted that she did. That she did not care about her husband's attention to someone else, as she once stated, is highly suspect for two reasons, one conjectural and the other factual.

First of all, it is unlikely that she did not care, since she subjected herself to the private misery of those "terrible" and "complicated" days in Nashville during the year before the divorce. Material comfort and social status alone cannot fully account for her actions, especially because by all accounts Larsen was a proud woman. Given her pride and the almost certain humiliation stemming from Imes's association with another women, it would appear that had she not cared for her husband, she would not have endured living with him, not even to build a case for a divorce. And the fifteen years of her knowing and being married to Imes nearly duplicated the number of years that she had spent growing up with her family, which she had left at age sixteen. The intimacy and companionship she had shared with him measured even more time than on an absolute scale of chronological years, because the period covered fifteen years of her adult life in which she had become much of what she dreamed possible for herself and her development.

Secondly, according to Elizabeth Shaffer Hull, the daughter of Van Vechten's sister and Larsen's friend in the early thirties, Larsen was "in love" with her husband and "cold reason" could not get her over it. Hull's marriage dissolved at the same time as Larsen's, and for a while the two spent more time together than usual, mainly talking about their situations and commiserating with each other. In November, 1933, shortly after Larsen's divorce and return to New York, Hull revealed to Grace Johnson: "Yesterday I saw Nella, from lunch until midnight. . . . Both Nella and I are ready for any insane asylum that will take us in. Grace, what do two gals do that are in love? . . . Aren't people, especially love sick people, messes?" Although in this account, Hull did not refer directly to Imes, she appeared to make her case analogous to Larsen's: "I'm in love with that old man of mine. And he's far away and I guess not in love with me."[41]

Following the divorce, the *Afro-American* presented Larsen, Imes, and Gilbert in extremely favorable terms, despite its tabloid style of covering the story in a front-page article, "Love Triangle Behind Fisk Univ. Divorce." Larsen gave an impartial statement to the press: "'There may be two or even three sides to this matter. . . . but I am not interested in sides. Important to me, was getting the divorce—the situation demanded it, and the exercise of care lest impudent tongues speculate on the situation to the discredit and the injury of the University.'" Her calmly rational and dispassionate remarks probably helped to diffuse the situation and alleviate embarrassment: "'we parted quite amiably, . . . and I should be surprised to learn that Dr. Imes had subsequently made any unflattering allegations.'"[42] In offering the press the image of a friendly divorce between amiable parties, Larsen deflated rumors of bitterness and vindictiveness and simultaneously assured that Imes could not publicly contradict the image that she presented of him without undermining his credibility.

While it is clear that none of the primary figures in such highly publicized events could escape without scars, Larsen emerged in the media as a stoical woman, readily admitting that "she had lost something, and that her life had been disrupted," but that nonetheless she intended to go on with her life and work. She admitted that loss and disruption may have occurred "perhaps because of 'weakness' and 'shiftiness,'" but she did not explain her meaning.[43] Appropriately, she would not address the allegations about her attempt to injure herself or speculations about her frustrations. Considering the adverse circumstances, Larsen demonstrated extraordinary control. She had developed style in the years since the publication of *Quicksand,* and she displayed it when public attention focused on her.

In fact, Larsen may well have sought out the media following her divorce. An earlier news story, entitled "Fisk Professor Divorced by N.Y. Novelist" and followed by three subheads ("Friends Think Love Cooled While Wife Wintered in Europe," "Recall 'Jump' From Window," and "Friendly Com-

---

41. Elizabeth Shaffer Hull to Grace Nail Johnson, November 22, 1933, in JWJ. In her conversation with Hull, Larsen may have been referring to Edward Donahoe, rather than to Elmer Imes, as her love interest; however, she was guarded in what she revealed about their relationship or her perception of it.

42. Larsen quoted in "Love Triangle," 2.

43. *Ibid.*

forter's Resignation Accepted"), contained information about Larsen's current writing project and recent achievements:

> Mrs. Imes, as Nella Larsen, wrote "Quicksand" and "Passing," two novels published by Knopf, and is understood to be now preparing a third novel, "Fall Fever." Mrs. Imes is now in the East. She is colored. One of her parents was white.
>
> Several years ago she spent a winter with her white relatives in Denmark. She spent the winter of 1931 with Dorothy Peterson, New York school teacher, in LaPalma, Majorca, in the Balearic Isles. She was then said to be working on a novel which she termed "Mirage."[44]

The details are congruent with Larsen's various attempts at self-fashioning. There is no basis in fact for her having spent a winter "several years ago," before 1933 with relatives in Denmark, and she is the most likely source for the representation of her connection to white relatives. It seems plausible that she released the information herself in an attempt to manipulate the press in order to salvage her image.

In private, too, she handled the events with equanimity, if not candor. Although Peterson was her closest personal friend, she was not immediately privy to Larsen's feelings about the divorce and the attendant publicity. What Larsen wrote to Peterson was as impersonal as her remarks to Grace and Jim Johnson, her Nashville neighbors. "Thank you both," she wrote to the Johnsons, "for your letters and for your quiet understanding friendship. . . . I terminated my domestic affairs just before I left. Very quickly, quietly and easily. But I didn't tell anyone. . . . I feel guilty about that but thought it better to say nothing to anyone. . . . I shall—or rather I may—be in Nashville a day or so a little later to settle about the household effects, though it seems silly to set any store on mere material things now." Her rituals of behavior and sense of personal decorum would not allow her to vent emotions in words. Self-contained and image-conscious, she would write little else of extended length to her friends after her letters of September 6, 1933, the week after the divorce. She effectively concluded her correspondence with a statement that was perhaps an emblem of her public stance and her private emotions: "The World's Fair is just as boring as the

44. "Fisk Professor Divorced by N. Y. Novelist," 1.

Paris Colonial Exposition. I said then I would never go inside one of the things again. Well, I did. And it was exactly the same."[45]

Years before, she had revealed that for her the "'unforgivable sin' is being bored."[46] At the end of her major correspondence, she admitted to allowing herself to be bored, which might be an indirect comment on her situation days after the divorce when she could not perhaps control her emotions or dictate her responses to the extent that she had believed possible and important. Her offhand reference to the 1930 Paris Colonial Exposition as comparable to the 1933 Chicago World's Fair ("A Century of Progress") repeated the kind of cosmopolitan and international perspective she sought for herself and her activities. Her comparison between Europe and America, and her inclusion that the symbolic displays of both were "boring," dismissed, in effect, any prospect for finding personal satisfaction in the projections of the larger world on either continent. It was perhaps her concession to the failure of external environments to provide private contentment and to confirm personal meaning. It marked, too, the conclusion of that phase of Larsen's life that had reached a climax in Paris.

The Chicago that Larsen returned to after the divorce was a city once again celebrating itself along with the "Century of Progress" fair. When she arrived on September 3, 1933, she found Automotive Week under way at the fair, and a special program in the court of the Hall of Science to commemorate Labor Day, September 4. The Hall of Science featured motion pictures on scientific topics, while the Hall of Religion had daily organ recitals at 2:00 in the afternoon. There was also a rodeo twice a day at Soldier Field, a floating theater near the Hall of Science with music and plays each evening, and "Wings of a Century," a Pageant of Transportation, at 7:00, 8:00, and 9:00 P.M. near 33rd Street. The fair offered a diverse selection of entertainments during Larsen's visit, but she was in no mood to enjoy any of them.[47]

Her choice of Chicago as a haven from the turmoil of the divorce is curious. She may have returned to Chicago to avoid New York and her certain-to-be-curious friends there. Her surviving family had long since left Chicago for California, and for years she had lacked intimacy with relatives. Despite

45. Nella Larsen Imes to Grace Nail and James Weldon Johnson, September 6, 1933, in JWJ; Larsen to Peterson, Wednesday 6th [postmarked September 6, 1933], *ibid.*

46. Rennels, New York *Telegram*, April 13, 1929.

47. Junior League of Chicago, *Chicago Calendar: Current and Cultural Events for Two Weeks, September 1st–15th, 1933* (N.p., n.d.).

her memories of an unhappy family life in Chicago, the city still represented an aspect of her youth that offered a measure of comfort and familiarity. She had returned not to family, but to friends who had known her since childhood. The retired Pullman porter John Mayo and his wife, Mattie, opened their home to her when she needed to escape Nashville. The parents of her girlhood friend Pearl offered her an unqualified emotional support. She wrote her letters to friends in the East from their home at 4732 Prairie Avenue, and asked that they write to her there in care of Mayo.[48] Yet even with the hospitality of friends who had cared about her as a child and who still cared enough to take her in though she had not visited Chicago for at least twenty years, Larsen did not choose to remain in Chicago. It was not only that the city was different from the one she had known as a youth, but also that she had become a New Yorker. There was no returning to the Midwestern environment. She did not consider remaining in Chicago, despite knowing that life in her adopted city would be difficult.

After returning east in 1933, Nella Larsen wrote only occasionally to her friends, and then primarily only to congratulate them on their achievements. For herself, there would be few public achievements to acknowledge. Yet she did not withdraw completely in the middle thirties; she severed some ties but maintained connection with a few members of her old circle of friends in New York. The practice of dashing off letters that had characterized exchanges of news among friends in the 1920s had been eroded, partly by more widespread use of the telephone, and partly by the dispersing of the social scene in which she had functioned. Upon her return to New York from Chicago, she lived with Dorothy Peterson—initially in Peterson's family home at 380 Monroe Avenue, Brooklyn, and then in the downtown 320 Second Avenue apartment that Peterson had maintained since the early 1920s—rather than in a place of her own.

There was no reason for her to resume residency in Harlem. She had spent long periods away from the city between 1930 and 1933, and the large concentration of lower-class African Americans in Harlem put her off. Her absences had partly alienated her from the social and cultural activities of the black middle class. Increasingly she relied upon her association with the ever-active Peterson for a social life, and Peterson, whether from her family home in Brooklyn or her Manhattan apartment, had become more involved with New York theater life and less with Harlem's middle class. These fac-

48. See Larsen to Peterson, Wednesday 6th [postmarked September 6, 1933], and Larsen Imes to Grace Nail and James Weldon Johnson, September 6, 1933, both in JWJ.

tors, combined with Larsen's divorce and its attendant publicity, account for her retreat from Harlem, which by 1933 was a completely different place from the one to which she had moved at the height of the New Negro Renaissance in 1927.

A few years had made an enormous difference in the quality of life in Harlem. In the same October 21, 1933, issue of the Baltimore *Afro-American* that had carried the news of Larsen's rather lucrative divorce settlement was an article, "Hungry Harlem Gay 'Neath Tears," reporting the findings of an Urban League survey of Harlem in the Depression. Out of a population of 250,000, only 12,500 Harlemites were employed, and 40,000 out of a potential working population of 62,500, or approximately 66 percent, were unemployed. In canvassing a typical block, 133rd Street between Seventh and Lenox avenues, the Urban League found that 70 percent of the tenants were unemployed, 18 percent ill, 60 percent behind in their rent, and 33 percent receiving aid from charitable organizations.[49] While the Urban League's survey may not have been "scientific," it aptly portrayed the poverty and dismal conditions in the community upon Larsen's return from Nashville.

The Depression was a reality that sophisticated New Yorkers could no longer avoid. Larsen herself, sometimes seemingly oblivious to the suffering of the masses, could not have ignored the changes that had taken place during the first few years of the 1930s. On Black Thursday, October 24, 1929, when the stock market had crashed, Larsen had been in New York, but Wall Street was far removed from everyday life in Harlem. While in Europe, she had received signals of the extent of the Depression, signals that directly affected her. When the Guggenheim Foundation denied her request for an extension of her fellowship on the bases of shortages of funds and of more applicants in need of opportunities, her immediate response to the foundation was: "I do agree that others should be given opportunity, especially in these hard times. My husband writes that America is quite a different place these days owing to the tightness of money there. So I do understand."[50]

Larsen's style of living and observations about her surroundings do not indicate, however, that the Depression was of critical concern to her. She was economically secure and capable of providing for herself. Her world,

---

49. "Hungry Harlem Gay 'Neath Tears," Baltimore *Afro-American*, October 21, 1933, p. 2.

50. Nella Larsen Imes to Henry Allen Moe, March 31, 1931, in John Simon Guggenheim Memorial Foundation files, New York.

nonetheless, was not insulated enough for her to escape evidences of changed conditions in the United States, especially in Harlem, where, following World War I, rural southern émigrés had converged in seeking economic opportunity. As early as 1931, while Larsen was in Europe, the *Report of the Committee on Negro Housing* had informed President Herbert Hoover that black populations in urban areas had little chance of improving their economic status because they were trapped in a cycle of disproportionately high rents and low-paying jobs or unemployment. Those African Americans who had the least possibility of transforming their lives were the undereducated and unskilled laborers who had flocked to urban areas from the South.

By 1933, the dim economic prospects for urban blacks had made an impact upon artists and white-collar professionals as well. A number of the middle-class African Americans whom Larsen had known in the 1920s had left Harlem to find work. Several had turned to the segregated schools in the South for employment. Arna Bontemps, for instance, had moved to Oakwood, a small Seventh-Day Adventist school in Alabama, to support his growing family. Others among the artists and writers had found that the depressed economy meant diminished opportunity for support, whether from white philanthropists, who had more pressing needs for their often-diminished resources, or from New York publishers, who had begun to rely increasingly on marketability in the face of limited budgets. The veneer of good race relations and assimilationist attitudes had not removed the marginal economic status from "New Negro" artists, or from the educated "talented tenth," so that both groups were particularly vulnerable to the adverse economic conditions, though they may not have suffered as much as their black counterparts among the domestic and day laborers.

Alain Locke, the stalwart and optimistic shaper of the Renaissance, sadly concluded in the mid-1930s: "No cultural advance is safe without some sound economic underpinning, the foundation of a decent and reasonably secure average standard of living; and no emerging elite—artistic, professional or mercantile—can suspend itself in thin air over an abyss of a mass of unemployment stranded in an over-expensive, disease- and crime-ridden slum. It is easier to dally over black Bohemia or revel in the hardy survivals of Negro art and culture than to contemplate this dark Harlem of semi-starvation, mass exploitation and seething unrest. But turn we must."[51]

Locke analyzed the devastating economic reality in the pages of the same

51. Alain Locke, "Harlem: Dark Weather-Vane," *Survey Graphic*, XXV (August, 1936), 457.

journal where ten years earlier he had announced a cultural awakening and the arrival of the "New Negro." Although he and others had not acknowledged the "deep undertow" existing in Harlem during "the few bright years of prosperity" in the 1920s, Locke was sobered into accepting that "there is no cure or saving magic in poetry and art, an emerging generation of talent, or in international prestige and interracial recognition, for unemployment or precarious marginal employment, for high rents, high mortality rates, civic neglect, capitalistic exploitation on the one hand and radical exploitation on the other." [52] He included the two key components of Nella Larsen's aesthetic vision, "international prestige" and "interracial recognition," that had fired her creativity and numbed her sensitivity to the masses of African Americans.

Yet while the Harlem riot of March 19 and 20, 1935, and, in its aftermath, the findings of Mayor Fiorello H. LaGuardia's commission of investigation forced Locke to confront an unavoidable truth, there is little evidence that Larsen faced its unwelcome reality. She, like other writers as diverse as H. L. Mencken, Joseph Hergesheimer, and James Branch Cabell (all of whom she admired), could not directly respond to the Depression or the social contexts of the 1930s. But unlike the situation of white writers in New York, Larsen's familiar territory was in dire straits. With 204,630 blacks crowded into Harlem by 1935, and over 76 percent of them restricted to jobs in domestic and personal service, the "city within a city" took on an edge of desperation and impoverishment that LaGuardia's commission linked directly to "a denial of the fundamental rights of a people to a livelihood," so that no "amount of charity, good will, social privileges, or political freedom [could] compensate for the enforced idleness and poverty." [53] Larsen feared that this combination of idleness and poverty would engulf her.

She had compelling reasons to escape Harlem and to turn her back on the problems it represented. Brooklyn and downtown Manhattan, which had always appealed to her, offered more amenable conditions and surroundings. Because she had also the difficult emotional task of overcoming and adjusting to her personal disappointments and miseries as a divorced woman alone, she found the Lower East Side environment a more receptive

---

52. *Ibid.,* 457–58.

53. *The Complete Report of Mayor LaGuardia's Commission on the Harlem Riot of March 19, 1935,* rpr. in *Mass Violence in America,* ed. Robert M. Fogelson and Richard E. Rubenstein (New York, 1969), 28, 30, 43.

space. It did not immediately display economic bleakness. There, moreover, she could function in a kind of anonymity impossible in Harlem, where, though the general African-American population was large, the group of upwardly mobile African Americans was small enough to encourage intimacy. Downtown she could live without the distraction of explaining her marital problems to those who were close associates of Dr. and Mrs. Elmer Imes, or of justifying her divorced status to those striving middle-class African Americans who were unaccustomed to the dissolution of marriages among their kind.

Nella Larsen Imes centered her life in a new circle, both spatially and emotionally. Known primarily as Nella Larsen, she did not completely drop her married name, because it added to her sense of respectability. Although she hinted at the possibility of another marriage, her main objective was the reestablishment of an independent life. Toward that end she settled on the periphery of a loosely connected group whose common denominator was that they were what she called "the artistic type."

Her mainstay was Dorothy Peterson, whose varied assortment of friends in New York and Connecticut made up Larsen's circle. Peterson and her brother, Sidney, who was then practicing medicine, remained almost familial in their relationship with Larsen. The others with whom Larsen associated were Elizabeth Shaffer Hull, who had become an aspiring writer; Edna Harris Thomas, an actress from the Lafayette Stock Company, and her husband, Lloyd Thomas; Josephine Leighton, an executive secretary at the Guggenheim Foundation; Fredi Washington, an actress who headed the Negro Actors Guild; Jimmy Daniels, a singer and nightclub performer; Olivia Wyndham, who used her farm in Sandy Hook, Connecticut, as a retreat for a number of New York artists; Kenneth McPherson, the husband of novelist Bryher (Winnifred Ellerman); and Andrew Meyer, who studied literature at New York University and worked in Wall Street. It was an interracial group with a decidedly bohemian and intellectual bent. Some in this circle of friends were openly lesbian and homosexual. During the mid- and late 1930s, Larsen's associates were still able to enjoy the best in arts and culture that New York had to offer, despite the general shortage of money.

For nearly five years, between 1933 and 1938, Larsen socialized with her artistic friends downtown and enjoyed excursions to Connecticut. Olivia Wyndham's house near Newtown became her summer home away from the city during the summers of 1935 and 1936; Nancy Cunard had given Wyndham and Edna Thomas, who had appeared in *Porgy* and "passed" as "Asiatic Indian" in Connecticut, the money to purchase the farm. Infrequently,

Larsen ventured back to Harlem for an evening's entertainment—benefits for the Negro Actors Guild, shows at the Hot Cha, where Billie Holiday sang, at Jimmy Daniels' Bronze Club, and at the Savoy, or late-night breakfasts at Clinton Moore's restaurant. She appeared then to be a "cultured, matured woman," who was "friendly and outgoing," but "a bit of a snob about non-intellectuals." Unemployed, she was known among her friends and acquaintances as a writer, despite the fact that she published nothing during the thirties and felt guilty about not having completed her Guggenheim project.[54]

There is no indication that Larsen attempted to pass for white. In *Intellectual Memoirs, New York 1936–1938,* Mary McCarthy uses race to contextualize a brief description of her friendship with Nella Larsen:

> Besides going to the Savoy Ballroom on Friday nights, John and I had black friends, who used to come to our apartment, nervously ushered by us past the elevator boys: Nella Larsen, the novelist (*Passing*), Dorothy Peterson, the actress (she played in the Negro *Macbeth*), and her brother, who was a doctor. They were high up in the black bourgeoisie. Nella Larsen told stories that always contained the sentence "And there I was, in the fullest of full evening dress." She lived downtown, near Irving Place. The Petersons lived in Brooklyn—we liked them, not simply because they were black, and were proud of the friendship.[55]

McCarthy, whose apartment on Beekman Place was a center for young intellectuals, racializes Larsen and positions her along with the Petersons in a class paradigm.

Larsen's frequent associates during the mid-1930s were mainly whites and her trips to Harlem were made with mixed groups of blacks and whites, which may have been perceived by some Harlemites as evidence that she had left the race. Her daytime activities in downtown Manhattan were usually conducted as well with whites. When Andrew Meyer's mother, Mayme Frye Meyer, moved from the Midwest in 1936, she became Larsen's frequent daytime companion for movies, sightseeing, gallery shows, and shop-

54. Andrew Meyer to Thadious M. Davis, January 27, 1982, in possession of Thadious M. Davis; Andrew Meyer to Thadious M. Davis, April 14, 1982, *ibid.*

55. Mary McCarthy, *Intellectual Memoirs: New York, 1936–1938* (New York, 1992), 27.

ping, because Nella Larsen was one of the few people that Meyer knew who was not working or seeking work. The pair ventured out on excursions almost daily. Both loved picture shows; they saw Greta Garbo in *Camille* twice at the Capitol Theater on Broadway and Fifty-first Street because that 1936 film, directed by George Cukor and based on a play by Alexandre Dumas *fils,* was a Larsen favorite. When they heard that a new Georgia O'Keeffe painting was at the Elizabeth Arden Fifth Avenue Salon, they went immediately to see it. They discovered that the painting was in Arden's private apartment, but were rewarded for their enthusiasm by an invitation to see it there and have tea with Arden.[56] Anyone from Harlem could easily have spotted Larsen around midtown Manhattan, in the theater district, or in Greenwich Village with Mayme Meyer or other whites and falsely assumed that she was passing.

Slipping across the color line was not uncommon in New York. In fact, during the 1920s, many of the fair-skinned women Larsen knew occasionally passed as white for convenience—for service in a restaurant, shop, or hotel. And in Harlem, stories of someone's passing downtown for a job or other opportunities circulated frequently. In a 1925 essay, "Color Lines," Walter White reported that one prominent "white" surgeon in New York was actually a black man from the South, and that one "white" woman well-placed in the world of the arts in the city was also a black southerner by birth. To these two primary examples, White added "at least one man high in the field of journalism, a certain famous singer, [and] several prominent figures of the stage," all of whom were passing "for wider opportunity and for freedom from race prejudice." Although many who crossed the color line were visibly white in appearance, many others were, like Larsen, swarthy in color but "passable" as Mediterranean Europeans, particularly Spanish and French, as Cubans, and as Latin or South Americans. Walter White's own wife, Gladys, had passed for "everything from a Spanish grande dame to an American Indian" during their 1927 trip to Europe.[57] Arnold Rampersad points to Elsie Roxborough, a one-time friend of Langston Hughes, who in the 1930s renamed herself "Pat Rico" and passed for white while modeling in New York; still living as a white in 1949, Roxborough, or "Mona Manet," died of a barbiturate overdose on Manhattan's

56. Meyer to Davis, April 14, 1982; Andrew G. and Kay Meyer, interview with author, May 25, 1982.

57. Walter White, "Color Lines," *Survey Graphic,* VI (March, 1925), 681; Walter White to Carl Van Vechten, July 30, 1927, in JWJ.

East Side.[58] Barrington Guy, one of the entertainers in Larsen's group of friends during the mid-1930s, did eventually cross the color line. Larsen, however, did not pass or assume a "white" identity during her years in lower Manhattan.

Years earlier, she had suggested one reason she would not pass: "with my economic status it's better to be a negro [*sic*]." She meant that the African-American middle class lived well above the status of their white counterparts. Claude McKay observed the same class phenomenon in Jessie Fauset: "She belonged to that closed decorous circle of Negro society, which consists of persons who live proudly like the better class of whites, except that they do so on much less money." There were, nevertheless, several instances of Larsen's casually passing, mainly for convenience or experiment. One she revealed in a 1932 letter written to Van Vechten from Nashville: "You will be amused that I who have never tried this much discussed 'passing' stunt have waited until I reached the deep south to put it over. Grace Johnson and I drove over fifty miles south of here the other day and then walked into the best restaurant in a rather conservative town called Murphreesbourough [*sic*] and demanded lunch and *got* it, plus all the service in the world and an invitation to return."[59] She enjoyed the idea of having deceived white people, especially southern whites, who based their conceptions of blacks on appearances without knowing the reality of black life.

The second incident of casual passing was revealed by an acquaintance who had heard the story from Tom Mabry and Larsen herself. It seems that Mabry, who was white, and Larsen were traveling together to Nashville, and along the way she pretended to be white whenever they arranged hotel accommodations. Mabry's race enabled them to carry out the deception without difficulty. Despite her getting away with passing on the car trip, "she was rather dark for success at that," according to Meyer, who thought Larsen was posturing while claiming to his mother that she frequently passed.[60]

In a third instance of passing, she was not so confident as she had been

---

58. Rampersad, *The Life of Langston Hughes*, I, 334. See also Kathleen A. Hauke, "The 'Passing' of Elsie Roxborough," *Michigan Quarterly Review*, XXIII (Spring, 1984), 155–70.

59. Rennels, New York *Telegram*, August 13, 1929; Claude McKay, *A Long Way From Home* (1937; rpr. New York, 1970), 112; Nella Larsen Imes to Carl Van Vechten, n.d. [postmarked May 14, 1932], in JWJ.

60. Andrew Meyer to Thadious M. Davis, January 17, 1982, in possession of Thadious M. Davis; Meyer to Davis, January 27, 1982.

with Mabry or Grace Johnson. John Becker, who was a friend of both Mabry and Edward Donahoe, recalled a story of a night ride in Donahoe's car in Nashville. When the police began to follow the car, Larsen panicked and hid on the floor to avoid detection, because she feared the officers would know that she was not white. In the excitement, she became hysterical, though the police did not stop the car.[61]

Becker, who ran an art gallery on Madison Avenue near Fifty-third Street in New York, was not a close associate of Larsen's, but he remembered her first visit to his gallery sometime during 1934: "I was busy and asked her to lunch the next day. Then when she left I turned to my secretary and said 'Now where I can take her?' I was told I was a damn fool, and that I should have thought of this first: the Ritz was suggested. But the Ritz was not my province. So I took Nella to Michel's a speakeasy on 52nd Street. The following day Michel appeared in my gallery to admonish me not to repeat the performance. He had nothing against Negroes etc. but many southern customers etc." Becker's account of an incident in the 1930s both underscores the reason why some blacks in New York did pass on occasion and reiterates the fact that Nella Larsen did not look white enough to pass. She had, however, the kind of personal style that might have enabled her to do so on occasion. Bruce Nugent, who occasionally passed in the 1920s in order to go to theaters and so forth, has pointed out that for an African American, passing is probably more accurately not disclosing, rather that renouncing, one's race.[62]

Although few old Harlem friends remained Larsen's intimate associates in the mid-1930s, she maintained contact for a time with Walter White and Rudolph Fisher. "Bud" Fisher became seriously ill with intestinal cancer during 1934 while completing his play *Conjur' Man Dies* for the Lafayette Theater. Caused by exposure to radiation in his work as an roentgenologist, the cancer debilitated him for six months. His death on December 26 was a particular blow to Larsen because Bud and his wife, Jane, had often made a foursome with the Imeses for bridge, theater, and dinner. Although he had been busy with both his medical and his literary careers between 1930 and 1934, Fisher had also served on the Literature Committee of the 135th Street YMCA and was active with the arts programs at the 135th Street branch of the New York Public Library.[63] His death just after Christmas

---

61. John Becker to Thadious M. Davis, July 14, 1982, in possession of Thadious M. Davis.
62. *Ibid.*; Richard Bruce Nugent, interview with author, April 30, 1983.
63. See "Rudolph Fisher," in *The Harlem Renaissance: A Historical Dictionary of the Era*,

deprived Larsen of one of her closest remaining ties with the literary community in Harlem.

Four days before Fisher's death, Wallace Thurman had died at City Hospital on Welfare Island. Although "Wally" had been closer to Dorothy Peterson and to A'Lelia Walker's "Dark Tower" crowd than to Larsen, he had been one of her New Negro associates, and his tragic death marked one end to the group's youthful promise.[64] Larsen's former brother-in-law, the Reverend William Lloyd Imes of St. James Presbyterian Church, led the memorial service on Christmas Eve. Thurman's death, along with Fisher's, cast an added pall over Larsen and the Harlem Renaissance artists remaining in New York during the Depression.

Walter White, who had become field secretary of the NAACP in 1931, was busy with the work of the association throughout the thirties, and his short career as a creative writer was over. Not long after Larsen's return to New York in 1933, White encouraged her to participate in the newly formed Writers' League Against Lynching and was instrumental in having her appointed assistant secretary.[65] In response to twenty-eight lynchings during the year, including two of white men in San Jose, California, Walter White, Lewis Gannett, Helen Woodward, and Benjamin Stolberg had sent telegrams to one hundred journalists, writers, editors, and publishers asking that they come together to combat lynching. Initially, eighty-one individuals responded; within a fortnight, the number reached two hundred, all willing to use their abilities and resources as writers to counter the increase in lynchings. Larsen held office with Harry Hansen, the elected chairman of the interracial organization, Lendre Marshall, the treasurer, and Suzanne LaFollette, the secretary. Her interests, however, had never been in political or social causes, and she had little commitment to organizations, not even the NAACP, so she soon drifted away from both White and the Writers' League. By 1935, she had few reasons to visit White or anyone uptown in Harlem.

When she first returned to New York in October of 1933, Larsen socialized most frequently with Dorothy Peterson. Peterson's high spirits kept Larsen preoccupied with matters other than her personal life. In particular,

---

ed. Bruce Kellner (New York, 1987), 123. See also "Rudolph Fisher," by Eleanor Q. Tignor, in *Dictionary of Literary Biography* (Detroit, 1987), LI, 86–96.

64. See Dorothy West, "Elephant's Dance: A Memoir of Wallace Thurman," *Black World*, II (November, 1970), 77–85.

65. Walter White, *A Man Called White* (New York, 1948), 166–67.

Peterson encouraged the contact that Larsen maintained with the James Weldon Johnsons during 1933 and 1934: "we have been dancing in the streets with pride because of you," they jointly wired James Weldon Johnson after the appearance of his autobiography *Along This Way* (1933). "Terribly flattering to be able to say that we know you well." The following summer, while still residing in the Peterson family home in Brooklyn, they took short excursions throughout the Northeast, one of which caused them to miss sending birthday greetings to Johnson and Van Vechten on June 17. "Jim's and Carl's birthday caught us on country road betwixt tiny hamlets whose telegraph offices were closed." Early in 1935 Larsen moved into Peterson's Second Avenue apartment. Although Peterson was teaching in Brooklyn, the two continued their close association. When they realized in February, 1935, that they had neglected to congratulate the Johnsons on the appearance of his book *Negro Americans: What Now?* (1934), they sent another of their hasty Western Union messages: "we dined tonight with Tennesseans one man a painter who had discovered Jim [Johnson] for himself with *God's Trombones* asked if we knew Jim we looked at each other not only with pride but with shame realizing that February was at its end but please at this late date take our blessings and admiration and all of our love."[66]

By summer, however, the two had begun to go their separate ways. The ever-active Peterson had started the involvement that would lead to her helping to found the Harlem Suitcase Theater and, subsequently, to her acting in Langston Hughes's play *Don't You Want to Be Free?* Although fond of the theater, Larsen had little interest in theatrical work, either on stage or behind the scene. In June she sent, without Peterson, the annual birthday greeting to Johnson at his summer home in Great Barrington, Massachusetts: "All good things for you this year and all the years to come my love and admiration to you both."[67]

During this same period (1933 to 1935), Larsen drew closer to several of her white acquaintances from the 1920s. Her editor at Knopf, Harry Block, and his wife, Malu, whom she had met through Van Vechten, continued to be part of her social life downtown. Van Vechten himself, despite having

---

66. Nella Larsen and Dorothy Peterson to James Weldon Johnson, October 4, 1933, in JWJ; Nella Larsen and Dorothy Peterson to Mrs. James Weldon Johnson, June 20, 1934, *ibid.*; Nella Larsen and Dorothy Peterson to Mr. and Mrs. James Weldon Johnson, February 27, 1935, *ibid.*

67. Nella Larsen to James Weldon Johnson, June 17, 1935, *ibid.*

turned his attention to photography, remained a loyal friend interested in Larsen personally and professionally; however, because of an unrelieved sense of guilt about incomplete works, Larsen kept at a distance from her former mentor, and their exchanges of letters and visits became less frequent. For his part, Van Vechten photographed her on occasion and celebrated her birthdays, though he no longer had weekly rounds of interracial parties. With his 1930 novel *Parties,* he had said farewell to his 1920s style of living. One of Larsen's last birthdays at the Van Vechtens was in 1934 when Edith, their cook, made a special birthday cake. Larsen, who was living with the Petersons, sent a thank-you note to Fania and Carl from Brooklyn: "I can't tell you how happy you made me last Friday night. It was the pleasantest birthday I have had for many a year—and I am glad that it happened to be this particular year.[68]

The year was one of transition and adjustment, as well as of recovery from the emotional stress of Nashville and divorce. On November 23, 1934, Van Vechten made the last of his Larsen photographs. The series of pictures shows the physical toll that the previous two years had taken on her. Her face is marked by age and stress lines; it is in noticeable contrast to the youthful, unlined face in the photographs taken upon her return from Europe (March 26, 1932) and those prior to her move to Nashville (August 17, 1932).[69]

Ironically, a few of her new associates in New York came by way of Nashville. Tom Mabry was a frequent visitor to the city as was his friend Edward Donahoe. Donahoe, in particular, was her frequent companion. Through him she met Carl and Zelma Corning Brandt, literary agents with offices on Park Avenue and a home in Connecticut. Donahoe's urbanity, wealth, and leisure fascinated her as much as did his interest in literature. Donahoe did not hold conventional views of class privilege: "That one class can dominate everything so brazenly appalls me, familiar as I am with the reason. I see all around me the brutality of the class to which I supposedly belong." Larsen had often been attracted to white men who ignored race as a basis for measuring individuals; Donahoe proved to be no exception. He presented himself as being without race prejudice and urged Langston Hughes to reconsider his view of the "disastrous results" of whites who "'go in for negroes [*sic*]'" and "to write a story about a white person

---

68. Nella Larsen Imes to Carl Van Vechten and Fania Marinoff, n.d. [postmarked April 18, 1934], *ibid.*

69. See Van Vechten's photographs of Nella Larsen, in JWJ.

wholly without race consciousness, and there are such people. I know several in the South alone. And, as you know, it isn't easy for such people in Nashville."[70]

During Larsen's difficult period in Nashville, Donahoe gained her confidence and her affection. After her divorce, she waited for his arrival in Chicago. She may, as well, have anticipated marrying him, because when she informed Dorothy Peterson of Donahoe's expected visit to Chicago, she added, "I haven't decided anything about my name yet. I wonder if there is much use in changing it back and then changing it again."[71] She did not change her name back to Larsen, and there are no records to indicate that she ever remarried. Nonetheless, marriage was very much on her mind following her divorce, and Donahoe was the likely partner.

Donahoe's correspondence, while mentioning his association with Larsen, suggested only that they were friends. For example, in August, 1934, he wrote to Langston Hughes: "(When we see one another I must tell you about the trip Nella Larsen and I took to Muscle Shoals. It would amuse you. We motored in my mother's majestic red Lincoln. Nella brought some sandwiches. I brought a quart of liquor and the set-ups for highballs. At Columbia Tennessee I had to 'pass' at a negro [sic] restaurant. We had a very exciting trip I assure you.)" Donahoe concluded the letter: "If you are in the East this Fall you can reach me through Nella or Dorothy Peterson. I usually stay at the Brevoort."[72] Obviously, he expected to see and to remain in close contact with Larsen.

Although neither Donahoe nor Larsen was forthright in revealing the nature of their relationship, the two remained friends throughout the middle thirties, but by 1937, when his novel *Madness in the Heart* appeared, they were no longer close, though he participated in a number of social affairs during the winter spring and in New York. Their collaborative writing projects had not materialized in print; while his first novel was being favorably reviewed by the *New York Times Book Review* and the *Herald Tribune* and his plans were developing for a second, Larsen had published nothing since the ill-fated "Sanctuary" in 1930. While under stress in Nashville, she had already claimed that Jessie Fauset had stolen her ideas for novels, and she may well have perceived Donahoe as doing the same, despite the fact that

70. Edward Donahoe to Langston Hughes, 27 VIII 34, in Langston Hughes Papers, Beinecke Rare Book and Manuscript Library, Yale University.

71. Larsen to Peterson, Wednesday 6th [postmarked September 6, 1933], in JWJ.

72. Donahoe to Hughes, 27 VIII 34, in Hughes Papers.

the subject of his novel was the intertwined stories of the "transition of an Oklahoma city from the gun-toting period to an era of culture . . . [and of] Timothy Wilson, weather-beaten old settler, who could not change with the times . . . [and of] the boy out of whom family pride tried to make something that he was not."[73]

The following summer, July, 1938, Donahoe bought a house near Georgetown, Connecticut; and despite describing himself at that time as "a bachelor . . . who has indulged himself outrageously," he was responsibly preparing himself to chair a League of American Writers' meeting on the topic "The Negro in American Literature," a subject he admitted was "very close to his heart," though he did not claim to be an authority. After that conference in November, at which Langston Hughes, Sterling Brown, Jessie Fauset, and others from the Harlem Renaissance spoke about the 1920s, Donahoe spent a "strange and disturbing winter" in what he called "lovely solitude" in Connecticut, but he was "unable to write or make much sense." By May, 1939, his life had, he said, "enormously changed," whereupon he revealed his intention to marry an old friend, Helen Bishop, in the fall. Bishop shared Donahoe's race and background in well-to-do Oklahoma society. After Donahoe's departure for Europe in June, he prepared for his marriage to Bishop. Late in the summer, Zelma Brandt reported that she had talked to his fiancée in London, where he was indeed planning to marry a woman who already had a child.[74]

Precisely what effect Donahoe's failure to continue his literary collaboration and the personal association with Larsen, his mental breakdown, departure for Europe, and impending marriage had on Nella Larsen cannot be determined from either his or her correspondence or conversations. Donahoe corresponded with Grace Nail Johnson throughout the 1930s to 1942, and then after a twenty-year hiatus, during which he suffered a series of mental breakdowns, he resumed writing in 1963; nevertheless, his letters fail to mention Larsen except as a friend of the Johnsons in Nashville, and they do not suggest that she had any particular connection to him. When he wrote infrequently to Grace Johnson from Mexico in the 1960s, his letters reflected that he was partly lucid and partly living in a confused version of

73. Houchins interviews, March 12 and December 30, 1984; A. G. Seiler, "First Distinction," Book of the Month pamphlet, in JWJ, Series I, 130, Edward Donahoe folder.

74. Edward Donahoe to Grace Nail Johnson, July 21, 1938, in JWJ; Edward Donahoe to Grace Nail Johnson, October 24, 1938, *ibid.*; Edward Donahoe to Grace Nail Johnson, May 30, 1939, *ibid.*; Zelma Corning Brandt to Grace Nail Johnson, August 10, 1939, *ibid.*

the past.[75] Curiously, however, there is one direct, isolated question: "Do you ever see Nella Larsen?"[76] Larsen was, if fact, the only person from the old Nashville group that Donahoe inquired about; he dismissed his other close associate, Tom Mabry, as not being a true friend.

While Donahoe's star was rising toward the end of the thirties, Larsen was withdrawing from her few remaining friends. In April, 1937, Elizabeth Shaffer Hull, then working in the theater, wrote Grace Johnson: "Nella told everyone she was taking a cruise to South America, the name of the boat, and the date of sailing, but she is in town, incognito or something." In exasperation, Hull concluded, "She is way past my understanding."[77] Always a private person, Larsen was beginning to conceal her whereabouts and activities just as Donahoe's novel was published, but her small circle all knew of her transparent attempts. Actual or imagined flight had throughout her life been a means of coping with difficulties. A week after Hull made her observation, Van Vechten, in sending one of his photograph postcards to Grace Johnson, flatly stated: "One report that Nella is in Brazil is slightly exaggerated."[78] Perhaps ironically, the photocard was a portrait of Edward Donahoe.

In the fall of 1937, Nella Larsen delivered "reverse farewell messages" to her friends. "On the night of the phone calls," as some of them came to call it, she telephoned all of her friends with the same message: "I arrive at once."[79]

She never arrived. After the dramatic message, she neither appeared nor was heard from again. When Andrew Meyer and Edna and Lloyd Thomas later compared the messages, they became concerned. Meyer had been in bed with a collapsed lung when Larsen phoned with the promise of delivering him a "basket of good mysteries," which she had selected from her collection. He was unaware then that she had telephoned her message of immediate arrival to everyone he knew who also knew her.[80]

75. See Edward Donahoe to Grace Nail Johnson, from September 16, 1963, to March 31, 1966, all *ibid.*

76. Donahoe to Johnson, October 16, 1965, *ibid.*

77. Elizabeth Shaffer Hull to Grace Nail Johnson, April 22, 1937, *ibid.* No subsequent references to Larsen appear in Hull's correspondence with Johnson.

78. Carl Van Vechten to Grace Nail Johnson, n.d. [postmarked April 28, 1937], in JWJ.

79. Meyer to Davis, January 17, January 27, and April 14, 1982; Andrew and Kay Meyer interview, May 25, 1982.

80. Meyer to Davis, January 27, 1982; Jean Blackwell Hutson, conversation with author, Hofstra University Conference on the Harlem Renaissance, May 3, 1985.

Following his convalescence, Meyer walked over from his apartment on East Twenty-fourth Street to the Second Avenue apartment that Larsen had taken over from Dorothy Peterson. He rang several times, but received no answer. Her name was still on the doorbell. He knew she had not moved and realized immediately that she was actually at home, because as he turned to leave he could see the curtain move in the window of her apartment. Why she refused to answer or to see him troubled him for months afterward. With the discovery of other "reverse farewell messages," Meyer remained puzzled by Larsen's actions, but reconciled to the idea that she did not want to see him or other friends, even though neither he nor they had angered or offended her. He knew that she loved mysteries and word puzzles. Later, he learned from Lloyd Thomas that Larsen, along with several others from his wife Edna's and Olivia Wyndham's group in Connecticut, was on drugs. Although unsubstantiated, the charge of drug addiction persisted well after the 1930s, according to Jean Blackwell Hutson. Passing and drug dependency functioned as explanations of her withdrawal from friends.[81]

After "the night of phone calls," Nella Larsen became an elusive figure who was seen by almost none of her former acquaintances. Nearly two years afterward, she was still an object of concern. Sidney Peterson sailed for Puerto Rico and a career in medicine on August 26, 1939, without a bon voyage from Larsen. In November, 1939, Lillian Alexander, who had nominated her for the Harmon Awards, reportedly approached Van Vechten at a theater party and lamented that she had "NO idea where Nella is and thinks it is about time somebody asked Elmer who *MUST* know, as he supports her."[82] Alexander had gotten it wrong: actually it was Dorothy Peterson who "must know," for she had turned the lease to her Second Avenue apartment over to her friend. Larsen evidently wanted to disappear; she intended that no one know her whereabouts, at least no one who would reveal them. Peterson sealed her letters from this period, so that whatever she knew has not yet been revealed.

Elmer Imes, who was paying her alimony, did not know and, as he made clear, was "NEVER allowed to have her address." His checks were sent directly to Larsen's bank, and she used no return address in writing to

---

81. Meyer to Davis, January 17, 1982, and April 14, 1982.

82. Dorothy Peterson to Grace Nail Johnson, August 15, 1939, in JWJ; Carl Van Vechten to Dorothy Peterson, November 21, 1939, *ibid.*

Imes.[83] In January, 1940, Imes insisted that he knew no one who had seen Larsen. Near the end of February, 1940, Imes, who had renewed his correspondence with Van Vechten following the death of James Weldon Johnson in 1938 and a memorial program for him at Fisk in 1939, revealed: "Nella seems to be o.k. as evidenced by typewritten and addressless note a few days ago about money. I replied in care of her bank which was the only way I could think of to reach her since her note implied that she had not received a letter addressed to 320 Second Avenue [Peterson's old apartment] in January (and not returned because of non-delivery)."[84] Even Johnson's death and Grace's serious injury in a car accident on June 26, 1938, which prompted Elmer Imes's renewed contact with old friends in Manhattan, did not rouse Nella Larsen from the East Side retreat. She was not detected among the 2,500 mourners attending Johnson's funeral at the Reverend Frederick Cullen's Salem Methodist Episcopal Church in New York.

From 1940 until 1941, when Elmer Imes returned to New York for treatment of what would prove to be terminal cancer, he insisted that he, like the others, was not privileged to information about his former wife and knew nothing of her whereabouts. Imes's fortune had been sinking since the 1933 divorce. Never financially secure, he had difficulty meeting the alimony arrangements and providing for his mother, who, after becoming seriously ill in Memphis, had come to live with him at 1804 Hermosa Street, the Fisk apartment that had been Ethel Gilbert's. During the summer of 1933 when the divorce was imminent, he had returned to Michigan for his annual research. From Ann Arbor he had requested permission from Fisk officials to give up the lease on the Morena Street house for three reasons: "The first was the smaller expense. The second was that it will simplify housekeeping for Mother and me. The third was that there will very probably be less chance of Mrs Imes' return to upset things." Because his mother had refused to move to the house as long as Larsen was there, Imes wanted an arrangement whereby he would take the apartment "furnished from Mrs Gilbert" ("that is, I have arranged to use her furniture so long as she does not need it elsewhere"), have his mother move there with a housekeeper in his absence, and "push the vacation of the house." He observed two problems, however: "it is settled that Mrs Imes takes the furniture from the house and

---

83. Carl Van Vechten to Dorothy Peterson, January 2, 1940, *ibid.* Van Vechten reports this information that Elmer Imes revealed in a telephone conversation with him.

84. Elmer Imes to Carl Van Vechten, February 24, 1940, in JWJ.

goes to New York. She will of course delay as long as possible"; and "in order to make ends meet I shall have to ask that I have use of the apartment rent free until at least Sept. 15 if it takes that long to vacate the house."[85]

Imes reiterated his request for use of the apartment without rent because, as he explained,

> I think I should tell you [President Jones] that apparently the only hitch in the program of immediate and final separation is my inability to meet some rather ambitious financial demands. I do not like to write a great deal of this personal matter but you have already agreed that for the sake of everybody and everything concerned it is wisest not to consider trying to go through another year of agony. I will not attempt it and am trying to make my readjustment with as little mess as possible, which means a certain amount of apparent catering to Mrs Imes' notions. She has agreed to leave on certain conditions which I couldn't quite meet but am trying to modify quietly and honorably.[86]

His appeal for assistance from Jones worked, but it was only the first of his attempts to augment his resources with help from Fisk. Much like his former wife, Imes had by the 1930s acquired tastes for expensive things and for quality living that he could not adequately accommodate on a Depression-era salary that had been cut by 10 percent the year before his divorce.

In the mid-1930s, Imes had begun to spend more time in New York City, usually during August and September, the period between his research in Michigan and his teaching in Nashville. He attempted to conceal his presence in the city from Larsen. By 1939, he was conducting some of his research in the Physics Department of New York University and seeing old friends and his brother's family in Harlem, but he usually departed quickly from any gathering that drew too many people, such as Lillian and Ernest Alexander's annual picnic at Green Pastures, their Long Island estate.[87] He was beginning to suffer from a serious illness that would soon prevent him from performing many of his academic responsibilities and that would add to his financial worries.

85. E. Imes to Jones, July 22, 1933, in Jones Papers.
86. *Ibid.*
87. Elmer Imes to Thomas E. Jones, September 5, 1939, in Jones Papers.

Incapacitated during much of the 1940–1941 school year, he engaged in gentlemanly disputes with the Fisk administration about his salary: "I should like here to express my deep appreciation of the manner in which my illness has been taken by the administration and of the concessions which have been cheerfully made. But I would like to point out that considering the extremely grave and painful nature of my illness, I have still managed to miss a very small part of my class room engagements and that I do not believe that our students have suffered at all on account of it."[88]

When his hospitalization at New York's Memorial Hospital occurred the following summer, Imes feared Larsen's discovery of his presence and his helpless condition. He worried that her demands for money would escalate, and he had none. His plane trip to New York had been paid for with a loan from one of his closest Nashville associates, Isaiah Creswell, who admired his strength not only in attempting that trip, but in inventing a device for voiding so that he could endure the time in the air. When Imes wired ahead for an ambulance service to meet his plane, American Airlines learned of the request and sent a representative to investigate. Imes then claimed good health to avoid having the airline cancel his trip, and when the time came, he walked unsupported onto the plane. According to Creswell, "No one impressed me more than Imes" in those last days and previously: "He was all-around, liked sports, literature, arts, bridge and women. . . . Money meant nothing to him."[89] Imes made provisions in his will to repay Creswell's loan.

Within days of his arrival in June, he began to contact some of his old friends to inform them that he had "been ill all year and [had not] had a day without pain since October." He revealed that his illness was cancer with "an ulcer in the throat" being "the primary lesion," which was "cured early in November after an extensive series of x-ray treatments with about the maximum dose ever given"; however, he had soon developed a persistent backache, which did not respond to "any treatment that the best men in Nashville could give" and which by summer was diagnosed as caused by malignant cells. Imes had been told by his doctors in Tennessee that he could be kept comfortable "only with sedatives" because the cancer had attacked his spinal column. Describing himself as a cripple since December of 1940, he cautioned Van Vechten, whom he wanted to see, "I am taking care that

88. Elmer Imes to Jesse F. Beale, March 1, 1941, *ibid.*
89. Isaiah Creswell interview, March 11, 1987.

Nella does not know that I am here."[90] Between June and September, when Imes died, he did not mention Larsen again, though he continued to write letters until late July.

His caution was due not only to his physical condition but also to his dire financial straits and the extraordinary effort that he was putting into making arrangements while hospitalized. He had asked that Fisk not deduct his rent from his June salary, in order to help defray his medical expenses in New York, and he had received a waiver of rent until the start of the new school year; however, when he requested a sabbatical leave for a half year with pay, he got an unexpected reply from Jones: "I certainly hope it will be possible for [the trustees] to grant this request. In case they do, would it be satisfactory to pro-rate your monthly rental indebtedness for both the past year and this year and deduct it from your monthly check?" The response upset Imes to the extent that he "lost a considerable portion of the gains" he had made during his four weeks of treatments, because he had already informed his doctor, George P. Pack, of his ability to pay "approximately $300 per month until December 1st." Imes asked instead that the university extend its assistance and accept a twelve-month note of indebtedness, to be paid either from his salary or from his estate.[91]

Imes believed until mid-July that his condition was improving. He had been confined to his hospital bed following his June 7 arrival, but radium treatments gave him hope of recovery. Even at the end of July he thought that there was "exceedingly slow but exceedingly real progress," and remarked that his blood counts were nearly normal at the beginning of August. He experienced weight loss and almost total helplessness, but had "the promise of permanent relief and perhaps total cure" at Memorial, where he could have and did encourage visitors.[92] He was overly optimistic.

In early July after hearing of his illness, Dorothy Peterson had contacted Ethel Gilbert for information about his condition. Peterson, who was out of the country at the time, wrote immediately to Van Vechten in New York: "I called Mrs. Gilbert who says that there is very little hope for Elmer. He is losing weight and is in great pain and the Doctor says he is infected through and through, even his lungs. He is feeling rather hopeless too and doesn't

90. Elmer Imes to Carl Van Vechten, Sunday, n.d. [postmarked June 9, 1941], in JWJ.
91. Thomas E. Jones to Elmer Imes, July 30, 1941, in Jones Papers; Elmer Imes to Thomas E. Jones, August 5, 1941, ibid.
92. E. Imes to Jones, August 5, 1941, ibid.; Elmer Imes to Carl Van Vechten, June 14, 1941, in JWJ.

seem to want to see people."[93] Gilbert was probably mistaken about his not wanting to see people, because he had received Van Vechten's visits in June and would see him again in July.

When Van Vechten first visited Imes at the hospital located at 444 East 68th Street, he brought along mountain laurel; a week later, he sent a radio for the hospital room. The gift so moved Imes that he was prompted to say, "It is grand to have good friends—even if I haven't always seemed to show it about mine." In one of his last notes to Van Vechten, he expressed appreciation for his friendship and announced a "slow but definite progress in the right direction." Imes was in a critical stage of throat cancer that, as his attending physician would observe, had already begun to spread throughout his body and infect his bones before his arrival at the New York facility.[94]

On the afternoon of September 11, the fifty-seven-year-old Imes died at Memorial Hospital. He had not seen Nella Larsen at any point during his illness and treatment. His brother, the Reverend William Lloyd Imes, handled the arrangements and signed the death certificate. Two days after his death, his body was cremated. A memorial service was held at Maspeth, Long Island. Larsen did not attend the service, though many of New York's prominent African Americans, such as Du Bois and Shelton Bishop, did. Dorothy Peterson, who managed to remain a loyal friend to Larsen and to Imes, especially during his illness, went to Long Island for the service. Ethel Gilbert later took Imes's ashes to Nashville, where she scattered them around a rose bush at the Hermosa Street apartment. The poet Robert Hayden would eventually live in the building and tend the bush in memory of Imes.[95]

Rev. William Lloyd Imes listed his brother as being divorced but did not provide the name of his former wife. It is not clear whether he referred to Elmer's divorce from Nella Larsen eight years earlier or to a more recent divorce from Ethel Gilbert. Gilbert had also been in New York City during Elmer's three-month hospitalization, and though there was no public acknowledgment, many believed that she had been married to Elmer Imes.[96]

93. Dorothy Peterson to Carl Van Vechten, July 11, 1941, in JWJ.

94. Imes to Van Vechten, June 14, 1941, *ibid.*; Elmer Imes to Carl Van Vechten, July 19, 1941, *ibid.*; Baltimore *Afro-American,* September 20, 1941, p. 1.

95. Certificate of Death no. 18457, in Bureau of Vital Records, Borough of Manhattan, New York City Department of Health; Baltimore *Afro-American,* September 20, 1941, p. 1; Pearl and Isaiah Creswell interviews, March 10 and 11, 1987.

96. Frankie Lea Houchins believed that the marriage had taken place around 1938, while Larsen had indicated in 1933 that it would occur within days of her divorce.

Imes's friend Isaiah Creswell, at Fisk, understood that the couple had made private vows to each other. Van Vechten pointed out that Elmer had not the nerve to tell him about his "marriage," and Dorothy Peterson, who had moved back to Brooklyn by 1941, alluded to the marriage.[97] She had initially heard of Imes's illness while visiting in Puerto Rico where her brother, Sidney, was practicing medicine. Because she was convinced that Gilbert was Imes's wife, Peterson had called her immediately for news of his condition.

After attending Imes's funeral, Peterson received a letter from Gilbert asking that they meet. In a quandary about how to address Gilbert and whether to see her, Peterson wrote immediately to Van Vechten for help. His response was partly humorous and partly serious:

> There are lots of ways of starting a letter without saying Dear Old Ethel . . . tho [sic] I don't see why you object to writing Dear Ethel Gilbert, which seems indicated by her address to you. Dear friend, doesn't mean very much. Dear friend of a friend is even better. Dear Lady has been done or you could start out jovially, Hello Folks? I am surprised at your lack of ingenuity. Obviously, she wants to see you. The question is do you want to see her? As I grow older this is a question of paramount importance to me. Less and less do I see people or read books or go to plays or what not unless I really desire to.[98]

Van Vechten, who did not attend Imes's memorial service, began to question Peterson about Larsen. "If Nella pops up, please let me know at once." He had heard that Imes wanted to see his former wife before he died. The story had originated in Nashville, where Grace Johnson, believing it true, had passed it along to Van Vechten in New York.[99] It was, however, nothing more than a rumor, according to Peterson, who apparently revealed what she knew of Larsen's whereabouts and response to Elmer's death.[100] Van Vechten replied, "Your Nella story is both funny and tragic but what can one do?"[101] That story never circulated among their mutual friends.

97. Isaiah Creswell interview, March 11, 1987; Carl Van Vechten to Dorothy Peterson, July 29 and 31, 1940, both in JWJ.

98. Carl Van Vechten to Dorothy Peterson, September 24, 1941, ibid.

99. Ibid.; Carl Van Vechten to Dorothy Peterson, October 2 and 30, 1941, both in JWJ.

100. See Carl Van Vechten to Dorothy Peterson, November 4 and 6, 1941, both ibid.

101. Carl Van Vechten to Dorothy Peterson, December 28, 1941, ibid.

Peterson, perhaps the only person who knew the truth about Larsen, would not admit openly to knowing anything at all about her friend's condition or location. In addition to knowing Larsen's whereabouts, Peterson may also have been aware that her friend's last close link to her childhood, John Mayo of Chicago, had died of cerebral hemorrhage on July 27, 1941, just as Elmer Imes began to lose his battle against cancer.[102] With the two deaths and the concomitant severing of major links to her past, Nella Larsen retreated into an elusive privacy that was already transforming her known self into an enigma.

Elmer Imes's death closed another period in Larsen's life. Their fourteen-year marriage coincided with her rise to social and literary prominence, as well as with the limited attainment of her expressed desire to become famous. The eight years between their divorce and his death marked her entrance into financial independence and security at the very time when many, including Imes, were losing economic stability. Freedom from earning a living during the stressful years between 1933 and 1941 allowed her to focus on herself, particularly on reordering her personal life while creating a social and physical environment supportive of her writing. Much of her energy went into attempts to regain emotional and psychic balance enough to concentrate on writing and to restore a necessary confidence in her artistic ability. Yet something other than the immediate crisis in her personal life conspired against her efforts.

When Larsen returned from Europe in 1932, the United States was in the middle of the Great Depression, and the Harlem Renaissance was mainly over. Larsen had taken little notice initially of the cultural changes, because the magnitude of her personal transitions obscured her vision of the larger world. Her writing took impetus from a glittering surface of wealth and comfort, but the class that she had chosen to portray was no longer in vogue. The harsher realities of life, which she had always preferred to ignore or suppress, were more pronounced in American society of the 1930s. Moreover, whether through misguidance or ambivalence, she had not recognized the significance of her own private view of society, and by selective exclusion of her own vital urges from her métier, she was left with little that she herself valued. Her specific life experiences, rooted in the urban poor and their struggle for survival and achievement and marked by the complexities of female identity, could have provided her with a unique oppor-

102. Certificate of Death no. 80774, in Records of Cook County, Office of the Cook County Clerk, Chicago.

tunity for meaningful explorations of race, gender, and class in her fiction. Instead, seduced by the glamour of the myth-world of Harlem in the 1920s, she buried much of the material available to her. The superficial reality and structures of privilege that she chose as a vehicle seemed less significant and consequential by the mid-1930s. She was not able to cast off that surface and explore the subterranean territory that had actually been her subtext in both novels. And she was unwilling to delve further into her female consciousness of the double blind of race and gender. Subterfuge and deception had combined with ambition and opportunism to prevent her from analyzing the matter and manner of her fiction.

She had created "Nella Larsen" and an identity that trapped her into acquiescence to situational contexts appropriate to the persona. Within that identity, she turned to writing that could not take full advantage of the substance that she knew, and knew more acutely after her divorce, motivated and drove women and blacks to strive for success, for position, for recognition that might somehow alleviate the reality of constriction and deprivation. The tensions in her own life and the interpretations of those tensions were fictional matter that she could not confront with the veracity and tenacity required in a transformed, sober society. By 1941 when Imes died, Larsen had not only isolated herself from other people, she had also alienated herself from her interior creative resources. The dreams she sowed perhaps without comprehending their significations had fallen on barren soil.

14

Resting on Headlands,
1941–1964

AFTER 1941, NELLA Larsen became once again Nella Imes. She also used *Mrs. Nella L. Imes* as her legal name.[1] Although she had assumed her maiden name in 1926 when the publication of *Quicksand* seemed certain, she rejected that name not long after the death of her former husband. The choice of *Imes* is a curious one at that point in her life if viewed only from the perspective of the enmity of the divorce and, thereafter, of the attempt to restructure an independent existence. However, the choice is understandable within the marketplace to which she would return once she lost the income from alimony. As "Mrs. Imes, widow," she could readily explain the long years of absence from work. Her last employment had been in 1926 as a librarian, but she had last worked as a nurse in the early 1920s, having completed her training a decade before that.

The resumption of the identity as Mrs. Imes signaled the end of her efforts to pursue a literary career. By the early 1940s, she had lost contact with those individuals who had fostered her career as a writer. Van Vechten, then more photographer than writer, was no longer as powerful a literary influence as he had been in the 1920s with New York publishers, though he

---

1. Nella L. Imes employment records, 1944–61, Gouverneur Hospital, in Personnel Office of the Beth Israel Medical Center and Hospital, New York; Nella L. Imes employment records, 1961–64, in Personnel Department, Metropolitan Hospital Center, New York. (The Gouverneur Hospital, though still in existence on the lower East Side of Manhattan, is now a clinic of the Beth Israel Medical Center and Hospital.) See also the listings for Imes, Nella L. Mrs., in the telephone directories for New York City, Borough of Manhattan, 1955–64.

was instrumental in facilitating the publishing of Langston Hughes's autobi-ography, *The Big Sea,* in 1940.[2] The death of his close friend James Weldon Johnson in 1938 redirected Van Vechten's interests to gathering "Negro" materials for the James Weldon Johnson Memorial Collection at Yale Uni-versity and to preparing his own papers for the Carl Van Vechten Personal Collection at the New York Public Library. As he told Dorothy Peterson in 1941, "I'm up to my ears in Negro doings," but these activities were very different from those of the 1920s.[3] The Knopfs, no longer publishing a spate of books by African-American authors, had sought out and found other literary talents for their publishing house. Walter White, enmeshed in the politics of the NAACP, was too busy with administrative responsibilities for ongoing involvement in publishing activity. Charles S. Johnson had long since left New York for Fisk in Nashville. Jessie Fauset, happily married in 1929, had returned to teaching, as had Countee Cullen. Dorothy Peterson, whose indefatigable energy and charm cemented connections at every level of the artistic and literary world, had invested most of her talent for orga-nizing others in productions for the Harlem Suitcase Theater. Throughout her active years as a writer, Larsen had depended upon these individuals for access to, or encouragement in, publishing.

Her decade of silence during the 1930s had generated neither a new co-terie of literary support nor a new audience for her voice. The advent of a fresh generation of African-American writers, forged out of the Depression era, did not bode well for her chances of renewed success as a published author, particularly given her approach to subject matter and its difference from that of Richard Wright, the writer who had emerged from the 1930s, with *Uncle Tom's Children* (1938) and *Native Son* (1940), as the best-selling and most popular African-American writer yet to appear on the lit-erary scene. Even Langston Hughes, the primary writer from the New Negro Renaissance to flourish in the 1930s, was overshadowed by Wright. Published the same year as *Native Son,* Hughes's *Big Sea,* which presented "Black Renaissance" as a main division, seemed dated to many critics, even to some on the Left who saw Hughes as a proletarian writer. Hughes's friend Arna Bontemps quipped about Wright: "That boy is sure kicking up the dust."[4] If Wright's "dust" could partly obscure a Langston Hughes, then

2. See Arnold Rampersad's discussion of Hughes's difficulties with Blanche Knopf over the Harlem materials in *The Big Sea,* and Van Vechten's assistance in resolving them, in *The Life of Langston Hughes* (2 vols.; New York, 1986), I, 376.

3. Carl Van Vechten to Dorothy Peterson, September 6, 1941, in JWJ.

4. Rampersad, *The Life of Langston Hughes,* I, 387–88; Arna Bontemps to Langston Hughes, June 21, 1941, quoted by Rampersad, 388.

Larsen's prospects for earning a living as a professional author at that time were considerably diminished.

Because of careful management of money, she was able to continue without regular employment for nearly three years after 1941. To supplement her savings, she occasionally worked as a private-duty nurse. Although there appears to be no extant record of her employment during the period before 1941, her Social Security number indicates that she obtained it in Connecticut after the advent of the Social Security Administration in 1935.[5] She may have done private duty or part-time work in that state in the late 1930s. To cut living expenses, she moved from 320 Second Avenue to a smaller, more economical studio apartment at 315 Second Avenue. After that move and the intermittent return to nursing, she made no effort to resume old friendships. The disappearance that she had so dramatically effected in the late 1930s became complete. All semblance of connection with her life as "Nella Larsen, novelist" was dropped. She apparently abandoned writing completely.

Like her character in "Freedom," she may well have wondered for a time about the impact of her dropping from sight on her former associates, but unlike her character, she did not die or commit suicide. Hers had always been an enormous will to live; that will took her through repeated transformations of her identity. Each instance of change required not only resilience but courage. Her courage in the face of overwhelming odds against her needs and wants as a woman of color was one of the defining aspects of her personality. That courage would finally not allow her to die, but would instead compel her to begin anew, like the phoenix, out of the ashes of old situations and identities.

Transformations of identity, a subtext in her apprentice stories and two novels, suggest the importance of the idea to her, most likely as a sign of the transformations in her own life that had taken place not merely on the level of career changes or choices. The Nellie Walker, Nellie Larson, and Nellye Larson who grew up in Chicago, the Nellie Marie Larsen who enrolled at Fisk, the Nella Marion Larsen who entered Lincoln and married Elmer Imes, the Nella Imes who attended the Library School and lived in Harlem, the Allen Semi who wrote romance stories, the Nella Larsen who wrote novels, and the Nella Larsen Imes who worked as a nurse were all the same person. Yet all of these identities were both transitions and transformations

---

5. Information on the region for Larsen's Social Security number was determined by the first three digits and was obtained from the Durham, North Carolina, office of the Social Security Administration, May 27, 1987.

emblematic of an incessant quest for meaning. All of the names reflected her atempt to integrate subconscious aspects of personality with the concious configurations of identity.

In 1944, Nella Larsen Imes began to work full-time at Gouverneur Hospital on Manhattan's Lower East Side. She chose night duty at the hospital, then located at South and Water streets. As a registered nurse, she soon became a supervising head nurse.[6] Her training at one of the best-known nursing institutions in the city enabled her to do what few women of her age would have been able to do: to find gainful, respectable employment at the age of fifty-three.

For seventeen years, she worked nights at Gouverneur. Well liked by her nursing colleagues, she was known as a strict but fair supervisor who took pride in her nurse's uniform and her appearance generally. "She held her head high," one co-worker recalled. Several of the other nurses thought that she was special, but also remembered that "Nella had quite a temper." Never timid about speaking her mind, she kept a sharp edge to her wit and sense of humor. It was not unusual to hear her humming under her breath as though she were happily at ease in her work. As the night supervisor of nurses, she was held in esteem for being a "good, dependable nurse," capable of meeting any crisis. "Most people liked her," especially as a supervisor, because she was competent and fair, and "never seemed to mind tending patients herself."[7]

During her years at Gouverneur, however, she lived reclusively, rarely associating with anyone outside the hospital setting. "Nothing strengthens the judgment and quickens the consciousness like individual responsibility," Elizabeth Cady Stanton believed. "Nothing adds such dignity to character as the recognition of one's self-sovereignty; the right to an equal place, everywhere conceded; a place earned by personal merit, not an artificial attainment by inheritance, wealth, family, and position." This period in Larsen Imes's life may well have been one of growing consciousness and recognition. She spent most of her free time reading in her Second Avenue studio, which she had appointed with a collection of beautiful objects from her travels in Europe and North Africa during her Guggenheim fellowship and with a selection of furniture from the house in Nashville. Her large room held a handsome bed and chest of drawers, but it was dominated by

6. N. Imes employment records, 1944–61, Gouverneur Hospital.
7. Alice L. Carper and Carolyn Lane, interview with author, May 5, 1985, and Alice L. Carper, interview with author, May 5, 1985.

books, which filled most of the wall space. Reading remained her great joy; she continued to buy and collect books of all sorts, and mysteries remained her special favorite. Alice Carper, one of the nurses from Gouverneur who grew the closest to her, remembered the first-floor, rear apartment as lovely, book-filled, and artistic, despite the kitchen's never being in order. Nella Imes cared little for cooking or for eating; she was conscious of her weight and of maintaining her trim appearance. In retrospect, her friend concluded, "Nella was a potential cardiac. She didn't eat as much as she should have. She was very pale."[8]

Carper, a registered nurse and graduate of Hampton Institute, had begun to work at Gouverneur Hospital shortly after Nella Larsen Imes. Previously she had spent ten years (1934 to 1944) at Harlem Hospital. Outgoing and social, she began to encourage Larsen Imes to visit her and to go on outings. Gradually, Carper became a trusted friend whose house on Oxford Street in Brooklyn served as a second home on holidays and special occasions. From 1945 through 1959, when Carper retired from the hospital, the two women shared a special friendship both in the workplace and outside of it. During those years, Carper and her sisters, especially her older sister, Hattie Carthan, became Larsen Imes's surrogate family, filling the void left by the Petersons. "She visited all the time," Carper recalled. "Nella was like family." Accepting her on her own terms, they reintroduced her to intimacy with others and with the outside world. They discovered, in the process, that their friend actually had a zest for living and being active, a zest that they believed had been suppressed by the sorrow of divorce and widowhood. Carper thought that the divorce had darkened and disillusioned her friend to the point where she broke all ties with other people and used her work to forget her disappointments: "Nella loved her husband, but he disappointed her by loving someone else. She still took care of him after he was sick and dying of cancer." Sensitive and observant, Carper may have had only Larsen Imes's version of her past, but she knew firsthand that her friend pushed herself to stay awake at work, that she took pills to help keep her alert during the night shifts, but that Nella was also an extremely proud woman who would not allow anyone to feel sorry for her.[9]

8. Elizabeth Cady Stanton, "Solitude of Self," in *Feminism: The Essential Historical Writings,* ed. Miriam Schneir (New York, 1972), 158f.; Alice L. Carper, telephone conversation with author, July 20, 1982; Andrew G. Meyer to Thadious M. Davis, January 17, 1982, in possession of Thadious M. Davis; Carper and Lane interview, May 5, 1985.

9. Carper interview, May 5, 1985; Carper, telephone conversations with author, July 20, 1982, and May 1, 1983.

In fact, as Larsen Imes ventured out of her isolation, she talked more and more. Animated, she unfolded her past as she wanted it remembered, while representing her present as a resting place from which to survey the world. She told of her experiences as a novelist, of her connections with famous, important people, of her travels in Europe, of her family in Denmark and her visit to her grandmother there. "Nella was a talker," according to Lane and Carper. Although she rarely spoke directly about her parents, she revealed to Lane, an immigrant from Czechoslovakia, that her parents were also immigrants, that her mother was born in Denmark but was German, and that her father was a light-skinned West Indian who had been a businessman in Chicago. Ironically, despite her misrepresentations of her past, Larsen Imes spoke more truthfully to Lane and her friends from Gouverneur about her parents than she had to many of the friends of her youth. She enjoyed contemplating past achievements, recreating and sharing them with new friends, perhaps because she was very much then a person who thrived on company and companionship, or perhaps because she needed to hear once again talk about herself. She enjoyed brandy along with conversation, a combination that encouraged spontaneous reflections on her past life. "She loved her brandy," Carper said, delicately glossing over Nella's drinking.[10]

She was appreciative and generous with those who listened. Over the years, she gave Alice Carper beautiful gifts: a set of thin crystal brandy glasses, a cashmere coat, a glass punch bowl and twelve glasses for eggnog at Christmas. The gifts signaled, Carper believed, that "she wanted to be loved," and in giving to others she reached out for the affection that first her family and later her husband had denied her. Yet the gifts may also be read as the endurance of her will to create herself and overcome the anxiety of aging by means of the image of self mirrored in the eyes of grateful others. In her enthusiasm for the company of those who cared about her, she would plan to take them on trips to Europe, to her house in Connecticut, or on excursions to shows, most of which for one reason or another never materialized. Larsen claimed to own a house in Connecticut; however, before she could take Carper and her sister Hattie for a visit there, the house was destroyed by a storm. The claim may have been an imaginative projection of the Sandy Hook, Connecticut, farm of Olivia Wyndham and Edna Thomas, and of the cottage near Georgetown, Connecticut, belonging to

10. Carper and Lane interview, May 5, 1985; Carolyn Lane, interview with author, May 5, 1985; Carper interview, May 5, 1985.

Edward Donahoe. On one outing that did occur, to a Broadway matinee of *South Pacific,* Larsen Imes was so tired from working at night that she slept through the performance.[11] The incident magnifies the contradictions inherent in her projected image of the privileged and leisured worldly woman.

Well into her fifties, Larsen Imes dressed in stylish and expensive clothing. She had long before developed a flair for clothes, which she often bought from secondhand stores where "she could spot quality faster then most other shoppers." Her collection of jewelry complemented her clothes: antique necklaces, diamond rings, and jade earrings. She could never hide her love of bright colors, especially rich, jewel-like colors. Her favorite color throughout her life was green. The purple cape that she wore over her nurse's uniform emphasized her dramatic side. Her colleagues all remarked upon the purple cape because it was so different from what the other nurses wore. "Nella was an actress; she knew how to pose for a picture," as Carolyn Lane, who was the operating room supervisor at Gouverneur, put it, remembering her exaggerated motions and gestures.[12]

In 1961, when she was already seventy years old, Larsen Imes left Gouverneur Hospital for Metropolitan Hospital. Gouverneur had been taken over by Beth Israel Medical Center and Hospital. She could have chosen retirement, but did not. She wanted to work; it still provided her greatest social contact, though her colleagues believed she "used work to try to forget . . . she was rejected twice by her husband and by her sister." After the move to Metropolitan, she began to retreat once again into herself, and to brood over her lost family. She did not travel to Brooklyn as much to see Alice Carper and Hattie Carthan. Preoccupied with the effects of aging, she did not like to be seen as old, though her employers and colleagues assumed that she was several years younger than she actually was. Her olive complexion turned pale, and she had become quite thin. Yet she made the daily journey to Metropolitan, where she worked in the evenings as she had at Gouverneur.[13]

Even while she was becoming frail, Nella Larsen Imes exhibited determination and courage. In the early 1960s while on her way to work, she was attacked by a mugger who snatched her purse and broke her arm.

11. Carper interview, May 5, 1985.

12. *Ibid.;* Alice L. Carper to Thadious M. Davis, April 3, 1985, in possession of Thadious M. Davis; Lane interview, May 5, 1985.

13. Carper and Lane interview, May 5, 1985; Carper, telephone conversation, July 20, 1982; Imes employment records, 1961–64, Metropolitan Hospital Center.

Nevertheless, she continued on to work that night and did not take time off after the incident. One of the other nurses called her "fearless" of the city's streets and dangers.[14] In effect, hers was a persistent self-determination to beat back antagonistic threats to her routine and order.

There were fears, nonetheless, that, internalized, were not about physical threats in the urban world. "Nella went bad into depression near the end of her life," Carper observed. Confronted with aging and loneliness, she sought out the sole surviving member of her immediate family, her sister Anna. Although she had not had personal contact with Anna Larsen Gardner for over thirty years, something propelled her to travel all the way to Santa Monica, California, to see her sister, who suffered from muscular dystrophy.[15]

In 1963, Larsen Imes experienced a bout of severe depression, apparently triggered by the visit to California. When she returned from California, she was never the same. She hinted that she had been rejected once again by her sister, who had not invited her into her home because Nella Larsen Imes was so obviously a black woman and Anna Gardner was white and without any visible connections to people of color. Later, Gardner denied knowing of Nella Larsen's existence: "Why, I didn't know that I had a sister." While Larsen Imes remained silent about the details of that trip, "she lost her air of confidence," Carper noticed thereafter.[16]

The self-imposed order of her world had been disrupted, ironically because she overestimated her own strength. She had more than once in her life felt a need to subdue the unpredictability of human beings, who acted out of a complex interplay of reason and emotion. Often she had succeeded. However, the force of racial imperatives in the attitudes and actions of "white" America, symbolized by her family, had not lessened by the time of her old age. Her white sister was lost to her. In the end Larsen could overcome neither her family's individual renunciation of a blood kinship nor its general rejection of the black race. She could not make peace with her past because she could not resolve the racial issue irrevocably separating her from her sister.

Although she had a male friend who, along with several of the nurses

14. Lane interview, May 5, 1985.

15. Carper interview, May 5, 1985; Carper, telephone conversation, July 20, 1982; Lane and Carper interview, May 5, 1985.

16. Carper interview, May 5, 1985; Anna Gardner quoted in Charles R. Larson, "Whatever Happened to Nella Larsen?," *Belles Lettres*, IV (Spring, 1989), 15.

from her years at Gouverneur, tried to cheer her out of her depressed state, nothing revived her spirits.[17] She felt more alone than ever, despite her condition's being in part the result of her own choices: her refusal to disengage from her longing for recognition by her blood kin and accept freely the friendship and affection offered by those who knew her as a nurse and liked her as a person. The journey to reclaim family had failed. The friendships from her happiest years during the 1920s had disappeared. Dorothy Peterson, the friend who had stood by her the longest, understood her best, and treated her as a sister, had long since lost connection with her. Suffering from arthritis throughout the 1950s, Peterson decided to leave New York for the better climate of Spain. She was featured in a 1958 *Ebony* magazine article on retired African Americans; photographed in her Manhattan apartment while reading up on Majorca, Peterson was reported to be negotiating the purchase of a house there. In 1959, she moved to Seville, where she converted to Catholicism, became more narrow-minded, and never revealed that she was African American. Peterson remained in Spain until the mid-1970s when poor health caused her return to the United States. She spent her last years in the Lathrop Nursing Home in Northampton, Massachusetts, which was near the home of her brother Sidney, and where she died on November 4, 1978. Before her death she refused to be interviewed about her involvement in the Harlem Renaissance; she called it a "frivolous, silly time in her youth," and would not discuss it even with her niece, Carla Peterson.[18] Peterson's personal papers and books remained in Spain, and her family was unable to recover them. Despite her assistance in helping Van Vechten establish the James Weldon Johnson Memorial Collection and in contributing letters to it, Peterson did not choose to record and preserve her personal memoirs.

Over seventy and still seeking reconciliation and acceptance, Larsen Imes turned inward and rejected the positive gestures of those who had come to care for her late in her life. A profound sense of isolation sealed off the possibility of emerging from depression. Toward the end of 1963, death may have been on her mind, as it had been in the fall of 1959 when she made a will naming Alice Carper as her beneficiary. Carper, however, believing that

17. Carper and Lane interview, May 5, 1985.

18. Carl Van Vechten to Dorothy Peterson, April 21 and October 30, 1959, both in JWJ; *Ebony*, XIII (June, 1958), 55; Carla L. Peterson to Thadious M. Davis, December 3, 1982, in possession of Thadious M. Davis; Carla Peterson, telephone conversation with author, January 11, 1989.

she should not keep the document, returned it. In fact, Carper sent it back several times before Larsen Imes accepted it, and then only by registered mail on October 8, 1959.[19]

Although she still worked as a night nurse, she no longer took care of her own apartment. Housework with its few rewards was labor that she had rejected after 1930 when she recognized how much of her self she had expended in cleaning and scrubbing floors. In aging, she had lost interest in doing anything at home except reading, which she still did voraciously with the aid of reading glasses. Her landlady in the front apartment used her key to enter and clean the studio. While not suffering from a debilitating physical illness, Larsen Imes was in a state of decline that took a toll on her body. Senility had also begun to affect her.[20]

By early 1964, she began refusing to see or accept calls from those few people who had grown close to her. Just as in the past, nearly twenty years earlier, no single incident prompted her dismissal of them, yet the finality of her refusal suggested injury, offense, or transgression. Once again her actions, though inexplicable, evoked rational explanations. Vanity, Carper believed, prevented her from accepting visitors, as Larsen Imes resented aging and having anyone see her growing old.[21] She may have been dimly or vaguely conscious of reasons behind her actions, or she may have actively battled against recognition and acknowledgment of her motivations. Whichever was the case, she was trapped within a pattern of behavior that had become, for her, predictable, especially in response to uncertainty and pain. Her last months revolved around sleeping and reading during the day and working at Metropolitan at night. The solitary pattern remained unbroken and unnoticed until, near the end of March, 1964, it became apparent that she had not reported to work for one week.

Nella Larsen Imes died while reading in bed, sometime before March 30, 1964, when her body was found. Although there was no autopsy, the cause of death was given as acute congestive heart failure due to hypertensive and arteriosclerotic cardiovascular disease.[22] She had died quickly and suddenly, perhaps nearly a week before the discovery. She had had a long Easter week-

---

19. Registered letter receipt no. 16.9390, Mrs. Alice Carper to Mrs. Nella Larsen Imes, October 8, 1959, copy in possession of Thadious M. Davis; Carper interview, May 5, 1985, and telephone conversation, July 20, 1982.

20. Carper and Lane interview, May 5, 1985; Carper telephone conversation, July 20, 1982.

21. Carper, telephone conversation with author, July 20, 1982.

22. Certificate of Death no. 156-64-107204, in Bureau of Records and Statistics, Borough of Manhattan, New York City Department of Health.

end off from work, so that when she did not appear before her time off, no one questioned her absence, despite its being uncharacteristic, but when she did not report the Monday after Easter, the hospital staff feared something had happened. Because she had become once again so private a person, she did not have a close enough association with anyone at the hospital who might have immediately become alarmed. She lay dead for days before the landlady, contacted by the hospital, discovered her body, notified the police, and called Alice Carper. [23]

By the time Carper arrived from Brooklyn, Larsen Imes's body had been taken to the First Avenue morgue. The apartment had been ransacked and most of the valuables taken. After providing information for the death certificate, Carper began the process of making funeral and burial arrangements for her friend. Although Larsen Imes had money in several bank accounts, she had failed to appoint someone to oversee her estate. Carper contacted Miles Funeral Home, 136 Decatur Street, Brooklyn, to handle the services, and she arranged for a burial plot in the Cypress Hills Cemetery at Jamaica Avenue and Crescent Street in Brooklyn, the same cemetery in which Langston Hughes had buried his mother, Carrie Hughes Clark, in June of 1938. [24] In the meantime, Carper hired a lawyer to assist with legal matters and with a search for Larsen Imes's sister in California.

On April 5, 1964, telegrams and flowers began to arrive at the funeral home. They came exclusively from Larsen Imes's nursing associates and hospital co-workers. The Alumnae Association of the Lincoln School for Nurses sent a telegram expressing "great sorrow"; Ruth Wasserman and the supervisors in maternity services of Metropolitan Hospital sent flowers, as did Pauline Cheeseborough for the night nursing supervisory office there, her co-workers from Gouverneur and Metropolitan hospitals, and the ambulatory care unit of Beth Israel. Carper, along with her sisters Hattie, Lottie, and Barbara, not only sent American Beauty roses and signed their card "Your dear friends," but also contacted former colleagues and collected information for the eulogy. [25]

The funeral services were held at Miles Funeral Home on April 6, 1964,

23. Information provided by Carper, telephone conversation, July 20, 1982.

24. *Ibid.*; Rampersad, *The Life of Langston Hughes,* I, 361. One of the remaining items in the ransacked apartment was Larsen's 1928 Harmon Awards bronze medal, which Carper retrieved and subsequently gave to the author.

25. Flower cards for Nella Larsen Imes, Miles Funeral Home, copies in possession of Thadious M. Davis.

with nearly fifty of her nursing colleagues and former co-workers in attendance. Carper read the eulogy she had written for her friend:

Nella Larsen Imes—
  Born April 13, 1893 in Chicago, Ill. to Mr. & Mrs. Larsen.
  Nella traveled as a child, visiting her grandparents in Denmark, her mother's home.
  She was a registered professional nurse, graduating from Lincoln School for Nurses—Bronx, N.Y. May 13, 1915. Her records then showed she was an excellent student nurse; she passed the state board with a score of 94%.
  The director of Lincoln School for Nurses stated at that time she showed great executive ability.
  After she was graduated she was retained as supervisor of Lincoln School for Nurses until October, when she accepted a position as Head Nurse at Tuskegee Normal and Industrial Institute, Tuskegee, Alabama.
  In 1916 she returned to Lincoln and held the position as Assistant Superintendent of Nurses until 1918.
  She functioned as a public health nurse until 1922. She then pursued a Liberal Arts course at the University of Copenhagen, Denmark.
  On her return to the United States she continued her education by completing a course in Library School at Columbia University, N. Y. C.
  In later years she worked as librarian in the New York Public Library system.
  In 1923 she entered into matrimony and traveled around the world with her husband.
  Much of Nella's time was devoted to the writing of novels, and magazine articles. Two known novels are *Quicksand* (1928) and *Passing* (1929).
  Still being a dedicated nurse, she returned to the field of nursing, to help alleviate the great shortage of nurses. In 1944 she became supervisor of nurses at Gouverneur Hospital, New York City and remained there until 1961 when she transferred to Metropolitan Hospital, N. Y. C. where she worked until her passing on March 30, 1964.
  Nella was greatly respected and loved by her co-workers and those with whom she came in contact.
  No task was ever too great for her to tackle. It was inspiring and encouraging the way she worked along with those in her charge.

Her passing is a great loss, and she will be missed by her co-workers and many friends.

God be with you, Nella.[26]

The eulogy rehearsed Nella Larsen Imes's life as she had presented it in the years after 1944. Specific details from her public life and vague references to family in the personal background mingle to create an impression of a woman of multiple interests and varied achievements. Nella Larsen Imes left intact what she wanted preserved of herself in the memory of those who had known her during the last twenty years of her life. She was buried in the Cypress Hills Garden of Memory, in a grave simply marked "Nella Imes."[27]

Throughout April and May, 1964, Carper and her lawyer, Irvin C. Maltz, worked to settle Larsen Imes's estate and to reimburse Carper for the funeral expenses. In accordance with her request in a lump-sum death claim filed with the Social Security Administration, Carper had the payment of $255 sent directly to Miles Funeral Home on April 29, 1964. With Maltz's assistance, she located Anna Larsen Gardner in Santa Monica, California, and forwarded a registered letter to her on May 25, 1964. Gardner, who was the legal heir, did not travel to New York, nor did she personally correspond with Alice Carper, who had made every effort to find her from information in Larsen Imes's employment records and personal papers. Gardner's reply to her sister's death and Carper's special delivery letters was through her attorney, David V. Easton of Hollywood, California.[28]

Not until September 9, 1964, did the public administrator of the County of New York forward to Carper's attorney two checks released from Larsen Imes's estate in the amounts of $64.38, which was to Alice Carper in payment for the grave, and $307, which was to Miles Funeral Home in payment on the funeral bill. According to Maltz, the question of the balance of the funeral bill would come up several months later after the final accounting by the public administrator. The public administrator was responsible for the "goods, chattels and credits" of the deceased, as Philip A. Donahue, the

---

26. Alice L. Carper, Eulogy for Nella Larsen Imes, April 6, 1964; Millicent H. Crawford, Miles Funeral Home, to Thadious M. Davis, August 23, 1982, in possession of Thadious M. Davis.

27. The grave site is 99 D, Block 4, Grave 3, Garden of Memory, Section 15. According to records at Cypress Hills, there is no perpetual care for the grave, only normal upkeep (information from Office of Cypress Hills Cemetery, April 29, 1983).

28. Registered letter receipt no. 381134, Alice L. Carper to Anna Gardner, May 25, 1964, copy in possession of Thadious M. Davis; Carper interview, May 5, 1985.

clerk of the Surrogate's Court, announced on December 15, 1964, in informing the general public and creditors that Larsen Imes's estate would be settled by the court on February 5, 1965.[29] His legal notice in the New York *Times* is the sole mention of Larsen Imes's death that might have reached some of her associates and intimates from the 1920s and 1930s, as none of the New York papers carried an obituary; however, very few apparently saw it or took notice of it, possibly because it was alphabetized under *I* for "Imes, Nella" with "Nella Larsen Imes" and "Nella L. Imes" as the alternate names, which almost none of them would have known she had reassumed in the 1940s.

On February 11, 1965, six days after the public administrator settled all accounts, Alice Carper, having been compensated for the debts encumbered for Larsen Imes's funeral, received her final bill from Maltz. Nearly eleven months after the death of Nella Larsen Imes, the public accounting was over. Throughout the legal transactions, Carper had asked for nothing for herself but had tried to settle the funeral expenses and to have the proceeds of the estate sent to Anna Larsen Gardner rather than allowing them to revert to the state. For her efforts, she received no word of thanks from Gardner, who acquired a sizable sum. In California, Gardner feigned surprise at the discovery of a sister and upon inheriting her estate.[30] In the end, the contact that family would have with Nella Larsen Imes even in death was starkly impersonal and minimal. Even at her death, race continued to isolate her from her kin.

Larsen Imes may fully have expected as much from her surviving "white" family, but she could not have anticipated the reclamation of her and her works by a new generation of African Americans, who in the period of her death were forging familial ties with the writers of the New Negro Renaissance and laying claim to Nella Larsen as one of their own. Out of the political activism and racial consciousness of the civil rights movement came a second black cultural renaissance that, in an effort to establish kinship and heritage, models and forebears, continuity and parallels, in essence to reaffirm traditions and legacies in black art and black identity, had "found" Nella Larsen, claimed her as kin, and asserted her fiction as forerunner.

---

29. Irvin C. Maltz to Alice L. Carper, September 9, 1964; Legal notices, New York *Times*, December 17, 1964.

30. Bill for Professional Services Rendered, Irvin C. Maltz to Alice Carper, February 11, 1965, in the amount of $50, copy in possession of Thadious M. Davis; Larson, "Whatever Happened to Nella Larsen?," 15.

Even in the wake of the historic March on Washington on August 28, 1963, she could not have foreseen that her longed for "place," with the attendant fame, recognition, and belonging that she so desired, would finally begin to come to her again within that very decade.

CONCLUSION

The Meaning of Nella Larsen

FOR A BRIEF time, Nella Larsen captured the spirit of a unique time for modern African-American writers. She praised the activity as "writing as if [one] didn't absolutely despise the age in which [one] lives. . . . [S]urely it is more interesting to belong to one's own time, to share its peculiar vision, catch that flying glimpse of the panorama which no subsequent generation can recover."[1] In mediating her own "peculiar vision," she saw a world of middle-class African Americans that became the basis for her fictional vision, but she saw, too, the complexities of personal identification with that world. While it cannot be claimed that she saw steadily and whole, it is clear that the angle and the scope of her vision partly resulted from her particular involvement with her times. Had she completed "Crowning Mercy," "Mirage" (or "Fall Fever"), "The Gilded Palm Tree," "The Wingless Hour," and her collaborative work "Adrian and Evadne," she might have emerged from her age with a more substantial canon, but that canon in all probability would have altered neither the achievement of the remarkable fiction in *Quicksand* and *Passing* nor the estimation of her limiting relationship to her milieu.

Larsen's movement from nurse to librarian to writer demonstrates her personal search for class position, meaningful work, social prestige, and full self-expression as an African-American female. Her movement, reconstituted through the lens of time, reflects the dual efforts of a woman con-

1. Nella Larsen Imes to Carl Van Vechten, Monday [1925], in CVV.

structing herself during the moment of the larger social construction of an African-American middle class and of a woman engendering herself during a period of confluence of race, gender, and art. Larsen's return to her first profession, nursing, underscores the dualism of her life and the problems created by gender and race marginality for her as a writer. Nursing in the 1940s and 1950s represented, as it had earlier in the century when Larsen trained at Lincoln Hospital, the profession exclusively for women that extended the roles of caretaker, wife, and mother outside the home and family environment. In caring for the sick, the nurse functioned as the male and, in Larsen's race-specific experiences, "white" doctor's helpmate who fed, medicated, cleansed, and nurtured. At the same time, nursing established a fixed routine, a regimented structure for conduct and relevancy that carried immediate rewards and assured approval. Although marked during that period by an emerging professionalism for African-American women, it also provided in work and associations a potentially absorbing, self-effacing order for one's life. Nursing also situated an individual woman within a woman-centered environment that fostered empathetic, caring relationships among females who, more often than not, became friends. Moreover, nursing provided a steady income, with opportunities for determining one's own work schedule, which Larsen did by choosing shifts as a night nurse. She no doubt had good reason to return to nursing, particularly after Elmer Imes's death in 1941.

Nonetheless, from the vantage point of today, her return to nursing is a kind of retreat that literally acts out the fears assigned to women characters in her fiction. She seems to have submitted, albeit reluctantly, to cultural restraints placed in her day upon African-American women writers and to have rejected autonomous and imaginative, though precarious, work as a professional writer. She was perhaps born too early, as it was not until the aftermath of the WPA Federal Writers' Project that black men and women in any numbers would become professional creative writers and earn their livings from that vocation. Her decision to return to nursing implies a need to simplify her existence and live securely and anonymously with money coming in, but also with demanding, rewarding work that would not challenge her sense of self. Acting as an agent rather than as a victim, she chose safety in a contained existence, rather than accepting the risks and the freedom in the life of a writer. That "choice," rooted in a complex subjectivity, at once conforms to and defies gender roles and expectations.

On the one hand, what seems to have been missing by the end of the 1930s from Larsen's artistic life were the security and reinforcement that women, such as her characters Helga Crane and Irene Redfield, are led to believe the family will offer. On the other hand, missing also were the courage and confidence of women such as Audrey Denny and Clare Kendry, her characters whose "having" natures demanded attention to their own needs first. Without the buffers of a supportive external environment and a resilient, determined personality, Larsen could not continue in the exposed, vulnerable career of a woman writer, but she could construct another gendered identity. Surely her inability to bring to completion her four novels, or if to completion, to have them accepted for publication, must have been an additional determining factor in her decision to resume work as a nurse.

While the stuff of Larsen's personal experience might have fueled her writing, she, like other African-American writers, was unable to slough off extensive personal pain compounded in direct conjunction with a vulnerability to racism. She seems to have lost sight of one impetus for writing: the need to heal the self. This need is especially visible in writers racialized within society. Larsen could not turn her need for expression and her experiences into fiction, for too closely had she allied her writing with the surfaces of "amusing" social experience and too little had she explored the psychological depths charted and sketched in her subtexts. "What things there are to write, if only one can write them," she mused in the mid-1920s. Her list of "things," meant to be extensive and tensile, revealed a limited, oddly vapid sense of material: "Boiler menders, society ladies, children, acrobats, governesses, business men, countesses, flappers, Nile green bath rooms, beautifully filled, gray moods and shivering hesitations, all presented in an intensely restrained and civilized manner and underneath the ironic survival of a much more primitive mood. Delicious."[2] Even her humor, a potential release from hurtful entrapments, became too shallow and affected to deflect her pain into meaningful satire or to emancipate her from her depression.

Unlike Zora Neale Hurston, whose dedication to her writing continued even when her powers had diminished along with her fortunes, Larsen did not persist. Her situation may have been similar to the one Georgia Douglas Johnson evoked in the poem "The Heart of a Woman":

> The heart of a woman falls back with the night,
> And enters some alien cage in its plight,

2. *Ibid.*

demand for jobs by college-educated individuals during the Depression, and given that African Americans were relegated to positions in only a few of the branch libraries. She had, perhaps, no other alternative than to return to nursing, which she had always equated somehow with work of a lower status, despite its professionalism. Embarrassed by her reduced circumstances and the concomitant move to a smaller studio apartment, she responded as she had in 1932 after her return from Europe when she refused to invite anyone to her West Eleventh Street apartment because she thought it too small. Given the reduction in her lifestyle and her need to work, she chose not to associate with her former acquaintances. In this decision, she was most unlike the valiant Georgia Douglas Johnson, who was candid about her desperate and unsuccessful search for employment in the 1930s; in the 1940s, when she was over sixty years old, Johnson did not hide her job in a civil service clerical pool or her many rejected applications for grants and awards.[7] Larsen's pride would not permit a conscious revelation of her position, even though she should have known that it mattered more to her than it would to those blacks and whites, such as Dorothy Peterson and Carl Van Vechten, who genuinely cared about her. The others who would mistake circumstance for substance should not have mattered, but they did.

Suppose too that she had a breakdown in the aftermath of the rejection by Edward Donahoe followed by the death of Imes. What resources for mental health were left? Neither Peterson nor Van Vechten, her closest friends, could understand her problem, because for them it was a false one, perverted by a value system that limited Larsen's possibilities. Her response was a characteristic decision to go it alone, perchance at some point to resume her writing or perhaps writing all the while but finally realizing that her old contacts with the publishing world were gone, that she did not know how to establish new ones, particularly when a different vogue of African-American writers had appeared during the Great Depression. Richard Wright's prominence, for example, would have made her style and her subject matter less significant or seemingly less urgent for publishers, emerging from the Depression themselves, to consider the financial risk of her passé type of novel. What a trap the modernist Larsen must have faced once she realized that she could not go back and that she had no room of her own from which to move forward. Would that her plight had ended with the

---

7. Gloria T. Hull, *Color, Sex and Poetry: Three Women Writers of the Harlem Renaissance* (Bloomington, 1987), 180–84.

ultimate quiet, joyful victory that Marita Bonner conjured up in "On Being Young—A Woman—And Colored" (1925):

> Still . . . "Perhaps Buddha is a woman."
> So you too. Still; quiet; with a smile, ever so slight, at the eyes so that Life will flow into and not by you. And you can gather, as it passes, the essences, the overtones, the tints, the shadows; draw understanding to your self.
> And then you can, when Time is ripe, swoop to your feet—at your full height—at a single gesture.
> Ready to go where?
> Why . . . Wherever God motions.[8]

Larsen's solution was a stasis in which no movement at all was necessary. She stopped in place and remained frozen there long enough to allow the problem to dissolve, to disappear as she herself had. When she began to move again, she concentrated on the smallest possible amount of space and motion so as to attract no notice to the self that had been Nella Larsen, novelist. She did not choose death by suicide; her choice was a life of her own making, just as that life of her youth and young womanhood had been of her making out of whatever resources were available. Much like the character she had created in "Freedom," she had walked away from one life and in its place had substituted one that satisfied few of her deepest longings, yet one that she alone created and controlled. In this aspect, she also seems somewhat comparable to Angelina Weld Grimké, who, without explanation, moved in 1930 to New York from Washington and, as Gloria T. Hull puts it, "buried herself" in an apartment until her death twenty-eight years later.[9] When she closed her door on the world, Grimké was fifty years old—ironically, precisely the same age that Larsen was in 1941 when she "disappeared" into a world bounded by her apartment. But Larsen's experience cannot be read simply in large emblematic terms but rather on the basis of a continual human struggle for individuality.

From her apartment on Second Avenue, Larsen could move quickly in the night to her job. At the hospital in uniform, she could become indistin-

---

8. Marita O. Bonner, "On Being Young—a Woman—and Colored," *Crisis*, XXI (December, 1925), 65, rpr. in Washington, *Invented Lives*, 173.
9. Hull, *Color, Sex and Poetry*, 192; see also 149–53.

And tries to forget it has dreamed of the stars,
While it breaks, breaks, breaks on the sheltering bars.[3]

Perhaps Larsen recognized that the harsh economic times demanded a realistic course for self-support. She is not to be criticized for her failure to persevere, to find anew a way of liberating her creative self; yet it seems that she gave in without a visible struggle, that despite her considerable courage her internal resources were not sufficient to allow her to continue to write. For Larsen, the writing of fiction, as Milton Nahm points out about art in general, might have "supplied . . . the energy, the courage, and the inspiration to direct the productivity which its profound symbols evoke for use in . . . [the] endless task of controlling [self] and nature."[4] Her failure is our loss, because Larsen's life after her divorce and after the death of Imes presented her with more of the substance of powerful fiction than any of her drawing-room dramas of the 1920s, or of the "delicious" subjects and moods she envisioned.

She was a woman who had the psychological perceptions and the detached stance to render insightful constructions of the impact of the Depression on African Americans in New York, particularly those independent females who were of the new fledgling middle class. She might well have been able to represent something of the transient nature of personal wealth and success for any individual. But the pain of that truth was one that she could not readily share with anyone, possibly not even with herself. Creative writing is after all a form of both transference and sublimation. Whatever she may have known and understood and felt on a deeper level during those traumatic years is lost to us today. Her tragedy is somehow also ours, because we do not have more of the writing that could at once express her personality and stand as an expressive medium for the commonly shared experience of others.

Perhaps her reality in writing at all was the one reflecting the female artist in Anne Spencer's "Sybil Warns Her Sister":

> It is dangerous for a woman to defy the gods;
> To taunt them with the tongue's thin tip,
> Or strut in the weakness of mere humanity,

---

3. Georgia Douglas Johnson, *The Heart of a Woman and Other Poems* (Boston, 1918), 1.
4. Milton Nahm, *Aesthetic Experience and Its Suppositions* (New York, 1946), 507.

Or draw a line daring them to cross;
The gods own the searing lightning,
The drowning waters, tormenting fears
And anger of red sins.

.   .   .   .

This you may do:
Lock your heart, then, quietly,
And lest they peer within,
Light no lamp when dark comes down
Raise no shade for sun.[5]

During the thirty-four years between the publication of "Sanctuary" and her death, silence replaced Larsen's voice, but in that silence is the story of an African-American woman writer unable to create in the face both of complex race and gender obstacles in society operating against her needs and of psychological dualism in her own personality fragmenting her responses to those needs. She was a proud, struggling woman who by means of work and effort made her own way up the social and class ladder, and who wrote out of a need to create herself and affirm her place. Her transitions from Nellie Marie Larson to Nella Marion Larsen to Nella Larsen Imes are inscriptions of her will to create and her determination to be—to become and mean all that she envisioned for her ideal self. The transformations in her identity are as well indicative of the complicated tangle of her earliest years with her "white" parents and sibling. Finally, however, illusions could not stay her changing fortunes, and sheer will could not sway her unchanging values. Measuring herself by appearances, possessions, and position, as first her parents and then her culture conditioned her to do, she assumed that others used and would use the same measures of her worth, which, with the altering of her material circumstance, was an untenable prospect for her future. She felt protected by money, along with class and marital and professional status; without these trappings, she became exposed and vulnerable. She refused to reenter Harlem without the public acclaim accorded her as a New Negro writer and without the sanction of Imes's name and connections, because she believed that she would sink into the desperate masses of Harlem during the Depression. Her distinction had come through her marriage, and self-validation had come through her pub-

5. Anne Spencer, "Sybil Warns Her Sister," in *Ebony and Topaz: A Collectanea*, ed. Charles S. Johnson (New York, 1927), 94.

lications; loss of the two negated her sense of achievement and meaning. The only option that she could envision for herself, disengagement, duplicated earlier patterns in her own life and in her fiction.

Complete disengagement from a personal past and social history left her in a marginal relationship to the rest of society and to her own ambitions. It seems that her ideas about class standing had as much to do with her disappearance as any possible desire to be white or to pass, or simply to escape contact with those who had known her as Mrs. Imes. Larsen's story, then, is a sad one because it reveals the complex tragedy of a more subtle racism that twists and undermines the individual's sense of who and what is valuable, all the while distorting the worth of the person into a sequence of material goods or public accolades. It is no accident that long after she began working again as a night nurse, she still insisted that she was a writer. This signature of identity is her representation of self-validation and meaning. In voicing her identity as a writer, she could also maintain some of her former prestige without what she construed as the embarrassment of being labeled a divorced woman working as a nurse. It is equally relevant that to the end of her life in 1964, she listed herself as a widow, never revealing that she had divorced Imes in 1933, eight years before his death.

In *Invented Lives,* Mary Helen Washington aptly concludes of Larsen:

> She did not solve her own problems, but Larsen made us understand as no one did before her that the image of the middle-class black woman as a coldly self-centered snob, chattering irrelevantly at bridge clubs and sorority meetings, was as much a mask as the grin on the face of Stepin Fetchit. The women in her novels, like Larsen, are driven to emotional and psychological extremes in their attempts to handle ambivalence, marginality, racism, and sexism. She has shown us that behind the carefully manicured exterior, behind the appearance of security is a woman who hears the beating of her wings against a walled prison.[6]

Although Larsen may have felt too keenly that her situation was so hopeless that her most viable way of coping was isolation, she perhaps had no

---

6. Mary Helen Washington, "The Mulatta Trap: Nella Larsen's Women of the 1920s," in *Invented Lives: Narratives of Black Women 1860–1960,* by Mary Helen Washington (Garden City, 1987), 166.

alternative, given the experiences she had throughout her life and the methods she developed for coping with them. Individual personal and social conflicts complicate a totalizing reconstruction of her racial and gendered experiences. Conjecturing her motivation and contextualizing her situation engage, not a static script of a woman's life, but rather dynamic processes that allow for an emergence of the logic of her actions.

Suppose that when her father and mother sent her to Fisk to enter an African-American world she had rebelled and decided to make her own way in New York. Upon her arrival in the city, she would have found that it was not as simple as she imagined to find a job and make a living. Suppose that she, like her character in "The Wrong Man," had found a benefactor who eventually enabled her to attend the Lincoln Training School for Nurses. If the suppositions are followed through, then Larsen had a history of past grievances and mistakes that she might wish not merely to hide but to avoid duplicating. Were she then confronted with the social embarrassment of having a messy divorce in which her husband's alienation of affection was the result of his affair with a white woman, she might then see the rejection and public knowledge of it as comparable to the loss of her father and mother and their rejection of her for a white world and a white daughter.

If Larsen's social position were even more compromised by her having relied too much on the attentions of a young white man who, prone to mental disorders, misled her in his intentions to marry her and write novels with her, then she might have felt that her last hope of resuming her writing career had disappeared, particularly because her writing had been undermined by the charge of plagiarism and her failure to produce the third novel either on her Guggenheim grant or in the years immediately after her return to the United States. When that man published his own novel in 1937 and announced his marriage in 1939 to a young woman of his own background, race, and class, he destroyed the expectations that Larsen had for her future as a writer and, possibly, as a person. What would that have done to her spirit, to her conception of her self, to her ability to write? What resources could she then muster in order to continue making a place for herself in a world that she then distrusted and perceived as hostile to her dreams and ambitions? What could she do?

She could perhaps continue for a time to exist as she had in the past. But financial necessities are real. With those as pressure, she could then resort to earning her living as she had before her marriage. However, she did not have the option of returning to the New York Public Library for a job, at least not one that paid adequately, given her qualifications and the greater demand for jobs by college-educated individuals during the Depression, and given that African Americans were relegated to positions in only a few of the branch libraries. She had, perhaps, no other alternative than to return to nursing, which she had always equated somehow with work of a lower status, despite its professionalism. Embarrassed by her reduced circumstances and the concomitant move to a smaller studio apartment, she responded as she had in 1932 after her return from Europe when she refused to invite anyone to her West Eleventh Street apartment because she thought it too small. Given the reduction in her lifestyle and her need to work, she chose not to associate with her former acquaintances. In this decision, she was most unlike the valiant Georgia Douglas Johnson, who was candid about her desperate and unsuccessful search for employment in the 1930s; in the 1940s, when she was over sixty years old, Johnson did not hide her job in a civil service clerical pool or her many rejected applications for grants and awards.[7] Larsen's pride would not permit a conscious revelation of her position, even though she should have known that it mattered more to her than it would to those blacks and whites, such as Dorothy Peterson and Carl Van Vechten, who genuinely cared about her. The others who would mistake circumstance for substance should not have mattered, but they did.

Suppose too that she had a breakdown in the aftermath of the rejection by Edward Donahoe followed by the death of Imes. What resources for mental health were left? Neither Peterson nor Van Vechten, her closest friends, could understand her problem, because for them it was a false one, perverted by a value system that limited Larsen's possibilities. Her response was a characteristic decision to go it alone, perchance at some point to resume her writing or perhaps writing all the while but finally realizing that her old contacts with the publishing world were gone, that she did not know how to establish new ones, particularly when a different vogue of African-American writers had appeared during the Great Depression. Richard Wright's prominence, for example, would have made her style and her subject matter less significant or seemingly less urgent for publishers, emerging from the Depression themselves, to consider the financial risk of her passé type of novel. What a trap the modernist Larsen must have faced once she realized that she could not go back and that she had no room of her own from which to move forward. Would that her plight had ended with the

7. Gloria T. Hull, *Color, Sex and Poetry: Three Women Writers of the Harlem Renaissance* (Bloomington, 1987), 180–84.

ultimate quiet, joyful victory that Marita Bonner conjured up in "On Being Young—A Woman—And Colored" (1925):

> Still . . . "Perhaps Buddha is a woman."
>
> So you too. Still; quiet; with a smile, ever so slight, at the eyes so that Life will flow into and not by you. And you can gather, as it passes, the essences, the overtones, the tints, the shadows; draw understanding to your self.
>
> And then you can, when Time is ripe, swoop to your feet—at your full height—at a single gesture.
>
> Ready to go where?
>
> Why . . . Wherever God motions.[8]

Larsen's solution was a stasis in which no movement at all was necessary. She stopped in place and remained frozen there long enough to allow the problem to dissolve, to disappear as she herself had. When she began to move again, she concentrated on the smallest possible amount of space and motion so as to attract no notice to the self that had been Nella Larsen, novelist. She did not choose death by suicide; her choice was a life of her own making, just as that life of her youth and young womanhood had been of her making out of whatever resources were available. Much like the character she had created in "Freedom," she had walked away from one life and in its place had substituted one that satisfied few of her deepest longings, yet one that she alone created and controlled. In this aspect, she also seems somewhat comparable to Angelina Weld Grimké, who, without explanation, moved in 1930 to New York from Washington and, as Gloria T. Hull puts it, "buried herself" in an apartment until her death twenty-eight years later.[9] When she closed her door on the world, Grimké was fifty years old—ironically, precisely the same age that Larsen was in 1941 when she "disappeared" into a world bounded by her apartment. But Larsen's experience cannot be read simply in large emblematic terms but rather on the basis of a continual human struggle for individuality.

From her apartment on Second Avenue, Larsen could move quickly in the night to her job. At the hospital in uniform, she could become indistin-

---

8. Marita O. Bonner, "On Being Young—a Woman—and Colored," *Crisis*, XXI (December, 1925), 65, rpr. in Washington, *Invented Lives*, 173.

9. Hull, *Color, Sex and Poetry*, 192; see also 149–53.

guishable from the rest of the nursing staff, even though she could also assert measured authority as a supervisor. Within her neighborhood, she could quietly go about taking care of her basic needs: doing shopping, laundry, shoe repair, all within her own block or a two-block radius of her apartment building. The reduction of her circumstances, as she perceived it, brought with it a reduction in her motion and mobility, and yet charting her years outside the limelight does not reveal a spiraling movement downward. She held herself in place, in check; she worked and read and lived in a different sphere but one that nonetheless was free of poverty or disgrace. While want and need were probably no less real psychological yearnings than they had been in her years of fame, they were not compelling enough to propel her into society, into sustained intimate interactions with people outside her workplace. Perhaps she achieved a measure of peace in her solitude, and perhaps it intensified her satisfaction in the few friendships that broke the pattern of her chosen routine. Both the constraints of social structure and the power of individual agency functioned interactively in Larsen's life, and understanding that interaction situates her story within the interpretive strategy identified by the Personal Narratives Group, who paraphrase Marx: "Women make their own lives . . . but they do so under conditions not of their own choosing." [10]

When Larsen's death came, it was in old age and from natural causes. Her heart simply gave out. No scrapbooks of clippings survived the ravage of her apartment after her death; her many books and papers seem to have vanished in the haste to clear her studio of the signs of death and decay. Yet her novels continue to have a life, to survive in a world neither Larsen nor her characters would recognize. Their existence today means that we remember yesterday, her and our conjoined past, when in the face of social constructions, Nella Larsen lived and wrote her own life in her own way.

10. Personal Narratives Group, *Interpreting Women's Lives: Feminist Theory and Personal Narratives* (Bloomington, 1989), 5.

Appendix A

Book Reviews of Quicksand

Bennett, Gwendolyn. "The Ebony Flute." *Opportunity*, VI (May, 1928).

"Book A Week." Baltimore *Afro-American*, May 15, 1928.

Bradford, Roark. "Books: Mixed Blood." New York *Herald Tribune*, May 13, 1928, p. 522.

Canadian Forum, VIII (1928), 730.

Chicago *Defender*, May 12, 1928. [Photograph with paragraph on novel.]

Cleveland *Open Shelf* (July, 1928), 91.

Du Bois, W. E. B. "The Browsing Reader: Two Novels." *Crisis*, XXXV (1928), 202.

Fauset, Arthur Huff. "Quicksand." *Black Opals*, I (June, 1928), 19.

Gordon, Barefield. "The Bookshelf." Chicago *Defender*, August 25, 1928.

G. W. K. "Two Novels." *New Statesman*, XXXI (June 2, 1928), 260.

Hayden, Katharine Shepard. *Annals of the American Academy of Political and Social Science*, CXL (November, 1928), 345.

Latimer, Margery. "The Book World." New York *World*, July 22, 1928.

Matthews, T. S. "What Gods! What Gongs!" *New Republic*, LV (May 20, 1928), 50.

"Miscegenation? Bah!" New York *Amsterdam News*, May 16, 1928.

Mortimer, Raymond. "New Novels." *The Nation and Athenaeum* [London] (June 23, 1928), 397.

"A Mulatto Girl." New York *Times*, April 8, 1928, pp. 16–17.

Opportunity, VII (January, 1929), 25.

Ovington, Mary White. "Book Chat" [NAACP press release], August 3, 1928, pp. 4–5.

Parsons, Alice Beal. "Three Novels." *Nation*, May 9, 1928, p. 540.

Pittsburgh *Monthly Bulletin*, XXXIII (June, 1928), 321.

"*Quicksand:* The Story of the Revolt of a Negro School Teacher." Boston *Transcript*, June 20, 1928, p. 2.

Root, E. Merrill. "Ebony Hour-Hand, Pointing to Midnight." *Christian Century,* October 18, 1928, pp. 1261–62.

Saturday Review of Literature, May 19, 1928, p. 896.

Thurman, Wallace. "High, Low, Past and Present." *Harlem,* I (November, 1928), 32.

Times Literary Supplement [London], July 26, 1928, p. 553.

Walton, Eda Lou. *Opportunity,* VI (July, 1928), 212–13.

World Tomorrow, XI (November, 1928), 474.

Yates, Ruth L. Pittsburgh *Courier,* May 26, 1928.

Appendix B

Book Reviews of Passing

"Beyond the Color Line." *New York Times Book Review*, April 28, 1929, p. 14.

"The Books of the Day—The Dilemma of Mixed Race: Another Study of the Color-Line in New York." New York *Sun*, May 1, 1929.

Bowser, Aubrey. "The Cat Came Back." New York *Amsterdam News*, June 5, 1929, p. 20.

Braithwaite, William Stanley. "Books and Magazines." *Dunbar News*, May 14, 1929, p. 4.

Cleveland *Open Shelf* (July, 1929), 110.

Dawson, Margaret Cheney. "The Color Line." New York *Herald Tribune*, April 28, 1929, p. 6.

"Do They Always Return?" New York *News*, September 28, 1929.

Du Bois, W. E. B. "The Browsing Reader." *Crisis*, XXXVI (1929), 234, 248–50.

Hyman, Esther. *Bookman*, LXIX (June, 1929), 427–28.

Labaree, Mary Fleming. *Opportunity*, VII (August, 1929), 255.

Seabrook, W. B. "Touch of the Tar-brush." *Saturday Review of Literature*, May 18, 1929, pp. 1017–18.

Times Literary Supplement [London], December 12, 1929, p. 1060.

Wilson Bulletin (December, 1929).

Chronological Listing of Works by Nella Larsen (Imes)

"Playtime: Three Scandinavian Games." *Brownies' Book,* I (June, 1920), 191–92.

"Playtime: Danish Fun." *Brownies' Book,* I (July, 1920), 219.

Review of *Certain People of Importance* by Kathleen Norris. *Messenger,* V (May, 1923), 713.

"The Wrong Man." *Young's Realistic Stories Magazine,* L (January, 1926), 243–46. (Published under pseudonym Allen Semi.)

"Freedom." *Young's Realistic Stories Magazine,* LI (April, 1926), 241–43. (Published under pseudonym Allen Semi.)

"Correspondence." *Opportunity,* IV (September, 1926), 295.

Quicksand. New York: Alfred A. Knopf, Inc., 1928.

Review of *Black Sadie* by T. Bowyer Campbell. *Opportunity,* VII (January, 1929), 24.

Passing. New York: Alfred A. Knopf, Inc., 1929.

"Moving Mosaic or N.A.A.C.P. Dance, 1929" (excerpt from *Quicksand*). In *All-Star Benefit Concert for the National Association for the Advancement of Colored People,* Forrest Theater, New York, program booklet, December 8, 1929.

"Sanctuary." *Forum,* LXXXIII (January, 1930), 15–18.

"The Author's Explanation." *Forum,* Supplement 4, LXXXIII (April, 1930), xli–xlii.

INDEX

African Americans: middle class of, 5, 7–8, 79, 171–72; in Chicago, 32–34, 38–39, 41–44, 48–49, 50, 52n; and racial tensions in Chicago, 39–40, 42–43; and segregation, 42, 52, 53; migration from the South, 44; as professionals, 50; at Fisk University, 52–68; in Nashville, 52, 52n, 356; illiteracy among, 55; attitudes toward skin color by, 62, 128–30, 141; employment opportunities for African-American women, 84–85, 127, 148; nursing profession for, 85–87, 138–39; and suffrage for women, 139; and education as key to upward mobility, 148; and importance of producing literature and art, 151–52; migration to Harlem, 157, 199, 223; chauvinism and misogyny against black women, 159–60; newspapers and magazines for, 171–72; and passing for white, 182–83, 200, 322–23, 421, 422–25; with doctorates, 222; Harlem residents, 227–29, 331, 417; and white patronage and interest in creative expression of, 239–42; during Depression, 418–20

Africana, 231

Alexander, Ernest R. "Scolly," 199, 227, 228, 302, 307, 434

Alexander, Lillian (Mrs. E. R.), 15, 125, 199, 227, 228, 285, 291, 302, 341, 432, 434

Alexander, Will, 155

Alfred A. Knopf, Inc.: records on Larsen, xvii, xviii, 22, 45, 110, 225; as publisher of black authors, 155, 166; Blue Jade Library of, 165–66, 259, 351; Larsen's view of, 186; rejection of Fauset's *There Is Confusion,* 186; publication of *Quicksand,* 219–21, 250–51, 281; Larsen as reader for, 226–27; publication of *Passing,* 293

Allen, Dever, 158

Allen, Frederick, 158

Allen, James, 302, 355

Allen, Samuel, 394–95

American Missionary Society, 52, 53